Mastering Social Psychology

Robert A. Baron
Rensselaer Polytechnic Institute

Donn Byrne
The University at Albany, State University of New York

Nyla R. Branscombe
University of Kansas

PEARSON

Boston   New York   San Francisco
Mexico City   Montreal   Toronto   London   Madrid   Munich   Paris
Hong Kong   Singapore   Tokyo   Cape Town   Sydney

Editor in Chief: Susan Hartman
Editorial Assistant: Courtney Mullen
Marketing Manager: Pamela Laskey
Editorial-Production Administrator:
  Karen Mason
Editorial-Production Service:
  Nesbitt Graphics, Inc.

Photo Editor: Annie Pickert
Design and Electronic Composition:
  Nesbitt Graphics, Inc.
Composition/Prepress Buyer: Linda Cox
Manufacturing Buyer: Megan Cochran
Cover Administrator: Kristina Mose-Libon

For related titles and support materials, visit our online catalog at www.ablongman.com.

Between the time website information is gathered and then published, it is not unusual for some sites to have closed. Also, the transcription of URLs can result in typographical errors. The publisher would appreciate notification where these errors occur so that they may be corrected in subsequent editions.

Library of Congress Cataloging-in-Publication Data

Baron, Robert A.
  Mastering social psychology / Robert A. Baron, Donn Byrne, Nyla R. Branscombe.
      p. cm.
    ISBN 0-205-49589-3
  1. Social psychology--Textbooks. I. Byrne, Donn Erwin. II. Branscombe, Nyla R. III. Title.
    HM1033.B33 2007
    302--dc22

                                    2006033619

Printed in the United States of America

10 9 8 7 6 5 4 3 2 1   VHP   10   09   08   07   06

Photo credits appear on pages C-1 and C-2, which constitute a continuation of the copyright page.

Mastering Social Psychology

BRIEF CONTENTS

CONTENTS

2 SOCIAL COGNITION:
Thinking about the Social World   29

3 SOCIAL PERCEPTION: Perceiving and Understanding Others 59

5 THE SELF:
Understanding "Who Am I?" 125

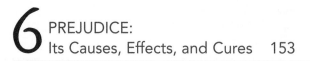

6 PREJUDICE: Its Causes, Effects, and Cures 153

7 INTERPERSONAL ATTRACTION:
Meeting, Liking, Becoming Acquainted 187

8 CLOSE RELATIONSHIPS:
Family, Friends, Lovers, and Spouses 213

10 PROSOCIAL BEHAVIOR: Helping Others 273

Contents

11 AGGRESSION: Its Nature, Causes, and Control 301

12 GROUPS AND INDIVIDUALS: The Consequences of Belonging 333

SPECIAL FEATURES

PREFACE

WELCOME

In our view, the pace of change—and progress—in social psychology has accelerated, so it is even more crucial than ever that any text seeking to represent the field stay in touch with what is happening *today;* failure to do so will result in a book that will be perceived as badly out of date by social psychologists and one that—because it has lost its sense of excitement with the field—is more likely to generate yawns than enthusiasm from students.

With this principle in mind, we created *Mastering Social Psychology*—the fundamentals version of our classic, best-selling text. Because social psychology advances at a dizzying pace, we have devoted special attention to the task of representing emerging new themes in the field. Among these are the following:

- The interface (and interplay) between social cognition and social behavior
- Social neuroscience
- The role of implicit (nonconscious) processes in both social thought and social behavior
- Growing attention to social diversity and the complex issues it involves

In addition to its cutting-edge coverage, *Mastering Social Psychology* retains the hallmark of the eleventh edition's success: strong pedagogy, emphasis on application, and a lively and engaging voice that will motivate students to take social psychology out of the classroom and into their lives.

Special Features Designed to Highlight the Value of Social Psychology

◀ *The Science of Social Psychology: Making Sense of Common Sense* boxes show how research findings are often counterintuitive—they have reversed or refined common sense ideas. For example: Can we be scared into changing our attitudes? Do opposites attract? Catharsis: Does getting it out of your system really help?

Ideas to Take with You—and Use! boxes at the end of every ▶ chapter highlight important concepts that affect students' daily lives well after the course is over.

▲*Connections* **tables** at the end of every chapter help explain the relationship between certain topics within the field of social psychology, with chapter cross-referencing. **Thinking about Connections"** questions follow the "Connections" tables.

Key Points at the end of every major section help students ▶ understand what they have read and **key terms** in bold help students look for definitions (both within the text and in the glossary at the end of the book).

◀ **Chapter summaries,** called "Summary and Review of Key Points" help students assess what they have read.

Supplementary Materials

All good texts should be supported by a complete package of supplementary material, both for the students and for the instructor. This book provides ample aid for both.

■ For the Instructor

Instructor's Manual

Michele Van Volkom, Monmouth University

Prepared by Michele Van Volkom of Monmouth University, this rich collection of teaching material can be used by first-time or experienced teachers. Each chapter includes an At-a-Glance Grid, with detailed pedagogical information linking to other available supplements; a comprehensive chapter outline and summary; teaching objectives covering major concepts within the chapter; a list of key terms; lecture material, classroom demonstrations, and activities; numerous handouts; and an updated list of web links. In addition, this manual includes a preface, a sample syllabus, and a comprehensive list of teaching resources.

Test Bank and Computerized Test Bank

Tina Burns, Florida International University

Tina Burns of Florida International University has created a comprehensive test bank with challenging questions that target key concepts. Each chapter includes over 100 questions, in multiple choice, true/false, short answer, and essay formats, each with an answer justification, page reference, difficulty rating, and type designation.

This product is also available in TestGen 5.5 computerized version, for ease in creating tests for the classroom.

PowerPoint Presentation

Philip Dunwoody, Juniata College

This dynamic multimedia resource pairs key points covered in the chapter with figures from the textbook to provoke effective classroom discussion.

MyPsychLab for Social Psychology

This interactive and instructive multimedia resource can be used to supplement a traditional lecture course or to administer a course entirely online. It is an all-inclusive tool, a text-specific e-book plus multimedia tutorials, audio, video, simulations, animations, and controlled assessments to completely engage students and reinforce learning. Fully customizable and easy to use, MyPsychLab meets the individual teaching and learning needs of every instructor and every student. Visit the site at www.mypsychlab.com.

Allyn and Bacon Transparencies for Social Psychology

Approximately 100 revised, full-color acetates to enhance classroom lecture and discussion. Includes images from Allyn and Bacon's major Social Psychology texts.

ABC Video for Social Psychology

A wonderful tool including 9 video clips. Clips cover topics such as self-esteem, plastic surgery, philanthropy, bullying, sororities, age discrimination, and more. Critical thinking questions accompany each clip. In addition, the video guide provides further critical thinking questions and Internet resources for more information.

■ For the Student

Grade Aid Study Guide

Philip Dunwoody, Juniata College

Written by Philip Dunwoody of Juniata College, this guide aids students in synthesizing the material they are learning and helping them prepare for exams. Each chapter includes "Before You Read," with a brief chapter summary and chapter learning objectives; "As You Read," a collection of demonstrations, in-depth activities, and exercises; "After you Read," containing three short practice quizzes and one comprehensive practice test; "When You Have Finished," with web links for further information; and crossword puzzles using key terms from the text. An appendix includes answers to all practice tests and crossword puzzles.

MyPsychLab for Social Psychology

This interactive and instructive multimedia resource can be used to supplement a traditional lecture course or to administer a course entirely online. It is an all-inclusive tool, a text-specific e-book plus multimedia tutorials, audio, video, simulations, animations, and controlled assessments to completely engage students and reinforce learning. Fully customizable and easy to use, MyPsychLab meets the individual teaching and learning needs of every instructor and every student. Visit the site at www.mypsychlab.com.

Companion Website for Social Psychology

A unique resource for connecting the Social Psychology course to the Internet. Each topic in our course table of contents includes flashcard glossary terms; online practice tests with multiple choice, true/false, and essay questions; and learning objectives.

Research Navigator Guide: Psychology, with access to Research Navigator™

Allyn & Bacon's new Research Navigator™ is the easiest way for students to start a research assignment or research paper. Complete with extensive help on the research process and three exclusive databases of credible and reliable source material including EBSCO's ContentSelect Academic Journal Database, New York Times Search by Subject Archive, and "Best of the Web" Link Library, Research Navigator™ helps students quickly and efficiently make the most of their research time. The booklet contains a practical and to-the-point discussion of search engines; detailed information on evaluating online sources and citation guidelines for web resources; web links for Psychology; and a complete guide to Research Navigator™.

To the Student

A textbook that is hard to read or understand is like a dull tool: it can't do what it is designed to do very well. Being well aware of this fact, we have tried our best to make this book easy to read, and have included a number of features designed to make it more enjoyable and useful for you. Following is an overview of the steps we've taken to make reading this book a pleasant and informative experience.

First, each chapter begins with an outline and ends with a summary. Within the text itself, key terms are printed in **dark type like this** and are followed by a defined. These terms are also defined in a running glossary in the margins, as well as in a glossary at the end of the book. To help you understand what you have read, each major section is followed by a list of **Key Points**—a brief summary of major points. All figures and tables are clear and simple, and most contain special labels and notes designed to help you understand them. Finally, each chapter ends with the section **Summary and Review of Key Points;** reviewing this section can be an important aid to your studying.

Second, this book has an underlying theme that can be stated as follows: Social psychology is much more than just a collection of interesting findings to be enjoyed for the moment, recalled on tests, and then quickly forgotten. On the contrary, we believe that social psychology provides a new way of looking at the social world that everyone should use long after this course is over. To emphasize this theme, we include a special feature that appears in each chapter. **The Science of Social Psychology: Making Sense of Common Sense** sections are designed to highlight how the scientific approach taken by social psychology has helped to resolve—or at least clarify—the contradictions often contained in common sense. Does absence make the heart grow fonder, or is it a case of out of sight out of mind? Does blowing off steam (expressing anger and aggressive impulses) help reduce those feelings? When a judge says to a jury, "Disregard that information," can the jurors really do that? We'll examine these and many other instances in which social psychology has helped resolve questions that have persisted through the ages.

Another special feature that will help you recognize the usefulness and value of social psychology appears at the end of each chapter: **Ideas to Take with You—and Use!** These features are designed to highlight important concepts you should remember—and use—long after this course is over. In our view, you may well them find useful in your life in the years ahead.

Finally, to help you understand how research in each area of social psychology is related to research in other areas, we've included special **Connections** tables at the end of each chapter. These tables provide a kind of global review, reminding you of related topics discussed elsewhere in the book. In addition, these tables emphasize that many aspects of social behavior and thought are closely linked: They do not occur in isolation.

We think that together, these features will help you get the most out of this book and from your first encounter with social psychology. Good luck! And may your introduction to social psychology prove to be a rich, informative, and valuable experience—and also, we hope, fun!

Some Concluding Comments

We have spared no effort to make *Mastering Social Psychology* the best it can be. While it's possible to *imagine* perfection, we fully realize that it is impossible to attain. So, we sincerely request your ideas and suggestions for further improvements. If there is something you feel can be better, please let us know. Write, call, e-mail, or fax us at the addresses below. We'll be genuinely glad to receive your input and—even more important—we will definitely listen! Thanks in advance for your help.

Robert A. Baron
Pittsburgh Building
Rensselaer Polytechnic Institute
Troy, NY 12180-3590
Phone: (518) 276-2864
E-mail: baronr@rpi.edu
Fax: (518) 276-8661

Donn Byrne
Department of Psychology
University at Albany, SUNY
Albany, NY 12222
Phone: (518) 768-2643
E-mail: vyaduckdb@aol.com
Fax: (518) 442-4867

Nyla R. Branscombe
Department of Psychology
University of Kansas
1415 Jayhawk Blvd.
Lawrence, KS 66045
Phone: 785-864-9832
E-mail: nyla@ku.edu
FAX: 785-864-5696

ACKNOWLEDGMENTS

WORDS OF THANKS

Each time we write a book, we gain a stronger appreciation of the following fact: We couldn't do it without the help of many talented, dedicated people. Although we can't possibly thank all of them here, we do wish to express our appreciation to those whose help has been most valuable.

First, our sincere thanks to the colleagues listed below. Their input was invaluable to us in planning this new edition.

Betty Bachman, Ph.D., Siena College

Birgit Bryant, Le Moyne College

Tina M. Burns, Florida International University

Robert Dushay, Morrisville State College

Marcia A. Finkelstein, University of South Florida

Karen Gasper, Pennsylvania State University

Andrew Geers, University of Toledo

David Gersh, Houston Community College

Barry Gillen, Old Dominion University

Peggy Moody, Ph.D., St. Louis Community College, Florissant Valle

Lisa Neff, University of Toledo

Marcus Patterson, University of Massachusetts, Boston

Miles L. Patterson, University of Missouri, St. Louis

Vicki Ritts, Ph.D., St. Louis Community College, Meramec

Eva Szeli, Ph.D., J.D., University of Miami

Second, we wish to offer our personal thanks to Susan Hartman, our editor at Allyn & Bacon. It has been a pleasure to work with her and get to know her, and we wish to thank her for her help, enthusiasm, and efforts to make this new edition terrific. Third, our sincere thanks to Erin Liedel, our developmental editor. Fourth, our thanks to Susan McIntyre for her very careful and constructive copyediting.

We also wish to offer our thanks to the many colleagues who provided reprints and preprints of their work. These individuals are too numerous to list here, but their input is gratefully acknowledged. Special thanks are also extended to Rebecca A. Henry for her insightful comments on several of the chapters, to Amy Le Fevre for her work on the references, and to Lindsey Kelley Byrne and Rebecka Byrne Kelley for their help in many different ways.

Finally, our sincere thanks to Michele Van Volkom for her work on the Instructor's Manual, to Philip Dunwoody for his work on the Grade Aid and the PowerPoint Presentation, and Tina Burns for her work on the Test Bank. To all of these truly outstanding people, and to many others, too, our warmest personal regards and thanks.

ABOUT THE AUTHORS

Robert A. Baron is Professor of Psychology and Wellington Professor of Management at Rensselaer Polytechnic Institute. He received his Ph.D. from the University of Iowa in 1968. Professor Baron has held faculty appointments at Purdue University, the University of Minnesota, the University of Texas, the University of South Carolina, and Princeton University. In 1982 he was a Visiting Fellow at Oxford University. From 1979 to 1981 he served as a Program Director at the National Science Foundation (Washington, DC). He has been a Fellow of the American Psychological Association and is also a Fellow of the American Psychological Society. In 2001, he was appointed an  Invited Senior Research Fellow by the French government, and held this post at the Université des Sciences Sociales at Toulouse, France.

Professor Baron has published more than one hundred articles in professional journals and thirty-five chapters in edited volumes. He is the author or coauthor of forty-two books, including *Behavior in Organizations* (8th ed.), *Psychology: From Science to Practice,* and *Entrepreneurship: A Process Perspective.* Professor Baron holds three U.S. patents based on his research, and served as president of his own company (Innovative Environmental Products, Inc.) from 1992 to 2000. Professor Baron's current research focuses mainly on the social and cognitive factors that influence entrepreneurs' success, and on various forms of workplace aggression.

 **Donn Byrne** holds the rank of Distinguished Professor of Psychology at the University at Albany, State University of New York. He received his Ph.D. in 1958 from Stanford University and has held academic positions at the California State University at San Francisco, the University of Texas, and Purdue University, as well as visiting professorships at the University of Hawaii and Stanford University. He was elected president of the Midwestern Psychological Association and of the Society for the Scientific Study of Sexuality. He headed the personality program at Texas, the social-personality programs at Purdue and at Albany, and was chair of the psychology department at Albany. Professor Byrne is a Fellow of the American Psychological Association and a Charter Fellow of the American Psychological Society.

During his career, Professor Byrne has published over 150 articles in professional journals, and twenty-nine of them have been republished in books of readings. He has authored or coauthored thirty-six chapters in edited volumes, and fourteen books, including *Psychology: An Introduction to a Behavioral Science* (four editions plus translations in Spanish, Portuguese, and Chinese), *An Introduction to Personality* (three editions), *The Attraction Paradigm,* and *Exploring Human Sexuality.*

He has served on the editorial boards of fourteen professional journals, and has directed the doctoral work of fifty-two Ph.D. students. He was invited to deliver a G. Stanley Hall lecture at the 1981 meeting of the American Psychological Association in Los Angeles and a state of the science address at the 1981 meeting of the Society for the Scientific Study of Sexuality in New York City. He was invited to testify at Attorney General Meese's Commission on Obscenity and Pornography in Houston in 1986 and to participate in Surgeon General Koop's Workshop on Pornography and Health in 1986 in Arlington, Virginia. He received the Excellence in Research Award from the University at Albany in 1987 and the Distinguished Scientific Achievement Award from the Society for the Scientific Study of Sexuality in 1989. In 2002, he participated in a Festschrift honoring his scientific contributions at the University of Connecticut organized by his graduate students (past and present) from Texas, Purdue, and Albany. He delivered the William Griffitt Memorial Lecture at Kansas State University in 2004. Professor Byrne's current research focuses on the determinants of interpersonal attraction, adult attachment styles, and sexually coercive behavior.

 **Nyla R. Branscombe** is Professor of Psychology at University of Kansas. She received her B.A. from York University in Toronto in 1980, a M.A. from the University of Western Ontario in 1982, and her Ph.D. from Purdue University in 1986. Professor Branscombe held a postdoctoral appointment at the University of Illinois at Urbana–Champaign in 1987. In 1993 she was a Visiting Fellow at Free University of Amsterdam. She served as Associate Editor of *Personality and Social Psychology Bulletin* for three years, and presently serves as Associate Editor of *Group Processes and Intergroup Relations.*

Professor Branscombe has published more than eighty articles and chapters in professional journals and edited volumes. In 1999, she was a recipient of the Otto Klienberg prize for research on Intercultural and International Relations from the Society for the Psychological Study of Social Issues. In 2004, she coedited the volume, *Collective Guilt: International Perspectives.* Professor Branscombe's current research focuses primarily on two main issues: the psychology of privileged groups, in particular when and why they may feel guilt about their advantages, and the psychology of disadvantaged groups, especially how they cope with prejudice and discrimination.

Mastering Social Psychology

1 THE FIELD OF SOCIAL PSYCHOLOGY
How We Think about and Interact with Others

When I (Robert Baron) was a junior in high school, I tried out for the track team—and made it. This didn't surprise me because I had always been one of the fastest runners in my neighborhood. Being on the track team meant that I could wear a special patch on my jacket and had a chance to win medals—and glory!—when my team competed. But it also meant a lot of hard work. We had training several times a week and our coach was really tough: While performing the exercises he gave us, I discovered muscles I didn't even know I had! But I stuck with it and won a few races before I quit in my senior year to take a job after school.

But what, you are probably wondering, does this have to do with social psychology? Actually, quite a lot. At first glance it might seem as though joining a high school track team has very little to do with the social side of life, but it really *does.* Consider this: Why did I try out for the team? The answer clearly involves *influence* from other people— friends who told me, "Baron, you are fast . . . you should go out for the team." Similarly, it involved key aspects of my *self-perceptions.* I knew that my friends were right: I *was* a fast runner. This was part of my self-concept (formed by comparing myself with others—what social psychologists term *social comparison*), and I believed it was true, just as I was certain that I was too short for the basketball team. Where does our self-concept come from? As you will discover in Chapter 5, it comes largely from information provided by other people; no one can really tell that he or she is smart, attractive, friendly, or anything else by looking into a mirror. Rather, we acquire such knowledge mainly from our contacts with other persons, who tell us—over and over—what we are really like. So my decision to join the team was shaped by important social factors, such as influence and socially derived self-perceptions.

But there's more to the story. I also realized that winning a spot on the team would make me a member of a fairly elite *group;* athletes of every kind were minor heroes or heroines in my school. In addition, I liked the idea of competing and, if I were lucky, winning. *Group processes* such as these are another key focus of social psychology—and a basic fact of social life.

Finally, I believed that being on the team would make me more *attractive* to the girls in my school, and especially to one named Linda

"This model is called the 'Aunt Edna.' The
support bar digs into one's back, assuring
that unwanted guests stay only one night."

Fisher, on whom I had a major crush. As I worked out each day, I imagined her in the audience, watching me win a race and then, perhaps,
showering me with approval. So, aspects of *social thought*—how we think
about other people and the effects this has on our behavior—certainly
played a role in my decision to try out for the team. As you will note
throughout this book, social thought is a major theme of modern social
psychology.

My brief foray into the world of high school athletics illustrates a basic
fact of life and a key theme of this book: *Virtually everything we do, feel, or
think is related in some way to the social side of life.* In fact, our relations with
other people are so central to our lives that it is hard to imagine existing
without them, although as the cartoon in Figure 1.1 suggests, we can certainly live without some of them. Survivors of shipwrecks or plane crashes who spend long
periods of time alone often state that not having relationships with other people was the
hardest part of their ordeal—more difficult to bear than lack of food or shelter. In short,
the social side of life is, in many ways, the core of our existence. It is this basic fact that
makes *social psychology*—the branch of psychology that studies all aspects of social behavior
and social thought—so fascinating and so essential.

Before getting started it's important to begin with some background information about
the scope, nature, and methods of our field. Why is such information useful? Because
research findings in cognitive psychology indicate that people have a much better chance
of understanding, remembering, and using new information if they are first provided with
a framework within which to organize it. In view of this fact, this introductory chapter is
intended to provide you with a framework for interpreting and understanding social psychology and everything about it that is contained in this book. Specifically, here's an outline of what we plan to do. (By the way, we provide this kind of outline at the start of each
chapter.)

First, we present a more formal *definition* of social psychology: what it is and what it
seeks to accomplish. Second, we describe some major, current trends in social psychology.
These are reflected throughout this book, so knowing about them at the start helps you recognize them and understand why they are important. Third, we examine some of the methods used by social psychologists to answer questions about the social side of life. A working
knowledge of these basic methods will help you to understand how social psychologists add
to our knowledge of social thought and social behavior, and will also be useful to you outside the context of this course.

Social Psychology: A Working Definition

Providing a formal definition of almost any field is a complex task. In the case of social psychology, this difficulty is increased by two factors: the field's broad scope and its rapid rate of
change. As you will note in each chapter, social psychologists have a wide range of interests.

Despite this fact, most social psychologists focus primarily on understanding how and why individuals behave, think, and feel as they do in social situations—ones involving the actual or imagined presence of other persons. Consistent with this basic fact, we define **social psychology** as *the scientific field that seeks to understand the nature and causes of individual behavior and thought in social situations.* We now clarify this definition by taking a closer look at several aspects of it.

Social Psychology Is Scientific in Nature

What is *science?* Many people seem to believe that this term refers only to fields such as chemistry, physics, and biology—ones that use the kind of equipment shown in the left photo in Figure 1.2. If you share this view, you may find our suggestion that social psychology is a scientific discipline somewhat puzzling. How can a field that studies the nature of love, the causes of aggression, and everything in between be scientific in the same sense as physics, biochemistry, or computer science? The answer is surprisingly simple.

In reality, the term *science* does not refer to a special group of highly advanced fields. Rather, it refers to two things: (1) a set of values and (2) several methods that can be used to study a wide range of topics. In deciding whether a given field is or is not scientific, therefore, the critical question is, "Does it adopt these values and methods?" To the extent that it does, it is scientific in nature; to the extent it does not, it falls outside the realm of science. We examine in detail the research procedures used by social psychologists in a later section, but here we focus on the core values that all fields must adopt to be considered scientific in nature. Four of the most important core values are:

1. *Accuracy:* A commitment to gathering and evaluating information about the world (including social behavior and thought) in as careful, precise, and error-free a manner as possible.

2. *Objectivity:* A commitment to obtaining and evaluating such information in a manner that is as free of bias as is humanly possible.

3. *Skepticism:* A commitment to accepting findings as accurate only to the extent that they have been verified repeatedly.

4. *Open-mindedness:* A commitment to changing one's views—even views that are strongly held—if existing evidence suggests that these views are inaccurate.

Social psychology, as a field, is deeply committed to these values and applies them in its efforts to understand the nature of social behavior and social thought. For this reason, it makes sense to describe social psychology as scientific in orientation. In contrast, fields that are *not* scientific make assertions about the world and about people that are not subjected to the careful testing and analysis required by the values listed above. In such fields (e.g., astrology and aromatherapy), intuition, faith, and unobservable forces are considered to be sufficient for reaching conclusions (see Figure 1.2).

■ "But Why Adopt the Scientific Approach? Isn't Social Psychology Merely Common Sense?"

All of us have spent our lives interacting with other people and thinking about them, so, in a sense, we are all amateur social psychologists. Why not rely on our own experience and intuition as a basis for understanding the social side of life? Our answer is straightforward: Because such sources provide an inconsistent and unreliable guide.

For instance, consider the following statement, suggested by common sense: "Absence makes the heart grow fonder." Do you agree? When people are separated from those they love, is it true that they miss them and so experience increased longing for them? Many people would agree. They would answer, "Yes, that's right. Let me tell you about the time I was separated from . . . ." But now consider the following statement: "Out of sight, out of mind." Is it true? When people are separated from those they love, do they quickly find another romantic interest? These two views—both suggested by common sense—are con-

Chapter 1 / The Field of Social Psychology

Figure 1.2 ■ What Is Science, Really?
Many people seem to believe that only fields that use sophisticated equipment such as that shown here (*left photo*) can be viewed as scientific. In fact, though, the term *science* simply refers to adherence to a set of basic values (e.g., accuracy, objectivity) and use of a set of basic methods that can be applied to almost any aspect of the world around us, including the social side of life. In contrast, fields that are *not* scientific in nature (*right photo*) do not accept these values or use these methods.

tradictory. The same is true for many informal observations about human behavior: They seem plausible but often suggest opposite conclusions. Common sense often suggests a confusing and inconsistent picture of human behavior. This is one important reason why social psychologists put their faith in the scientific method: It yields much more conclusive evidence. In fact, the scientific method is designed to help us determine not only *which* of the opposite sets of predictions listed previously is correct, but also *when* and *why* one or the other might apply. We think this principle is so important that we call attention to it throughout the book in special sections titled **The Science of Social Psychology: Making Sense of Common Sense,** designed to show how careful research by social psychologists has helped to refine—and in some cases, to refute—the conclusions offered by common sense.

Another reason for being suspicious of common sense relates to the fact that humans are not perfect information-processing machines. On the contrary, as we note (e.g., in Chapters 2, 3, 4, and 6), our thinking is subject to several forms of error that can lead us seriously astray. Here's one example: Think back over major projects on which you have worked in the past (writing term papers, cooking a complicated dish, painting your room). Now, try to remember two things: (1) your initial estimates about how long it would take you to complete these jobs and (2) how long it actually took. Is there a gap between these two numbers? In all likelihood there is, because most of us fall victim to the *planning fallacy*—a strong tendency to believe that projects will take less time than they actually do or that we can accomplish more in a given period of time than is really true. Moreover, we are susceptible to this bias in our thoughts, despite repeated experiences that tell us that everything will take longer than we think it will.

Why are we subject to this kind of error? Research by social psychologists indicates that part of the answer involves a tendency to think about the future when we are estimating how long a job will take. This prevents us from remembering how long similar tasks took in the past, and that in turn leads us to underestimate the time we will need to accomplish the current task (e.g., Buehler, Griffin, & Ross, 1994). This is just one of the many ways in which we can—and often do—make errors in thinking about other people (and ourselves); we consider others in Chapter 3. Because we are prone to errors in our informal thinking about the social world, we cannot rely on it—or on common sense—to solve the mysteries of social behavior. Rather, we need scientific evidence; and that, in essence, is what social psychology is all about.

Social Psychology Focuses on the Behavior of Individuals

Societies differ in terms of their views concerning courtship and marriage; yet, it is still individuals who fall in love. Similarly, societies vary in terms of their overall levels of violence; yet, it is individuals who perform aggressive actions or refrain from doing so. The same argument applies to virtually all other aspects of social behavior, from prejudice to helping. Due to this basic fact, the focus in social psychology is strongly on individuals. Social psychologists realize, of course, that we do not exist in isolation from social and cultural influences—far from it. As you will see throughout this book, much social behavior occurs in group settings, and these can exert powerful effects on us. But the field's major interest lies in understanding the factors that shape the actions and thoughts of individuals in social settings.

Social Psychology Seeks to Understand the Causes of Social Behavior and Social Thought

Social psychologists are interested primarily in understanding the many factors and conditions that shape the social behavior and social thought of individuals—their actions, feelings, beliefs, memories, and inferences concerning other persons. Obviously, a huge number of variables play a role in this regard. Most variables, though, fall under the following five headings.

■ The Actions and Characteristics of Other Persons

Imagine the following events:

> *You are attending a concert in a theater when a person seated nearby receives a call on his cell phone and begins a loud conversation about very private topics.*

> *You are in a hurry and notice that you are driving far above the speed limit. Suddenly, up ahead, you see the blinking lights of a state trooper who has pulled another driver over and is giving him a ticket.*

Will these actions by other persons have any effect on your behavior and thoughts? Absolutely. You will probably become annoyed with the person speaking on the cell phone and may even say something to him. And the second you spot the state trooper's blinking light, you will almost certainly slow down. These instances indicate that other persons' behaviors often have a powerful impact on us (see Figure 1.3).

In addition, we are often affected by others' appearance. Be honest: Have you ever felt uneasy in the presence of a person with a physical disability? Do you ever behave differently toward attractive persons than toward less attractive ones? Toward elderly persons than toward young ones? Toward persons belonging to racial and ethnic groups different from your own? Your answer to some of these questions is probably "yes," because we often react to others' visible characteristics, such as their appearance (e.g., McCall, 1997; Twenge & Manis, 1998). In fact, findings reported by Hassin and Trope (2000) indicate that we cannot ignore others' appearance, even when we consciously try to do so. So, despite warnings to avoid "judging books by their covers," we are often strongly affected by other persons' outward appearance—even if we are unaware of such effects and might deny their existence.

■ Cognitive Processes

Suppose that you have arranged to meet a friend, and this person is late. In fact, after thirty minutes you begin to suspect that your friend will never arrive. Finally, she or he does appear and says, "Sorry . . . I forgot all about meeting you until a few minutes ago." How do you react? Probably with considerable annoyance. Imagine that instead your friend says, "I'm so sorry to be late. There was a big accident, and the traffic was tied up for miles." Now how

Figure 1.3 ■ **Reacting to the Actions of Other Persons**
The behaviors of other persons often exert powerful effects on our own behaviors and social thoughts.

do you react? Probably with less annoyance—but not necessarily. If your friend is often late and has used this excuse before, you may be suspicious. In contrast, if this is the first time your friend has been late, or if your friend has never used such an excuse in the past, you may accept it. In other words, your reactions depend strongly on your *memories* of your friend's past behavior and your *inferences* about whether her or his explanation is actually true. Situations such as these call attention to the fact that *cognitive processes* play a crucial role in social behavior and social thought. We are always trying to make sense out of the social world, and this effort leads us to engage in lots of social cognition—to think long and hard about other persons: what they are like, why they do what they do, how they might react to our behaviors, and so on (e.g., Shah, 2003). Social cognition is one of the most important areas of research in the field (e.g., Killeya & Johnson, 1998; Swann & Gill, 1997).

■ Environmental Variables: Impact of the Physical World

Do we become more irritable and aggressive when the weather is hot and steamy than when it is cool and comfortable (Anderson, Bushman, & Groom, 1997; Rotton & Cohn, 2000)? Does exposure to a pleasant smell in the air make people more helpful (Baron, 1997)? Research indicates that the physical environment does influence our feelings, thoughts, and behaviors, so environmental variables fall within the realm of modern social psychology.

■ Cultural Context

Have you ever seen the old TV program *Leave It to Beaver*? What about *I Love Lucy*? If so, you know that they painted a picture of a very happy world, one in which parents were kind and understanding, children loved and respected them, and divorce was nonexistent. These programs exaggerated; life in the 1950s and 1960s was not all sunshine and roses. It is true, though, that divorce rates were lower than they are at present. Why? This is a complex question, but an important part of the answer involves changing *cultural beliefs* and *values*. In previous decades, divorce was viewed as a drastic action—something done under extreme conditions (e.g., an abusive or repeatedly unfaithful spouse). Further, divorce was viewed in negative terms; cultural beliefs suggested that it was better to suffer in silence than to break up a home and family.

Although divorce is still viewed as an unhappy event, cultural beliefs have changed. Personal unhappiness is now considered adequate grounds for ending a marriage, and divorced persons are no longer viewed as unusual or somehow flawed.

These changes in beliefs concerning divorce are only one illustration of an important and basic fact: Social behavior does not occur in a cultural vacuum. On the contrary, social behavior is often strongly affected by *cultural norms* (social rules concerning how people should behave in specific situations; see Chapter 9), membership in various groups, and changing societal values. Cultural norms say a lot about important life decisions, such as when people should marry and who, how many children they should have and so on. Clearly, social behavior and social thought can be, and often are, strongly affected by cultural factors. (The term *culture* refers to the system of shared meanings, perceptions, and beliefs held by persons belonging to some group [Smith & Bond, 1993].) As you'll soon discover, attention to the effects of cultural factors is an important trend in social psychology as the field attempts to take account of the growing cultural diversity in many countries.

Social Psychology: A Working Definition

■ Biological Factors

Do biological processes and genetic factors influence social behavior? In the past, most social psychologists would have answered "no," at least to the genetic part of this question. Now, however, many have come to believe that our preferences, behaviors, emotions, and even attitudes are affected, to some extent, by our biological inheritance (Buss, 1999; Buss & Schmitt, 1993; Schmitt, 2004; Nisbett, 1990).

The view that biological factors play an important role in social behavior comes from the field of **evolutionary psychology** (e.g., Buss, 1999; Buss & Shackelford, 1997). This new branch of psychology suggests that all species have been subjected to the process of biological evolution throughout history, and that as a result of this process, we now possess a large number of *evolved psychological mechanisms* that help (or once helped) us deal with important survival problems. How do these mechanisms become part of our biological inheritance? It happens through the process of evolution, which, in turn, involves three basic components: *variation, inheritance,* and *selection.* Variation refers to the fact that organisms belonging to a given species vary in different ways. Human beings, as you know, come in a wide variety of shapes and sizes, and they vary on an almost countless number of dimensions. Inheritance refers to the fact that some of these variations can be passed from one generation to the next through complex mechanisms that we are only now beginning to fully understand. Selection refers to the fact that some variations give the individuals who possess them an edge in terms of reproduction: They are more likely to survive, find mates, and pass these variations on to succeeding generations. The result is that, over time, more members of the species possess these variations. This change in the characteristics of a species over time—often immensely long periods of time—is the concrete outcome of evolution (see Figure 1.4).

Social psychologists who adopt the evolutionary perspective suggest that this process applies to at least some aspects of social behavior. For instance, why do we find some people attractive? According to the evolutionary perspective, the characteristics they show—symmetrical facial features; well-toned, shapely bodies (e.g., a relatively large waist-to-hip ratio in women; Schmitt & Buss, 2001; Tesser & Martin, 1996); clear skin; lustrous hair—are associated with reproductive capacity. Thus, a preference for these characteristics in mates among our ancestors increased the chances that they would reproduce successfully; this, in turn, contributed to our preference for these aspects of appearance.

A related question involves what evolutionary psychologists term *short-term mating strategies*—how many sexual partners people would prefer to have without commitment. Informal observation suggests that a gender difference may exist, with men preferring many partners and women preferring a smaller number. An evolutionary perspective suggests that such differences, if they exist, are the result of evolutionary pressures. For instance, although men can father an almost infinite number of children and therefore pass their genes on to many offspring, women can have a limited number, no matter how many sexual partners they have (e.g., Barash & Lipton, 2001; Buss & Schmitt, 1993).

Consider a recent study by Schmitt (2004) that involved more than sixteen thousand people living

evolutionary psychology
A new branch of psychology that seeks to investigate the potential role of genetic factors in various aspects of human behavior.

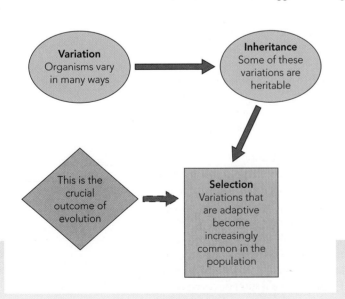

Figure 1.4 ■ Evolution: An Overview
As shown here, evolution involves three major components: variation, inheritance, and selection.

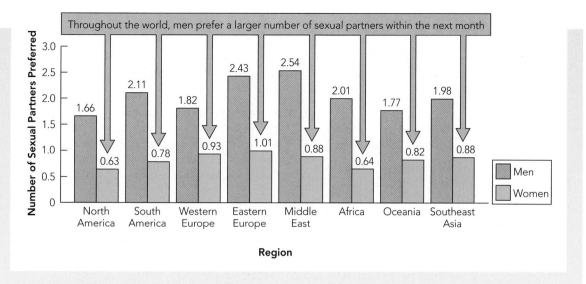

Figure 1.5 ■ Gender Differences in Short-Term Mating Strategies
As shown here, men preferred a larger number of sexual partners within the next month than did women. The fact that this finding occurs in many cultures throughout the world indicates that genetic factors may play a role in its occurrence, as an *evolutionary* perspective suggests. (*Source: Based on data from Schmitt, 2003b.*)

in virtually every major region of the world (North America, South America, Western Europe, Eastern Europe, Africa, the Middle East, Oceania, Southeast Asia, East Asia). Participants were asked questions relating to how many different sexual partners they would like to have over varying periods of time (from one month to their entire lifetimes), and how long they would want to know someone before having sexual relations with that person. Regardless of the measures used and across every region studied, men indicated a preference for more partners than did women (see Figure 1.5) and reported that they would require knowing someone for a shorter period of time. The fact that these differences in the desired number of partners occur in different cultures points to the possibility that this difference between men and women may have some genetic component.

Many other topics have been studied from the evolutionary perspective (e.g., helping others, and preferences for various ways of attracting persons who are already in a relationship—*mate poaching* [e.g., Schmitt, 2004; Schmitt & Shackelford, 2003]), and we will consider such research in Chapters 10 and 11. Here, however, we emphasize an important fact: The evolutionary perspective does *not* suggest that we inherit specific patterns of social behavior. Rather, it contends that we inherit tendencies or predispositions that may or may not be translated into reality, depending on the environments in which we live. Similarly, this perspective does *not* suggest that we are "forced" or driven by our genes to act in specific ways. It merely suggests that because of our genetic inheritance, we have tendencies to behave in certain ways that, at least in the past, enhanced the chances that our ancestors would survive and pass their genes on to us. These tendencies, however, can be reduced or overridden by cognitive factors and the effects of experience (i.e., learning). For example, recent findings (Pettijohn & Jungeberg, 2004) indicate that men's preferences for certain facial and body characteristics in women may change with shifting economic conditions. When economic conditions are bad, men's preferences tend to shift toward more mature-looking women (e.g., ones with smaller eyes, larger chins, and fuller figures), as compared to when economic conditions are good. These findings suggest that even if we do have biologically based tendencies to find others with certain traits attractive, these tendencies can readily be overridden by other factors. So, the evolutionary perspective does *not* accept the view that biology is destiny— far from it.

KEY POINTS

★ *Social psychology* is the scientific field that seeks to understand the nature and causes of individual behavior and thought in social situations.

★ *Social psychology* is scientific in nature because it adopts the values and methods used in other fields of science.

★ Social psychologists adopt the scientific method because common sense provides an unreliable guide to social behavior and because our thoughts are influenced by many potential sources of bias.

★ *Social psychology* focuses on the behavior of individuals and seeks to understand the causes of social behavior and thought, which can involve the behavior and appearance of others, social cognition, environmental factors, cultural values, and even biological and genetic factors.

Social Psychology: Its Cutting Edge

We feel strongly that any textbook should reflect the field it covers in an accurate and up-to-date manner. The remainder of this text is devoted to describing some of the key findings of social psychology. This information is fascinating, so we're certain that you will find it of interest. We're equally sure, however, that you will also find some of it surprising, and that it will challenge many of your ideas about people and social relations.

Cognition and Behavior: Two Sides of the Same Social Coin

In the past, social psychologists could be divided into two groups: those who were interested primarily in social behavior (how people act in social situations) and those who were interested primarily in social thought (how people attempt to make sense out of the social world and to understand themselves and others). This division has largely disappeared. In modern social psychology, there is virtually universal agreement in the field that we cannot hope to understand how and why people behave in certain ways in social situations without considering their thoughts, memories, intentions, attitudes, and beliefs. Similarly, virtually all social psychologists agree that we cannot hope to fully understand how people think about the social world without considering how such social cognition affects their behavior and their relations with others. Perhaps a concrete example of what we mean will be helpful.

Consider the following question: Who would you like better—someone who seems to be very similar to you in many ways or someone who is different? Decades of research point to the conclusion that, in general, the more similar others are to us, the more we tend to like them. But is this always true? We all have a mental picture of what we are like right now—our *actual self*—and a mental picture of the kind of person we would like to be—our *ideal self.* Suppose that someone is not merely similar to you as you view yourself but is more similar to what you'd like to be in the future. In other words, he or she is closer to your ideal self than you are. Would you like this person? Perhaps, but it is also possible that you would find the situation a little threatening; after all, he or she is currently where you want to be in the future.

Recent research by Herbst, Gaertner, and Insko (2003) has confirmed this kind of effect. They asked participants to rate themselves on thirty different dimensions (e.g., talkative—reserved; generous—stingy) both in terms of how they were right now (their actual self) and how they would like to be in the future (their ideal self). During a second session, a week later, participants received information indicating that on the basis of their earlier ratings, a computer program had derived a key defining dimension for them. They also received information about a stranger they would supposedly meet later. This stranger appeared to vary in terms of similarity to a participant's ideal self.

In three conditions, he or she was increasingly similar but lower than a participant's ideal self on the key dimension. In one condition, however, the stranger was actually higher than a participant; in other words, the stranger's current actual self was higher than a participant's ideal self. After receiving this information, the participants in the study rated their liking for the stranger. The researchers predicted that increasing similarity to a participant's ideal self would lead to greater liking for the stranger until this person surpassed the participant's ideal self, but then liking would decrease and this is precisely what happened.

The findings illustrate the main point we wish to make: There is a continuous, complex interplay between social thought (how people think about themselves and others) and social behavior (how people act in social situations). For example, do they like or dislike others they meet for the first time? This perspective is now a given in modern social psychology, and it is a major theme in this book.

Social Neuroscience: Where Social Psychology and Neuroscience Meet

Do you understand these words as you read them? If so, that ability is the result of activity in your brain. Do you feel happy? Sad? Excited? Calm? Again, whatever you feel derives from activity in your brain and other biological events. Can you remember what your psychology professor looks like? What your first kiss felt like? Once more, that ability is the result of activity in several areas of your brain. In recent years, powerful tools such as magnetic resonance imaging (MRI) and PET scans (see Figure 1.6) have allowed psychologists and other scientists to peer into the human brain as people engage in various activities (e.g., while solving problems, looking at emotion-provoking photos or films, etc.). As a result, we now know more about the complex relationships between neural events and psychological ones (feelings, thoughts, and overt actions).

In recent years, social psychologists have begun to search for the neural foundations of social thought and social behavior. In fact, the volume of research on this topic has increased greatly (e.g., Harmon-Jones & Devine, 2003). In conducting this research, social psychologists use the same basic tools as other scientists: They study events in the brain (through the use of MRI and other kinds of brain scans), other neural activity, and even changes in the immune system (e.g., Taylor et al., 2003) to determine how these events are related to important social processes.

Consider a recent study by Ito and Urland (2003) concerning *social categorization*—how we decide whether individuals belong to one social category or another (e.g., black or white, male or female, liberal or conservative, etc.). These researchers studied the neural basis of this process by recording special kinds of electrical activity in the brain known as *event-related potentials*. Such events can occur very soon after people see a stimulus (e.g., another person) and reflect immediate

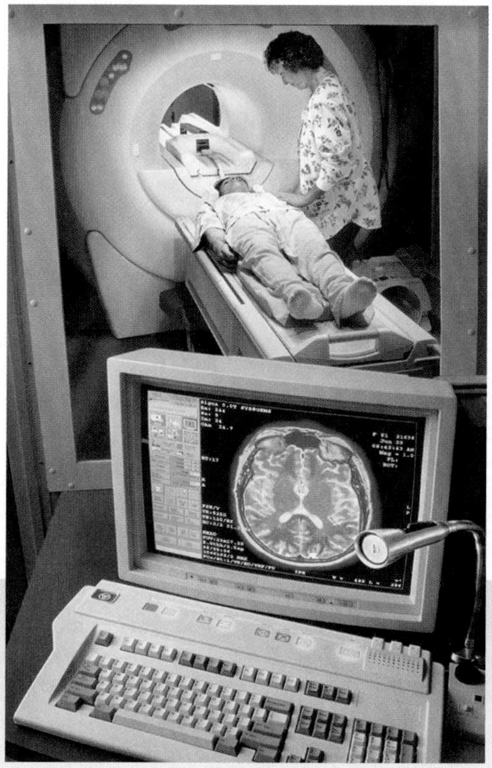

Figure 1.6 ■ Modern Techniques for Studying the Functioning Brain: One Foundation for Social Neuroscience
In recent years, techniques for studying activity in the functioning human brain have been devised (e.g., MRIs, PET scans). These techniques have allowed social psychologists to begin a scientific search for the neural roots of social processes.

reactions to the stimulus, while others occur later and seem to reflect more complex cognitive events, such as the operation of memory processes. In their study, Ito and Urland asked college students (almost all of whom were white) to indicate whether people shown in photographs were black or white and male or female. The photos were shown for one second each, and participants in the study indicated their judgment by pushing keys labeled "black," "white," "female," and "male." While they performed this task, recordings were made of several kinds of event-related brain potentials. Results indicated that, initially, attention was directed more to black than to white targets (i.e., photographs of black persons elicited larger potentials, indicating more attention). Later, but still relatively early in the process of social categorization, attention shifted to gender, with female targets inducing larger reactions than male targets. Only later did more complex factors relating to social context come into play, such as whether black persons were shown among other black persons or among white persons, and whether females were shown with other females or with males. Overall, the findings indicate that social categorization occurs very quickly—within one hundred milliseconds of seeing another person—and that people seem to pay attention to racial identity before they direct attention to gender. In other words, social categorization is not only fast, it also follows a distinct order in which we first pay attention to some kinds of information, then to others, and so on.

social neuroscience
An area of research in social psychology that seeks knowledge about the neural and biological bases of social processes.

Research in the growing field of **social neuroscience** has investigated many topics—everything from how alcohol and other drugs affect our perceptions of other persons (Bartholow et al., 2003) to ways in which social thought can affect our health (e.g., people who view themselves in positive ways tend to be more resistant to stress than persons who do not engage in such self-enhancement) (Taylor et al., 2003). However, as noted by several experts (e.g., Cacioppo et al., 2003), social neuroscience cannot provide the answer to every question we have about social thought or behavior. For example, as Willingham and Dunn (2003) note, there are many aspects of social thought that cannot easily be related to activity in specific areas of the brain—aspects such as stereotypes, attitudes, attributions, and reciprocity. In principle, these components of social thought reflect activity in the brain, but this does not necessarily mean that it is best to try to study them in this way. Social psychology does not have to seek to understand all of its major topics in terms of activities in the brain or nervous system; other approaches (described in later chapters) are still useful and provide important new insights. Throughout this book, therefore, we describe research that uses a wide range of methods, from brain scans to direct observations of social behavior—methods that reflect the current, eclectic nature of social psychology.

The Role of Implicit (Nonconscious) Processes

Have you ever met someone for the first time and taken an immediate liking or disliking to that person? Afterward, you may have wondered, "Why do I like (dislike) this person?" You probably didn't wonder for long, because we are all experts at finding good reasons to explain our own actions or feelings. This explanation in no way implies, however, that we really *do* understand why we behave or think in certain ways. In fact, a growing theme of recent research in social psychology is this: In many cases, we really don't know why we think or behave as we do in social contexts. On the contrary, our thoughts and actions are shaped by factors and processes of which we are only dimly aware at best, and that often take place automatically, without any conscious thought or intention on our part. This is one more reason why social psychologists are reluctant to trust common sense as a basis for reliable information about social behavior or social thought: We are unaware of many of the factors that influence how we think and how we behave and so cannot report on them accurately.

A very dramatic—and intriguing—illustration of this basic principle is provided by Pelham, Mirenberg, and Jones (2002) in a paper entitled, "Why Susie Sells Seashells by the Seashore. . . ." In this research, the authors argued that as a result of *implicit egotism*—an unconscious tendency toward self-enhancement—our feelings about almost anything are influenced by its relationship to our self-concept. The closer someone or something is to our self-concept, the more we will tend to like them or it. As a result, people will tend to live, at a higher rate than chance would predict, in places (cities or states) whose names resemble their own (e.g., people named Louis are more likely to live in St. Louis). Similarly, they will tend to live, at a greater than expected rate, in cities whose names begin with the numbers of their birthdays (e.g., Three Corners; Seven Springs) and will tend to choose careers whose names resemble their own (e.g., people named Dennis or Denise will be overrepresented among dentists, while people named Lawrence or Laura will be overrepresented among lawyers). In ten separate studies, Pelham, Mirenberg, and Jones found evidence for these predictions. While questions have been raised about the validity of these findings (Gallucci, 2003), additional evidence offers support for the original conclusion: Our preferences for the places in which we live and the careers we choose can be influenced by reactions and feelings we don't even realize we have (Pelham et al., 2003).

Research on the role of implicit (nonconscious) processes in our social behavior and thought has examined many other topics, such as the impact of our moods on what we tend to remember about other persons or complex issues (e.g., Ruder & Bless, 2003); how negative attitudes toward members of social groups other than our own, which we deny having, can still influence our reactions toward them (e.g., Fazio & Hilden, 2001); how we automatically evaluate persons belonging to various social groups once we have concluded that they belong to that group (Castelli, Zogmaister, & Smith, 2004); and how our tendency to assume that other people's behavior reflects their underlying traits rather than their reactions to the present situation can interfere with our ability to tell when they are lying (O'Sullivan, 2003). In short, the more deeply social psychologists delve into this topic, the broader and more general the effects of nonconscious factors in our social behavior and thought seem to be. We examine such effects in several subsequent chapters because they are clearly on the cutting edge of progress in this field.

Taking Full Account of Social Diversity

There can be no doubt that the United States is undergoing a major social and cultural transformation. The census of 2000 indicates that 67 percent of the population identifies itself as white (of European heritage), while fully 33 percent identifies itself as belonging to some other group (13 percent African American, 4.5 percent American Indian, 13 percent Hispanic, 4.5 percent Asian/Pacific Islander, and 7 percent some other group). This represents a tremendous change from the 1960s, when approximately 90 percent of the population was of European descent. Indeed, in several states (e.g., California, New Mexico, Texas, Arizona), persons of European heritage are no longer a clear majority. In response to these tremendous shifts, psychologists recognize the importance of taking cultural factors and differences into account in everything they do—teaching, research, counseling, and therapy. Social psychologists have been increasingly sensitive to the fact that individuals' cultural, ethnic, and racial heritages often play key roles in their self-identities, which can exert important effects on their behaviors. This contrasts the point of view that prevailed in the past, which suggested that cultural, ethnic, and gender differences are relatively unimportant. Psychology in general and social psychology, too, now adopt a **multicultural perspective**—one that carefully and clearly recognizes the potential importance of gender, age, ethnicity, sexual orientation, disability, socioeconomic status, religious orientation, and many other social and cultural dimensions.

multicultural perspective
A focus on understanding the cultural and ethnic factors that influence social behavior.

This perspective led to important changes in the focus of social psychological research. Recent studies conducted by social psychologists focus on ethnic and cultural differences in a wide range of social processes, including recognizing faces of persons belonging to one's own race versus those belonging to another race (e.g., Twenge & Crocker, 2002), cultural differences in binge drinking (Luczak, 2001), ethnic differences in optimism and pessimism (Chang & Asakawa, 2003), cultural and ethnic differences in reactions to sexual harassment (Cortina, 2004), and even cultural differences in attraction and love (e.g., Langlois et al., 2000). Increased recognition of diversity is a hallmark of modern social psychology, and we discuss research highlighting the importance of such factors at many points in this book.

KEY POINTS

★ Social psychologists currently recognize that social thought and social behavior are two sides of the same coin and that there is a continuous, complex interplay between them.

★ Another major field of study involves growing interest in *social neuroscience*—efforts to relate activity in the brain and other biological events to key aspects of social thought and behavior.

★ Often our behavior and thoughts are shaped by factors of which we are unaware. Growing attention to such implicit (nonconscious) processes is another major theme of modern *social psychology*.

★ *Social psychology* currently adopts a *multicultural perspective*, which recognizes the importance of cultural factors in social behavior and thought.

Answering Questions about Social Behavior and Social Thought: Research Methods in Social Psychology

Now that we've described the current state of social psychology, we can turn to the third major task mentioned at the beginning of this chapter: explaining how social psychologists attempt to answer questions about social behavior and social thought—how they conduct their research. First, we will describe several *methods of research in social psychology*. Next, we consider the role of *theory* in such research. Finally, we touch on some of the complex *ethical issues* relating to social psychological research. Before beginning, though, we need to consider one other question about which you may already be wondering: Why should you bother to learn about the research methods used by social psychologists?

Understanding Research Methods: What's in It for You

Do you plan to become a psychologist? A social psychologist? If so, it is obvious why you need to know something about the basic methods of research. But even if you do not plan a career in social psychology, there are several reasons why it is very useful to know about these methods.

First, understanding how research is actually conducted will help you to understand many of the discussions in this text. Often, we will describe specific studies and what they tell us about the topics being considered. In this effort, we will assume that you have a working knowledge of the basic methods of research used by social psychologists. So, clearly, this information will be useful to you in this respect.

Second, and perhaps more important, understanding the nature of research will help you to be a more informed consumer of knowledge. Almost every time you pick up a newspaper or magazine, you will find articles dealing with some aspect of the social side of life: Why do people fall in love? Why do they join cults? Are they affected by violent movies and video games? What are their attitudes toward the president, new fashion trends, or almost anything else? How should you interpret the findings reported? In part, by asking "How was this information obtained?" Some methods provide answers in which you can have more confidence than others, and understanding the nature of research—and its basic rules—will help you to decide what you should believe and what you should reject.

Finally, a working knowledge of research methods will help you avoid some tempting logical traps into which most people fall. For instance, many people do not seem clear about the difference between correlations and causation; they assume that if two variables seem to be related, one must cause the other. As you will discover, this assumption is wrong, and a working knowledge of research methods will help you avoid this and other common errors people make. Overall, then, knowing about the methods used by social psychologists is useful in ways that go far beyond this book and course.

Systematic Observation: Describing the World around Us

One basic technique for studying social behavior involves **systematic observation**—carefully observing behavior as it occurs. Such observation is not the kind of informal observation we all practice from childhood. Rather, in a scientific field such as social psychology, it is observation accompanied by careful, accurate measurement. For example, suppose that a social psychologist wanted to find out how frequently people touch each other in different settings (see Chapter 3). The researcher could study this topic by going to shopping malls, airports, college campuses, and so on and observing in those settings who touches whom, how they touch, and with what frequency. Such research uses what is known as *naturalistic observation*—observation of behavior in natural settings (Linden, 1992). Note that, in such observation, the researcher simply notices what is happening in various contexts; she or he makes no attempt to change the behavior of the subjects being observed. Such observation requires that the researcher take great pains to *avoid* influencing the subjects observed in any way. Thus, the psychologist tries to remain as inconspicuous as possible.

Another technique that is often included under the heading of systematic observation is known as the **survey method.** Researchers ask large numbers of persons to respond to questions about their attitudes or behavior. Surveys are used for many purposes: to measure attitudes toward specific issues, to find out how voters feel about various political candidates, and even to assess student reactions to professors. Social psychologists sometimes use this method to measure attitudes concerning social issues—for instance, national health care or affirmative action programs.

Surveys offer several advantages. Information can be gathered about thousands or even hundreds of thousands of persons with relative ease. In fact, surveys are now often conducted online. For instance, one of us (Robert Baron) has been conducting one such study to find out how consumers who work with Microsoft and other large companies to help these companies develop better new products feel about the experience, and whether they would repeat it. (This is known as *co-innovation,* because consumers and companies work together to develop something new; see Figure 1.7.)

To be useful as a research tool, though, surveys must meet certain requirements. First, the persons who participate must be *representative* of the larger population about which conclusions are to be drawn—the issue of *sampling*. If this condition is not met,

systematic observation
A method of research in which behavior is systematically observed and recorded.

survey method
A method of research in which large numbers of persons answer questions about their attitudes or behavior.

Figure 1.7 ■ Surveys on the Internet: An Example
The page shown here is from a survey conducted on the Internet. The survey is concerned with reactions individuals have to *co-innovation*—helping large companies develop better products—by targeting people in online product communities.

Instructions: Please answer the survey questions based on your experience or interactions in an online product community (e.g. Microsoft Windows XP newsgroup). The term 'product' in the survey questions refers to the product (or, products) that the online community is based on (e.g. Windows XP). The term 'product vendor' relates to the manufacturer of that product (e.g. Microsoft, HP). Once again, thank you!

1. Nature of your interactions in the online community

The following statements relate to the nature of your interactions in the online product community. For each item, please mark the box that best describes your interactions.

	S. Disagree				S. Agree
1.1. The amount of information about product design, features, and usage contained in my interactions in the online community is very large.	○	○	○	○	○
1.2. The amount of information about new product and product versions contained in my interactions in the online community is very large.	○	○	○	○	○
1.3. The amount of information about competing or other similar products contained in my interactions in the online community is very large.	○	○	○	○	○
1.4. The amount of information about the product vendor (e.g. Microsoft, HP) and their product plans contained in my interactions in the online community is very large.	○	○	○	○	○
1.5. The amount of information relevant to my profession/work that is contained in my interactions in the online community is very large.	○	○	○	○	○
1.6. The amount of information about other community members' personal/social issues contained in my interactions in the online community is very large.	○	○	○	○	○
1.7. The amount of information about hobbies, sports, politics, and other general interest topics contained in my interactions in the online community is very large.	○	○	○	○	○

serious errors can result. Yet another issue that must be carefully addressed with respect to surveys is this: The way in which the items are worded can exert strong effects on the outcomes obtained. For example, suppose a survey asked, "Do you think that persons convicted of multiple murders should be executed?" Many people might answer "yes"; after all, the convicted criminals have murdered several victims. But if the survey asked, "Are you in favor of the death penalty?" a smaller percentage might answer "yes." So, the way in which questions are posed can strongly affect the results.

Correlation: The Search for Relationships

You have probably noticed that some events appear to be related to each other: As one changes, the other changes, too. For example, perhaps you've noticed that people who drive new, expensive cars tend to be older than people who drive old, inexpensive ones, or that when interest rates rise, the stock market often falls. When two events are related in this way, they are said to be *correlated,* or that a correlation exists between them. The term *correlation* refers to a tendency for one event to change as the other changes. Social psychologists refer to such changeable aspects of the natural world as *variables,* because they can take different values.

From the scientific point of view, the existence of a correlation between two variables can be very useful. When a correlation exists, it is possible to predict one variable from information about one or more other variables. The ability to make such *predictions* is one important goal of all branches of science, including social psychology. For instance, imagine that a correlation is observed between certain attitudes on the part of individuals (one variable) and the likelihood that they will later engage in workplace violence against coworkers or their bosses (another variable). This correlation could be useful in identifying potentially dangerous persons so that companies can avoid hiring them.

How accurately can such predictions be made? The stronger the correlation between the variables in question, the more accurate the predictions. Correlations can range from zero to −1.00 or +1.00; the greater the departure from zero, the stronger the correlation. Positive numbers mean that as one variable increases, the other increases as well. Negative numbers indicate that as one variable increases, the other decreases. For instance, there is a negative correlation between age and the amount of hair on the heads of males: The older they are, the less hair they have.

These basic facts underlie an important method of research sometimes used by social psychologists: the **correlational method.** In this approach, social psychologists attempt to determine whether and to what extent different variables are related to each other. This method involves making careful observations of each variable and then performing appropriate statistical tests to determine whether and to what degree the variables are correlated.

Here is a concrete example: A social psychologist wants to find out if, as common sense seems to suggest, people who are in a good mood are more likely to be helpful to others than are persons in a bad mood. How could research on this **hypothesis**—an as-yet-unverified prediction—be conducted? The researcher might ask people to complete a questionnaire that measures their typical mood during the course of the day. Participants in the research would also be asked to report how many times they are helpful to others each day. If positive correlations are obtained between these two factors—between mood and helpfulness—this would provide evidence for the hypothesis that being in a good mood is indeed related to helping.

If the finding obtained in the research was a correlation of +.51 between mood and helpfulness, what could we conclude? That being in a good mood causes people to help others? Although it's tempting to jump to this conclusion, it may be false. Here's why: *The fact that two variables are correlated in no way guarantees that changes in one cause changes in the other.* On the contrary, the relationship between them may be due to chance, to random factors, or to the fact that changes in *both* variables are related to a third variable (see Figure 1.8). For instance, in this case, it is possible that being in a good mood doesn't really make people more helpful; rather, it may simply be that people who are often in a good mood are friendlier than people who are not often in a good mood, and it is *this* factor that results in their showing higher levels of helpfulness. Why? Because their friendliness encourages oth-

correlational method
A method of research in which a scientist systematically observes two or more variables to determine whether changes in one are accompanied by changes in the other.

hypothesis
An as-yet-unverified prediction.

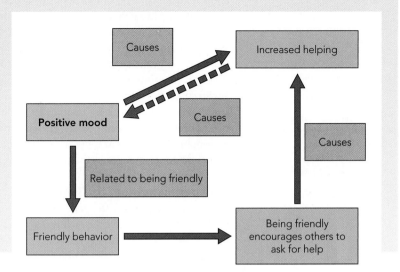

Figure 1.8 ■ Why Correlation Does Not Necessarily Mean Causation
Suppose that a correlation is found between mood and helping: The better people's moods, the more instances of helping. Does this mean that being in a good mood causes increased helpfulness (*upper path*)? Not necessarily. As shown here, people who are often in a good mood also tend to be friendlier than others. This, in turn, encourages others to ask them for help. So, they are more helpful not *because* they are in a good mood, but because of this other factor (their increased friendliness; *lower path*). In addition, helping others may cause boosts in our mood rather than vice versa (*dotted arrow*).

ers to ask them for favors or other kinds of help. After all, would you be more likely to ask a smiling person for a favor or one who is frowning? Thus, the fact that people in a good mood engage in more helping than do persons who are not in a good mood may stem from this factor—not from any direct connection between mood and helpfulness.

There is still one further complication: It is also possible that helping others *puts us in a good mood.* In other words, it's not that being in a good mood causes increased helpfulness, but that helping produces boosts in our mood. Correlations simply tell us that two variables are related; they do *not* indicate the directions of these effects. For additional illustrations of strong correlations between two variables, see the **Ideas to Take with You— and Use!** section at the end of this chapter.

Despite this major drawback, the correlational method of research is sometimes very useful to social psychologists. It can be used in natural settings, and it is often highly efficient: A large amount of information can be obtained in a relatively short period of time. However, the fact that it is generally not conclusive with respect to cause-and-effect relationships is a serious drawback, which leads social psychologists to prefer a different method. It is to this approach that we turn next.

KEY POINTS

★ In *systematic observation,* behavior is carefully observed and recorded. In naturalistic observation, such observations are made in settings in which the behavior naturally occurs.

★ In the *survey method,* large numbers of persons respond to questions about their attitudes or behavior.

★ In the *correlational method* of research, two or more variables are measured to determine if they are related to one another.

★ The existence of correlations between variables does not indicate that they are causally related to each other.

The Experimental Method: Knowledge through Systematic Intervention

As we have just seen, the correlational method of research is useful from the point of view of one important goal of science: making accurate predictions. The correlational method is less useful, though, in attaining another important goal: *explanation.* This is sometimes known as the "why" question, because scientists do not merely wish to describe the world and relationships among variables in it: They want to be able to *explain* these relationships, too. For instance, continuing with the mood and helpfulness example, if a link between being in a good mood and a tendency to help others does exist, social psychologists would want to know *why* this is so. Does being in a good mood automatically trigger kindness, without any conscious thought? Does it make us less able to say no to others? Or does it make us feel good about ourselves?

To attain the goal of explanation, social psychologists employ a method of research known as **experimentation,** or the **experimental method.** As the heading of this section suggests, experimentation involves the following strategy: One variable is changed systematically, and the effects of this change on one or more other variables are carefully measured. If systematic changes in one variable produce changes in another variable (and if the two additional conditions we describe below are also met), it is possible to conclude with reasonable certainty that there is a causal relationship between these variables: that changes in one do *cause* changes in the other.

■ Experimentation: Its Basic Nature

In its most basic form, the experimental method involves two key steps: (1) The presence or strength of some variable believed to affect an aspect of social behavior or thought is systematically changed, and (2) the effects of such changes (if any) are carefully measured. The factor systematically varied by the researcher is termed the **independent variable,** while the aspect of behavior studied is termed the **dependent variable.** In a simple experiment, different groups of participants are exposed to contrasting levels of the independent variable (such as low, moderate, and high). The researcher carefully measures their behavior to determine whether it varies with these changes in the independent variable. If it does—and if two other conditions are also met—the researcher can tentatively conclude that the independent variable causes changes in the aspect of behavior being studied.

To illustrate the basic nature of experimentation in social psychology, let's return to the mood and helpfulness example. How could a social psychologist study this topic through experimentation? The researcher could arrange for participants to come to a laboratory or other setting, where two things happen: (1) They are exposed to experiences designed to change their mood (to put them either in a good, a neutral, or a bad mood), and (2) they then have one or more opportunities to act in a helpful way. For instance, to vary their moods, the participants might be asked to perform some task and then receive either strong praise of their performance (which would induce a positive mood), neutral feedback (which would not change their mood much), or harshly negative feedback (which would induce a negative mood). Notice the word *either* in the preceding sentence—it is important because it means that participants would be put in either a good mood, a neutral mood, or a negative mood. Soon after the mood-changing procedures, they might be asked to make a donation to a charitable organization or to volunteer their time for more research or to help someone (e.g., another participant) in various ways.

If the results of this study look like those in Figure 1.9, the researcher could tentatively conclude that being in a good mood does produce increased helpfulness. Why? Because if the study were done correctly, the only difference between the experiences of participants assigned to the good mood, neutral mood, or negative mood conditions is that they receive contrasting feedback designed to alter their moods. As a result, any difference in their behaviors (i.e., in their helpfulness) must be due to this factor. It's important to note that in experimentation, such knowledge is obtained through direct intervention: A participant's mood—the independent variable—is systematically changed by the

experimentation (experimental method)
A method of research in which one or more factors (the independent variables) are systematically changed to determine whether such variations affect one or more other factors (dependent variables).

independent variable
The variable that is systematically changed (i.e., varied) in an experiment.

dependent variable
The variable that is measured in an experiment.

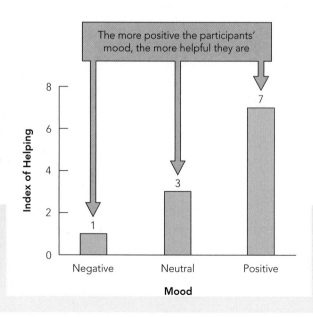

Figure 1.9 ■ Experimentation: A Simple Example
In the study shown here, the participants were exposed to feedback designed to induce a positive, a neutral, or a negative mood. Then they were given an opportunity to act in a helpful way. Results indicated that the more positive their mood, the greater their helpfulness.

Chapter 1 / The Field of Social Psychology

researcher. In the correlational method, in contrast, variables are *not* altered in this manner; rather, naturally occurring changes in them are simply observed and recorded.

■ Experimentation: Two Requirements for Its Success

Earlier, we referred to two conditions that must be met before a researcher can conclude that changes in an independent variable have caused changes in a dependent variable. The first involves what is termed **random assignment of participants to experimental conditions,** meaning that all participants in an experiment must have an equal chance of being exposed to each level of the independent variable. The reason for this rule is simple: If participants are *not* randomly assigned to each condition, it may later be impossible to determine whether differences in their behavior stem from differences they brought with them to the study, from the impact of the independent variable, or both. For instance, imagine that in the study just described, one of the assistants decides to collect all the data for the positive mood condition on one day and all the data for the negative mood condition on the next day. On the first day, perhaps a very sad event occurred—there was an explosion on a space shuttle, and it seems likely that all the astronauts on board will die—while on the second day, a miracle occurred and the crew returned safely. Results indicate that participants in the good mood condition are actually *less* helpful than those in the negative mood condition. Can you see why this might happen? All participants on the first day are in such a negative mood that the positive feedback fails to make them happy, while all those the next day are in such a happy mood that even the negative feedback seems unimportant and doesn't lower their moods. So, we can't tell *why* the results occurred, because the principle of random assignment of participants to experimental conditions has been violated.

The second condition essential for successful experimentation is as follows: Insofar as is possible, all factors other than the independent variable that might also affect participants' behavior must be held constant. Consider what would happen if, in the study on mood and helping, the research is conducted in rooms in which the temperature varies greatly. Sometimes the rooms are comfortable, and sometimes they are hot and stuffy. As a result, there are no effects of mood on helping. What causes this? It is possible that mood really has no impact on helpfulness. It is also possible, however, that changes in temperature play a role. Uncomfortable conditions put people in a bad mood, and because this factor is not being systematically varied by the researcher, it is impossible to determine what effects, if any, it has had on the results. In situations such as this, the independent variable is said to be *confounded* with another variable—one that is *not* under systematic investigation in the study. When such confounding occurs, the findings of an experiment may be largely meaningless (see Figure 1.10).

random assignment of participants to experimental conditions A basic requirement for conducting valid experiments. According to this principle, research participants must have an equal chance of being exposed to each level of the independent variable.

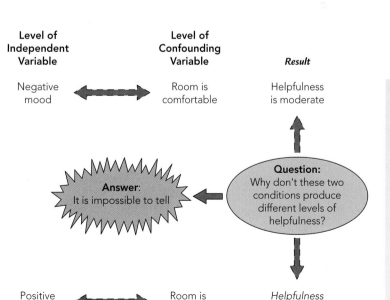

Figure 1.10 ■ Confounding of Variables: A Fatal Flaw in Experimentation
In a hypothetical experiment designed to investigate the effects of mood on helping, mood—the *independent variable*—is confounded with another variable: temperature in the rooms where the study is conducted. Sometimes, the room is very hot and sometimes the room is comfortable. Results indicate no effects of mood on helping. Why? It is impossible to tell because the *independent variable* (mood) is confounded with a variable not systematically varied or controlled by the researcher (temperature).

In sum, experimentation is, in several respects, the crown jewel among social psychology's methods but it certainly isn't perfect. For example, because experimentation is often conducted in laboratory settings, which are quite different from the locations in which social behavior actually occurs, the question of **external validity** often arises: To what extent can the findings of experiments be generalized to real-life social situations and perhaps to persons different from those who participated in the research? When experimentation is used with skill and care, however, it can yield results that help us answer complex questions about social behavior and social thought. Why, if this is so, don't social psychologists use it all the time? The reason is that, in some situations, experimentation cannot be used because of practical or ethical considerations: It is impossible to vary the independent variables systematically, or doing so would violate ethical principles. For example, imagine that a researcher has good reason to believe that exposure to certain kinds of television programs encourages teenagers to engage in unprotected sex. Could the researcher ethically conduct an experiment on this topic, exposing some teenagers to lots of these programs and others to none and then comparing their rates of unprotected sex? Such research is possible, but no ethical social psychologist would perform it because it might cause harm.

KEY POINTS

★ *Experimentation* involves systematically altering variables (*independent variables*) to determine whether changes in these variables affect some aspect of behavior (*dependent variables*).

★ Successful use of the *experimental method* requires *random assignment of participants to experimental con-*

ditions and holding other factors that might influence behavior constant to avoid confounding of variables.

★ The *experimental method* is not perfect—questions concerning its *external validity* often arise. Further, it cannot be used in some situations because of practical or ethical considerations.

Interpreting Research Results: The Use of Statistics, and Social Psychologists as Perennial Skeptics

Once a research project has been completed, social psychologists must turn their attention to another crucial task: interpreting the results. The key question is: How much confidence can we place in the findings? Are correlations between variables, or observed differences between experimental conditions, real ones we can accept as accurate? To answer this question, social psychologists generally employ **inferential statistics**—a special form of mathematics that evaluates the likelihood that a given pattern of research results occurred by chance alone. To determine whether the findings of a study are indeed real—unlikely to be a chance event—psychologists perform appropriate statistical analyses on the data. If these analyses suggest that the likelihood of obtaining the observed findings by chance is low (usually fewer than five times in one hundred), the results are described as *significant*. Only then are they interpreted as being of value in helping us understand some aspect of social behavior or thought. The findings reported in this book have passed this basic test, so you can be confident that they refer to real (i.e., significant) results.

It's important to realize, however, that the likelihood that a given pattern of findings is a chance event is *never* zero. It can be very low—one chance in ten thousand, for instance—but never zero. For this reason, a specific finding is always viewed as tentative in nature until it is replicated—reported again by different researchers in different laboratories. Only when findings have passed this additional test are they viewed with confidence by social psychologists. But here is where a serious problem arises: Only rarely do the results of social psychological research yield totally consistent findings. A more common pattern is that some studies offer support for a given hypothesis, but others fail to offer such support. Why do such discrepancies arise? In part, because different researchers use different methods and measures of social behavior and thought. For instance, continuing with the mood and help-fulness example, some might use feedback on a task to vary participants' moods, while others might use exposure to happy or sad films. Both techniques are designed to vary mood, but it is possible that they also produce other, different effects. For instance, the content of the films, not just whether they are happy or sad, might affect participants' thoughts as well as their moods. The dependent measures employed in such research might vary, too. One researcher might measure helpfulness in terms of willingness to donate to charity, another in terms of willingness to volunteer for another experiment, and still another might measure it in terms of whether participants help the experimenter pick up papers that spilled on the floor. Whatever the reason for contrasting research results, social psychologists must decide which results should be accepted as most valid.

■ Interpreting Diverse Results: The Role of Meta-Analysis

What do social psychologists do when confronted with this problem? One answer involves the use of a technique known as **meta-analysis** (e.g., Bond & Smith, 1996). This procedure allows the results of many studies to be combined to estimate both the direction and the magnitude of the effects of independent variables. Meta-analytic procedures are mathematical in nature, so they eliminate potential sources of errors that might arise if researchers attempted to examine the findings of several studies in a more informal manner. Overall, meta-analysis is an important tool for interpreting the results of social psychological research, and we refer to it often in later chapters.

meta-analysis
A statistical technique for combining data from independent studies in order to determine whether specific variables (or interactions among variables) have significant effects across these studies.

The Role of Theory in Social Psychology

There is another aspect of social psychological research we should consider. As noted earlier, social psychologists seek to do more than simply describe the world: They want to be able to explain it, too. For instance, social psychologists don't want merely to state that racial prejudice is common in the United States: They want to be able to explain *why* some persons hold these negative views. In social psychology, as in all branches of science, explanation involves the construction of **theories**—frameworks for explaining various events or processes. The procedure involved in building a theory goes like this:

theories
Efforts by scientists in any field to answer the question "Why?" Theories involve attempts to understand why certain events or processes occur as they do.

1. On the basis of existing evidence, a theory reflecting this evidence is proposed.

2. This theory, which consists of basic concepts and statements about how these concepts are related, helps to organize existing information and makes predictions about observable events.

3. These predictions, known as *hypotheses,* are then tested by actual research.

4. If the results are consistent with the theory, confidence in its accuracy is increased. If they are not, the theory is modified and further tests are conducted.

5. Ultimately, the theory is either accepted as accurate or rejected as inaccurate. Even if the theory is accepted as accurate, however, it remains open to further refinement as improved methods of research are developed and additional evidence relevant to the theory's predictions is obtained.

This procedure may sound a bit abstract, so let's turn to a concrete example. Suppose that a social psychologist formulates the following theory: When people believe that they hold a view that is in the minority, they will be slower to state it (something known as the *minority slowness* effect). This stems not from the strength of their views, but from reluctance to state minority opinions publicly (where others could hear them and perhaps disapprove). This theory would lead to specific predictions; for instance, the minority slowness effect is reduced if people can state their opinions privately (e.g., Bassili, 2003). If research findings are consistent with this prediction and with others derived from the theory, confidence in the theory is increased. If findings are *not* consistent with the theory, it will be modified or perhaps rejected, as noted previously. (See Chapter 6 for a discussion of the causes of racial prejudice and research testing this specific theory; Crandall et al., 2001.)

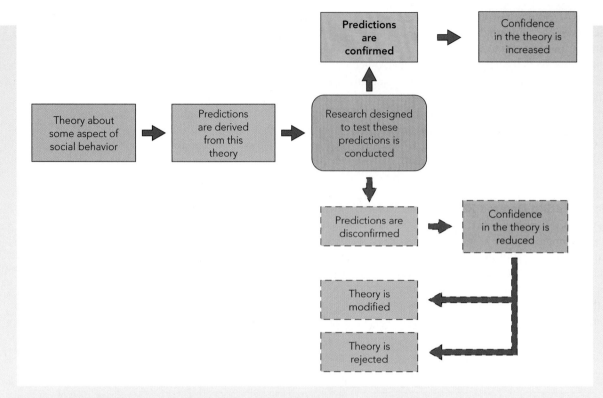

Figure 1.11 ■ The Role of Theory in Social Psychological Research
Theories both organize existing knowledge and make predictions about how various events or processes will occur. Once a theory is formulated, *hypotheses* are tested through careful research. If results agree with the predictions, confidence in the theory is increased. If results disagree, the theory may be modified or, ultimately, rejected as false.

This process of formulating a theory, testing it, modifying the theory, testing it again, and so on, lies close to the core of the scientific method, so it is an important aspect of social psychological research (see Figure 1.11). Thus, different theories relating to important aspects of social behavior and social thought are presented in this book.

Two final points need to be made: First, theories are never *proved* in any final, ultimate sense. Rather, they are always open to testing and are accepted with more or less confidence depending on the weight of the available evidence. Second, research is *not* undertaken to prove or verify a theory; it is performed to gather evidence relevant to the theory. A researcher who sets out to "prove" her or his pet theory would be in serious violation of the principles of scientific skepticism, objectivity, and open-mindedness described on page 6.

KEY POINTS

★ To determine whether the results of a research project are real or due to chance, social psychologists use *inferential statistics*.

★ If the chances are small that research results occurred by chance (less than five times in one hundred), results are described as significant.

★ To assess the direction and magnitude of the effects of *independent variables* across different studies, social psychologists use a statistical technique known as *meta-analysis*.

★ *Theories* are frameworks for explaining various events or processes and play a key role in social psychological research.

The Quest for Knowledge and Rights of Individuals:
Seeking an Appropriate Balance

In their use of experimentation, correlation, and systematic observation, social psychologists do not differ from other researchers. One technique, however, does seem to be unique to social psychology: **deception.** This technique requires researchers to withhold or conceal information from participants about the purposes of a study. The reason for deception is simple: Many social psychologists believe that if participants know the true purposes of a study, their behavior will be changed and the research will not yield valid information about social behavior or social thought.

Some kinds of research seem to require the use of temporary deception. For example, consider the minority slowness effect described previously. If participants know that a study is investigating this effect, isn't it possible that they will lean over backward to avoid showing it? In this and many other cases, social psychologists feel compelled to employ temporary deception in their research (Suls & Rosnow, 1988). However, the use of deception raises ethical issues that cannot be ignored.

First, there is the chance, however slim, that deception may result in some kind of harm to the persons exposed to it. They may be upset by the procedures used or by their own reactions to them, which raises complex ethical issues about just how far researchers can go. For example, participants may receive a request for help from a stranger who is actually an accomplice of the researchers, or they may be informed that other students hold certain views when in fact they do not. Still, even in such mild cases of deception, the potential for some kind of harmful effect to participants exists and is a potentially serious drawback.

Second, participants may resent being fooled during a study and, as a result, will acquire negative attitudes toward social psychology and psychological research in general. For instance, they may become suspicious about information presented by researchers (Kelman, 1967). To the extent such reactions occur—and recent findings indicate that they do, at least to a degree (Epley & Huff, 1998)—they have disturbing implications for the future of social psychology.

Because of such possibilities, the use of deception poses a dilemma to social psychologists. On one hand, deception seems essential to their research. On the other, its use raises serious problems. How can this issue be resolved? Although opinion remains somewhat divided, most social psychologists agree on the following points. First, deception should *never* be used to persuade people to take part in a study; withholding information about what will happen in an experiment or providing misleading information in order to induce people to take part in it is not acceptable (Sigall, 1997). Second, temporary deception may sometimes be acceptable, provided two basic safeguards are employed. One of these is **informed consent**—providing as much information as possible about the procedures to be followed before people decide to participate. The second safeguard is careful **debriefing**—providing a full description of the purposes of a study after their participation. Such information should also include an explanation of deception and why it was necessary.

A growing body of evidence indicates that informed consent and thorough debriefing can substantially reduce the potential dangers of deception (Smith & Richardson, 1985). Overall, existing evidence seems to suggest that most research participants do not react negatively to temporary deception as long as its purpose and necessity are clear. However, these findings do not mean that the safety or appropriateness of deception should be taken for granted (Rubin, 1985). On the contrary, the guiding principles for researchers planning to use this procedure should be as follows: (1) Use deception only when it is absolutely essential—when no other means for conducting the research exists; (2) always proceed with caution; and (3) make certain that every possible precaution is taken to protect the rights, safety, and well-being of participants.

deception
A technique whereby researchers withhold information about the purposes or procedures of a study from persons participating in it.

informed consent
A procedure in which research participants are provided with as much information as possible about a research project before deciding whether to participate in it.

debriefing
Procedures at the conclusion of a research session in which participants are given full information about the nature of the research and the hypothesis or hypotheses under investigation.

KEY POINTS

★ *Deception* involves efforts by social psychologists to withhold or conceal information about the purposes of a study.

★ Social psychologists view *deception* as acceptable only when important safeguards are used: *informed consent* and thorough *debriefing*.

Summary and Review of Key Points

Social Psychology: A Working Definition

■ *Social psychology* is the scientific field that seeks to understand the nature and causes of individual behavior and thought in social situations.

■ *Social psychology* is scientific in nature because it adopts the values and methods used in other fields of science.

■ Social psychologists adopt the scientific method because common sense provides an unreliable guide to social behavior, and because our thoughts are influenced by many potential sources of bias.

■ *Social psychology* focuses on the behavior of individuals and seeks to understand the causes of social behavior and social thought, which can involve the behavior and appearance of others, social cognition, environmental factors, cultural values, and even biological and genetic factors.

Social Psychology: Its Cutting Edge

■ Social psychologists currently recognize that social thought and social behavior are two sides of the same coin, and that there is a continuous, complex interplay between them.

■ Another major field of study involves growing interest in *social neuroscience*—efforts to relate activity in the brain and other biological events to key aspects of social thought and behavior.

■ Our behavior and thought are often shaped by factors of which we are unaware. Growing attention to such implicit (nonconscious) processes is another major theme of modern social psychology.

■ *Social psychology* currently adopts a *multicultural perspective*, which recognizes the importance of cultural factors in social behavior and thought.

Answering Questions about Social Behavior and Social Thought: Research Methods in Social Psychology

■ In *systematic observation*, behavior is carefully observed and recorded. In naturalistic observation, such observations are made in settings in which the behavior naturally occurs.

■ In the *survey method*, large numbers of persons respond to questions about their attitudes or behavior.

■ In the *correlational method* of research, two or more variables are measured to determine if they are related to one another.

■ The existence of correlations between variables does not indicate that they are causally related to each other.

■ *Experimentation* involves systematically altering variables (*independent variables*) in order to determine whether changes in these variables affect some aspect of behavior (*dependent variables*).

■ Successful use of the *experimental method* requires *random assignment of participants to experimental conditions* and holding all other factors that might influence behavior constant to avoid confounding of variables.

■ The *experimental method* is not perfect. Questions concerning its *external validity* often arise. Further, it cannot be used in some situations because of practical or ethical considerations.

■ To determine whether the results of a research project are real or due to chance, social psychologists use *inferential statistics*.

■ If the chances are small that research results occurred by chance (less than five times in one hundred), results are described as significant.

■ To assess the direction and magnitude of the effects of *independent variables* across different studies, social psychologists use a statistical technique known as *meta-analysis*.

■ *Theories* are frameworks for explaining various events or processes. They play a key role in social psychological research.

■ *Deception* involves efforts by social psychologists to withhold or conceal information about the purposes of a study.

■ Social psychologists view *deception* as acceptable only when important safeguards are used: *informed consent* and thorough *debriefing*.

That two variables are correlated—even strongly correlated—does not necessarily mean that changes in one cause changes in the other. This is true because changes in both variables may actually be related to, or caused by, a third variable. Here is one example.

Observation: The more violent television and movies people watch, the more likely they are to engage in dangerous acts of aggression. (These two variables are positively correlated.)

Possible Interpretations:

1. Exposure to media violence is one factor that increases aggression.

Exposure to Media Violence → Causes → Increased Aggression

2. People who prefer a high level of stimulation have little control over their impulses; thus, they choose to watch displays of violence and also act aggressively more often than other people. Both variables are related to a need for certain kinds of stimulation.

Need for Certain Kinds of Stimulation → Watching Violent TV Programs, Films / Behaving Aggressively ← Correlation

3. High Levels of Aggressiveness → Preference for Watching Violent TV Programs and Films

Key Conclusion: Even if two variables are strongly correlated, this does not necessarily mean that changes in one cause changes in the other.

KEY TERMS

correlational method (p. 18)
debriefing (p. 25)
deception (p. 25)
dependent variable (p. 20)
evolutionary psychology (p. 10)
experimentation (experimental method) (p. 20)

external validity (p. 22)
hypothesis (p. 18)
independent variable (p. 20)
inferential statistics (p. 22)
informed consent (p. 25)
meta-analysis (p. 23)
multicultural perspective (p. 15)

random assignment of participants to experimental conditions (p. 21)
social neuroscience (p. 14)
social psychology (p. 6)
survey method (p. 17)
systematic observation (p. 17)
theories (p. 23)

2 SOCIAL COGNITION
Thinking about the Social World

There's an old saying that goes something like this: "We choose our friends, but our relatives are inflicted upon us." This sentiment certainly applied to one relative I used to have, but who now—thank goodness—has left my family. He was probably the most opinionated person I have ever known. Even worse, many of his views seemed to be set in stone. I remember one conversation with him about safety belts. "I never wear them," he said with a smug grin. "If I'm in an accident, I want to be able to get out of the car fast, and belts slow you down." I tried to point out that more people are hurt when they are thrown out of their cars than are injured by remaining in them after an accident, and that many thousands of people are alive today because they were wearing safety belts during serious accidents, but it was of no use. His mind was made up, and he wouldn't even consider the possibility that safety belts could be helpful.

Another time, he tried to persuade me that refusing to hire women as firefighters was *not* discrimination against them—on the contrary, it was a very good thing because it protected them from unnecessary danger. When I tried to point out that if women are capable of performing this job, it is wrong to refuse to hire them, he answered by stating that no woman would *ever* be capable of being a firefighter and walked away. Argument over!

I could continue with other examples, but you get the idea. I found this particular relative to be obnoxious not because he disagreed with me or because he liked to argue, but because his ideas seemed to be totally fixed: Nothing—no facts, no evidence, nothing—could affect them. Truly, he was not someone I would have chosen to be around!

Although I did not enjoy interacting with my former relative, he does have something to contribute to this discussion: His actions illustrate several important points about **social cognition**—the ways in which we interpret, analyze, remember, and use information about the social world; how, in other words, we think about other people, our relations with them, and the social environments in which we live.

First, my relative's behavior demonstrates that social thought is not always rational. Instead, it is subject to a wide range of tendencies and "tilts" that can lead us into serious errors, including the tendency to stick to views and beliefs we have formed even in the face of evidence indicating that they are wrong (see Figure 2.1). Why do we do this? Many factors play a role, but one of the most important illustrates another key fact about social cognition: Thinking about the social world often involves hard work, so we avoid it—or at least

social cognition
The manner in which we interpret, analyze, remember, and use information about the social world.

Figure 2.1 ■ Social Cognition: Far from Error-Free
As shown in this cartoon, once we have made a decision, we are often reluctant to change it, or even to consider information contrary to it. So, like the boss shown here, our thinking about the social world is often far from totally rational. (*Source: DILBERT reprinted by permission of United Features Syndicate, Inc.*)

try to minimize it. Once our ideas and beliefs are formed, it takes a lot of effort to change them, so we don't, even if it makes little or no sense from a purely rational perspective.

Second, other aspects of my relative's behavior illustrate that we often process social information in a seemingly *automatic* manner. Consider his view that no woman could ever be qualified to be a firefighter. How could he hold such a narrow-minded, baseless opinion? In part because he had a very strong stereotype of women, one suggesting that they were too small and weak to be effective firefighters. This stereotype led him to conclude, in a seemingly automatic manner, that women should be excluded from this job because they could not perform it (e.g., Bargh et al., 1996; Greenwald et al., 1998). He didn't have to examine this view carefully or systematically; he just held it! If you are a woman, he believed, you cannot be a firefighter—period.

Finally, I often noticed that if someone *did* challenge my relative's views, he would become emotional about them and that would tend to make him more unreasonable. This observation illustrates that there are important links between cognition and affect—how we think and how we feel. In other words, our thoughts often shape our feelings and our feelings, in turn, can strongly influence our thoughts. This interplay between cognition and affect is complex—far more complex than merely intensifying views we already hold (e.g., Forgas, 1995a)—and such interplay, too, is an important aspect of social thought.

In this chapter we examine key aspects of social cognition. As noted in Chapter 1, a cognitive perspective is central to modern social psychology, and we consider it throughout this book. Thus, it makes good sense to examine some of the basic principles of social thought before turning to other aspects of social psychology.

First, we examine a basic component of social thought—*schemas*. These are mental frameworks that allow us to organize large amounts of information in an efficient manner. Once formed, these frameworks exert strong effects on social thought—effects that are not always beneficial in terms of accuracy. Second, we consider *heuristics*—simple rules of thumb we often use to make decisions or draw inferences quickly, and with minimal effort. In other words, heuristics are another means of reducing cognitive effort, the mental work we do to make sense out of the social world (e.g., Kunda, 1999). After discussing heuristics, we return to the important point that, often, social thought unfolds in a quick and relatively effortless manner rather than in a careful, systematic, and more effortful one. Next, we examine several specific tendencies or "tilts" in social thought—tilts that can lead us to false conclusions about others or to additional errors in our efforts to understand the social world. Finally, we focus on the complex interplay between **affect**—our current feelings or moods—and various aspects of social cognition (e.g., Forgas, 1995a). Note that we also examine important aspects of social thought in Chapter 3, which considers several aspects of *person perception* (how we perceive others and try to understand them), and in Chapter 5, which examines key aspects of our social *self*.

affect
Our current feelings and moods.

Schemas: Mental Frameworks for Organizing—and Using—Social Information

What happens when you visit your doctor? Probably something like this: You enter and sign in. Then you sit and wait. If you are lucky, the wait is not long and a nurse takes you into an examining room. Once there, you wait some more. Eventually, the doctor enters and talks to you and perhaps examines you. Finally, you leave and perhaps pay some part of your bill on the way out. It doesn't matter who your doctor is or where you live. This sequence of events, or something like it, will take place. None of this surprises you; in fact, you expect these events to occur. Why? Because through past experience, you have built up a mental structure or framework for visiting a doctor. Similarly, you have other mental structures for going to restaurants, taking exams, shopping for groceries, and so on (see Figure 2.2).

You don't simply have such frameworks for situations; you also have them for people, occupations, social roles, specific social groups, and many other aspects of the social world. In each case, your experience enables you to build a mental framework that allows you to organize your knowledge and assumptions about each of the subjects or themes in question. Social psychologists describe such frameworks as **schemas** and define them as mental structures that help us to organize social information. Once schemas are formed, they exert powerful effects on several aspects of social cognition. We examine these because they are an important aspect of social cognition and our efforts to make sense out of the social world around us.

schemas
Mental frameworks centering around a specific theme that help us to organize social information.

The Impact of Schemas on Social Cognition: Attention, Encoding, Retrieval

How do schemas influence social thought? Research suggests that they influence three basic processes: attention, encoding, and retrieval. *Attention* refers to what information we notice. *Encoding* refers to the processes through which information we notice is stored in memory. Finally, *retrieval* refers to the processes through which we recover information from memory in order to use it in some manner.

Figure 2.2 ■ Schemas: Mental Frameworks for Organizing Information about the Social World
Through experience, we acquire *schemas*—mental frameworks for organizing, interpreting, and processing social information. For instance, you almost certainly have well-developed schemas for taking an exam (*left photo*) and shopping for groceries (*right photo*). In other words, you know what to expect in these situations and are prepared to behave in certain ways.

Schemas have been found to influence all of these aspects of social cognition (Wyer & Srull, 1994). With respect to attention, schemas often act as a filter: Information consistent with them is more likely to be noticed and to enter our consciousness. Information that does not fit is often ignored (Fiske, 1993), unless it is so extreme that we can't help but notice it.

Encoding works to store the information that becomes the focus of our attention in long-term memory. In general, information that is consistent with our schemas gets encoded. However, information that is sharply inconsistent with our schemas—information that does *not* agree with our expectations in a given situation—may be encoded into a separate memory location and marked with a unique "tag." After all, such information is so unexpected that it literally seizes our attention and almost forces us to make a mental note of it (Stangor & McMillan, 1992). Here's an example: You have a well-developed schema for the role of "professor." You expect professors to come to class, lecture, answer questions, give and grade exams, and so on. Suppose that a professor comes to class and reads poetry or does magic tricks. You will certainly remember these experiences because they are so inconsistent with your professors schema.

That leads us to the third process: retrieval from memory. What information is most readily remembered—information that is consistent with our schemas or information that is inconsistent with them? This is a complex question that has been investigated in many studies (e.g., Stangor & McMillan, 1992). Overall, this research suggests that people tend to report remembering and using information that is consistent with schemas to a greater extent than information that is inconsistent. However, this effect could stem from differences in actual memory or, alternatively, from simple response tendencies. In other words, information inconsistent with schemas might be present in memory as strongly, or even more strongly, than information consistent with schemas, but people simply tend to report (describe) information consistent with their schemas. In fact, this appears to be the case. When measures of memory are corrected for this response tendency, or when individuals are asked to actually *recall* information rather than simply use it or indicate whether they recognize it, a strong tendency to remember information that is incongruent with schemas appears. So, there is no simple answer to the question "Which do we remember better—information consistent or inconsistent with our schemas or expectations?" Rather, the answer depends on the measure of memory employed.

It's important to note that the effects of schemas on social cognition (e.g., what we notice and remember, and how we use this information to make decisions or judgments) are strongly influenced by several other factors. For instance, such effects are stronger when schemas are strong and well developed (e.g., Stangor & McMillan, 1992; Tice, Bratslavsky, & Baumeister, 2000), and they are stronger when *cognitive load*—how much mental effort we are expending—is high rather than low (e.g., Kunda, 1999). In other words, when we are trying to handle a lot of social information at one time, we rely on schemas because they allow us to process this information with less effort.

We must call attention to the fact that although schemas are based on our past experiences and are often helpful, they have a serious downside, too. By influencing what we notice, enter into memory, and later remember, schemas can produce distortions in our understanding of the social world. For example, as we'll discover in Chapter 6, schemas play an important role in prejudice, forming one basic component of stereotypes about specific social groups. And, unfortunately, once they are formed, schemas are often very resistant to change. They show a strong **perseverance effect,** remaining unchanged even in the face of contradictory information (e.g., Kunda & Oleson, 1995). For instance, when we encounter information inconsistent with our schemas, such as an engineer who is a wonderful cook, we do not alter our schema for "engineers." Rather, we may place such persons in a special category or *subtype* consisting of persons who do not confirm the schema or stereotype (e.g., Richards & Hewstone, 2001). Perhaps even worse, schemas can sometimes be *self-fulfilling:* They influence the social world in ways that *make* it consistent with the schema. Let's take a closer look at this process, known in social psychology as the self-fulfilling prophecy, or *the self-confirming nature* of schemas.

perseverance effect
The tendency for beliefs and schemas to remain unchanged, even in the face of contradictory information.

The Self-Confirming Nature of Schemas: When—and Why—Beliefs Shape Reality

self-fulfilling prophecies
Predictions that, in a sense, make themselves come true.

During the 1930s depression, many banks faced rumors that they were not in excellent financial shape. As a result, many depositors lined up to withdraw their funds and ultimately, the banks really did fail. They didn't have enough money on hand to meet the demands (Figure 2.3).

Interestingly, schemas, too, can produce such effects, which are sometimes described as **self-fulfilling prophecies**—predictions that, in a sense, make themselves come true. Robert Rosenthal and Lenore Jacobson (1968) provided classic evidence for such effects during the turbulent 1960s. During that period, there was concern over the possibility that teachers' beliefs about minority students—their schemas—were causing them to treat these children differently (less favorably) than majority-group students and as a result, the minority group students were falling further behind.

To gather evidence on the possible occurrence of such effects, Rosenthal and Jacobson conducted an ingenious study that exerted a powerful effect on subsequent research in social psychology. They went to an elementary school in San Francisco and administered an IQ test to all students. They told the teachers that some of the students had scored very high and were about to "bloom" academically. In fact, this was not true: They chose the names of these students randomly. But Rosenthal and Jacobson predicted that this information might change the teachers' expectations (and schemas) about these children, and hence their behavior toward them. The teachers were not given such information about other students, who constituted a control group.

To find out whether their predictions were self-fulfilling, Rosenthal and Jacobson returned eight months later and tested the children again. Results were clear and dramatic: Those who had been described as "bloomers" showed significantly larger gains on the IQ test than those in the control group. The teachers' beliefs about the students had operated in a self-fulfilling manner: The students that teachers believed would bloom academically actually did.

How did such an effect occur? In part, through the impact of the schemas on the teachers' behaviors. Further research (Rosenthal, 1994) indicated that the teachers gave the students they expected to bloom more attention, more challenging tasks, more and better feedback, and more opportunities to respond in class. In short, the teachers acted in ways that benefited the students they expected to bloom, and they did excel.

This early research inspired social psychologists to search for other self-confirming effects of schemas in many settings—education, therapy, and business, to name a few. They soon uncovered evidence that schemas often shape behavior in ways that lead to their confirmation. Further, studies indicated that the self-confirming effects of schemas do not result from deliberate attempts by people to confirm these mental frameworks (Chen & Bargh, 1997). On the contrary, these self-confirming effects occur even when individuals attempt to avoid letting their expectations shape their behavior toward others. So, schemas are definitely a two-edged sword: They help us make sense out of the social world and process information quickly and with minimal effort, but they can also lock us into perceiving the world in ways that may not be accurate. We consider these effects again in our discussion of prejudice in Chapter 6.

Figure 2.3 ■ The Self-Confirming Nature of Beliefs
During the 1930s, many people believed rumors that their banks would soon fail. As a result, many rushed to withdraw their money, and thus actually *caused* the collapse of the banks.

KEY POINTS

★ Because we have limited cognitive capacity, we often attempt to reduce the effort we expend on *social cognition*—how we think about other persons. This can increase efficiency but reduce our accuracy.

★ One basic component of social cognition is *schemas*—mental frameworks centering on a specific theme that help us to organize social information.

★ Once formed, schemas exert powerful effects on what we notice (attention), enter into memory (encoding), and later remember (retrieval). Individuals report remembering more information consistent with their schemas than information that is inconsistent with them. However, inconsistent information is strongly represented in memory.

★ Schemas help us process information, but they often persist even in the face of disconfirming information, thus distorting our understanding of the social world.

★ Schemas can also exert self-confirming effects, causing us to behave in ways that confirm them.

Heuristics and Automatic Processing: How We Reduce Our Effort in Social Cognition

Several states have passed or are considering laws that ban talking on handheld cell phones while driving. Why? Because it has been found that when drivers are distracted, they are more likely to be involved in accidents, and talking on the phone can be highly distracting. This illustrates a basic principle concerning our cognitive abilities: They are definitely limited. At any given time, we are capable of handling a certain amount of information; additional input beyond this level places us into a state of **information overload.** The demands on our cognitive system are greater than its capacity. In addition, our processing capacity can be depleted by high levels of stress or other demands (e.g., Chajut & Algom, 2003). To deal with such situations, we adopt various strategies designed to "stretch" our cognitive resources—to let us do more, with less effort, than would otherwise be the case. To be successful, such strategies must meet two requirements: (1) They must provide a quick and simple way of dealing with large amounts of information, and (2) they must work. Many potential shortcuts for reducing mental effort exist, but among these, perhaps the most useful are **heuristics**—simple rules for making complex decisions or drawing inferences in a rapid and efficient manner.

Another means of dealing with the fact that the social world is complex yet our information processing capacity is limited is to put many activities, including some aspects of social thought and social behavior, on *automatic* (or *automatic processing,* as psychologists term it; e.g., Ohman et al., 2001). After discussing several heuristics, we consider such automatic processing and its implications for social thought.

information overload
Instances in which our ability to process information is exceeded.

heuristics
Simple rules for making complex decisions or drawing inferences in a rapid and seemingly effortless manner.

Representativeness: Judging by Resemblance

Suppose that you have just met your neighbor for the first time. While chatting, you notice that she is dressed conservatively, is neat in her personal habits, has a large library in her home, and seems to be gentle and a little shy. Later you realize that she never mentioned what she does for a living. Is she a business manager, a physician, a waitress, an attorney, a dancer, or a librarian? One quick way of guessing is to compare her with other members of these occupations. How well does she resemble persons you have met in these fields or, perhaps, the typical member of these fields? You may quickly conclude that she is probably a librarian; her traits seem closer to those associated with this profession than they do to traits associated with being a physician, dancer, or executive. If you made a judgment about her

representativeness heuristic
A strategy for making judgments based on the extent to which current stimuli or events resemble other stimuli or categories.

occupation in this manner, you would be using the **representativeness heuristic.** In other words, you would make your judgment on the basis of a relatively simple rule: *The more similar an individual is to typical members of a given group, the more likely she or he is to belong to that group.*

Are such judgments accurate? Often they are, because belonging to certain groups affects the behavior and style of persons in them, and because people with certain traits are attracted to particular groups. But sometimes, judgments based on representativeness are wrong, mainly for the following reason: Decisions or judgments made on the basis of this rule tend to ignore *base rates*—the frequency with which given events or patterns (e.g., occupations) occur in the total population (Tversky & Kahneman, 1973; Koehler, 1993). In fact, there are many more business managers than librarians. Thus, even though your neighbor seems more similar to librarians than to managers the chances are actually higher that she is a manager. Yet, because of our strong tendency to use the representativeness heuristic, we tend to ignore such base rate information and base our judgments on similarity to typical members of a group or category. In this and related ways, the representativeness heuristic can lead to errors in our thinking about others.

Availability: "If I Can Think of It, It Must Be Important."

Which are more common: words that start with the letter *k* (e.g., *king*) or words with *k* as the third letter (e.g., *awkward*)? In English there are more than twice as many words with *k* in the third position as there are with *k* in the first position. Despite this fact, when asked this question, most people guess incorrectly (Tversky & Kahneman, 1982). Why? In part because of the operation of another heuristic—the **availability heuristic,** which suggests that the easier it is to bring information to mind, the greater its impact on subsequent judgments or decisions. This heuristic, too, makes good sense. After all, that we can bring some information to mind quite easily suggests that it must be important and *should* influence our judgments and decisions. Relying on availability in making social judgments, however, can also lead to errors. For instance, it can lead us to overestimate the likelihood of events that are dramatic but rare, because they are easy to bring to mind. Consistent with this principle, many people fear travel in airplanes more than automobiles, even though the chances of dying in an auto accident are much higher.

availability heuristic
A strategy for making judgments on the basis of how easily specific kinds of information can be brought to mind.

Interestingly, research suggests that there is more to the availability heuristic than merely the subjective ease with which relevant information comes to mind. In addition, the *amount* of information we bring to mind seems to matter (e.g., Schwarz et al., 1991). The more information we can think of, the greater its impact on our judgments. Which of these two factors is more important? The answer appears to involve the kind of judgment we are making. If it involves emotions or feelings, we tend to rely on the "ease" rule, but if it involves facts or information, we tend to rely on the "amount" rule (e.g., Rothman & Hardin, 1997; Ruder & Bless, 2003).

■ Priming: Some Effects of Increased Availability

The availability heuristic plays a role in many aspects of social thought, such as stereotyping (see Chapter 6). In addition, the availablility heuristic relates to another important process: **priming**—increased availability of information resulting from exposure to specific stimuli or events.

priming
Increased availability in memory or consciousness of specific types of information held in memory due to exposure to specific stimuli or events.

Here's a clear example: During the first year of medical school, many experience the "medical student syndrome." They begin to suspect that they or others have serious illnesses. An ordinary headache may lead them to wonder about a brain tumor, and a mild sore throat may lead to anxiety over some rare but fatal type of infection. What accounts for such an effect? The explanation favored by social psychologists is that the students are exposed to descriptions of diseases day after day in their classes and assigned readings. As a result, such information increases in availability and leads them to imagine the worst.

Chapter 2 / Social Cognition

Figure 2.4 ■ Priming in Action
After watching a horror movie, many find that they are easily frightened by unexpected sights (e.g., moving shadows) and sounds. Thoughts of fear-inducing events have been *primed* by the content of the film. Priming plays an important role in social cognition in many contexts.

Priming effects occur in many contexts. For example, the magnified fears people experience after watching a horror film cause them to see every shadow as a potential monster and to jump at every sound (see Figure 2.4). Thus, priming effects are an important aspect of social thought (e.g., Higgins & King, 1981; Higgins, Rohles, & Jones, 1977). In fact, research indicates that priming may occur even when individuals are unaware of the priming stimuli—an effect known as *automatic priming* (e.g., Bargh & Pietromonaco, 1982). In other words, the availability of certain kinds of information can be increased by priming stimuli, even though we are not aware of being exposed to them. Suppose that while waiting for a movie to start, you are thinking about something important. As a result, you do not notice that a message urging you to "eat popcorn" has appeared on the screen. A few minutes later, you have a strong urge to buy popcorn. Why? Perhaps because you are hungry and like popcorn; but it is also possible that your urge to buy popcorn stems, in part, from your being primed to do so by the message you did not consciously notice.

In sum, it appears that priming is a basic fact of social thought. External events and conditions—or even our own thoughts—can increase the availability of specific types of information. And increased availability influences our judgments with respect to such information. "If I can think of it," we seem to reason, "then it must be important."

Anchoring and Adjustment: Where You Begin Makes a Difference

Suppose you are in the market for a used car. You check the papers and find one that sounds promising. The ad says, "Best offer," so no price is listed. When you meet the owner, she names a figure that is much higher than you had in mind. What do you do? Do you counter with the price you want to pay, or do you offer something higher, in between what she has asked and your original price? Unless you are highly skilled in negotiation, you will probably offer more than you originally planned. Why? Because we often use a number or value as a starting point (an anchor) from which we then make adjustments. Her asking price is the anchor in this situation, and you then make adjustments to it, offering something lower, but still above what you originally had in mind. Why? Because, the adjustments you make to the anchor are insufficient. Logically, they should be larger, but usually they are not (e.g., Epley & Gilovich, 2004). Our tendency to make decisions in this way stems from another important heuristic, known as **anchoring and adjustment.** This heuristic involves the tendency to use a number or value as a starting point and to which we then make adjustments.

Anchoring and adjustment can be seen in many situations, not only ones involving money or other figures. For instance, we often allow our personal experiences to serve as an anchor for our views, even if we know our experiences are unique or unusual in some way (e.g., Gilovich, Medvec, & Savitsky, 2000). Here's an example: Imagine that you visit Paris for the first time and find that the streets are filled with trash, the metro (public transportation) is not running, and the streets are choked with cars (see Figure 2.5 on page 38). Your conclusion: Paris does not live up to its reputation of beauty and romance, and you never want to return. Here's the surprising part: You may continue to feel this way, even if you later learn that you arrived during the worst strike in many years—a time when almost all public

anchoring and adjustment heuristic
A heuristic that involves the tendency to use a number or value as a starting point, to which we then make adjustments.

Figure 2.5 ■ Anchoring and Adjustment: A Failure to Adjust Our Thinking
We often allow our personal experiences to serve as an anchor for our views, even if we know that these experiences are unusual or unreliable. If you visited Paris during a major strike and found it to be dirtier and less pleasant than you had originally expected, you might fail to adjust your thinking about the city to reflect the impact of the strike. In other words, you might continue to view it negatively, even though you realize that you saw it at its worst.

employees had walked off their jobs. Normally, the streets are clean and the metro runs just fine. But even though you have this information and know that your experience was unusual, you merely adjust your initial impression to make it a little more positive. You do not return to your initial expectations about Paris being a beautiful city.

Why do we let heuristics influence our thinking? Because they save us mental effort and that, it seems, is a guiding principle of social cognition—just as it is in other aspects of life.

Automatic Processing in Social Thought: Saving Effort—But at a Cost!

As noted earlier, a central dilemma we face with social cognition is this: Our capacity to process information (including social information) is limited, yet daily life floods us with large amounts of information and requires us to deal with it both effectively and efficiently. Heuristics offer one means of solving this problem. In fact, however, heuristics represent just one aspect of a more general tendency: to engage in **automatic processing,** or *automatic modes of thought.* This refers to processing of social information that is nonconscious (recall the discussion in Chapter 1), unintentional, involuntary, and relatively effortless. Automatic processing tends to develop after we have extensive experience with a task or type of information and reach the stage at which we can perform the task or process the information without giving it conscious thought—and sometimes without even meaning to do so. Do you remember learning to ride a bicycle? At first, you had to devote a lot of attention to this task, otherwise you would fall. But as you mastered it, riding required less attention until you could do it while thinking of different topics, or engaging in other tasks, such as talking to a friend. In these situations the shift from *controlled processing* (which is effortful and conscious) to automatic processing is something we *want* to happen.

To an extent, this is true for social thought as well as learning new skills. For instance, once we have a well-developed schema for a social group (e.g., doctors), we can think in shorthand ways about members of that group. We can, for instance, assume that all doctors will be busy, so it's necessary to get right to the point with them, that they are intelligent but not always considerate, and so on. But, as is usually the case, these gains in efficiency or ease are offset by potential losses in accuracy. For instance, evidence indicates that one type of schema—*stereotypes*—can be activated in an automatic and nonconscious manner by the physical features associated with the stereotyped group (e.g., Pratto & Bargh, 1991). Thus, dark skin may automatically trigger a negative stereotype about African Americans, even if the person in question has no intention of thinking in terms of this stereotype. Similarly, attitudes (beliefs and evaluations of some aspect of the social world) may be triggered automatically by the mere presence of the focus of the attitude in question (e.g., Wegner & Bargh, 1998). Such automatic processing of social information can lead to serious errors.

Perhaps even more surprising, research findings indicate that schemas, once activated, may exert seemingly automatic effects on behavior. Research by Bargh, Chen, and Burrows (1996) provides a clear illustration of such effects. They first activated either the schema for the trait of *rudeness* or the schema for the trait of *politeness* through priming by having participants work on the task of unscrambling scrambled sentences. The sentences contained

automatic processing
After extensive experience with a task or type of information, the stage at which we can perform the task or process the information in a seemingly effortless, automatic, and nonconscious manner.

words related either to rudeness (e.g., *rude, impolitely, bluntly*) or to politeness (*cordially, patiently, courteous*). Exposure to words related to schemas was found, in past research, to prime or activate these mental frameworks. Persons in a third (control) group unscrambled sentences containing words unrelated to either trait (e.g., *exercising, flawlessly, occasionally, normally*). After finishing, participants in the study were asked to report to the experimenter for more instructions. When they approached the experimenter, he or she was engaged in a conversation with another person (an accomplice). The experimenter continued this conversation, ignoring the participant. The major dependent measure was whether the participant interrupted the conversation. Bargh and colleagues (1996) predicted that persons primed for the trait *rudeness* would be more likely to interrupt than those primed for the trait *politeness*. This is precisely what happened. Even more revealing is the fact that these effects occurred despite the fact that participants' ratings of the experimenter in terms of politeness did not differ across the three experimental conditions. In other words, the differences in their behavior—how willing they were to interrupt—seemed to occur in a nonconscious, automatic manner.

These results and those of other studies (e.g., Fazio & Hilden, 2001; O'Sullivan, 2003) indicate that, often, social cognition is *not* the rational, reasonable, orderly process we would like it to be. On the contrary, schemas and other mental structures we have acquired through experience can strongly affect our behaviors, and our overt actions in ways that we do not fully recognize, and might, in some cases, wish to change. As we'll see in detail in Chapter 6, once stereotypes are activated, individuals may think about the social groups who are the targets of such stereotypes in negative ways and may treat these groups in a hostile or rejecting manner, *even if they do not intend to do so, and would be upset to realize that they are acting in these ways.* In these and other situations, automatic processing is an important aspect of social thought, one well worth considering in our efforts to understand how we think about others and as we attempt to make sense out of the social world.

Controlled versus Automatic Processing in Evaluating the Social World: Evidence from Social Neuroscience

A very basic dimension of our reactions to the social world is *evaluation*—the extent to which we view events, people, or situations as good or bad. A large body of evidence suggests that we often make such evaluations in an automatic manner, without conscious thought or awareness. Fazio and his colleagues (1986) found that individuals were able to classify words as having a good or bad meaning more quickly if these words had been preceded by other words with similar meanings. Research participants responded more quickly to words with a good meaning, such as *beautiful,* if these words had been preceded by other words with a good meaning, such as *triumph,* than if they had been preceded by words with a bad meaning, such as *murder.* Additional studies (e.g., Bargh et al., 1992) indicated that such effects occurred even if participants did not have to decide whether the words had a good or bad meaning but were merely asked to pronounce them. Good words preceded by other good words were pronounced more quickly than were good words preceded by words with a bad meaning, and vice versa. These findings indicate that evaluations often occur in an automatic manner. In contrast, evaluations of words, people, or any other aspect of the world can also occur in a controlled or reflective manner, one in which we think about the judgments we are making carefully and consciously (e.g., Greenwald & Banaji, 1995). This is especially likely to occur when we are dealing with more complex information, or aspects of the social world toward which we have ambivalent reactions—ones that are both positive and negative.

These findings suggest that we may have two systems for evaluating various aspects of the social world: one that operates in an automatic manner and another that operates in a systematic and controlled manner. Do these systems involve different parts of the brain? If so, there would be strong evidence for their existence and for the distinction between them. In fact, studies conducted from the perspective of *social neuroscience* (see Chapter 1) indicate that these differences exist. Certain parts of the brain, especially the amygdala, may be involved in automatic evaluative reactions—simple good–bad judgments that occur in a rapid and nonconscious manner (Phelps et al., 2001). In contrast, portions of the prefrontal cortex (especially the medial prefrontal cortex and ventrolateral prefrontal cortex) may play a key role in more controlled evaluative reactions—the kinds about which we think carefully and consciously (e.g., Duncan & Owen, 2000).

Research by Cunningham and colleagues (2003) provides clear evidence for these conclusions. Participants were shown the names of famous people (e.g., Adolf Hitler, Bill Cosby) and asked to judge whether these persons were good or bad (an evaluative judgment) or whether the names referred to historical or present-day people (a nonevaluative judgment). As participants did this, activity in their brains was recorded by means of functional magnetic resonance imaging (fMRI). The researchers reasoned that because the names were the same for both tasks, the *automatic* component of evaluation would be present in both. That is, the names would evoke evaluative reactions automatically, regardless of whether participants were asked to rate them as good or bad, or as historical versus present-day. Additional brain activation occurring during the good–bad task would then reflect more controlled evaluative processing—processing that took place *only when the conscious goal of participants was that of evaluating these names.*

Results indicated that such controlled processing occurred primarily in several areas of the prefrontal cortex—areas of the brain long known to be associated with our higher mental processes. In other words, activation in these areas increased when participants performed the evaluative task, relative to when they were judging the names in a nonevaluative manner. In contrast, automatic processing seemed to occur primarily in the amygdala. Perhaps of greater interest, when the names referred to people toward whom participants had ambivalent reactions—both positive and negative (e.g., Bill Clinton, Yasser Arafat)—rather than to ones toward whom they had nonambivalent reactions (e.g., Adolf Hitler, Mahatma Gandhi; see Figure 2.6), increased activity occurred in the prefrontal cortex during the good–bad (evaluative) task. Ambivalent names generated a greater amount of activity reflecting controlled processing than did the nonambivalent names, and this increased activity occurred mainly in the prefrontal cortex.

Overall, these results and those of other studies support the view that we have distinct systems for evaluating social stimuli: one that responds quickly, automatically, and without conscious intention or effort, and another that comes into play when we engage in more controlled, systematic processing.

Figure 2.6 ■ Evaluation of Social Stimuli: Two Neural Systems
Recent research conducted in social neuroscience suggests that we have two distinct systems for evaluating social stimuli. One system, located primarily in the amygdala, evaluates stimuli quickly and automatically. Another system, located mainly in the prefrontal cortex, evaluates stimuli in a more controlled and systematic manner. Additional findings indicate that when we evaluate social stimuli toward which we have mixed feelings (e.g., *photo on left*), the second (systematic thought) system shows greater activity than when we evaluate social stimuli toward which we have nonambivalent feelings (e.g., *photo on right*). (*Source: Based on findings reported by Cunningham et al., 2003.*)

Chapter 2 / Social Cognition

KEY POINTS

★ Because our capacity to process information is limited, we often experience *information overload*. To avoid this, we make use of *heuristics*—rules for making decisions in a quick and relatively effortless manner.

★ One such heuristic is *representativeness*, which suggests that the more similar an individual is to typical members of a given group, the more likely she or he is to belong to that group.

★ Another heuristic is *availability*, which suggests that the easier it is to bring information to mind, the greater its impact on subsequent decisions or judgments. In some cases, availability may involve the amount of information we bring to mind.

★ A third heuristic is *anchoring and adjustment*, which leads us to use a number or a value as a starting point from which we make adjustments. These adjustments may not be sufficient to reflect actual social reality.

★ *Priming* refers to increased availability of information resulting from exposure to specific stimuli or events.

★ In a sense, heuristics are just one aspect of a more general tendency: to engage in *automatic processing*, or automatic thought, which refers to processing of social information that is nonconscious, unintentional, and relatively effortless. Such processing is a basic fact of social cognition and can affect both our thoughts and our overt actions.

★ Evidence indicates that the distinction between automatic and controlled processing is basic. In fact, different regions of the brain appear to be involved in these two types of processing, especially with respect to evaluations of the social world.

Potential Sources of Error in Social Cognition: Why Total Rationality Is Rarer Than You Think

Human beings are definitely not computers. Although we can *imagine* being able to reason in a logical way, we know that we often fall short of this goal. This is true with respect to many aspects of social thought. In our efforts to understand others and make sense out of the social world, we are subject to a wide range of tendencies that, together, can lead us into serious error. In this section, we consider some of these "tilts" in social cognition. Before doing so, however, we must emphasize the following point: Although these aspects of social thought sometimes result in errors, they are also quite adaptive. They can help us focus on the kinds of information that are most informative, and they reduce the effort required for understanding the social world. So, these tendencies in social thought are something of a mixed bag, supplying us with tangible benefits as well as exacting important costs.

Negativity Bias: The Tendency to Pay Extra Attention to Negative Information

Imagine that in describing someone new, your friend mentions many positive things about this person: He or she is pleasant, intelligent, good-looking, friendly, and so on. Then, your friend mentions one negative piece of information: This person is also somewhat conceited. What are you likely to remember? Research indicates that, probably, the negative information will stand out in your memory (e.g., Kunda, 1999). Because of this, the negative information will have a stronger influence on your desire to meet this person than any equivalent piece of positive information. This suggests that we show a strong **negativity bias**—greater sensitivity to negative information than to positive information. This bias applies to both social information and information about other aspects of the world as well.

negativity bias
A greater sensitivity to negative information than to positive information.

Why do we have this tendency? From an evolutionary perspective, it makes a great deal of sense. Negative information reflects features of the external world that may threaten our well-being. For this reason, it is especially important that we be sensitive to such stimuli and thus able to respond quickly. Consider our ability to recognize facial expressions in others.

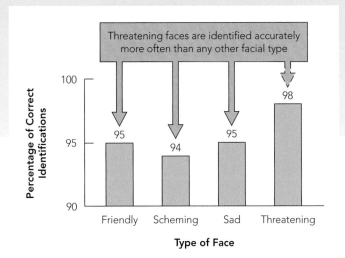

Threatening faces are identified accurately more often than any other facial type

Type of Face

Figure 2.7 ■ Evidence for the Negativity Bias: Which Face Do You Notice First?
Threatening faces shown among a background of neutral faces were identified more quickly and accurately than friendly, scheming, or sad faces. These findings provide evidence for the existence of the *negativity bias*—enhanced sensitivity to negative stimuli or information. (*Source: Based on data from Ohman, Lundqvist, and Esteves, 2001.*)

Study results indicate that we are faster and more accurate in detecting negative facial expressions (e.g., ones showing anger or hostility) than positive facial expressions (e.g., ones showing friendliness).

Studies by Ohman, Lundqvist, and Esteves (2001) provide a clear illustration. These researchers asked participants to search for neutral, friendly, or threatening faces among other faces with discrepant expressions (e.g., the friendly face was shown among neutral or threatening faces; the threatening face was shown among friendly or neutral faces; and so on). Results indicated that regardless of the background, participants were faster and more accurate in identifying threatening faces. In an additional study, participants were asked to search for several kinds of faces—threatening, friendly, scheming, or sad—among an array of neutral faces. Again, the threatening faces were identified faster and more accurately than any of the others (see Figure 2.7).

This tendency to show enhanced sensitivity to negative information seems to be a basic aspect of social thought and may be built into the structure and functioning of our brains (Ito et al., 1998; Cacioppo et al., 2003). In this respect, it is an important "tilt" in our social cognition, and one worth noting.

The Optimistic Bias: Our Tendency to See the World through Rose-Colored Glasses

optimistic bias
Our predisposition to expect things to turn out well overall.

overconfidence barrier
The tendency to have more confidence in the accuracy of our judgments than is reasonable.

planning fallacy
The tendency to make optimistic predictions concerning how long a given task will take for completion.

Although the tendency to notice negative information is strong, don't despair. Despite the existence of the negativity bias, we also have a seemingly opposite tendency, known as the **optimistic bias.** This refers to a predisposition to expect things to turn out well overall. In fact, research indicates that most people believe they are *more* likely than others to experience positive events and *less* likely to experience negative events (e.g., Shepperd, Ouellette, & Fernandez, 1996). Similarly, we often have greater confidence in our beliefs or judgments than is justified—an effect known as the **overconfidence barrier** (Vallone, Ross, & Lepper, 1985). Our leaning toward optimism is seen in other contexts, too: Most people believe they are more likely than others to get a good job, have a happy marriage, and live to a ripe old age, but less likely to experience negative outcomes such as being fired, becoming seriously ill, or being divorced (e.g., Schwarzer, 1994).

Yet another illustration is the **planning fallacy**—our tendency to believe that we can get more done in a given period of time than we actually can. Because of this aspect of the optimistic bias, governments frequently announce overly optimistic schedules for public works (e.g., new airports, new bridges; see Figure 2.8), and individuals adopt unrealistic schedules for their work. If you estimated that a project would take a certain amount of time but then found that it took longer, you are familiar with the planning fallacy.

Why do we fall prey to this kind of optimism? According to Buehler, Griffin, and Ross (1994), several factors play a role. One is that when individuals make predictions about how long it will take to complete a given task, they enter a *planning* or *narrative* mode of thought in which they focus primarily on the future and how to perform the task. This prevents them from remembering how long similar tasks took them in the past. As a result, one important

Chapter 2 / Social Cognition

Figure 2.8 ■ The Planning Fallacy in Action
Tunnel construction in Boston took several years longer and cost billions of dollars more than originally projected. This is not a rare occurrence. Public projects routinely take longer to complete than initially planned. This may reflect effects of the planning fallacy—the tendency to believe that we can accomplish more than we actually can in a given period of time.

"reality check" that might help them avoid being overly optimistic is removed. When individuals *do* consider past experiences in which tasks took longer than expected, they tend to attribute such outcomes to factors outside their control. The result is that they tend to overlook potential obstacles when predicting how long a task will take and fall prey to the planning fallacy. These predictions have been confirmed in several studies (e.g., Buehler et al., 1994), so they seem to provide important insights into the origins of the tendency to make optimistic predictions about task completion.

This is not the entire story, though. Research suggests that another factor may play an important role in the planning fallacy: *motivation* to complete a task. When predicting what will happen, individuals often guess that is what they *want* to happen (e.g., Johnson & Sherman, 1990). In cases in which they are strongly motivated, therefore, they make overly optimistic predictions about when they will attain this goal. Research offers support for this reasoning (e.g., Buehler, Griffin, & MacDonald, 1997), so it appears that our estimates of when we will complete a task are influenced by our desires: We want to finish early or on time, so we predict that we will. The result? Unfounded optimism strikes again!

■ The Rocky Past versus the Golden Future: Optimism at Work!

Think back over your past. Did it have peaks (times when things were going great for you) and valleys (times when things were not good)? Now try to imagine your future. How do you think it will unfold? If you are like most people, you may notice a difference in these descriptions. Although most of us recognize that our pasts have been mixed in terms of highs and lows, we tend to forecast a very rosy future—one in which we will be happy and few negative events will happen. In fact, research by Newby-Clark and Ross (2003) indicates that this tendency is so strong that it occurs even when people have just recalled negative episodes from their pasts. What accounts for this difference? One possibility is that when we think about the past, we recall failures, unpleasant events, and other disappointments. When we think about the future, we tend to concentrate on desirable goals, personal happiness, and doing things we have always wanted to do. The result? Because our thinking is dominated by positive thoughts, we make optimistic predictions about the future and tend to perceive it as indeed golden, at least in its promise or potential. In short, the optimistic bias seems to occur not only for specific tasks or situations, but in our future projections as well.

■ Bracing for Loss: An Exception to the Optimistic Rule

Though optimism seems to be the general rule for most people, there is an important exception to this pattern. When individuals expect to receive feedback or information that may be negative and has important consequences for them, they seem to *brace for loss* (or for the worst) and show a reversal of the optimistic pattern. They tend to be *pessimistic*, showing an enhanced tendency to anticipate *negative* outcomes (e.g., Taylor & Shepperd, 1998).

Why does this occur? Shepperd and his colleagues (Shepperd et al., 2000) suggest that it is due to the desire to be ready—braced—for the worst. In related studies, Shepperd et al. (2000) asked students to estimate the likelihood that they would receive an additional bill (a negative outcome) or a refund (a positive outcome) from the registrar. (Supposedly, the registrar had made a number of errors, resulting in 25 percent of the students receiving incorrect bills for tuition and fees.) Shepperd and his colleagues predicted that students who were financially needy—for whom the additional bill would be a problem—would show a stronger *brace for loss* effect than would those who were not financially needy. Results confirmed this prediction. In several studies, financially needy students estimated the likelihood that they would receive an additional bill at between 40 and 67 percent—much higher than the 25 percent chance figure and significantly higher than for students who were not financially needy. Further, the financially needy students showed such pessimism only for themselves, not for a friend, and regardless of whether they were primed to think about past financial losses.

Together, these findings suggest that people brace for the worst and turn pessimistic when they anticipate possible news that will have strong negative effects on them. Research (e.g., Shepperd & McNulty, 2002) indicates that this tendency can have important effects on long-term personal relationships as well. For instance, it may help newly wed couples who are not high in social skills to avoid the bitter disappointments that may occur if their expectations for marital happiness are unrealistically high (McNulty & Karney, 2004). But again, we should emphasize that this is the exception to a general rule of optimism. In most situations, we tend to be overly optimistic about our lives and social outcomes, but we can switch to pessimism when this protects us from unexpected bad news.

KEY POINTS

★ We show a strong *negativity bias*—a tendency to be highly sensitive to negative stimuli or information. This basic tendency may be built into the functioning of our brains. Thus, it may be the result of evolutionary factors.

★ We also show a strong *optimistic bias*, expecting positive events and outcomes in many contexts. In addition, we tend to make overly optimistic predictions about how long it will take to complete a given task, an effect known as the *planning fallacy*.

★ The optimistic bias also shows up in our tendency to assume that we are more likely than others to experience positive outcomes, but less likely than others to experience negative ones.

★ The optimistic bias is also evident when we compare our past and future: Although we perceive the past as mixed in terms of highs and lows, we tend to perceive the future in highly optimistic terms.

★ The optimistic bias may be reversed and turn to pessimism, however, when we anticipate receiving bad news; in such cases, we brace for loss and show an enhanced tendency to predict negative outcomes.

Counterfactual Thinking: The Effects of Considering What Might Have Been

Suppose that you take an important exam; when you receive your score, it is a C–, much lower than you had hoped. What thoughts enter your mind? If you are like most people, you may quickly imagine what might have been—a higher grade—along with thoughts about how you could have obtained it. "If only I had studied more, or come to class more often," you may think. And then you may begin to formulate plans for doing better on the next test.

Such thoughts about what might have been—known in social psychology as **counterfactual thinking**—occur in a wide range of situations, not only disappointing experiences (see Figure 2.9). Suppose you read an article about someone who left work at the normal time and was injured in a car accident in which another driver ran a stop sign. You would feel sympathetic and would probably recommend compensation for him. Now imagine the same story with a slight difference: The same person was injured in the same kind of accident, but he had left work early. Because the accident is the same, you should rationally feel

counterfactual thinking
The tendency to imagine other outcomes in a situation than the ones that actually occurred ("what might have been").

Chapter 2 / Social Cognition

Figure 2.9 ■ Counterfactual Thinking: An Example
General Halftrack is engaging in counterfactual thinking: He is imagining what might have been and is experiencing intense regret. This is a common aspect of social cognition—a kind of thinking most of us engage in at least occasionally. (*Source: Reprinted with special permission of King Features Syndicate.*)

the same amount of sympathy. In fact, though, you may not, because given that he left work early, it is easy to imagine him *not* being in the accident. In other words, counterfactual thoughts about what might have happened (or not have happened) influence your sympathy—and perhaps your recommendations concerning compensation.

Why do such effects occur? Because counterfactual thoughts seem to occur automatically; we can't help imagining that things might have turned out differently. To overcome these automatic tendencies, we must try to correct for their influence, and this requires active processing in which we both suppress the counterfactual thoughts or discount them if they occur. If this reasoning is correct, then anything that reduces our information-processing capacity might strengthen the impact of counterfactual thoughts on our judgments and behavior (Bargh & Chartrand, 1999). Growing evidence suggests that this is so. For instance, Goldinger and his colleagues (2003) first measured participants' working memory capacity—an index of information-processing capacity. Then they asked participants to read stories designed to induce counterfactual thoughts or not to induce such thoughts. One story involved a person who had a season basketball ticket. One night, he is sitting in his usual seat and a light fixture falls, injuring him severely. This is the control version that would *not* be expected to trigger counterfactual thoughts. In another version, he is also injured, but sitting in a different seat that happened to be empty that night. This version would be expected to induce counterfactual thoughts. Goldinger et al. also asked participants to perform an additional task (memorizing and recalling nonsense words such as *flozick* and *nucade*). They performed this memory-loading task at various times—before reading the stories or after reading them.

After reading the stories, participants indicated how much monetary compensation the victim of the accident should receive. Results indicated that asking them to perform a memory task that loaded their memories (reduced their information-processing capacity) greatly strengthened the impact of counterfactual thoughts, especially for those who had low capacity to begin with (i.e., those with a low working memory capacity). Because they could readily imagine situations in which the victim was *not* injured (e.g., he sat in his regular seat), they recommended much smaller compensation. These findings suggest that counterfactual thoughts tend to occur automatically in many situations and that resisting their effects requires hard, cognitive work.

These are not the only effects of counterfactual thinking. As noted by Roese (1997), engaging in such thoughts can yield a wide range of effects, some of which are beneficial and some of which are costly to the persons involved. If individuals imagine *upward counterfactuals,* comparing their current outcomes with more favorable ones than they experienced, the result may be strong feelings of dissatisfaction or envy, especially if they do not feel capable of obtaining better outcomes in the future (Sanna, 1997). Olympic athletes who win a silver medal but imagine winning a gold experience such reactions (e.g.,

Potential Sources of Error in Social Cognition

Medvec, Madey, & Gilovich, 1995). Alternatively, if individuals compare their current outcomes with less favorable ones, or if they contemplate various ways in which disappointing results could have been avoided and positive ones attained, they may experience positive feelings of satisfaction or hopefulness. Such reactions have been found among Olympic athletes who win bronze medals, and who therefore imagine what it would be like to have won no medal whatsoever (e.g., Gleicher et al., 1995).

In addition, it appears that we often use counterfactual thinking to mitigate disappointments. After tragic events, such as the death of a loved one, people often find solace in thinking, "Nothing more could be done; the death was inevitable." They adjust their view concerning the inevitability of the death to make it seem more certain and therefore unavoidable. In contrast, if they have different counterfactual thoughts—"If only the illness had been diagnosed sooner" or "If only we had gotten him to the hospital quicker"—their suffering may be increased. So, by assuming that negative events or disappointments are inevitable, we tend to make these events more bearable (Tykocinski, 2001). We'll have more to say about such effects in a later section.

KEY POINTS

★ In many situations, when individuals imagine what might have been, they engage in *counterfactual thinking*. Such thoughts can affect our sympathy for persons who have experienced negative outcomes, and can cause us to experience strong regret over missed opportunities.

★ Counterfactual thoughts seem to occur automatically and their effects can be reduced only through hard, cognitive work in which they are suppressed or discounted.

★ By assuming that disappointing or tragic events are unavoidable, individuals can make them more bearable. This is an adaptive function of counterfactual thinking.

Thought Suppression: Why Efforts to Avoid Thinking Certain Thoughts Sometimes Backfire

thought suppression
Efforts to prevent certain thoughts from entering consciousness.

In our discussion of counterfactual thinking, we noted that such thoughts occur automatically in many situations and that to prevent them from influencing our judgments, we must try to suppress them. You have probably tried to do this in other contexts, too. For example, if you have been on a diet, you probably tried to avoid thinking about desserts or other forbidden foods. And if you ever felt nervous about giving a speech, you probably tried to avoid thinking about how you could fail at this task (see Figure 2.10).

How do we accomplish such **thought suppression,** and what are the effects of this process? According to Daniel Wegner (1992b), efforts to keep certain thoughts out of consciousness involve two components. First, there is an automatic *monitoring process* that searches

Figure 2.10 ■ Thought Suppression: Can We Really Avoid Thinking about Things We Don't Want to Think About? Yes, But It's Not Easy!
Often we engage in *thought suppression:* We try not to think about unpleasant events or outcomes (e.g., ones that frighten us, such as looking foolish in front of an audience). Although we sometimes succeed in driving such thoughts from our minds, it is no easy task.

for evidence that unwanted thoughts are about to intrude. When such thoughts are detected by the first process, a second one, which is more effortful and less automatic (i.e., more controlled), swings into operation. This *operating process* involves effortful, conscious attempts to distract oneself by finding something else to think about. In a sense, the monitoring process is an early-warning system that tells the person that unwanted thoughts are present, and the second process is an active prevention system that keeps such thoughts out of consciousness through distraction.

Normally the two processes do a good job of suppressing unwanted thoughts. When information overload occurs or when individuals are fatigued, however, the monitoring process continues to identify unwanted thoughts, but the operating process no longer has the resources to keep them from entering consciousness. The result is a pronounced *rebound* effect in which the unwanted thoughts occur at an even higher rate than was true before efforts to suppress them began. As we'll soon discover, the rebound effect can have serious consequences for the persons involved.

The operation of the two processes described by Wegner (1992a, 1994) has been confirmed in numerous studies (e.g., Wegner & Zanakos, 1994), and with respect to thoughts ranging from strange or unusual images (e.g., a white elephant) to thoughts about former lovers (Wegner & Gold, 1995). This model of thought suppression therefore appears to be accurate.

Now for the second question posed earlier: What are the effects of engaging in thought suppression—and of failing? Generally, people engage in thought suppression to influence their feelings and behaviors. For example, if you want to avoid feeling angry, it's best not to think about incidents that cause you to feel resentment toward others. Similarly, if you want to avoid feeling depressed, it's useful to avoid thinking about events that make you feel sad. But sometimes, people engage in thought suppression because they are told to do so by someone else—for instance, a therapist who is trying to help them cope with personal problems. A therapist may tell a woman with a drinking problem to avoid thinking about the pleasures of alcohol (e.g., how good drinking makes her feel). If she succeeds in suppressing such thoughts, she will overcome her drinking problem. But consider what happens if the individual fails in her efforts. She may think, "What a failure I am—I can't even control my thoughts!" As a result, her motivation to continue these efforts—or even to continue therapy—may decline (e.g., Kelly & Kahn, 1994).

Unfortunately, because some persons possess certain personal characteristics, they seem especially likely to experience such failures. Individuals who are high in *reactance*—those who react very negatively to perceived threats to their personal freedom—may be especially at risk. Such persons often reject advice from others because they want to "do their own thing," so they may find instructions to suppress certain thoughts hard to follow. Personal characteristics can play a role in thought suppression, and persons high in reactance may not be very good candidates for forms of therapy that include suppressing unwanted thoughts as part of their procedures.

Limits on Our Ability to Reason about the Social World: Magical Thinking and Ignoring Moderating Variables

Please answer the following questions truthfully:

If you are in class and don't want the professor to call on you, do you try to avoid thinking about being called on?

Imagine that someone offered you a piece of chocolate shaped like a cockroach— would you eat it?

On the basis of purely rational considerations, you know that your answers should be "no" and "yes," respectively, but are those the answers you actually gave? If you are like most people, perhaps not. Research findings indicate that we are quite susceptible to what has been termed **magical thinking** (Rozin & Nemeroff, 1990). Such thinking makes assumptions that

magical thinking
Thinking involving assumptions that don't hold up to rational scrutiny—for example, the belief that things that resemble one another share fundamental properties.

Figure 2.11 ■ Magical Thinking: An Example
Would you eat the candy shown here? Many would not, even though they realize that the shape has nothing to do with its taste. This illustrates the *law of similarity*—one aspect of what social psychologists term *magical thinking*.

don't hold up to rational scrutiny but are compelling nonetheless. One principle of magical thinking assumes that one's thoughts can influence the physical world in a manner not governed by the laws of physics; for example, if you think about being called on by your professor, you will be! Another is the *law of similarity,* which suggests that things that resemble one another share basic properties. So, people won't eat a chocolate shaped like a cockroach, even though they know, rationally, that its shape has nothing to do with its taste (see Figure 2.11).

■ Failure to Take Account of Moderating Variables

Suppose that you read a story indicating that female professors at your university receive 25 percent less pay, on average, than male professors. This angers you because you feel that gender should have no effect on people's salaries. You read further and learn that male professors also have, on average, eight years more experience than female professors. This suggests that the difference in their pay may reflect a difference in number of years on the job rather than discrimination. You don't know whether this inference is accurate, but at least it's a possibility.

This kind of reasoning, in which we take account of the fact that an effect that seems to stem from one factor can, in fact, stem from another, is a type we are called on to perform in many social situations, so you might expect that we can do it very well. Findings reported by Fiedler and his colleagues (2003), however, suggest that we are *not* very adept at such thinking. In this research, Fiedler et al. presented participants with information about thirty-two women and thirty-two men who had applied for admission to two universities. Overall, nineteen men were accepted and thirteen rejected. For women, the opposite was true: thirteen were accepted and nineteen rejected. Additional information, however, suggested that this difference was due to the fact that most of the women applied to a university with higher rejection rates (about 60 percent), while most men applied to a university with lower rejection rates (about 40 percent). The key question was, "Would participants be aware of the effects of this moderating variable?" Results from this study and several others indicated that they were not. They tended to assume that women were at a disadvantage simply because they were women, not because they chose to apply to a university with higher admissions standards. This tendency was evident even when steps were taken to help participants recognize the impact of this third variable (university selectivity) by, for instance, calling attention to the third variable or giving participants more time to examine the relevant information.

Overall, then, the following conclusion seems justified: Though our thinking about the social world *can* be rational, and we *can* reason effectively about it, our desire to save mental effort, the existence of many mental shortcuts, and our limited processing capacity all work against total rationality. To put it simply, we are capable of more accurate and reasoned social cognition than we often show.

Social Cognition: Some Words of Optimism

The *negativity bias, optimistic bias, counterfactual thinking, magical thinking, thought suppression*—having discovered these sources of error in social thought, you may be ready to lose hope: Can we ever get it right? The answer, in fact, is *absolutely.* No, we are definitely not perfect information processing machines. We have limited cognitive capacities, and we can't

Chapter 2 / Social Cognition

increase these by buying pop-in memory chips. And, yes, we are somewhat lazy where social thought is concerned: We generally do the least amount of cognitive work possible in any situation. Despite being flooded by truly enormous amounts of social information, we manage to sort, store, remember, and use a large portion of this input in an intelligent and highly efficient manner. Our thinking is subject to many potential sources of bias, and we do make errors. For the most part, however, we do a very good job of processing social information and making sense out of the social world around us.

KEY POINTS

★ Individuals often engage in *thought suppression*—trying to prevent themselves from thinking about certain topics (e.g., desserts, alcohol, cigarettes).

★ These efforts are often successful, but sometimes they result in a rebound effect, in which such thoughts increase in frequency. Persons who are high in reactance are more likely to experience such effects.

★ There are important limits on our ability to think rationally about the social world. One involves *magical thinking*—

thinking based on assumptions that don't hold up to rational scrutiny.

★ Another limitation involves our inability to take account of moderating variables in many situations.

★ Although social cognition is subject to many sources of error, we generally do an excellent job of understanding the social world.

Affect and Cognition: How Feelings Shape Thought and Thought Shapes Feelings

In our discussion of the optimistic bias, we used the phrase "seeing the world through rose-colored glasses" to reflect our tendency to expect positive outcomes in many situations. But there's an additional way in which these words apply to social cognition: They also illustrate the effect that being in a good mood has on our thoughts and perceptions (see Figure 2.12). Think of a time in your life when you were in a very good mood. Didn't the world seem to be a happier place? And didn't you view everything and everyone with whom you came into contact more favorably? Experiences such as this illustrate that there is often a complex interplay between *affect*—our current moods—and *cognition*—the ways in which we process,

Figure 2.12 ■ The Influence of Affect on Cognition
Because Mr. Dithers is in a good mood, he is not upset by Dagwood's negative news; in fact, it seems unimportant to him. This is an illustration of the potentially powerful effect of our current moods on our social thoughts. (*Source: Reprinted with special permission of King Features Syndicate.*)

store, remember, and use social information (Forgas, 1995a; Isen & Baron, 1991). We use the term *interplay* because research on this topic indicates that the relationship is very much a two-way street: Our feelings and moods strongly influence several aspects of cognition, and cognition exerts strong effects on our feelings and moods (e.g., McDonald & Hirt, 1997; Seta, Hayes, & Seta, 1994). What are these effects like? Let's see what research findings tell us.

The Influence of Affect on Cognition

We have mentioned the impact of moods on our perceptions of the world around us. Such effects apply to people as well as objects. Imagine, for instance, that you have just received good news: You did much better on an important exam than you expected. As a result, you are feeling great. Now, you run into one of your friends and she introduces you to someone you don't know. You chat with this person and then leave for another class. Will your first impression of the stranger be influenced by the fact that you are feeling good? The findings of several studies suggest strongly that it will (Bower, 1991; Mayer & Hanson, 1995; Clore, Schwarz, & Conway, 1993). In other words, our current moods can strongly affect our reactions to new stimuli, whether these are people, foods, or even geographic locations, causing us to perceive them more favorably than we would if we were not in a good mood. Indeed, recent evidence indicates that we are more likely to judge statements as true when we are in a positive mood than when we are in a more neutral mood (Garcia-Marques et al., 2004).

Such effects have important practical implications. Consider the impact of moods on job interviews—a context in which interviewers meet many people for the first time. Evidence indicates that even experienced interviewers can't avoid being influenced by their current moods: They assign higher ratings to persons they interview when they are in a good mood than when they are in a bad mood (e.g., Baron, 1993a; Robbins & DeNisi, 1994).

Another way in which affect influences cognition involves its impact on memory. Here, two different but related kinds of effects seem to occur. One is known as **mood-dependent memory,** which refers to the fact that what we remember while in a given mood may be determined, in part, by what we learned when previously in that mood. For instance, if you stored some information into long-term memory when in a good mood, you are more likely to remember it when in a similar mood. Your current mood serves as a kind of *retrieval cue* for memories stored while you were in a similar mood in the past. A second kind of effect is known as **mood congruence effects,** which refers to the fact that we tend to notice or remember information that is congruent with our current moods (Blaney, 1986). So, if we are in a good mood, we tend to notice and remember information congruent with this mood, and if we are in a bad mood, we tend to notice and remember information that matches *that* mood. A simple way to think about the difference between mood-dependent memory and mood congruence effects is this: In mood-dependent memory, the nature of the information doesn't matter—only your mood at the time you learned it and your mood when you try to recall it are relevant. In mood congruence effects, the affective nature of the information—whether it is positive or negative—is crucial. When we are in a positive mood, we tend to remember positive information and when we are in a negative mood, we tend to remember negative information (see Figure 2.13).

Our current moods influence another component of cognition—creativity. The results of several studies suggest that being in a happy mood can increase creativity, perhaps because being in a happy mood activates a wider range of ideas of associations than being in a negative mood, and because creativity consists, in part, of combining such associations into new patterns (e.g., Estrada, Isen, & Young, 1995).

Additional findings indicate that information that evokes affective reactions may be processed differently than other kinds of information. Specifically, because emotional reactions are often diffuse in nature, information relating to them may encourage heuristic or automatic processing rather than systematic processing or thought. As a result, it may be almost impossible to ignore or disregard information relating to moods once it has been introduced into a situation (e.g., Edwards, Heindel, & Louis-Dreyfus, 1996; Wegner & Gold, 1995). This finding has important implications for the legal system. Often, attorneys introduce emotion-laden

mood-dependent memory
The effect that what we remember while in a given mood may be determined, in part, by what we learned when previously in that mood.

mood congruence effects
Effects that we are more likely to store or remember positive information when in a positive mood, and negative information when in a negative mood.

Chapter 2 / Social Cognition

Figure 2.13 ■ The Effects of Mood on Memory
Our moods influence what we remember through two mechanisms: *mood-dependent memory*, which refers to the fact that what we remember while in a given mood is determined, in part, by what we learned when previously in that mood; and *mood congruence effects*, which refers to the fact that we are more likely to store or remember positive or negative information consistent with our current mood.

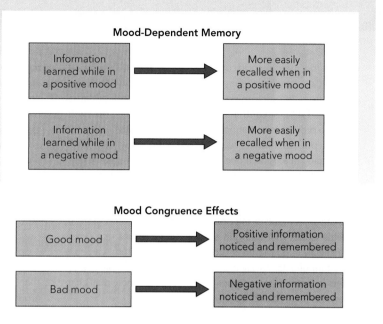

information into their statements to juries. They may mention previous crimes by the defendant or other negative information. The opposing side quickly objects, and the judge may then instruct the jury to ignore this information. Can the jury actually do so? Because of its emotional content, ignoring the information may be virtually impossible. The findings of several studies (e.g., Edwards & Bryan, 1997) indicate that attempts to ignore or suppress such information may lead to a *rebound effect* in which jurors actually think about such information *more* than would otherwise be the case. (Recall our earlier discussion of thought suppression.) Clearly, we process emotional information differently from other kinds of social information and that can have important effects. (Common sense suggests that feeling happy is a very good thing. Is this actually true? For a discussion of this intriguing issue, please see the **Making Sense of Common Sense** section.)

MAKING SENSE OF COMMON SENSE

Is Being in a Good Mood Always a Plus? The Potential Downside of Feeling "Up"

Everyone wants to feel happy, and there is no doubt that, for most of us, being in a good mood is more pleasant. So, common sense strongly suggests that we should do everything we can to enhance our moods. Consistent with this belief, research indicates that when people are in a good mood, they tend to be more creative and more helpful to others than when they are in a negative mood (e.g., Baron, 1997; Isen, 1984; Isen & Levin, 1972). But is being in a good mood always a plus? Does it always produce positive effects? In fact, growing evidence suggests that in this respect, common sense may be throwing us a curve. Being in a good mood may have some real drawbacks that are worth considering.

First, there is no doubt that being in a good mood increases our willingness to help others; this tendency has been demonstrated in many studies (e.g., Isen, 1984). The other side of the coin, however, is that when we are in a good mood, we are more susceptible to efforts by others to get us to do what they want. We discuss such social influence in Chapter 9, but here, we should note that others who want to change our behaviors or attitudes don't always have our best interests at heart. Advertisers, salespersons, and sometimes politicians want to influence us because it is beneficial to them. So, in this respect, being in a good mood can be risky: It increases our tendency to say "yes" to requests or other forms of influence from others, and that can sometimes be downright dangerous!

An additional downside to being in a good mood relates to the effects of such positive, happy feelings on social cognition. Evidence suggests that one effect of being in a good mood is that it tends to encourage heuristic thinking—a

3

SOCIAL PERCEPTION
Perceiving and Understanding Others

*S*uppose that after a serious accident, an individual suffers from profound amnesia. The patient can speak normally and recognizes friends and family members but has lost almost all memory for general knowledge—facts about the world, important dates in history, and the names of famous people. Now, imagine that we conduct the following experiment with this person. We show her photos of three evil tyrants—Adolf Hitler, Josef Stalin, and Saddam Hussein (see Figure 3.1). In all the photos, these despots are shown demonstrating positive emotions and acting in friendly ways toward other people. Now, you ask the patient to describe the personalities and traits of these monstrous dictators. What would she be likely to say? Because she has no memory of who these people are, she might offer comments such as, "He has a nice warm smile," "I think he's probably kind and friendly," and "Look at how he is giving flowers to those children—he must be really nice."

How wrong could she get! These tyrants were responsible for the torture, imprisonment, and murder of many of their own countrymen and women. How can our patient see them as good, kind, and friendly? The answer is obvious: Given the limited information she has—their appearance in photos—she has reached reasonable conclusions. After all, in the photos they *do* appear to be friendly, happy, and kind. The moral? **Social perception**—perceiving others and understanding what makes them tick—is a complicated task, more complex and uncertain than you probably guess.

social perception
The process through which we seek to know and understand other persons.

Although social perception is a complex task, it is one we simply must perform: Other people play such an important role in our lives, we can't help but devote a lot of effort to trying to understand them.

Figure 3.1 ■ Social Perception: Trickier Than You Might Guess
Because all we can observe is others' outward appearances and overt behaviors, perceiving them accurately is often difficult. Like the tyrants shown here, people may act in ways that do *not* reflect their underlying traits or motives, and this can lead us seriously astray.

Sometimes these efforts succeed, but as we'll see in later sections, this is not always so, and we often make errors in those efforts. Why is accurately perceiving other persons so difficult? Because, in performing this task, we have to behave like a detective. All we can observe is others' overt actions and outward appearances; we must then use this information as a basis for *inferring* how they are feeling, what kind of persons they are (what lasting traits they possess), why they have acted in various ways (their motives or goals), and how they will act in the future (their plans and intentions). Clearly, this is a complex task, and although we generally perform it well, we are also open to many forms of error.

Social perception has long been recognized by social psychologists as a central aspect of social thought and an important foundation of social behavior, so it has been the topic of careful study for several decades. To acquaint you with the key findings of this research, we focus on several major topics. First, we examine the process of *nonverbal communication*—communication between individuals involving an unspoken language of facial expressions, eye contact, body movements, and postures (e.g., Zebrowitz, 1997).

Next, we examine *attribution,* the complex process through which we attempt to understand the reasons behind others' behavior. Third, we examine the nature of *impression formation*—how we form first impressions of others—and *impression management (*or *self-presentation)*—how we try to ensure that these impressions are favorable. In this discussion, we consider the role of our implicit beliefs about what traits or characteristics typically go together—what social psychologists describe as *implicit theories of personality.* These implicit beliefs can exert strong effects on our impressions of others, and on other aspects of social perception.

Nonverbal Communication: The Language of Expressions, Gazes, and Gestures

Changing moods, shifting emotions, fatigue, illness, and drugs can all influence the ways in which we think and behave. Because such temporary factors exert important effects on social behavior and thought, we are often interested in them: We try to find out how others are feeling *right now.* How do we go about this? Sometimes we ask other persons directly. Unfortunately, this strategy often fails, because others may be unwilling to reveal their inner feelings. Or, they may actively seek to conceal such information or even lie about their current emotions (e.g., DePaulo et al., 2003; Forrest & Feldman, 2000). For example, negotiators often hide their reactions and salespersons frequently show more liking and friendliness toward potential customers than they really feel.

In situations such as these, we often fall back on another, less direct method for gaining information about others' reactions: We pay careful attention to *nonverbal cues* provided by changes in their facial expressions, eye contact, posture, body movements, and other expressive actions. As noted by DePaulo et al. (2003), such behavior is relatively *irrepressible*—difficult to control—so that even when others try to conceal their inner feelings, these often "leak out" through nonverbal cues. The information conveyed by such cues, and our efforts to interpret this input, are often described by the term **nonverbal communication.** In this section, we first examine the basic channels through which nonverbal communication takes place. Then we turn to some interesting findings concerning how we use nonverbal cues to cut through *deception*—efforts by others to mislead us about their true feelings or beliefs (e.g., DePaulo, 1994). Before beginning, though, we must make one point: Nonverbal cues emitted by other persons can affect our feelings, even if we are not consciously paying attention to these cues or trying to figure out how these persons feel. For instance, Neumann and Strack (2000) found that when individuals listen to another person read a speech, the tone of this person's voice (happy, neutral, or sad) can influence the listeners' moods even though they are concentrating on the content of the speech. Neumann and Strack refer to such effects as *emotional contagion*—a mechanism through which feelings are transferred in a seemingly automatic way from one person to another.

nonverbal communication
Communication between individuals that does not involve the content of spoken language. It relies instead on an unspoken language of facial expressions, eye contact, and body language.

Nonverbal Communication: The Basic Channels

Think for a moment: Do you act differently when you are feeling happy than when you are feeling sad? Most likely, you do. People tend to behave differently when experiencing different emotional states. But precisely how do differences in your emotions, feelings, and moods show up in your behavior? This question relates to the *basic channels* through which such communication takes place. Research indicates that five of these channels exist: facial expressions, eye contact, body language, posture, and touching.

■ Unmasking the Face: Facial Expressions as Clues to Others' Emotions

It appears that six basic emotions are represented clearly, and from a very early age, on the human face: anger, fear, happiness, sadness, surprise, and disgust (Izard, 1991; Rozin, Lowery, & Ebert, 1994). Additional findings suggest that another expression—contempt—may also be basic (e.g., Ekman & Heider, 1988). However, agreement on what specific facial expression represents contempt is less consistent than the other six emotions.

It's important to realize that these findings do not imply that human beings can show only a small number of facial expressions. On the contrary, emotions occur in many combinations (e.g., surprise combined with fear), and each of these reactions can vary in strength. Thus, while there may be only a small number of basic facial expressions, the number of variations on these themes is immense (see Figure 3.2).

Are facial expressions universal? In other words, if you traveled to a remote part of the world and visited a group of people who had never met an outsider, would their facial expressions resemble your own? Would they smile in reaction to events that made them happy, frown when exposed to conditions that made them angry, and so on? Further, would you be able to recognize these distinct expressions as readily as the ones shown by persons belonging to your own culture? Early research on this question seemed to suggest that facial expressions *are* universal in both respects (e.g., Ekman & Friesen, 1975). However, some findings have called this conclusion into question (Russell, 1994). The results of more recent studies (e.g., Russell, 1994; Carroll & Russell, 1996) indicate that while facial expressions may reveal much about others' emotions, our judgments in this respect are also affected by the context in which the facial expressions occur and various situational cues. For instance, if individuals view a photo of a face showing what would normally be judged as *fear* but also read a story suggesting that this person is actually showing *anger,* many describe the face as showing anger, not fear (Carroll & Russell, 1996). These findings suggest that facial expressions may not be as universal in terms of providing clear signals about underlying emotions as was previously assumed. However, additional evidence (e.g., Rosenberg & Ekman, 1995) provides support for the view that when

Figure 3.2 ■ Facial Expressions: The Range Is Huge
Although only six basic emotions are represented in distinct facial expressions, these emotions can occur in many combinations and be shown to varying degrees. The result? The number of unique facial expressions any one person can show is truly immense.

situational cues and facial expressions are *not* inconsistent, others' facial expressions do provide an accurate guide to their underlying emotions.

■ Gazes and Stares: Eye Contact as a Nonverbal Cue

Have you ever had a conversation with someone wearing dark sunglasses? If so, you realize that this can be an uncomfortable situation. Because you can't see the other person's eyes, you are uncertain about how she or he is reacting. Taking note of the importance of cues provided by others' eyes, ancient poets often described the eyes as "the windows to the soul." We often learn much about others' feelings from their eyes. For example, we interpret a high level of gazing from another as a sign of liking or friendliness (Kleinke, 1986). In contrast, if others avoid eye contact, we may conclude that they are unfriendly, don't like us, or are simply shy (Zimbardo, 1977).

While a high level of eye contact is usually interpreted as a sign of liking or positive feelings, there is an exception. If another person gazes at us continuously and maintains such contact regardless of what we do, she or he can be said to be **staring.** A stare is often interpreted as a sign of anger or hostility—as in *cold stare*—and most people find this particular nonverbal cue disturbing (Ellsworth & Carlsmith, 1973). In fact, we may quickly terminate social interaction with someone who stares at us and may even leave (Greenbaum & Rosenfield, 1978).

staring
A form of eye contact in which one person continues to gaze steadily at another regardless of what the recipient does.

■ Body Language: Gestures, Posture, and Movements

Try this simple demonstration. First, remember some incident that made you angry, the angrier the better. Think about it for a minute. Now, try to remember another incident, one that made you feel sad—again, the sadder the better. Compare your behavior in the two contexts. Did you change your posture or move your hands, arms, or legs as your thoughts shifted from the first event to the second? There is a good chance that you did, because our current moods or emotions are often reflected in the position, posture, and movement of our bodies. Together, such nonverbal behaviors are termed **body language,** and they, too, can provide useful information about others.

First, body language often reveals others' emotional states. Large numbers of movements, especially ones in which one part of the body does something to another part (touching, rubbing, scratching), suggest emotional arousal. The greater the frequency of such behavior, the higher the level of arousal or nervousness.

body language
Cues provided by the position, posture, and movement of others' bodies or body parts.

Larger patterns of movements, involving the whole body, can also be informative. Statements such as "She adopted a *threatening posture*" and "he greeted her with *open arms*" suggest that different body orientations or postures indicate contrasting emotional states. In fact, research by Aronoff, Woike, and Hyman (1992) confirms this possibility. These researchers first identified two groups of characters in classical ballet: ones who played a dangerous or threatening role (e.g., Macbeth, the Angel of Death, Lizzie Borden) and ones who played warm, sympathetic roles (Juliet, Romeo). Then they examined dancing by these characters in actual ballets to see if they adopted different kinds of postures. Aronoff and his colleagues predicted that the dangerous, threatening characters would show more diagonal or angular postures, while the warm, sympathetic characters would show more rounded postures. Their results strongly confirmed this hypothesis. These and related findings indicate that large-scale body movements or postures can sometimes provide important information about others' emotions, and even about their apparent traits.

More specific information about others' feelings is often provided by gestures. These fall into several categories, but perhaps the most important are *emblems*—body movements carrying specific meanings in a given culture. Do you recognize the gestures shown in Figure 3.3? In the United States and several other countries, these movements have clear and definite meanings. However, in other cultures, they might have no meaning, or even a different meaning. For this reason, it is wise to be careful about using gestures while traveling in cultures different from your own: You may offend the people around you without meaning to do so!

Figure 3.3 ■ Gestures: One Form of Nonverbal Communication
Do you recognize the gestures shown here? Can you tell what they mean? In the United States and other western cultures, each of these gestures has a clear meaning. However, they might have no meaning, or entirely different meanings, in other cultures.

Interestingly, research (e.g., Schubert, 2004) indicates that specific gestures can have different meanings for women and men. For instance, for men, gestures associated with bodily force, such as a clenched fist, seem to signal increased power (or efforts to obtain it); for women, such bodily actions seem to signal *loss* of power or reduced hope of gaining it. This may reflect the fact that men are physically stronger than women, and so often seek to gain power through force, while for women, force is more often defensive and has much less chance of success.

■ Touching: Is a Firm Handshake Really a Plus?

Suppose that during a conversation with another person, she or he touched you briefly. How would you react? What would this behavior convey? The answer to both questions is *it depends*. It depends on several factors relating to who does the touching (a friend, a stranger, a member of your own or the other gender), the nature of this physical contact (brief or prolonged, gentle or rough, what part of the body is touched), and the context in which the touching takes place (a business or social setting, a doctor's office). Given such factors, touch can suggest affection, sexual interest, dominance, caring, or even aggression. Despite such complexities, existing evidence indicates that when touching is considered appropriate, it often produces positive reactions in the person being touched (e.g., Alagna, Whitcher, & Fisher, 1979; Smith, Gier, & Willis, 1982).

One acceptable way in which people in different cultures touch strangers is through handshaking. Pop psychology and even books on etiquette (e.g., Vanderbilt, 1957) suggest that handshakes reveal much about other persons—for instance, their personalities—and that a firm handshake is a good way to make a favorable first impression. Are such observations true? Is this form of nonverbal communication actually revealing? Research findings (e.g., Chaplin et al., 2000) suggest that it is. The firmer, longer, and more vigorous others' handshakes are, the higher we tend to rate them in terms of extraversion and openness to experience. Further, the firmer and longer the handshakes are, the more favorable our first impressions tend to be.

Recognizing Deception: The Role of Nonverbal Cues

Why do people lie? For many reasons: to avoid hurting others' feelings, to conceal their real feelings or reactions, to avoid punishment for misdeeds. In short, lying is an all-too-common part of social life (see Figure 3.4). This raises two important questions: (1) How good are we at recognizing deception by others? And (2) how can we do a better job at this

"In my ad, I lied about my age."

task? The answer to the first question is somewhat discouraging. In general, we do only a little better than chance in determining whether others are lying or telling the truth (e.g., Malone & DePaulo, 2003; Ekman, 2001). There are many reasons why this is so, including the fact that we tend to perceive others as truthful and so don't search for clues to deception (Ekman, 2001); our desire to be polite, which makes us reluctant to discover or report deception by others; and our lack of attention to nonverbal cues that might reveal deception (e.g., Etcoff et al., 2000). Recently, another compelling explanation has been added to this list: We tend to assume that if people are truthful in one situation or context, they will be truthful in others, which can prevent us from realizing that they might lie on some occasions (e.g., O'Sullivan, 2003). We return to this possibility in more detail in our later discussion of *attribution*. We should add that trying to "read" others' nonverbal cues accurately does not always center on efforts to determine whether they are telling the truth. Recent findings (e.g., Pickett, Gardner, & Knowles, 2004) indicate that accuracy in decoding nonverbal cues is also related to the desire to be liked and accepted by others—the more individuals *need to belong,* the better they tend to be at reading nonverbal cues because they pay careful attention to others and *want* to understand them.

Given that nearly everyone engages in deception at least occasionally, the question of how we might do a better job of recognizing lies when they occur is an important one. The answer seems to involve careful attention to both nonverbal and verbal cues that can reveal that others are trying to deceive us.

With respect to nonverbal cues, the following information is very helpful (e.g., DePaulo et al., 2003):

1. *Microexpressions:* These are fleeting facial expressions that last only a few tenths of a second. Such reactions appear on the face after an emotion-provoking event and are difficult to suppress, thus revealing others' true feelings or emotions. For instance, if you ask others whether they like something (e.g., an idea you have expressed, something you have just purchased), watch their faces closely as they respond. One expression (e.g., a frown) followed quickly by another (e.g., a smile) can be a useful sign that they are lying.

2. *Interchannel discrepancies:* These are inconsistencies among nonverbal cues from different basic channels, resulting from the fact that persons who are lying often find it difficult to control all of these channels at once. (The term *channel* refers to a type of nonverbal cue; for instance, facial expressions are one channel, and body movements are another.) For instance, they may manage their facial expressions but have difficulty looking you in the eye.

3. *Eye contact:* Efforts at deception are often revealed by certain aspects of eye contact. Liars often blink more and show more dilated pupils. They may also show an unusually low level of eye contact or—surprisingly—an unusually high level, as they attempt to fake being honest by looking others right in their eyes.

4. *Exaggerated facial expressions:* Persons who are lying sometimes show exaggerated facial expressions. They may smile more—or more broadly—than usual or may show greater sorrow than is typical. A prime example: Someone says "no" to a request you've made

microexpressions
Fleeting facial expressions lasting only a few tenths of a second.

KEY POINTS

★ *Social perception* involves the processes through which we seek to understand others. It plays a key role in social behavior and thought.

★ To understand others' emotional states, we often rely on *nonverbal communication*—an unspoken language of facial expressions, eye contact, and body movements and postures.

★ Although facial expressions may not be as universal as once believed, they can provide useful information about others' emotional states. Useful information is also provided by eye contact, body language, and touching.

★ Recent findings indicate that handshakes provide useful nonverbal cues about others' personalities and can influence first impressions.

★ If we pay careful attention to certain nonverbal cues, we can recognize efforts at deception by others.

★ Women are better than men at sending and interpreting nonverbal cues. This gives them an important advantage in many situations and may account for the widespread belief in "women's intuition."

Attribution: Understanding the Causes of Others' Behavior

attribution
The process through which we seek to identify the causes of others' behavior and so gain knowledge of their stable traits and dispositions.

Accurate knowledge of others' current moods or feelings can be very useful. Yet, where social perception is concerned, this knowledge is often the first step. In addition, we usually want to know more—to understand others' lasting traits and to know the causes behind their behavior. Social psychologists believe that our interest in such questions stems from our basic desire to understand cause-and-effect relationships in the social world (Pittman, 1993; Van Overwalle, 1998). In other words, we don't simply want to know *how* others have acted; we want to understand *why* they have done so, too, because this knowledge can help us predict how they will act in the future. The process through which we seek such information is known as **attribution.** More formally, *attribution* refers to our efforts to understand the causes behind others' behavior and, on some occasions, the causes behind *our* behavior. Social psychologists have studied attribution for several decades, and their research has yielded many intriguing insights (e.g., Graham & Folkes, 1990; Heider, 1958; Read & Miller, 1998).

Theories of Attribution: Frameworks for Understanding How We Attempt to Make Sense of the Social World

Because attribution is complex, many theories have been proposed to explain its operation. Here, we focus on two classic views that have been especially influential.

correspondent inference (theory of)
A theory describing how we use others' behavior as a basis for inferring their stable dispositions.

■ From Acts to Dispositions: Using Others' Behavior as a Guide to Their Lasting Traits

The first—Jones and Davis's (1965) theory of **correspondent inference**—asks how we use information about others' behavior as a basis for inferring that they possess various traits. At first glance, this might seem simple. Others' behavior provides us with a rich source of information to draw on, so if we carefully observe the behavior of others, we should be able to learn a lot about them. Up to a point, this is true. The task is complicated, however, because individuals often act in certain ways, not because doing so reflects their own preferences or traits, but rather because *external factors* leave them little choice. For example, suppose you observe a customer acting rudely toward a salesperson. Does this mean that the customer is a nasty person who often treats others rudely? Not necessarily. She may simply be responding to the fact that the salesperson ignored her and waited on two other customers even though she was first in line. So, her behavior may be the exception, not the rule. Situations such as this are common, and in them, using others' behavior as a guide to their lasting traits or motives can be misleading.

How do we cope with such complications? According to Jones and Davis's theory (Jones & Davis, 1965; Jones & McGillis, 1976), we focus our attention on certain types of actions—those most likely to prove informative. First, we consider only behavior that seems to have been chosen freely, while largely ignoring ones that were somehow forced on the person in question. Second, we pay attention to actions that show what Jones and Davis term **noncommon effects**—effects that can be caused by one specific factor but not by others. (Don't confuse *noncommon* with *uncommon,* which simply means "infrequent.") Why are actions that produce noncommon effects informative? Because they allow us to zero in on the causes of others' behavior. For example, imagine that one of your friends has just become engaged. His future spouse is very attractive, has a great personality, is wildly in love with your friend, and is very rich. What can you learn about your friend from his decision to marry this woman? Not much. There are so many good reasons for his decision that you can't choose among them. In contrast, imagine that your friend's fiancée is very attractive but that she treats him with indifference and is known to be extremely boring; also, she is deeply in debt and is known to live far beyond her means. Does the fact that your friend is marrying this woman tell you anything about him under these conditions? Definitely. You can probably conclude that he cares more about physical beauty than personality or wealth. As you can see from this example, then, we can usually learn more about others from actions on their part that yield noncommon effects than from ones that do not.

Finally, Jones and Davis suggest that we also pay greater attention to actions by others that are low in *social desirability* than to actions that are high on this dimension. In other words, we learn more about others' traits from actions they perform that are somehow out of the ordinary than from actions that are very much like those of most people.

In sum, according to the theory proposed by Jones and Davis, we are most likely to conclude that others' behavior reflects their stable traits (i.e., we are likely to reach *correspondent* inferences about them) when that behavior (1) is freely chosen; (2) yields distinctive, noncommon effects; and (3) is low in social desirability.

noncommon effects
Effects produced by a particular cause that could not be produced by any other apparent cause.

■ Kelley's Theory of Causal Attributions: How We Answer the Question "Why?"

Consider the following events:

> *You arrange to meet someone for lunch, but he doesn't show up.*

> *You leave several messages for a friend, but she doesn't call back.*

> *You expect a promotion in your job but don't receive it.*

In all of these situations, you would probably wonder *why* these events occurred: *Why* didn't your lunch date show up? *Why* has your friend failed to return your messages? *Why* didn't you get the promotion? We want to know why other people have acted as they have or why events have turned out in a specific way. Such knowledge is crucial, because only if we understand the causes behind others' actions or events can we hope to make sense out of the social world. Obviously, the number of specific causes behind others' behavior is large. To make the task more manageable, therefore, we often begin with a preliminary question: Did others' behavior stem mainly from *internal* causes (their own traits, motives, intentions), mainly from *external* causes (some aspect of the social or physical world), or from a combination of the two? For example, you might wonder whether you didn't receive the promotion because you really haven't worked very hard (an internal cause), because your boss is unfair and biased against you (an external cause), or perhaps because of both factors.

A theory proposed by Kelley (Kelley, 1972; Kelley & Michela, 1980) provides important insights into this process. According to Kelley, in our attempts to answer the question *Why?* about others' behavior, we focus on three major types of information. First, we consider **consensus**—the extent to which others react to a given stimulus or event in the same manner as the person we are considering. The higher the proportion of people who react in the same way, the higher the consensus. Second, we consider **consistency**—the extent to which the person reacts to the stimulus or event in the same way on other occasions. And third, we examine **distinctiveness**—the extent to which this person reacts in the same manner to other stimuli or events.

According to Kelley's theory, we are most likely to attribute another's behavior to *internal* causes under conditions in which consensus and distinctiveness are low but consistency is high. In contrast, we are most likely to attribute another's behavior to *external* causes when consensus, consistency, and distinctiveness are all high. Finally, we usually attribute another's behavior to a combination of internal and external factors when consensus is low but consistency and distinctiveness are high. Perhaps a concrete example will help illustrate these ideas.

Imagine that you see a server in a restaurant flirt with a customer. This behavior raises an interesting question: Why does the server act this way? Because of internal causes or external causes? Is she simply someone who likes to flirt (an internal cause)? Or is the customer extremely attractive (an external cause)? According to Kelley's theory, your decision (as an observer) would depend on information relating to the three factors mentioned previously. First, assume that the following conditions prevail: (1) You observe other servers flirting with this customer (consensus is high); (2) you have seen this server flirt with the same customer on other occasions (consistency is high); and (3) you have *not* seen this server flirt with other customers (distinctiveness is high). Under these conditions—high consensus, consistency, and distinctiveness—you would probably attribute the server's behavior to external causes: This customer is very attractive, and that's why the server flirts with him.

Now, in contrast, assume these conditions: (1) No other servers flirt with the customer (consensus is low); (2) you have seen this server flirt with the same customer on other occasions (consistency is high); and (3) you have seen this server flirt with many other customers, too (distinctiveness is low). In this case, Kelley's theory suggests that you would attribute the server's behavior to internal causes: The server is simply a person who likes to flirt (see Figure 3.7).

The basic assumptions of Kelley's theory have been confirmed in a range of social situations, so it seems to provide important

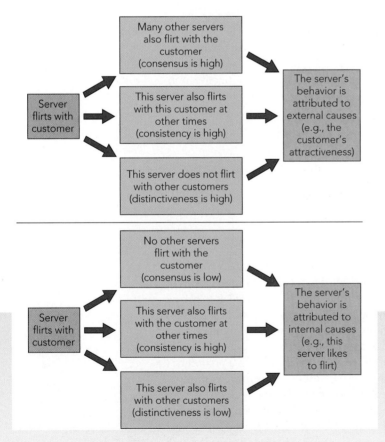

Figure 3.7 ■ Kelley's Theory of Causal Attribution: An Example
Under the conditions shown in the top of this figure, we would attribute the server's behavior to external causes. Under the conditions shown in the bottom, however, we would attribute the server's behavior to internal causes.

insights into the nature of causal attributions. However, research on the theory also suggests the need for certain modifications or extensions, as described below.

■ Other Dimensions of Causal Attribution

Although we are often very interested in knowing whether others' behavior stemmed mainly from internal or external causes, this is not the entire story. We are also concerned with two other questions: (1) Are the causal factors that influenced their behavior likely to be *stable* over time or to change, and (2) are these factors *controllable*—can the individual change or influence them if she or he wishes to do so (Weiner, 1993, 1995)? These dimensions are independent of the internal–external dimension we considered. For instance, some internal causes of behavior tend to be stable over time— personality traits and temperament (e.g., Miles & Carey, 1997). In contrast, other internal causes can, and often do, change greatly—for instance, motives, health, fatigue. Similarly, some internal causes are *controllable*—individuals can learn to hold their tempers in check; other internal causes, such as chronic illnesses or disabilities, are not controllable. Some external causes of behavior are stable over time (e.g., laws or social norms that indicate how we should behave in various situations), while others are not (e.g., bad luck). A large body of evidence indicates that in trying to understand the causes behind others' behavior, we take note of all three of these dimensions— internal–external, stable–unstable, controllable–uncontrollable (Weiner, 1985, 1995). Moreover, our thinking in this respect strongly influences our conclusions concerning important matters, such as whether others are *personally responsible* for their own actions (e.g., Graham, Weiner, & Zucker, 1997).

■ Augmenting and Discounting: How We Handle Multiple Potential Causes

Suppose that your boss stops by your desk and praises your work, telling you that you are doing a wonderful job and that she is glad to have you working with her. She does this in front of several employees, who all congratulate you after she leaves. For the rest of the morning, you feel great. Then, after lunch, she calls you into her office and asks if you would take on an extra, difficult work assignment. Now you begin to wonder: Why did she praise your work? Because she really wanted to thank you for doing a good job *or* because she was going to ask you to take on extra work? There are two possible causes behind her behavior, and because there are, you may well engage in what social psychologists term **discounting**—you view the first possible cause (her desire to give you positive feedback) as less important or likely because another possible cause for this action exists, too (i.e., she wanted to set you up to do extra work). Studies indicate that discounting is a common occurrence and exerts a strong effect on our attributions in many situations (e.g., Gilbert & Malone, 1995; Morris & Larrick, 1995; Trope & Liberman, 1996). However, discounting is far from universal. For instance, suppose that you have a very thrifty friend—he literally pinches pennies. He is also a member of several proenvironmental groups. You visit his home during the winter and find that he has set his thermostats very low. In this situation, you can't use one of your attributions about him (e.g., he is thrifty) to discount the other (he is strongly in favor of protecting the environment; McClure, 1998).

Now, imagine the previous situation with one difference: Your boss has a strong policy against giving employees feedback in front of others. What will you conclude about her behavior now? Probably that the feedback was really motivated by a genuine desire to tell you that she is pleased with your work. After all, she has done so despite the presence of another factor that would be expected to *prevent* her from doing this (her own policy against public feedback). This illustrates what social psychologists describe as **augmenting**—the tendency to assign added weight or importance to a factor that might facilitate a given behavior when this factor and another factor that might *inhibit* such

discounting principle
The tendency to attach less importance to one potential cause of some behavior when other potential causes are also present.

augmenting principle
The tendency to attach greater importance to a potential cause of behavior if the behavior occurs despite the presence of other, inhibitory causes.

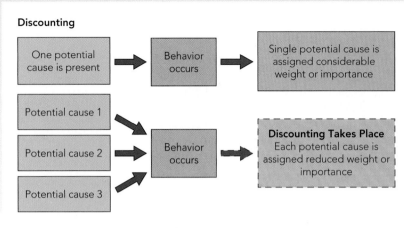

Discounting

Augmenting

Figure 3.8 ■ **Augmenting and Discounting in Causal Attribution**
According to the *discounting* principle (*upper diagram*), we attach less weight or importance to a given cause of some behavior when other potential causes of that behavior are also present. According to the *augmenting* principle (*lower diagram*), we attach greater weight to a potential cause of some behavior if that behavior occurs despite the presence of another factor that would tend to inhibit its occurrence.

behavior are both present, *yet the behavior still occurs* (see Figure 3.8 for an overview of both attributional discounting and augmenting). In this case, you conclude that your boss actually is pleased with your behavior.

Evidence for the occurrence of attributional augmenting and discounting is found in many studies (e.g., Baron, Markman, & Hirsa, 2001), so it seems clear that these principles help explain how we deal with situations in which others' behavior could stem from several different causes.

KEY POINTS

★ To obtain information about others' lasting traits, motives, and intentions, we often engage in *attribution*— efforts to understand why they have acted as they have.

★ According to Jones and Davis's theory of *correspondent inference,* we attempt to infer others' traits from observing certain aspects of their behavior, especially behavior that is freely chosen, produces *noncommon effects,* and is low in social desirability.

★ Kelley's theory of causal attribution asks whether others' behavior stems from internal or external causes. To answer this question, we focus on information relating to *consensus, consistency,* and *distinctiveness.*

★ Two other dimensions of causal attribution relate to whether specific causes of behavior are stable over time and are controllable or not controllable.

★ When two or more potential causes of another person's behavior exist, we tend to downplay the importance of each—an effect known as *discounting.* When a cause that facilitates a behavior and a cause that inhibits it exist, but the behavior still occurs, we assign added weight to the facilitative factors—an effect known as *augmenting.*

Attribution: Some Basic Sources of Error

A basic theme we develop in this book is that although we generally do a good job in terms of thinking about the social world, we are far from perfect in this respect. In fact, our efforts to understand other persons—and ourselves—are subject to several types of errors that can lead us to false conclusions about why others have acted as they have and how they will behave in the future. Let's take a look at several of these errors now.

■ The Correspondence Bias: Overestimating the Role of Dispositional Causes

Imagine that you witness the following. A man arrives at a meeting one hour late. On entering, he drops his notes on the floor. While trying to pick them up, his glasses fall and break. Later, he spills coffee on his tie. How would you explain these events? The chances are good that you would reach a conclusion such as "This person is disorganized and clumsy." Is such an attribution accurate? Perhaps; but it is also possible that the man was late because of unavoidable delays at the airport, that he dropped his notes because they were printed on slick paper, and that he spilled his coffee because the cup was too hot. The fact that you would be less likely to consider such potential *external* causes of his behavior illustrates what Jones (1979) labeled **correspondence bias**—the tendency to explain others' actions as stemming from (corresponding to) dispositions, even in the presence of clear situational causes (e.g., Gilbert & Malone, 1995). This bias seems to be so general in scope that many social psychologists refer to it as the *fundamental attribution error*. In short, we tend to perceive others as acting as they do because they are "that kind of person," rather than because of the many external factors that may influence their behavior. This tendency occurs in a wide range of contexts, but research (e.g., Van Overwalle, 1997) indicates that it is strongest in situations in which consensus and distinctiveness are low, as predicted by Kelley's theory, and when we are trying to predict others' behavior in the far-off future rather than in the immediate future (Nussbaum, Trope, & Liberman, 2003). Why? Because when we think of the far-off future, we tend to do so in abstract terms, and this leads us to think about others in terms of global traits resulting in overlooking potential external causes of their behavior.

Social psychologists have conducted many studies to find out why this bias occurs (e.g., Robins, Spranca, & Mendelsohn, 1996), but the answer is still unclear. One possibility is that when we observe another person's behavior, we tend to focus on his or her actions; hence potential situational causes of his or her behavior often fade into the background. As a result, dispositional causes (internal causes) are easier to notice (they are more *salient*) than situational ones. From our perspective, the person we are observing is high in *perceptual salience* and is the focus of our attention, while situational factors that might have influenced this person's behavior are less salient and seem less important. Another explanation is that we notice such situational causes but give them insufficient weight in our attributions. Still another explanation is when we focus on others' behavior, we tend to begin by assuming that their actions reflect their underlying characteristics. Then, we attempt to correct for any possible effects of the external world by taking these into account. (This involves a kind of mental shortcut known as *anchoring and adjustment,* covered in Chapter 2.) This correction, however, is often insufficient: We don't make enough allowance for the impact of external factors or give enough weight to the possibility of delays at the airport or a slippery floor, for example, when reaching our conclusions (Gilbert & Malone, 1995).

Evidence for this two-step process—a quick, automatic reaction followed by a slower, more controlled correction—has been obtained in many studies (e.g., Gilbert, 2002; Chaiken & Trope, 1999), so it seems to offer a compelling explanation for the correspondence bias (i.e., fundamental attribution error). In fact, it appears that most people are aware of this process, or are at least aware of the fact that they start by assuming other people behave as they do because of internal causes (e.g., their personality, their true beliefs), but then correct this assumption, at least to a degree, by taking account of situational constraints.

Perhaps even more interesting, we tend to assume that *we* adjust our attributions to take account of situational constraints more than others do. In other words, we perceive that we are less likely to fall victim to the correspondence bias than are others. This tendency is illustrated in studies by Van Boven et al. (2003). In one investigation, participants were asked to rate the extent to which a terrible crime (the massacre of twelve students and one teacher by students at a high school in Colorado) was due to the evil nature of the boys who performed this atrocity

correspondence bias (fundamental attribution error) The tendency to explain others' actions as stemming from dispositions, even in the presence of clear situational causes.

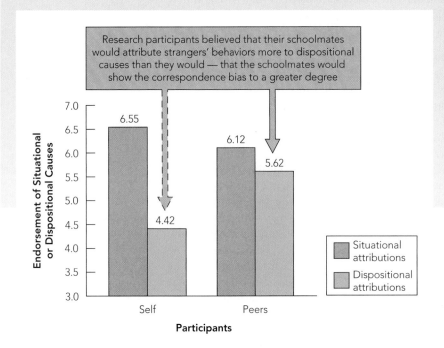

Research participants believed that their schoolmates would attribute strangers' behaviors more to dispositional causes than they would — that the schoolmates would show the correspondence bias to a greater degree

Figure 3.9 ■ **"You Fall Victim to the Correspondence Bias; I Avoid (or at Least Minimize) It"** Research participants assumed that they would show the correspondence bias to a lesser extent than would others. Specifically, they believed that their schoolmates would attribute strangers' behavior to dispositional causes to a greater extent than they would. (*Source: Based on data from Van Boven et al., 2003.*)

(internal causes) or external factors such as harassment by fellow students and problems in their families. Participants were asked to estimate how other students in their school would rate these causes. Figure 3.9 indicates that participants felt that they would show the correspondence bias to a much lesser degree than other students at their school. In other words, they felt that they would attribute this crime more to situational (external) causes and less to dispositional (internal) causes than would other persons. Not only do we tend to overestimate the importance of internal causes in shaping others' behavior, we tend to believe that we correct for this error to a greater extent than do other persons.

■ Cultural Factors in the Fundamental Attribution Error

Is this tendency to emphasize dispositional causes truly universal, or is it influenced by cultural factors? Research indicates that while this tendency is somewhat universal, culture does play a role. Specifically, the fundamental attribution error appears to be more common in cultures that emphasize individual freedom—*individualistic* cultures such as those in Western Europe, the United States, or Canada—than in *collectivistic* cultures that emphasize group membership, conformity, and interdependence (e.g., Triandis, 1990). This difference seems to reflect that in individualistic cultures, there is a *norm of internality*—the view that people should accept responsibility for their own outcomes. In collectivistic cultures, in contrast, this norm is weaker or absent (Jellison & Green, 1981). We return to this topic in Chapter 5.

One of the studies carried out by Van Boven et al. (2003) provides support for the role of cultural factors in the fundamental attribution error. In one of their experiments, they asked students in the United States and Japan to imagine that they read an essay or heard a speech by a stranger who had been told to support a particular point of view on various controversial issues (e.g., abortion, the death penalty). Participants were asked to estimate how much they would correct their initial impression of the stranger's real attitudes after learning that he had been told to write the essay in a specific way, and how much other persons would correct *their* impressions. The researchers predicted that students in the United States would assume that they would correct for the correspondence more than other persons. However, Japanese students would not show this effect and, in fact, would demonstrate the correspondence bias to a lesser degree. In other words, they would attribute the stranger's behavior primarily to external causes (the fact that he was told to write the essay to support a particular point of view). Results confirmed these predictions, thus suggesting that cultural differences matter where the correspondence bias is concerned. Similar findings—more correspondence bias in western, individualistic countries than in Asian and more collectivistic ones—have been reported in other studies (e.g., Choi and Nisbett, 1998).

Figure 3.10 ■ Attributions about Groups: The Correspondence Bias Revisited Jewish research participants attributed German atrocities during World War II to internal causes (Germans' aggressiveness) to a greater extent than did German participants. Germans, in contrast, tended to explain these atrocities in terms of external causes (e.g., historical events and contexts). (*Source: Based on data from Doosje & Branscombe, 2003.*)

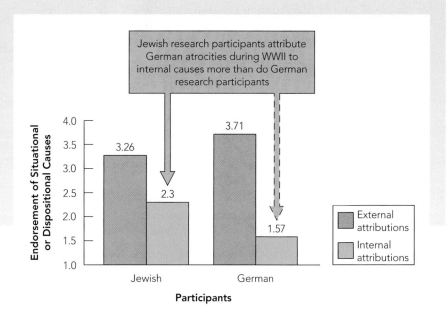

■ The Correspondence Bias in Attributions about Groups

Not only do we make attributions about the behavior of individuals, we also sometimes make attributions about the behavior of groups. For instance, we try to understand why one group seems to dislike another—why, for example, did the Tutsis and Hutus (groups living in Rwanda) hate each other to the point that it erupted into open genocide? And why did so many Germans hate Jews in pre–World War II Germany? Are our attributions about why various groups behave as they do also subject to the correspondence bias? Research conducted by Doosje and Branscombe (2003) suggests that it is. These researchers asked visitors to Anne Frank's home in Amsterdam to rate the extent to which German atrocities against Jews during World War II were due to the aggressive nature of Germans (an internal cause) or to the historical context in which these actions occurred (external factors). Participants were either Jewish or German. The researchers predicted that Jewish people would show a greater tendency to attribute German atrocities to internal causes than would Germans, and, in fact, this is what was found (see Figure 3.10). While neither group showed a strong tendency to explain these events in terms of internal causes, Jewish people—whose group had been harmed—showed this tendency to a greater extent than Germans, thus demonstrating that attributions can be strongly affected by group membership, an effect we consider again in Chapters 6 and 12. It seems clear that attributional processes—and errors—can operate for social groups or even entire nations with respect to perceptions of individuals.

■ The Actor–Observer Effect: "You Fell; I Was Pushed."

The fundamental attribution error, powerful as it is, applies mainly to attributions we make about others—we don't tend to "overattribute" our own actions to external causes. This helps explain another, closely related type of attributional error known as the **actor–observer effect** (Jones & Nisbett, 1971), which involves our tendency to attribute our behavior to situational (external) causes but that of others to dispositional (internal) ones. Thus, when we see another person fall, we tend to attribute this to his or her clumsiness. If *we* trip, however, we are more likely to attribute this event to situational causes, such as ice on the sidewalk.

Why does the actor–observer effect occur? In part because we are aware of the external factors affecting our own actions but less aware of such factors when we turn our attention to others' actions. Thus, we tend to perceive our behavior as arising largely from situational causes but that of others as deriving mainly from their traits or dispositions.

■ The Self-Serving Bias: "I'm Good; You Are Lucky."

Suppose you write a term paper and when you get it back, you find the following comment on the first page: "An outstanding paper—one of the best I've seen in years. A+." To what will

actor–observer effect
The tendency to attribute our own behavior mainly to situational causes but the behavior of others mainly to internal (dispositional) causes.

Figure 3.11 ■ The Self-Serving Bias in Action
As shown in this cartoon, we have a strong tendency to attribute negative outcomes to external causes (e.g., other persons, society) while attributing positive outcomes to internal causes (e.g., our own characteristics). (*Source:* NON SEQUITUR © 1994 Wiley Miller. Dist. By UNIVERSAL PRESS SYNDICATE. Reprinted with permission. All rights reserved.)

self-serving bias
The tendency to attribute positive outcomes to internal causes (e.g., one's own traits or characteristics) but negative outcomes or events to external causes (e.g., chance, task difficulty).

you attribute this success? Probably you will explain it in terms of internal causes: your high level of talent, the effort you invested in writing it, and so on. Now imagine when you get the paper back, *these* comments are written on it, "Horrible paper—one of the worst I've seen in years. D–." How will you interpret *this* outcome? The chances are good that you will be tempted to focus on external (situational) factors: the difficulty of the task, the unfairly harsh grading standards, the fact that you didn't have enough time to do a good job, and so on.

This tendency to attribute our own positive outcomes to internal causes but our negative ones to external factors is known as the **self-serving bias,** and it appears to be both general in scope and powerful in its effects (see Figure 3.11; Brown & Rogers, 1991; Miller & Ross, 1975).

Why does this tilt in our attributions occur? Several possibilities have been suggested, but most fall into two categories: cognitive and motivational explanations. The cognitive model suggests that the self-serving bias stems mainly from certain tendencies in the way we process social information (see Chapter 2; Ross, 1977). Specifically, it suggests that we attribute positive outcomes to internal causes but negative ones to external causes because we *expect* to succeed and have a tendency to attribute expected outcomes to internal causes more than to external ones. In contrast, the motivational explanation suggests that the self-serving bias stems from our need to protect and enhance our self-esteem or the related desire to look good to others (Greenberg, Pyszczynski, & Solomon, 1982). While both cognitive and motivational factors may play a role in this kind of attributional error, research evidence seems to offer more support for the motivational view (e.g., Brown & Rogers, 1991).

Whatever the origins of the self-serving bias, it can be the cause of interpersonal friction. It often leads persons who work with others on a joint task to perceive that *they*, not their partners, have made the major contributions. I see this effect in my classes every semester when students rate their contribution and that of the other team members in a required term project. The result? Most students take lots of credit for themselves when the project has gone well but tend to blame (and downrate) their partners if it has not.

Interestingly, the results of several studies indicate that the strength of the self-serving bias varies across cultures (e.g., Oettingen, 1995; Oettingen & Seligman, 1990). In particular, the self-serving bias is weaker in Asian cultures that place a greater emphasis on group outcomes and harmony than it is in western cultures, in which individual accomplishments are emphasized and it is considered appropriate for winners to gloat (at least a little) over their victories (see Figure 3.12). For example, Lee and Seligman (1997) found that Americans of European descent showed a larger self-serving bias than either Chinese Americans or mainland Chinese. Once again, therefore, we see that cultural factors often play an important role, even in very basic aspects of social behavior and thought.

Figure 3.12 ■ The Self-Serving Bias: Stronger in Some Cultures Than in Others
Research findings indicate that the self-serving bias is stronger in western cultures than in Asian ones. This is why western athletes or politicians seem to gloat after their victories, while Asian athletes or politicians are less likely to show such reactions.

Before concluding, we should note that despite the errors described here, growing evidence suggests that social perception *can* be accurate—we do, in many cases, reach accurate conclusions about others' traits and motives from observing their behaviors. We examine some of the evidence pointing to this conclusion as part of our discussion of the process of impression formation. (Please see the **Ideas to Take with You—and Use!** section at the end of this chapter for some tips on how to avoid various attributional errors.)

KEY POINTS

★ *Attribution* is subject to many potential sources of error. One of the most important is the *correspondence bias*—the tendency to explain others' actions as stemming from dispositions, even in the presence of situational causes. This tendency seems to be stronger in western cultures than in Asian cultures and can occur for attributions for groups as well as for individuals.

★ Two other attributional errors are the *actor–observer effect*—the tendency to attribute our behavior to external (situational) causes but that of others to internal causes—and the *self-serving bias*—the tendency to attribute positive outcomes to internal causes but negative ones to external causes.

★ The strength of the self-serving bias varies across cultures, being stronger in western societies than in Asian cultures.

Applications of Attribution Theory: Insights and Interventions

Kurt Lewin, one of the founders of modern social psychology (see Chapter 1), often remarked, "There's nothing as practical as a good theory." By this he meant that once we obtain scientific understanding of some aspect of social behavior or social thought, we can potentially put this knowledge to use. In attribution theory, this has definitely been the case. As basic knowledge about attribution has grown, so, too, has the range of practical problems to which such information has been applied (Miller & Rempel, 2004; Graham & Folkes, 1990). Here, we examine two important, and timely, applications of attribution theory.

■ Attribution and Depression

Depression is the most common psychological disorder. Estimates show that almost half of all humans experience such problems at some time in their lives (e.g., Blazer et al., 1994). Although many factors play a role in depression, one that has received increasing attention is what might be termed a *self-defeating* pattern of attributions. In contrast to most people, who show the self-serving bias described previously, depressed individuals tend to adopt an opposite pattern. They attribute *negative* outcomes to lasting, internal causes, such as their traits or lack of ability, but attribute *positive* outcomes to temporary, external causes, such as good luck or favors (see Figure 3.13). As a result, such persons perceive that they have little control over what happens to them—they are mere chips in the

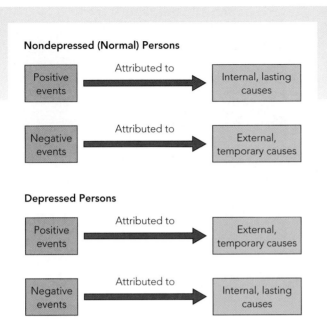

Nondepressed (Normal) Persons

Positive events → Attributed to → Internal, lasting causes

Negative events → Attributed to → External, temporary causes

Depressed Persons

Positive events → Attributed to → External, temporary causes

Negative events → Attributed to → Internal, lasting causes

Figure 3.13 ■ Attribution and Depression
While most persons tend to attribute positive events to internal, lasting causes and negative events to external, temporary ones, depressed persons show the opposite pattern.

winds of unpredictable fate. It is little wonder that they become depressed and tend to give up on life. And once they *are* depressed, the tendency to engage in this self-defeating pattern is strengthened, often initiating a vicious cycle. Fortunately, several forms of therapy that focus on changing such attributions have been developed and appear to be successful (e.g., Bruder et al., 1997; Robinson, Berman, & Neimeyer, 1990). These forms of therapy focus on getting depressed persons to take personal credit for successful outcomes, to stop blaming themselves for negative outcomes (especially ones that can't be avoided), and to view some failures as the result of external factors beyond their control.

■ Attribution in Workplaces: Understanding Reactions to Sexual Harassment

sexual harassment
Unwanted contact or communication of a sexual nature.

There is little doubt that **sexual harassment**—unwanted contact or communication of a sexual nature—is an all-too-common occurrence in work settings (see Figure 3.14; e.g., O'Donohue, 1997). In fact, surveys find almost one third of all working women report that they have had such experiences (Greenberg & Baron, 2002). A key issue relating to sexual harassment is that it is perceived differently by different social groups. For instance, men are less likely to define various actions as sexual harassment than are women (e.g., Runtz & O'Donnell, 2003). In part, such differences seem to involve the perceived motives and intentions behind the actions. For instance, men may view a comment on a woman's appearance as an inoffensive compliment, while women may view it as harassment. This difference suggests that attribution plays a key role in how people perceive and judge sexual harassment. Evidence that attribution theory can be helpful in dealing with this problem has been provided by several studies (e.g., Wayne, Riordan, & Thomas, 2001). Among these, a study conducted recently by Smirles (2004) offers especially revealing findings.

In this study, male and female students read a brief description of an employer who threatened the career of an employee if this person did not consent to having a relationship. The gender of both the employer and the victim was systematically varied so that different groups of participants were exposed to all possible combinations (a male harassing a male, a male harassing a female, a female harassing a female, a

Figure 3.14 ■ Sexual Harassment: Insights from Attribution Theory
Sexual harassment is a serious problem. Attribution theory helps explain why men and women differ in their perceptions of this problem, and suggests potential ways of reducing its occurrence.

female harassing a male). After reading this information, they rated the extent to which the employer and the empolyee were responsible for what had happened. Results from this portion of the study indicated that male participants held the employee more responsible and the employer less responsible than did female participants, regardless of the gender of the victim or the perpetrator. Why did this occur? One aspect of attribution theory—*defensive attribution*—offers an intriguing possibility.

Defensive attribution occurs when we notice that we are similar to someone who has experienced negative outcomes (e.g., a victim of sexual harassment). This causes us distress because we reason that since we are similar, we might experience these outcomes, too. To reduce these negative reactions, we attribute blame to external causes—the perpetrator—while minimizing blame for the victim. Because women are more often the victims of sexual harassment than men, women would be expected to perceive greater similarity to the victim (regardless of this person's gender) and blame the victim less for the negative events.

In a second part of the study, participants read a description of the victim's response: acquiescence (giving in to the demands of the employer) or resistance (threatening to report the employer to a supervisor); a control group received no information on the victim's reaction. Attribution theory predicts that a victim who gives in to the demands of an employer will be held more responsible for the harassment than one who resists, because it is clear that victims *can* resist; if they don't, this is attributed, at least in part, to internal factors such as weakness on their part. These predictions, too, were confirmed: Victims who acquiesced were held more responsible by both women and men than ones who resisted.

Overall, these findings, and those of related research, suggest that attribution theory can offer important insights into the causes, and perhaps prevention, of sexual harassment. For instance, increasing males' awareness of their similarity to the victims of such treatment may cause them to blame persons who engage in sexual harassment more and victims less. Because most sexual harassment is performed by men, this could lead to reductions in such behavior. In this and other ways, knowledge regarding attributions can be valuable.

KEY POINTS

★ *Attribution* has been applied to many practical problems. Depressed persons often show a pattern of attributions opposite to that of the self-serving bias: They attribute positive events to external causes and negative ones to internal causes. Therapy designed to change this pattern has proved highly effective.

★ Attribution theory also helps explain reactions to *sexual harassment* and can be used to reduce such actions in workplaces.

Impression Formation and Impression Management: How We Integrate Social Information

Do you care about making a good first impression (see Figure 3.15 on page 80)? Research indicates that you should, because such impressions seem to exert strong and lasting effects on others' perceptions of us; and as we've seen throughout this chapter, the way others perceive us can strongly influence their behavior toward us (e.g., Fiske, Lin, & Neuberg, 1999; Swann & Gill, 1997).

But what, exactly, *are* first impressions? How are they formed? And what steps can we take to make good first impressions on others? Let's consider these questions. First, we'll examine some classic research and then we'll turn to more modern findings about the nature of first impressions.

Figure 3.15 ■ **First Impressions Really Do Matter**
Research findings confirm what common sense suggests: First impressions really do matter. They tend to persist and can influence our thinking about and interactions with others.

A True Classic in Social Psychology: Asch's Research on Central and Peripheral Traits

As we have seen, some aspects of social perception, such as attribution, require lots of hard mental work: It's not always easy to draw inferences about others' motives or traits from their behavior. In contrast, forming first impressions seems to be relatively effortless. As Solomon Asch (1946), one of the founders of experimental social psychology, put it, "We look at a person and immediately a certain impression of his character forms itself in us. A glance, a few spoken words are sufficient to tell us a story about a highly complex matter . . ." (1946, p. 258). How do we manage this feat? How, in short, do we form unified impressions of others in the quick and seemingly effortless way that we often do? This is the question Asch set out to study.

At the time Asch conducted his research, social psychologists were heavily influenced by the work of *Gestalt psychologists*—specialists in the field of perception. A basic principle of Gestalt psychology is this: "The whole is often greater than the sum of its parts," which means that what we perceive is often more than the sum of individual sensations. Asch applied these ideas to understanding impression formation, suggesting that we do *not* form impressions simply by adding together all of the traits we observe in other persons. Rather, we perceive these traits *in relation to one another,* so that the traits cease to exist individually and become part of an integrated, dynamic whole. How could these ideas be tested? Asch gave individuals lists of traits supposedly possessed by a stranger and then asked them to indicate their impressions of this person by putting check marks next to traits (on a much longer list) that they felt fit their overall impression of the stranger. For example, in one study, participants read one of the following two lists:

intelligent—skillful—industrious—warm—determined—practical—cautious

intelligent—skillful—industrious—cold—determined—practical—cautious

As you can see, the lists differ only with respect to two words: *warm* and *cold.* Thus, if people form impressions merely by adding together individual traits, the impressions formed by persons exposed to these two lists shouldn't differ very much. This was *not* the case. Persons who read the list containing *warm* were much more likely to view the stranger as generous, happy, good-natured, sociable, popular, and altruistic than were people who read the list containing *cold.* The words *warm* and *cold,* Asch concluded, described *central traits*—ones that strongly shaped overall impressions of the stranger and colored the other adjectives in the lists. Asch obtained additional support by substituting the words *polite* and *blunt* for *warm* and *cold.* When he did this, the two lists yielded highly similar impressions of the stranger. So, *polite* and *blunt,* it appeared, were *not* central traits that colored the entire impressions of the stranger.

On the basis of more studies, Asch concluded that forming impressions involves more than simply combining individual traits. As he put it: "There is an attempt to form an impression of the *entire* person. . . . As soon as two or more traits are understood to belong to one person they cease to exist as isolated traits, and come into immediate . . . interaction. . . . The subject perceives not this *and* that quality, but the two entering into a particular relation . . ." (1946, p. 284). Although research on impression formation has become far more sophisticated since Asch's early work, many of his basic ideas about impression formation have withstood the test of time.

Chapter 3 / Social Perception

Implicit Personality Theories: Schemas That Shape First Impressions

Suppose your friend described someone new as *helpful* and *kind.* Would you assume that this person is also sincere? Probably. And what if your friend described this stranger as *practical* and *intelligent?* Would you assume that she or he is also ambitious? Again, the chances are good that you might. But why, in the absence of information on these specific traits, would you assume that this person possesses them? In part because we all have what social psychologists describe as **implicit personality theories**—beliefs about what traits or characteristics tend to go together (e.g., Sedikides & Anderson, 1994). These theories, which can be viewed as a specific kind of *schema,* suggest that when individuals possess some traits, they are likely to possess others. These theories or expectations are strongly shaped by culture. For instance, in many societies it is assumed that beautiful is good—that people who are attractive also possess other positive traits, such as good social skills and an interest in enjoying the good things in life (e.g., Wheeler & Kim, 1997).

These tendencies to assume that certain traits or characteristics go together are common and can be observed in many contexts. For instance, you may have implicit beliefs about the characteristics related to birth order. Research findings indicate that we expect first-borns to be high achievers who are aggressive, ambitious, dominant, and independent, while we expect middle-borns to be caring, friendly, outgoing, and thoughtful. Only-children, in contrast, are expected to be independent, self-centered, selfish, and spoiled (e.g., Nyman, 1995).

The strength and generality of these implicit beliefs about the effects of birth order are illustrated in research conducted by Herrera et al. (2003). These researchers asked participants to rate first-borns, only-children, middle-borns, last-borns, and themselves on various trait dimensions: agreeable–disagreeable, bold–timid, creative–uncreative, emotional–unemotional, extraverted–introverted, responsible–irresponsible, and several others. Results indicated clear differences in expectations about the traits supposedly shown by each group. First-borns were seen as more intelligent, responsible, obedient, stable, and unemotional; only-children were seen as the most disagreeable; middle-borns were expected to be envious and the least bold; last-borns were seen as the most creative, emotional, disobedient, and irresponsible. So, clearly, implicit beliefs about links between birth order and important traits existed.

Going further, the same researchers asked other participants to rate the extent to which first-borns and last-borns would work in various occupations. As shown in Figure 3.16, birth order was significantly related to these expectations,

implicit personality theories Beliefs about what traits or characteristics tend to go together.

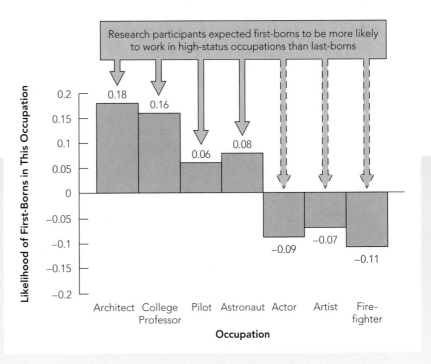

Figure 3.16 ■ Implicit Beliefs about the Effects of Birth Order When asked to rate the extent to which first-borns and last-borns would work in various occupations, participants perceived significant differences between the two groups. They expected first-borns to be more likely to work in high-status occupation. In contrast, they expected last-borns to be more likely to work in lower-status occupations. (*Source: Based on data from Herrera et al., 2003.*)

too. Participants in the study expected first-borns to be more likely to work in high-status occupations such as accountant, pilot, architect, astronaut, college professor, dentist, lawyer, physician, and high school teacher. In contrast, they expected last-borns to be more likely to work as an actor, artist, firefighter, journalist, musician, photographer, social worker, or stunt man.

Perhaps most surprising, additional findings indicated that birth order was actually related to important life outcomes: In a large sample from Poland, the earlier individuals' position in their families' birth order, the higher their occupational status and the more education they completed. This illustrates an important point we made in Chapter 2: Beliefs and expectations are often self-fulfilling, at least to a degree. More generally, the findings by Herrera et al. (2003) and other researchers indicate that our beliefs about birth order can be viewed as one important kind of implicit personality theory: We *do* strongly believe that an individual's birth order is related to different traits.

This implicit personality theory is not the only kind we hold. In addition, we have beliefs about how many other traits and characteristics tend to vary together. For instance, recall the correspondence bias discussed earlier in this chapter. In the classic research, participants were asked to read essays supporting one or the other side in a controversial issue. Some were told that the persons who wrote the essays chose to do this, while others were told that they were assigned to write the essay in support of one particular view. Even when they knew that the essay writers had been told what view to support, participants in many studies still assumed that the essay represented the writers' views—they attributed their behavior to their true beliefs, even though they knew this was not the case (e.g., Jones & Harris, 1967). So far, this finding seems to have little bearing on implicit personality theories. But consider this: What if the essays varied in quality or persuasiveness? It is possible that we have an implicit belief (implicit personality theory) that suggests that no one can write a persuasive essay in favor of a position unless that person really believes it, at least to some extent. In contrast, we may implicitly believe that almost anyone can write a weak or unpersuasive essay in favor of views they don't believe. This leads to the intriguing prediction that the tendency to attribute the essay to the writer's views will be strong when the essay is persuasive and eloquent, because we implicitly believe that only people who really hold these views can be so passionate about them. When the essay is not very persuasive, we will be less likely to attribute the essay to the writer's views; after all, anyone can write a weak essay in support of a position they don't really believe. Findings reported by Gawronski (2003) have confirmed these predictions, thus indicating that we have implicit beliefs about links between underlying beliefs and eloquence or persuasiveness—something that can be viewed as yet another kind of implicit personality theory. (These findings also provide additional evidence that there are indeed limits to the **fundamental attribution error**—our tendency to attribute other persons' behavior to internal causes.)

In sum, our impressions are often shaped by our beliefs about what traits or characteristics go together. These beliefs may be so strong that we sometimes bend our perceptions of others to be consistent with them. The result? We form impressions that reflect our implicit beliefs more than others' actual traits.

Impression Formation: A Cognitive Perspective

Since Asch's classic research, social psychologists have made progress toward understanding the nature of **impression formation**—the process through which we form impressions of others (e.g., Fiske, Lin, & Neuberg, 1999). A major reason for this progress has been adoption of a *cognitive perspective* on this topic. Briefly, social psychologists have found it useful to examine impression formation in terms of basic cognitive processes. For instance, when we meet others for the first time, we don't pay equal attention to all kinds of information about them; rather, we focus on certain kinds—the kinds of input we view as being most useful (e.g., De Bruin & van Lange, 2000). Further, to form lasting first impressions, we enter various kinds of information into memory so that we can recall it later. And, of course, our first impressions will depend, to a degree, on our own characteristics. In fact,

fundamental attribution error (correspondence bias) The tendency to overestimate the impact of dispositional cues on others' behavior.

impression formation The process through which we form impressions of others.

Chapter 3 / Social Perception

we can't help but see others through the lens of our own traits, motives, and desires (Vinokur & Schul, 2000).

Early work that adopted a cognitive perspective grappled with this question: How do we combine diverse information about others into unified impressions of them? Two possibilities seemed to exist: We could form unified impressions of others by *adding* discrete pieces of information about them, or we might form our impressions by *averaging* available information in some way (e.g., Anderson, 1965, 1968). Results were complex but generally pointed to the conclusion that averaging was the better explanation. The findings that led to this conclusion went something like this: If participants were given information suggesting that a stranger possessed two highly favorable traits (e.g., truthful, reasonable), they formed a more favorable impression of this person than if they were given information suggesting that he or she possessed two highly favorable traits *and* two moderately favorable ones (e.g., truthful, reasonable, painstaking, persuasive). Researchers reasoned that if people combine the information they received simply by adding it together, they would like the second person more than the first because he was described as possessing more positive characteristics (two very favorable traits and two moderately favorable traits). If people combined the information through averaging, they would like the first one better, because the average of two highly favorable traits is higher than the average of two highly favorable *and* two moderately favorable traits. On the basis of these and related results, it was concluded that we form our impressions of others on the basis of a relatively simple kind of "cognitive algebra" (e.g., Anderson, 1973).

Research on impression formation has gone beyond this initial approach. For instance, one question that was not addressed by early studies was this: What kind of information, exactly, do people focus on when meeting others for the first time? This question has many answers, depending on the precise context in which we encounter strangers. For instance, we might want different kinds of information about a physician we meet as a patient than we would about someone we meet at a party. Many studies, however, find that, across a wide range of contexts, we focus first on information concerning others' traits, values, and principles and then turn to information about their competence—how well they can do various tasks (e.g., De Bruin & van Lange, 2000). Wouldn't you find information about whether another person is considerate and interested in people more revealing than information about this person's ability to master various tasks quickly? Many studies confirm this prediction: We do find certain kinds of information more informative than others, and it is this kind of information on which we tend to focus when meeting others for the first time. Of course, the context in which we meet others is important, too. In job interviews, for instance, we might well give competence more attention. Across many situations, though, we seem to assume that competence can be acquired, while traits, values, and principles are harder to change, and so offer more value information about others.

Other Aspects of Impression Formation: The Nature of First Impressions and Our Motives for Forming Them

The cognitive perspective has provided important insights into the basic nature of first impressions (e.g., Wyer et al., 1994; Ruscher & Hammer, 1994). For instance, most social psychologists agree that impressions of others involve two major components: concrete examples of behaviors they have performed that are consistent with a given trait—*exemplars* of this trait—and mental summaries that are based on repeated observations of others' behavior—*abstractions* (e.g., Klein, Loftus, & Plog, 1992; Smith & Zarate, 1992). Some models of impression formation stress the role of behavioral exemplars. These models suggest that when we make judgments about others, we recall examples of their behavior and base our judgments—and our impressions—on these. In contrast, other models stress the role of abstractions (sometimes called *categorical judgments*). Such views suggest that when we make judgments about others, we simply bring our previously formed abstractions to mind and use these as the basis for our impressions and decisions. For instance, we recall that we have previously judged a person to be kind or unkind, friendly or hostile, optimistic or pessimistic, and then combine these traits into an impression of this individual.

Evidence suggests that both exemplars and mental abstractions play a role in impression formation (e.g., Budescheim & Bonnelle, 1998; Klein & Loftus, 1993; Klein et al., 1992). It appears that the nature of impressions may shift as we gain increasing experience with others. Our first impression of someone consists largely of exemplars (concrete examples of behaviors he or she has performed). Later, as our experience with this person increases, our impression comes to consist mainly of mental abstractions derived from many observations of the person's behavior (Sherman & Klein, 1994).

The cognitive perspective has also shed new light on another important issue—the influence of our motives (what we are trying to accomplish in a given situation) on the kind of impressions we form, and even the processes through which we form them. As we saw in Chapter 2, people generally do the least cognitive work they can, and impression formation is no exception. Usually, then, we form impressions in the simplest way possible: by placing people into large social categories with which we are already familiar (e.g., "She is an engineer," "He is an Irish American," etc.). Then we base our impressions, at least in part, on what we know about these social groups. If we are motivated to be more accurate, though, we may focus on people we meet more as individuals possessing a unique collection of traits (e.g., Fiske, Lin, & Neuberg, 1999; Stevens & Fiske, 2000).

Overall, modern research on impression formation employing a cognitive perspective has added to our understanding of this process. Because first impressions are often lasting and can strongly shape our future relations, this knowledge is valuable from a theoretical and practical perspective. Perhaps the best way of illustrating the latter point is by considering impression formation from the point of view of the person about whom the impression is being formed. This leads us to a discussion of the intriguing process of *impression management* (or *self-presentation*).

KEY POINTS

★ Most people are concerned with making good first impressions because they believe that these impressions will exert lasting effects.

★ Research on *impression formation*—the process through which we form impressions of others—suggests that this belief is true. Asch's classic research on impression formation indicated that impressions of others involve more than simple summaries of their traits.

★ Modern research conducted from a cognitive perspective has confirmed and extended this view, suggesting that in forming impressions we emphasize certain kinds of information (e.g., about others' traits and values rather than their competence).

★ Additional research indicates that impressions of others consist of examples of both behavior relating to specific traits (exemplars) and mental abstractions based on observations of behavior.

Impression Management: The Fine Art of Looking Good

impression management (self-presentation)
Efforts by individuals to produce favorable first impressions on others.

The desire to make a favorable impression on others is strong, so most of us do our best to "look good" to others when we meet them for the first time (see Figure 3.17). Social psychologists use the term **impression management** (or *self-presentation*) to describe these efforts, and the results of their research suggest that persons who perform impression management successfully *do* often gain important advantages (e.g., Sharp & Getz, 1996; Wayne & Liden, 1995). What tactics do people use to create favorable impressions? Which work best? Let's see what research indicates about these questions.

■ Tactics of Impression Management and Their Relative Success
Although individuals use many techniques for boosting their image, most of these fall into two major categories: *self-enhancement*—efforts to increase their appeal to others—and *other-enhancement*—efforts to make the target person feel good.

Figure 3.17 ■ Impression Management: Not Always
Effective!
Nearly everyone engages in impression management from time to
time, but most people do a better job at this important task than
the character shown here! (*Source:* HERMAN *reprinted by
permission of Newspaper Enterprise Association, Inc.*)

HERMAN   **By Unger**

© 1986 United Press Syndicate

*"I always wear my lucky hat for
job interviews."*

With respect to self-enhancement, specific strategies include
efforts to boost one's physical appearance through style of dress,
personal grooming, and the use of various props (e.g., eyeglasses,
have been found to encourage impressions of intelligence; Terry &
Krantz, 1993). Additional tactics involve efforts to appear highly
skilled, or describing oneself in positive terms, explaining, for
instance, how he or she (the person engaging in impression management) overcame daunting obstacles (Stevens & Kristof, 1995).
Other findings (e.g., Rowatt, Cunningham, & Druen, 1998) indicate that many use this tactic to increase their appeal to potential
dating partners describing themselves in very favorable terms,
bending the truth to enhance their appeal.

Turning to *other-enhancement,* individuals use different tactics
to induce positive moods and reactions in others. Research findings
suggest that such reactions play an important role in generating
liking for the person responsible for them (Byrne, 1992). The most commonly used tactic is
flattery—making statements that praise the target person, his or her traits or accomplishments, or the organization with which the person is associated (Kilduff & Day, 1994). Such
tactics are often successful, provided they are not overdone. Additional tactics of other-
enhancement involve expressing agreement with the target person's views, showing a high
degree of interest in this person, doing small favors for them, asking for their advice and feedback in some manner (Morrison & Bies, 1991), or expressing liking for them nonverbally
(e.g., through eye contact, nodding in agreement, and smiling; Wayne & Ferris, 1990).

Do these tactics of impression management succeed in generating positive feelings and
reactions? The answer provided by a growing body of literature is clear: *yes,* provided they
are used with skill and care. For example, in one study involving more than 1,400 employees, Wayne et al. (1997) found that social skills (including impression management) were
the single best predictor of job performance ratings and assessments of potential for promotion in a wide range of jobs. These findings and those of related studies (e.g., Wayne &
Kacmar, 1991; Witt & Ferris, 2003; Paulhus, Bruce, & Trapnell, 1995) indicate that impression management tactics often succeed in enhancing the appeal of persons who use them
effectively. However, we hasten to add that the use of these tactics involves potential pitfalls:
If they are overused or used ineffectively, they can backfire and produce negative rather than
positive reactions. For instance, Vonk (1998) found strong evidence for what she terms the
slime effect—a tendency to form very negative impressions of others who "lick upward but
kick downward"—persons in a work setting who play up to their superiors but treat subordinates with disdain and contempt. The moral is clear: Although tactics of impression
management often succeed, sometimes they can boomerang, adversely affecting reactions
to the persons who use them. (We return to this effect in Chapter 5.)

slime effect
A tendency to form negative
impressions of others who
play up to their superiors but
who treat subordinates with
disdain.

■ Impression Management: The Role of Cognitive Load

That we try to make a favorable impression on others in many situations is obvious; this
effort makes a great deal of common sense. We have strong reasons for wanting to "look
good" in job interviews, on first dates, and in many other contexts. Generally, we can do
quite a good job in this respect because we have practiced impression management skills
for many years. As a result, we can engage in positive self-presentation in a relatively

Figure 3.18 ■ Cognitive Overload and Impression Management
Research findings indicate that for some (e.g., persons who are shy or uncomfortable in social situations), cognitive overload can be a "plus," helping them to make good impressions on others. For most people, however, the opposite is true: When overloaded cognitively, they do a worse job at impression management. This is one reason why famous politicians make public blunders: They are so overloaded, they can't continue to maintain their "good image."

automatic and effortless manner—we are simply following well-practiced scripts (see Schlenker & Pontari, 2000). Some situations in which we try to make a good first impression, however, are demanding. For instance, consider politicians seeking the presidential nomination from their party. Often, they face a grueling schedule of meetings, speeches, and travel. As a result, they often become fatigued and experience cognitive overload—they are trying to handle more tasks and information than they can. What effect does such extra *cognitive load* have on the ability to present oneself in a favorable light?

You might guess that the effect would always be detrimental: When we are busy performing other tasks, we can't do as good a job at presenting ourselves, and, in general, this appears to be true (e.g., Tice et al., 1995). In fact, political candidates often *do* make serious blunders when fatigued or otherwise overloaded (see Figure 3.18). But consider this: Some persons are very uncomfortable in social situations because they feel anxious and tend to worry about how others will perceive them. For such persons, being busy with other tasks may distract them from such thoughts and so actually *enhance* their ability to present themselves favorably. In fact, research by Pontari and Schlenker (2000) indicates that this is true. These researchers had extraverts (outgoing, friendly, sociable) and introverts (reserved, shy, withdrawn) take part in a mock job interview in which participants tried to present themselves either as they were (extraverted or introverted) or as the opposite. During the interview, participants were either busy performing another task (trying to remember an eight-digit number) or were not busy. Results indicated that for the extraverts, cognitive busyness interfered with their ability to present themselves as introverts (i.e., to appear shy, withdrawn, etc.). For introverts, however, the opposite was true: Trying to remember the eight-digit number actually improved their ability to appear to be extraverts. Pontari and Schlenker (2000) interpreted these findings as indicating that being busy with other tasks prevented introverts from feeling anxious and focusing on their fear of doing poorly. Thus, cognitive distraction was actually a plus—it helped them to do a better job at self-presentation. But as interesting as this finding is, it does not negate the fact that, in most situations and for most people, cognitive overload can interfere with their efforts to "look good" in the eyes of others.

KEY POINTS

★ To make a good impression, individuals often engage in *impression management* (self-presentation).

★ Many techniques are used for this purpose, but most fall under two major headings: self-enhancement—efforts to boost one's appeal to others—and other-enhancement—efforts to induce positive moods or reactions in others.

★ *Impression management* is something we practice throughout life, so we can usually perform it in a fairly effortless manner. When other tasks require our cognitive resources, however, *impression management* can suffer—unless such tasks distract us from anxiety and fears over performing poorly.

Chapter 3 / Social Perception

Nonverbal Communication: The Language of Expressions, Gazes, and Gestures

- *Social perception* involves the processes through which we seek to understand others. It plays a key role in social behavior and thought.

- To understand others' emotional states, we often rely on *nonverbal communication*—an unspoken language of facial expressions, eye contact, and body movements and postures.

- Although facial expressions may not be as universal as once believed, they can provide useful information about others' emotional states. Useful information is also provided by eye contact, *body language,* and touching.

- Recent findings indicate that handshakes provide useful nonverbal cues about others' personalities and can influence first impressions.

- If we pay careful attention to certain nonverbal cues, we can recognize efforts at deception by others.

- Women are better than men at sending and interpreting nonverbal cues. This ability gives women an important advantage in many situations and may account for widespread belief in "women's intuition."

Attribution: Understanding the Causes of Others' Behavior

- To obtain information about others' lasting traits, motives, and intentions, we often engage in *attribution*—efforts to understand why they have acted as they have.

- According to Jones and Davis's theory of *correspondent inference,* we attempt to infer others' traits from observing certain aspects of their behavior—especially behavior that is freely chosen, produces *noncommon effects,* and is low in social desirability.

- Kelley's theory of causal *attribution* asks the question of whether oth-

ers' behavior stems from internal or external causes. To answer, we focus on information relating to *consensus, consistency,* and *distinctiveness.*

- Two other dimensions of causal attribution relate to whether specific causes of behavior are stable over time and controllable or not controllable.

- When two or more potential causes of another person's behavior exist, we tend to downplay the importance of each—an effect known as *discounting.* When a cause that facilitates a behavior and a cause that inhibits it exist, but the behavior still occurs, we assign added weight to the facilitative factors—an effect known as *augmenting.*

- *Attribution* is subject to many potential sources of error. One of the most important is the *correspondence bias*—the tendency to explain others' actions as stemming from dispositions, even in the presence of situational causes. This tendency seems to be stronger in western cultures than in Asian cultures, and can occur for attributions for groups as well as individuals.

- Two other attributional errors are the *actor–observer effect*—the tendency to attribute our behavior to external (situational) causes but that of others to internal causes—and the *self-serving bias*—the tendency to attribute positive outcomes to internal causes but negative ones to external causes.

- The strength of the *self-serving bias* varies across cultures, being stronger in western societies than in Asian cultures.

- *Attribution* has been applied to many practical problems. Depressed persons often show a pattern of attributions opposite to that of the *self-serving bias:* They attribute positive events to external causes and negative ones to internal causes. Therapy designed to change this pattern has proved highly effective.

- *Attribution* theory also helps explain reactions to *sexual harassment* and can potentially be used to reduce such actions in workplaces.

Impression Formation and Impression Management: How We Integrate Social Information

- Most people are concerned with making good first impressions because they believe that these impressions will exert lasting effects.

- Research on *impression formation*—the process through which we form impressions of others—suggests that this belief is true. Asch's classic research on *impression formation* indicated that impressions of others involve more than simple summaries of their traits.

- Modern research conducted from a cognitive perspective has confirmed and extended this view, suggesting that in forming impressions, we emphasize certain kinds of information (e.g., about their traits and values rather than their competence.)

- Additional research indicates that impressions of others consist of examples of both behavior relating to specific traits (exemplars) and mental abstractions based on observations of behavior.

- To make a good impression, individuals often engage in *impression management* (self-presentation).

- Many techniques are used for *impression management,* but most fall under two major headings: self-enhancement—efforts to boost one's appeal to others—and other-enhancement—efforts to induce positive moods or reactions in others.

- *Impression management* is something we practice throughout life, so we can usually engage it in a fairly effortless manner. When other tasks require our cognitive resources, however, *impression management* can suffer—unless such tasks distract us from anxiety and fears over performing poorly.

In this chapter, you read about . . .	In other chapters, you will find related discussions of . . .
basic channels of nonverbal communication	the role of nonverbal cues in interpersonal attraction (Chapter 7), persuasion (Chapter 4), prejudice (Chapter 6), and charismatic leadership (Chapter 12)
theories of attribution	the role of attribution in persuasion (Chapter 4), social identity and self-perception (Chapter 5), prejudice (Chapter 6), long-term relationships (Chapter 8), prosocial behavior (Chapter 10), and aggression (Chapter 11)
first impressions and impression management	the role of first impressions in interpersonal attraction (Chapter 7)

Thinking about Connections

1. As we'll point out in Chapters 4 (Attitudes) and 9 (Social Influence), influence is an important fact of social life: Each day, we attempt to change others' attitudes or behavior and they attempt to change ours. Having read about attribution in this chapter, do you think that influence attempts that conceal their true goals will be more successful than ones that do not? If so, why? If not, why?

2. In Chapter 11 (Aggression), we'll see that some persons experience more than their share of aggressive encounters. Such persons, it appears, are lacking in basic social skills, such as the ability to accurately read nonverbal cues. On the basis of the discussion of nonverbal cues in this chapter, can you explain how this could contribute to their problems?

3. Suppose you were preparing for an important job interview. On the basis of information presented in this chapter, what steps could you take to improve your chances of actually getting the job?

4. Suppose you compared happy couples with unhappy ones. Do you think that these couples would differ in their attributions concerning their partners' behavior? For instance, would the happy couples attribute their partners' behavior to more positive causes than the unhappy couples?

Ideas to Take with You—and Use! · MINIMIZING THE IMPACT OF ATTRIBUTIONAL ERRORS

Attribution is subject to many errors, and these can prove costly, so it's well worth the effort to avoid such pitfalls. Here are our suggestions for recognizing—and minimizing—several important attributional errors.

The Correspondence Bias: The Fundamental Attribution Error

We have a strong tendency to attribute others' behavior to internal (dispositional) causes, even when external (situational) factors that might have influenced their behavior are present. To reduce this error, try to put yourself in their shoes. In other

words, try to see the world through their eyes. If you do, you will probably realize that, from their perspective, there are many external factors that played a role in their behavior.

The Actor–Observer Effect: "I behave as I do because of situational causes; you behave as you do because you are that kind of person."

Consistent with the fundamental attribution error, we have a tendency to attribute our own behavior to external causes but that of others to internal causes. This tendency can lead us to false generalizations about others and the traits they possess. To minimize this error, try to imagine yourself in their place and ask yourself, "Why would I have acted that way?" If you do, you'll quickly realize that external factors might have influenced your behavior. Similarly, ask yourself, "Did I behave that way because of traits or motives of which I'm not very aware?" This exercise may help you to appreciate the internal causes of your behavior.

The Self-Serving Bias: "I'm good; you're lucky."

Perhaps the strongest attributional error we make is that of attributing positive outcomes to internal causes, such as our abilities, but negative outcomes to external factors, such as luck. This error can have many harmful effects, but among the worst is a strong tendency to believe that the rewards we receive (raises, promotions, share of the credit) are smaller than we deserve. I (Robert Baron) had first-hand experience with this effect when I was a department chair; virtually every faculty member seemed to feel they deserved a bigger raise than I recommended! Simply being aware of this attributional error can help you reduce it; such awareness may help you to realize that all your positive outcomes don't stem from internal causes, and that you may have played a role in producing negative ones. In addition, try to remember that other people are subject to the same bias; doing so can help remind you that they want to take as much credit for positive outcomes as possible but shift the blame for negative ones to external causes—such as you!

4 ATTITUDES
Evaluating the Social World

In May 2004, the Massachusetts Supreme Court ruled that it is a violation of gay and lesbian people's constitutional rights to deny them the right to marry. With this ruling, Massachusetts became the first state to legally permit same-sex marriages. When we examine the attitudes of the U.S. public, we see a substantial generation gap in support for same-sex marriage (*Newsweek* Poll, 2004).

Legal changes that affect U.S. institutions often precede widespread public opinion change. Consider Americans' views on racial segregation. Before the *Brown vs. Topeka Board of Education* U.S. Supreme Court ruling in May 1954, which ordered that public schools be desegregated because "separate is inherently unequal," most White Americans were in favor of racial segregation in schools (Pettigrew, 2004). Fifty years after this groundbreaking legal decision, the majority of Americans favor racial desegregation in the public schools. On both of these issues concerning matters of social justice, the opinions of younger people have tended to be more liberal than those of older people, but both groups hold strong opinions of which they are certain.

People do, however, hold many attitudes about which they feel some ambivalence—that is, they have both positive and negative responses, or have both approach and avoidance tendencies regarding the object or issue. For example, people may feel positively disposed toward particular foods (e.g., desserts) but simultaneously avoid them because of their high fat content. Likewise, people can positively evaluate a particular brand of automobile but not purchase it because it is too expensive for their budget. The point is that for some attitudes we have no ambivalence toward the object or issue, but for others we have considerable ambivalence. As you'll see, the issue of strength and clarity of an attitude has important implications for our actions.

attitude
Evaluation of various aspects of the social world.

Social psychologists use the term **attitude** to refer to people's evaluation of virtually any aspect of the social world (e.g., Olson & Maio, 2003; Petty, Wheeler, & Tormala, 2003). People can have favorable or unfavorable reactions to issues, ideas, specific individuals, entire social groups, and objects. Yet attitudes in many domains are not always as uniformly positive or negative as they are for same-sex marriage and school desegregation; on the contrary, our evaluations are often mixed (e.g., Priester & Petty, 2001).

Chapter 4 / Attitudes

Figure 4.1 ■ Attitudes That Lack Ambivalence Often Predict Behavior
Our evaluations of various issues, people, groups, and objects can contain both positive and negative components. Many of us tend to confront our purchasing decisions with ambivalence (*left*). Strong attitudes (*right*) are often a better guide to predicting our future actions than ambivalent attitudes.

By definition, ambivalent attitudes are easier to change than those that reflect a uniform position on an issue; as a result, behavioral responses tend to be unstable when attitudes are mixed (Armitage & Conner, 2000). Consider my friend's dilemma. She had limited funds and had "pre-decided" to purchase a modestly priced vehicle. However, at one car dealership, she saw a Lexus and decided to take it for a test drive. It was love on the first drive! In this case, can you guess which component of her attitude toward autos won out—her feelings about affordability or her desire for this luxurious car? As Figure 4.1 illustrates, like many people in the market for a new car, my friend convinced herself that she could manage the large monthly payments and she ended up taking the Lexus home. Although I pointed out to her that there were many very nice, less expensive vehicles that she might consider, she was convinced that the Lexus was the car for her (and the financial sacrifices she would be making for several years by purchasing it were already seen as "not so bad"). When attitudes are ambivalent, they are more susceptible to change, compared with when they are uniformly positive or negative. In contrast, attitudes that lack ambivalence are difficult to change—and, like the issue of school desegregation and same-sex marriage, may only be altered in response to behavioral changes across time or among those who are younger and lack a life-long commitment to a particular attitude position (Sears, 1986). Thus, strong attitudes tend to be better predictors of behavior in domains to which they are relevant than ambivalent attitudes.

Social psychologists view the study of attitudes as central to their field for several reasons. First, attitudes influence our thoughts, even if they are not always reflected in our overt behavior. Growing evidence suggests that attitudes, as evaluations of the world around us, represent a basic aspect of social cognition. As we saw in Chapter 2, the tendency to evaluate stimuli as positive or negative—something we like or dislike—appears to be an initial step in our effort to make sense out of the world. Such reactions occur almost immediately, before we attempt to integrate new stimuli with our previous experience (Ito et al., 1998). When stimuli are evaluated in terms of our attitudes, we experience different brain wave activity, compared with when we respond to the same stimuli in nonevaluative terms (Crites & Cacioppo, 1996). So, in a sense, attitudes truly reflect an essential building block of social thought (Eagly & Chaiken, 1998).

Second, attitudes often affect our behavior. This is especially likely to be true when attitudes are strong, well established, and accessible (Ajzen, 2001; Fazio, 2000; Petty & Krosnick, 1995). What is your attitude toward the current U.S. president? If positive, you are likely to have voted for him in the 2004 election, but if negative, you are unlikely to have done so. Because attitudes influence behavior, knowing something about them helps us predict people's behavior in many contexts. As we'll see in Chapter 6, people hold attitudes toward various social

CLOSE TO HOME

© 1997 John McPherson/Dist. by Universal Press Syndicate

BUT THEN AGAIN, IF BEING HERE BY 8:30 IS CRAMPING YOUR STYLE, 10:30 OR 11:00 IS JUST FINE! AND, HEY! LIKE THE TV! NICE HOMEY TOUCH!

Todd's relationship with management improved dramatically once he started bringing his new pet to work.

groups—for example, we may like or dislike particular groups; as a consequence, we may be positively or negatively predisposed to act in particular ways toward them. Clearly, attitudes can play a crucial role in our behavioral responses.

Attitudes have been a central concept in social psychology since its earliest days (e.g., Allport, 1924). In this chapter, we provide you with an overview of what social psychologists have discovered about attitudes. First, we consider the ways in which attitudes are *formed,* and why we construct them—in other words, what functions they serve. Next, we consider the question: When do attitudes influence behavior? The answer: sometimes but not always. Recent research provides important insights concerning the complex issue of when attitudes and behavior are connected. Third, we turn to the question of how attitudes are changed—the process of *persuasion.* Changing attitudes, though, can be difficult. In fact, changing them is far more difficult than advertisers, politicians, salespersons, and many other would-be persuaders assume. Still, as suggested in Figure 4.2, such persons have many tricks and make use of them in their effort to change our views. Fourth, we examine some of the reasons *why* attitudes are often so resistant to change. Finally, we consider the intriguing fact that on some occasions, our actions shape our attitudes rather than vice versa. The process that underlies such effects is known as *cognitive dissonance,* and it has fascinating implications for many aspects of social behavior.

Attitude Formation: How Attitudes Develop

How do you feel about the U.S. role in the war in Iraq, the legalization of marijuana, people who cover their bodies with tattoos, fraternities and sororities on campus, or people who talk on their cell phones while driving? Most people have attitudes about these issues, but where, precisely, did these views come from? Did you acquire them as a result of your experiences, or from people with whom you interact frequently? Are people's group memberships (e.g., racial, age, gender) important predictors of social attitudes? Why do we form attitudes—in other words, what functions do attitudes serve? Almost all social psychologists believe that attitudes are *learned,* and much of our discussion focuses on the processes through which attitudes are acquired. Turning to the second question—*why* do we form attitudes (i.e., what functions do they serve?), we'll soon see that attitudes serve several functions, and they are useful to us in many respects.

Social Learning: Acquiring Attitudes from Others

social learning
The process through which we acquire new information, forms of behavior, or attitudes from other persons.

One way our attitudes develop is through the process of **social learning.** In other words, many of our views are acquired in situations in which we interact with others or observe their behavior. Such learning occurs through several processes outlined below.

Chapter 4 / Attitudes

Classical Conditioning: Learning Based on Association

It is a basic principle of psychology that when one stimulus regularly precedes another, the first one can become a signal for the second. Over time, people learn that when the first stimulus occurs, the second will soon follow. For example, suppose you are allergic to cats. Whenever you go to visit one of your friends who has cats, you end up with watery eyes. As a result of classical conditioning, over time you associate the first stimulus (e.g., going to your friend's house) with the second stimulus (e.g., watery eyes), and you gradually acquire the same kind of reactions to the first stimulus as you show to the second stimulus, especially if the second is one that induces fairly strong and automatic reactions. Because visiting that friend reliably predicts these negative responses, the idea of going to your friend's house (and perhaps even that person) eventually will automatically elicit a negative response from you.

This process—known as **classical conditioning**—has important implications for attitude formation. To see how this process might influence attitudes toward an entire social category, consider the following. A young child sees her mother show signs of displeasure each time she encounters a member of a particular ethnic group. At first, the child is neutral toward this group and their visible characteristics (e.g., skin color, style of dress, accent). She has not yet learned to categorize this particular variation in people in terms of group membership. After these cues are paired repeatedly with the mother's negative emotional reactions, classical conditioning occurs, and the child comes to react negatively to members of this particular ethnic group (see Figure 4.3). This reaction can occur without the child having conscious access to the role that her mother's subtle facial changes have had on what attitude she forms. The result is that the child acquires a negative attitude toward members of a particular group—an attitude that may form the core of prejudice (see Chapter 6).

Not only can classical conditioning contribute to shaping our attitudes, it can also occur when we are not even aware of the stimuli that serve as the basis for this kind of conditioning. In one experiment (Krosnick et al., 1992), students saw photos of a stranger engaged in routine daily activities such as shopping in a grocery store or walking into her apartment. While these photos were shown, other photos known to induce positive or negative feelings were shown for periods of time so brief that participants were not aware of their presence. Participants who were nonconsciously exposed to photos that induced positive feelings (e.g., a newlywed couple, people playing cards and laughing) liked the stranger better than did participants exposed to photos that nonconsciously induced negative feelings (e.g., open-heart surgery, a werewolf). Even though participants were not aware of their exposure to the second group of photos, these stimuli significantly influenced the attitudes they formed toward the stranger. Those exposed to the positive photos reported more favorable attitudes than those exposed to the negative photos. These findings suggest that attitudes can be influenced by **subliminal conditioning**—classical conditioning that occurs in the absence of conscious awareness of the stimuli involved.

Once formed, attitudes relevant to discrimination against a particular category of people are most likely to affect people's behavior when they feel threatened (Stephan & Stephan, 2000).

classical conditioning
A basic form of learning in which one stimulus, initially neutral, acquires the capacity to evoke reactions through repeated pairing with another stimulus. In a sense, one stimulus becomes a signal for the presentation or occurrence of the other.

subliminal conditioning
Classical conditioning of attitudes by exposure to stimuli that are below individuals' threshold of conscious awareness.

Figure 4.3 ■ Classical Conditioning of Attitudes
Initially, a young child may have little or no emotional reaction to the visible characteristics of members of different social groups. If, however, the child sees her mother showing negative reactions when in their presence, she may gradually acquire a negative reaction too, as a result of the process of *classical conditioning.*

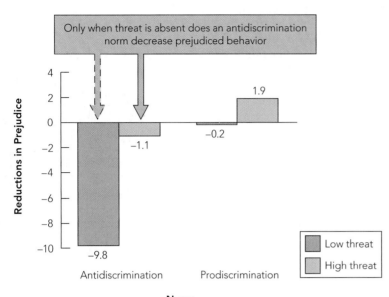

Only when threat is absent does an antidiscrimination norm decrease prejudiced behavior

Figure 4.4 ■ Feelings of Threat Can Result in Prejudiced Action Toward Foreigners, Even When Norms Are Antidiscriminatory
An antidiscrimination norm against showing prejudice toward foreigners is only effective at reducing favoritism toward members of one's own group when people are feeling little threat. Regardless of feelings of threat, if a prodiscrimination norm is present, people discriminate by showing favoritism toward their own group members. (*Source: Based on data from Falomir-Pichastor et al., 2004.*)

For example, since the terrorist attacks on the United States on September 11, 2001, many Americans have felt increasingly threatened and, as a result, favor greater surveillance of foreigners. Research (Falomir-Pichastor et al., 2004) has revealed that even when the norms in a cultural setting are antidiscriminatory, it is only when feelings of threat from foreigners are low that prejudice is reduced (see Figure 4.4). As this research indicates, **social norms**—beliefs about how people should or are likely to behave—against discrimination are crucial for nonprejudiced behavior, but they are not sufficient. Rather, when perceived threat from foreigners is high, discrimination is still likely, even when the norm is antidiscriminatory.

social norms
Expectations about how people will or should behave in a particular context.

Instrumental Conditioning: Rewards for the "Right" Views

Have you ever heard a seven-year-old child state, with great conviction, that she or he is a Republican or a Democrat? Children have little understanding of what these categories mean or the ways in which they differ. Yet they sometimes confidently make such claims. Why? They have been praised or rewarded in various ways by their parents for stating such views. As a result, children learn which views are seen as "correct" among the people with whom they identify. Behaviors that are followed by positive outcomes are strengthened and tend to be repeated, whereas behaviors that are followed by negative outcomes are weakened or decrease. Thus, another way in which attitudes are acquired from others is through **instrumental conditioning.** By rewarding children with smiles, approval, or hugs for stating the "right" views—the ones they favor—parents and other adults play an active role in shaping youngsters' attitudes. It is for this reason that until they reach their teen years—when peer influences become especially strong—most children express political, religious, and social views that are highly similar to those of their family members.

instrumental conditioning
A basic form of learning in which responses that lead to positive outcomes or that permit avoidance of negative outcomes are strengthened.

As adults, we may expect to be rewarded for expressing support for a particular attitude with some audiences, but at the same time, we know that we would be rewarded for expressing a different view to other audiences. Indeed, elections are won and lost on this premise. Politicians who are constantly shifting their responses to accommodate those they believe represent the majority of their audience may hurt themselves by looking as though they are not taking a firm stand on anything.

One way of assessing whether people's reported attitudes vary depending on the expected audience reaction is to alter the audience that is expected to receive the message. For example, people seeking membership in a fraternity or sorority differ in the attitudes they report toward other fraternities and sororities, depending on whether they believe their attitudes will remain private or whether they think that the well-established members of their group who will be controlling their admittance will know the attitude position they advocated (Noel, Wann, & Branscombe, 1995). When those who are attempting to gain membership in an organization believe that other members will learn of their responses, they derogate other fraternities or sororities as a means of communicating that the particular organization to which they want to be admitted is seen as the most desirable. Yet when they believe their responses will be private, they do not derogate other fraternities or sororities.

Observational Learning: Learning by Example

A third process through which attitudes are formed can operate even when parents have no desire to directly transmit specific views to their children. **Observational learning** occurs when individuals acquire new forms of behavior or thought by observing the actions of others (e.g., Bandura, 1997). Where attitude formation is concerned, observational learning appears to play an important role. In many cases, children hear their parents say things that are not intended for their ears, or observe their parents engaging in actions their parents tell them not to perform. Parents might even explicitly say, "Don't do what I do." For example, parents who smoke often warn their children against this habit (see Figure 4.5). What message do children actually learn from such instances? The evidence is clear: They generally learn to do as their parents *do,* not as they *say.*

In addition, both children and adults acquire attitudes from exposure to mass media—magazines, films, and so on. Just think about how much observational learning most of us are doing as we watch television! For instance, the characters in many American action films routinely exhibit high levels of violence that, in the past, would have evoked stress and been perceived as frightening by viewers. However, young people who have grown up watching horror films (e.g., *Halloween; Friday the 13th,* the "Scream" series) do not find such graphic violence as distressing as do older persons. Interestingly, we tend to think that it is *other* people who will be harmed by viewing violent or pornographic material, while we believe that we are not affected by doing so (Gunther, 1995). This has been referred to as the **third-person effect** of media exposure—the impact on others' attitudes and behaviors is overestimated, and the impact on the self is underestimated. See Chapter 11 for more on violence in the media and its effect on aggression.

Role of Social Comparison

Why do people often adopt the attitudes that they hear others express or acquire the behaviors they observe in others? One answer involves **social comparison**—the tendency to compare ourselves with others in order to determine whether our view of social reality is correct (Festinger, 1954). That is, to the extent that our views agree with those of others, we tend to conclude that our ideas and attitudes are accurate; after all, if others hold the same views, they must be right! But are we equally likely to adopt all others' attitudes, or does it depend on our relationship to them?

People often change their attitudes to hold views closer to those of people they value and with whom they identify. Imagine that you heard persons you like and respect expressing negative views toward a group with whom you have had no contact. Would this influence your attitudes? While it might be tempting to say, "Absolutely not!" research findings indicate that hearing others state negative views about a group can

observational learning
A basic form of learning in which individuals acquire new forms of behavior as a result of observing others.

third-person effect
Effect that occurs when the impact of media exposure on others' attitudes and behaviors is overestimated and the impact on the self is underestimated.

social comparison
The process through which we compare ourselves to others in order to determine whether our views of social reality are or are not correct.

Figure 4.5 ■ Observational Learning in Action
Children learn many things from their parents, including attitudes and behaviors that their parents may not wish for them to acquire, such as a positive view of smoking.

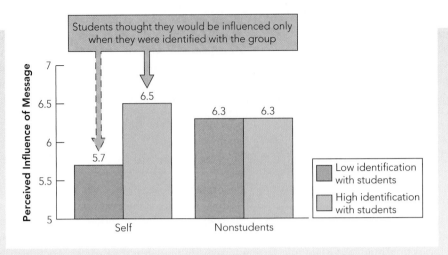

Figure 4.6 ■ Evidence for the Importance of Social Identity Influences on Attitudes
When judging how much the self would be influenced by a message aimed at members of one's group (e.g., students), students thought they would be personally influenced when they highly identified with their student group but not when they were low in identification with their group. Identification with the group did not influence the message when it was nonstudents being estimated. (*Source: Based on data from Duck, Hogg, & Terry, 1999.*)

lead you to adopt similar attitudes—without your ever meeting any members of that group (e.g., Maio, Esses, & Bell, 1994; Terry, Hogg, & Duck, 1999). In such cases, attitudes are shaped as a result of social information, coupled with our desire to be similar to people we like.

Indeed, people expect to be influenced by others' attitude positions differentially, depending on how much they identify with those others. When a message concerning safe sex and AIDS prevention was created for university students, those who identified with their university's student group believed that they would be personally influenced by the position advocated in the message, whereas those who were low in identification did not expect to be personally influenced by the message (Duck, Hogg, & Terry, 1999). As shown in Figure 4.6, nonstudents were expected to be equally influenced by the message regardless of how identified with the student group the rater was. Thus, when we identify with a group, we expect to take on the attitudes advocated by that group.

KEY POINTS

★ *Attitudes* are evaluations of any aspect of the social world. Often, attitudes are strong and unambivalent, which makes them resistant to change. Other attitudes are ambivalent, which means they are based on conflicting beliefs and such attitudes are less likely to predict behavior consistently.

★ Attitudes are often acquired from others through *social learning*. Such learning can involve *classical conditioning*, *instrumental conditioning*, or *observational learning*.

★ Attitudes are also formed on the basis of *social comparison*—the tendency to compare ourselves with others to determine whether our views of social reality are

or are not correct. To be similar to others we like, we often adopt the attitudes that they hold.

★ Attitudes are influenced by exposure to mass media. We tend to believe, however, that only other people are affected by such exposure (e.g., to violence), but not ourselves—the *third-person effect*.

★ When we identify with a group, we expect to be influenced by messages that are aimed at that group. We do not expect to be personally influenced when we do not identify with the group to which the attitude-relevant message is aimed.

Attitude Functions: Why We Form Attitudes in the First Place

Each of us holds attitudes on a wide array of issues; in fact, it is safe to say that we are rarely completely neutral toward any aspect of the world. Indeed, **mere exposure** to an object—having seen it before but not necessarily remembering having seen it—can result in attitude formation. Even among patients with advanced Alzheimer's disease, who cannot remember having been exposed to an object, new attitudes are formed (Winograd et al., 1999). But why do we bother to form so many attitudes? Attitudes can be viewed as almost automatic reactions to the world around us. As noted earlier, research employing sophisticated techniques for observing activity in the human brain suggests that we seem to classify stimuli we encounter as either positive or negative almost immediately, and show different responses in the brain to the same object, depending on whether we are evaluating it (e.g., Crites & Cacioppo, 1996; Ito et al., 1998).

Having an already formed attitude toward a class of stimuli serves a number of useful functions. We now consider the knowledge, identity, self-esteem, ego-defensive, and impression motivation functions that attitudes can serve (Shavitt, 1990).

mere exposure
By having seen an object previously, but not necessarily remembering having done so, attitudes toward an object can become more positive.

The Knowledge Function of Attitudes

Attitudes serve a **knowledge function** by aiding our interpretation of new information and influencing basic approach or avoidance responses. For example, Chen and Bargh (1999) found that positive attitudes toward an object were more quickly expressed when a lever had to be pulled toward the self, whereas negative attitudes were more readily expressed when a lever had to be pushed away from the self. This suggests that attitudes color our perceptions and responses. Research indicates that we view new information that offers support for our attitudes as more convincing and accurate than information that refutes our attitudes (Munro & Ditto, 1997). Likewise, we perceive information that is weak as relatively strong when it is consistent with our existing attitudes, compared with when it is inconsistent (Chaiken & Maheswaran, 1994). Conversely, there is considerable evidence that we view sources that provide evidence contrary to our views as highly suspect—biased and unreliable (Giner-Sorolla & Chaiken, 1994, 1997).

knowledge function
Attitudes aid in the interpretation of new stimuli and enable rapid responding to attitude-relevant information.

The Identity Function of Attitudes

Attitudes permit us to express our central values and beliefs—they can serve an **identity** or **self-expression function.** If being politically liberal is crucial for a person's identity, that individual may find it important to express his or her proenvironmental attitudes by wearing Sierra Club T-shirts, because this allows the person to express a central belief. In fact, those people wearing their Sierra Club T-shirts might find that they are more well received by others wearing similar proenvironmental slogan T-shirts as opposed to those wearing pro–National Rifle Association T-shirts, which tend to represent the other side of the political spectrum. Likewise, the person wearing the pro–NRA T-shirt is unlikely to endear him- or herself to a person wearing a "Have you hugged a tree?" T-shirt. Indeed, we are more likely to adopt the attitude of someone with whom we share an important identity (McGarty et al., 1994). Suppose you have to form an attitude concerning a new product. How might the identity relevance of the message influence your attitude? To address this question, Fleming and Petty (2000) first selected students who reported being high or low in identification with their gender group. Then, they introduced a new snack product ("Snickerdoodles") to men and women as either one that is "women's favorite snack food" or "men's favorite snack food." As Figure 4.7 on page 100 illustrates, among those who were highly identified with their gender group, a more favorable attitude toward this new product was formed when the message was framed in terms of their own group liking that food. Among both men and women who were low in gender group

identity or self-expression function
Attitudes can permit the expression of central values and beliefs and thereby communicate who we are.

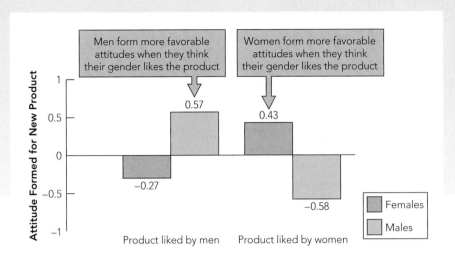

Figure 4.7 ■ Attitude Formation among Those Who Are Highly Identified with Their Gender Group
Men formed more positive attitudes when they thought other men liked a new product, and women formed more positive attitudes when they thought other women liked it. (*Source: Based on data from Fleming & Petty, 2000.*)

identification, no differences in attitudes toward the product were found as a function of who was said to favor it. By what means did the identity group information influence the formation of new attitudes among the highly identified participants? By examining the thoughts that the participants listed as they reviewed the information about the new food product, Fleming and Petty found that a greater proportion of positive thoughts were induced when the product was said to be favored by members of the participant's own gender group among those who were highly identified. Thus, the thoughts people have when they encounter a new object and form an attitude toward it can depend on their own group membership and how important it is to them.

The Self-Esteem Function of Attitudes

self-esteem function
Function in which holding particular attitudes can help maintain or enhance feelings of self-worth.

A third function that attitudes often serve is a **self-esteem function.** Holding particular attitudes can help us maintain or enhance our feelings of self-esteem or self-worth. This function is consistent with social comparison theory, which states that it can feel good to "know we are right," because our attitudes are validated by other people. For attitudes with a strong moral component, it can be self-validating to hold and act on those attitudes (Manstead, 2000). Indeed, a variety of emotions can be experienced as a result of expressing and acting on our attitudes. People can take pride in not cheating when they have an opportunity to do so, to the extent that their attitudes are based on moral principles. Considerable research has revealed that attitudes based on a moral conviction are good predictors of behavior. Does this mean that people never violate attitudes that they deem to be "right"? No, but violations of this sort can be more psychologically painful than attitude–behavior inconsistencies with which our moral selves are less strongly linked.

The Ego-Defensive Function of Attitudes

ego-defensive function
Protecting ourselves from unwanted or unflattering views of ourselves by claiming particular attitudes.

Attitudes sometimes serve an **ego-defensive function** (Katz, 1960), helping people to protect themselves from unwanted information about themselves. For instance, many persons who are quite bigoted express the view that they are against prejudice and discrimination. By stating such attitudes, they protect themselves from recognizing that they are actually highly prejudiced against members of various social groups. Indeed, because most of us want to be "cool" and accepted, we may claim to have more accepting or positive attitudes toward issues (e.g., same-sex marriage, marijuana use, alcohol consumption) than we actually do—because we assume that our peers do and we want to defend our self-view as "like everyone else" (Miller & Prentice, 1996).

Figure 4.8 ■ Attitudes: Their Impression Motivation Function

We sometimes use attitudes to make a good impression. In this study, participants whose impression motivation was high generated more new arguments in support of their attitudes than did participants whose impression motivation was moderate or low. (*Source: Based on data from Nienhuis, Manstead, & Spears, 2001.*)

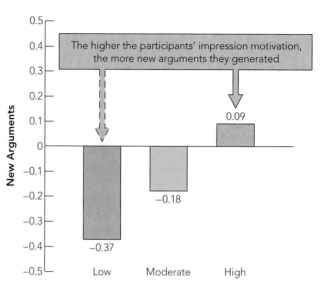

The Impression Motivation Function of Attitudes

Finally, attitudes often serve an **impression motivation function.** As you may recall from Chapter 3, we often wish to make a good impression, and expressing the "right" views is one way of doing so (Chaiken, Giner-Sorolla, & Chen, 1996). Research indicates that the extent to which attitudes serve this function can strongly affect how social information is processed. Such effects are clearly demonstrated in a study by Nienhuis, Manstead, and Spears (2001). These researchers reasoned that when attitudes serve an impression motivation function, individuals tend to generate arguments that support their attitudes, and the stronger the motivation to impress others, the more arguments generated. To test this prediction, they asked Dutch college students to read a message arguing in favor of the legalization of hard drugs. Then, the participants were told that they would be asked to defend this position. To vary the level of participants' impression motivation, some were told that their performance in this role would not be evaluated (low motivation), others were told that their performance would be evaluated by one other person (the moderate motivation condition), and still others were informed that their performance would be evaluated by three other people (high motivation). After receiving this information and reading the message, participants reported their attitudes and also indicated to what extent they had generated new arguments in favor of drug legalization. As predicted, those in the high-motivation condition generated more new arguments and also reported that they would be more likely to use those arguments to convince others (see Figure 4.8). Thus, the attitudes we express can depend on the social context in which we find ourselves, and this situation can alter the amount of cognitive work we are willing to do (Schwarz & Bohner, 2001).

impression motivation function Using attitudes to lead others to have a positive view of us. When motivated to do so, the attitudes we express can shift in order to create the desired impression on others.

KEY POINTS

★ Attitudes can be viewed as almost automatic reactions to the world. They can form rapidly as we are exposed to the attitude object and can influence basic approach or avoidance responses. Attitudes can serve different functions.

★ Attitudes can serve a *knowledge function* and provide an interpretative framework for understanding the world.

★ Attitudes can provide a means for expressing who we are and who we are similar to, thereby serving an *identity or self-expression function.*

★ The *self-esteem function* can be observed when we feel we are right and moral by expressing and behaving according to our attitudes.

★ Attitudes can serve an *ego-defensive function* by allowing us to defend our self-view as like others and not deviant.

★ When attitudes serve an *impression motivation function,* they guide the arguments constructed and, for this reason, may be difficult to change. Attitudes can allow us to manage how others perceive us.

Role of the Social Context in the Link between Attitudes and Behavior

More than seventy years ago, a classic study concerning ethnic prejudice (attitudes) and discrimination (behavior) was conducted by Richard LaPiere (1934). He wondered whether persons holding various prejudices—negative attitudes toward the members of specific social groups (see Chapter 6)—would, in fact, act on their attitudes. To find out, he spent two years traveling the United States with a young Chinese couple. They stopped at 184 restaurants and 66 hotels and motels. In the majority of cases, they were treated courteously. In fact, they were refused service only once, and LaPiere reported that they received what he considered to be above-average service in most instances. After his travels were completed, LaPiere wrote to all of the businesses where they had stayed or dined and asked whether they would or would not offer service to Chinese visitors. The results were startling: Of the 128 businesses that responded, 92 percent of the restaurants and 91 percent of the hotels said "No to Chinese customers!" These results seemed to indicate that there is often a sizable gap between attitudes and behavior— that is, what people say and what they do can be quite different.

Many continue to expect that such social attitudes will directly predict behavior. For example, people think that those who hold bigoted attitudes will consistently behave in a prejudicial fashion, and that nonprejudiced people will not. However, there is a host of norms and laws that make many prejudicial actions illegal, and such actions are likely to be seen as immoral (e.g., cross burning, some forms of hate speech), so that even the most prejudicial people will not always act on their attitudes. In addition, there are social conditions under which people who do not think of themselves as prejudiced may find themselves advocating discriminatory treatment of people based on group membership. Consider some Americans' responses to Arabs or Muslims after September 11. Despite not seeing themselves as prejudiced, their exclusionary actions are perceived as legitimate because of heightened safety concerns provoked by terrorism. Therefore, although it might seem reasonable to expect that attitudes toward a given ethnic group will directly predict discriminatory behavior, the matter is considerably more complicated.

Many factors can alter the degree to which attitudes and behavior are related. You have probably experienced a gap between your own attitudes and behaviors on many occasions— this is because the social context can also affect our behavior. What would you say if one of your friends shows you a new possession of which he or she is proud and asks for your opinion? Would you state that you think the object is not attractive, if that is your view? Perhaps, but the chances are good that you would try to avoid hurting your friend's feelings by saying that you *like* his or her new possession, even though you do not. In such cases, there can be a sizable gap between our attitudes and behavior, and we are often clearly aware of our conscious choice not to act on our "true" attitude. As this example illustrates, social contextual factors can limit the extent to which attitudes alone determine behavior. Your attitude might be a very good predictor of whether *you* would purchase that product, but the fact that your friend already has the product influences what you say to your friend. Depending on the degree to which the action is public and there are potential social consequences, attitudes will differentially predict behavior.

Because of the important role that the social context plays in determining the relationship between attitudes and behavior, research has focused on the factors that determine *when* attitudes influence behavior, as well as the issue of *why* such influence occurs.

When and Why Do Attitudes Influence Behavior?

Several factors determine the extent to which attitudes influence behavior. As discussed, aspects of the situation can strongly influence the extent to which attitudes influence behavior. Features of the attitudes themselves are also important. After considering these influences on the attitude–behavior relationship, we examine the question of *how* attitudes influence behavior—the underlying mechanisms involved in this process.

Situational Constraints That Affect Attitude Expression

Have you ever worried about what others would think if you expressed your "true" attitude toward an issue? If so, you understand the dilemma that Princeton University students experienced when studied by Miller, Monin, and Prentice (2000). The private attitudes of the students toward heavy alcohol consumption were relatively negative; however, they believed that other students' attitudes toward heavy alcohol consumption were more positive (an instance of **pluralistic ignorance,** in which we erroneously believe others have different attitudes). When these students were placed in a discussion with other students, they expressed more comfort with campus drinking than they actually felt, and their beliefs about what others would think about them predicted their behavior in the group discussion better than their actual attitudes. Such constraints on revealing our private attitudes can occur even when we are talking with members of a group with whom we highly identify. For example, members of attitude groups that were either "pro-choice" or "pro-life" were studied. In both groups, respondents were reluctant to publicly reveal the ambivalence they actually felt about their political position for fear that members of their own group would see them as disloyal. Thus, important forms of situational constraints of this sort can moderate the relationship between attitudes and behavior, and prevent attitudes from being expressed in overt behavior (Fazio & Roskos-Ewoldsen, 1994; Olson & Maio, 2003).

pluralistic ignorance
When we collectively misunderstand what attitudes others hold, and believe erroneously that others have different attitudes than ourselves.

Strength of Attitudes

Consider the following: A large timber company signs a contract with the government that allows the company to cut trees in a national forest. Some of the trees are ancient giants, hundreds of feet tall. A group of conservationists objects to the cutting of the trees and quickly moves to block this action. They join hands and form a human ring around the largest trees, preventing the loggers from cutting them down. Indeed, such tactics can often work: Because so much negative publicity results, the contract is revoked and the trees are saved, at least temporarily.

Why might people take such drastic and potentially risky action (i.e., the blocking of logging activity)? The activists hold very strong attitudes, which are important determinants of their behavior. Such events are far from rare. For example, residents of my (Nyla Branscombe) city have repeatedly and successfully prevented construction of a large mall that would drain business from the downtown area as has happened in many U.S. towns and cities. A dedicated few, and the possibility of negative publicity against government or business policies, can result in political actions that are consistent with such activists' attitudes. Such incidents call attention to the fact that whether attitudes predict sustained behavior depends on the strength of the attitudes. Let's consider why attitude strength has this effect.

The term *strength* captures the *extremity* or intensity of an attitude (how strong the emotional reaction provoked by the attitude object is), as well as the extent to which the attitude is based on *personal experience*. Both of these affect **attitude accessibility** (how easily the attitude comes to mind in various situations; Fazio, Ledbetter, & Towles-Schwen, 2000). As Figure 4.9 on page 104 illustrates, research indicates that all of these components are interrelated, and each plays a role in attitude strength (Petty & Krosnick, 1995).

attitude accessibility
The ease with which specific attitudes can be remembered and brought into consciousness.

Attitude Extremity

Let's consider attitude *extremity*—the extent to which an individual feels strongly about an issue (Krosnick, 1988). One of its key determinants is what social psychologists term *vested interest*—the extent to which the attitude is relevant to the concerns of the individual who holds it, which

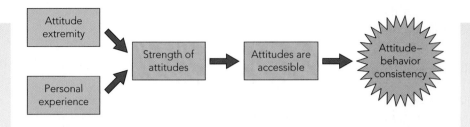

Figure 4.9 ■ How Attitude Strength Influences Attitude–Behavior Consistency
Attitudes that are formed on the basis of personal experience with the attitude object and extremity of the attitude combine to determine attitude strength. Strong attitudes are more likely to be accessible when a behavioral response is made, which results in greater attitude–behavior consistency than when attitudes are weak. (*Source: Based on suggestions by Petty & Krosnick, 1995.*)

typically amounts to whether the object or issue might have important consequences for this person. Study results indicate that the greater such vested interest, the stronger the impact of the attitude on behavior (Crano, 1995). For example, when students at a large university were telephoned and asked if they would participate in a campaign *against* increasing the legal drinking age from eighteen to twenty-one, their responses depended on whether they would be affected by the change (Sivacek & Crano, 1982). Students who would be affected—those younger than twenty-one—had a stronger vested interest than those who would not be affected by the law because they were already twenty-one or would reach this age before the law took effect. Thus, it was predicted that those in the first group—whose vested interests were at stake—would be more likely to join a rally against the proposed policy change than would those in the second group. This is exactly what happened: While more than 47 percent of those with high vested interest agreed to take part in the campaign, only 12 percent of those in the low vested interest group did so.

Not only do people with a vested interest behave in a way that supports their cause, they are also likely to elaborate on arguments that favor their position. By doing so, attitude-consistent thoughts come to mind when an issue is made salient. For example, Haugtvedt and Wegener (1994) found that when participants were asked to consider a nuclear power plant being built in their state (high personal relevance), they developed more counterarguments against the plan than if it might be built in a distant state (low personal relevance). Thus, attitudes based on vested interest are more likely to be thought about carefully, be resistant to change, and be an accessible guide for behavior.

Role of Personal Experience

Depending on how attitudes are formed initially, the link between attitudes and behavior can differ. Considerable evidence indicates that attitudes formed on the basis of direct experience can exert stronger effects on behavior than ones formed indirectly. This happens because attitudes formed on the basis of direct experience are easier to bring to mind when in the presence of the attitude object, which increases the likelihood that they will influence behavior (Tormala, Petty, & Brunol, 2002). Similarly, attitudes based on personal relevance are more likely to be elaborated in terms of supporting arguments, making them resistant to change (Wegener et al., 2004). Consider the difference between a friend telling you that a particular car model, Brand X, is a lemon versus experiencing several failures with this brand yourself. When looking at new models of Brand X, would your friend's opinion come to mind? Maybe not. Would your experiences come to mind? Probably. Thus, when you have direct experience with an attitude object, it is likely to be quite personally relevant, and your attitude is likely to predict your behavior toward it in the future.

Chapter 4 / Attitudes

KEY POINTS

How Do Attitudes Guide Behavior?

Researchers have found several basic mechanisms through which attitudes shape behavior. We first consider behaviors that are driven by attitudes based on reasoned thought, and then examine the role of attitudes in more spontaneous behavioral responses.

Attitudes Based on Reasoned Thought

In some situations, we give careful, deliberate thought to our attitudes and their implications for our behavior. Insight into the nature of this process is provided by the **theory of reasoned action,** a theory developed further and later known as the **theory of planned behavior,** first proposed by Icek Ajzen and Martin Fishbein in 1980. The theory of reasoned action begins with the notion that the decision to engage in a particular behavior is the result of a rational process. Various behavioral options are considered, the consequences or outcomes of each are evaluated, and a decision is reached to act or not act. That decision is then reflected in *behavioral intentions,* which often predict how we act in a given situation (Ajzen, 1987). According to the theory of planned behavior, intentions are determined by two factors: *attitudes toward a behavior*—people's positive or negative evaluations of performing the behavior—and *subjective norms*—people's perceptions of whether others will approve or disapprove. A third factor, *perceived behavioral control*—people's appraisals of their ability to perform the behavior—was subsequently added (Ajzen, 1991). A specific example helps to illustrate these ideas.

Suppose a student is considering getting a body piercing—for instance, a nose ornament. Will she go to the shop and take this action? The answer depends on her intentions, which are strongly influenced by her attitude toward body piercing. Her decision, though, is based on perceived norms and the extent to which she has control over the decision. If the student believes that a body piercing will be relatively painless and will make her look fashionable (she has positive attitudes toward the behavior), and also believes that the people whose opinions she values will approve (subjective norms) and that she can readily do it (she knows an expert who does body piercing), her intention to carry it out may be quite strong. On the other hand, if she believes that getting the piercing will be painful, it might not improve her appearance, her friends will disapprove, and she will have trouble finding an expert to do it safely, then her intentions to get the nose ornament will be weak. Of course, even the best of intentions can be thwarted by situational factors, but, in general, intentions are an important predictor of behavior.

Research suggests that these two theories are useful for predicting whether individuals will use Ecstasy, a dangerous drug used by a growing number of people between the ages of fifteen and twenty-five. Orbell et al. (2001) approached young people in various locations and asked them to complete a questionnaire designed to measure (1) their

theory of reasoned action
A theory suggesting that the decision to engage in a particular behavior is the result of a rational process in which behavioral options are considered, consequences or outcomes of each are evaluated, and a decision is reached to act or not to act. That decision is then reflected in behavioral intentions, which strongly influence overt behavior.

theory of planned behavior
An extension of the *theory of reasoned action,* suggesting that in addition to attitudes toward a given behavior and subjective norms about it, individuals also consider their ability to perform the behavior.

attitudes toward Ecstasy (e.g., is this drug enjoyable–unenjoyable, pleasant–unpleasant, beneficial–harmful, and so forth), (2) their intention to use it in the next two months, (3) subjective norms (whether their friends would approve), and (4) two aspects of perceived control over using this drug—whether they could obtain it and whether they could resist taking it if they had it. Two months later, the same persons were contacted and asked whether they had used Ecstasy. The results indicated that having a positive attitude toward Ecstasy, seeing its use as normatively accepted by one's peer group, and perceived control over using it were all significant predictors of the intention to use. Indeed, attitudes, subjective norms, and intentions were all significant predictors of actual Ecstasy use. Thus, overall, the findings were consistent with the theories of reasoned action and planned behavior.

Attitudes and Spontaneous Behavioral Reactions

Our ability to predict behavior in situations in which people have the time and opportunity to reflect carefully on possible actions that they might undertake is quite good. However, in many situations, people have to act quickly and their reactions are more spontaneous. In such cases, attitudes seem to influence behavior in a more direct and seemingly automatic manner, with intentions playing a less important role. According to one theoretical view—Fazio's **attitude-to-behavior process model** (Fazio, 1989; Fazio & Roskos-Ewoldsen, 1994)—the process works as follows. Some event activates an attitude; that attitude, once activated, influences how we perceive the attitude object. At the same time, our knowledge about what's appropriate (our knowledge of various social norms) is also activated (see Chapter 9). Together, the attitude and the previously stored information about what's appropriate or expected shape our definition of the event. This perception influences our behavior. Let's consider a concrete example.

Imagine that someone cuts you off in traffic (see Figure 4.10). This triggers your attitude toward people who engage in dangerous and discourteous behavior and, at the same time, your understanding of how people are expected to behave on the road. As a result, you perceive this behavior as nonnormative, or unexpected, which influences your definition of and your response to the event. You might think, "Who does this person think she/he is? What nerve!" or perhaps your response is more situational: "Gee, this person must be in a big hurry; or maybe she/he is a foreigner who doesn't know that you should signal before pulling in front of someone." Indeed, when norms are violated by a foreigner, local people may respond differently, depending on their interpretation of the nonnormative behavior. For example, when I (Nyla Branscombe) was living in Amsterdam, I went to a local bank to conduct some business. I immediately went and stood behind the person talking to the teller and ignored everyone else milling around the lobby. When the teller began to serve me, to

attitude-to-behavior process model
A model of how attitudes guide behavior that emphasizes the influence of attitudes and stored knowledge of what is appropriate in a given situation on an individual's definition of the present situation. This definition, in turn, influences overt behavior.

Figure 4.10 ■ Spontaneous Attitude-to-Behavior Process Effects
According to the *attitude-to-behavior process* model, events trigger our attitudes and, simultaneously, our understanding of how people are expected to behave or the appropriate norms for a given situation. In this case, being cut off in traffic by another driver triggers our attitudes toward such persons and our knowledge that this action is nonnormative. This interpretation, in turn, determines how we behave. Thus, attitudes are an important factor in shaping our overt behavior. (*Source: Based on Fazio, 2000.*)

my puzzlement, one Dutch person commented loudly on the "rudeness of Americans" (my nationality apparently was obvious from my accent), while another suggested that maybe I just didn't know the norms there: While waiting, there is a queue, but everyone waiting is supposed to *know* where they are in the line, making a literal queue unnecessary). Thus, people's definition of the event shapes their behavior—in one case, the assumption made was that I knew the norms and was ignoring them, and in the other, there was an acknowledgment that precisely because I was a foreigner I might not be familiar with this odd (to me) version of a line-up. Several studies support this perspective on how attitudes can influence behavior by affecting the interpretation given to the situation.

Under hectic everyday conditions, we often don't have time for deliberate weighing of alternatives. In such cases, our attitudes seem to spontaneously shape our perceptions of events, and thereby our immediate behavioral reactions to them (Bargh, 1997; Dovidio et al., 1996).

KEY POINTS

★ Several factors affect the strength of the relationship between attitudes and behavior; some of these relate to the situation in which the attitudes are activated, and some to aspects of the attitudes themselves.

★ Attitudes seem to influence behavior through two different mechanisms. The theories of *reasoned action* and *planned behavior* predict behavior when the decision to engage in an action is consciously and deliberately

assessed. When we can give careful thought to our attitudes, intentions derived from our attitudes, norms, and perceived control over the behavior all predict behavior. When we do not engage in such deliberate thought, as described in the *attitude-to-behavior process model*, attitudes influence behavior by shaping our perceptions of the situation, which, in turn, dictate our behavior.

The Fine Art of Persuasion: How Attitudes Are Changed

How many times during the past day has someone tried to change your attitude? If you stop and think for a moment, you may be surprised, for it is clear that each day we are bombarded with such attempts, some of which are illustrated in Figure 4.11. Billboards, television commercials, newspaper and magazine ads, appeals from charities, pop-up ads on our computers, our friends, even university professors—the list of potential "would-be persuaders" seems endless. To what extent are such attempts at **persuasion**—efforts to change our attitudes through the use of various messages—successful? And what factors determine whether they succeed or fail? Social psychologists have studied these issues for decades, and

persuasion
Efforts to change others' attitudes through the use of various kinds of messages.

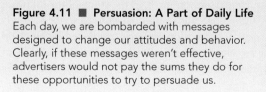
Figure 4.11 ■ Persuasion: A Part of Daily Life
Each day, we are bombarded with messages designed to change our attitudes and behavior. Clearly, if these messages weren't effective, advertisers would not pay the sums they do for these opportunities to try to persuade us.

Fear Appeals: Do They Really Work?

Many believe that the best method of getting people to change their attitudes (and behavior) is to frighten them about the consequences of not changing. When I (Nyla Branscombe) smoked cigarettes, people assumed that simply telling me about the dangers of smoking would scare me enough to make me quit. People's assumption seemed to be that I'd be persuaded by their arguments, be frightened of the likely consequences, and then "just say no!" Governments appear to think this method will be effective as well. In Canada, all tobacco products carry very large warnings of the sort, "Smoking KILLS" (see Figure 4.12). Indeed, Canada spends millions of dollars creating fear-based commercials showing diseased lungs and other grotesque long-term consequences of smoking. Social psychologists have conducted much research addressing the question of whether fear appeals effectively change attitudes, and they have come up with some surprising answers about how ineffective such fear appeals can be if used under the wrong circumstances.

Common sense would seem to suggest that if fear appeals present compelling arguments that frighten us with the reality of what will happen if we don't change, they should be effective at inducing change. It is more complicated than this, however. If the message is so fear arousing that people feel threatened, they are likely to react defensively and argue against the threat, or else dismiss its applicability (Liberman & Chaiken, 1992; Taylor & Shepperd, 1998). In this case, people are likely to say to themselves, "The evidence isn't that strong," "I'll quit before those consequences occur," or "It won't happen to me," all of which can undermine the effectiveness of

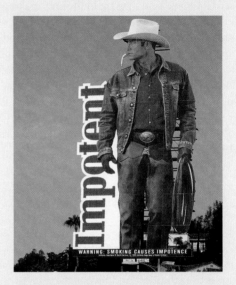

Figure 4.12 ■ Attempting to Frighten Us into Change
Many frightening images have been used in an attempt to scare people into changing their attitudes and behavior. Research indicates that this approach can be surprisingly ineffective because people have a variety of defenses they can use that allow them to dismiss the message.

truly frightening messages. Smokers attending the funerals of their loved ones who died of lung cancer—and who are presumably feeling considerable fear—can be heard to utter just these sorts of defensive responses as they light up.

Might inducing more moderate levels of fear work better? There is some evidence for this, but only when it is paired with specific information about how to reduce the fear and methods of behavioral change that allow the negative consequences to

as we'll soon see, their efforts have yielded important insights into the cognitive processes that play a role in persuasion (e.g., Eagly, Wood, & Chaiken, 1996; Petty et al., 2003). We illustrate the important progress made by social psychologists in understanding whether a particular persuasion technique—using fear appeals—is or is not effective in the **Making Sense of Common Sense** section.

Persuasion: Communicators and Audiences

Early research efforts aimed at understanding persuasion involved the study of the following elements: Some *source* directs some type of *message* (the *communication*) to some person or group (the *audience*). Following World War II, persuasion research conducted by Hovland, Janis, and Kelley (1953) focused on these key elements, asking "*Who* says *what* to *whom* with what effect?" This approach yielded a number of important findings, with the following being the most consistent.

be avoided (Petty & Krosnick, 1995). After all, if people do not know how to change, do not know where to get help to do so, do not know it will be a long process, or do not believe they can succeed (see Chapter 5 for research on self-efficacy), then fear will do little except induce avoidance and defensive responses.

Might health messages of various sorts be more effective if they were framed in a positive manner (e.g., how to attain good health) rather than in a negative manner (e.g., risks and undesirable consequences? For example, any health message can be framed positively as "Do this and you will feel better" (e.g., "Having an annual mammogram may allow you to live a long life"). Negative framings for the same messages might be "If you don't do this behavior, you may become ill" (e.g., "Not getting a mammogram may shorten your life"). The point is that the same health information can be framed either positively or negatively. Broemer (2004) has provided evidence that when health messages are framed positively and when it

is relatively easy to imagine ourselves having the rather serious symptoms described (so that fear is experienced), more change occurs than when health messages are framed negatively. In contrast, when it is easy to imagine experiencing only trivial symptoms (so that less fear is elicited), more attitude change was observed when the message was framed negatively than positively (see Figure 4.13).

Thus, fear appeals appear to be most effective when the symptoms of a potential illness are trivial, not when they are serious. Therefore, using them to induce change in order to prevent a serious illness, such as lung cancer, might be ineffective. In contrast, positively framed appeals seem to be most effective at inducing attitude change when the symptoms are serious. Thus, social psychological research shows how such commonsense notions of "Just scare people and they'll change" may be misleading. Indeed, positively framed messages can be even more effective when they concern serious health warnings.

Figure 4.13 ■ Effectiveness of Positively versus Negatively Framed Health Messages
When serious symptoms that could occur because of one's own health-related behavior are easy to imagine, a positively framed message is most effective at inducing change. However, when, trivial symptoms are easy to imagine because of one's own health-related behavior, a negatively framed message is most effective at inducing change. (*Source: Based on data from Broemer, 2004.*)

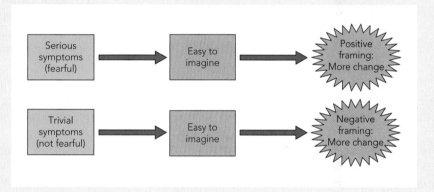

- Communicators who are *credible*—who seem to know what they are talking about or who are expert with respect to the topics or issues they are presenting—are more persuasive than nonexperts. For instance, in a famous study, Hovland and Weiss (1951) asked participants to read communications dealing with various issues (e.g., atomic submarines, the future of movie theaters—remember, this was back in 1950!). The supposed source of these messages was varied to be high or low in credibility. For instance, for atomic submarines, a highly credible source was the scientist Robert J. Oppenheimer, while the low-credibility source was *Pravda*, the newspaper of the Communist party in the Soviet Union (notice, though, that the credible source was an ingroup member for Americans, but the low credible source was an outgroup source). Participants expressed their attitudes toward these issues a week before the experiment and then immediately after receiving the communications. Those who were told that the source of the messages they read was a highly credible ingroup member showed significantly greater attitude change than those who thought the message was from the

outgroup member. So, as Figure 4.14 suggests, source credibility is an important factor in persuasion, and members of our own group are typically seen as more credible and produce greater influence than those with whom we do not share group membership (Turner, 1991).

"A word to the wise, Benton, Don't squander your credibility."

- Communicators who are attractive in some way (e.g., physically) are more persuasive than unattractive communicators (Hovland & Weiss, 1951). This is one reason why advertisements often include attractive models. Frequently, advertisers are attempting to suggest that if we use their product, we will be perceived as attractive (see Figure 4.15).

- Messages that do not appear to be designed to change our attitudes are often more successful than those that seem to be designed to achieve this goal (Walster & Festinger, 1962). A recent meta-analysis of research concerning forewarning that a message will be aimed at changing our attitudes has revealed that such forewarning typically lessens the extent to which attitude change occurs (Benoit, 1998). So, simply knowing that a sales pitch is coming your way helps you resist it.

- People are sometimes more susceptible to persuasion when they are distracted by an extraneous event than when they are paying full attention to what is being said (Allyn & Festinger, 1961). This is one reason why political candidates often arrange for spontaneous demonstrations or large crowds during their speeches. The distraction generated among the audience may enhance acceptance of the speaker's message. As you'll see later, research in the elaboration–likelihood tradition has demonstrated how distraction can enhance persuasion by preventing systematic processing of the message content.

- When an audience holds attitudes contrary to those of a would-be persuader, it is often more effective for the communicator to adopt a *two-sided approach,* in which both sides of the argument are presented rather than a *one-sided approach* that discusses only one side. This is especially true when, within the message, arguments are included that refute the side of which the speaker is not in favor (Crowley & Hoyer, 1994). Well-educated listeners in particular are more likely to be persuaded by two-sided messages (Faison, 1961). With a two-sided approach, we can feel that we've heard both sides of the argument but that the evidence strongly supports the position being advocated by the communicator.

Figure 4.15 ■ **Role of Attractiveness of Communicator in Persuasion**
It is no accident that advertisers attempt to pair their product (everything from autos to beer) with an attractive woman (particularly when their target market is young men). The assumption is that the attractiveness of the model will be linked with the product.

- People who speak rapidly are often more persuasive than those who speak slowly (Miller et al., 1976). Presumably, this works by influencing the perceived credibility of the communicator.

- People who exhibit greater confidence in what they are saying, regardless of its validity, are often more persuasive than those who appear to be less confident.

- Across the life span, people differ in the extent to which they are likely to be persuaded by a communicator. Specifically, young people (between the ages of eighteen and twenty-five) are especially likely to be influenced, whereas older people are more resistant to changing their attitudes (Sears, 1986).

Early research on persuasion provided important insights into the factors that influence persuasion. What such work *didn't* do, however, was offer a comprehensive account of *how* persuasion occurs. In recent years, social psychologists have recognized that it is necessary to examine the cognitive factors and processes that underlie persuasion—in other words, what goes on in people's minds while they listen and why they are influenced or not influenced. It is to this highly sophisticated work that we turn next.

The Cognitive Processes Underlying Persuasion

What happens when you are exposed to a persuasive message—for instance, when you watch a television commercial or listen to a political speech? Your first answer might be something like "I think about what's being said," and in a sense, that's correct. But as we saw in Chapter 3, social psychologists know that, in general, we often do the least amount of cognitive work that we can in a given situation. Indeed, people may *want* to avoid listening to such commercial messages—and thanks to VCRs, DVDs and TiVo, people can tape a program and skip the commercials! But when you are subjected to a message, the central issue—the one that seems to provide the key to understanding the entire process of persuasion—is really "How do we process (absorb, interpret, evaluate) the information?" The answer that has emerged from hundreds of studies is that, basically, we process persuasive messages in two distinct ways.

■ Systematic versus Heuristic Processing

The first type of processing we can use is known as **systematic processing** or the **central route to persuasion,** and it involves careful consideration of message content and the ideas it contains. Such processing requires effort, and it absorbs much of our information-processing capacity. The second approach, known as **heuristic processing,** or the **peripheral route to persuasion,** involves the use of simple rules of thumb or mental shortcuts, such as the belief that "experts' statements can be trusted," or the idea that "if it makes me feel good, I'm in favor of it." This kind of processing requires less effort and allows us to react in an automatic manner. It occurs in response to cues in the message or situation that evoke various mental shortcuts (e.g., beautiful models evoke the "What's beautiful is good and worth listening to" heuristic).

When do we engage in each of these modes of thought? Modern theories of persuasion such as the **elaboration–likelihood model** (ELM for short; e.g., Petty & Cacioppo, 1986; Petty, Wheeler, & Tormala, 2003) and the heuristic–systematic model (e.g., Chaiken, Liberman, & Eagly, 1989; Eagly & Chaiken, 1998) provide the following answer. We engage in the most effortful and systematic processing when our motivation and capacity to process information relating to the persuasive message is high. This type of processing occurs if we have a lot of knowledge about the topic, a lot of time to engage in careful thought, or the issue is sufficiently important to us and we believe it is essential to form an accurate view (Maheswaran & Chaiken, 1991; Petty & Cacioppo, 1990). In contrast, we engage in the type of processing that requires less effort (heuristic processing) when we lack the ability or capacity to process more carefully (we must make up our minds very quickly, or we have little

systematic processing
Processing of information in a persuasive message that involves careful consideration of message content and ideas.

central route to persuasion
Attitude change resulting from systematic processing of information presented in persuasive messages.

heuristic processing
Processing of information in a persuasive message that involves the use of simple rules of thumb or mental shortcuts.

peripheral route to persuasion
Attitude change that occurs in response to peripheral persuasion cues, often based on information concerning the expertise or status of would-be persuaders.

elaboration–likelihood model (of persuasion)
A theory suggesting that persuasion can occur in either of two distinct ways—systematic versus heuristic processing, which differ in the amount of cognitive effort or elaboration they require.

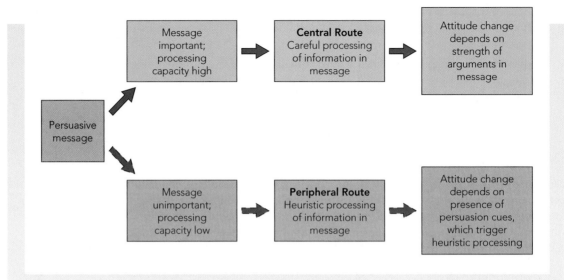

Figure 4.16 ■ The ELM Model: A Cognitive Theory of Persuasion
According to the *elaboration–likelihood* model (ELM), persuasion can occur in two ways. First, we can be persuaded by carefully and systematically processing the information contained in the persuasive messages (the central route), or second, through less systematic processing based on heuristics or mental shortcuts. Systematic processing occurs when the message is important to us and we have the cognitive resources available to think about it carefully. Heuristic processing is most likely when the message is not important to us or we do not have the cognitive resources (or time) to engage in careful thought. (*Source: Based on suggestions by Petty & Cacioppo, 1986.*)

knowledge about the issue) or when our motivation is low (the issue is unimportant to us or has little potential effect on us). Advertisers, politicians, salespersons, and others wishing to change our attitudes prefer to push us into the heuristic mode because, for reasons we describe below, it is often easier to change our attitudes when we think in this mode than when we engage in more careful and systematic processing. (See Figure 4.16 for an overview of the ELM model.)

The discovery of these two contrasting modes provide an important key to understanding the process of persuasion, because the existence of these two modes of thought helps us solve several intriguing puzzles. For instance, when persuasive messages are not interesting or relevant, the degree of persuasion they produce is *not* strongly influenced by the strength of the arguments these messages contain. When such messages are highly relevant, however, they are more successful in inducing persuasion when the arguments they contain *are* strong and convincing. Can you see why this so? According to modern theories, such as the ELM and the heuristic–systematic model, when relevance is low, individuals tend to process messages through the heuristic mode by means of cognitive shortcuts. Thus, argument strength has little impact on them. When relevance is high, they process persuasive messages more systematically, and in this mode, argument strength *is* important (e.g., Petty & Cacioppo, 1990).

Similarly, the systematic versus heuristic distinction explains why people are more easily persuaded when they are somewhat distracted than when they are not. Under these conditions, the capacity to process the information in a persuasive message is limited, so people adopt the heuristic mode of thought. If the message contains the "right" cues that will induce heuristic processing (e.g., attractive or seemingly expert communicators), persuasion may occur because people respond to these cues and *not* to the arguments being presented. In summary, the modern cognitive approach seems to provide a crucial key to understanding many aspects of persuasion.

Chapter 4 / Attitudes

KEY POINTS

★ Early research on *persuasion*—efforts to change attitudes through the use of messages—focused primarily on characteristics of the communicator (e.g., expertise, attractiveness), message (e.g., one-sided versus two-sided), and audience.

★ Modern theories of persuasion include the *elaboration-likelihood model (ELM)* and the *heuristic–systematic model*.

Research has sought to understand the cognitive processes that play a role in persuasion and to illuminate how we process persuasive messages in two distinct ways: through *systematic processing* or the *central route to persuasion*, which involves careful attention to message content, or through *heuristic processing* or the *peripheral route to persuasion*, which involves the use of mental shortcuts.

Resisting Persuasion Attempts

Based on the studies we are discussing, it should be clear that we tend to be highly resistant to persuasive messages. Why are we sometimes such a "tough sell" where efforts to change our attitudes are concerned? The answer involves several factors that, together, enhance our ability to resist even highly skilled efforts at persuasion.

Reactance: Protecting Our Personal Freedom

Have you ever experienced someone who increasingly mounts pressure on you to change your attitude on some issue? As they do, you may experience a growing level of annoyance and resentment. The final outcome: Not only do you resist, you may actually lean over backward to adopt views that are *opposite* to those of the would-be persuader. This is an example of what social psychologists call **reactance**—a negative reaction to efforts by others to reduce our freedom by getting us to do what *they* want us to believe or do what they want. Research indicates that, in such situations, we often change our attitudes and behavior in the opposite direction of what we are being urged to believe or do. This effect is known as *negative attitude change* (Brehm, 1966; Rhodewalt & Davison, 1983). When we are feeling reactance, strong arguments in favor of attitude change can produce greater opposition to the advocated position than when moderate or weak arguments are presented (Fuegen & Brehm, 2004).

The existence of reactance is one reason why hard-sell attempts at persuasion often fail. When individuals perceive such appeals as direct threats to their personal freedom (or their image of being independent), they are motivated to resist. For example, some people are raised with the expectation that they will become a member of a particular occupational or religious group. Reactance can be experienced, though, from such pressure, which can then virtually assure that the individual's family or other would-be persuaders will fail in their mission.

reactance
Negative reactions to threats to one's personal freedom. Reactance often increases resistance to persuasion and can even produce negative attitude change or that opposite to what was intended.

Forewarning: Prior Knowledge of Persuasive Intent

When we watch television, we expect commercials, and we know that these messages are designed to persuade us to purchase various products. Similarly, we know that when we listen to a political speech, the speaker is attempting to persuade us to vote for him or her. Does the fact that we know in advance about the persuasive intent behind such messages help us resist them? Research on the effects of such advance knowledge—known as **forewarning**—indicates that it does (e.g., Cialdini & Petty, 1979; Johnson, 1994). When we know that a speech, taped message, or written appeal is designed to alter our views, we are often less likely to be affected than when we do not possess such knowledge. Why? Because forewarning influences several cognitive processes that play an important role in persuasion.

First, forewarning provides us with more opportunity to formulate *counterarguments* and that can lessen the message's impact. In addition, forewarning provides us with more time in

forewarning
Advance knowledge that one is about to become the target of an attempt at persuasion. Forewarning often increases resistance to the persuasion that follows.

which to recall relevant facts and information that may prove useful in refuting a persuasive message. Those who want to persuade others and who want to counter the effects of forewarning should try distracting individuals between the time of the warning and receipt of the message; this tactic can prevent participants from counterarguing. In fact, those who have been forewarned, when distracted, are no more likely to resist the message than those who were not forewarned of the upcoming persuasive appeal. Wood and Quinn (2003) found that forewarning was generally effective at increasing resistance, and that simply *expecting* to receive a persuasive message (without actually receiving it) can influence attitudes in a resistant direction. The benefits of forewarning are more likely to occur with respect to attitudes we consider important (Krosnick, 1989), but they seem to occur to a smaller degree even for attitudes we view as fairly trivial. In many cases, it appears that to be forewarned is indeed to be forearmed where persuasion is concerned.

There are instances, though, in which forewarnings can encourage attitude shifts toward the position advocated, but this effect appears to be a temporary response to people's desire to defend their view of themselves as not gullible or easily influenced (Quinn & Wood, 2004). In this case, because people make the attitude shift before they receive the persuasive appeal, they can convince themselves that they were not influenced at all! We can be assured that this effect is motivated because people are especially likely to show it when they know that the "future persuader" is an expert or will be highly persuasive. Furthermore, distraction after the forewarning was received—which presumably inhibits thought—had no effect on the extent to which attitudes were changed in the direction of the expected message. Thus, people appear to be using a simple heuristic (e.g., "This person will be an expert and I'll look stupid if I don't agree with what he/she says") and change their attitudes before receiving the message.

Selective Avoidance of Persuasion Attempts

Still another way we resist attempts at persuasion is through **selective avoidance**—a tendency to direct our attention away from information that challenges our existing attitudes. As explained in Chapter 2, selective avoidance is one of the ways in which schemas guide the processing of social information, and attitudes often operate as schemas. Television viewing provides a clear illustration of the effects of selective avoidance. People channel surf, mute the commercials, tape their favorite programs, or simply cognitively tune out when confronted with information contrary to their views. The opposite effect occurs as well. When we encounter information that *supports* our views, we tend to give it our full attention. Such tendencies to ignore or avoid information that contradicts our attitudes while actively seeking information consistent with them constitute two sides of what social psychologists term *selective exposure*. Such selectivity in what we make the focus of our attention helps ensure that our attitudes remain largely intact for long periods of time.

Actively Defending Our Attitudes: Counterarguing against the Competition

Ignoring or screening out information incongruent with our current views is certainly one way of resisting persuasion. Growing evidence suggests that, in addition to this kind of passive defense of our attitudes, we also use a more active strategy as well: We actively counterargue against views that are contrary to our own (e.g., Eagly et al., 1999). Doing so makes the opposing views more memorable, but it reduces their impact on our attitudes. Eagly and her colleagues have reported clear evidence for such effects (2000).

These researchers exposed students previously identified as either for (pro-choice) or against (pro-life) abortion to persuasive messages delivered by a female communicator; the messages were either consistent with the participants' attitudes or were contrary. After hearing the messages, participants reported their attitudes toward abortion, indicated how sure they were of their views (a measure of attitude strength), and listed all the message's arguments they could recall (a measure of memory). In addition, they listed their thoughts while listening to

Chapter 4 / Attitudes

Figure 4.17 ■ Counterarguing against Counterattitudinal Messages
Participants reported having more oppositional thoughts about a counterattitudinal message, but they reported having more supportive thoughts about a proattitudinal message. These findings are consistent with the view that one reason we are so good at resisting persuasion is that we actively defend our attitudes against opposing views by counterarguing against them. (*Source: Based on data from Eagly et al., 2000.*)

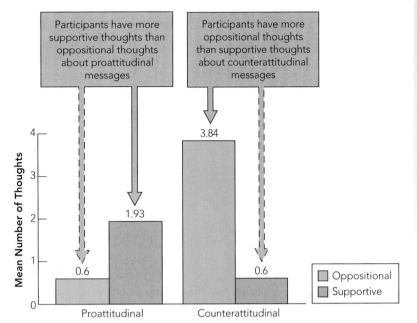

the message; this provided information on the extent to which they counterargued internally against the message when it was contrary to their views.

As expected, the results indicated that the counterattitudinal message and the pro-attitudinal message were equally memorable. However, participants reported thinking more systematically about the counterattitudinal message, and reported having more oppositional thoughts about it—a clear sign that they were counterarguing against this message. In contrast, they reported more supportive thoughts in response to the proattitudinal message (see Figure 4.17). Therefore, one reason we are so good at resisting persuasion is that we not only ignore information that is inconsistent with our current views, but also carefully process counterattitudinal input and argue actively against it. In a sense, we provide our own strong defense against efforts to change our attitudes.

Inoculation against "Bad Ideas"

The idea that resistance to persuasion stems, in part, from generating arguments against the views presented in persuasive messages is far from new. More than forty years ago, William McGuire (1961) suggested that people could be inoculated against persuasion if they were first presented with views that opposed their own, along with arguments that refuted these counterattitudinal positions. He reasoned that when people were presented with counter-arguments, they would be stimulated to generate additional counterarguments of their own, and this would make them more resistant to attitude change.

To test this prediction, he conducted several studies (e.g., McGuire & Papageorgis, 1961) in which individuals received attitude statements (e.g., truisms such as "Everyone should brush his or her teeth after every meal") along with one of two sets of arguments. One set of arguments supported this truism (the *supportive defense* condition), and the other set refuted the truism (the *refutational defense* condition). Two days later, participants received additional messages that attacked the original truisms with new arguments. Finally, participants were asked to report their attitudes toward these views. As predicted, the refutational defense was more effective in preventing persuasion. In other words, exposure to arguments opposed to our attitudes can serve to strengthen the views we already hold, making us more resistant to subsequent efforts to change them. (Please see the **Ideas to Take with You—and Use!** section at the end of this chapter for advice on how to resist persuasion.)

KEY POINTS

★ Several factors contribute to our ability to resist persuasion. One factor is *reactance*—negative reactions to efforts by others to reduce or limit our personal freedom, which can produce greater overall opposition to the message.

★ Resistance to persuasion is often increased by *forewarning*—the knowledge that someone is trying to change our attitudes—and by *selective avoidance*—the tendency to avoid exposure to information that contradicts our views.

★ When we are exposed to persuasive messages that are contrary to our existing views, we actively counterargue against them.

★ If we receive arguments against our views along with arguments that refute these counterattitudinal positions, our resistance to subsequent persuasion attempts increases; this is known as inoculation against counterattitudinal views.

Cognitive Dissonance: What It Is and How We Reduce It

cognitive dissonance
An internal state that results when individuals notice inconsistency among two or more attitudes or between their attitudes and their behavior.

When we first introduced the questions of whether and to what extent attitudes and behavior are linked, we noted that there is a sizable gap between what we feel on the inside (positive or negative reactions to some object or issue) and what we show on the outside. Social psychologists term this **cognitive dissonance**—an unpleasant state that occurs when we notice that various attitudes we hold, or our attitudes and behavior, are somehow inconsistent.

You have probably experienced cognitive dissonance in your everyday social life. Any time you say things you don't really believe (e.g., praise something you don't actually like just to be polite), make a difficult decision that requires you to reject an alternative you find attractive, or discover that something you've invested effort or money in is not as good as you expected, you may experience dissonance. In all of these situations, there is a gap between your attitudes and your actions, and such gaps tend to make us quite uncomfortable. Most important from the present perspective, cognitive dissonance sometimes leads us to change our attitudes—to shift them so that they *are* consistent with our overt behavior. Let's take a closer look at cognitive dissonance and its intriguing implications for attitude change.

Dissonance theory begins with a very reasonable idea: People find inconsistency between their actions and attitudes uncomfortable. In other words, when we notice that our attitudes and our behaviors don't match, we are motivated to do something to reduce the dissonance. How do we accomplish this goal? In its early forms, dissonance research (Aronson, 1968; Festinger, 1957) focused on three basic mechanisms:

- First, we can change either our attitudes or behavior so that they are more consistent with each other.

- Second, we can reduce cognitive dissonance by acquiring new information that supports our attitude or behavior. People who smoke, for instance, search for evidence suggesting that the harmful effects are minimal or occur only for heavy smokers, or that the benefits (e.g., reduced tension, improved weight control) outweigh the costs (Lipkus et al., 2001).

- Third, we can decide that the inconsistency doesn't matter; in other words, we engage in **trivialization**—concluding that the attitudes or behaviors in question are not important, so any inconsistency between them is of no importance (Simon, Greenberg, & Brehm, 1995).

trivialization
A technique for reducing dissonance in which the importance of attitudes or behaviors that are inconsistent with each other is cognitively reduced.

All of these strategies can be viewed as *direct* methods of dissonance reduction: They focus on the attitude–behavior discrepancy that is causing the dissonance. Research by Steele and his colleagues (Steele & Lui, 1983; Steele, 1988) also indicates that dissonance can be reduced via *indirect* means—that the basic discrepancy between the attitude and behavior is left intact, but the unpleasant or negative feelings generated by dissonance can be reduced. According to this view, adoption of indirect tactics to reduce dissonance is most likely when the attitude–behavior discrepancy involves *important* attitudes or self-beliefs. Under these conditions, individuals experiencing dissonance may not focus so much on reducing the gap between their attitudes and behavior, but focus instead on other methods that will allow them to feel good about themselves despite the gap (Steele, Spencer, & Lynch, 1993). Specifically, *self-affirmation*—restoring positive self-evaluations that are threatened by the dissonance (e.g., Elliot & Devine, 1994; Tesser, Martin, & Cornell, 1996) can be accomplished by focusing on positive self-attributes.

In summary, dissonance can be reduced in many ways—through indirect tactics, as well as direct strategies aimed at reducing the attitude–behavior discrepancy. As you'll see, the choice between various alternatives may be a function of what's available and the specific context in which dissonance occurs (Aronson, Blanton, & Cooper, 1995; Fried & Aronson, 1995).

Is Dissonance Really Unpleasant?

When, without sufficient justification, we say or do things that are contrary to our true beliefs, we feel uncomfortable as a result. Until recently, however, there was little direct scientific evidence relating to this issue. That dissonance is arousing in a physiological sense was well documented (e.g., Elkin & Leippe, 1986; Losch & Cacioppo, 1990; Steele, Southwick, & Crichtlow, 1981), but there was little evidence that dissonance itself is unpleasant, although this is a central assumption of dissonance theory. To examine this, Eddie Harmon-Jones (2000) first had participants write counterattitudinal essays under conditions in which expressing views contrary to their real ones could not produce aversive consequences. That is, participants wrote essays in which they described a boring paragraph as actually interesting, and they were told to throw their essays away after writing them. Participants wrote their essays under one of two conditions: low choice (they were simply told to describe the boring paragraph as interesting) or high choice (they were told that they could describe the boring paragraph in any way they wished, but that the experimenter would really appreciate it if they wrote that the dull paragraph was interesting). Only in the high-choice condition, in which they felt responsible for what they wrote, would they be expected to experience dissonance.

After completing their essays, participants reported their attitude toward the paragraph they read, the discomfort they felt (e.g., how uneasy or bothered they were), and general negative affect (e.g., how tense, distressed, and irritable they felt) on a questionnaire. The results were as expected: Those in the high-choice condition rated the dull paragraph as more interesting than did those in the low-choice condition. People in this condition also reported feeling more discomfort and more general negative affect than did those in the low-choice condition (see Figure 4.18). Because their essays could not have any aversive consequences, these findings suggest that the experience of dissonance indeed produces negative affect, as Festinger (1957) originally proposed.

Is Dissonance a Universal Human Experience?

According to cognitive dissonance theory, human dislike experiencing cognitive inconsistency. As discussed, people feel uncomfortable when they perceive their attitudes and behaviors as inconsistent, and this often leads them to engage in active efforts

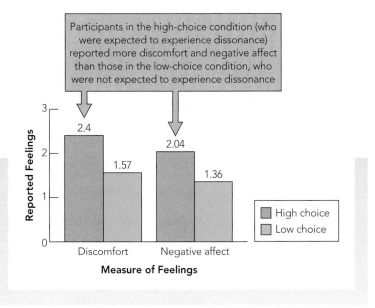

Figure 4.18 ■ Evidence That Dissonance Generates Negative Affect
Persons who wrote statements counter to their own attitudes under conditions in which they freely chose to do this reported higher levels of discomfort and general negative affect than those who wrote such statements because they were told to do so. (*Source: Based on data from Harmon-Jones, 2000.*)

Participants in the high-choice condition (who were expected to experience dissonance) reported more discomfort and negative affect than those in the low-choice condition, who were not expected to experience dissonance to reduce the discomfort. A large body of evidence offers support for these ideas, so dissonance theory appears to be a source of important insights into several aspects of social thought. It's important to note, though, that the vast majority of studies on dissonance have been conducted in North America and Western Europe. This raises an important question: Does cognitive dissonance occur in other cultures? Although initial studies in Japan yielded mixed results (e.g., Takata & Hashimoto, 1973; Yoshida, 1977), more recent findings by Heine and Lehman (1997) point to the conclusion that dissonance is indeed a universal aspect. However, the factors that produce dissonance, and even its magnitude, can be influenced by cultural factors.

Consider the study conducted by Heine and Lehman (1997). They reasoned that although dissonance might occur all around the world, it may be less likely to influence attitudes in some cultures than in others. Specifically, they suggested that after making a choice between closely ranked alternatives, persons from cultures such as those in the United States and Canada would be more likely to experience post-decision dissonance than would persons from cultures in Asian countries. Why? Because in western cultures, the *self* is linked to individual actions, such as making correct decisions, so after making a choice between alternatives (different courses of action, different objects), individuals in western cultures can experience considerable dissonance. The possibility of having made an incorrect choice poses a threat to their self-esteem. In many Asian cultures, in contrast, the self is not as closely linked to individual actions or choices. Rather, the self is more strongly tied to roles and status—an individual's place in society and their obligations. Thus, persons in such cultures should be less likely to perceive the possibility of making an incorrect decision as a threat to their selves. If this were the case, they should also be less likely to experience dissonance.

To test this reasoning, Heine and Lehman (1997) had Canadian and Japanese students (who were temporarily living in Canada) choose ten CDs from a group of forty that they would most like to own. The students also evaluated how much they would like each of these ten CDs. Then, participants were told that they could only have *either* the CD they ranked first or the one they ranked sixth. After choosing, participants rated these two CDs again. Previous research suggests that to reduce dissonance, individuals who must make a decision between two options often downrate the item they did not choose, while raising their ratings of the item they did choose— an effect known as **spreading of alternatives** (Steele et al., 1993). The researchers predicted that such effects would be stronger for Canadians than for Japanese participants, and this is precisely what happened. The Canadian students showed the spreading of alternatives effect that results from dissonance reduction to a significant degree, while the Japanese students did not.

These findings suggest that cultural factors influence how dissonance affects people in different cultures. Although all human are made somewhat uneasy by inconsistencies among their attitudes and their behaviors, the intensity of such reactions, the precise conditions under which they occur, and the strategies used to reduce them may all be influenced by cultural factors.

Dissonance and Attitude Change: The Effects of Induced or Forced Compliance

As noted repeatedly, there are many occasions when we say or do things that are inconsistent with our true attitudes. Social psychologists refer to these situations as involving **induced or forced compliance**—we are induced, somehow, to say or do something contrary to how we really feel. Dissonance is then aroused, and when it is, we may change our attitudes so that they are more consistent with our actions. In a sense, we produce attitude change in ourselves when dissonance is experienced. We are especially likely to change our attitudes when other techniques for reducing dissonance are unavailable or require great effort.

■ Dissonance and the Less-Leads-to-More Effect

Will the reasons you engaged in the behavior that is inconsistent with your attitudes matter? We can engage in attitude-discrepant behavior for many reasons, and some are more compelling than others. When will our attitudes change more: When there are "good" reasons for engaging in attitude-discrepant behavior or when there is no real justification for doing so? Cognitive dissonance theory offers an unexpected answer: Dissonance will be stronger when we have

---

spreading of alternatives
When individuals make a decision between two options, they tend to reduce the rating of the item they did not choose and increase the rating of the item they did choose.

induced or forced compliance
Situations in which individuals are somehow induced to say or do things inconsistent with their true attitudes.

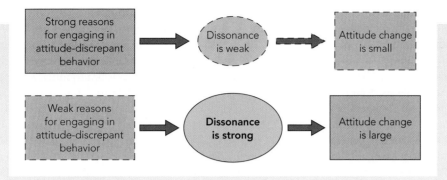

Figure 4.19 ■ Why Less (Smaller Inducements) Often Leads to More (Greater Attitude Change) after Attitude-Discrepant Behavior
When individuals have strong reasons for engaging in attitude-discrepant behavior, they experience relatively weak dissonance and weak pressure to change their attitudes. In contrast, when they have little apparent justification for engaging in the attitude-discrepant behavior, they will experience stronger dissonance and stronger pressure to change their attitudes. The result: Less justification leads to more dissonance following attitude-discrepant behavior.

few reasons for engaging in attitude-discrepant behavior. When we have little justification, and therefore cannot explain away our actions to ourselves, dissonance will be most intense.

- As Figure 4.19 illustrates, cognitive dissonance theory predicts that it will be easier to change individuals' attitudes by offering them *just barely enough* to get them to engage in the attitude-discrepant behavior. This ensures that they will feel there is little justification for their behavior. On the other hand, additional reasons or rewards would help to reduce dissonance and result in little subsequent attitude change. Social psychologists sometimes refer to this surprising prediction as the **less-leads-to-more effect**—having fewer reasons or rewards for an action often leads to greater attitude change. This effect has been confirmed in studies (Riess & Schlenker, 1977; Leippe & Eisenstadt, 1994). Indeed, contrary to what many might think, more money or other rewards offered to people to behave in a particular way can act as a justification for their actions, which then undermines the likelihood that attitude change will occur.

- First, the less-leads-to-more effect occurs only when people believe they have a choice as to whether or not to perform the attitude-discrepant behavior. Strong forms of coercion undermine dissonance.

- Second, small rewards lead to greater attitude change only when people believe that they are personally responsible for the chosen course of action and any negative effects it produces. For instance, when ordered by an authority to do a particular behavior, we may not feel responsible for our actions or dissonance.

- And third, the less-leads-to-more effect does not occur when people view the payment they receive as a bribe rather than as a payment for services rendered. To the extent that we believe we are being bribed, more may be required.

Because such conditions often exist, the strategy of offering others just barely enough to induce them to say or do things contrary to their true attitudes can often be an effective technique for inducing attitude change.

less-leads-to-more effect
The fact that offering individuals small rewards for engaging in counterattitudinal behavior often produces more dissonance, and so more attitude change, than offering them larger rewards.

When Dissonance Is a Tool for Beneficial Changes in Behavior

People who don't wear safety belts are much more likely to die in accidents than those who do. . . . People who smoke heavily are much more likely to suffer from lung cancer and heart disease than those who don't. . . . People who engage in unprotected sex are much more likely than those who engage in safe sex to contract dangerous diseases, including AIDS.

Cognitive Dissonance: What It Is and How We Reduce It

Most of us know that these statements are true, so our attitudes are generally favorable toward using seat belts, quitting smoking, and engaging in safe sex (Carey, Morrison-Beedy, & Johnson, 1997). Yet, these attitudes are often *not* translated into overt actions: Some people continue to drive without seat belts, to smoke, and to have unprotected sex. To address these major social problems, what's needed is not so much a change in attitudes as a shift in overt behavior. Can dissonance be used to promote beneficial behavioral changes? A growing body of evidence suggests that it can (Batson, Kobrynowiez et al., 1997; Gibbons, Eggleston, & Benthin, 1997; Stone et al., 1994), especially when it is used to generate feelings of **hypocrisy**—the public advocating of some attitude and then making it salient to the person that they have acted in a way that is inconsistent with their own attitudes. Such feelings might be sufficiently intense that only actions that reduce dissonance directly, by inducing behavioral change, may be effective. These predictions concerning the possibility of dissonance-induced *behavior change* have been tested in several studies. In one interesting study, Jeff Stone and his colleagues (1997) asked participants to prepare a videotape advocating the use of condoms (safe sex) to avoid contracting AIDS. Next, participants were asked to think about reasons why they hadn't used condoms in the past (*personal reasons*) or reasons why people in general fail to use condoms (*normative reasons* that didn't center on their own behavior). The researchers predicted that dissonance would be maximized in the personal reasons condition, in which participants had to come face to face with their own hypocrisy. Finally, all participants were given a choice between a direct means of reducing dissonance—purchasing condoms at a reduced price—or an indirect means—making a donation to a program to aid homeless persons. The results indicated that when participants had been asked to focus on the reasons why they didn't engage in safe sex in the past, an overwhelming majority chose to purchase condoms, suggesting that their future behavior would be different—the direct route to dissonance reduction. In contrast, when asked to think about reasons why people in general didn't engage in safe sex, more participants chose the indirect route to dissonance reduction—a donation to the aid-the-homeless project—and didn't change their behavior.

These findings suggest that using dissonance to make our hypocrisy salient can be a powerful tool for changing behavior in desirable ways. For maximum effectiveness, however, such procedures must involve several elements: The persons in question must publicly advocate the desired behaviors (e.g., using condoms, wearing safety belts), must be induced to think about their past behavioral failures, and must be given access to direct means for reducing their dissonance. When these conditions are met, dissonance can bring about beneficial changes in behavior.

hypocrisy
The public advocating of some attitudes or behaviors and then acting in a way that is inconsistent with these attitudes or behaviors.

KEY POINTS

★ *Cognitive dissonance* is an unpleasant state that occurs when we notice discrepancies between our attitudes and our behaviors. Recent findings indicate that dissonance produces negative affect and attitude change.

★ Dissonance often occurs in situations involving *induced or forced compliance*, in which we are led to say or do things that are inconsistent with our true attitudes.

★ Dissonance appears to be a universal aspect of social thought, but the conditions under which it occurs and tactics individuals choose to reduce it appear to be influenced

by cultural factors. In western cultures, the individual self is valued for correct decisions, but this is less so in Asian cultures.

★ Dissonance can lead to attitude change when we have reasons that are barely sufficient to get us to engage in attitude-discrepant behavior. Stronger reasons (or larger rewards) produce less attitude change—the *less-leads-to-more effect*.

★ Dissonance induced through *hypocrisy* can be a powerful tool for effecting behavioral changes.

Attitude Formation: How Attitudes Develop

- *Attitudes* are evaluations of any aspect of the social world. Often, attitudes are strong and unambivalent, which makes them resistant to change.
- Other attitudes are ambivalent, which means they are based on conflicting beliefs, and such attitudes are less likely to predict behavior consistently.

Social Learning: Acquiring Attitudes from Others

- Attitudes are often acquired from others through *social learning*. Such learning can involve *classical conditioning*, *instrumental conditioning*, or *observational learning*.
- Attitudes are also formed on the basis of *social comparison*—the tendency to compare ourselves with others to determine whether our views of social reality are or are not correct. To be similar to others we like, we accept the attitudes that they hold.
- Attitudes are influenced by exposure to mass media. We tend to believe, however, that only other people are affected by such exposure (e.g., to violence), but not ourselves—the *third-person effect*.
- When we identify with a group, we expect to be influenced by messages that are aimed at that group. We do not expect to be personally influenced when we do not identify with the group toward which the attitude-relevant message is aimed.

Attitude Functions: Why We Form Attitudes in the First Place

- Attitudes can be viewed as almost automatic reactions to the world. They can form rapidly as we are exposed to the attitude object and can influence basic approach or avoidance responses. Attitudes can serve different functions.
- Attitudes can serve a *knowledge function* and provide an interpreta-

tive framework for understanding the world.
- Attitudes can provide a means for expressing who we are and who we are similar to, thereby serving an *identity* or *self-expression function*.
- The *self-esteem function* can be observed when we feel we are right and moral by expressing and behaving according to our attitudes.
- Attitudes can serve an *ego-defensive function* by allowing us to defend our self-view as like others and not deviant.
- When attitudes serve an *impression motivation function*, they guide the arguments constructed and, for this reason, may be difficult to change. Attitudes can allow us to manage how others perceive us.

Role of the Social Context in the Link between Attitudes and Behavior

- Attitudes toward a group or object will not always predict behavior.

When and Why Do Attitudes Influence Behavior?

- There are situational constraints that affect our willingness to express our true attitudes. Not wanting to offend others and concerns about what others may think are important factors that can limit the extent to which attitudes and behavior are linked. We also often show *pluralistic ignorance* and erroneously believe others have attitudes that are different than ours, and this can limit the extent to which we express our attitudes in public.
- Strong attitudes are more likely to be accessible at the time we take action, so they are likely to influence behavior. Strong attitudes are most likely when they are based on extreme beliefs and personal experience with the attitude object.
- Extreme attitudes are ones to which we are committed and have elaborate arguments to support them. These attitudes often predict behavior.

- People whose attitudes are formed via direct and personal experience are likely to have their attitudes come to mind and thereby affect their behavior.

How Do Attitudes Guide Behavior?

- Several factors affect the strength of the relationship between attitudes and behavior; some of these relate to the situation in which the attitudes are activated, and some to aspects of the attitudes themselves.
- Attitudes seem to influence behavior through two different mechanisms. The theories of *reasoned action* and *planned behavior* predict behavior when the decision to engage in an action is consciously and deliberately assessed. When we can give careful thought to our attitudes, intentions derived from our attitudes, norms, and perceived control over the behavior all predict behavior. When we don't engage in such deliberate thought, as described in the *attitude-to-behavior process model*, attitudes influence behavior by shaping our perceptions of the situation.

The Fine Art of Persuasion: How Attitudes Are Changed

- Early research on *persuasion*—efforts to change attitudes through the use of messages—focused primarily on characteristics of the communicator (e.g., expertise, attractiveness), message (e.g., one-sided versus two-sided argument), and audience.
- Modern theories of persuasion include the *elaboration–likelihood model (ELM)* and the *heuristic–systematic model*. Research has sought to understand the cognitive processes that play a role in persuasion. We process persuasive messages in two distinct ways: through *systematic processing*, which involves careful attention to message content, or through *heuristic processing*, which involves the use of mental shortcuts.

Resisting Persuasion Attempts

■ Several factors contribute to our ability to resist persuasion. One factor is *reactance*—negative reactions to efforts by others to reduce or limit our personal freedom, which can produce greater overall opposition to the message.

■ Resistance to persuasion is often increased by *forewarning*—the knowledge that someone is trying to change our attitudes and by *selective avoidance*—the tendency to avoid exposure to information that contradicts our views.

■ When we are exposed to persuasive messages that are contrary to our existing views, we actively counterargue against them.

■ If we receive arguments against our views along with arguments that refute these counterattitudinal positions, our resistance to subsequent persuasion increases; this is known as inoculation against counterattitudinal views.

Cognitive Dissonance: What It Is and How We Reduce It

■ *Cognitive dissonance* is an unpleasant state that occurs when we notice discrepancies between our attitudes and our behaviors. Recent findings indicate that dissonance produces negative affect—and attitude change.

■ Dissonance often occurs in situations involving *induced* or *forced compliance*, in which we are led to say or do things inconsistent with our true attitudes.

■ Dissonance appears to be a universal aspect of social thought, but the conditions under which it occurs and tactics individuals choose to reduce it appear to be influenced by cultural factors. In western cultures, the individual is valued for correct decisions, but this is less so in Asian cultures.

■ Dissonance can lead to attitude change when we have reasons that are barely sufficient to get us to engage in attitude-discrepant behavior. Stronger reasons (or larger rewards) produce *less* attitude change—the *less-leads-to-more effect*.

■ Dissonance induced through *hypocrisy* can be a powerful tool for effecting behavioral changes.

Connections   INTEGRATING SOCIAL PSYCHOLOGY

In this chapter, you read about . . .	In other chapters, you will find related discussions of . . .
the role of social learning in attitude formation	the role of social learning in several forms of social behavior—the self (Chapter 5), attraction (Chapter 7), helping (Chapter 10), and aggression (Chapter 11)
persuasion and resistance to persuasion	other techniques for changing attitudes and behavior and why they are effective or ineffective (Chapter 9) and leadership (Chapter 12)

Thinking about Connections

1. Suppose you wanted to launch a campaign to persuade adults of all ages to engage in safe sex (e.g., use condoms). What specific features would you include to maximize its effectiveness?

2. If we are so resistant to persuasion, why does advertising work? Think about heuristic processing when we are not cognitively engaged. Provide an example of how heuristic processing can lead to persuasion and then explain why.

3. If attitudes are learned, it is reasonable to suggest that mass media (television, films, magazines) are important factors in attitude formation. What do you think the media is teaching children about key aspects of social behavior—love and sexual relations (Chapters 7 and 8), aggression (Chapter 11), honesty and integrity (Chapter 12)? Would you change any of this if you could? Why or why not?

Each day, we are exposed to many attempts to change our attitudes. Advertisers, politicians, and charities all seek to exert this kind of influence on us. How can you resist? Here are some suggestions based on social psychology research findings.

View Attempts at Persuasion as Assaults on Your Personal Freedom

No one likes being told what to do but, in a sense, this is what advertisers and politicians are trying to do. So, when you are on the receiving end of such appeals, remind yourself that you are in charge, and there's no reason to listen to, or accept, what these would-be persuaders tell you.

Recognize Attempts at Persuasion When You See Them

Knowing that someone is trying to persuade you—being forewarned— is often useful to resist efforts at persuasion. So, whenever you encounter someone who seeks to influence your views, remind yourself that no matter how charming or friendly they are, persuasion is their goal. This will help you to resist.

Remind Yourself of Your Own Views and How These Differ from the Ones Being Urged on You

While biased assimilation—the tendency to perceive views different from our own as unconvincing and unreliable—can prevent us from absorbing potentially useful information, it is also a means for resisting persuasion. So when others offer views different from yours, focus on how different these ideas are from your own. The rest will often take care of itself!

Actively Counterargue in Your Own Mind against the Views Being "Pushed" on You by Others

The more arguments you can generate against such views, the less likely these views are to influence you.

KEY TERMS

attitude (p. 92)

attitude accessibility (p. 103)

attitude-to-behavior process model (p. 106)

central route (p. 111)

classical conditioning (p. 95)

cognitive dissonance (p. 116)

ego-defensive function (p. 100)

elaboration–likelihood model (p. 111)

forewarning (p. 113)

heuristic processing (p. 111)

hypocrisy (p. 120)

identity or self-expression function (p. 99)

impression motivation function (p. 101)

induced or forced compliance (p. 118)

instrumental conditioning (p. 96)

knowledge function (p. 99)

less-leads-to-more effect (p. 119)

mere exposure (p. 99)

observational learning (p. 97)

peripheral route (p. 111)

persuasion (p. 107)

pluralistic ignorance (p. 103)

reactance (p. 113)

selective avoidance (p. 114)

self-esteem function (p. 100)

social comparison (p. 97)

social learning (p. 94)

social norms (p. 96)

spreading of alternatives (p. 118)

subliminal conditioning (p. 95)

systematic processing (p. 111)

theory of planned behavior (p. 105)

theory of reasoned action (p. 105)

third-person effect (p. 97)

trivialization (p. 116)

5

THE SELF
Understanding "Who Am I?"

When I (Nyla Branscombe) was young, the American space program was big news. Family and friends would gather to watch the unfolding of this riveting scientific endeavor. I remember watching the lunar launches on television and Neil Armstrong's walks on the moon with great excitement. I was truly fascinated by the idea that humans could fly such distances, and that there were other worlds that might be explored.

I remember the night that I announced to my father at dinner that when I grew up I wanted to be an astronaut. He smiled and said, "Girls *can't* be astronauts," but, perhaps to placate me, he added that I "*could* be an airline stewardess." At the time, they seemed similar enough to me—with flying being the crucial element that had captured my imagination—so I was not too upset to learn that I could expect to be forever barred from my favorite career option because of a part of myself that I could not change. This incident quite effectively conveyed very important information about the nature of the world and my place in it. I learned that there were positions that my gender might prevent me from occupying, and more generally, that my category membership was sufficiently important that it was likely to have a pervasive influence on the course of my life.

You might be tempted to think that this story reflects a very different time and that gender-based exclusion and discrimination is a thing of the past. And, to a certain extent, you'd be right. Legal barriers that prevented women from entering many occupations have been dismantled; there have even been female astronauts. But, as you'll see, differential treatment based on gender is not history, although it may operate in a considerably more subtle fashion than my father's certainty that women simply were not *allowed* to be in some occupations.

People's stereotypes about women have changed over time, due, in part, to the actual changes in the roles that women occupy (Diekman & Eagly, 2000). Although it may be amusing to look at how previous generations thought about women's work, as illustrated in "The Good Wife's Guide" in Figure 5.1, it would be erroneous to conclude that women no longer experience discrimination in the workplace. Nor are the consequences of being a target of discrimination as easy to accept as an eleven-year-old's perception that exclusion from one occupation is OK because any job that involves flying can be interchanged with any other. To realize that no matter what you do, your gender may consistently result in undesirable consequences can harm psychological well-being (see Nolen-Hoeksema, 1987; Schmitt & Branscombe, 2002a). As the research shows, there are negative emotional, cognitive, and behavioral consequences of perceiving the self as a target of prejudice.

In this chapter, we examine what social psychologists have learned about the nature of the self. Some have suggested that the self is the heart of social psychology; consequently, the self has been the focus of much systematic research. Not only does how we think about ourselves influence our choices and behaviors, but it also serves as a reference point for how we perceive and interact with others. First we consider whether we have just one "self" or many

Figure 5.1 ■ **The 1945 Stereotype of a Good Woman**
Looking back more than a half century, it is difficult to believe that these were the normative expectations for women. Clearly expectations of employment outside the home for married women was absent, although most college-educated women in the United States today will be in the labor force for much of their adult lives. (*Source:* Housekeeping Monthly, *May 13, 1945.*)

The Good Wife's Guide

- Have dinner ready. Plan ahead, even the night before, to have a delicious meal ready, on time for his return. This is a way of letting him know that you have been thinking about him and are concerned about his needs.

- Prepare yourself. Take 15 minutes to rest so you'll be refreshed when he arrives. Touch up your makeup, put a ribbon in your hair and be fresh-looking. He has just been with a lot of work-weary people.

- Clear away the clutter. Make one last trip through the main part of the house just before your husband arrives.

- Listen to him. You may have a dozen important things to tell him, but the moment of his arrival is not the time. Let him talk first—remember, his topics of conversation are more important than yours.

- Don't ask him questions about his actions or question his judgment or integrity. Remember, he is the master of the house and as such will always exercise his will with fairness and truthfulness. You have no right to question him.

- A good wife always knows her place.

selves. The issue of whether one aspect of the self is more "true" or predictive of behavior than another, or if it depends on the nature of the situation in which people find themselves, is one with which we will grapple. What does it mean to be *self-aware*, and does that influence how we evaluate ourselves and others? Do we experience ourselves the same way all the time, or does our experience depend on the context and the nature of the comparison it evokes? If we do categorize and think about ourselves in terms of different identities, what consequences does this have for our judgments about ourselves? Do our perceptions of ourselves depend on whether we have high or low self-esteem? Do people have methods of knowing themselves that allow them to feel positive, even when others perform better than they do? After considering these questions, we will examine the effects of being a target of prejudice for a number of self-related processes, including the emotional, cognitive, and performance consequences that can ensue when people face rejection by others because of their group membership.

Thinking about the Self: Personal versus Social Identity

One of the most fundamental principles of the social identity perspective (Tajfel & Turner, 1986; Turner, 1985) is that individuals can perceive themselves differently depending on where they are at a particular moment in time on what is known as the **personal–social identity continuum**. The personal identity end of this continuum refers to when we think of ourselves primarily as *individuals*. The social identity end refers to when we think of ourselves as members of specific *social groups*. Because we do not experience all aspects of our self-concept simultaneously, which aspect of our identity is salient at any given moment will influence how we think about ourselves, and this, in turn, has consequences for our behavior. When we think of ourselves as unique individuals, our personal identities are salient, and this is likely to result in self-descriptions that emphasize how we are different from others. For example, you might describe yourself as fun when thinking of yourself at the personal identity level, to emphasize your self-perception as having more of this attribute than other individuals you are using as the comparative referent. Because personal identity self-description can be thought of as **intragroup** in nature—involving comparisons with other individuals who share our group membership—*which* group is the implicit referent used when describing the personal self can affect the content of self-descriptions (Oakes, Haslam, & Turner, 1994). For example, if you were asked to describe how you are different from other Americans, you might characterize

personal–social identity continuum
The two distinct ways that the self can be categorized. At the personal level, the self can be thought of as a unique individual, whereas at the social identity level, the self is thought of as a member of a group.

intragroup comparisons
Judgments that result from comparisons between individuals who are members of the same group.

yourself as particularly liberal, but if you were indicating how you are different from other college students you might say that you are rather conservative. For personal identity, the content we generate depends on some comparative reference, and this can result in different self-descriptors coming to mind, depending on the context.

At the other end of the personal–social identity continuum, we can perceive ourselves as members of a group, which means we emphasize the ways in which we are similar to other group members. When we think of ourselves at the social identity level, we describe ourselves in terms of the attributes that members of our group share and what differentiates "our group" from other groups. That is, descriptions of the self at the social identity level are **intergroup** in nature—they involve contrasts between groups. For example, you may think of yourself in terms of your social identity as a fraternity or sorority member. On other occasions, you might think of yourself in terms of a different social identity, that of your gender group. If you are female, you might emphasize the attributes that you share with other women (e.g., warm and caring) and that you perceive as differentiating women from men. What's important to note here is that when you think of yourself as an *individual,* the *content* of your self-description is likely to differ from when you are thinking of yourself as a member of a *category* that you share with others. Of course, as these examples indicate, most of us are members of a variety of groups (e.g., occupation, age group, sexual orientation, nationality, sports teams), but not all of these will be salient at the same time. Thus, there may be a number of situational factors that will alter how we define ourselves, and the actions that stem from those self-definitions will also differ.

Can we say that one of these "selves" is the "true" self—either the personal self or any one of a person's potential social identities? Not really. All of these could be accurate portraits of the self, and accurately predict behavior, depending on the context and comparison dimension (Oakes & Reynolds, 1997). Note, too, how some ways of thinking about the self could imply behaviors that are opposite of those that would result from other self-descriptions (e.g., fun versus scholarly).

Despite such potential variability in self-definition, most people manage to maintain a coherent image of the self, while recognizing that they may define themselves and behave differently in different situations (see Figure 5.2). For example, when you are at home with your parents, your self-image as a responsible adult might come into question. You might not pick up after yourself, or you might expect that someone else will do your laundry, and so forth. When, however, you are away at college, you perform these tasks competently and feel like a responsible adult. Despite such readily admitted pockets of irresponsibility, does that mean you will generally see yourself in this way? No, definitely not. You may maintain an image of yourself as responsible, either because the domains in which you are irresponsible are not particularly important to you, or they are not salient when you think of yourself as a college student (Patrick, Neighbors, & Knee, 2004). When people face such mixed evidence for a valued self-perception as a function of context or audience, they can reduce the importance of competence in a given domain, or, alternatively, they can decide that only some reference groups are important for self-definition. Thus, some people may be affected by their families' perceptions of their competence, but not their professors', while others may show the reverse (Crocker & Wolfe, 2001).

Who I Am Depends on the Situation

College students' answers to the question, "Who am I?" typically consist of references to social identities (e.g., nationality, race, gender, university affiliation), interpersonal

intergroup comparisons
Judgments that result from comparisons between our group and another group.

Figure 5.2 ■ Seeing the Self as Competent Can Depend on the Context
This woman may define herself as competent in her role as executive but not so competent in her parental role (at least some days)!

relationships (e.g., Karen's boyfriend, daughter of Howard and Rose), and a variety of personal traits such as honest or kind (Rentsch & Heffner, 1994). People describe themselves differently, depending on whether the question asked implies situational specificity or not. This effect was clearly illustrated in research by Mendoza-Denton and colleagues (2001). In their study, participants were given one of two different types of sentence completion tasks. When open-ended prompts, such as "I am a (an) . . . person," implied self-definition as an individual. In this condition, participants' responses were primarily traitlike or global (e.g., "I am an ambitious person"). When, however, the prompt implied particular social settings, "I am a (an) . . . when . . . ," the responses were more contingent on the situation considered by the participant (e.g., "I am an ambitious person when a professor provides me with a challenge").

Our tendency to see the self differentially, depending on what relationships with others we consider, and according to the context, increases with age (Byrne & Shavelson, 1996; Roccas & Brewer, 2002). We also differ across the life span in the extent to which we have multiple aspects of our self-concepts that are important to us. This has consequences for how we view the self when we experience stress. For instance, Linville (1987) found that people with more aspects of the self that are distinct (e.g., self as professional, mother, baseball fan) were less responsive to threats to any given identity (e.g., following a professional setback) than people for whom those same identities were intertwined and not distinct. When important aspects of the self are distinct from one another—so that **self-complexity** is high—a failure in any one domain is less likely to affect how one feels about one's self overall. Indeed, those whose self-concepts are organized less complexly exhibit more variability in how they feel about themselves than do those whose self-concepts are more complexly organized. Stress is likely to be experienced by people when two important aspects of the self are perceived as being in conflict with each other, creating **identity interference.** For example, Settles (2004) found that women in stereotypically masculine fields such as physics and astronomy who experienced interference between their identities as women and as scientists reported poorer well-being than those who did not perceive their identities as being in conflict.

Aspects of the self that are associated with a particular cultural tradition may be activated, depending on subtle context changes, and this can lead to different self-perceptions. For example, it is well known that North American culture emphasizes highly *individualistic norms* and an **independent self-concept,** whereas Asian cultures emphasize *collectivist norms* and an **interdependent self-concept** (Markus & Kitayama, 1991). Because of this difference, the self-concepts of people who spend their lives in one cultural context might be expected to differ from those from another cultural context. Such culture-based self-concept differences may be reflected in systematic differences in what is assumed to be "personal" tastes and preferences.

To test this idea, Kim and Markus (1999) showed Koreans and Americans abstract figures, each composed of nine different parts, and participants were asked to say which they liked better. Koreans selected more of the figures wherein the parts fit together, whereas Americans chose more of the figures for which some part of the figure was distinctive or different. Such cultural differences in the choices people make may reflect contrasting interdependent and independent self-conceptions. However, it could also be that subtle aspects of the context simply cue one aspect of the self over another—the interdependent or independent component—because everyone is some of both. In support of the latter possibility, research with bicultural individuals (people who belong to two different cultures) finds that they behave differently, depending on which identity is made salient. People who are experienced with both Asian and western cultural traditions might express their "Asian-ness" in contexts that cue that aspect of the self, but express their "western-ness" in contexts that cue that aspect of the self. This notion that bicultural individuals possess both Asian and western identities, and can respond according to either, was tested with students in Hong Kong who were fluent in both Chinese and English (Trafimow et al., 1997). The students were asked to answer the question, "Who am I?" in either language. The Hong Kong students who responded to the question in English described themselves in terms of personal traits that differentiate them from others, which reflects an individualistic self-construal, while those

self-complexity
How the self-concept is organized. For those whose self-concepts are organized complexly, important aspects of the self are distinct from one another. For those whose self-concept is low in complexity, there is greater overlap in different components of the self.

identity interference
When two important social identities are perceived as being in conflict, such that acting on the basis of one identity interferes with performing well based on the other identity.

independent self-concept
In individualistic cultures, the expectation is that people will develop a self-concept as separate from or independent of others. Men are expected to have an independent self-concept more so than women.

interdependent self-concept
In collectivist cultures, the expectation is that people will develop a self-concept in terms of their connections or relationships with others. Women are expected to have an interdependent self-concept more so than men.

who answered the question in Chinese described themselves in terms of group memberships, reflecting a more interdependent self-construal. Thus, important group-based differences in the self-concept may emerge primarily when that group identity is activated, as it is when using a particular language (for those who have more than one).

Recently, Ryan, David, & Reynolds (2004) illustrated the importance of how the self is categorized for the ways in which men and women describe themselves. Their study examined when gender differences in such self-descriptions are present and when they are not. In their research, when *both* men and women were first asked to focus on groups to which they belonged (i.e., they were asked to think about similarities between the self and others), they tended to describe themselves in terms of interdependent traits such as "dependable" and "understanding." When *both* men and women had first focused on groups to which they did not belong (i.e., they were asked to think about differences between the self and others), they were more likely to describe themselves in terms of independent traits such as "unique" and "objective." Gender differences in self-definition *only* emerged when the participant's gender group membership was salient, but gender differences were not present in contexts such as those in which other identities were activated.

Such context shifts in self-definition have been shown to affect moral reasoning—a domain in which men and women have been supposed to fundamentally differ. Ryan, David, and Reynolds (2004) showed that people's responses to a standard moral dilemma in which another person is in need depended on how they categorized themselves in relation to that other person. As shown in Figure 5.3, when the participant categorized the person in need as a university student and that person was therefore seen as a member of the participant's category, men and women were *equally* likely to display care-oriented responses toward the person in need. In contrast, when the participants categorized themselves in terms of gender, women displayed significantly more care-oriented responses than men. In fact, men reduced their care-oriented responses in the gender condition compared with the shared university-identity condition. Thus, both the self-concept and moral reasoning believed to stem from it appear to be flexible and context dependent. Gender differences in both the self-concept and moral reasoning depended on gender being a salient self category when the response was made. Nevertheless, gender is a powerful social category that is likely to be activated often(Fiske & Stevens, 1993). As a result, gender may be expected to influence perceptions of the self as well as responses to others with some frequency.

What determines *which* aspect of the self will be most influential at any given moment, if how we define ourselves can differ according to the context? First, one aspect of the self might be especially relevant to a particular context (e.g., thinking of ourselves as fun at a party, but as hard working when we are at work). Second, features of the context can make one aspect

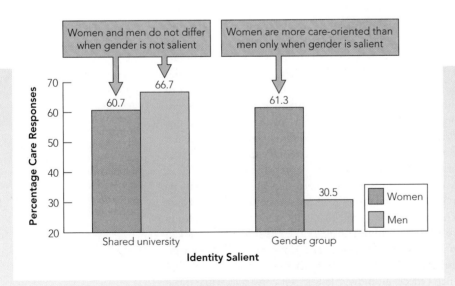

Figure 5.3 ■ Gender Differences Depend on What Identity Is Salient
When a shared identity with another in need is salient, both men and women display care-oriented responses. However, when one's gender group (and its differing norms) is salient, then men display fewer care-oriented responses to the same need situation compared with women. (*Source: Based on data from Ryan, David, & Reynolds, 2004.*)

Chapter 5 / The Self

of the self highly distinctive, with that aspect of identity forming the basis of self-perception. Suppose an office is composed of only one woman among several men. The woman's gender distinguishes her from her colleagues. In such contexts, the lone woman is likely to feel "like a woman" and she may be treated as representative of that group (Fuegen & Biernat, 2002; Yoder & Berendsen, 2001). Similarly, African American students at predominantly white universities and other contexts in which other minority group members are rare are likely to think of themselves in terms of their race (Pollak & Niemann, 1998; Postmes & Branscombe, 2002). Third, some people may categorize themselves in terms of a particular personal trait (e.g., intelligence) or group identity and its associated attributes (e.g., gender) because of its importance to the self. The more a personal attribute or social identity is valued, the more self-verification on that dimension will be sought (Hogg & Turner, 1987; Swann, 1990). Fourth, other people, including how they refer to us linguistically, can cue us to think of ourselves in personal versus social identity terms. Bernd Simon (2004) has noted that aspects of the self-concept that are referred to as nouns (e.g., woman, psychologist) are likely to activate social identities. Nouns suggest discrete categories, which trigger perceptions of members of those categories as sharing a fundamental nature or essence that is different than that of members of other categories (Lickel, Hamilton, & Sherman, 2001). In contrast, aspects of the self that are referred to with either adjectives or verbs (e.g., weak, taller, supportive) reference perceived differences between people within a category (Turner & Onorato, 1999) and are likely to elicit self-perceptions at the personal identity level.

Who I Am Depends on Others' Treatment

How others treat us, and how we believe they will treat us in the future, has important implications for how we think about ourselves. When it comes to self-perception, no person is truly an island. When we expect that others will reject us because of some aspect of ourselves, we can choose from a few possible responses (Tajfel, 1978). To the extent that it is possible to change an aspect of the self and avoid being rejected by others, we could choose to do that. In fact, we could choose to change *only* that feature when we anticipate being in the presence of others who will reject us because of it. As the U.S. military policy of "Don't ask, don't tell" on homosexuality suggests, there are group memberships that we can choose to reveal or not. However, this option can be impossible for some social identities. We can't easily hide or change our race, gender, or age. In some cases, even if we *could* alter the part of the self that brings rejection, we may rebel against those rejecting us and make that feature *even more* self-defining. In effect, by emphasizing that feature, we are publicly communicating that we value something different than those who might judge us because of it.

This point was illustrated in research by Jetten and colleagues (2001). They studied young people who elect to get body piercings in visible parts of the body other than earlobes (e.g., navel, tongue, eyebrow). How we dress and alter our bodies can be conceptualized as important identity markers—ways of communicating to the world who we are. Although some identity markers may bring acceptance into peer groups, they may be perceived by other groups as weird. Today, body piercings may be comparable to wearing blue jeans and men having long hair in the 1960s. These latter identity markers were the visible indicators of a "hippie" identity, a self-perception as a rebel against the establishment. Like their 1960s' counterparts, young people who opt for visible body piercings appear to be engaged in a similar form of rebel identity construction. Even though they know that they are likely to be discriminated against because of their piercings, this expectation can lead them to greater self-definition in terms of a group that is actively rejecting the dominant culture's standards of beauty. This research found that those with body piercings who were led to expect rejection from the mainstream because of their piercings identified more strongly with other people who have body piercings than did those who were led to expect acceptance from the mainstream. Such expected rejection and devaluation on the part of the culture as a whole can result in increasingly strong identification with a newly forming cultural group. As Figure 5.4 on page 132 illustrates, people with body piercings seem to be creating an identity that communicates to all that "we are different from the mainstream." If, over time,

Figure 5.4 ■ Claiming an Identity That Is "Nonmainstream"
Many forms of body adornment and body modification are visual indicators of social identity. This young woman may be conveying to the "mainstream" that she is not one of them.

getting body piercings ultimately becomes diffused throughout the culture, with almost everyone adopting the practice, then those who are attempting to convey their collective difference from the mainstream may be compelled to become more extreme to achieve the same identity end.

This sort of identity dilemma may be especially likely to be provoked when a person moves from one social context to another. Consider the dilemma experienced by Hispanic students as they leave their home environment to attend a primarily Anglo university. Social psychologists have examined the different strategies that such students can employ during their first year at college (Ethier & Deaux, 1994). Evidence shows that people facing this identity dilemma use one of two strategies—movement away from the identity or increased movement toward it. Among those for whom a Hispanic identity was initially not important, when they moved to a non-Hispanic environment, they emphasized their Hispanic identity to a lesser degree. In contrast, for those who initially valued their Hispanic identity, in this new context, they increased the emphasis they placed on their ethnic identity. Interestingly, it was those students who emphasized their Hispanic identity and who took pride in their differences from others in this new environment whose self-esteem was better during the transition to college. Those who chose to distance themselves from their Hispanic identity suffered reduced self-esteem when they faced rejection based on that identity.

As we saw with the body piercing research, whether others devalue an identity one might hold is typically not correlated with how important that identity is to the self (Ashmore, Deaux, & McLaughlin-Volpe, 2004). In other words, it is not solely those identities that might be widely regarded as negative that the individual must decide whether to give up or strengthen as shifts in context are made. Consider someone who moves from a context in which royalty is a valued identity to a new poorer setting in which it might not be. That person would be faced with a similar choice about whether to retain value in and emphasize the former "blue blood" identity or distance from it.

Self-Awareness

Constantine Sedikides and John Skowronski (1997) argue that the first level of self to emerge in terms of our evolutionary history and during the individual's life span is **subjective self-awareness.** Such awareness allows organisms to differentiate themselves from the physical environment. Clearly, plants don't possess this quality, but most animals do. For example, my cat knows where his paw ends and my arm begins, as do quite young human children. A few animals (primates) also develop **objective self-awareness**—the organism's capacity to be the object of its own attention (Gallup, 1994). As shown in Figure 5.5, a chimp can inspect itself in a mirror and "know it knows" that it is seeing the self (Lewis, 1992, p. 124). Only humans, however, seem to have reached the third level of self-functioning—**symbolic self-awareness**—the ability to form an abstract representation of the self through language.

Possible Selves: The Self over Time

Although we generally experience ourselves as relatively consistent over time, it is nonetheless true that people change. It is often gratifying to compare one's past self with the present self, for doing so will suggest that there has been improvement (Wilson & Ross, 2000). In fact, thinking about a future **possible self** that you may become can inspire you to forego current activities that are enjoyable but will not help, or might

subjective self-awareness
The first level of self to emerge. It is the recognition that the self is separate from other objects in one's physical environment.

objective self-awareness
The organism's capacity to be the object of its own attention—to know that it is seeing its own self in a mirror, for example.

symbolic self-awareness
The uniquely human capacity to form an abstract representation of the self through language.

possible selves
Images of how the self might be in the future—either "dreaded" possible selves to be avoided or "desired" potential selves that can be strived for.

Figure 5.5 ■ Objective Self-Awareness: Recognizing the Self
Only among primates, such as the chimp shown here, does there seem to be *objective self-awareness*—the capacity to be aware of the self as an object. When a red spot is placed on the chimp's forehead, it can only be detected in a mirror. The fact that seeing this image in the mirror leads the chimp to touch its forehead is powerful evidence that there is some recognition that the reflected image is of the self.

hinder, bringing about this improved self (Markus & Nurius, 1986). Instead, you may invest in less immediately enjoyable activities in order to achieve the goal of becoming your desired possible self. Think about what is involved in attaining a variety of social identities. We give up years of "having fun" to attain the status of a "college graduate," complete years of schooling and long internships to call ourselves "doctors," and put grueling hours into law school and studying for state bar exams to become "lawyers." Lockwood and Kunda (1999) have found that *role models*—other people we wish to imitate or be like—can inspire us to invest in such long-term achievements, but, to do so, we must see the possible self that the role model represents as being potentially attainable. The image of a possible future self can influence our motivation to study harder, give up smoking, or invest in child-care and parenting classes, to the extent that we can imagine that a new and improved self will result from such changes.

People often consider new possible selves of this sort, as well as how to avoid negative and feared future possible selves, when they are making New Year's resolutions. Envisioning such self-changes can induce feelings of control and optimism, but failing to keep those resolutions is a common experience and repeated failures can lead to unhappiness (Polivy & Herman, 2000). As we saw in Chapter 2, people appear to be generally *unrealistically optimistic* (Helweg-Larsen & Shepperd, 2001) about the extent to which they can achieve a host of positive outcomes and avoid negative outcomes. The truth is, having confidence and efficacy in our ability to change is important but overconfidence in our ability can lead to false hope and, ultimately, disappointment. Although our ability to remake our physical selves may have limits, the photos in Figure 5.6, like those seen on the TV program *Extreme Makeover,* suggest that rather dramatic changes are possible.

Successful performance in physical, academic, and job tasks is enhanced by feelings of **self-efficacy** (Courneya & McAuley, 1993; Huang, 1998; Sanna & Pusecker, 1994). It is necessary to believe that we *can* achieve a goal as a result of our own actions in order to even try (Bandura, 1997). Indeed, people high in self-efficacy tend to prefer to allocate their time and effort to tasks that *can* be solved, and they stop

self-efficacy
The belief that one can achieve a goal as a result of one's own actions. Collective self-efficacy is the belief that by working together with others, a goal can be achieved.

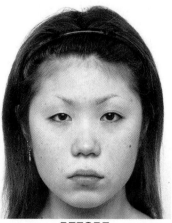

Figure 5.6 ■ There May Be Limits to Our Ability to Change Ourselves, but Some Extreme Makeovers Suggest That Incredible Change Is Possible
These photos make the point that if we make extreme changes to ourselves, including cosmetic surgery, there might not seem to be much of the original "self" left.

BEFORE   AFTER

working on tasks that cannot be solved more quickly than those who are low in self-efficacy. A defining feature of entrepreneurs is their high levels of perceived self-efficacy (Markman, Balkin, & Baron, 2002).

When a task can be successfully accomplished only by working together with others, *collective self-efficacy* may be critical. Some successes critically depend on the team's performance as a whole—which is not equivalent to the self-efficacy that the individual members of the team may feel. Among basketball players, a shared belief in the collective efficacy of the team (measured at the beginning of the season) is associated with the team's overall success by the end of the season (Watson, Chemers, & Preiser, 2001). Likewise, collective self-efficacy can lead to political activism, such as persuading people to vote or joining a protest movement to bring about social change (Bandura, 2000; Simon & Klandermans, 2001).

Although we can bring about self-change as a result of our desire for self-improvement, many of these changes occur because of situational factors. Change can occur as we age, for example, because different demands are made on us as we occupy different roles throughout the life span. Consistent with this, much self-change occurs in response to relocating to a different community, where we begin to conform to new norms (Kling, Ryff, & Essex, 1997). Entering a new occupation also tends to bring about changes in our self-concept. Equally dramatic changes in the self-concept occur as one moves from civilian life to the armed forces and face combat (Silverstein, 1994), as well as when college students graduate and leave the academic environment to become attorneys, engineers, or parents. In addition, very negative effects on our self-concept can occur as a result of major life changes, such as losing a job (Sheeran & Abraham, 1994), contracting a serious illness (Taylor, Buunk, & Aspinwall, 1990), or losing someone close to us through death (Stroebe et al., 1995). Such identity changes can be conceptualized as either the addition of a new but not necessarily sought after identity or the deletion of a prior valued identity.

KEY POINTS

★ Our self-conceptions can vary in terms of their emphasis on the *personal self* or the *social self*, with the resulting behavior being *intragroup* or *intergroup* in nature. We have multiple social identities, which could have different implications for behavior, depending on which one is activated.

★ The context in which we find ourselves can alter the aspect of the self that is salient. Gender differences tend to be exhibited most when our gender group identity is salient, but may be absent when another one is salient.

★ A frequent response to perceived rejection by others is to choose to emphasize the aspect of one's identity that differentiates the self from those rejecting us. To create a self-perception as a "rebel," one can "take on" a feature that differentiates members of one's peer group from the mainstream.

★ Images of future *possible selves* can inspire us to make difficult changes in the present in order to achieve this more desirable self.

★ To succeed in changing something about ourselves, we need to have *self-efficacy*, or feelings that we can accomplish a goal. Some goals, however, can be accomplished only by joining with others—in these cases, it is important to feel *collective self-efficacy*.

★ Self-change can occur as we find ourselves in a new social context. Such change can occur because we have moved, taken a new job, or become a parent. It can also result from negative events, such as illness, loss of a loved one, or loss of a job.

Self-Esteem: Attitudes toward the Self

self-esteem
The degree to which the self is perceived positively or negatively; one's overall attitude toward the self.

So far we have considered some ways that people attempt to protect their self-esteem when they feel threatened, but we haven't discussed how self-esteem is routinely assessed. **Self-esteem** has been conceptualized by social psychologists as the individual's overall attitude

Figure 5.7 ■ Measurement: The Rosenberg Self-Esteem Scale
Each of the items with an asterisk is reverse-scored, and then an average of all ten items is computed so that higher numbers indicate greater self-esteem. (*Source: Based on Rosenberg, 1965.*)

1. I feel that I am a person of worth, at least on an equal basis with others.
2. I feel that I have a number of good qualities.
3. All in all, I am inclined to feel that I am a failure.*
4. I am able to do things as well as most other people.
5. I feel I do not have much to be proud of.*
6. I take a positive attitude toward myself.
7. On the whole, I am satisfied with myself.
8. I wish I could have more respect for myself.*
9. I certainly feel useless at times.*
10. At times I think I am no good at all.*

toward the self. What kind of attitude do you have toward yourself—is it positive or negative? Is that attitude stable, or does the situation affect how you feel, with self-esteem varying across contexts?

The Measurement of Self-Esteem

The most common method of measuring self-esteem as a general traitlike evaluation is with the ten-item Rosenberg (1965) scale. As shown in Figure 5.7, this scale has rather straightforward items. People who agree strongly with such items are said to have high self-esteem, whereas those who disagree have low self-esteem. Given that most people can guess what is being assessed with such items, it is not surprising that this measure correlates very highly with responses to the simple item, "I have high self-esteem" (Robins, Hendin, & Trzesniewski, 2001). On this measure, using a scale ranging from 1 (*not very true of me*) to 5 (*very true of me*), people are asked to provide their own explicit attitude. There are also more specific measures that are used on occasion to assess self-esteem in particular domains such as academics, personal relationships, appearance, and athletics. In general, overall trait self-esteem, as measured with the Rosenberg scale, typically reflects the average of these more specific domains.

Self-esteem can also be responsive to specific situations. As Figure 5.8 illustrates, when we achieve important goals, self-esteem can improve, whereas failures can harm self-esteem. Such short-term increases in *state* self-esteem—how an individual feels about the self at a particular moment in time—can be induced easily in a laboratory setting. For example, simply giving people false feedback about their positive score on a personality test can raise self-esteem (Greenberg et al., 1992), and positive feedback about being accepted by other people has a similar effect (Leary, 1999). Self-esteem can be temporarily enhanced by wearing clothing that you like (Kwon, 1994) or by directing your thoughts toward desirable aspects of yourself (McGuire & McGuire, 1996).

Likewise, self-esteem can be temporarily undermined in laboratory settings. When people are reminded of the ways they fall short of their ideals, self-esteem can decrease (Eisenstadt & Leippe, 1994). In fact, for women who place importance on their physical appearance, simply being required to put on a swimsuit can undermine their self-esteem (Fredrickson et al., 1998). Being ostracized, excluded, or ignored by other people, even in Internet chat rooms or while playing cybergames that lack long-term importance to the individual, can lower self-esteem (Williams, 2001).

Figure 5.8 ■ Self-Esteem: Attitudes toward the Self
One's self-esteem, or attitude about oneself, can range from very positive to very negative. At least temporarily, the individuals shown here would seem to be expressing a very positive (*left*) and a very negative (*right*) attitude about themselves.

Researchers have attempted to measure self-esteem with greater subtlety. They believed that attitudes toward the self might be better revealed using unconscious assessment procedures, compared with the explicitly conscious methods such as the Rosenberg scale. Such implicit measures of self-esteem might be less susceptible to bias due to people's self-presentation concerns (e.g., their desire to present themselves to others in the best possible light). Given the **self-reference effect** in information processing, in which people seem to prefer stimuli that are associated with the self (e.g., we like the letters in our own name better than other letters), researchers have investigated whether this preference for self-relevant information is sufficiently automatic that it occurs rapidly and without a conscious intention. To assess this possibility, Gray and colleagues (2004) measured brain responses (known as *event-related potentials*—ERPs) to self-relevant words versus non-self-relevant words. They found that people automatically allocate their attention to self-relevant information. Because such basic and unconscious processes appear to be involved in the self-reference effect, it suggests that strategies designed to improve self-esteem might be effective when administered at the unconscious level.

In an attempt to assess whether implicit self-esteem can be improved without the participant's conscious awareness, Dijksterhuis (2004) used the logic of *classical conditioning* procedures (see Chapter 4). After repeatedly pairing representations of the self (*I* or *me*) with positively valenced trait terms (e.g., *nice, smart, warm*) that were presented subliminally, implicit self-esteem was found to be significantly higher compared with those in a control group who were not exposed to such pairings. In addition, such subliminal conditioning prevented participants from suffering a self-esteem reduction when they were later given negative false feedback about their intelligence. Thus, consistent with research on explicit self-esteem (such as studies using the Rosenberg scale) that shows people with high self-esteem are less vulnerable to threat following a failure, this subliminal training procedure appears to provide similar self-protection in the face of threat to the self.

Self-Serving Biases

People want to feel positive about themselves, and most manage to see themselves favorably much of the time. The fact that most of us show the **above-average effect**—which is thinking we are better than the average person on almost every dimension imaginable—is strong evidence of our desire to see the self relatively positively (Alicke et al., 2001; Klar, 2002; Taylor & Brown, 1988). Even when we are directly provided with negative social feedback that contradicts our rosy view, we show evidence of forgetting such instances and emphasizing information that supports our favored positive self-perceptions (Sanitioso, Kunda, & Fong, 1990; Sanitioso & Wlodarski, 2004).

As described in Chapter 3, people reliably show self-serving biases when explaining their personal outcomes. Information that might imply we are responsible for negative outcomes is assessed critically, and our ability to refute such arguments appears to be rather remarkable (Greenwald, 2002; Pyszczynski & Greenberg, 1987). As children we adopt the mantra, "It's not my fault," which we take into adulthood. We can use this when it comes to explanations for outcomes for which we might be blamed, regardless of whether we are innocent or guilty. Overusing this excuse, though, can have important consequences for how others evaluate us.

In contrast to our resistance to accepting responsibility for negative outcomes, we easily accept information that suggests we are responsible for our successes. This is especially true for people with high self-esteem (Schlenker, Weigold, & Hallam, 1990). Not only do people show self-serving biases for their personal outcomes, but also for their group's achievements. Fans of sports teams often believe that their presence and cheering was responsible for their team's success (Wann & Branscombe, 1993). There are, however, culture-based limits on people's willingness to "grab the credit." For example, in China, modesty is an important basis for self-esteem (Bond, 1996). Accordingly, Chinese students attribute their school success to their teachers, whereas American students attribute it to their own skills and intelligence. Conversely, when it comes to failure, Chinese students are more likely to explain their failure as stemming from their own flaws, while Americans explain it as being someone else's fault.

self-reference effect
People's orientation toward stimuli that are associated with the self. People show a preference for objects owned by and reflective of the self.

above-average effect
The tendency for people to rate themselves as above the average on most positive social attributes.

Is High Self-Esteem Always Positive?

Given the many techniques that people have for maintaining self-esteem, it is reasonable to ask whether high self-esteem is a crucial goal for which we should all strive. Some social scientists have suggested that the lack of high self-esteem (or presence of low self-esteem) is the root of many social ills, including drug abuse, poor school performance, depression, and various forms of violence, including terrorism. Some have argued that low self-esteem might be an important cause of aggression and general negativity toward others (Crocker et al., 1987; Nunn & Thomas, 1999). However, strong evidence has now accumulated in favor of the opposite conclusion—that high self-esteem is more strongly associated with bullying, narcissism, exhibitionism, self-aggrandizing, and interpersonal aggression (Baumeister, Smart, & Boden, 1996). For example, it is men with high self-esteem who are most likely to commit violent acts when someone disputes their favorable view of themselves. Why might this be? To the extent that high self-esteem implies superiority to others, that view of the self may need to be defended whenever the individual's pride is threatened. It may even be that high self-esteem coupled with instability results in the most hostility and defensive responding (Kernis et al., 1993). When those with unstable high self-esteem experience failure, their underlying self-doubt is reflected in physiological responses indicative of threat (Seery et al., 2004). Thus, while there are clear benefits for individuals to have a favorable view of themselves, there also appears to be a potential downside.

Do Women and Men Differ in Their Levels of Self-Esteem?

Who do you think, on average, has higher or lower self-esteem—women or men? Most might guess that men have higher self-esteem than women. Why might social psychologists predict this, too? Because women occupy positions of lower status and are frequently targets of prejudice, their social structural position should have negative consequences for their self-esteem. Beginning with George Herbert Mead (1934), who first suggested that self-esteem is affected by how important others in our sociocultural environment see us, women have been expected to have lower self-esteem overall because self-esteem is responsive to the treatment we receive from others. To the extent that women have been traditionally viewed as less competent than men in the larger social world, their self-esteem should be, on average, lower. How important the dimensions are on which women are devalued in the larger society, and how aware women are of their devalued status, should influence the extent to which a gender-based self-esteem difference is observed.

Williams and Best (1990) conducted a fourteen-nation study of the self-concepts of women and men to provide support for these predictions. In nations such as India and Malaysia, where women are expected to remain in the home in their roles as wives and mothers, women have the most negative self-concepts. In nations such as England and Finland, where women are most active in the labor force and are valued participants in life outside the home, women and men tend to perceive themselves equally favorably. This research suggests that when women are excluded from important life arenas, they feel more strongly devalued and, as a result, have worse self-concepts than men. Longitudinal research with employed women in the United States similarly finds that women in jobs in which gender discrimination is most frequent exhibit increasingly poorer emotional and physical health over time (Pavalko, Mossakowski, & Hamilton, 2003). Harm to women—as a function of employment in a discriminatory work environment—can be observed in comparison to health status before their employment began.

A meta-analysis comparing the global self-esteem of women and men in 226 samples collected in the United States and Canada from 1982 to 1992 has likewise found that men have reliably higher self-esteem than women (Major et al., 1999). Consistent with the reasoning of the earlier cross-nation research, Major and his colleagues (1999) found that the self-esteem difference between men and women was less among those in the professional class and greatest among those in the middle and lower classes. Again, those women who have attained culturally desirable positions suffer less self-esteem loss than those who are more likely to experience the greatest devaluation. Interestingly, it was among white North Americans that the largest overall difference between men and women was observed, whereas no reliable difference in self-esteem by gender was obtained for minority Americans. For minority groups, members of *both* genders are likely to experience broad social devaluation based on their racial category, whereas only among whites are women likely to be discriminated against in important aspects of life. Consistent with this finding that the degree of gender discrimination matters, among preadolescents, there was no reliable gender difference in self-esteem, but beginning in puberty, when girls' options become increasingly limited (remember the opening vignette), a reliable self-esteem difference emerges that continues through adulthood, with women's self-esteem levels being lower than men's.

KEY POINTS

★ *Self-esteem* is the attitude we have toward ourselves and can range from very positive to negative. Self-esteem is most frequently measured with Rosenberg's scale, which uses explicit items that capture people's perceptions that they do or do not have high self-esteem. Other more implicit measures assess the strength of the positive or negative association between the self and stimuli associated with it, including trait terms such as *warm* and *honest*.

★ Most people feel relatively positive about themselves. This is reflected in the *above-average effect,* in which people see themselves as above the average on most positive dimensions.

★ People maintain their positive view of themselves, in part, with self-serving biases in the explanations they provide

for their outcomes. Americans especially accept credit for positive outcomes and refute their responsibility for negative outcomes, whereas Chinese people tend to show the reverse pattern.

★ Low self-esteem may not be predictive of the social ills many had thought. In fact, high self-esteem is predictive of violent reactions when one's superior view of the self is threatened.

★ There is a small but reliable gender-based difference in self-esteem. Women's self-esteem is worse than men's to the extent that they live in a nation with more exclusion of women from public life (lower labor force participation by women) and in the United States when they work in occupations in which discrimination is more likely.

Social Comparison: Knowing the Self

How do we know ourselves—whether we're good or bad in various domains, what our best and worst traits are, and how likable we are to others? Some social psychologists have suggested that *all* human judgment is relative to *some* comparison standard (Kahneman & Miller, 1986). There is considerable evidence that how we think and feel about ourselves depends on the standard of comparison we use. If we compare our ability to complete a puzzle with a five-year-old's ability to solve it, we'll probably feel pretty good about our ability. This represents a **downward social comparison,** in which our own performance is compared with that of someone who is less capable than we are. On the other hand, if we compare our performances on the same task with that of a puzzle expert, we might not fare so well, nor feel so good about ourselves. This is the nature of **upward social comparisons,** which tend to be threatening to our self-image. As the amateur musician in Figure 5.9 suggests, protecting our self-image can depend on choosing the right standard of comparison.

You might be wondering why we compare ourselves with other people at all. Festinger's (1954) **social comparison theory** suggests that we compare ourselves with others because, for many domains and attributes, there is no objective yardstick with which to evaluate ourselves; other people are therefore highly informative. Indeed, feeling uncertain about themselves in a particular domain is among the most crucial conditions that lead people to engage in social comparison (Wood, 1989).

With whom do we compare ourselves, and how do we decide what standard to use? It depends on our motive for the comparison. Do we want an accurate assessment of ourselves,

downward social comparison
A comparison with someone who does less well than the self.

upward social comparison
A comparison with someone who does better than the self.

social comparison theory
Festinger (1954) suggested that people compare themselves to others because, for many domains and attributes, there is no objective yardstick with which to evaluate the self, so other people are therefore highly informative.

or do we want to simply feel good about ourselves? In general, the desire to see the self positively appears to be more powerful than either the desire to accurately assess the self or to verify strongly held beliefs about the self (Sedikides & Gregg, 2003). But, suppose, that we really do want an accurate assessment. As Festinger (1954) originally suggested, we might gauge our abilities most accurately by comparing our performance with that of someone who is similar to us. But, what determines similarity? Do we base it on age, gender, nationality, occupation, year in school, or something else? Similarity tends to be based on broad social or demographic categories such as gender, race, or experience in a particular domain—which might include time spent playing the flute, or number of cooking classes taken (Goethals & Darley, 1977; Wood, 1989).

Often, by using comparisons with others who share a social category with us, we can judge ourselves more positively than when we compare ourselves with others who are members of a different social category (especially a more advantaged one). This is partly because there are different performance expectations for members of different categories in particular domains (e.g., children versus adults). To the extent that the context encourages a person to categorize the self as a member of a category with relatively low expectations in a particular domain, the individual will be able to conclude that he or she measures up rather well. For example, a woman could console herself by thinking that her salary is "pretty good for a woman," while she would feel considerably worse if she made the same comparison with men, who on average are paid more (Reskin & Padavic, 1994; Vasquez, 2001). Thus, self-judgments are often less negative when the standards of our ingroup are used (see Biernat, Eidelman, & Fuegen, 2002). Some have suggested that such ingroup comparisons protect members of disadvantaged groups from negative and painful social comparisons with more advantaged groups (Crocker & Major, 1989; Major, 1994).

Many have suggested that the goal of perceiving the self positively is human beings' "master motive" (Baumeister, 1998). Social comparison is an important means by which this powerful motive is served (Wood & Wilson, 2003). How the generally positive self-perception that most of us have of ourselves is achieved depends on how we categorize the self in relation to the other to whom we are comparing. Such self-categorization influences how particular comparisons affect us by influencing the *meaning* of the comparison. Two influential perspectives on the self—the **self-evaluation maintenance model** and **social identity theory**—both build on Festinger's (1954) original social comparison theory to describe the consequences of social comparison in different contexts. Self-evaluation maintenance (Tesser, 1988) applies when we categorize the self at the personal level and we compare ourselves as an individual with another individual. Social identity theory (Tajfel & Turner, 1986) applies when we categorize the self at the group level, and the comparison other is categorized as sharing the same category. When the context encourages comparison at the group level, the same other person will be responded to differently than when the context suggests a comparison between individuals.

Let's consider first what happens in an interpersonal comparison context. When someone with whom you compare yourself outperforms you in an area that is important to you, you will be motivated to distance yourself from that person. Such a situation has the potential to be a relatively painful interpersonal comparison. Conversely, when you are comparing yourself with another person in an area that is important to you and that individual performs similarly or worse, then you will be more likely to seek closeness to that person because the comparison is positive. By performing worse than you, this person makes you look good by comparison. Such psychological movement toward and away from a

self-evaluation maintenance model
The perspective that suggests that in order to maintain a positive view of the self, we distance ourselves from others who perform better than we do on valued dimensions, but move closer to others who perform worse. This view suggests that doing so will protect our self-esteem.

social identity theory
Our response when our group identity is salient. Suggests that we will move closer to positive others with whom we share an identity, but distance ourselves from other ingroup members who perform poorly or otherwise make our social identity negative.

comparison other who performs better or worse than you illustrates an important means by which positive self-evaluations are maintained.

A study by Pleban and Tesser (1981) illustrates this effect. They had participants compete in a game with another person (the experimenter's accomplice). When the questions being asked were on a dimension of importance to the self, participants reported disliking the accomplice who outperformed them more than the accomplice who performed worse than they did. Mussweiler, Gabriel, and Bodenhausen (2000) similarly paired participants with an individual who either performed better or worse than they did. They found that the upward comparison led participants to focus less on an aspect of the self that they shared with the comparison other, while the downward comparison resulted in a greater focus on an aspect of the self that they shared with the comparison. Supporting the idea that such shifts in focus are self-protective, participants who scored high on a measure of self-esteem were more likely to exhibit these shifting focus effects compared with those low in self-esteem.

When, if ever, should we want to align ourselves with another person who outperforms us? Do we always dislike others who do better on identity-relevant dimensions? No, not at all—it depends on how we categorize ourselves in relation to the other. According to social identity theory, people are motivated to perceive their groups positively, and this should especially be the case for those who value a particular social identity. Therefore, another person who is categorized as a member of the same group as the self can help make our group positively distinct from other groups, and, as a result, those fellow group members who perform well can enhance our group's identity instead of threatening it.

To show that both of the self-protective processes described by the self-evaluation maintenance and social identity perspectives can occur, depending on whether personal or social identity is at stake, Schmitt, Silvia, and Branscombe (2000) manipulated the nature of the comparative context. When the performance dimension is relevant to the self—which was achieved by selecting people for the study who said that being creative was relevant to their own identity—then responses to a target who performs better than or equally poorly as the self will depend on the nature of the categorization context. As shown in Figure 5.10, when participants believed that their performance as an individual would be compared with the other target, they liked the poor-performing target better than the high-performing target, who represented a threat to their positive personal self-image. In contrast, when participants categorized themselves in terms of the gender group that they shared with the target

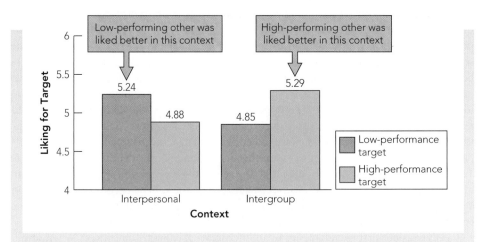

Figure 5.10 ■ How Do We Evaluate Another Who Performs Better or Worse Than We Do?
Research indicates that it depends on whether the context is interpersonal, whereby the personal self is at stake, or intergroup, with the social self at stake. As shown here, the low-performing target is liked best in an interpersonal context. The high-performing target is liked best in an intergroup context. (*Source: Based on data from Schmitt, Silvia, & Branscombe, 2000.*)

Chapter 5 / The Self

and the expected comparison was intergroup in nature (between women and men), the high-performing other woman was evaluated more positively than the similar-to-self poor-performing other. Why? Because this person made the participants' group look good. In another study, these investigators showed that such positive evaluation of the high-performing target in the intergroup condition occurred most for those who highly valued their gender identity. Thus, different comparative contexts can induce us to categorize ourselves at varying degrees of inclusiveness, and this has important implications for the effects that upward and downward social comparisons have for self-evaluation.

Another important implication of group dynamics for how we evaluate ourselves and others is reflected in the **black sheep effect**—the rejection of negative ingroup members who threaten the group's positive image. Members of our group who perform poorly can be intensely derogated (Marques & Paez, 1994). To the extent that their actions have implications for the positivity of our group's identity, members of our group may be derogated more severely than members of another group who behave in the same way. People who value a particular group identity (e.g., highly identified fans of the University of Kansas basketball team) are especially likely to show the black sheep effect by derogating a disloyal Kansas fan (Branscombe et al., 1993). Such derogation of black sheep casts the unfavorable ingroup member as nonrepresentative of one's group, and this effectively protects the ingroup's overall identity (Castano et al., 2002).

black sheep effect
When a member of the ingroup behaves in a way that threatens the value of the group identity and is intensely derogated as a means of protecting the group identity.

Self-Presentation and Self-Regulation

As previously described, we all have a strong desire for others to perceive us positively. To ensure this, we often attempt to manage the impressions that they form of us. In Chapter 3 we noted how people attempt to ensure that others form impressions of them based on their most favorable self-aspects—that is, we engage in *self-promotion*. However, we also seem to know that an important way to induce others to like us is to convey positive regard for them. People like to feel respected, and we really like those who convey this to us (Tyler & Blader, 2000). To achieve this, you can present yourself to others as someone who particularly values or respects them. People who are newcomers to a group, for example, may be especially motivated to present themselves to powerful others as a "good person." An important means of doing so is to communicate loyalty to the group and a willingness to conform to the group's norms (Noel, Wann, & Branscombe, 1995).

In general, when we want to make a good impression, we use **ingratiation.** That is, we can make others like us by praising them. This is generally quite effective, unless we overdo it and others suspect our sincerity, which can bring the risk of being seen as "slime" by those who witness our "sucking up" (Vonk, 1999). We can also try to present ourselves to others as superbly competent or otherwise having desirable attributes. The tendency to use this strategy depends on our cultural background. When Kanagawa, Cross, and Markus (2001) asked Japanese and American students to describe themselves, the Americans tended to describe themselves in terms of their strengths (e.g., "I am good at math"), while the Japanese students were self-critical (e.g., "I am not good at music"). In both instances, people are conforming to norms about how to make a good impression and be liked by others, although the norms of how best to accomplish this can vary from culture to culture.

Some people are more adept at monitoring their behavior and conforming to what others expect or will see as desirable than others (Snyder & Ickes, 1985). One individual difference variable—**self-monitoring**—captures people's willingness and ability to regulate their behavior. High self-monitoring means that people are concerned with how others will react, and involves a focus on external cues such as others' expectations. Low self-monitoring involves a focus on internal cues such as their own beliefs or attitudes as a basis for behavior. Low self-monitors tend to be less responsive to situational norms (whatever those are in a given context), whereas high self-monitors tend to change as the situation changes (Koestner, Bernieri, & Zuckerman, 1992). Degree of self-monitoring is assessed with items such as "I can only argue for ideas that I already believe," with low self-monitors tending to agree more than high self-monitors with this idea. Indeed, differences in self-monitoring are reflected in how people use language (Ickes, Reidhead, & Patterson, 1986). High self-monitors

ingratiation
The attempt to make others like us by praising them.

self-monitoring
The monitoring by people of their behavior in response to others' expectancies. Low self-monitors are not very effective at doing this and instead prefer to act consistently according to their personal views. High self-monitors are quite effective at monitoring their behavior and adjust their actions according to others' expectations or the situation.

Is Looking Inward the Best Route to Self-Insight?

Self-help books tell us time and again to get to know ourselves by looking inward. Indeed, many people believe that the more people introspect about themselves, the better they will understand themselves. As shown in Figure 5.11, pop psychology authors repeatedly tell us that the road to self-knowledge runs through such self-inspection. Is this really the best way to accurately understand ourselves? Not necessarily.

First, often we do not know or have conscious access to the reasons for our actions, although if pressed we can certainly generate what appear to be logical theories. For example, in early research on this issue, Richard Nisbett and Timothy Wilson (1977) presented participants with a choice situation: They were shown a variety of different pairs of socks from which they were to choose their favorite. After selecting participants were asked *why* they chose the pair they did. Although people came up with various reasons, the researchers knew that their choices were actually based on an entirely different factor (the order of the items on the table—the more to the right the pair was, the better it was liked, regardless of which pair that was). Although the participants could and did introspect about why they liked one pair of socks over another, and they came up with seemingly logical

Figure 5.11 ■ Self-Help Books Recommend Introspection
The titles of pop psychology books imply that the route to self-understanding may lie in introspection, but research reveals that this can be misleading. Depending on the nature of the factors that are actually driving our behavior, introspection may misdirect us.

reasons, they apparently did not have conscious access to the factor that actually predicted their affective responses to the various pairs of socks.

In fact, subsequent research has revealed that attempting to analyze our reasons for liking something or acting in

---

tend to use third-person pronouns (*they, them*) when they speak, which reflects their outward focus on others. Low self-monitors, on the other hand, tend to use first-person pronouns (*I, me*) more frequently.

High self-monitors know how to obtain positive evaluations from others; this can be quite useful in many occupations. Politicians, actors, and salespeople are especially likely to be high in self-monitoring (Lippa & Donaldson, 1990). Overall, high self-monitors tend to have higher self-esteem than low self-monitors. This may stem from the higher levels of social approval that high self-monitors receive compared with low self-monitors (Leary et al., 1995). Indeed, the basis on which self-esteem rests and can be undermined differs for these two types (Gonnerman et al., 2000). For low self-monitors, depression results when there is a discrepancy between the self and what the individual thinks he or she should be. For high self-monitors, depression results when there is a discrepancy between the self and what he or she thinks other people expect. How do high self-monitors manage to be successful in controlling the impressions others form of them? They seem to give others both what they expect and what they want!

So far, we have illustrated how we get to know ourselves by comparing how we perform on various tasks with others. By presenting ourselves in a particular way to others, we come to see what we value about ourselves and what we hope others will perceive positively. Another important method that people have assumed is useful for learning about the self is to engage in **introspection**—to privately think about "who we are." Is looking inward the best route to understanding ourselves—to gaining self-insight? For a discussion of this intriguing issue, see the **Making Sense of Common Sense** section.

introspection
Attempts to understand the self by self-examination; turning inward to assess one's motives.

a particular way can mislead us when we have to make a subsequent choice. Because we often genuinely don't know why we feel a particular way, generating reasons (that are likely to be inaccurate) could result in changing our minds about how we feel based on those reasons. Wilson and Kraft (1993) illustrated this process in a series of studies concerning introspection on topics ranging from "Why I Feel as I Do about My Romantic Partner" to "Why I Like One Type of Jam over Another." They found that after analyzing the reasons for their feelings, people changed their attitudes, at least temporarily, to match their reasons. As you might imagine, this can lead to regrettable choices, because the original feelings that are based on other factors entirely are still there.

Another way in which introspection might be rather misleading is when we attempt to predict our future feelings. Try imagining how you would feel living in a new city, being fired from your current job, or living with another person for many years. When you are not in these specific circumstances, you might not be able to accurately predict how you will respond. This applies to both positive and negative future circumstances. Gilbert and Wilson (2000) suggest that when we think about something terrible happening to us and try to predict how we would feel one year into the future, we focus exclusively on the awful event and neglect all the other factors that will contribute to our happiness level. People predict that they would feel much worse than they actually would when this future time arrives. Likewise, for positive events, if we focus on only its occurrence, we will mispredict our happiness as being higher than the actual moderate feelings that are likely one year later. Again, this would occur because we would not focus on all the daily hassles and other factors that would moderate how we feel at some future point in time.

Does all this mean that introspection is inevitably misleading, and is in fact potentially harmful? It depends on *what* we analyze about ourselves. When the behavior in question is based on a conscious decision-making process—and is not based on unconscious affective factors—thinking about those reasons might lead to accurate self-judgments. In addition, if we introspect about our behavior frequency in a particular domain, it is likely to be a very good cue to our preferences. When we find ourselves working on a particular task for long periods of time without any external rewards or constraints, we are likely to conclude that we are intrinsically motivated by the task and enjoy it. On the other hand, if we only perform a task when we are being monitored or rewarded for doing so, we can accurately conclude that our reasons for performing those actions may be *extrinsic* and not due to sheer liking of the task. So, although looking *inward* can be helpful, it may not be, as popular books suggest, helpful under all circumstances. Research has revealed that we may be "asking ourselves" more than we actually know!

KEY POINTS

★ *Downward social comparison* refers to instances in which we are compared with someone of lesser ability than ourselves. *Upward social comparison*, in contrast, refers to someone who outperforms us in areas central to the self. We often find these people threatening in interpersonal comparative contexts, but they are tolerated to the extent that we believe we, too, can achieve the other's more favorable position. We tend to like those who outperform us, particularly when we share a social category with them and the context implies an intergroup comparison. Then, the better-performing other is making our group identity more positive and is not experienced as threatening as the same target would be if the comparison were interpersonal.

★ *Social comparison theory* spawned two perspectives on the consequences of negative or upward social comparisons for the self—the *self-evaluation maintenance model* and *social identity theory*.

★ Presenting ourselves as liking or admiring others is often an effective way of ingratiating ourselves with them and being liked in return. There are cultural differences in the way people present themselves, as a function of the valued norm of modesty in Asian cultures and self-promotion norms in American culture.

★ The *black sheep effect* proposes that we will derogate a member of our own group more than a member of another group when we think that person reflects badly on our group's image.

★ Individuals differ in the extent to which they engage in *self-monitoring*. Low self-monitors are keen to be true to themselves and show cross-situational consistency, whereas high self-monitors want to be what others want and adapt themselves to different people and situations.

The Self as Target of Prejudice

Although the experience of not getting what you want, or getting what you don't want, is generally negative, how you explain these outcomes has important implications for how you feel about yourself. As you saw in Chapter 3, attributions affect the *meaning* derived from events, and some attributions for a negative outcome are more psychologically harmful than others (Weiner, 1985). How people explain and respond to one class of negative outcomes—prejudice-based negative treatment stemming from one's group membership—has been the focus of considerable research. Although overt discrimination against women and minorities has generally declined in the United States since the end of World War II, it is sufficiently prevalent (although often subtle) that it may explain the more frequent undesirable outcomes that members of devalued groups experience. As Figure 5.12 suggests, the mere presence of devalued group members is not the same thing as their being able to feel comfortable in an environment in which they can feel assured that discrimination will be absent.

Emotional Consequences: How Well-Being Can Suffer

As discussed earlier, social psychologists have long been interested in the self-esteem consequences of being a member of a devalued social group. George Herbert Mead (1934) initially suggested that our self-appraisals depend on how others see us. Given that members of devalued groups are more likely to experience negative responses from others compared with mainstream group members, self-esteem processes between these two have been closely examined.

To account for how targets of prejudice maintain their self-esteem, Crocker and Major (1989) suggested that attributing negative outcomes to prejudice might be self-protective among those who are devalued and discriminated against. Specifically, they argued that an attribution for a negative outcome that points to another person's prejudice as the cause

"To begin with, I would like to express my sincere thanks and deep appreciation for the opportunity to meet with you. While there are still profound differences between us, I think the very fact of my presence here today is a major breakthrough."

Figure 5.12 ■ Progress toward Group Equality Can Be Measured in Degrees
As this cartoon illustrates, women's (or the dragon's) presence in male-dominated professions (the knights' domain) represents a "good start," but it can hardly be said to represent "a warm and welcoming environment." (*Source: © The New Yorker Collection 1983 William Miller from cartoonbank.com. All Rights Reserved.*)

should be considered *external*. For this reason, attributing a negative outcome to something outside the self should be self-protective. These theorists speculated that because an attribution to prejudice is a sufficiently self-protective explanation for poor outcomes that it "may not only be used in response to negative evaluations or outcomes that do, in fact, stem from prejudice against the stigmatized group, but also in response to negative outcomes that do not stem from prejudice" (Crocker & Major, 1989, p. 612). This implies that there could be a self-esteem protection motivation that encourages attributions to prejudice among devalued group members. Yet there is overwhelming correlational evidence that the more disadvantaged group members perceive discrimination against their group, the worse their well-being. Therefore, negative outcomes that are seen as stemming from stable factors such as one's group membership are not predicting positive self-esteem. Such relationships between perceived discrimination and negative well-being have been obtained among members of different social groups, including women (Schmitt et al., 2002), black Americans (Branscombe, Schmitt, & Harvey, 1999), homosexuals (Herek, Gillis, & Cogan, 1999), Jewish Canadians (Dion & Earn, 1975), and people who are overweight (Crocker, Cornwell, & Major, 1993). Let's consider the evidence that experimental research has generated concerning these dual propositions: (1) that attributions to prejudice are external and can therefore discount internal causes for negative outcomes, and (2) that attributions to prejudice for a *specific* negative outcome protect the well-being of devalued group members.

Should our group memberships be considered truly external to the self? As this chapter has revealed, our social identities as group members can be an important aspect of the self. Use of Kelley's "covariation principle" (see Chapter 3) suggests that when something about the self (group membership) covaries with an outcome (discrimination), the attribution made will have a substantial internal component. To illustrate the previously unidentified internal component of attributions to prejudice, Schmitt and Branscombe (2002b) compared this attribution with a situation in which a clear external attribution for the same exclusionary outcome was plausible. These researchers had participants think about a situation in which a professor refused their request to let them into a course that required the professor's permission for enrollment. This exclusion could be due to different reasons that would have differing implications for how the person would feel. By varying information about the professor and who was or was not let in to the class, prejudice or an exclusively external cause for the participant's rejection was made plausible. In the "prejudice plausible" condition, participants learned that the professor had a reputation for being hostile toward their gender and that only members of the other gender were admitted. In the "everyone excluded" condition, participants learned that the professor had a reputation of being hostile toward all students and that no one was given the special permission. To what did the students attribute their failure to be admitted to the class? In the prejudice condition, they perceived the cause of their rejection as both due to something about the professor *and* due to something about themselves. Only when everyone was excluded was the internal attributional component essentially absent. The finding that the self is implicated when a prejudice attribution is made (e.g., one's group membership is a part of the self, so internality is high), compared with when an attribution that does not involve prejudice is made, was subsequently replicated (Major, Kaiser, & McCoy, 2003).

Given that we know that attributions to prejudice have a substantial internal component, we can ask whether they are likely to be self-protective. Indeed, Schmitt and Branscombe (2002b) found that, for women, making an attribution to the professor's prejudice against women harmed their well-being, compared with when everyone was excluded and the exclusion could not be attributed to prejudice. Using the same experimental materials involving the professor who refuses a student admittance to a course, Major, Kaiser, and McCoy (2003) found that there is an even worse attribution that can be made than either an attribution to prejudice or the professor's refusal to admit anyone. When the professor viewed the participant as *uniquely* stupid and, for this reason, the participant was the *only* person excluded from the class, this situation caused the participants' feelings about the self to be most negative.

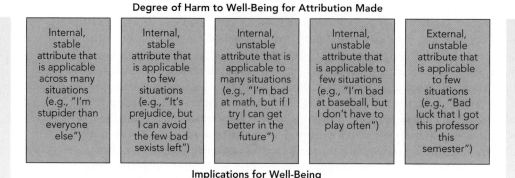

Degree of Harm to Well-Being for Attribution Made

| Internal, stable attribute that is applicable across many situations (e.g., "I'm stupider than everyone else") | Internal, stable attribute that is applicable to few situations (e.g., "It's prejudice, but I can avoid the few bad sexists left") | Internal, unstable attribute that is applicable to many situations (e.g., "I'm bad at math, but if I try I can get better in the future") | Internal, unstable attribute that is applicable to few situations (e.g., "I'm bad at baseball, but I don't have to play often") | External, unstable attribute that is applicable to few situations (e.g., "Bad luck that I got this professor this semester") |

Implications for Well-Being

Worst ⟶ Best

Figure 5.13 ■ Attributions for an Outcome Differ in How Harmful They Are for Well-Being
The worst attribution a person can make for well-being is that there is something unique about themselves that is stable and applicable to many situations. The best attribution—will be that the outcome is due entirely to something external that is unstable and is unlikely to be encountered in many situations.

The conclusions drawn about the emotional consequences of perceiving one's negative outcomes as stemming from prejudice against one's group clearly depend on the attribution to which it is compared. When negative outcomes are attributed to prejudice, this reflects an internal and relatively stable cause for disadvantaged group members. When compared with *another* important internal and stable feature of the self, such as one's lack of intelligence, an attribution to prejudice might be self-protective. To the extent that the other internal explanation is relevant to more situations or outcomes (is even more pervasive; Major, Kaiser, & McCoy, 2003), making that attribution could cause greater harm to well-being than attributing the outcome to prejudice. On the other hand, when compared with an actual external attribution, such as the professor's generally negative disposition, then attributions to prejudice are relatively harmful for well-being (Schmitt & Branscombe, 2002b). As Figure 5.13 illustrates, attributions for the same unfavorable outcome can be differentiated along a continuum in terms of the extent to which they have negative implications for psychological well-being.

An attribution to prejudice can reflect pervasive discriminatory circumstances, or it can be perceived as reflecting a rare or unusual instance. In effect, for any given experience, an attribution to prejudice could be seen as reflecting wider social circumstances or could be seen as an encounter with a lone bigot. Schmitt, Branscombe, and Postmes (2003) illustrated the importance of the perceived pervasiveness of prejudice for psychological well-being in women. Participants believed that they were taking part in a study concerning job interviewing skills and that one of the twenty male businesspeople involved in the study would give them feedback. Each participant received the *identical* negative feedback from the interviewer. However, while waiting for their interviewing feedback, the experimenter ostensibly confided to the participant either that (1) "your interviewer is a real jerk and seems to give everyone a negative evaluation" (the nonsexist external attribution); (2) "your *particular* interviewer is really sexist and gives the women negative evaluations, but is positive toward the men" (the lone sexist); or (3) "*all* of the interviewers, including yours, are really sexist" (pervasive sexism). Both feelings of self-esteem based on their gender and overall positive mood worsened when the prejudicial outcome was seen as also likely to occur in other situations (prejudice was seen as pervasive across the twenty interviewers), compared with either when prejudice could be seen as limited to the lone sexist or when a prejudice attribution was not made at all. When discrimination was seen as isolated, self-esteem and mood did not differ from when a "nonsexist jerk" delivered the negative feedback. Thus, all attributions to prejudice are not equal. What is fundamentally important for how an event is coped with and whether psychological well-being will be harmed or not is the perception of how likely it is that such discriminatory treatment will be encountered in the future.

Cognitive Consequences: Performance Deficits

Perceived prejudice can not only affect psychological well-being, but can also interfere with our ability to learn and acquire new skills. Several studies have found that when people fear that others will discover their devalued group membership, as might be the case for conceal-able stigmas, this fear can negatively affect people's ability to learn (Frable, Blackstone, & Scherbaum, 1990; Lord & Saenz, 1985). When we are in a position in which we feel we need to hide our identity and worry about how others might perceive us, it can be rather distracting. Studies measuring attention allocation reveal that when such distractions weigh on disadvantaged group members, their cognitive abilities are impaired and performance suffers.

Behavioral Consequences: Stereotype Threat

Stereotype threat occurs when people believe they might be judged in light of a negative stereotype about their social identity or that they may inadvertently act in some way to confirm the stereotype of their group (Steele, 1997). When people value their ability in a certain domain (e.g., math), but it is one in which their group is stereotyped as performing poorly (e.g., women), stereotype threat may occur. When those who are vulnerable to stereotype threat are reminded in some overt or subtle way that the stereotype might apply to them, performance in that domain may be undermined.

Stereotype threat effects seem to be fairly difficult to control. For example, simply telling women before they take a math test that men do better than women (Spencer, Steele, & Quinn, 1999) or having African Americans indicate their race before taking a difficult verbal test (Steele & Aronson, 1995) is sufficient to evoke stereotype threat and hurt their performance. Indeed, because women are negatively stereotyped as being worse at math than men, women tend to perform more poorly when they simply take a difficult math test in the presence of men, whereas they tend to perform better when the same test is taken in the presence of women only (Inzlicht & Ben-Zeev, 2000). It is worth noting that these decrements in performance occur *only* with respect to stereotype-relevant dimensions—it is not all types of performances that are harmed. Thus, women are vulnerable on math, but African Americans are vulnerable on tests of verbal ability.

Precisely because such stereotype threat effects have been difficult to eliminate, investigators have considered the response options that are available to devalued group members when they are in settings in which they experience stereotype threat. One option that has been suggested is disidentification with the domain (Steele, Spencer, & Aronson, 2002). People could try to distance themselves from domains in which they are stereotypically vulnerable. Such an option, though, is likely to be rather problematic for people who strongly value performing well in a given domain. In this research, the women who are selected are strongly concerned about doing well in math; likewise, African Americans who are selected are keen to do well in occupations requiring strong verbal skills. Another option that might be used in a stereotype threat situation is to attempt to distance the self from the group identity as a whole. That is, women could decrease how much they identify with their gender group, or African Americans might do the same with their race. However, this option also comes with long-term risks—minority group identification is known to be important for psychological well-being (Postmes & Branscombe, 2002).

Research has revealed a third option that is available to those subjected to stereotype threat conditions. People who are vulnerable to stereotype threat can maintain their overall level of identification with their group, and distance themselves only from the stereotypic dimensions that represent a threat to their performance in a particular valued domain. Consider the dilemma of women who have taken a lot of math classes and who perceive math to be an important aspect of their self-concept. They also value their identity as women. When they find themselves exposed to information that suggests there are reliable

stereotype threat
People's belief that they might be judged in light of a negative stereotype about their group or that they may, because of their performance, in some way confirm a negative stereotype of their group.

sex differences in math ability, with men doing better than women, these women experience threat. How then do they manage to cope *without* simultaneously distancing from either the domain or their group? One possibility is suggested by Pronin, Steele, and Ross (2004), who found that high math-identified women distanced themselves only from gender stereotypic dimensions that are deemed to be incompatible with math success (e.g., leaving work to raise children, being flirtatious) but did not do so for gender stereotypic dimensions deemed to be irrelevant to math success (e.g., being empathic, being fashion conscious). Disidentification from such aspects of their gender group occurred only in the stereotype threat condition but not when it was absent, suggesting it was a motivated process designed to alleviate the threat experienced.

Why do stereotype threat–based performance decrements occur? Some researchers suggest that anxiety is evoked in women, blacks, and Latinos when their group membership is portrayed as predictive of poor performance (Osborne, 2001). As a result of such anxiety, their actual performance is disrupted. If this is the case, when stress-based anxiety is prevented, as occurs among women who use humor as a coping strategy, then performance decrements may be avoided (Ford et al., 2004).

Some studies have, however, failed to find increased self-reported anxiety among stigmatized group members in stereotype threat conditions (Aronson et al., 1999). This could be because members of stigmatized groups are reluctant to admit their feelings of anxiety in conditions in which they realize they will be compared with dominant group members, or it may be that they do not actually realize they are feeling anxious or aroused and so cannot accurately report those feelings.

Research that examines nonverbal measures of anxiety has revealed that anxiety can play a crucial role in stereotype threat effects. Although measures of self-reported anxiety have frequently failed to reveal the important role of anxiety, nonverbal measures of anxiety illustrate clearly the role that anxiety plays in stereotype threat effects. In a clever test of the hypothesis that anxiety does cause stereotype threat performance deficits, Bosson, Haymovitz, and Pinel (2004) first either reminded or did not remind gay and straight participants of their category membership before videotaping their interactions with young children in a nursery school. Participants were reminded of their sexual orientation by asking them to indicate their sexual orientation on a form just before they interacted with the children. After this subtle reminder that their group is stereotyped as one that is dangerous to children, the gay participants' child-care skills (as rated by judges blind to the hypotheses and procedure) suffered compared with when they were not reminded of their category membership. This same group membership reminder had no effect on the straight participants because there is no such stereotype of danger to children. Consequently, straight participants were not at risk of potentially confirming a negative stereotype in the performance situation.

Is it only for groups that are historically devalued in the culture that stereotype threat effects have been observed? No, definitely not. Such effects occur with men who are not a devalued group as a whole, but who are stereotyped as being less emotional than women (Leyens et al., 2000). When men were reminded of the stereotype concerning their emotional deficits, their performance on a task requiring them to identify emotions suffered. Stone and colleagues (1999) found that stereotype threat effects can occur among dominant group members as long as the implied comparison is based on dimensions on which their group is perceived less favorably. In their research, white men who were being compared with black men performed more poorly on an athletic performance task when they believed it reflected natural athletic ability. The reverse occurred when white men believed the exact same task reflected sports intelligence, which is a dimension on which white men expect to excel. Likewise, although there is no stereotype that whites perform poorly on math, when they are threatened by a potentially negative comparison to Asians, who are stereotyped as performing better than whites in this domain, whites show math performance deficiencies (Aronson et al., 1999). Thus, the comparative context matters for stereotype threat effects, and these effects are not limited to members of historically disadvantaged groups. Stereotype threat effects illustrate the importance of group membership for the experience of psychological threat, and how this can easily disrupt performance.

Chapter 5 / The Self

KEY POINTS

★ Emotional responses to a negative outcome depend on the attribution made for it. If you believe that bad outcomes happen because you are uniquely stupid and this is a characteristic that predicts many negative outcomes, you will feel even worse than when an attribution to prejudice is made. When the identical outcome is attributed to pervasive prejudice, then well-being will be harmed more than if it is seen as isolated or rare. When an attribution for a negative outcome reflects an external cause, rather than prejudice against the person's group membership, well-being is protected.

★ The fear of being "found out" by others in terms of having a negatively valued group identity can disrupt performance. Deficits occur only when the identity is devalued in the culture as a whole, and such deficits are absent when the same identity is valued.

★ *Stereotype threat* effects involve the undermining of performance in a domain a person values. This occurs when a person is a member of a group that is negatively stereotyped in a particular domain. Stereotype threat effects can be difficult to control, and they can be induced easily. Simply requiring people to indicate their group membership before taking a test in a domain in which they are vulnerable is enough to undermine performance.

★ When people experience stereotype threat, they can distance themselves from the task domain or they can distance themselves from the group as a whole. However, both of these options present long-term problems. One option that has received support is to disidentify with *only* the negative part of the group's stereotype.

★ Anxiety appears to be the mechanism by which stereotype threat effects occur. However, self-report measures of anxiety often fail to reveal its importance, but use of nonverbal measures has illustrated its importance.

SUMMARY AND REVIEW OF KEY POINTS

Thinking about the Self: Personal versus Social Identity

■ How we think about ourselves varies depending on where we are on the *personal–social identity* continuum at any given moment in time. We can think of ourselves in terms of attributes that differentiate us from other individuals, and are therefore based on *intragroup comparison*. Or, the self can be thought of as a member of a social group, with perceptions of the self being based on attributes shared with other group members; this perception of the self stems from *intergroup comparison* processes.

■ Self-definitions can vary across situations, with each being valid predictors of behavior in those settings. How the self is conceptualized can also depend on how others expect us to be and how we believe they will treat us.

■ Other selves, besides who we are currently, can motivate us to attempt self-change. Dreaded possible selves can lead us to give up certain behaviors (e.g., smoking), while desired possible selves can lead us to work long hours to attain them.

Self-Esteem: Attitudes toward the Self

■ How we feel about ourselves can be assessed directly, as well as with more implicit or indirect methods. Most people show self-serving biases, such as the *above-average effect,* in which we see ourselves more positively (and less negatively) than we see most other people.

■ High self-esteem comes with risks. It is correlated with an increased likelihood of interpersonal aggression, which appears to be in response to the greater need to defend one's superior self-view.

■ Women do, on average, have lower self-esteem than men. This is particularly the case in nations in which women do not participate in the labor force, and in the United States among middle- and lower-class women who work in environments in which gender-based devaluation is most frequent.

Social Comparison: Knowing the Self

■ *Social comparison* is a vital means by which we judge and know ourselves. *Upward social comparisons* at the personal level can be painful, and *downward social comparisons* at this level of identity can be comforting. When we self-categorize at the group level, though, the opposite is true. Ingroup members who perform poorly threaten the positive view of our group identity, while ingroup members who perform well reflect positively on our group identity. Indeed, we are likely to derogate ingroup members who behave disloyally (the *black sheep effect*), and doing so protects the positive view of our group identity.

- People often present themselves to others in an ingratiating manner, in order to be liked, although this tendency can depend on the cultural norms that guide our behavior. Individual differences in *self-monitoring* predict people's ability and willingness to adapt their behavior according to differing situational norms.

The Self as Target of Prejudice

- Some researchers have suggested that, among devalued group members, attributions to prejudice are external and therefore have the potential to protect self-esteem. Not only are such attributions to prejudice not perceived by the individual as external to the self (my group membership is about me), they generally are not protective—except when compared with the very worst possible attribution (an important-dimension that is applicable to a wide range of situations and reflects both internal and stable aspects of the self). Indeed, perceiving the self as a target of discrimination can have negative consequences for well-being, particularly when the discrimination is seen as pervasive.

- Suspecting that prejudice might be operating and affecting one's outcomes can be distracting, deplete cognitive resources, and create anxiety. As a result, *stereotype threat* effects can occur in historically devalued groups when members are simply reminded of their group member-

ship and fear they might confirm negative expectancies about their group. Stereotype threat can undermine performance in dominant group members as well, when they fear a negative comparison with members of another group. This undermining of performance occurs only on dimensions relevant to the stereotype.

- People cope with stereotype threat by distancing themselves from the performance domain (e.g., math) or from their group as a whole (e.g., women), but both of these options are emotionally costly. Distancing from only the stereotypic dimensions relevant to high performance in a domain appears to be preferable.

Connections   INTEGRATING SOCIAL PSYCHOLOGY

In this chapter, you read about . . .	In other chapters, you will find related discussions of . . .
the role of norms in social functioning	the nature of norms and their role in social influence (Chapter 9) and aggression (Chapter 11)
the nature of attribution and social explanation	self-serving biases in attribution (Chapter 3)
individuals' concern with others' evaluations of their performance	the effects of others' evaluations on our liking for others (Chapter 7) and self-presentation (Chapter 3)
the importance of the situation or context for judgment	audience effects on attitudes (Chapter 4)
the role of stereotyping and discrimination	the nature of prejudice (Chapter 6), and various forms of social influence (Chapter 9)

Thinking about Connections

1. Do you see any connection between perceiving yourself as a member of a group (in social identity terms) and stereotype threat? (Hint: Have you ever suspected that

other people might see your group negatively?)

2. Most of us are motivated to protect our self-esteem. What would be the most favorable attribution you could make when you explain a bad outcome that has happened to you? What would be the worst? How might others respond to you if

you voiced aloud either of those attributions?

3. We all want to know ourselves. How do we attempt this? Can you think of instances in which you compared unfavorably to another person and attempted to distance yourself from that person? Can you think of instances in which you

compared favorably and liked being around the downward social comparison other? How did these different performances affect your relationship with that person?

4. If images of "new possible selves" can motivate us to change ourselves, can you identify a "desired possible self" and a "feared possible self" that might suggest useful changes in yourself? If so, describe the changes you would make to avoid your feared possible self and then consider the changes you would make to achieve your desired possible self.

5. Have you ever experienced a change in your self-perception as you move from one situation or group to another? If so, does one self-perception seem more accurate than another? Or are they equally true, depending on the situation?

Ideas to Take with You—and Use! MAXIMIZING YOUR OWN WELL-BEING

■ Find a role model whose accomplishments seem attainable. If you think you can achieve his or her position or accomplishments ultimately, such an upward comparison can be inspiring.

■ Present yourself as liking and valuing others if you want them to like you. People like others who value them.

■ Avoid making attributions to prejudice for your own outcomes if you want to feel good about your future, because they are relatively internal and stable attributions, which are predictive of poor well-being. On the other hand, preju-

dicial treatment is likely to persist when complaints of discrimination are avoided. If you do perceive an outcome as due to unjust discrimination, then seek social support from other members of your group.

■ Avoid making public attributions that blame others for negative outcomes, for there will be social costs.

■ *Stereotype threat* occurs when persons fear confirming a negative stereotype about their group. You can attempt to undermine its likelihood of occurring by suggesting to vulnerable others that group differences are absent on a particular

task. Here's how you can help prevent others from experiencing stereotype threat:

■ Avoid making their group membership salient.

■ *Self-definition* can shift as the situation changes. Notice how you think about yourself when you are sitting in a classroom, in your dorm or apartment, when on a date, at your job versus when you are with your family.

■ Think about what others expect of you and consider how that affects how you feel about yourself.

■ Practice thinking about yourself positively.

KEY TERMS

6

PREJUDICE
Its Causes, Effects, and Cures

I (Nyla Branscombe) travel internationally frequently, commuting between the United States and Europe, in addition to trips to Canada and Australia. For flights departing from the United States—since the terrorist attacks of September 11, 2001—I, like other Americans, have encountered dramatic increases in airport security procedures. Now, in U.S. airports, we routinely see indicators that we live in a nation "on alert." During various trips, I have wondered about the extent to which experiencing such security procedures—including removal of shoes and body searches with metal detectors—affects travelers. Some might expect that such increased security will make us feel more "secure" and reduce feelings of threat because it serves as a reminder that our government is actively trying to stop other would-be attackers. However, much social psychological research suggests that the experience of such security procedures, which have long been common in nations such as Israel, may have the opposite effect. Such reminders that our safety is in jeopardy can make death salient, heighten anxiety, and have the potential to increase prejudice toward the group representing the threat (Pyszczynski et al., 2004). This psychological consequence is consistent with reports of Muslim Americans' airport experiences since 9/11, and, more generally, with those of people who appear to be of Arab origin (Fries, 2001; Gerstenfeld, 2002). As you will see in this chapter, feelings of threat and vulnerability have played a critical role in theories of prejudice.

While traveling with a Middle Eastern friend, I noticed that he received special scrutiny from U.S. security personnel, as well as some wary glances from other passengers. Do you think such additional scrutiny stems from prejudice? Do we perceive the actions of our own group members—for example, its treatment of Arab and Muslim Americans or citizens of other nations—as prejudicial? Or are we more likely to perceive such scrutiny as legitimate when we feel our own group is under threat? In this chapter, we will consider when prejudicial treatment is seen as legitimate, and when it is seen as illegitimate.

Chapter 6 / Prejudice

Figure 6.1 ■ The Evil Results of Prejudice
At one time or other, all of us come face to face with prejudice, although hopefully not in such extreme forms as the atrocities depicted here. Some of the devastating effects of ethnic cleansing, slavery, and prejudice against Americans on the part of al Qaeda are illustrated here.

At some time or other, virtually everyone comes face to face with prejudice—as the target, as an observer of someone else's treatment of members of another group, or as a perpetrator—when we recognize that we do feel and act less positively toward members of some groups compared with how we respond to members of our own group. Prejudice is not limited to the extreme forms shown in Figure 6.1—atrocities such as ethnic cleansing in Europe and Africa, the institution of slavery, or the attacks on the World Trade Center on September 11, 2001. As you will see, the *roots* of such prejudice can be found in the cognitive and emotional processes that social psychologists have measured with reference to a number of different social groups.

Even if less extreme, prejudice can be consequential for its victims when it is based on category memberships, including age, occupation, gender, religion, language spoken and regional accent, sexual orientation, or body weight, to name just a few. Discriminatory treatment based on such category memberships can be blatant or relatively subtle (Devine, Plant, & Blair, 2001; Swim & Campbell, 2001). Prejudice may be perceived by its perpetrators as acceptable and justified (Crandall, Eshleman, & O'Brien, 2002), or it can be seen as illegitimate and something that individuals should actively strive to prevent, both in themselves and in others (Devine & Monteith, 1993). In other words, all inequality and differential treatment is *not* perceived and responded to in the same way. Some forms of inequality are perceived as justified, and when norms concerning its legitimacy begin to change, threat can be aroused. Under these conditions, those high in prejudice may attempt to maintain the status quo, and even show a backlash against those seeking change. Those low in prejudice, may strive to accelerate social change in those same changing social conditions, in the belief that doing so is how social justice is best achieved. Under such unstable and changing conditions, social conflict will be felt most intensely, with public opinion likely to be polarized concerning how relations among the groups should be (Hogg & Abrams, 1988).

In this chapter, we will examine the nature of *stereotyping* and consider how it is related to *discrimination,* particularly against women in the workplace. Although there is a high degree of interpersonal contact between men and women, which tends to be absent in other cases, such as racial and religious groups (Jackman, 1994), it is a group membership in which we all have a stake. We then turn to perspectives on the origins and nature of *prejudice* and consider why it is so persistent. Lastly, we explore various successful strategies to reduce prejudice.

The Nature and Origins of Stereotyping, Prejudice, and Discrimination

In everyday conversation, the terms *stereotyping, prejudice,* and *discrimination* are often used interchangeably. However, social psychologists have drawn a distinction between them by building on the more general attitude concept (see Chapter 4). That is, stereotypes are considered the cognitive component of attitudes toward a social group, and they consist of beliefs about what a particular group is like. Prejudice is considered the affective component, or the feelings we have about particular groups. Discrimination concerns the behavioral component, or differential actions taken toward members of specific social groups.

Stereotyping: Beliefs about Social Groups

stereotypes
Beliefs about social groups in terms of the traits or characteristics that they are deemed to share. Stereotypes are cognitive frameworks that influence the processing of social information.

gender stereotypes
Stereotypes concerning the traits possessed by females and males, and that distinguish the two genders from each other.

Like other attitudes, **stereotypes** about groups concern the beliefs and expectations that we have concerning what members of those groups are like. Stereotypes can include more than just traits; physical appearance, activity preferences, and likely behaviors are common components of stereotypic expectancies (Biernat & Thompson, 2002; Deaux & LaFrance, 1998; Twenge, 1999). The traits thought to distinguish between the groups can be either positive or negative attributes, they can be accurate or inaccurate, and can be agreed with or rejected by members of the stereotyped group.

Gender stereotypes—beliefs concerning the characteristics of women and men—contain positive and negative traits (see Table 6.1). Stereotypes of each gender are typically the converse of each other. On the positive side of the gender stereotype for women, they are viewed as being kind, nurturant, and considerate. On the negative side, they are viewed as being dependent, weak, and overly emotional. Thus, as Susan Fiske and her colleagues (Fiske et al., 2002) noted, our collective portrait of women is that they are high on warmth but low on competence. Indeed, perceptions of women are similar on these two dimensions to other groups who are seen as relatively low in status and *not* a threat to the high-status group (Conway & Vartanian, 2000; Eagly, 1987; Stewart et al., 2000). As you will see, when a group—such as Jews in Nazi Germany—is perceived as a threat to the high-status group (which is sometimes referred to as "envious prejudice"), those groups are frequently stereotyped as low in warmth but high in competence (see Glick, 2002).

Men are also assumed to have positive and negative stereotypic traits—they are viewed as decisive, assertive, and accomplished, but also as aggressive, insensitive, and arrogant. Such a portrait reflects men's relatively high status. Interestingly, because of the strong emphasis on warmth in the stereotype for women, people tend to feel somewhat more positively about women—a finding described by Eagly and Mladinic (1994) as the "women are wonderful" effect.

Despite this greater perceived likeability, women face a key problem: The traits they supposedly possess tend to be viewed as less appropriate for high-status positions than the traits supposedly possessed by men. Women's traits tend to make them seem appropriate for "support roles," which is reflected in the occupational roles of women in the United States today. The vast majority are in clerical, nursing, or service occupations, all of which bring less status and monetary compensation than comparably skilled male-dominated occupations (Jacobs &

Table 6.1 ■ Common Traits Stereotypically Associated with Women and Men

As this list of stereotypic traits implies, women are seen as "nicer and warm," whereas men are seen as "competent and independent."

FEMALE TRAITS	MALE TRAITS
Warm	Competent
Emotional	Stable
Kind/polite	Tough/coarse
Sensitive	Self-confident
Follower	Leader
Weak	Strong
Friendly	Accomplished
Fashionable	Nonconforming
Gentle	Aggressive

(*Source: Based on Deaux & Kite, 1993; Eagly & Mladinic, 1994; Fiske et al., 2002.*)

Steinberg, 1990; Peterson & Runyan, 1993). Although women comprise more than half the U.S. population, the power structure remains heavily male dominated: Men own and control most of the wealth, as well as the political power (Ridgeway, 2001). Again, because men and women are intimately intertwined in personal relationships, we often fail to recognize this structural fact concerning gender group membership.

■ Stereotypes and the "Glass Ceiling"

Between the 1970s and the 1990s, the proportion of female managers rose from 16 percent to more than 42 percent (U.S. Department of Labor, 1992). Yet, the proportion of high-level female managers changed very little—from 3 percent to 5 percent (Glass Ceiling Commission, 1995), reflecting what Schein (2001) has called the "think manager—think male" bias. Many authors have suggested that a **glass ceiling**—a final barrier that prevents women, as a group, from reaching top positions in the workplace— may explain these differential outcomes.

glass ceiling
Barriers based on attitudinal or organizational bias that prevent qualified women from advancing to top-level positions.

Several studies have confirmed that a glass ceiling exists (Heilman, 1995; Stroh, Langlands, & Simpson, 2004). For example, we know that although subordinates often *say* much the same things to female and male leaders, they actually exhibit more negative *nonverbal behaviors* toward women (Butler & Geis, 1990). When women serve as leaders, they tend to receive lower evaluations from subordinates, even when they act similarly to men (Butler & Geis, 1990; Eagly, Makijani, & Klonsky, 1992). Indeed, those women who have been rather successful in competitive, male-dominated work environments are most likely to report experiencing gender discrimination, compared with those in gender stereotypic occupations (Redersdorff, Martinot, & Branscombe, 2004), and they are especially likely to be evaluated negatively when their leadership style is task-focused or authoritarian (Eagly & Karau, 2002).

When women violate stereotypic expectancies concerning warmth and nurturance and instead act according to the prototype of a leader, particularly in masculine domains, they are likely to be rejected. For example, between 1978 and 1998, in 1,696 state executive office elections, Fox and Oxley (2003) found that women were less likely to put themselves forth as candidates, and were less successful when they did so, if they ran for stereotype-inconsistent offices (e.g., financial comptroller or attorney general) than if they ran for stereotype-consistent offices (e.g., education or human services). Violating stereotype-based expectancies appears to have been the problem for Ann Hopkins, who had acquired multi-million-dollar projects for Price Waterhouse but was declined partnership in part because she was deemed insufficiently feminine (Hopkins, 1996). In her case, the senior partners suggested in her evaluations that she "wear more make-up" and act more "like a woman" should! Such explicit stereotyping may be one reason why the amicus brief on stereotyping research that was written by social psychologists influenced the U.S. Supreme Court, which ruled against Price Waterhouse and ordered that Ann Hopkins be given the partnership that she had earned (Fiske et al., 1991).

Female professors at the prestigious Massachusetts Institute of Technology discovered that they were systematically awarded less research support and lower salaries than their male colleagues (*MIT-report*, 1999). When the data that clearly illustrated the case were presented to the institution's officials, they did make corrections, although they had failed to see the gender-based differences that were occurring before the data were combined across departments by gender. As Faye Crosby and her colleagues have demonstrated (Crosby et al., 1986), when individual cases are examined in isolation, people can easily generate explanations for differential treatment. It is only by combining the same case information across multiple instances that the clear pattern of differential treatment by gender is even noticed.

The overlap of stereotypes about men and stereotypes about leaders leads to the converse of the glass ceiling effect for men when they enter predominantly female occupations. In such cases, men tend to be given a ride to the top on a "glass escalator" (Williams, 1992) and rapidly become managers and executives in nursing and other traditionally female-dominated fields. Thus, the bias against people rising to the top when they enter stereotype-inconsistent work roles appears to be primarily against women.

On the other hand, there is some basis for optimism for women presently entering the workforce. Lyness and Thompson (1997) compared the outcomes of men and women in a large company. The two groups were carefully matched in terms of education, work experience, and other factors. Very few differences were found in terms of their salaries, bonuses, or other benefits. However, the women reported supervising fewer subordinates and encountering more obstacles. In a subsequent study, Lyness and Thompson (2000) looked more closely at the nature of the barriers that prevent women from attaining success. Again, the women and men in the study were closely matched in terms of their current job, years with the company, and performance ratings to assure that differences in these factors could not account for the results.

What emerged was evidence that although women and men may ultimately arrive at the same levels in a specific company, they differentially face obstacles along the way. Women reported experiencing greater difficulties with not fitting into the male-dominated culture, being excluded from informal networks, and greater difficulties in securing developmental assignments—ones that would help increase their skills and advance their careers. Again, relatively few gender differences in actual career success emerged. However, two factors—having a mentor and receiving assignments with a lot of responsibility—were strongly related to tangible measures of career success. Overall, then, while these women in management did experience more obstacles to success than men, they nevertheless appeared to surmount those obstacles and ultimately attained comparable levels of success. So, is there a glass ceiling? *Yes,* in the sense that women must overcome greater obstacles than men to arrive at similar levels of success. But the fact that a few, ultimately, arrive at high levels of management suggests that some cracks have begun to appear in the glass ceiling. Although a lot remains to be done, it does seem that some change has occurred in the world of work, and some women do overcome the obstacles that gender stereotyping places in their way.

■ Consequences of Token Women in High Places

We can reasonably ask if the success of those individual women who have managed to break through the glass ceiling (see Figure 6.2) makes discrimination seem less plausible as an

Figure 6.2 ■ Do Visible and High-Status Women Lead Us to Believe That Discrimination Is a Thing of the Past? Condoleeza Rice, U.S. Secretary of State. Her presence in this role might seem to suggest that "anyone can make it to the top" and that group membership is no longer important. Research suggests that gender and racial discrimination are alive and well, however, in American workplaces.

explanation for other women's relative lack of success. To the extent that the success of such token high-status women is taken as evidence that gender no longer matters (Ely, 1994; Geis, 1993; Greenhaus & Parasuraman, 1993), people may infer that the relative absence of women in high places is due to their lacking the necessary qualities to succeed. For this reason, the success of token high-status women may obscure the structural nature of the disadvantages that women on the whole face. As a result of a few successful tokens, those women who do not achieve similar success may believe that they have only themselves to blame (Schmitt, Ellemers, & Branscombe, 2003). A number of laboratory experiments have confirmed that tokenism can be a highly effective strategy for deterring collective protest by disadvantaged groups. For instance, allowing even a small percentage (e.g., 2 percent) of low-status group members to advance into a higher-status group deters collective resistance and leads disadvantaged group members to favor individual attempts to overcome barriers (Lalonde & Silverman, 1994; Wright, Taylor, & Moghaddam, 1990).

Growing evidence indicates that persons who are hired as token representatives of their groups are perceived quite negatively by other company members (Yoder & Berendsen, 2001). In a sense then, such tokens are set up to be marginalized and disliked by their coworkers (Fuegen & Biernat, 2002). For example, job applicants who are identified as "affirmative action hirees" are perceived as less competent by people reviewing their files (Heilman, Block, & Lucas, 1992). Such a designation seems to imply to perceivers that the hiree is not qualified, which is not a happy situation for any prospective employee!

Hiring persons as token members of their group is just one form of **tokenism.** Performing trivial positive actions for the targets of prejudice can serve as an excuse or justification for later discriminatory treatment (Wright, 2001). In this case, perpetrators can point to their prior positive actions as a credential that indicates their "nonprejudiced" treatment of the target group. In whatever form it occurs, research indicates that tokenism can have at least two negative effects. First, it lets prejudiced people off the hook; they can point to the token as public proof that they aren't really bigoted, and the presence of a token helps to maintain perceptions that the existing system is legitimate and fair, even among members of the disadvantaged group (Ellemers, 2001). Second, it can be damaging to the self-esteem and confidence of the targets, including those few who are selected as tokens.

■ Do Targets Agree with Stereotyped Portrayals of Their Group?

Are women around the world as likely to, if not more so than men, concur with what they perceive to be positive stereotypic images of their group? For example, in what Peter Glick and his colleagues (2000) describe as **benevolent sexism**—views suggesting that women are superior to men in various ways and that they play a necessary role in men's happiness—women often agree more strongly with the idea that their group has such positively distinct attributes than do men. Low-status groups are especially likely to show such **social creativity responses**—in which alternative dimensions are chosen as a means of differentiating their group from the higher-status group—when inequality between the groups is stable (Tajfel

tokenism
Tokenism can refer to hiring based on group membership. It also can concern instances in which individuals perform trivial positive actions for members of out-groups that are later used as an excuse for refusing more meaningful beneficial actions for members of these groups.

benevolent sexism
Views suggesting that women are superior to men in various ways and are truly necessary for men's happiness.

social creativity responses
When low-status groups attempt to achieve positive distinctiveness for their group on alternative dimensions that do not threaten the high-status group (e.g., *benevolent sexism*).

The Nature and Origins of Stereotyping, Prejudice, and Discrimination

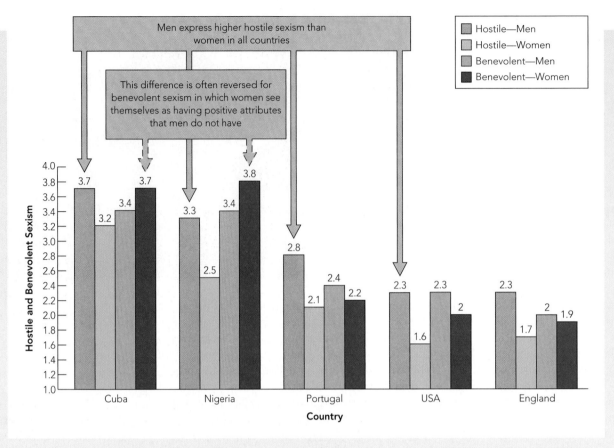

Figure 6.3 ■ Hostile and Benevolent Sexism around the Globe
Two forms of sexism have been identified—hostile (e.g., seeing women as a threat to men's position) and benevolent (e.g., seeing women as possessing uniquely positive attributes that are not shared by men). Men generally show *hostile sexism* more strongly than women, but this difference is often reversed with respect to *benevolent sexism*. (*Source: Based on data from Glick et al., 2000.*)

hostile sexism
The view that women are a threat to men's position.

& Turner, 1986). As shown in Figure 6.3, in a massive study involving more than 15,000 participants in nineteen different countries, Glick et al. (2000) showed that such positive distinctiveness beliefs about women's finer qualities, which those researchers label *benevolent sexism,* are often agreed with more by women, whereas men uniformly show higher **hostile sexism** than do women.

You can substitute almost any disadvantaged group label in the items on the hostile sexism measure and have a reasonable assessment of prejudice toward that specific group. Indeed, such items are very similar to how most measures of "modern prejudice" are worded, regardless of the group referenced in the measure. That is not the case for the benevolent sexism items, however, which refer to the positive attributes of the disadvantaged group. Indeed, many disadvantaged groups show this sort of favoritism toward their own group on dimensions that do not challenge the high-status group's position; they *self-stereotype* by agreeing with what they perceive to be *positive* descriptions of their group (Ellemers et al., 1997; Jetten & Spears, 2003; Mummendey & Schreiber, 1984; Oakes, Haslam, & Turner, 1994).

In addition to the gender differences in hostile and benevolent sexism scores that Glick et al. (2000) report, the degree to which gender inequality is present in the participants' countries, based on data from the United Nations, was recorded. These researchers found that the greater the gender inequality in a nation (in terms of women not being found in high-status jobs, having few educational opportunities and a poor standard of living), the more both forms of sexism were present. However, only hostile sexism predicted negative stereotyping of women. Overall, then, **sexism**—or perceiving and treating the gender groups differently—may not simply refer to hostility toward women; it can also mean greater perceived gender stereotypic differences that might seem to favor women. Although the latter could appear to suggest a kinder, gentler face of stereotyping, as Glick et al. (2000) note, benevolent sexism may keep women in a subordinate role by suggesting that their attributes make them uniquely suited for roles that are subordinate to men.

sexism
Prejudice based on gender; it typically refers to biases and negative responses toward women.

■ Gender Stereotypes and Differential Respect

Though gender stereotypes are an important part of persistent sexism and the glass ceiling effect, they are not the only factor affecting the experiences of women, especially in the workplace. Jackson, Esses, and Burris (2001) suggest that differential **respect** is critical for women attaining high-status positions. Precisely because men occupy positions of greater power and have higher status, people may infer that they are more *deserving* of respect than women, who are more likely to be found in relatively low-status positions.

respect
The quality of being seen positively and as having worth.

To determine whether differential respect actually plays a role in discrimination against women, Jackson, Esses, and Burris (2001) conducted studies in which male and female participants evaluated applicants for relatively high-status or low-status jobs. The applicants were either men or women, and participants rated them on the basis of information contained in job applications they had, supposedly, completed. In addition to rating the applicants in terms of whether they should be hired, participants also completed a standard measure of masculine and feminine stereotyping. Finally, they indicated their level of respect for the applicants.

The researchers predicted that men would receive higher ratings in terms of both hiring recommendations and respect, and this was the case, particularly for the higher-status jobs. In addition, they found that only ratings of respect for the job applicants significantly predicted hiring recommendations; gender stereotypes did *not* predict such ratings. In other words, the more respect participants in the study expressed for the applicants, the higher their ratings in terms of hiring recommendations. In contrast, the extent to which participants rated the applicants as showing traits consistent with gender stereotypes did *not* predict hiring recommendations. Because men, across the board, received higher ratings of respect, the results suggested that this factor plays an important role in at least some forms of discrimination against women.

■ Are Gender Stereotypes Accurate?

Do men and women really differ in the ways that gender stereotypes suggest? This question is complex, because such gender differences, even if observed, may be more a reflection of the *impact* of stereotypes and their self-confirming nature than of basic differences between females and males (Chen & Bargh, 1997; Claire & Fiske, 1998; Eagly, 1987). Existing evidence, however, points to the following conclusion: There are some differences between males and females with respect to various aspects of behavior, but in general, the magnitude is much smaller than prevailing gender stereotypes might suggest (Bettencourt & Miller, 1996; Plant et al., 2000; Swim, 1994). Gender stereotypes can be exaggerations that reflect behaviors that are typical of the roles occupied by men and women. As these roles have shifted, so, too, have the behaviors most typical of both genders (Eagly & Wood, 1999). In the section **The Science of Social Psychology: Making Sense of Common Sense,** we consider how stereotyping might still be operating, despite people often showing no differences in the evaluations given to women and men.

Why Do People Form and Use Stereotypes?

Stereotypes often function as **schemas,** which, as we saw in Chapter 2, are cognitive frameworks for organizing, interpreting, and recalling information (Wyer & Srull, 1994). Also noted in Chapter 2, human beings are "cognitive misers"—investing the least amount of

schemas
Cognitive frameworks developed through experience that affect the processing of new social information.

Shifting Standards: Does No Difference in Evaluations Indicate No Difference in Meaning?

At present, overt discrimination on the basis of gender, race, and religious affiliation is illegal in many countries. Does this mean that stereotype-based discrimination has been eliminated? Not necessarily. Although overt and blatant discrimination may be substantially reduced, other more subtle forces continue in ways that perpetuate discrimination in even well-meaning people (Crosby, 2004).

When people appear to evaluate members of two different groups similarly, does that mean that stereotypes are not operating, and, if not, how can we know that is the case? Common sense suggests that when no differences in evaluations are obtained, it means that discrimination is absent. However, social psychologists have documented how there might be more going on and that we would be wrong if we conclude that stereotypes are not continuing to affect behavior.

In a fascinating line of research by Monica Biernat and her colleagues on the **shifting standards** phenomena, we have learned that even when the same evaluation ratings are given to targets who are members of different groups, it does *not* mean that stereotypes are not influencing those ratings. Nor will those identical evaluation ratings translate into the same behavioral expectations.

According to Biernat and Vescio (2002), identical scores on **subjective scales**—which are open to interpretation and lack an externally grounded referent in reality, including scales labeled from good to bad or weak to strong—can take on different meanings depending on the group membership of the person being evaluated. These different meanings are revealed when judgments about the targets are also made on **objective scales**—those that are tied to measurement units that mean the same thing regardless of category membership. For example, dollars earned per year means the same thing regardless of whether you are male or female, but rating oneself as "earning a lot" might take more dollars if you are male than if you are female. In this case, because women tend to compare themselves with other women, and because women are known to earn less than men, women may conclude that they are doing pretty well when they make less (Major, 1994). In other words, if stereotypes lead people to make **within-group comparisons**, subjective ratings can be the same for members of different groups, although those evaluations translate into something quite different in reality for members of those groups.

So, what happened when Biernat and Vescio asked people to evaluate on subjective scales nine men and nine women from photographs that were prerated as "looking similarly athletic" in terms of their likely batting and fielding abilities from "good" to "poor?" Did those ratings closely reflect the participants' responses on more "objective" measures when they were also asked to choose thirteen of the eighteen people to be on their team, and to decide the batting order for ten players (with the other three on the supposed team to be benched)? The argument was that they would not, because with such "zero-sum" behavioral

shifting standards
When people use one group as the standard but shift to another group as the comparison standard when judging members of a different group.

subjective scales
Response scales that are open to interpretation and lack an externally grounded referent, including scales labeled from good to bad or weak to strong. They are said to be subjective because they can take on different meanings, depending on the group membership of the person being evaluated.

cognitive effort possible. Thus, one important reason people hold stereotypes is that it can save considerable cognitive effort—the effort required to perceive the person complexly as an individual. We don't have to bother engaging in careful, systematic processing, because we "know" what members of this group are like; we can rely on quicker, heuristic-driven processing and use these preconceived beliefs when making behavioral choices. Several studies offer support for this view of stereotyping (Bodenhausen, 1993; Macrae, Milne, & Bodenhausen, 1994). This is not the only purpose served by stereotypes, however. As you'll see, stereotypes can serve important motivational purposes; in addition to providing us with a sense that we understand the world, they can help us feel positive about our group identity in comparison with other social groups. For now, though, let's consider what the cognitive miser perspective has illustrated in terms of how stereotypes are used.

■ Stereotypes: How They Operate

Consider the following groups: Korean Americans, homosexuals, Native Americans, artists, homeless people. Suppose you were asked to list the traits most characteristic of each. You would probably not find this difficult. Most people can easily construct a list for each group, and, moreover, they could probably do so for groups with whom they have had limited personal contact. Stereotypes provide us with information about the typical or "modal" traits

Chapter 6 / Prejudice

choices, which involve an allocation of limited resources, like other objective scales, they require the respondent to use an absolute standard that has the same meaning regardless of category membership ("You're on the team or you are not"). How would you rate the targets shown in Figure 6.4? Were you aware that you might be thinking, "She could be pretty good . . . *for a girl?*" What happens when you evaluate both the male and female targets using a common standard (e.g., how often will each hit home runs)?

On the subjective scales concerning good to poor batting and fielding ability ratings, participants actually displayed a tendency to favor women over men. This would seem to imply that the stereotype concerning women's lesser skill in sports was not operating. However, when the objective scale or zero-sum judgments were considered (e.g., team selections, batting order, and benching decisions), a very different pattern emerged. On each of these measures, men were consistently given preference over women. This research therefore suggests that "same" does not necessarily mean "equal" or the absence of stereotyping. In fact, on measures in which the meaning of "good" can differ depending on group membership, such ratings can often mask stereotyping effects, while objective measures can reveal them.

Figure 6.4 ■ Shifting Standards: Do Similar Ratings of Girls and Boys Mean the Same Thing?
Gender stereotypes may induce us to equivalently rate members of different groups by leading us to use different standards of comparison. Male and female targets may be similarly rated on subjective rating scales, but when it comes time to pick the team, the male player will more likely be selected. (*Source: Based on Biernat & Vescio, 2002.*)

supposedly possessed by these groups (Judd, Ryan, & Parke, 1991), and, once activated, these traits come automatically to mind. This explains the ease with which you can construct such lists, even though you may not have had much direct experience with any of these social groups.

Stereotypes act as theories, guiding what we attend to and exerting strong effects on how we process social information (Yzerbyt, Rocher, & Schradron, 1997). Information relevant to an activated stereotype is often processed more quickly and remembered better than information unrelated to it (Dovidio, Evans, & Tyler, 1986; Macrae et al., 1997). Similarly, stereotypes lead persons holding them to pay attention to specific types of information—usually, information consistent with the stereotypes. Furthermore, when information *inconsistent* with stereotypes manages to enter consciousness, it may be actively refuted or changed in subtle ways that makes it seem *consistent* (Kunda & Oleson, 1995; Locke & Walker, 1999; O'Sullivan & Durso, 1984).

How do we make such stereotype-inconsistent information make sense when we encounter it? Suppose you learn that a well-known liberal politician has come out in favor of a large tax cut. This information is inconsistent with your stereotype of liberals, so you quickly draw another inference that will permit you to make sense of the unexpected information—for instance, you might conclude that this politician did so because most of the tax cut will go to people with low incomes. This is consistent with your stereotype of liberal

objective scales
Scales with measurement units that are tied to external reality so that they mean the same thing regardless of category membership.

within-group comparisons
Comparisons made between a target and other members of that same category only.

politicians' concern with helping the poor. Such inferences can help keep your stereotype intact, despite the presence of disconfirming information. In view of such effects, two social psychologists, Dunning and Sherman (1997) have described stereotypes as *inferential prisons:* Once they are formed, they shape our perceptions so that new information is interpreted as confirming our stereotypes, even if this not the case.

Research findings also indicate that when we encounter someone who belongs to a group about whom we have a stereotype, and this person does not seem to fit the stereotype (e.g., a highly intelligent and cultivated person who is also a member of a low-status occupational group), we do not necessarily alter our stereotype about what is typical of members of that occupational group. Rather, we place such persons into a special category or **subtype** consisting of persons who do not confirm the schema or stereotype (Richards & Hewstone, 2001; Queller & Smith, 2002). It is only when the person who disconfirms the stereotype in one specific way is otherwise seen as a typical group member that stereotype revision seems to occur (Locke & Johnston, 2001). This is especially the case when we repeatedly encounter members of the stereotyped group who consistently show this one deviation from our stereotype. When the disconfirming target is seen to be atypical of the group as a whole, or the target represents an extreme disconfirmation of the stereotype, stereotypes are not revised.

Think about what effect encountering a taxi driver who dresses fashionably, has Shakespeare's sonnets on the front seat, and speaks elegantly would have on your stereotype of taxi drivers. Would she lead you to stop expecting taxi drivers to be aggressive men who are not well educated and who dress casually? Not likely. Instead, you would simply think she's atypical, and her extreme atypicality on a variety of dimensions might even confirm the "validity" of your initial stereotype about *most* taxi drivers. Now suppose I told you that I met this woman in Germany? Ah, you say, no wonder—the stereotype doesn't apply in foreign countries—and your stereotype of *American* taxi drivers remains unchanged.

■ Forming Illusory Correlations

Suppose you were asked to evaluate the criminal tendencies of two groups: Would your ratings differ depending on the group size? Your first answer is probably, "Of course not—why should they?" Let's assume that the actual rate of criminal behavior is 10 percent in both a majority and a minority group. Surprisingly, research suggests that you might form more negative stereotypes and perceive the minority group less favorably than the majority group with exactly the same rates of negative behaviors (Johnson & Mullen, 1994; McConnell, Sherman, & Hamilton, 1994). Social psychologists refer to this tendency to overestimate the rate of negative behaviors in relatively small groups as the formation of **illusory correlations.** This term makes a great deal of sense, because such effects involve perceiving links between variables that aren't really there—in this case, links between being in a minority group and the tendency to engage in criminal behavior.

As you can see, illusory correlations can have important implications. In particular, the formation of illusory correlations can help explain why negative behaviors are often attributed to members of various minority groups. For example, some social psychologists have suggested that illusory correlation effects help explain why many whites in the United States overestimate crime rates among African American men (Hamilton & Sherman, 1989). For many complex reasons, young African American men are arrested for various crimes at higher rates than young white men or those of Asian descent (United States Department of Justice, 1994). But white Americans tend to *overestimate* this difference, and this can be interpreted as an instance of illusory correlation. Mark Schaller and Anne Maass (1989) have shown that illusory correlation effects do not occur among minority-group members, or when forming an illusory correlation would result in one's own group being negatively stereotyped.

Why, then, do such effects occur among majority-group members? One explanation is based on the distinctiveness of infrequent events or stimuli. According to this view, infrequent events are distinctive and readily noticed. For this reason, they may be encoded more extensively than other items when they are encountered, and so become more accessible in memory. When judgments about the groups involved are made later, the distinctive events come readily to mind, and lead us to overinterpret their importance. Consider how this explanation applies to the tendency of white Americans to overestimate crime rates among

---

subtype
A subset of a group that is not consistent with the stereotype of the group as a whole.

illusory correlation
The perception of a stronger association between two variables than actually exists.

African Americans. African Americans are a minority group; for this reason, they are high in distinctiveness. Many criminal behaviors, too, are highly distinctive (relatively rare). When news reports show African Americans being arrested for such crimes, this becomes highly accessible in memory. It also is highly consistent with existing stereotypes about African American men, and this, too, is a condition known to increase the size of illusory correlation effects (McArthur & Friedman, 1980). Thus, because of the multiple forms of distinctiveness and consistency with existing stereotypes, white Americans may tend to believe such illusory correlation–based information (Hamilton & Sherman, 1989; Stroessner, Hamilton, & Mackie, 1992).

■ Out-Group Homogeneity: "They're All the Same"—or Are They?

Do stereotypes, in effect, lead us to conclude that members of another group are "all the same"? To what extent do we see members of groups we do not belong to as more similar to one another (e.g., as more homogeneous) than the members of our own group? The tendency to perceive persons belonging to groups other than one's own as all alike is known as the **out-group homogeneity** effect (Linville et al., 1989). Its mirror image is **in-group differentiation**—the tendency to perceive members of our own group as being different from one another (as being more heterogeneous) than those of other groups.

Out-group homogeneity has been demonstrated for a variety of groups. For example, individuals tend to perceive older people as more similar to one another than persons in their own age group—an intriguing type of "generation gap" (Linville, Fischer, & Salovney, 1989). People also perceive students from another university as more homogeneous than students at their own university, especially when these persons appear to be biased against *them* (Rothgerber, 1997).

The converse—an **in-group homogeneity** effect—in which "we" are seen as all similar to each other often emerges among minority groups (Simon, 1992; Simon & Pettigrew, 1990), and this is particularly likely in social contexts in which the minority is preparing to respond to perceived injustices (Simon, 1998). Indeed, both effects (in-group and out-group homogeneity) have been observed in one study. By assessing stereotypical perceptions of the in-group and the out-group among gay and straight men, Simon, Glassner-Bayerl, and Stratenwerth (1991) found that straight participants exhibited an out-group homogeneity effect, while the gay participants exhibited an in-group homogeneity effect.

What accounts for the tendency to perceive members of other groups as more homogeneous than members of our own group and the less frequent but equally important tendency to perceive members of the in-group as similarly united and homogeneous? One explanation that has been offered for the out-group homogeneity effect involves the fact that we have a great deal of experience with members of our own group, and so are exposed to a wider range of individual variation within that group. In contrast, we generally have much less experience with other groups, and hence less exposure to their individual variations (Linville, Fischer, & Salovney, 1989). Another explanation has emerged recently because the differential familiarity notion cannot explain why in-group homogeneity would occur. That is, depending on the perceiver's purposes in a given setting, they may be motivated to emphasize their similarities with each other (e.g., when those perceptions are useful for mobilizing against a majority group) or their differences from each other (e.g., when majority groups want to emphasize their own individuality, and the lack thereof in out-groups). Because either the in-group or the out-group can be perceived as relatively more homogeneous, it suggests that stereotyped perception may have strategic elements, with stereotypes being recruited in the service of social motives (Oakes, Haslam, & Turner, 1994; Simon, 2004).

■ Do Stereotypes Ever Change?

We have reviewed evidence that stereotypes can be automatically activated, that we interpret new information in ways that allow us to maintain our stereotypes, and that we form illusory correlations concerning the negativity of minority groups. Does this mean that we can never change stereotypes? We must first consider whether stereotypes might serve other purposes besides efficiency, conserving mental effort, and helping maintain preexisting beliefs. If so, these motivations could provide us with clues about when and why stereotypes might change.

out-group homogeneity
The tendency to perceive members of an out-group as "all alike" or more similar to each other than members of the in-group.

in-group differentiation
The tendency to perceive members of our own group as showing much larger differences from one another (as being more heterogeneous) than members of other groups.

in-group homogeneity
In-group members are seen as more similar to each other than out-group members are. This tends to occur most among minority-group members.

Figure 7.3 ■ Affect Varies in Direction and in Strength
The underlying dimensions of affect involve direction in that they can be positive or negative. They also vary in intensity from weak to strong.

important characteristics of affect are *intensity*—the strength of the emotion—and *direction*—whether the emotion is positive or negative (see Figure 7.3).

Why is affect a basic aspect of human behavior? Social psychologist John Cacioppo has provided an explanation based on evolutionary principles. He suggests, "The affect system is responsible for guiding our behavior toward whole classes of stimuli. The most fundamental discrimination animals must be able to make [in order to] survive is to discriminate hostile from hospitable events" (quoted by Volpe, 2002, p. 7). Our ancestors were best able to live long enough to reproduce if they could avoid the unpleasant and seek out the pleasant. In effect, we are "built for pleasure" because the chances of survival and reproduction are enhanced by such tendencies. This generalization is useful whether the discrimination involves evaluations of unfamiliar food, a new environmental setting, or a stranger.

It was once assumed that all emotions fall along a single dimension (positive feelings on one end and negative feelings on the other). We now know, however, that affect consists of at least two separate dimensions that activate somewhat different portions of the brain (Drake & Myers, 2001; George et al., 1995). The presence of two separate kinds of affect means that we can feel both positive and negative at the same time. We often respond to situations with ambivalence. This, too, has evolutionary significance because positive affect motivates us to seek out and explore novel aspects of the environment, while negative affect simultaneously warns us to be vigilant, watching out for possible danger (Cacioppo & Berntson, 1999). Depending on the specific circumstances and on individual predispositions, positive and negative affect can be equally important in determining our evaluations. In different situations, sometimes positive and sometimes negative emotions may predominate (Eiser et al., 2003; Gable, Reis, & Elliot, 2000).

Besides simply a positive and negative dimension, there seem to be additional affective subdivisions (Egloff et al., 2003). For example, positive affect includes joy, interest, and activation. It may be that positive evaluations based on joy (for example) are different than positive evaluations based on interest.

Affect and Attraction

However complex positive and negative affect may turn out to be, a basic principle remains. The presence of positive affect leads to positive evaluations of other people (liking), while negative affect leads to negative evaluations (disliking) (Byrne, 1997a; Dovidio et al., 1995).

■ The Direct Effect of Emotions on Attraction

Emotions have a *direct effect* on attraction when another person says or does something that makes you feel good or bad. You will not be surprised that you tend to like someone who makes you feel good and dislike someone who makes you feel bad (Ben-Porath, 2002; Shapiro, Baumeister, & Kessler, 1991). Many experiments have confirmed such an effect. For example, attraction toward another person is less if he or she provides punishments in rating one's performance on a task rather than rewards (McDonald, 1962), and less toward a stranger who invades one's personal space than one who remains at a comfortable distance (Fisher & Byrne, 1975). Many such findings allow us to predict with confidence that a stranger will like you better if you do or say something pleasant as opposed to something unpleasant.

■ The Associated Effect of Emotions on Attraction

A phenomenon that is perhaps more surprising than the *direct effect* of emotions on attraction is the *associated effect*. This effect occurs when another person is simply present when one's emotional state is aroused by something or someone else. Though the individual toward whom you express like or dislike is not in any way responsible for what you are feeling, you nevertheless tend to evaluate him or her more positively when you are feeling good and more negatively when you are feeling bad. For example, if you come in contact with a stranger shortly after you receive a low grade, you tend to like that person less than someone you meet shortly after you receive your paycheck.

These associated (or indirect) influences of one's affective state have been demonstrated in many experiments involving emotional states based on a variety of quite diverse external causes. Examples include the subliminal presentation of pleasant versus unpleasant pictures—kittens versus snakes (Krosnick et al., 1992); the presence of background music that college students perceived as pleasant versus unpleasant—rock and roll versus classical (May & Hamilton, 1980); and the positive versus negative mood states that the research participants express when they first report for an experiment (Berry & Hansen, 1996).

The general explanation for such effects on attraction rests on classical conditioning. When a neutral stimulus is paired with a positive stimulus, it is evaluated more positively than a neutral stimulus that is paired with a negative stimulus, even when the person is not aware that the pairing occurred (Olson & Fazio, 2001). Figure 7.4

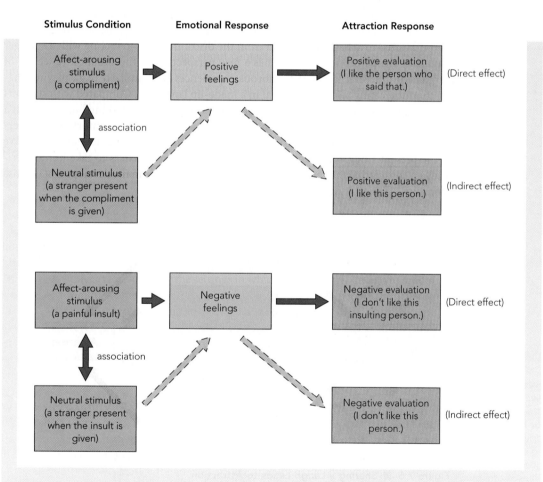

Figure 7.4 ■ Affect and Attraction: Direct Effects and Associated Effects
When any stimulus (including another person) arouses an individual's positive affect, the stimulus is liked. If the stimulus arouses negative affect, it is disliked. Such positive and negative arousal is defined as the direct effect of affect on attraction. Indirect effects occurs when any neutral stimulus (including another person) is present at the same time that affect is aroused by some other, unrelated source. The neutral stimulus becomes associated with the affect and is therefore either liked or disliked as a result. An indirect or associated effect is a form of classical conditioning. (*Source: Based on material in Byrne & Clore, 1970.*)

Figure 7.6 ■ Proximity: Repeated Interactions in Everyday Life Facilitate Attraction
At school, at work, or where you live, proximity results in repeated contact with specific others simply on the basis of the physical arrangement of a classroom, workplace, or dwelling place. Repeated exposure most often leads to recognition, an increasingly positive evaluation, and a greater likelihood that two people will become acquainted.

Palmade, & Fourment, 1952; Segal, 1974). In addition to proximity in the classroom, investigations conducted throughout the twentieth century indicated that people who live or work in close proximity are likely to become acquainted, form friendships, and even marry (Bossard, 1932; Couple repays . . . , 1997; Festinger, Schachter, & Back, 1950). Despite the many examples of proximity resulting in attraction, you might wonder *why* proximity results in attraction.

repeated exposure
Zajonc's finding that frequent contact with any mildly negative, neutral, or positive stimulus results in an increasingly positive evaluation of that stimulus.

mere exposure effect
Another term for the *repeated exposure* effect, emphasizing the fact that exposure to a stimulus is all that is necessary to enhance the positive evaluation of that stimulus.

The answer has been provided by numerous experiments showing that **repeated exposure** to a new stimulus results in an increasingly positive evaluation of that stimulus (Zajonc, 1968). This finding is sometimes called the **mere exposure effect** because the positive response to a stranger, a drawing, or whatever else that is observed multiple times occurs simply on the basis of exposure. Even infants tend to smile at a photograph of someone they have seen before but not at a photograph of someone they are seeing for the first time (Brooks-Gunn & Lewis, 1981).

A clear demonstration of the effects of repeated exposure on attraction is provided by an experiment conducted in a classroom setting (Moreland & Beach, 1992). In a college course, one female assistant attended class fifteen times during the semester, a second assistant attended class ten times, a third attended five times, and a fourth did not attend the class at all. None of the assistants interacted with the other class members. At the end of the semester, the students were shown slides of the four assistants and asked to indicate how much they liked each one. As shown in Figure 7.7, the more times an assistant attended class, the more she was liked. In this and other experiments, repeated exposure was found to have a positive effect on attraction.

Zajonc (2001) explains the effect of repeated exposure by suggesting that we ordinarily respond with at least mild discomfort when we encounter anyone or anything new. It

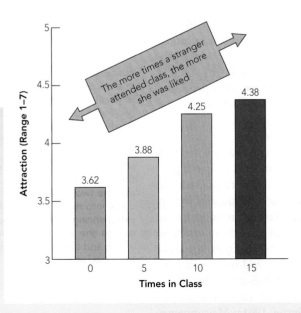

Figure 7.7 ■ Frequency of Exposure and Liking in the Classroom
To test the repeated exposure effect in a college classroom, Moreland and Beach (1992) employed four female assistants to pretend to be fellow students. One of them did not attend class all semester, another attended five times, a third attended ten times, and a fourth fifteen times. None of them interacted with the actual students. At the end of the semester, the students were shown photos of the assistants and asked to indicate how much they liked each one. It was found that the more times the students had been exposed to an assistant, the more they liked her. (*Source: Based on data from Moreland and Beach, 1992.*)

is reasonable to suppose that it was adaptive for our ancestors to be wary of approaching anything or anyone for the first time. With repeated exposure, however, in the absence of harmful consequences, negative emotions decrease and positive emotions increase—familiarity with a stimulus reduces feelings of uncertainty, suggesting that it is safe (Lee, 2001). A familiar face, for example, elicits positive affect, is evaluated positively, and activates facial muscles and brain activity in ways associated with positive emotions (Harmon-Jones & Allen, 2001). Not only does familiarity elicit positive affect, but positive affect elicits the perception of familiarity (Monin, 2003). For example, even when seen for the first time, a beautiful face is perceived as being more familiar than an unattractive one.

Many animals, too, appear to categorize specific individuals in their social encounters as friends or foes (Schusterman, Reichmuth, & Kastak, 2000). It may be helpful to remember that the word *familiar* is related to the word *family*. In a way, repeated exposure allows us to include new individuals and new aspects of the environment in our expanded "family."

■ Extensions of the Repeated Exposure Effect

Repeated exposure results in a more positive evaluation of a stimulus, even when a person is not aware of the exposure. In fact, the effect is stronger under these conditions (Bornstein & D'Agostino, 1992). In addition, the positive affect generated by repeated exposure to subliminal stimuli *generalizes* to other, similar stimuli and even to new, different stimuli (Monahan, Murphy, & Zajonc, 2000).

Not all individuals are equally responsive to the repeated exposure effect. People differ in their need for structure, and people high on this dimension are apt to organize their surroundings in simple rather than complex ways and to rely more heavily on stereotypes and categories when making judgments (Neuberg & Newsom, 1993). Hansen and Bartsch (2001) proposed that familiarity would have the greatest effect on liking among those with a high need for structure. When unfamiliar Turkish words were first presented to American students, they were rated more negatively by students high in need for structure than by those low in this need. After the participants were shown these words multiple times, the words were rated more positively by most of the participants, but the effect was greatest among students high in the need for structure.

As powerful as the repeated exposure effect has been found to be, it fails to operate when a person's initial reaction is extremely negative. Repeated exposure in this instance not only fails to bring about a more positive evaluation, it can lead to greater dislike (Swap, 1977). You may have experienced this yourself when a song or a commercial you disliked at first seems even worse when you hear it over.

Observable Characteristics: Instant Evaluations

Though positive affect from any source and the positive affect aroused by repeated exposure tend to result in attraction, it doesn't always work out that way. Sometimes people do not interact with the person sitting next to them or the person living in the next apartment. And, sometimes you may be attracted to someone who is not in close proximity—you might see a stranger "across a crowded room" and still be attracted. What might account for these contradictory behaviors? Instant likes and dislikes (first impressions) can arouse strong affect, sometimes strong enough to overcome the proximity effect.

How could a person we don't know elicit a strong emotional reaction? Whenever we like—or dislike—someone at first sight, this reaction suggests that something about that person has elicited positive or negative affect. Presumably, the affect is based on past experiences, stereotypes, and attributions that often are inaccurate and irrelevant (Andreoletti, Zebrowitz, & Lachman, 2001). For example, if a stranger reminds you of someone you know and like, you probably will respond positively to that person (Andersen & Baum, 1994). Or if the stranger belongs to a category of people about whom you hold a generalized attitude (e.g., individuals with a Southern accent), you may tend to like the stranger if you like that kind of accent or express dislike if you react to such an accent negatively. As discussed in

Figure 7.8 ■ A Negative Reaction to Observable Characteristics Can Prevent You from Knowing the Actual Person
In the movie *Shallow Hal*, Hal (Jack Black) only responds to the external appearance of women. When he is granted the power to see the "inner person," he perceives an overweight Gwyneth Paltrow as a beautiful woman.

Chapter 6, stereotypes about people are poor predictors of their behavior. Despite that fact, most people react strongly on the basis of their stereotypes.

■ Physical Attractiveness: Judging Books by Their Covers

You know that your reaction to the cover of this textbook is not a good indicator of how much you will like or dislike its contents. (We hope, by the way, that you like both.) Each of us has learned since childhood "not to judge books by their covers" and that "beauty is only skin deep" and "pretty is as pretty does." Nevertheless, it is repeatedly found that people are most likely to respond positively to those who are most attractive and negatively to those who are least attractive (Collins & Zebrowitz, 1995). Thus, a pervasive factor that influences one's initial response to others is **physical attractiveness** (Maner et al., 2003), as illustrated in Figure 7.8.

In experiments and the real world, physical appearance determines many types of interpersonal evaluations, including guilt or innocence in the courtroom and the grade on an essay (Cash & Trimer, 1984). People even respond more positively to attractive infants (Karraker & Stern, 1990). As we will discuss in Chapter 8, appearance also plays a major role in mate selection. One of the reasons we focus on appearance is that we hold stereotypes based on how people look. Before you read any further, take a look at Figure 7.9, and follow the instructions.

Most people tend to believe that attractive men and women are more poised, interesting, sociable, independent, dominant, exciting, sexy, well adjusted, socially skilled, successful, and more masculine (men) or more feminine (women) than unattractive individuals (Dion & Dion, 1987; Hatfield & Sprecher, 1986a). Altogether, as social psychologists documented over three decades ago, most people assume that "what is beautiful is good" (Dion, Berscheid, & Hatfield, 1972). Despite the powerful effects of attractiveness, people are not very accurate in estimating how they are perceived by others (Gabriel, Critelli, & Ee, 1994). The appearance issue seems to be more acute for women than for men, but some members of both genders experience

physical attractiveness
The combination of characteristics that are evaluated as beautiful or handsome at the positive extreme and as unattractive at the negative extreme.

Figure 7.9 ■ How Would You Describe These People?
Make a list of the personality characteristics that you think might describe these individuals. For example, what do you think about each person's sociability, adjustment, intelligence, poise, independence, masculinity–femininity, popularity, vanity, potential for success, integrity, concern for others, sexual appeal, and other qualities? When you are finished, return to the text to find out whether your perceptions correspond to those of most people and what has been found in psychological research.

appearance anxiety—an undue concern with how one looks. Those with the greatest anxiety agree with test items such as "I feel that most of my friends are more physically attractive than myself" and disagree with test items such as "I enjoy looking at myself in the mirror" (Dion, Dion, & Keelan, 1990). It probably comes as no surprise that when women watch TV commercials dealing with appearance, they begin focusing on how they look and express anger and dissatisfaction with themselves (Hargreaves & Tiggemann, 2002). A woman's comparison between herself and the women in the ads has the most negative effect if she perceives herself to be relatively unattractive (Patrick, Neighbors, & Knee, 2004).

appearance anxiety
Apprehension or worry about whether one's physical appearance is adequate and about the possible negative reactions of other people.

Although cross-cultural research indicates that positive stereotypes about attractiveness are universal, the *specific content* of the stereotypes depends on the characteristics most valued by each culture (Dion, Pak, & Dion, 1990). In a collectivist culture such as Korea, attractiveness is assumed to be associated with integrity and concern for others, but these attributes do not appear among the stereotypes that are common among individualistic North Americans (Wheeler & Kim, 1997).

Despite widespread acceptance of attractiveness as an important cue to personality and character, most of the widely held appearance stereotypes are *incorrect* (Feingold, 1992; Kenealy et al., 1991). Note that extraordinarily unpleasant individuals can be good looking, and many people who do not look like movie stars—Bill Gates, for example—are often intelligent, amusing, and so forth. Though the stereotypes about attractive people tend to be invalid, attractiveness actually *is* associated with popularity, good interpersonal skills, and high self-esteem (Diener, Wolsic, & Fujita, 1995; Johnstone, Frame, & Bouman, 1992). A probable reason for this association is that very attractive people have spent their lives being liked and treated well by other people who are responding to their appearance (Zebrowitz, Collins, & Dutta, 1998). And, those who are very attractive are aware that they are pretty or handsome (Marcus & Miller, 2003).

People who are beautiful are usually seen as "good," but attractiveness is also associated with a few negative assumptions. For example, beautiful women are sometimes perceived as vain and materialistic (Cash & Duncan, 1984). Also, handsome male political candidates are more likely to be elected than unattractive ones, but an attractive female candidate is *not* helped by her appearance (Sigelman et al., 1986). Possibly, being "too feminine" is assumed to be inappropriate for someone in a legislative, judicial, or executive position, although being "too masculine" is OK.

■ What, Exactly, Constitutes "Attractiveness"?

Judgments of one's own attractiveness may not match the judgments of others very well, but there is surprisingly good agreement when two people are asked to rate a third person (Cunningham et al., 1995; Fink & Penton-Voak, 2002). The greatest agreement occurs when men are judging the attractiveness of women (Marcus & Miller, 2003). Despite the consensus as to who is and is not attractive, it has proved difficult to identify the precise cues that determine these judgments.

In attempting to discover just what these cues might be, investigators have used two different procedures. One approach is to identify individuals who are perceived to be "attractive" and then to determine what they have in common. Cunningham (1986) asked male undergraduates to rate photographs of young women. The women who were judged to be most attractive fell into one of two groups. Some had "childlike features" consisting of large, widely spaced eyes and a small nose and chin. Women in this category are considered "cute" (Johnston & Oliver-Rodriguez, 1997; McKelvie, 1993a). The other category of attractive women had mature features, with prominent cheekbones, high eyebrows, large pupils, and a big smile. These same two general facial types are found among fashion models, and they appear with equal frequency among white, African American, and Asian women (Ashmore, Solomon, & Longo, 1996).

A second approach to the determination of what is meant by attractiveness was taken by Langlois and Roggman (1990). They began with several facial photographs and then used computer digitizing to combine multiple faces into one face. The image in each photo is divided into microscopic squares, and each square is assigned a number that represents a specific shade. Then the numbers are averaged across two or more pictures, and this average

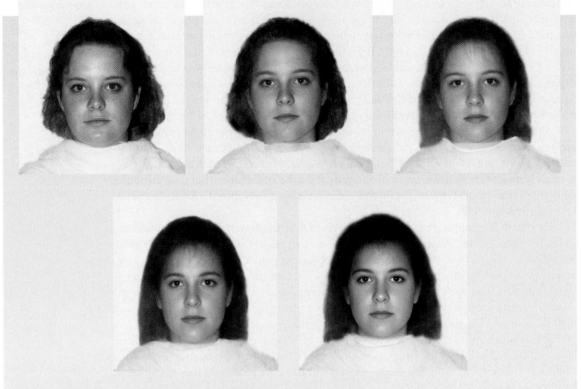

Figure 7.10 ■ Averaging Multiple Faces Results in an Attractive Face
When computer images of several different faces are combined to form a composite, the resulting average face is seen as more attractive than the individual faces that were averaged. As the number of faces contributing to the average increases, the attractiveness of the composite increases. (*Source: Lemley, 2000, p. 47.*)

is translated back into a corresponding shade. The overall result is assembled into a composite image of the combined faces.

You might guess that a face created by averaging would be rated as average in attractiveness. Instead, composite faces are rated as *more* attractive than most of the individual faces (Langlois, Roggman, & Musselman, 1994; Rhodes & Tremewan, 1996). In addition, the more faces that are averaged, the more beautiful the resulting face. As shown in Figure 7.10, when you combine as many as thirty-two faces, "you end up with a face that is pretty darned attractive" (Judith Langlois, as quoted in Lemley, 2000, p. 47).

It is possible to create an even more attractive face by taking initial attractiveness into account. For example, if you start with fifteen extremely attractive faces, their composite is more attractive than a composite of fifteen average faces (Perrett, May, & Yoshikawa, 1994). Another way to enhance the attractiveness of a composite face is to rate each face going into the mix and then to assign more weight to the most attractive faces. When biopsychologist Victor Johnston did this with a series of twenty generations of composites rated by ten thousand visitors to his website, the final face was extremely attractive and perceived to be more feminine than average (Lemley, 2000). With respect to male and female faces, a relatively feminine composite is preferred (Angier, 1998a).

Why should composite faces be especially attractive? It is possible that each person's schema of women and men is created in our cognitions in much the same way that the averaged face is created. We form such schemas on the basis of our experiences with different images, so a composite face is closer to that schema than any specific face. If this analysis is accurate, a composite of other images should also constitute the most attractive alternative, but it does *not* work with composite dogs or birds (Halberstadt & Rhodes, 2000). It may be that our perception of human composites is different because it was historically more

Chapter 7 / Interpersonal Attraction

important to our species to recognize potential friends, enemies, and mates than to recognize specific, individual dogs and birds.

In addition to the details of facial features, perceptions of attractiveness are also influenced by the situation. When research participants have been shown pictures of very attractive people, they then rate a stranger as less attractive than do participants who have not been looking at attractive pictures (Kenrick et al., 1993). Why? The difference creates what is known as a *contrast effect*. In a similar way, men rate their female partners less positively if they have just been looking at photos of very attractive women (Kenrick & Gutierres, 1980).

Other aspects of context also matter. As suggested by Mickey Gilley's song about searching for romance in bars, "the girls all get prettier at closing time." Research in bars indicates that "girls" (and "boys," too) are perceived as more attractive by members of the opposite sex as the evening progresses (Nida & Koon, 1983; Pennebaker et al., 1979). Ratings of same-sex strangers by heterosexuals do not improve as closing time approaches, so alcohol consumption does not explain the effects (Gladue & Delaney, 1990). Rather, as people pair off and the number of available partners decreases, the resulting scarcity results in a more positive evaluation of those who remain.

■ Other Aspects of Appearance and Behavior That Influence Attraction

When we meet someone for the first time, we usually react to a variety of factors. Any observable cue, no matter how superficial, may evoke a stereotype, and the resulting emotional reactions lead to instant likes and dislikes. One of the factors that has been studied is clothing (Cheverton & Byrne, 1998; Jarrell, 1998). Beyond such factors as neatness (Mack & Rainey, 1990), clothing colors seem to have an effect. People make an automatic association between brightness and affect; specifically, bright equals good, and dark equals bad (Meier, Robinson, & Clore, 2004). Attraction is also influenced by the presence of observable disabilities (Fichten & Amsel, 1986), behaviors that suggest mental illness (Schumacher, Corrigan, & Dejong, 2003), perceived age (McKelvie, 1993b), the presence of eyeglasses (Lundberg & Sheehan, 1994), and a man's facial hair (Shannon & Stark, 2003).

Among other observable characteristics, a person's physique is associated with stereotypes that trigger emotional reactions and differential attraction. It was once thought that body type provided information about personality (Sheldon, Stevens, & Tucker, 1940), but decades of research indicated that this assumption was inaccurate. Nevertheless, people respond to others as if physique provided useful information. Though these observations are untrue, people believe that a round and fat body indicates a sad and sloppy person, that a hard and muscular body indicates good health and lack of intelligence, and a thin and angular body indicates intelligence and fearfulness (Gardner & Tockerman, 1994; Ryckman et al., 1989).

In these and other investigations, a consistent finding is that the least liked physique is one characterized by excess fat (Harris, Harris, & Bochner, 1982; Lundberg & Sheehan, 1994), as in Figure 7.11. Obesity even functions as a stigma, and the stigma can rub off onto others—a man sitting with an overweight woman is evaluated more negatively than a man sitting with a woman of average weight (Hebl & Mannix, 2003). Once again, it is important to remember that stereotypes associated with weight do not lead to accurate predictions about how an individual can be expected to behave (Miller et al., 1995a).

Crandall (1994) equates prejudice against obesity with racial prejudice, and he developed a measure of antifat prejudice consisting

Figure 7.11 ■ Obesity as a Stigma
Along with facial attractiveness, weight is an observable characteristic that elicits consistent stereotypes. In many cultures, negative attitudes about obesity influence various aspects of interpersonal behavior. As with others who are the object of stereotyping, overweight individuals sometimes fight back with anger or humor. Shown here is a rally for the Million Pound March in southern California.

of such statements as "I really don't like fat people much" and "Fat people tend to be fat pretty much through their own fault." Though there is a prevailing prejudice in the United States against overweight people, in Mexico and other collectivist cultures there is much less concern about weight and a less negative reaction to those who are overweight (Crandall & Martinez, 1996; Crandall et al., 2001).

Observable differences in overt behavior also elicit stereotypes that influence attraction. A youthful walking style elicits a more positive response than an elderly style, regardless of gender or actual age (Montepare & Zebrowitz-McArthur, 1988). A person with a firm handshake is perceived as being extroverted and emotionally expressive (Chaplin et al., 2000). People respond positively to someone whose behavior is animated (Bernieri et al., 1996), who actively participates in class discussions (Bell, 1995), and who acts modestly rather than arrogantly (Hareli & Weiner, 2000).

In initial encounters, men who behave in a dominant, authoritative, competitive way are preferred to those who seem submissive, noncompetitive, and less masculine (Friedman, Riggio, & Casella, 1988). When subsequent interactions provide additional information about the individual, however, the preference shifts to men who are prosocial and sensitive (Jensen-Campbell, West, & Graziano, 1995; Morey & Gerber, 1995). It might be said that nice guys finish first when you get to know them.

Interpersonal judgments are also influenced by what a person eats (Stein & Nemeroff, 1995). Regardless of factors such as height and weight, a person who eats "good food" (e.g., oranges, salad) is perceived as more likeable and morally superior to one who eats "bad food" (e.g., French fries, donuts, double-fudge sundaes).

One final, and perhaps most surprising, influence on interpersonal perceptions is a person's first name. Familiar names activate a category of experience and information that provides us with a stereotype (Macrae, Mitchell, & Pendry, 2002). And, various male and female names elicit widely shared positive and negative stereotypes (Mehrabian & Piercy, 1993), as shown in Table 7.1. A distinctive first name for a highly publicized individual (real or

Table 7.1 ■ What's in a Name? The Answer Is Stereotypes

Initial impressions are sometimes based on a person's first name. Once again, stereotypes lead to inaccurate assumptions, which influence interpersonal behavior.

MALE NAMES	FEMALE NAMES	ATTRIBUTIONS ABOUT THE INDIVIDUAL
Alexander	Elizabeth	Successful
Otis	Mildred	Unsuccessful
Joshua	Mary	Moral
Roscoe	Tracy	Immoral
Mark	Jessica	Popular
Norbert	Harriet	Unpopular
Henry	Ann	Warm
Ogden	Freida	Cold
Scott	Brittany	Cheerful
Willard	Agatha	Not cheerful
Taylor	Rosalyn	Masculine
Eugene	Isabella	Feminine

(*Source:* Based on information in Mehrabian & Piercy, 1993.)

fictional) becomes associated with some of the characteristics of that individual; the resulting stereotype then transfers to anyone else who has that name. What would your first thought be if you met someone named Osama, Bart, Whoopi, or Gwyneth?

KEY POINTS

★ The initial contact between two people is often based on the *proximity* that is the result of such physical aspects of the environment as seating assignments, residence locations, and workplaces.

★ Proximity leads to the *repeated exposure* of two individuals to one another. Repeated exposure usually results in positive affect, which results in attraction—a process known as the *mere exposure effect*.

★ Interpersonal attraction and judgments based on stereotypes are strongly affected by various observable char-

acteristics, including *physical attractiveness*. People like and make positive attributions about attractive men and women, despite the fact that assumptions based on appearance are usually inaccurate.

★ In addition to attractiveness, other observable characteristics influence initial interpersonal evaluations, including physique, weight, behavioral style, food preferences, first names, and other superficial characteristics.

Interactive Determinants of Attraction: Similarity and Mutual Liking

We have learned that the formation of any kind of relationship between two people is facilitated by the need for affiliation, positive affect, physical proximity, and a positive reaction to the observable characteristics of one another. The next steps toward interpersonal closeness involve communication: the extent to which the interacting individuals discover their degree of *similarity* and the extent to which they indicate *mutual liking* by what they say and do.

Similarity: Birds of a Feather Actually Do Flock Together

The role of similarity in fostering interpersonal attraction is now generally accepted. This phenomenon has been observed and discussed for over two thousand years, beginning with Aristotle's (330 B.C./1932) essay on friendship. Empirical support for the "similarity hypothesis" was not provided, however, until Sir Francis Galton (1870/1952) obtained correlational data on married couples, indicating that spouses resemble one another in many respects. In the first half of the twentieth century, additional correlational studies continued to find that friends and spouses were more similar than would occur by chance (e.g., Hunt, 1935). Such similarity could have meant either that liking led to similarity or vice versa, but Newcomb (1956) studied university transfer students and found that similar attitudes (assessed before the students met) predicted subsequent liking. In addition, later experiments manipulated similarity and then assessed attraction, coming to the same conclusion (Byrne, 1961b; Schachter, 1951). As Aristotle and others had speculated, the data indicate clearly that two people who find that they are similar like each other *because* they are similar.

Before we describe some of the research on similarity, you may be asking, "What about the 'fact' that opposites attract?" Do they? Most people, including especially those who write scripts for movies and television, clearly believe that the answer is "yes." In the realm of empirical evidence, however, similarity is found to be the rule. See **The Science of Social Psychology: Making Sense of Common Sense** section that follows.

MAKING SENSE OF COMMON SENSE

Complementarity: Do Opposites Attract?

The idea that "opposites attract" is nearly as ancient as the idea that "birds of a feather flock together" and as new as the last movie you saw in which two very different people become friends, roommates, or romantic partners. In plays, movies, and television series, a familiar story line is one in which two very different people are attracted to one another. Think, for example, of Will and Grace, the couples in *Maid in Manhattan* and *Along Came Polly*, not to mention Marge and Homer Simpson, plus many others. In contrast, real-life examples of such pairings are relatively rare (Angier, 2003; Buston & Emlen, 2003). Even when opposites do form a relationship (e.g., a married couple

Figure 7.12 ■ With Rare Exceptions, Opposites Don't Attract
Though the belief that opposites attract is a familiar one in fiction, similarity is a much better predictor of attraction. Even when seemingly opposite people do attract one another (as with Democrat James Carville and his wife, Republican Mary Matalin), they still have a great deal in common.

like Democratic strategist James Carville and Republican strategist Mary Matalin; see Figure 7.12), one can guess that despite their opposing political views, they have a great deal in common. For example, both are intensely interested in the political process, and party differences represent only a relatively limited set of disagreements.

In the early days of research on this topic, the proposed attraction of opposites was often phrased in terms of complementarity. It was suggested that dominant individuals would be attracted to submissive ones, talkative people to quiet ones, sadists to masochists, and so on. The idea was that such complementary characteristics would be mutually reinforcing and hence a good basis for a relationship. Direct tests, however, failed to support complementarity as a determinant of attraction, even with characteristics like dominance and submissiveness (Palmer & Byrne, 1970). With respect to attitudes, values, personality characteristics, bad habits, intellectual ability, income level, and even minor preferences, similarity results in attraction (Byrne, 1971). On the basis of multiple experiments over several decades, one can only conclude that there is no evidence that opposites attract.

There is, however, consistent evidence that complementarity *sometimes* operates in a specific situation (e.g., when a male and female are interacting). Specifically, when one person engages in dominant behavior, the other then responds in a submissive fashion (Markey, Funder, & Ozer, 2003; Sadler & Woody, 2003). This situation-specific kind of complementarity leads to greater attraction than when the second person copies the first (Tiedens & Fragale, 2003). With other kinds of interaction (e.g., a verbally withdrawn person interacting with a verbally expressive and critical person), opposite styles not only fail to attract, they are especially incompatible and more likely to bring about rejection and avoidance (Swann, Rentfrow, & Gosling, 2003).

similarity–dissimilarity effect
The consistent finding that people respond positively to indications that another person is similar to themselves and negatively to indications that another person is dissimilar from themselves.

attitude similarity
The extent to which two individuals share the same attitudes about a range of topics. In practice, the term also includes similarity of beliefs, values, and interests—as well as attitudes.

■ Similarity–Dissimilarity: A Consistent Predictor of Attraction

Much of the early work on the **similarity–dissimilarity effect** focused on **attitude similarity,** but this phrase was generally used as a short-hand term that included not only similarity of attitudes, but also beliefs, values, and interests. The initial experiments on this topic consisted of two steps: First, participants' attitudes were assessed, and second, these individuals were exposed to a stranger's attitudes and asked to evaluate him or her (Byrne, 1961b). The results were straightforward in that people consistently liked similar strangers much better than dissimilar ones. Not only do we like people who are similar to ourselves, we also judge them to be more intelligent, better informed, more moral, and better adjusted. As you might suspect on the basis of our discussion of affect earlier in this chapter, similarity arouses positive feelings and dissimilarity arouses negative feelings.

Many such investigations with a variety of populations, procedures, and topics, revealed that people respond to similarity–dissimilarity in a surprisingly precise way. Attraction is determined by the **proportion of similarity.** That is, when the number of topics on which

Chapter 7 / Interpersonal Attraction

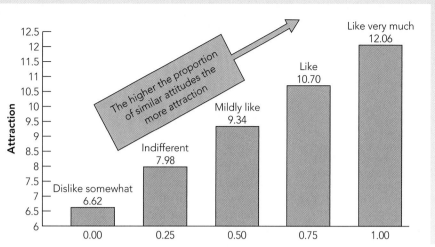

Figure 7.13 ■ As Proportion of Similar Attitudes Increases, Attraction Increases
The relationship between proportion of similar attitudes and attraction is consistent and highly predictable. The greater the proportion of similar attitudes, the greater the attraction. The relationship can be expressed in a simple linear formula, and it holds true for both genders and across age groups, cultures, and educational levels.

two people express similar views is divided by the total number of topics on which they have communicated, the resulting proportion can be inserted in a simple formula that allows us to predict their attraction to one another (Byrne & Nelson, 1965). The higher the proportion of similarity, the greater the liking, as illustrated in Figure 7.13. No one knows exactly how attitudinal information is processed to produce that outcome, but it is *as if* people automatically engage in some kind of cognitive addition and division, manipulating the units of positive and negative affect they experience.

The effect of attitude similarity on attraction is strong, and it holds true regardless of the number of topics on which people express their views and how important or trivial the topics may be. It holds equally true for males and females, regardless of age, educational, or cultural differences (Byrne, 1971).

The most serious challenge to the validity of such findings was offered by Rosenbaum (1986) when he proposed that using proportion as the independent variable made it impossible to separate the effect of similarity from the effect of dissimilarity. Based on data he gathered, the **repulsion hypothesis** was put forth as an alternative to the *similarity–dissimilarity effect*. The basic idea is that information about similarity has no effect on attraction—people are simply repulsed by information about dissimilarity. Later research showed that the idea is wrong (Smeaton, Byrne, & Murnen, 1989), but there was a grain of truth in the repulsion hypothesis. Under most circumstances information about dissimilarity has a *slightly stronger effect* on attraction than the same amount of information about similarity (Chen & Kenrick, 2002; Singh & Ho, 2000; Tan & Singh, 1995).

Beyond attitudes, values, and so forth, many kinds of similarity–dissimilarity have been investigated, and in each instance, people prefer those who are similar to themselves. Examples include similarity–dissimilarity with respect to physical attractiveness (Zajonc et al., 1987), smoking marijuana (Eisenman, 1985), religious practices (Kandel, 1978), self-concept (Klohnen & Luo, 2003), being a "morning person" versus an "evening person" (Watts, 1982), and finding the same jokes amusing (Cann, Calhoun, & Banks, 1995).

Is it possible that people seek similarity with their pets as well? It has often been suggested that people resemble their dogs, but is that true? This proposition has recently been tested, and it seems to be accurate. Roy and Christenfeld (2004) took separate photographs of dogs and of pet owners. College students (who didn't know the people in the pictures) were shown an owner along with two dog pictures—one was that person's dog and the other was a picture of an other dog. The students were asked to guess which dog was the person's pet, and the matches were correct more often than would have occurred by chance. Note that this finding holds only for purebred dogs and not mixed breeds, presumably because people are unconsciously seeking a pet similar to themselves, but a puppy's eventual appearance can consistently be predicted only for pure breeds.

proportion of similarity
The number of specific indicators that two people are similar divided by the number of specific indicators that two people are similar plus the number of specific indicators that they are dissimilar.

repulsion hypothesis
Rosenbaum's provocative proposal that attraction is not increased by similar attitudes but is simply decreased by dissimilar attitudes. This hypothesis is incorrect as stated, but it is true that dissimilar attitudes tend to have negative effects that are stronger than the positive effects of similar attitudes.

There a few partial exceptions to the similarity effect. One example is the degree to which two people are similar with respect to ideal self. Similarity to ideal self has a positive effect (as is true of other types of similarity), but discovering that someone is closer to your ideal than you are is also threatening (Herbst, Gaertner, & Insko, 2003). Leaving aside such minor exceptions, why do people usually respond to similarity and dissimilarity in a positive versus negative way?

■ Explaining the Effect of Similarity–Dissimilarity on Attraction

To ask the general question another way, *why* does similarity elicit positive affect, while dissimilarity elicits negative affect? The oldest explanation—**balance theory**—was proposed independently by Newcomb (1961) and Heider (1958). This formulation states that people naturally organize their likes and dislikes in a symmetrical way (Hummert, Crockett, & Kemper, 1990). When two people like each other and discover they are similar in some specific respect, this constitutes a state of *balance,* and balance is emotionally pleasant. When two people like each other and find they are dissimilar in some specific respect, the result is *imbalance.* Imbalance is emotionally unpleasant, causing the individuals to strive to restore balance by inducing one of them to change and thus create similarity, by misperceiving the dissimilarity, or by deciding to dislike one another. Whenever two people dislike one another, their relationship involves *nonbalance.* This is not especially pleasant or unpleasant, because each individual is indifferent to the other person's similarities or dissimilarities.

These aspects of balance theory are correct, but they do not deal with the question of why similarity should matter in the first place. So, a second level of explanation is needed. Why should you care if someone differs from you with respect to musical preferences, belief in God, or anything else? One answer is provided by aspects of Festinger's (1954) *social comparison theory.* Briefly stated, you compare your attitudes and beliefs with those of others because the only way you can evaluate your accuracy and normality is by finding that other people agree with you. This is not a perfect way to determine the truth, but it is often the best we can do. For example, if you are the *only one* who believes that invisible Martians have landed and are living in your attic, the odds are that you are incorrect and perhaps delusional. No one wants to be in that position, so we turn to others to obtain *consensual validation* (see Chapter 9). When you learn that someone else shares your attitudes and beliefs, it feels good, because such information suggests that you have sound judgment, are normal and in contact with reality. Dissimilarity suggests the opposite, and that creates negative affect. We all are anxious to be "right, sensible, and sane," but we each have some degree of self-doubt. You may have observed two people arguing and getting angry about issues for which there is no way to prove that either is correct—"It is when we are not sure that we are doubly sure" (Niebuhr, as quoted by Beinart, 1998, p. 25).

A third approach to an explanation of the similarity–dissimilarity effect rests on an evolutionary perspective as an **adaptive response** to potential danger. Gould (1996) suggests that our negative reaction to dissimilar others may have originated when humans were living in small groups of hunters and gatherers on the savannas of Africa. A great deal of human animosity is based on reactions to dissimilarity. In the words of Howard Stern, "If you're not like me, I hate you" (Zoglin, 1993). It seems that the worst acts of barbarism are directed toward those who differ in race, ethnicity, language, religious beliefs, sexual orientation, political affiliation, and so on: "Programmed into the human soul is a preference for the near and familiar" (McDonald, 2001).

Imagine what it was like when a band of our primitive ancestors accidentally encountered another band. Horney (1950) described three basic alternative reactions: Our ancient relatives could have moved *toward* them with a friendly intent; *away from* them, out of fear, with a self-protective intent; or *against* them with an aggressive intent. Under specific circumstances, monkeys have been observed to engage in each of these three patterns when they spot an unfamiliar monkey (Carpenter, 2001a).

Potential consequences are associated with the response choices. If the strangers are good and kind, a friendly approach could benefit both. If, however, the strangers posed a threat (perhaps most likely), then greeting them with friendliness and trust would be the most dangerous and least adaptive response. Survival, and hence reproduction, would best be enhanced by either retreating or attacking, and the latter is probably the most effective way to survive. Humans are not the only species to aggress against strangers. Male

---

balance theory
The formulations of Heider and of Newcomb that specify the relationships among (1) an individual's liking for another person, (2) his or her attitude about a given topic, and (3) the other person's attitude about the same topic. Balance (liking plus agreement) results in a positive emotional state. Imbalance (liking plus disagreement) results in a negative state and a desire to restore balance. Nonbalance (disliking plus either agreement or disagreement) leads to indifference.

adaptive response
Any physical characteristic or behavioral tendency that enhances the odds of reproductive success for an individual or for other individuals with similar genes.

chimpanzees, for example, band together to kill chimps from a different group. By destroying the outsiders, the killers weaken the rival band, expand their territory, and provide additional food for their mates and offspring (Wilson & Wrangham, 2003; Wade, 2003). Similar behavior is common even among mice (Stowers et al., 2002): "Male mice are genetically programmed to follow a simple rule when a strange mouse enters their territory. If it's a male, attack it; if female, seduce it" (Wade, 2002, p. F3).

This general account at least seems plausible. If it is accurate, we may be programmed to fear and hate those who are different, especially if they are males. There is increasing evidence that we are automatically vigilant in reacting to cues that alert us to positive or negative consequences of interaction and therefore to approach or avoid those cues (Bargh, 1997; Wentura, Rothermund, & Bak, 2000). Though these various reactions may have been crucial to survival and reproductive success for our species, today they form the basis for prejudice, hate crimes, terrorism, genocide, and a general dislike of anyone "different."

Attraction: Progressing from Bits and Pieces to an Overall Picture

Throughout this chapter, we have stressed that attraction is based on positive and negative affective responses that lead us to make evaluations. This general formulation is known as the **affect-centered model of attraction.** The emphasis on affect does not mean, however, that cognitive processes are irrelevant. As shown in Figure 7.14, Person B's affective state (either directly aroused by Person A or simply associated with Person A) is conceptualized as playing a major role in determining how B evaluates A, as well as B's subsequent behavior toward A. It is also necessary, however, for B to engage in cognitively processing all available information about A. Such information includes stereotypes, beliefs, and factual knowledge and can therefore have an additional influence on affective arousal, enhancing or mitigating B's initial evaluation (Montoya & Horton, 2004).

As an example of the interplay of affect and cognition, let's return to the issue of responding aggressively to those who are dissimilar. Cognitive and language skills enable us to dehumanize whomever we attack, and this helps justify our aggression. Compared with the behavior of predators such as lions, however, human aggression is notably vicious. Bandura (1999a) makes the point that it is all too easy to disengage moral control and thus justify

affect-centered model of attraction
A conceptual framework in which attraction is assumed to be based on positive and negative emotions. These emotions can be aroused directly by another person or simply associated with that person. The emotional arousal can also be enhanced or mitigated by cognitive processes.

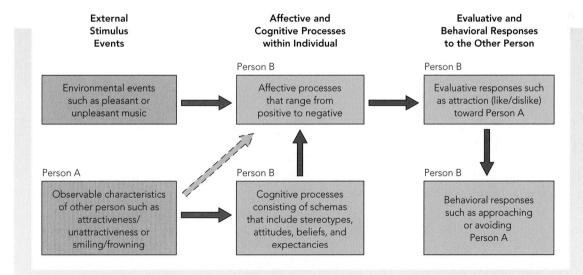

Figure 7.14 ■ The Affect-Centered Model of Attraction
Attraction toward a given person is based on the relative number of positive and negative affective responses that are aroused by that person, by other external events, or by internal factors, including cognitive processes. The net affective state forms the basis of an evaluative response such as like or dislike and also of a behavioral response such as approach or avoidance. (*Source: Based on material in Byrne, 1992.*)

cruel and inhumane acts. It is easy, for example, to attribute one's angry, fear-inspired, violent impulses to others: "It is justifiable to harm them, because they intend to harm me" (Schimel et al., 2000). And once the violent, harmful, evil behavior begins, it grows increasingly intense (Staub, 1999). Though the initial dislike of a stranger may be based on affective factors, the justification for that affect and the subsequent decision about the most appropriate way to respond are based on cognitive factors. (Keep in mind that dissimilarity is only one source of provocation to aggress. As we discuss in Chapter 11, there are multiple determinants of human aggression.)

Mutual Evaluations: Reciprocal Liking or Disliking

Note that Person B in Figure 7.14 is not the only one experiencing arousal, processing information, and making evaluations. Person A is engaged in reciprocal reactions to Person B. The specific details of such a dyadic interaction can result in moving the two people toward a relationship based on mutual liking, as described in Chapter 8, or away from a relationship. We will focus on mutual liking—the intermediate step between *initial attraction* and the establishment of an *interpersonal relationship*.

When each interacting individual communicates a positive evaluation of the other, this realization of mutual attraction is an added positive experience for each of them. Most of us are pleased to receive positive feedback and displeased to receive negative feedback (Gordon, 1996).

Not only do we enjoy being evaluated positively, we welcome such an evaluation when it is inaccurate or an insincere attempt at flattery. To an outside observer, false flattery may be perceived accurately, but to the person being flattered, it is likely to appear honest and accurate (Gordon, 1996; Vonk, 1998, 2002). Using this type of ingratiation technique to deal with a boss or supervisor may disgust one's coworkers, but pay off in raises and promotions (Orpen, 1996). In 1831, Tocqueville observed that Americans had a special talent for ingratiating themselves with anybody and everybody who could help them in any way (Lapham, 1996).

At times, the first sign of attraction is nonverbal. If an acquaintance sits next to you in class, you reasonably interpret this as a positive sign of his or her feelings. In this instance, liking leads to proximity rather than the reverse (Byrne, Baskett, & Hodges, 1971). Another example is when a woman maintains eye contact while talking to a man and leans toward him. The man tends to interpret these acts (sometimes incorrectly) to mean that she likes him. Her positive signals may lead him to like her (Gold, Ryckman, & Mosley, 1984).

In a more general sense, our lives are made more pleasant by genuine, sincere communication of positive feelings about one another—and sometimes even by positive messages that are not entirely genuine and sincere. In contrast, negative interpersonal communications almost always elicit unpleasant reactions. Put simply, it never hurts to be nice, but it always hurts to be nasty.

KEY POINTS

★ One of the many factors determining attraction toward another person is similarity of attitudes, beliefs, values, and interests.

★ Despite the continuing popularity of the idea that opposites attract, especially in fiction, it rarely occurs in the real world.

★ Though dissimilarity tends to have a greater impact on attraction than similarity, we respond to both, and the larger the *proportion of similarity*, the greater the attraction.

★ The *similarity–dissimilarity effect* has been explained by *balance theory*, social comparison theory, and by an

evolutionary perspective as an adaptive response to potential danger.

★ An overall summary of the major determinants of attraction is provided by the *affect-centered model of attraction*, which stipulates that attraction is determined by direct and associated sources of affect, often mediated by cognitive processes.

★ We especially like other people who indicate in word or deed that they like and positively evaluate us. We dislike those who dislike and negatively evaluate us.

Internal Determinants of Attraction: The Need to Affiliate and the Basic Role of Affect

- *Interpersonal attraction* refers to the evaluations we make of other people—the positive and negative attitudes we form about them.

- Human beings are apparently born with a *need for affiliation*, the motivation to interact with other people in a cooperative way, often relying on shared laughter to smooth the way.

- Positive and negative affective states influence attraction both directly and indirectly. Direct effects occur when another person is responsible for arousing the emotion. Indirect effects occur when the source of the emotion is elsewhere and another person is simply associated with its presence.

External Determinants of Attraction: Proximity and Observable Characteristics

- The initial contact between two people is often based on the *proximity* that is the result of such physical aspects of the environment as seating assignments, residence locations, and workplaces.

- Proximity leads to the *repeated exposure* of two individuals to one another. Repeated exposure usually results in positive affect, which results in attraction—a process known as the *mere exposure effect*.

- Interpersonal attraction and judgments based on stereotypes are strongly affected by various observable characteristics, including *physical attractiveness*. People like and make positive attributions about attractive men and women, despite the fact that assumptions based on appearance are usually inaccurate.

- In addition to attractiveness, other observable characteristics influence initial interpersonal evaluations, including physique, weight, behavioral style, food preferences, first names, and other superficial characteristics.

Interactive Determinants of Attraction: Similarity and Mutual Liking

- One of the many factors determining attraction toward another person is similarity of attitudes, beliefs, values, and interests.

- Despite the continuing popularity of the idea that opposites attract, especially in fiction, it rarely occurs in the real world.

- Though dissimilarity tends to have a greater impact on attraction than similarity, we respond to both, and the larger the *proportion of similarity information*, the greater the attraction.

- The *similarity–dissimilarity effect* has been explained by *balance theory*, social comparison theory, and by an evolutionary perspective as an adaptive response to potential danger.

- An overall summary of the major determinants of attraction is provided by the *affect-centered model of attraction*, which stipulates that attraction is determined by direct and associated sources of affect, often mediated by cognitive processes.

- We especially like other people who indicate in word or deed that they like and positively evaluate us. We dislike those who dislike and negatively evaluate us.

Connections INTEGRATING SOCIAL PSYCHOLOGY

In this chapter, you read about . . .	In other chapters, you will find related discussions of . . .
attitudes about people	attitudes (Chapter 4)
conditioning of affect/attraction	conditioning of attitudes (Chapter 4)
similarity and attraction	similarity and friendship, love, and marriage (Chapter 8)
effects of physical attractiveness	attractiveness and love (Chapter 8)
appearance and stereotypes	prejudice and stereotypes (Chapter 6)

Thinking about Connections

1. Pick one person you know very well. Can you remember exactly how you met? When did you decide that you liked this individual? Why do you think you liked him or her? Are there any connections between your personal experience and the chapter discussion about the factors influencing attraction?

2. Give some thought to the physical appearance of someone you don't know very well but see in class, in your neighborhood, or at work. On the basis of the person's attractiveness, physique, accent, clothing, or whatever else you have observed, what can you conclude? Have you ever talked to him or her? Why, or why not? Do you perceive any connections between prejudice and your evaluation of this individual?

3. Consider some issues about which you have strong attitudes and beliefs. Do you ever discuss these topics with your acquaintances or friends? How do you react when others agree? What happens when they disagree? Have disagreements ever caused you to stop interacting with someone you once liked? Think about why agreement and disagreement might matter to you.

4. What is your first reaction when you see a stranger? Do you feel friendly, fearful, angry? Does it matter if this person is different from you in appearance, clothing, or accent?

5. Do you ever compliment other people, tell them you like them, or comment favorably on something they have done? If so, how did they respond? Describe what you believe is going on in this kind of interaction. Consider also the opposite situation, in which you have criticized someone, indicated your dislike, or given a negative evaluation. What happens in that kind of interaction?

Ideas to Take with You—and Use!

WHAT CAN YOU DO TO MAKE PEOPLE LIKE YOU?

Most of us would rather be liked than disliked, and attraction research provides a lot of information that can be helpful when we interact with other people.

Make Proximity Work for You
Whenever possible, don't passively accept the accidental demands of the environment. Instead, play an active role by taking advantage of proximity opportunities. In a lunchroom, for example, sit near other people with whom you can talk instead of sitting by yourself.

Make the Most of Your Own Appearance and Look Beyond the Appearance of Others
Within reasonable limits, do what you can to look your best with respect to weight, hair, clothing, and so on. At the same time, try not to judge others on the basis of inaccurate stereotypes. Get to know people as they actually are and not on the basis of skin color, height, accent, or whatever.

Create Positive Affect
Do your best to create a positive mood. If you can, say something to make others laugh, and avoid criticizing others. Smile!

Emphasize Similarities and Minimize Differences
You don't need to lie about your attitudes and beliefs, but there is no reason to concentrate on disagreements and dissimilarities. When you don't agree, deal with it in an open-minded and nondogmatic way that doesn't sound like an attack on the other person.

KEY TERMS

adaptive response (p. 206)

affect (p. 191)

affect-centered model of
  attraction (p. 207)

appearance anxiety (p. 199)

attitude similarity (p. 204)

balance theory (p. 206)

interpersonal attraction (p. 189)

mere exposure effect (p. 196)

need for affiliation (p. 190)

physical attractiveness (p. 198)

proportion of similarity (p. 204)

proximity (p. 195)

repeated exposure (p. 196)

repulsion hypothesis (p. 205)

similarity–dissimilarity effect (p. 204)

8 CLOSE RELATIONSHIPS
Family, Friends, Lovers, and Spouses

The following story is based on actual experiences, but the events described by a variety of couples have been combined to avoid embarrassment for specific couples.

Greg and Linda met when they were in college, sitting in the same row of an introductory course in anthropology. They talked a few times, and when she had to miss class once, Linda asked if she could borrow Greg's notes. Soon after, they began hanging out at various campus events. One night during a keg party at Greg's fraternity house, they went to an empty room and, without actually saying much, simply had sex. The next week they met for coffee and began talking seriously about their feelings, love, and the future. From then on, they were a "couple"—two people in an exclusive relationship that includes physical intimacy and joyful, exciting conversations about the future and marriage. They didn't talk about money, careers, or parenthood—why should two people in love spoil everything with details?

Shortly after graduation, they had a beautiful wedding, went to Jamaica for what they agreed was a perfect honeymoon, and returned to a small apartment near the university where Greg would attend graduate school. The first several months were a continuation of their life before marriage, but more convenient, more exciting, and more "grown up." They were happy, and their future seemed bright and endless.

Over time, a few problems began to arise. Linda had been an excellent student with plans to attend law school, but there was no law school at Greg's new university. Her plans would have to be postponed. Greg worked hard as a graduate student and spent a good deal of time in the library and in the lab where he was a research assistant. Sometimes he had to work on the weekends, and some evenings he came home late, with beer on his breath. One night, Linda brought up her desire to have kids—at least two but maybe more. Greg told her, for the first time, that he had no desire to be a father. They more or less compromised on a "substitute baby" by adopting a kitten. Greg's late nights became more frequent, and Linda worried that he might be seeing someone else. She feared that Greg would dump her because she was "just a housewife," while he was surrounded by women working on advanced degrees. He believed that Linda was "too possessive."

Figure 8.1 ■ Love Is Often Blind
In choosing a romantic partner or a spouse, we often see what we want to see and believe what we want to believe, just like this snail. Eventually, the lover comes to his or her senses and perceives the loved one more accurately. (*Source: © The New Yorker Collection 1998 Sam Gross from cartoonbank.com. All Rights Reserved.*)

"I don't care if she is a tape dispenser. I love her."

They drifted steadily apart. Without telling Greg, she shopped around for a lawyer; one day he came home to find a note telling him that she had filed for divorce. What happened, and why did a romantic, loving relationship turn into an unpleasant year of arguments, insults, and accusations?

We hope to answer some of these questions. You might want to look back at the story of Linda and Greg from time to time whenever you find possible explanations for the things that went wrong. One familiar sort of problem is illustrated in Figure 8.1. Love (as well as lust) is often blind, in that we see what we want to see and believe what we want to believe. What do you think—will the relationship between the snail and the tape dispenser work out?

The study of *interpersonal attraction* has been a major focus of social psychology since early in the twentieth century, but the investigation of *interpersonal relationships* was largely ignored until the second half of that century. Social psychologists have made up for lost time by turning their attention to relationships in general (Berscheid & Reis, 1998), relationships within families (Boon & Brussoni, 1998), love and intimacy (Hatfield & Rapson, 1993), and marriage (Sternberg & Hojjat, 1997).

In this chapter, we describe what psychologists have learned about relationships. One's first experiences with *interdependent relationships* are with family members. During infancy and early childhood, *attachment patterns* develop, and these can affect one's interpersonal behavior throughout life. We then discuss the establishment of friendships and one of the consequences of not being able to form such relationships—*loneliness*. We also examine *romantic relationships* and what is meant by *love*. The final topic is *marriage,* and we describe the major factors involved in the success or failure of such a union, as well as the often painful consequences of divorce.

Interdependent Relationships with Family and Friends versus Loneliness

All close relationships share one common characteristic: **interdependence.** This term refers to an interpersonal association in which two people consistently influence each other's lives (Holmes, 2002). They often focus their thoughts and emotions on one another and regularly engage in joint activities. Interdependent relationships with family members, friends, and romantic partners include a sense of commitment to the relationship itself (Fehr, 1999). Interdependence occurs across age groups and different interactions. The importance of forming such bonds with other people is emphasized by Ryff and Singer (2000, p. 30), who propose, "Quality ties to others are universally endorsed as central to optimal living."

interdependence
The characteristic that is common to all close relationships. Interdependence refers to an interpersonal association in which two people influence each others' lives. They often focus their thoughts on one another and regularly engage in joint activities.

Figure 8.2 ■ Humans and Our Closest Primate Relatives Evolved as Social Beings
There is a good deal of evidence that the human need for close relationships was adaptive for our ancestors, human and otherwise. DNA studies show that chimpanzees and bonobos are our closest primate relatives, and they are similar to us in much of their social behavior, including mother–infant bonding and the formation of cooperative friendships.

The affection felt by mothers for their offspring ("mother love") appears to be based in part on specific hormones (Maestripieri, 2001). Do other interpersonal bonds (e.g., between friends and lovers) also rest on biological factors? As discussed in Chapter 7 with respect to the *need for affiliation,* there is good reason to believe that our need for companionship is an adaptive mechanism that benefited our ancestors, increasing the odds that they would survive and reproduce. Animal studies provide evidence that social attachment depends on specific neurochemical systems (Curtis & Wang, 2003). DNA evidence indicates that chimpanzees and bonobos are our closest nonhuman relatives, and they are more closely related to us than they are to gorillas or orangutans (Smuts, 2000/2001). Field studies of these primates reveal that they interact socially much as we do. They hug, kiss, and form long-term social bonds such as mother–offspring, friendship pairs, and mates (see Figure 8.2).

We now take a closer look at human relationships, beginning with the family.

Family: Where Relationships and Attachment Styles Begin

Parent–child interactions are of basic importance because this is usually one's first contact with another person. It is logical to suppose that our attitudes and expectancies about relationships begin to form in this context. We come into the world ready to interact with others, but the specific characteristics of those interactions differ from person to person and from family to family. It is those details that seem to have important implications for our later interactions.

During their first year, human infants are extremely sensitive to facial expressions, bodily movements, and the sounds people make. The mother typically takes care of the baby, and she is equally sensitive to what the infant does (Kochanska et al., 2004). As they interact, the two individuals communicate and reinforce each other's actions (Murray & Trevarthen, 1986; Trevarthen, 1993). The adult shows interest in the infant's communication, such as engaging in baby talk and displaying exaggerated facial expressions. The infant shows interest in the adult by attempting to make appropriate sounds and expressions. Such reciprocal interactions tend to be a positive educational experience for both (see Figure 8.3). There is even evidence that a mother's "baby talk" is "incredibly systematic and rhythmical"—much like poetry and song lyrics (Miall & Dissanayake, 2004; Selim, 2004). In addition to interpersonal bonding, these interactions may form the basis for the emotional response to music and other artistic expressions.

■ The Lasting Importance of Parent–Child Interactions

The study of early relationships has been conducted primarily by developmental psychologists. Because the nature of these relationships affects the nature of later interpersonal behavior, social psychologists have begun to look more closely at early childhood.

As a very brief overview, it appears that the quality of the interaction between a mother (or other caregiver) and her infant determines the infant's future interpersonal attitudes and

attachment style
The degree of security experienced in interpersonal relationships. Differential styles initially develop in the interactions between infant and caregiver when the infant acquires basic attitudes about self-worth and *interpersonal trust.*

self-esteem
The self-evaluation made by each individual. It represents one's attitude about oneself along a positive–negative dimension.

interpersonal trust
An attitudinal dimension underlying *attachment styles* that involves the belief that other people are generally trustworthy, dependable, and reliable as opposed to the belief that others are generally untrustworthy, undependable, and unreliable.

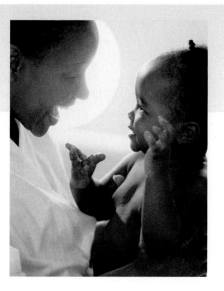

Figure 8.3 ■ Infants and Their Mothers Communicate
Beginning in early infancy, babies are sensitive to the sounds, facial expressions, and bodily movements of their mothers (or caregivers). Mothers are equally sensitive to their infants' sounds, expressions, and movements. The result is interactive communication between the two. Such exchanges constitute the earliest form of social interaction.

actions (Oberlander, 2003). People are found to be consistent with respect to their interaction patterns in different relationships—parent–child, friends, and romantic partners (Foltz et al., 1999).

Bowlby's (1969, 1973) studies of mothers and infants led him to the concept of **attachment style**—the degree of security an individual feels in interpersonal relationships. It is assumed that an infant acquires two basic attitudes during its earliest interactions with an adult. The first is an attitude about self that we label **self-esteem**. The behavior and the emotional reactions of the caregiver provide information that he or she is a valued, important, loved individual or, at the other extreme, someone without value. The second basic attitude acquired by an infant is about other people, involving general expectancies and beliefs. This attitude is labeled **interpersonal trust**. It is based on whether the caregiver is perceived as trustworthy, dependable, and reliable or as untrustworthy, undependable, and unreliable. Research findings suggest that we develop these basic attitudes about self and others long before we acquire language skills. As adults, it often seems that we were "just born with" a given level of self-esteem and a given level of trust, but it is likely that these dispositions were learned at such an early age that we simply cannot remember their origins.

Based on the two basic attitudes about self and others, people can be roughly classified as having a particular interaction style. There is some disagreement as to the number of attachment styles, but there *is* general agreement about their overall effects (Bartholomew & Horowitz, 1991; Bowlby, 1982). If we conceptualize self-esteem as one dimension and interpersonal trust as another, it follows that a person could be high on both dimensions, low on both, or high on one but low on the other. This yields four attachment styles. A **secure attachment style** is characterized by a person who is high in self-esteem and trust. Secure individuals are best able to form lasting, committed, satisfying relationships (Shaver & Brennan, 1992). A secure style is ideal not only with respect to relationships, but also as associated with a high need for achievement, low fear of failure, and the desire to learn about and explore one's world (Elliot & Reis, 2003; Green & Campbell, 2000). Being low in both self-esteem and interpersonal trust results in a **fearful–avoidant attachment style.** Fearful–avoidant individuals tend to avoid close relationships or to establish unhappy partnerships (Mikulincer, 1998a; Tidwell, Reis, & Shaver, 1996). A negative self-image combined with high interpersonal trust produces a **preoccupied attachment style.** These individuals want closeness (sometimes excessively so), and they readily form relationships. They cling to others but are often depressed because they expect eventually to be rejected (Davila et al., 2004; Lopez et al., 1997; Whiffen et al., 2000). Those with a **dismissing attachment style** are high in self-esteem and low in interpersonal trust. This combination leads to the belief that one is very much deserving of good relationships, while expecting the worst of others. As a result, dismissing individuals fear genuine closeness (Onishi, Gjerde, & Block, 2001).

It is sometimes assumed that the attachment style one develops in infancy and childhood remains constant (Klohnen & Bera, 1998), and styles frequently *are* stable from infancy (Fraley, 2000). Nevertheless, there is considerable evidence that very good or very bad relationship experiences can lead to a change in style (Brennan & Bosson, 1998; Cozzarelli et al., 2003; Davila & Cobb, 2003). For example, a relationship breakup is likely to reduce

secure attachment style
A style characterized by high *self-esteem* and high *interpersonal trust*. This is the most successful and most desirable attachment style.

fearful–avoidant attachment style
A style characterized by low *self-esteem* and low *interpersonal trust*. This is the most insecure and least adaptive attachment style.

preoccupied attachment style
A style characterized by low *self-esteem* and high *interpersonal trust*. This is a conflicted and somewhat insecure style in which the individual strongly desires a close relationship but feels that he or she is unworthy of the partner and is thus vulnerable to being rejected.

dismissing attachment style
A style characterized by high *self-esteem* and low *interpersonal trust*. This is a conflicted and somewhat insecure style in which the individual feels that he or she "deserves" a close relationship but is frustrated because of mistrust of potential partners. The result is the tendency to reject the other person at some point in the relationship in order to avoid being the one who is rejected.

(sometimes only temporarily) the extent of one's secure attachment, while a positive, lasting relationship is likely to increase the possibility of feeling securely attached (Ruvolo, Fabin, & Ruvolo, 2001).

■ Relationships between and among Siblings

Approximately 80 percent of us have grown up with at least one sibling, and sibling interactions are important with respect to what we learn about interpersonal behavior (Dunn, 1992). Among elementary school children, those who have no siblings are found to be less liked by their classmates and to be more aggressive (or to be more victimized by aggression). Such differences presumably exist because having brothers or sisters provides useful interpersonal learning experiences (Kitzmann, Cohen, & Lockwood, 2002). Sibling relationships, unlike those between parent and child, often combine feelings of affection, hostility, and rivalry (Boer et al., 1997). A familiar theme is some version of "Mom always liked you best." Parents, though, seldom admit any such favoritism.

Most of us have experienced (or observed) multiple examples of sibling rivalry, as in Figure 8.4. In fact, though, most siblings get along fairly well. An affectionate relationship between siblings is most likely if each has a warm relationship with the parents, and if the mother and father are satisfied with their marriage (McGuire, McHale, & Updegraff, 1996).

The nature of sibling relationships is important in part because the positive or negative affect associated with siblings is likely to be aroused over and over again in interactions with peers, romantic partners, and spouses (Klagsbrun, 1992). For example, schoolyard bullies (see Chapter 11) tend to have had negative relationships with their siblings (Bowers, Smith, & Binney, 1994). Boys who exhibit behavior problems in school are likely to have had intense conflicts with a sibling plus a rejecting, punitive mother (Garcia & Shaw, 2000).

Siblings who feel close are able to share attitudes and memories, protect one another from outsiders, enjoy being together, and provide support when problems arise (Floyd, 1996). Siblings tend to grow apart in adolescence and young adulthood, even if they were very close as children (Rosenthal, 1992). By the time they reach middle age, however, most reestablish positive relationships. These same general patterns are true for twins, with identical twins experiencing the greatest closeness, followed by fraternal twins, and then ordinary brothers and sisters (Neyer, 2002). Sibling relationships sometimes involve one taking the parent role and the other functioning as the child. Siblings may interact as casual acquaintances, they may become close buddies, or they may simply maintain contact only because they believe that is what family members are supposed to do (Stewart, Verbrugge, & Beilfuss, 1998). About 20 percent of adult siblings never establish any degree

Figure 8.4 ■ Sibling Rivalry Can Last a Lifetime
Sibling relationships are often based on a mixture of affection, hostility, and rivalry. Remnants of these childhood emotions and reactions sometimes continue beyond childhood and influence other relationships. (*Source:* © Grimmy, Inc. Reprinted with special permission of King Features Syndicate.)

of closeness—about half of these are simply indifferent to their siblings, and half actively dislike them (Folwell et al., 1997).

Beyond the Family: Friendships

Beginning in early childhood, most of us establish casual friendships with peers who share common interests. Such relationships generally begin on the basis of proximity, as described in Chapter 7, or because the respective parents know one another. If two children have mutual interests and they have positive rather than negative experiences together, they may maintain a friendship over a relatively long period of time. Positive affect tends to be a simple matter of having fun together, and negative affect is most likely to be aroused by verbal or physical aggression (Hartup & Stevens, 1999). A simple truth is that, regardless of age, we prefer pleasant interactions to unpleasant ones.

■ Close Friendships

Many childhood friendships simply fade away. At times, however, a relationship from early childhood can mature into a **close friendship** (see Figure 8.5) that involves increasingly mature types of interaction. What, exactly, is involved in close friendships?

Such friendships have several distinctive characteristics. Many individuals tend to engage in self-enhancing behavior (such as bragging) when interacting with a wide range of other people, but they exhibit modesty with their close friends (Tice et al., 1995). Friends are less likely to lie to one another, unless the lie is designed to make the friend feel better (DePaulo & Kashy, 1998). And, friends begin to speak of "we" and "us" rather than "she and I" or "he and I" (Fitzsimmons & Kay, 2004). Once established, a close relationship results in the two individuals spending a great deal of time together, interacting in varied situations, self-disclosing, and providing mutual emotional support (Laurenceau, Barrett, & Pietromonaco, 1998; Matsushima & Shiomi, 2002). A close friend is valued for his or her generosity, sensitivity, and honesty—someone with whom you can relax and be yourself (Urbanski, 1992).

Culture also influences what is meant by *friendship*. Among Japanese college students, a best friend was described as someone in a give-and-take relationship, a person with whom it is easy to get along, who does not brag, and is considerate and not short-tempered (Maeda & Ritchie, 2003). American students describe friends in a similar way except that, unlike those in Japan, they also value a spontaneous and active friend.

close friendship
A relationship in which two people spend a great deal of time together, interact in a variety of situations, and provide mutual emotional support.

Figure 8.5 ■ A Lasting Childhood Friendship
Children are often brought together by proximity—living in the same neighborhood or attending the same preschool. If they enjoy the same activities and interact pleasantly, they are likely to become friends. These friendships frequently come to an end when interests change or when one's family moves. The two young ladies in these photographs, Lindsey Byrne and Chanda Brown, lived across the street from each other and played together from the time they were toddlers (*left photo*). The right photo was taken almost two decades later.

■ Gender and Friendships

Women indicate that they have more close friends than men do (Fredrickson, 1995). Women also place more importance on intimacy (characterized by self-disclosure and emotional support) than men (Fehr, 2004). Do conversations of two male friends differ from those of two female friends? Martin (1997) identified several gender-specific aspects of what friends talk about. Two men often talk about women and sex, being trapped in a relationship, sports, and alcohol. Two women tend to talk about relationships with men, clothes, and problems with roommates.

Can a man and a woman become friends without having a romantic or sexual relationship? Men and women differ in their expectations about opposite-sex friendships (Bleske-Rechek & Buss, 2001). Men tend to initiate such friendships when the woman is attractive, and they assume that a sexual relationship will eventually develop. If that does *not* happen, they usually end the relationship. Women, in contrast, initiate such a friendship because they want a man who can protect them. As with men who lose interest without sex, women are likely to end a relationship if the man does not fill a protective role.

Loneliness: Life without Close Relationships

loneliness
The unpleasant emotional and cognitive state based on desiring close relationships but being unable to attain them.

Despite a biological need to establish relationships and despite the rewards of being in a relationship, many individuals find they are unable to achieve that goal. The result is **loneliness**—an individual's emotional and cognitive reaction to having fewer and less satisfying relationships than he or she desires (Archibald, Bartholomew, & Marx, 1995). In contrast, people who simply are uninterested in having friends do not experience loneliness (Burger, 1995). It is also possible for an individual to desire solitude for very positive reasons (Long et al., 2003).

Loneliness appears to be a common human experience, as shown by studies of Americans and Canadians (Rokach & Neto, 2000), British Asians (Shams, 2001), Spaniards (Rokach et al., 2001), Portuguese (Neto & Barrios, 2001), Chinese Canadians (Goodwin, Cook, & Yung, 2001), and Turks and Argentines (Rokach & Bacanli, 2001).

■ The Consequences of Being Lonely

If a child has only *one* friend, that is enough to diminish feelings of loneliness (Asher & Paquette, 2003). In the absence of close friends, people who feel lonely tend to spend their leisure time in solitary activity, have very few dates, and have only casual friends or acquaintances (R. A. Bell, 1991; Berg & McQuinn, 1989). Lonely individuals feel left out and believe they have very little in common with those they meet (B. Bell, 1993).

Loneliness is, of course, unpleasant, and the negative affect includes feelings of depression, anxiety, unhappiness, dissatisfaction, pessimism about the future, self-blame, and shyness (Anderson et al., 1994; Jackson, Soderlind, & Weiss, 2000). From the perspective of others, lonely individuals are perceived as maladjusted (Lau & Gruen, 1992; Rotenberg & Kmill, 1992).

■ Why Are Some People Lonely?

The origins of dispositional loneliness include a combination of genetics, attachment style, and the opportunity for early social experiences with peers. In an intriguing study designed to examine the possible role of genetic factors in loneliness, McGuire and Clifford (2000) conducted a behavioral genetic investigation of loneliness among children aged nine to fourteen. The participants included pairs of biological siblings, unrelated siblings raised in adoptive homes, and identical and fraternal twins. The data consistently indicated that loneliness is based, in part, on inherited factors. For example, identical twins are more similar in loneliness than fraternal twins, indicating that greater genetic similarity is associated with greater similarity with respect to loneliness. Nevertheless, loneliness was also found to be influenced by environmental factors—unrelated siblings raised in adoptive homes are more similar in loneliness than random pairs of children. As the investigators point out, the fact that there is a genetic component to loneliness does not fully explain how it operates. For example, the relevant genes might affect feelings of depression or hostility; if so, differences in loneliness could be the result of rejection based on genetically determined differences in interpersonal behavior.

Another possible source of loneliness can be traced to attachment style (Duggan & Brennan, 1994). Both dismissing and fearful–avoidant individuals fear intimacy and tend to avoid establishing relationships (Sherman & Thelen, 1996). Such individuals do not have sufficient trust in others to risk seeking closeness. Shyness and loneliness are related, in part, because lonely individuals expect to be rejected, and shyness can provide protection from that possibility (Jackson et al., 2002). Loneliness is also associated with failure to self-disclose because others might react negatively to one's disclosures (Matsushima & Shiomi, 2001). In general, insecure attachment is associated with social anxiety and loneliness (Vertue, 2003). A study of Dutch students by Buunk and Prins (1998) suggests that a preoccupied attachment style may also lead to loneliness when such individuals believe they are giving more than they are receiving. This perceived lack of reciprocity leads to feelings of loneliness and being underappreciated.

A third possible factor that results in loneliness is the failure to develop appropriate social skills, and this can occur for many reasons (Braza et al., 1993). In part, children learn interpersonal skills by interacting with peers. Because they have such opportunities, children who attend preschool are better liked in elementary school than those who lack such experiences (Erwin & Letchford, 2003). Also, loneliness is more likely to occur among those who did not have a close relationship with a sibling, especially if the relationship is characterized by conflict (Ponzetti & James, 1997). Without the necessary social skills, a child may engage in self-defeating behaviors such as avoiding others, engaging in verbal aggression such as teasing, or aggressing physically. As a consequence of these behaviors, the child is rejected by potential playmates (Johnson, Poteat, & Ironsmith, 1991; Kowalski, 2000; Ray et al., 1997). Inappropriate interpersonal behavior leads to rejection and unpopularity and thus to increased loneliness—the individual is caught in a seemingly endless self-destructive cycle (Carver, Kus, & Scheier, 1994). The determinants of loneliness are summarized in Figure 8.6.

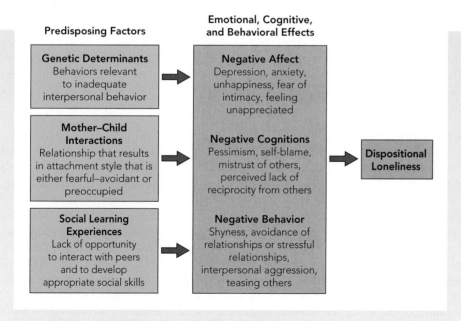

Figure 8.6 ■ The Origins of Dispositional Loneliness
Loneliness is most often studied as a personality disposition. Dispositional loneliness can develop as the result of genetic factors, the early acquisition of specific attachment styles, and/or the failure to learn appropriate social skills. These predisposing factors result in a combination of negative emotions, cognitions, and behaviors that increases the odds that an individual will be unable to establish close relationships and will thus develop dispositional loneliness.

Without some form of intervention to alter this behavior, interpersonal difficulties typically continue throughout childhood and adolescence and into adulthood. These interpersonal problems do not simply go away with the passage of time (Asendorpf, 1992; Hall-Elston & Mullins, 1999).

■ Loneliness as a Response to External Factors

Most of the research on loneliness is based on the assumption that it represents a personality disposition. In addition to dispositional loneliness, situational loneliness can result from external factors. For example, a move to a new location usually means that a person is surrounded by strangers and without friends. Loneliness can also arise when a student goes away to college. As he or she meets new people and makes new friends, however, the problem most often goes away. A study of North American college students studying in Israel revealed that they were lonely, but only for a few weeks, by which time new relationships had been established (Wiseman, 1997).

A more difficult situation arises in response to **social rejection**—when another individual has no interest in establishing a relationship with you. The rejection is not based on something you have done or said but on the prejudices, stereotypes, and attitudes held by the rejecting individual. The tactics of rejection involve three basic strategies to discourage a personal relationship (Hess, 2002): *avoidance* (failing to interact, ignoring the other person, cutting short the interaction), *disengagement* (not disclosing information about self, not paying attention, interacting in an impersonal way), and, the most direct of all, *cognitive dissociation* (derogating and degrading the other person). Each of these behaviors communicates a lack of interest in establishing a relationship.

Social exclusion occurs when the rejection comes not from one individual, but an entire group. The devastating effects of being rejected by a group were shown in an experiment in which undergraduates interacted with several strangers. After the interaction, each participant was asked to name two group members with whom they would like to interact again (Twenge, Catanese, & Baumeister, 2003). The experimenters provided (false) information to some that they were named by everyone in the group as a choice for future interactions, while others were supposedly rejected by everyone. Not only did it create a negative mood, the rejected students functioned badly afterward. They felt tired, judged time to be passing more slowly, and were more likely to express the belief that "life is meaningless."

■ Reducing Loneliness

Are there any satisfactory ways to deal with loneliness? Once loneliness develops, it is not possible to change the individual's history by providing new genes or altering early mother–child interactions. It is possible, however, to acquire new and more appropriate social skills. Such intervention concentrates on a number of fairly specific behaviors. The major intervention procedures are *cognitive therapy* (Salmela-Aro & Nurmi, 1996) and *social skills training* (Hope, Holt, & Heimberg, 1995), and they can be used simultaneously. The goal of cognitive therapy is to disrupt the pattern of negativity and encourage new cognitions, perceptions, and expectations about social interactions. In social skills training, the lonely person is provided with examples of socially appropriate behavior on videotape and then given the opportunity to practice in role play. Finally, there are instructions to try out the new skills in actual situations. The person can learn to interact with others in a friendly way, avoid expressing anger and hostility, and make casual conversation (Keltner et al., 1998; Reisman, 1984). Lonely individuals are instructed to express interest in the other person and make fewer self-references (Kowalski, 1993), and they learn to self-disclose in an acceptable way (R. A. Bell, 1991; Rotenberg, 1997). Just as people can be taught mathematics, table manners, and how to drive a car, they can also be taught social skills.

---

social rejection
Rejection by one individual of another individual, not on the basis of what he or she has done, but on the basis of prejudice, stereotypes, and biases.

social exclusion
Social rejection of an individual by an entire group of people, not on the basis of what he or she has done, but on the basis of prejudice, stereotypes, and biases.

KEY POINTS

★ Close relationships are characterized by *interdependence,* in which two people influence each other's lives, share their thoughts and emotions, and engage in joint activities.

★ Evolutionary theory proposes that emotional bonding with other humans increased the odds of survival and reproductive success. As a result of this selective process, modern humans and other primates are hard-wired to seek emotional closeness.

★ The first relationships are within the family, and we acquire an *attachment style* (a combination of *self-esteem* and *interpersonal trust*) based on interactions with a caregiver. Children also learn what to expect from other people and how to interact as a result of their interactions with parents, siblings, and other family members.

★ Friendships outside the family begin in childhood and are based initially on common interests and other sources of positive affect, resulting in attraction. With increasing maturity, it becomes possible to form *close friendships* that involve spending time together, interacting in many situations, providing mutual social support, and engaging in self-disclosure.

★ *Loneliness* occurs when a person has fewer and less satisfying relationships than he or she desires. The result is depression and anxiety. Dispositional loneliness originates in a combination of genetics, an insecure attachment style based on mother–child interactions, and the lack of early social experiences. Situational loneliness is brought about by external factors such as a move to a new location or social rejection and is based on factors unrelated to the behavior of the rejected individual. A helpful intervention involves a combination of cognitive therapy and social skills training.

Romantic Relationships and Falling in Love

We discussed attraction in Chapter 7 and friendship in this chapter. What factors might lead two individuals to an even closer relationship, one involving romance, love, and sometimes sex? In a developing relationship, one or any combination of these aspects of closeness may occur, in any sequence. Even in early adolescence, romantic relationships often develop, and they tend to focus on affiliation needs and sexual feelings (Furman, 2002). Most of the existing research on these topics deals with heterosexual couples, but we will note here whenever relevant data involving gays and lesbians are available. It appears that most of what we know about heterosexual couples applies equally well to homosexual couples (Kurdek, 2003). Regardless of sexual orientation, people expect that a romantic relationship will include sexual attraction, similarity of attitudes and values, spending time together, and, very often, the belief that two people share something special (Baccman, Folkesson, & Norlander, 1999).

Romance: Moving beyond Friendship

Among the most obvious differences between friendship and romance are sexual attraction and some level of physical intimacy, as suggested in Figure 8.7 on page 224. Depending on what is acceptable in one's cultural subgroup, the sexual attraction may or may not lead to some form of sexual behavior and the physical intimacy may be limited to holding hands, hugging, and kissing, or it can include more explicitly sexual interactions. At least one of the partners is likely to believe that he or she is in love and to expect that the relationship may lead to marriage (Hendrick & Hendrick, 2002).

■ Similarities and Differences between Friendship and Romance

Most often, romantic attraction begins the same way that all interpersonal attraction does: a combination of affiliation need, affect arousal, proximity, reactions to observable characteristics, similarity, and mutual liking. Among college students, an ideal romantic partner is one who is similar to oneself and has a secure attachment style (Dittmann, 2003; Klohnen & Luo, 2003). A primary feature of romance is the interpretation of one's emotional arousal as an indicator of a strong attraction that includes the potential for love and sex. In addition,

Figure 8.7 ■ **Romantic Relationships Include Physical Intimacy**
Unlike friendships, romantic relationships usually include some degree of physical intimacy. Depending on cultural norms and individual differences, intimacy can range from holding hands to sexual interactions.

men and women set higher standards for romantic partners than for friends with respect to physical attractiveness, social status, and characteristics such as warmth and intelligence (Sprecher & Regan, 2002). A spirit of playfulness also is important in romantic relationships (Aune & Wong, 2002).

Beyond the overtones of sexuality, other aspects of a romantic relationship differ from those of a friendly relationship. Swann, De La Ronde, and Hixon (1994) report that among friends, dormitory roommates, and even married couples, most people prefer a partner who provides accurate feedback. We appreciate being with someone who knows us well enough to point out our good and bad characteristics. In contrast, at least at the beginning of a romantic relationship, the two individuals are not looking for accuracy and truth as much as they are looking for approval and acceptance. In a romantic relationship, we want to like and to be liked unconditionally, and we need to be reassured by compliments, praise, and frequent demonstrations of affection.

It may be helpful to think about a romantic relationship in terms of three overlapping schemas (Fletcher et al., 1999), as in Figure 8.8. There is a self schema, as was described in Chapter 5, a second schema that is a person's perception of the partner, and a third schema that encompasses the relationship between self and partner. The schema involving one's partner is often unrealistic and inaccurate. Each individual wants to believe that the other person represents the perfect partner, and each wants uncomplicated, totally positive feedback from that partner (Katz & Beach, 2000; Simpson, Ickes, & Blackstone, 1995). The closer the partner is to one's ideal, the better and more lasting the relationship is perceived to be (Campbell et al., 2001; Fletcher, Simpson, & Thomas, 2000). That person's virtues are emphasized, and possible faults are dismissed as unimportant (Murray & Holmes, 1999). Remember the cartoon snail attracted to a tape dispenser in Figure 8.1? Many of us seem to behave like that snail from time to time.

Romance is built, in part, on fantasies and illusions that may be crucial to men and women in creating the relationship (Martz et al., 1998; Murray & Holmes, 1997). Women seem to fantasize on a general basis, while men must be strongly committed to a specific relationship before the fantasies kick in (Gagne & Lydon, 2003). Studies in various countries indicate that couples believe their relationship is better than the relationships of other people (Buunk & van der Eijnden, 1997; Endo, Heine, & Lehman, 2000). To the extent that two people like one

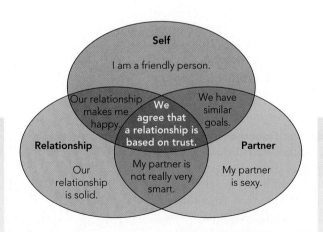

Figure 8.8 ■ **Schemas for Self, Partner, and the Romantic Relationship**
A romantic relationship involves three overlapping schemas: for self, for one's partner, and for the relationship. There is overlapping content between pairs of schemas and a central area of content involving all three schemas. (*Source: Based on concepts from Fletcher et al., 1999.*)

another and believe that their relationship is special, this affection and this belief may actually help maintain the relationship (Franiuk, Cohen, & Pomerantz, 2002; Knee, 1998).

Selecting a Potential Mate: Different Criteria for Men and Women

Dreams of romance may not include the desire to become a parent, but some evolutionary psychologists suggest that our genetic history is a crucial aspect of romantic attraction (Geary, Vigil, & Byrd-Craven, 2004). Our motives need not be conscious, but our search for a romantic partner involves something different than the search for a friend. What matters most in seeking a romantic partner? As we will discuss, men stress the physical attractiveness of a potential mate, and women stress a mate's status and resources (Fletcher et al., 2004). For both genders, personality and character matter. Men and women say that finding a kind and intelligent mate is important (Li et al., 2002), as is avoiding a mate with a history of infidelity (Hanko, Master, & Sabini, 2004).

■ Men Seek Female Attractiveness: Youth and Beauty Equals Reproductive Fitness

From the perspective of evolutionary determinants, female beauty is believed to be sexually attractive to men because beauty is associated with youth, health, and fertility. The basic principle is that the reproductive success of our male ancestors was enhanced by selecting female mates on the basis of such cues. Though men in a dating relationship are not ordinarily interested in reproduction (sex, maybe, but not reproduction), they *are* predisposed to respond positively to beauty. Over hundreds of thousands of years, males who were attracted to youthful beauty were more likely to pass on their genes to the next generation than were males for whom youth and beauty were irrelevant (Buss, 1994, 1998).

Men are attracted not only to beauty, but also to other specific characteristics that indicate youth and health. A woman's long hair is one example (Jacobi & Cash, 1994), presumably because healthy, shiny hair is a sign of youth and health (Etcoff, 1999; Hinsz, Matz, & Patience, 2001). Another positive cue is a face that exhibits **bilateral symmetry** (having identical left and right sides). A symmetrical face is perceived as more attractive than an unsymmetrical one (Hughes, Harrison, & Gallup, 2002). Beyond the face, bodily symmetry in general is associated with genetic fitness, health, and fertility (Manning, Koukourakis, & Brodie, 1997; Scutt et al., 1997).

bilateral symmetry
The alikeness of the left and the right sides of the body (or parts of the body).

■ Women Seek Men with Resources: Power Equals Ability to Raise and Protect Offspring

In Chapter 7, we pointed out that women respond positively to physical appearance, though not as strongly as men. In seeking a romantic partner, women pay more attention to a man's resources, whether that consists of a warm cave and the strength to fight off predators in prehistoric times or economic and interpersonal power in today's world. The reason that women are relatively unconcerned about male youth and attractiveness—as explained by evolutionary theorists—is that, unlike women, men are usually able to reproduce from puberty into old age. For a prehistoric female, reproductive success was enhanced by being young and healthy and by choosing a mate who had the ability to protect and care for her and for their offspring (Kenrick et al., 1994, 2001).

Many studies of contemporary men and women suggest that mate preferences are consistent with this evolutionary description. A study in the Netherlands of men and women between twenty and sixty years of age reported that men preferred women who were more attractive than themselves, while women preferred men who were higher in income, education, self-confidence, intelligence, dominance, and social position (Buunk et al., 2002).

As compelling as the evolution-based explanation of gender differences may be, it is far from universally accepted. Miller, Putcha-Bhagavatula, and Pedersen (2002) discuss culture-based explanations of gender differences in mate selection. With respect to resources, for example, *both* men and women prefer a wealthy mate, and these findings make more sense

and commitment by way of religious teachings, civil laws, and the way we depict love and marriage in songs and stories (Allgeier & Wiederman, 1994).

■ The Components of Love

Though passionate love is a common experience, it is too intense and too overwhelming to be maintained. There are other kinds of love, however, that *can* be long lasting. Hatfield describes **companionate love** as the "affection we feel for those with whom our lives are deeply entwined" (1988, p. 205). Unlike passionate love, companionate love is based on a very close friendship in which two people are sexually attracted, have a great deal in common, care about each other's well-being, and express mutual liking and respect (Caspi & Herbener, 1990). It's not quite as exciting as passionate love nor as interesting a theme for music and fiction, but it *is* a crucial aspect of a satisfying and lasting relationship.

In addition to these two aspects, four other styles have been identified. Game-playing love includes behavior such as having two lovers at once, possessive love concentrates on the fear of losing one's lover, logical love is based on decisions as to whether a partner is suitable, and selfless love is a rare phenomenon in which an individual would rather suffer than have a lover suffer (Hendrick & Hendrick, 1986). Among the many findings with respect to style differences, men are more likely to engage in game-playing love, but the reverse is true for logical and possessive love (Hendrick et al., 1984). In general, people agree that companionate love and selfless love are the most desirable, while game-playing is the least desirable (Hahn & Blass, 1997).

A different conception of the meaning of love is provided by Sternberg's (1986) **triangular model of love**, as depicted in Figure 8.10. This formulation suggests that each love

companionate love
Love that is based on friendship, mutual attraction, shared interests, respect, and concern for one another's welfare.

triangular model of love
Sternberg's conceptualization of love relationships consisting of three basic components: *intimacy, passion,* and *decision/commitment.*

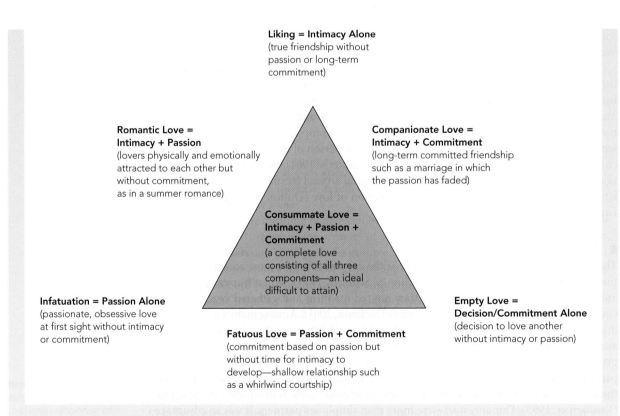

Figure 8.10 ■ Sternberg's Triangular Model of Love
Sternberg's model of love has three basic components: *intimacy, passion,* and *decision/commitment.* For a couple, love can be based on any one of these three components, a combination of any two of them, or all three. As shown, these various possibilities yield seven types of relationships, including the ideal (*consummate love*) that consists of all three components equally represented.

Chapter 8 / Close Relationships

relationship is made up of three basic components that are present in varying degrees in couples (Aron & Westbay, 1996). One component is **intimacy**—the closeness two people feel and the strength of the bond that holds them together. Intimacy is essentially companionate love. Partners high in intimacy are concerned with each other's welfare and happiness, and they value, like, count on, and understand each other. The second component, **passion,** is based on romance, physical attraction, and sexuality—in other words, passionate love. Men are more likely to stress this component than women (Fehr & Broughton, 2001). The third component, **decision/commitment,** represents cognitive factors such as the decision that you love and want to be associated with the other person, along with a commitment to maintain the relationship on a permanent basis.

Actual lovers subjectively experience these three elements as overlapping and related components of love. Many relationships can be categorized primarily by a single component or by a combination of two of the components (as described in Figure 8.10). When all three angles of the triangle are equally strong, the result is **consummate love**—defined as the ideal but difficult to attain.

Although attraction research (see Chapter 7) has long stressed the effects of physical attractiveness on liking, its effect on love has been somewhat overlooked. In Spain, almost two thousand individuals ranging from age eighteen to sixty-four were asked about physical attractiveness, falling in love, and the components of Sternberg's model (Sangrador & Yela, 2000). The findings suggest that appearance is important not only with respect to passion, but also with intimacy and decision/commitment. Surprisingly, attractiveness is as important in the later stages of a relationship as in the beginning. This focus on external appearance may not be wise, but these investigators suggest that we should at least acknowledge the reality of the influence of physical attractiveness on long-term relationships.

■ Romance, Love, and Sex

Despite a long history of religious, legal, and commonsense pressures to avoid premarital sex, there is an equally long history of couples whose behavior defied these pressures. Early in the twentieth century, attitudes about sexuality became increasingly permissive, and sexual interaction became common and widely accepted (Coontz, 1992; Jones, 1997; Michael et al., 1994). These changes in attitude and behavior were sufficiently dramatic to be characterized as a "sexual revolution" (see Figure 8.11). Gender differences in sexuality have essentially disappeared (Weinberg, Lottes, & Shaver, 1995), but men and women vary widely in their sexual knowledge, attitudes, and practices (Byrne, 1997b; Fisher & Barak, 1991; Simpson & Gangestad, 1992).

The "flower children" of the 1960s and 1970s were described by some as representing the future, with permissive sexuality providing the solution to problems as varied as world peace and establishing lasting relationships. As the twentieth century ended and the twenty-first century began, there were many signs that the sexual revolution was fading. The reasons included the growing realization that sexual "freedom" often meant sexual "conformity" to social pressure (Townsend, 1995). Two other, unrelated issues contributed to a decrease in permissiveness: the explosive number of teenage pregnancies (Byrne & Fisher, 1983) and the rise of the sexually transmitted human immunodeficiency virus (HIV) infection, which can develop into acquired immunodeficiency syndrome (AIDS). Though this disease first spread from apes to humans

intimacy
In Sternberg's *triangular model of love*, the closeness felt by two people—the extent to which they are bonded.

passion
In Sternberg's *triangular model of love*, the sexual motives and sexual excitement associated with a couple's relationship.

decision/commitment
In Sternberg's *triangular model of love*, these are the cognitive processes involved in deciding that you love another person and are committed to maintaining the relationship.

consummate love
In Sternberg's *triangular model of love*, a complete and ideal love that combines *intimacy, passion,* and *decision/commitment.*

Figure 8.11 ■ In Turbulent Times—The Sexual Revolution
In the 1960s and 1970s, the United States was the scene of experiments with illegal drugs, new music, the demand for sexual freedom, and protests against the Vietnam War. Change was the goal, and the status quo was unacceptable to many young people. Among the lasting effects is a shift toward permissiveness and tolerance with respect to sexual attitudes and behavior.

Romantic Relationships and Falling in Love

as early as the seventeenth century, it was identified as an epidemic in the 1980s (Boyce, 2001). A growing realization of the dangers posed by sexual pressure, unwanted pregnancies, and incurable diseases gradually led to changes in sexual practices. Teenage birth rates in the United States dropped to a record low (Schmid, 2001) and the incidence of HIV infections has decreased in several parts of the world, though it continues to increase in the United States, the Caribbean, and sub-Saharan Africa (Fang, 2001; Whitelaw, 2003).

The permissiveness that characterized the revolution did have some lasting effects. Though free love in the park has not become the norm, it is nevertheless true that most married couples in the early twenty-first century have engaged in some form of premarital sexual intimacy with each other and often with others as well. It also is true that premarital sex, including cohabitation, is not related to the probability of marriage taking place, and it has no effect on subsequent marital satisfaction or on marital success or failure (Cunningham & Antill, 1994; Stafford, Kline, & Rankin, 2004).

KEY POINTS

★ One defining characteristic of romantic relationships is some degree of physical intimacy, ranging from holding hands to sexual interactions.

★ As is true for attraction and friendship, romantic attraction is influenced by factors such as physical proximity, appearance, and similarity. In addition, romance includes sexual attraction, the desire for total acceptance, and an acceptance of positive fantasies about such relationships.

★ The reproductive success of our ancestors was enhanced by male attraction to young, fertile females; female attraction to males with resources; and by bonding between mates and between parents and their offspring.

★ *Love* consists of multiple components. *Passionate love* is a sudden, overwhelming emotional response to

another person. *Companionate love* resembles a close friendship that includes caring, mutual liking, and respect. Sternberg's *triangular model of love* includes these two components plus a third—*decision/commitment*—a cognitive decision to love and be committed to a relationship.

★ Widespread changes in sexual attitudes and practices in the 1960s and 1970s have been described as a "sexual revolution" that, among other changes, resulted in premarital sex becoming the norm. Because of reactions against pressures to conform to the new sexual norms, unwanted pregnancies, and the fear of sexually transmitted diseases, there has been a partial backlash against the sexual revolution toward safer and more discriminating sexual behavior.

Marriage: Happily Ever After—and Otherwise

As you might expect, all of the factors that have been discussed with respect to attraction, friendship, romance, love, and sex are also relevant to the selection of a marital partner. Marriage does bring challenges, such as economic issues, parenthood, and careers that can conflict with the task of maintaining a long-term relationship.

Before we discuss how marriage is affected by such challenges, we turn to a relatively recent phenomenon that has created a major conflict in the United States. In May 2004, the first same-sex couples in the United States were legally married in Massachusetts. Simultaneously, the Massachusetts state legislature worked to draft an amendment to the state constitution that would make such marriages *illegal* (see Figure 8.12), and President George W. Bush supported an amendment to the U.S. Constitution confining marriage to the union of a man and a woman. In Belgium, the Netherlands, and three Canadian provinces, gay marriages have been legal for some time and are not the subject of controversy (Haslett, 2004; Kisner, 2004).

Figure 8.12 ■ Gay Marriage: A Threat or a Civil Right?
When the ban on gay marriage was declared unconstitutional by a Massachusetts court, officials in the United States began issuing marriage licenses to nonheterosexual couples. The result was an outpouring of gay and lesbian couples who wanted to marry and heated protests by those who viewed it as a threat to the institution of marriage. Shown here is one of the confrontations taking place at the San Francisco Court House. (*Source:* The New Republic, *May 3, 2004, p. 18.*)

Marital Success and Satisfaction: Similarity, Personality, and Sexuality

Given the fact that most people get married and that half or more of these marriages fail, it would be helpful if we knew as much as possible about the factors that differentiate marital success and failure. Though the importance of commitment to the relationship is often stressed, note that commitment based on fear of a breakup is not as effective as commitment based on the rewards of a continuing relationship (Frank & Brandstatter, 2002).

In a long-term relationship, many problems can arise, and we discuss this shortly. Other predictive factors are present even before the wedding, and they can be useful indications of the probability that a marriage will succeed or fail.

■ Similarity and Assumed Similarity

Not surprisingly, over a century of research has consistently indicated that spouses are similar in their attitudes, beliefs, values, interests, ages, attractiveness, and other attributes (Galton, 1870/1952; Pearson & Lee, 1903; Terman & Buttenwieser, 1935a, 1935b). Further, a longitudinal study of couples from the time they were engaged through twenty years of marriage indicates little change in the degree of similarity (Caspi, Herbener, & Ozer, 1992). Greater than chance similarity is also found for pairs of friends and for dating couples, but husbands and wives are even more similar (Watson, Hubbard, & Wiese, 2000). As emphasized in Chapter 7, opposites don't attract. Also, because there is a positive relationship between the degree of similarity and the success of the relationship, a couple contemplating marriage might do well to pay greater attention to their similarities and dissimilarities and less attention to attractiveness and sexuality.

Not only do similar people marry, but happily married couples *believe* they are more similar than they are—a phenomenon known as **assumed similarity** (Byrne & Blaylock, 1963; Schul & Vinokur, 2000). Both actual and assumed similarity increases marital satisfaction. Interestingly, dating couples have even higher assumed similarity than married couples.

■ Dispositional Factors

Beyond similarity, marital success is affected by some specific personality dispositions. Some individuals are better able to maintain a positive relationship than others, and they are better bets as marriage partners.

For example, **narcissism** refers to an individual who feels superior to most other people, someone who seeks admiration and lacks empathy (American Psychiatric Association, 1994). Narcissists report feeling less commitment to a relationship (Campbell & Foster, 2002). As one exception to the similarity rule, two narcissists are not likely to have a happy relationship (Campbell, 1999).

Other important personality dispositions that affect the success of a relationship are associated with interpersonal behavior and attachment styles. Thus, individuals with

assumed similarity
The extent to which two people believe they are similar with respect to specific attitudes, beliefs, values, and so forth, as opposed to the extent to which they are actually similar.

narcissism
A personality disposition characterized by unreasonably high *self-esteem*, a feeling of superiority, a need for admiration, sensitivity to criticism, a lack of empathy, and exploitative behavior.

preoccupied or fearful–avoidant styles have less satisfying relationships than those with secure or dismissing styles (Murray et al., 2001). In general, secure attachment is associated with marital satisfaction (Banse, 2004).

It seems clear that, over time, the expression of negative affect results in disillusionment as love fades, overt affection declines, and ambivalence increases. When marital partners *do not express* negative emotions such as fear, anxiety, and anger, the relationship has a greater chance of success (Robins, Caspi, & Moffitt, 2000). The longer a couple has been together, the less likely the individuals are to keep their opinions to themselves (Stafford, Kline, & Rankin, 2004). Despite what you may have heard, it is usually *not* a good idea to "let it all hang out." When a partner is inconsiderate or hostile, the other individual usually responds by pointing out the lack of consideration or expressing hostility in return. The relationship suffers from the original negative behavior and the resultant negative behavior of the other partner. Holding back requires more self-control than many of us are able to master (Finkel & Campbell, 2001).

■ Marital Sex

Surveys of married couples reveal that sexual interactions become less frequent as time passes, and that the most rapid decline occurs during the first four years of marriage (Udry, 1980); this decreased frequency of sexual interaction over time is equally true for cohabiting couples. Surprisingly, studies show that neither full-time nor part-time employment has a negative effect on a couple's sex life.

Regardless of sexual *frequency,* the degree of *similarity* of sexual attitudes and preferences predicts marital compatibility (Smith et al., 1993). Also, men are more likely than women to equate sexual satisfaction with the quality of the relationship (Sprecher, 2002).

Love and Marriage: Careers, Parenthood, and Family Composition

The ongoing realities of a marital relationship present a more complex challenge than falling in love, having a ceremony, and living happily every after. Two people must interact daily and find ways to deal with an almost endless list of potential problems, such as dividing up chores, dealing with unexpected events, meeting demands of those outside the relationship (e.g., family and friends), and juggling a job. In addition, economic concerns (Conger, Rueter, & Elder, 1999), the stresses of parenthood (Kurdek, 1999), and the complications of a nontraditional family composition can bring unexpected complications. Such factors are likely to contribute to the fact that relationship quality begins to decline shortly after the bride and groom say, "I do."

■ Is It Better to Be Married or to Be Unmarried?

If marriage does not promise eternal bliss, should people avoid it? Although more Americans are remaining single, 90 percent of adults are (or were) married (Edwards, 2000; Households, 2001). Most adults want to get married and most *do* get married (Frazier et al., 1996; People, 2001). Compared with single individuals, men who are married consistently report being happier and healthier, but for women, only a satisfactory marriage provides health benefits (DeNoon, 2003; Steinhauer, 1995). A Norwegian study found that married people report a greater sense of well-being and have a lower suicide rate than singles—at least until their late thirties. After that, the advantages of being married begin to disappear (Mastekaasa, 1995).

■ Love and Marriage

In song, these two concepts may "go together like a horse and carriage," but what really happens? Usually, passionate love decreases over time (Tucker & Aron, 1993), although women who continue to feel intense love toward their husbands are more satisfied than those who do not. Male satisfaction with marriage is unrelated to feelings of passionate love (Aron & Henkemeyer, 1995). Companionate love is, however, important for both—sharing activities, exchanging ideas, laughing together, and cooperating on projects.

■ Work Inside and Outside of the Home

Although the patterns are gradually changing, men do most of the repairs and women do most of the cooking and cleaning, even if they have careers (Yu, 1996). Marital conflict and dissatisfaction often involve the perceived unfairness in the way such chores are divided (Grote & Clark, 2001). Similar problems arise in gay households, but lesbian partners report being able to share household labor in a fair and equitable way (Kurdek, 1993).

With respect to work, there is always the potential for conflict between job demands and the demands of the marriage. This conflict can easily lead to alienation and eventually to emotional exhaustion (Senecal, Vallerand, & Guay, 2001). For men and women, this results in dissatisfaction with one's job and one's life (Perrew & Hochwarter, 2001). When both spouses work outside the home, the potential for conflict is greater, and no one has devised a satisfactory way to solve the problems created by a two-career family (Gilbert, 1993). Spouses with secure attachment styles deal with these competing demands best, while fearful–avoidant individuals have the most difficulty. Individuals with dismissing or preoccupied styles fall in between (Vasquez, Durik, & Hyde, 2002).

■ Parenthood

Bell (2001) suggests that evolution has produced a neurobiological basis for the emotional bond between parents and children that goes beyond logic or other cognitive considerations (see Figure 8.13). Despite these biological pressures favoring parenthood, along with social disapproval of childlessness (LaMastro, 2001), becoming a parent creates unexpected problems. Becoming a parent is likely to interfere with marital sexuality, beginning during pregnancy (De Judicibus & McCabe, 2002; Regan et al., 2003), and having children can bring additional sources of conflict to the relationship (Alexander & Higgins, 1993; Hackel & Ruble, 1992). Parenthood is often associated with a decline in marital satisfaction, but less so if the couple has a strong, companionate relationship (Shapiro & Gottman, 2000) and if the parents have secure attachment styles (Alexander et al., 2001; Berant, Mikulincer, & Florian, 2001).

Despite the difficulties, parents consistently report that they are glad they have children (Feldman & Nash, 1984). With larger families, however, men and women differ somewhat. The more children they have, the more women express dissatisfaction with the marriage, while men express greater satisfaction (Grote, Frieze, & Stone, 1996). Perhaps this is because women spend more time taking care of their expanding brood (Bjorklund & Shackelford, 1999).

■ Changes in Family Composition

Marriage rates are down in the United States and several European countries, while cohabitation rates are up (Montgomery, 2004). Nevertheless, when most people think of marriage, parenthood, and families, they have an idealized image of a traditional household with a mother and father plus children.

Figure 8.13 ■ Parenthood Can Be a Challenge
Although most couples want to have children, the transition to parenthood presents an unending series of potential challenges.

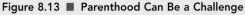

By the early 1970s, only 45 percent of American families consisted of a married couple and their offspring, and that dropped to 23.5 percent over the next thirty years (Irvine, 1999; Schmitt, 2001). Comparing U.S. Census Bureau figures for 1990 and 2000, the greatest increase has been in the number of households consisting of a single mother; such families grew five times faster in the 1990s than families with a married couple (Schmitt, 2001).

In addition to single-parent households, there has been an increase in the number of remarriages in which the wife, the husband, or both have offspring from a previous marriage; the number of cohabiting couples who became parents; and the number of gay and lesbian couples with children (McLaughlin, 2001a; Stacy & Biblarz, 2001). We don't know the possible ramifications of these relatively new family arrangements.

When Relationships Fail: Causes, Preventives, and Consequences

People usually enter marriage with high hopes, and they tend to be optimistic about their chances of success (McNulty & Karney, 2004). More than 50 percent of marriages in the United States end in divorce, and the figure for those marrying today is expected to reach 64 percent. In an attempt to point out the discrepancy between positive expectancies and negative reality, Chast (2004) created a mock "marital adjustment test" that suggests a high frequency of marital discord. For example, the first question asks,

When did you realize that you couldn't stand your partner?

A minute ago ___ About an hour ago ___

Last night when I was watching "E. R." ___

Sometime in the last month ___ Before that even ___

Despite statistics to the contrary, unmarried respondents estimate only a 10 percent chance of divorce when they marry (Fowers et al., 2001). People expect their own marriages to succeed, despite the fact that at least half of all marriages fail. Why is it that couples fail to succeed at marriage, no matter how optimistic they may be?

■ Costs and Benefits of Marital Interactions

Before we discuss specific problems, it may be useful to consider each marital interaction in terms of costs and benefits. It is assumed that the greater the number of benefits relative to the number of costs, the higher the quality of the relationship.

Clark and Grote (1998) identified several types of costs and benefits, some of which are intentionally positive or negative and some of which are unintentional. From the viewpoint of attempting to maintain a good relationship, it is possible to engage in intentionally positive acts and to avoid intentionally negative acts, but both partners have to consider the consequences of what they say and do and be motivated to exercise self-control. Even more difficult is being willing to engage in difficult or undesired behavior in order to meet the needs of one's partner. These acts constitute **communal behavior**—a "cost" for one individual that is a "benefit" for the partner. As you might expect, a communal orientation is associated with a partner's marital satisfaction (Mills et al., 2004). Altogether, relationship satisfaction depends on maximizing benefits and minimizing costs, as outlined in Figure 8.14.

communal behavior
Benevolent acts in a relationship that "cost" the one who performs those acts and "benefit" the partner and the relationship itself.

■ Problems between Spouses

What happens to transform a loving relationship into an unhappy one, often characterized by mutual hate? Why do costs begin to rise and benefits drop? One factor is the failure to understand the reality of a relationship. That is, no spouse (including oneself) is perfect. No matter how ideal the other person may have seemed, it eventually becomes

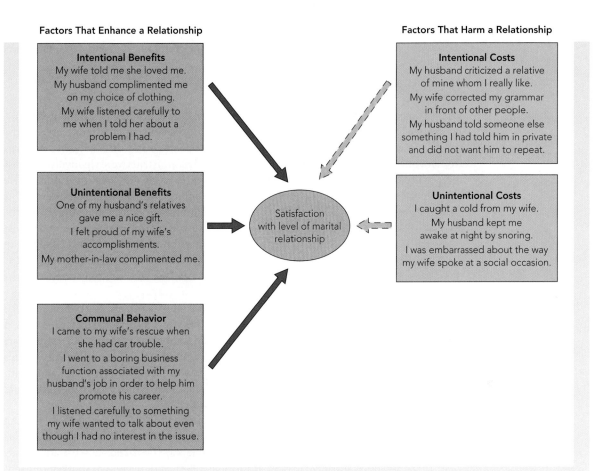

Factors That Enhance a Relationship

Intentional Benefits
My wife told me she loved me.
My husband complimented me on my choice of clothing.
My wife listened carefully to me when I told her about a problem I had.

Unintentional Benefits
One of my husband's relatives gave me a nice gift.
I felt proud of my wife's accomplishments.
My mother-in-law complimented me.

Communal Behavior
I came to my wife's rescue when she had car trouble.
I went to a boring business function associated with my husband's job in order to help him promote his career.
I listened carefully to something my wife wanted to talk about even though I had no interest in the issue.

Satisfaction with level of marital relationship

Factors That Harm a Relationship

Intentional Costs
My husband criticized a relative of mine whom I really like.
My wife corrected my grammar in front of other people.
My husband told someone else something I had told him in private and did not want him to repeat.

Unintentional Costs
I caught a cold from my wife.
My husband kept me awake at night by snoring.
I was embarrassed about the way my wife spoke at a social occasion.

Figure 8.14 ■ Marital Relationships as a Matter of Costs and Benefits
Relationship success and failure can be conceptualized as the result of the relative number of costs and benefits present. Here are some of the possible intentional and unintentional costs and benefits. In addition, there is *communal behavior*, which represents a cost to the spouse engaging in the behavior but a benefit to the partner and the relationship. Marital satisfaction depends on the relative number of costs and benefits that spouses experience in their marriage. (*Source: Based on information in Clark & Grote, 1998.*)

obvious that he or she has negative qualities as well. There is the disappointing discovery that the *actual* similarity between spouses is less than the *assumed* similarity (Silars et al., 1994). Over time, the negative personality characteristics (discussed earlier in this chapter) become less tolerable. Minor behavioral flaws that once seemed cute can be perceived as annoying and unlikable (Felmlee, 1995; Pines, 1997). If you are initially drawn to someone because that person is different from you or even unique, chances are good that disenchantment will eventually set in (Felmlee, 1998).

A special problem in any intimate relationship is jealousy, the negative reaction to a partner's real or imagined attraction to someone else. Some propose that men are most threatened by a partner's sexual attraction to a rival man, while women are most threatened by a partner's emotional attraction to a rival woman. The difference presumably results from biological differences, in that men fear having to raise some other man's offspring, while women fear losing a mate's resources if he transfers his affection (Berscheid & Reis, 1998). Although the possibility of such sex differences is both interesting and plausible, research suggests that men and women are equally threatened by either type of infidelity (DeSteno et al., 2002; Harris, 2002, 2003; Levy & Kelly, 2002).

The ultimate step in sexual attraction toward someone else is infidelity. It has long been known that extramarital sex is associated with marital dissolution, but which occurs first?

A longitudinal study by Previti and Amato (2004) indicates that the events can go either way. Individuals in an unhappy marriage often engage in extramarital sex, and extramarital sex often leads to a marriage breaking up.

■ Dealing with Marital Problems

When there are marital arguments or disagreements, it is not helpful to focus on winning versus losing or being right versus being wrong. In videotaped interactions of husbands and wives discussing marital problems, one positive and three negative patterns were identified (McNulty & Karney, 2004). A positive, constructive style involves focusing on the topic under discussion and attempting to resolve it. Negative, destructive behaviors consisted of avoidance (changing the subject), direct negative interactions (faulting, rejecting, or criticizing the partner), and indirect negative interactions (making attributions, avoiding responsibility, or asking hostile questions). Avoidance is most often practiced by men, and it simply postpones any effort to solve problems (Bodenman et al., 1998), but the most maladaptive response to conflict is for the disagreeing partners to lash out in a directly or indirectly negative way. This behavior only intensifies the conflict.

In addition, it seems to be true that "people do a lot of mean and nasty things to one another" (Kowalski et al., 2003, p. 471). A variety of aversive interpersonal behaviors such as lying, cheating, complaining, and teasing are familiar examples. At the opposite extreme are positive interpersonal behaviors that communicate commitment to the relationship, including showing affection, providing support and companionship, showing respect, and maintaining a positive atmosphere (Weigel & Ballard-Reisch, 2002). Which set of behaviors would you guess are more likely to help maintain a relationship?

If partners pause and consider the long-term effects of what they say and do, this can often lead to a constructive response (Yovetich & Rusbult, 1994). It is important to be able to disagree and yet deal with problems in an agreeable way (Graziano, Jensen-Campbell, & Hair, 1996), to show empathy (Arriaga & Rusbult, 1998), and to avoid hostility and defensiveness (Newton et al., 1995; Thompson, Whiffen, & Blain, 1995).

A more comprehensive way of characterizing these various patterns of interacting can be summarized simply: Whatever is said or done that creates negative affect is bad for a relationship, and whatever is said or done that creates positive affect is good for a relationship (Levenson, Carstensen, & Gottman, 1994). Videotapes of interactions between satisfied and dissatisfied partners reveal much more negative verbal and nonverbal behavior in the latter pairs than in the former (Halford & Sanders, 1990). As the amount of negative affect increases and the amount of positive affect decreases, the relationship becomes less and less satisfactory (Kurdek, 1996, 1997).

Jeff Herring (2001), marriage and family therapist, provides ten tips to strengthen a marriage, and his suggestions (see Table 8.2) are consistent with what is known about avoiding and dealing with problems. A successful marriage is one that emphasizes friendship, commitment, trust, social support, similarity, and a consistent determination to create positive affect (Adams & Jones, 1997; Cobb, Davila, & Bradbury, 2001; Wieselquist et al., 1999).

■ The Consequences of a Failed Relationship

When it is clear that a relationship has severe problems, partners can respond either actively or passively to the situation (Rusbult & Zembrodt, 1983). An active response consists of either ending the relationship as quickly as possible or working to improve it. A passive response involves simply waiting and hoping that things will get better. Men and women with secure attachment styles are more likely to work actively to save a relationship, while those with insecure attachment styles are more likely to end the relationship or simply wait for it to get worse (Rusbult, Morrow, & Johnson, 1990).

It is difficult, though possible, to reverse a deteriorating relationship. A couple is most able to reconcile if (1) the needs of each partner can be satisfied, (2) each is committed to continuing the relationship, and (3) alternative lovers are not readily available (Arriaga

Chapter 8 / Close Relationships

Table 8.2 ■ Ten Tips for Spouses

A marriage and family therapist provides these suggestions as ways to maintain a positive marital relationship.

1. You can be right or you can be happy—not both. Choose wisely.

2. Learn the gentle art of cooperation.

3. Talk about the important stuff.

4. Forgive as much or more than you would like to be forgiven.

5. Celebrate what you want to see more of. Appreciation can go a long way.

6. Listen to the heart more than you listen to the words. This can lead to conflict resolution and to taking care of each other.

7. Don't be like Darren in *Bewitched* who wanted Samantha to stop using her magic witch powers. Encourage your partner in her or his gifts.

8. Check out your communication. It's easy to talk, but it's more difficult to communicate.

9. Take responsibility for your contributions to the problems.

10. Don't assume that just because you are married, you know how to be married.

(Source: Based on information from Herring, May 20, 2001, Knight Ridder.)

& Agnew, 2001; Rusbult, Martz, & Agnew, 1998). When children are part of the marriage, they become the innocent victims of relationship failure. Approximately one out of three American children has this experience (Bumpass, 1984). The negative consequences of divorce for boys and girls include long-term effects on their health and well-being (Friedman et al., 1995; Vobejda, 1997), behavior problems at school (O'Brien & Bahadur, 1998), a higher risk of mortality, and a greater likelihood of getting a divorce themselves (Tucker et al., 1997). And the negative effects of divorce on children are worse if either of the parents moves to a new location (Braver, Ellman, & Fabricius, 2003). Despite the numerous problems, sociologist Constance Ahrons (2004) points out that this does not mean that *all* children of divorce are doomed to have serious problems. "The reality is that although a minority of children will indeed suffer negative consequences, the great majority do not" (quoted by Carroll, 2004, p. D1). Divorce is not solely to blame for unpleasant effects. Even if unhappily married parents stay together, their negative interactions are predictive of future marital problems for their offspring (Amato & Booth, 2001). Among the specific parental behaviors associated with a harmful effect on their children's future are expressing jealousy, being easily angered, making critical remarks, and refusing to talk to one another. Parental conflicts, whether or not they lead to divorce, are bad for their offspring (Doucet & Aseltine, 2003; Riggio, 2004). Anyone who considers marriage and plans to have children might do well to give more than a passing thought to the consequences of marital failure.

Despite the shattered hopes of living happily ever after and despite the emotional and often financial pain of a marital breakup, it must be noted that most divorced individuals, especially men, marry again. In fact, almost half of all marriages in the United States are remarriages for one or both partners (Koch, 1996). The desire for love and happiness in a relationship seems to have a greater influence on what people do than any negative experiences with a former spouse.

KEY POINTS

★ In the United States, about 50 percent of marriages end in divorce, but people do not believe that their marriages will fail.

★ Most married couples have some degree of conflict and disagreement. When difficulties can be resolved constructively, the marriage is likely to endure. When problems are made worse by destructive interactions, the marriage is likely to fail.

★ Constructive responses include attempts to understand the partner's point of view, not threatening his or her

self-esteem; compromising; increasing the benefits and decreasing the costs of the marriage; being agreeable; and, above all, maximizing positive affect and minimizing negative affect.

★ If dissatisfaction becomes too great, individuals tend to respond either actively or passively.

★ Divorce is usually a painful process with negative emotional and economic effects. The most vulnerable victims are the children. Despite what they have experienced, those who divorce are likely to marry again.

SUMMARY AND REVIEW OF KEY POINTS

Interdependent Relationships with Family and Friends versus Loneliness

■ Close relationships are characterized by *interdependence,* in which two people influence each other's lives, share their thoughts and emotions, and engage in joint activities.

■ Evolutionary theory proposes that emotional bonding with other humans increased the odds of survival and reproductive success. As a result of this selective process, modern humans and other primates are hard-wired to seek emotional closeness.

■ The first relationships are within the family, and we acquire an *attachment style* (a combination of *self-esteem* and *interpersonal trust*) based on interactions with a caregiver. Children also learn what to expect from other people and how to interact as a result of their interactions with parents, siblings, and other family members.

■ Friendships outside the family begin in childhood and are initially based simply on common interests and other sources of positive affect, resulting in attraction. With increasing maturity, it becomes possible to form *close friendships* that involve spending time together, interacting in many situations, providing mutual social support, and engaging in self-disclosure.

■ *Loneliness* occurs when a person has fewer and less satisfying relationships than he or she desires. The result is depression and anxiety. Dispositional loneliness originates in a combination of genetics, an insecure attachment style based on mother–child interactions, and the lack of early social experiences. A helpful intervention involves a combination of cognitive therapy and social skills training. Situational loneliness is brought about by external factors such as a move to a new location or social rejection and is based on factors unrelated

to the behavior of the rejected individual.

Romantic Relationships and Falling in Love

■ One defining characteristic of romantic relationships is some degree of physical intimacy, ranging from holding hands to sexual interactions.

■ As is true for attraction and friendship, romantic attraction is influenced by factors such as physical proximity, appearance, and similarity. In addition, romance includes sexual attraction, the desire for total acceptance, and an acceptance of positive fantasies about such relationships.

■ The reproductive success of our ancestors was enhanced by male attraction to young, fertile females; female attraction to males with resources; and bonding between mates and between parents and their offspring.

- *Love* consists of multiple components. *Passionate love* is a sudden, overwhelming emotional response to another person. *Companionate love* resembles a close friendship that includes caring, mutual liking, and respect. Sternberg's *triangular model of love* includes these two components plus a third—*decision/commitment*—a cognitive decision to love and to be committed to a relationship.

- Widespread changes in sexual attitudes and practices in the 1960s and 1970s have been described as a "sexual revolution" that, among other changes, resulted in premarital sex becoming the norm. Because of reactions against feeling the pressure to conform to sexual pressures, unwanted pregnancies, and the fear of sexually transmitted diseases, there has been a partial backlash against the sexual revolution and toward safer and more discriminating sexual behavior.

Marriage: Happily Ever After—and Otherwise

- In the United States, about 50 percent of marriages end in divorce, but people do not believe that their marriages will fail.

- Most married couples have some degree of conflict and disagreement. When difficulties can be resolved constructively, the marriage is likely to endure. When problems are made worse by destructive interactions, the marriage is likely to fail.

- Constructive responses include attempts to understand the partner's point of view, not threatening his or her self-esteem; compromising; increasing the benefits and decreasing the costs of the marriage; being agreeable; and, above all, maximizing positive affect and minimizing negative affect.

- If dissatisfaction becomes too great, individuals tend to respond either actively or passively.

- Divorce is usually a painful process with negative emotional and economic effects. The most vulnerable victims are the children. Despite what they have experienced, those who divorce are likely to marry again.

Connections INTEGRATING SOCIAL PSYCHOLOGY

In this chapter, you read about . . .	In other chapters, you will find related discussions of . . .
the association between self-esteem and attachment and the effects of love on self-esteem	self-esteem (Chapter 5)
similarity as a factor in friendships, romantic relationships, and marriage	similarity and attraction (Chapter 7)
love as emotional misattribution	misattribution and emotions (Chapter 3)
affect and relationships	affect and attraction (Chapter 7)

Thinking about Connections

1. Do you believe that your relationship with your parents has anything to do with how you relate to other people? Did your mother and father make you feel good about yourself? Do you still feel the same way? In your childhood, were the adults in your life dependable? Do you think of them as kind? How do you feel about most of the people you meet? Do you believe the average person is more or less trustworthy?

2. Think of someone who is (or was) your closest friend. What was it about that person that first attracted you? Did proximity, similarity, posi- tive affect, or appearance play a role in your getting to know one another? How do (or did) you spend your time together? Are there any parallels between your childhood friendships and your current friendships?

3. Think about yourself in a close romantic relationship—in the past, present, or possible future. What is it about the other person that

you find appealing? Do you think romance is something that develops gradually, or is it love at first sight? Is there any match between your experience and research topics such as the role of misattributed emotions, evolution-related reproductive strategies, or expectancies based on stories about love you first heard in childhood? Write down the lyrics of a love song that you believe express a realistic perspective.

4. When you find yourself disagreeing with a romantic partner, a friend, or anyone else, what do you do and say? Is the interaction constructive, or do you just get mad and exchange insults? Have you ever ended a relationship with someone with whom you once felt very close? Why? Who initiated the breakup, and how was it done? Could either of you have handled the situation more constructively?

ARE YOU IN LOVE?

At some point in a relationship, individuals often ask themselves questions about their feelings with respect to love, sex, and marriage. You might find it useful to consider what social psychologists have discovered.

Love or Just Arousal?

When you are near someone who appeals to you, it is easy to confuse a variety of arousal states with feelings of "love." Social psychologist Elaine Hatfield once suggested that people often fall in lust and interpret it as love. More generally, research on emotional misattribution indicates that the physiological arousal associated with general excitement, fear, happiness, and even anger can be mislabeled. If you are with someone nice and find yourself surging with emotion, don't automatically assume that you are madly in love. Take a deep breath and consider other possible explanations for your feelings.

Be Informed about Your Partner

You don't have to administer a questionnaire to every potential date, lover, or spouse, but try to learn as much as you can. Pay attention to personal details when you interact. If any particular topic is especially important to you (e.g., religion, politics, abortion rights, sex, vegetarianism, having children), it is essential to discover incompatibilities early, no matter how awkward it may be to ask about such matters.

Know What You (and the Other Person) Mean by "Love"

Look back in the chapter to remind yourself of the different kinds of love identified and determine just what each of you has in mind when you say, "I love you." If the two of you have different definitions or if you differ with respect to your beliefs about true love, you both need to evaluate this information and think about what incompatibility might mean to your relationship.

Think about You and Your Partner in Terms of Companionate Love

Set aside your feelings of passionate love and try to picture yourselves engaging in friendly interactions having nothing to do with love or sex. Do you have enough interests in common that you would enjoy spending time together playing games, hiking, traveling, gardening, or whatever? If so, the two of you have a better chance of building a lasting relationship than if your feelings consist primarily of passionate love.

Chapter 8 / Close Relationships

KEY TERMS

assumed similarity (p. 233)
attachment style (p. 217)
bilateral symmetry (p. 225)
close friendship (p. 219)
communal behavior (p. 236)
companionate love (p. 230)
consummate love (p. 231)
decision/commitment (p. 231)
dismissing attachment style (p. 217)

fearful–avoidant attachment style (p. 217)
interdependence (p. 215)
interpersonal trust (p. 217)
intimacy (p. 231)
loneliness (p. 220)
love (p. 227)
narcissism (p. 233)
passion (p. 231)

passionate love (p. 228)
preoccupied attachment style (p. 217)
secure attachment style (p. 217)
self-esteem (p. 217)
social exclusion (p. 222)
social rejection (p. 222)
triangular model of love (p. 230)
unrequited love (p. 229)

9 SOCIAL INFLUENCE
Changing Others' Behavior

W hen I (Robert Baron) was a teenager, my parents were pretty relaxed: They didn't set many rules for me to follow because, I'd like to believe, they trusted me and felt I was responsible. But there was one rule they did state over and over: "Never drive with someone who is drunk." My father repeated this because he had a favorite cousin who was killed while driving with friends who were intoxicated. I rarely had reason to consider this rule, but one New Year's Eve, I did. I was at a party and everyone was drinking heavily. When the party broke up, my friend Stan offered me a ride home. It was snowing heavily and I knew I'd never get a city bus at that time, so I accepted. As we walked to the car with several friends, I could see that Stan was very unsteady on his feet, so remembering my parents' repeated warnings, I said, "Hey Stan, I don't think you are in any condition to drive. I'll walk home." This brought hoots of derision from my friends, who told me, very directly, that I was acting like a "scared chicken"—Stan could handle it. Sad to relate, I gave in and got into the car with the others. As soon as we started out, I could see that Stan was truly drunk. He weaved all over the street and had major problems making turns. Soon, I was pretty scared, and the more scared I got, the more clearly I could hear my father's voice saying, "Don't risk your life—if someone is drunk, don't drive with them. Remember what happened to my cousin." When Stan pulled up at a red light, I jumped out of the car, saying, "I'll walk from here. See you guys tomorrow." I arrived home soaked and freezing—but in one piece. As it turns out, Stan drove off the road after a near accident and got stuck in a ditch. So although no one was hurt, Stan and my friends didn't get home any sooner than I did. I've never regretted resisting social pressure from my friends that night; who knows—it might have saved my life.

A lthough this incident happened many years ago, it still clearly reflects several major themes we consider in this chapter. First, it illustrates the process of **social influence**—efforts by one or more individuals to change the attitudes, beliefs, perceptions, or behaviors of one or more others. Social influence is a common feature of everyday life, and like the character in Figure 9.1, we either try to influence others or are influenced by them many times each day.

Because social psychologists have long recognized the importance of social influence, it has been a central topic in our field since the beginning. We have already considered some of this work in Chapter 4, in which we examined the process of *persuasion*. We expand on that earlier discussion by examining other aspects of social influence. First, we focus on the topic of **conformity**—pressure to behave in ways that are viewed as acceptable or appropriate by

social influence
Efforts by one or more individuals to change the attitudes, beliefs, perceptions, or behaviors of one or more others.

conformity
A type of social influence in which individuals change their attitudes or behavior in order to adhere to existing social norms.

Chapter 9 / Social Influence

Figure 9.1 ■ Social Influence: A Part of Everyday Life
Each day, we try to influence others—and are also on the receiving end of influence attempts from them. As you can see from this cartoon, such *social influence* can take many different forms. (*Source:* CLOSE TO HOME © 1998 John McPherson. Reprinted with permission of UNIVERSAL PRESS SYNDICATE. All rights reserved.)

our group or society. As we'll discover, such pressures can be hard to resist. Next, we turn to **compliance**—efforts to get others to say "yes" to various requests. Third, we examine influence that occurs when other persons are not present and are not making any direct attempts to affect our behavior. For instance, in the opening story, it was my parents' earlier warnings that caused me to get out of Stan's car; my mother and father weren't there to enforce this rule. Research indicates that thoughts of other persons, or simply being reminded of them or our relationships with them, are often sufficient to change our current behavior (e.g., Fitzsimons & Bargh, 2003). We refer to such effects as *symbolic social influence* to reflect that it results from our mental representations of others rather than their actual presence or overt actions. After considering this indirect form of social influence, we'll examine another kind that is, in some respects, its direct opposite: **obedience**—social influence in which one person simply orders others to do what they want. Finally, we briefly consider forms of social influence that occur in many *real-life settings,* especially workplaces (e.g., Yukl, Kim, & Chavez, 1999).

Conformity: Group Influence in Action

Have you ever found yourself in a situation in which you felt that you stuck out like the famous sore thumb? If so, you have had direct experience with pressures toward *conformity.* You probably experienced a strong desire to get back into line—to fit in with the people around you. Such pressures toward conformity stem from the fact that in many contexts, there are explicit or unspoken rules indicating how we should behave. These rules are known as **social norms,** and they often exert powerful effects on our behavior. (There are several kinds of social norms, but we are discussing primarily one type, known as *injunctive norms*—the kind that tells us what we *should* do in a given situation. We consider other types in later sections; Kallgren, Reno, & Cialdini, 2000.)

In some instances, social norms are detailed and stated explicitly. Governments generally function through written constitutions and laws; athletic contests are usually regulated by written rules; and signs in many public places describe expected behavior in considerable detail (e.g., *Speed Limit: 55; No Swimming; No Parking; Keep Off the Grass*).

In contrast, other norms are unspoken or implicit, and may have developed in an informal manner. For instance, when people work together, they gradually converge in their perceptions of how much time has passed—even though they never set out to influence one another in this way and may not intend to do so (Conway, 2004). Similarly, most of us obey such unwritten rules as "Don't stare at strangers" and "Don't arrive at parties exactly on time." We are often influenced by current standards of dress, speech, and grooming. Regardless of whether social norms are explicit or implicit, though, one fact is clear: Most people obey them most of the time. For instance, few persons visit restaurants without leaving a tip, and virtually everyone, regardless of personal political beliefs, stands when the national anthem of their country is played (see Figure 9.2 on page 248).

At first glance, this strong tendency toward conformity may strike you as objectionable. After all, it places restrictions on personal freedom. Actually, though, there is a strong basis

compliance
A form of social influence involving direct requests from one person to another.

obedience
A form of social influence in which one person simply orders one or more others to perform some action(s), and the persons then comply.

social norms
Rules indicating how individuals are expected to behave in specific situations.

for so much conformity: Without it, we would quickly find ourselves facing social chaos. Imagine what would happen outside movie theaters, stadiums, or at supermarket checkout counters if people did *not* obey the norm "Form a line and wait your turn." And consider the danger to both drivers and pedestrians if there were not clear traffic regulations. In many situations, then, conformity serves a useful function.

Given that strong pressures toward conformity exist in many social settings, it is surprising to learn that conformity, as a social process, received relatively little attention in social psychology until the 1950s. At that time, Solomon Asch (1951), whose research on impression formation we considered in Chapter 3, carried out a series of experiments on conformity that yielded dramatic results. Because Asch's research had a strong influence on later studies of this aspect of social influence, it's worth a close look here.

Asch's Research on Conformity: Social Pressure— The Irresistible Force?

Life is filled with instances in which we discover that our own judgments, actions, or conclusions are different than those reached by others. What do we do in such situations? Important insights into our behavior were provided by studies conducted by Solomon Asch (1951, 1955), research that is viewed as a true "classic" in social psychology.

In his research, Asch asked participants to respond to a series of simple perceptual problems such as the one in Figure 9.3. On each problem, they indicated which of three comparison lines matched a standard line in length. Several other persons (usually six to

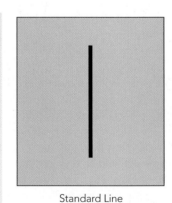

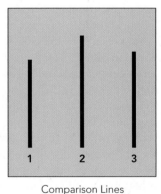

Standard Line   Comparison Lines

Figure 9.3 ■ **Asch's Line Judgment Task**
Participants in Asch's research were asked to report their judgments on problems such as this one. Their task was to indicate which of the comparison lines (1, 2, or 3) best matched the standard line in length. To study conformity, Asch had participants make these judgments out loud, only after hearing the answers of several other people—all of whom were Asch's assistants. On certain critical trials, the assistants all gave wrong answers. These wrong answers exposed participants to strong pressures to conform.

eight) were also present, but unknown to the real participant, all were assistants of the experimenter. On certain occasions known as *critical trials* (twelve out of the eighteen problems), the accomplices offered answers that were wrong: They unanimously chose the wrong line as a match for the standard line. Moreover, they stated their answers *before* the real participants responded. Thus, on these critical trials, the persons in Asch's study faced a dilemma: Should they go along with the other individuals present or stick to their own judgments? A large majority of the persons in Asch's research chose conformity. Across several different studies, fully 76 percent of those tested went along with the group's false answers at least once; and overall, they voiced agreement with these errors 37 percent of the time. In contrast, only 5 percent of the participants in a control group, who responded to the same problems alone, made such errors.

Of course, there were large individual differences in this respect. Almost 25 percent of the participants *never* yielded to the group pressure. At the other extreme, some went along with the majority nearly all the time. When Asch questioned them, some of them stated, "I am wrong; they are right." They had little confidence in their own judgments. Others, however, said they felt that the other present were suffering from an optical illusion or were merely sheep following the responses of the first person. Yet, when it was their turn, these people, too, went along with the group.

In further studies, Asch (1956) investigated the effects of shattering the group's unanimity by having one of the accomplices break with the others. In one study, this person gave the correct answer, becoming an "ally" of the real participant; in another study, this person chose an answer in between the one given by the group and the correct one; and in a third, he chose the answer that was even more incorrect than that chosen by the majority. In the latter two conditions, he broke from the group but still disagreed with the real participants. Results indicated that conformity was reduced under all three conditions. However, somewhat surprisingly, this reduction was greatest when the dissenting assistant expressed views even more extreme (and wrong) than the majority. Together, these findings suggest that it is the unanimity of the group that is crucial; once it is broken, no matter how, resisting group pressure becomes much easier.

There's one more aspect of Asch's research that is important to mention. In later studies, he repeated his basic procedure but with one change: Instead of stating their answers, participants wrote them down. As you might guess, conformity dropped sharply because there was no way for the real participants to know what the others were doing. This finding points to the importance of distinguishing between *public conformity*—doing or saying what others around us say or do—and *private acceptance*—actually coming to feel or think as others do. Often, it appears, we follow social norms overtly but don't actually change our private views (Maas & Clark, 1984). This distinction between public conformity and private acceptance is important, and we refer to it at several points in this book.

Asch's research was the catalyst for much activity in social psychology, as other researchers sought to investigate the nature of conformity to identify factors that influence it and to establish its limits (e.g., Crutchfield, 1955; Deutsch & Gerard, 1955). Indeed, such research continues, and still adds to our understanding of this crucial form of social influence (e.g., R. S. Baron, Vandello, & Brunsman, 1996; Bond & Smith, 1996; Buehler & Griffin, 1994).

KEY POINTS

★ *Social influence*—efforts by one or more persons to change the attitudes or behavior of one or more others—is a common part of life.

★ Most people behave in accordance with *social norms* most of the time; they show strong tendencies toward *conformity*.

★ Conformity was first systematically studied by Solomon Asch, whose classic research indicated that many persons will yield to social pressure from a unanimous group.

Factors Affecting Conformity: Variables That Determine the Extent to Which We "Go Along"

Asch's research demonstrated the existence of powerful pressures toward conformity, but a moment's reflection suggests that conformity does not occur to the same degree in all settings. What factors determine the extent to which individuals yield to conformity or resist it? Research suggests that many factors play a role; here, we examine the ones that appear to be most important.

■ Cohesiveness and Conformity: Being Influenced by Those We Like

cohesiveness
All of the factors that bind group members together into a coherent social entity.

Cohesiveness refers to all of the factors that bind group members together into a coherent social entity. When cohesiveness is high pressures toward conformity are magnified. After all, we know that one way of gaining the acceptance of such persons is to be like them in various ways. On the other hand, when cohesiveness is low, pressures toward conformity are low; why should we change our behavior to be like other people we don't especially like or admire? Research findings indicate that cohesiveness exerts strong effects on conformity (Crandall, 1988; Latane & L'Herrou, 1996); therefore, it is one important determinant of the extent to which we yield to this type of social pressure.

■ Conformity and Group Size: Why More Is Better with Respect to Social Pressure

A second factor that exerts important effects on the tendency to conform is the size of the influencing group. Asch (1956) and other early researchers (e.g., Gerard, Wilhelmy, & Conolley, 1968) found that conformity increases with group size but only up to about three members; beyond that point, it appears to level off or even decrease. However, more recent research failed to confirm these early findings (e.g., Bond & Smith, 1996). Instead, these later studies found that conformity tended to increase with group size of up to eight group members and beyond. So, it appears that the larger the group, the greater our tendency to go along with it, even if this means behaving differently than we'd really prefer.

■ Descriptive and Injunctive Social Norms: How Norms Affect Behavior

descriptive norms
Norms that simply indicate what most people do in a given situation.

injunctive norms
Norms specifying what *ought* to be done—what is approved or disapproved behavior in a given situation.

Social norms, we have already seen, can be formal or informal—as different as rules printed on large signs and informal guidelines such as "Don't leave your shopping cart in the middle of a parking spot." This is not the only way in which norms differ, however. Another important distinction is that between **descriptive norms** and **injunctive norms** (e.g., Cialdini, Kallgren, & Reno, 1991; Reno, Cialdini, & Kallgren, 1993). Descriptive norms are ones that simply describe what most people do in a given situation. They influence behavior by informing us about what is generally seen as effective or adaptive in that situation. In contrast, injunctive norms specify what *ought* to be done—what is approved or disapproved behavior in a given situation. Both kinds of norms can exert strong effects on our behavior (e.g., Brown, 1998). However, Cialdini and his colleagues believe that in certain situations—especially ones in which antisocial behavior (behavior not approved of by a given group or society) is likely to occur—injunctive norms may exert stronger effects. This is true for two reasons. First, such norms tend to shift attention away from *how* people are acting in particular situation (littering) to how they *should be* behaving (putting trash into containers). Second, such norms may activate the social motive to do what's right in a given situation, regardless of what others have done or are doing.

normative focus theory
A theory suggesting that norms will influence behavior only to the extent that they are focal for the persons involved at the time the behavior occurs.

When, precisely, do injunctive norms influence behavior? It is clear that injunctive norms don't always produce such effects. For instance, although there is an injunctive norm stating, "Clean up after your dog," and many towns and cities have laws requiring such behavior, many dog owners choose to look the other way when their pets obey the call of nature. Why do people sometimes disobey or ignore even strong injunctive norms? One answer is provided by **normative focus theory** (e.g., Cialdini, Kahlgren, & Reno, 1991). This theory suggests that norms will influence behavior only to the extent that they are *salient* (i.e., relevant, significant) to the persons involved at the time the behavior occurs. This prediction

Figure 9.4 ■ **Social Norms: They Affect Our Behavior Only When They Are Salient to Us**
Why do some people park in handicapped parking spots, even though they are not physically challenged? While there may be many reasons for such socially objectionable behavior, one factor may be that such persons do not view this rule (norm) as applying to them; they feel that, somehow, they are exempt and that the rule is irrelevant to them.

has been verified in many studies (e.g., Kallgren, Reno, & Cialdini, 2000). In a study on this issue conducted by Reno, Cialdini, and Kallgren (1993), individuals crossing a parking lot encountered an accomplice walking toward them. In the experimental condition of most interest here, the accomplice stopped to pick up a fast-food bag that had been dropped by someone else. (In a control condition, the accomplice did not engage in this behavior.) The researchers reasoned that seeing another person actually pick litter up from the ground would remind participants of society's disapproval of littering, and so make this norm very salient to them. To test the effects of this norm on their later behavior, Reno et al. (1993) placed handbills on the windshields of the participants' cars and observed what they did when they found them there. As predicted, those who had seen another person pick up the fast-food bag were significantly less likely to toss the handbills on the ground than were those who had not seen this action, and so had not been reminded of the injunctive norm against littering.

The fact that we tend to follow injunctive norms only to the degree that they are salient to us raises an interesting point: Many persons are members of a number of different groups, and some of these groups may have opposing norms. For instance, should women who are executives behave in ways that are consistent with their gender or with their role as someone in authority? We examined this issue in detail in Chapter 5.

These findings and those of related studies (e.g., Kallgren, Reno, & Cialdini, 2000) suggest that norms influence our actions primarily when they are made salient. When we do not think about them or view them as irrelevant (i.e., as not applying to us), their effects are much weaker or nonexistent. One reason why people sometimes disobey even very strong injunctive norms is that they don't see these norms as applying to them. For instance, I have a friend who sometimes parks in spots reserved for handicapped people (see Figure 9.4). I think this behavior is indefensible and I avoid driving with her. She is a very considerate and law-abiding person overall, so why does she disobey this particular injunctive norm? She believes that because she is from another country where this is no such rule, it does not apply to her! In other words, she views this particular norm as irrelevant, so it does not influence her behavior, just as normative focus theory predicts.

Situational Norms: Automaticity in Normative Behavior

When you enter a museum or hospital, do you lower your voice? And when you are in a sports stadium, do you raise it? If so, you are showing adherence to what social psychologists describe as *situational norms*—norms that guide behavior in a certain situation or environment (e.g., Cialdini & Trost, 1998). But do you have to be aware of these norms—or any others—for them to influence your behavior? Research findings indicate that such awareness is not necessary. Norms can be activated in an automatic manner without your consciously thinking of them; and when they are, they can still strongly affect your overt actions. A clear illustration of such effects, and of the powerful effects of situational norms, is provided by research conducted by Aarts and Dijksterhuis (2003). They first asked participants to look at photographs of a library or an empty railway station. Some of the people who saw the library photo were told that they would be visiting this location later; others were not given this information. Then, they were instructed to read out loud ten words from a computer screen. The volume of their voices was measured as they performed this task.

Conformity: Group Influence in Action

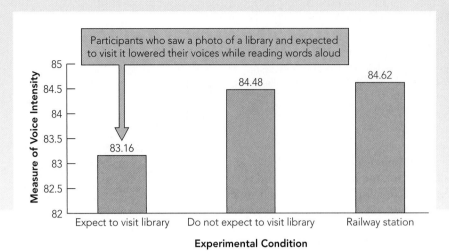

Figure 9.5 ■ The Effects of Situational Norms on Behavior
Participants who saw a photo of a library and expected to visit this location lowered the intensity of their voices relative to persons who saw a photo of a library but did not expect to visit it, or those who saw a photo of a railway station. This illustrates the effects of situational norms ("Be quiet in libraries") on overt behavior. (*Source: Based on data from Aarts & Dijksterhuis, 2003.*)

The researchers predicted that when individuals expected to visit the library, the situational norm of being quiet would be activated and that they would read the words less loudly. They also predicted that such effects would not occur when the individuals did not expect to visit the library or when they saw a photo of the railway station—a place in which the "Be quiet" norm does not apply. As you can see from Figure 9.5, this is precisely what was found: Participants lowered their voices in the expect-to-visit library condition relative to the other two.

In additional studies, Aarts and Dijksterhuis (2003) found similar effects with respect to acting polite in a fancy restaurant, thus indicating that situational norms operate in many locations, and that they can automatically influence our behavior in these settings. Participants for whom this norm had been activated actually ate a biscuit more neatly than those for whom this norm had not been primed! Overall, then, two facts seem clear: (1) Situational norms that tell us how to behave in a given environment or location often strongly affect our behavior, and (2) such norms—like other norms—can exert such effects in a relatively automatic manner, even if we do not consciously recognize their impact.

The Bases of Conformity: Why We Often Choose to "Go Along"

As noted, several factors determine whether and to what extent conformity occurs. Yet, this does not alter the essential point: Conformity is a basic fact of social life. Most people conform to the norms of their groups or societies much, if not most, of the time. Why do people often choose to go along with these social rules or expectations instead of resisting them? The answer seems to involve two powerful motives: the desire to be liked or accepted by others and the desire to be right—to have an accurate understanding of the social world (Deutsch & Gerard, 1955; Insko, 1985)—plus cognitive processes that lead us to view conformity as justified after it has occurred (e.g., Buehler & Griffin, 1994).

■ Normative Social Influence: The Desire to Be Liked

How can we get others to like us? As we saw in Chapters 3 and 7, many tactics can prove effective. One of the most successful ways is to appear to be as similar to others as possible. From our earliest days, we learn that agreeing with the persons around us, and behaving as they do, causes them to like us. Parents, teachers, friends, and others often heap praise and approval on us for showing such similarity (see the discussion of attitude formation in Chapter 4). A reason we conform, therefore, is this: We have learned that doing so can help us win approval and acceptance. This source of conformity is known as **normative social influence,** because it involves altering our behavior to meet others' expectations.

normative social influence
Social influence based on the desire to be liked or accepted by other persons.

Chapter 9 / Social Influence

■ The Desire to Be Right: Informational Social Influence

If you want to know your weight, you can step onto a scale. If you want to know the dimensions of a room, you can measure them. But how can you establish the accuracy of your political or social views or decide which hairstyle suits you best? There are no simple physical tests or measuring devices for answering these questions. Yet we want to be correct about such matters, too. The solution to this dilemma is obvious: To answer such questions, we refer to other people. We use *their* opinions and actions as guides for our own. Such reliance on others is often a powerful source of the tendency to conform. Other people's actions and opinions define social reality for us, and we use these as a guide for our own actions and opinions. This basis for conformity is known as **informational social influence,** because it is based on our tendency to depend on others as a source of information about the social world.

Research evidence suggests that because our motivation to be correct or accurate is strong, informational social influence is a powerful source of conformity. However, as you might expect, such motivation is more likely to be present in situations in which we are highly uncertain about what is "correct" or "accurate" than in situations in which we have more confidence in our decisions. That this is so is clearly illustrated by the results of a study conducted by Robert S. Baron, Vandello, and Brunsman (1996). In this investigation, the researchers used a modification of the Asch line-drawing task. They showed participants a drawing of a person and asked them to identify this person from among several others in a simulated eyewitness line-up. In one condition, the drawing was shown for only 0.5 seconds; this made the identification task difficult. In another condition, it was shown for 5.0 seconds, and the task was much easier. Another aspect of the study involved the importance of making an accurate decision. Half of the participants were told that the study was only preliminary in nature, so results were not very important. The others were told that results were very important to the researchers.

To measure conformity, participants were exposed to the judgments of two assistants who identified the *wrong* person before making their choice in the simulated line-up. The overall prediction was that when the study was described as being very important, participants would be more likely to conform when the task was difficult (when they saw them for only 0.5 seconds) than when the task was easy (when they saw them for 5.0 seconds). This is because under the former conditions, participants would be uncertain of their decisions and would rely on the judgments of the assistants. When the study was described as being relatively unimportant, however, task difficulty wouldn't matter: Conformity would be the same in both conditions. Results offered clear support for these predictions, suggesting that our desire to be correct or accurate can be a strong source of conformity, but primarily when we are uncertain about what is correct or accurate in a given situation.

How powerful are the effects of social influence when we are uncertain about what is and is not correct? Research suggests a chilling answer: extremely powerful. In one study with disturbing results (Apanovitch, Hobfoll, & Salovey, 2002), participants viewed a video showing a gang rape of a woman. After watching, participants discussed it and then rated the victim's pain, their empathy for her, and the extent to which the men were responsible for the rape. Unknown to the participants, one of the people present was an assistant of the experimenter who, as in Asch's research, expressed prearranged opinions. This person indicated that he either held the men responsible for the rape, held the woman responsible for the rape, or offered no clear opinion. Even though the participants then made their judgments privately, they were strongly influenced by the assistant's behavior, viewing the men as more responsible when the assistant expressed this view than when he blamed the woman for the rape (see Figure 9.6 on page 254). Why was this so? Rape, after all, is an atrocious behavior that everyone finds disturbing, so how could people's judgments about it be influenced so readily? The answer seems to be that the participants were uncertain about how they should react in an unfamiliar situation, and as a result, they were highly susceptible to influence. In other words, the results of this study provide a strong and disturbing illustration of the powerful impact social influence can have on our perceptions, behavior, and judgments.

informational social influence
Social influence based on the desire to be correct (i.e., to possess accurate perceptions of the social world).

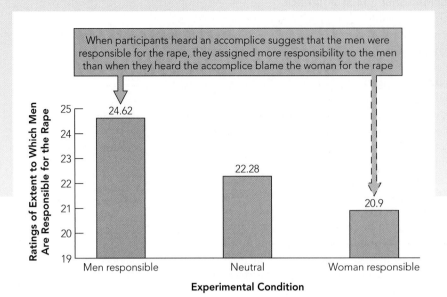

When participants heard an accomplice suggest that the men were responsible for the rape, they assigned more responsibility to the men than when they heard the accomplice blame the woman for the rape

Figure 9.6 ■ The Powerful Effects of Social Influence
When participants who had seen a videotape of a gang rape heard an accomplice blame the men for this appalling event, they assigned more responsibility to the men than when they heard the accomplice blame the woman, or when the accomplice voiced no clear opinion. (*Source: Based on data from Apanovitch, Hobfoll, & Salovey, 2002.*)

KEY POINTS

★ Many factors determine whether, and to what extent, conformity occurs. These include *cohesiveness*—degree of attraction felt by an individual toward some group, group size, and type of social norm operating in that situation (*descriptive* or *injunctive*).

★ Norms tend to influence our behavior primarily when they are relevant to us.

★ Situational norms, like other norms, can influence our behavior in an automatic manner, even when we are not consciously aware of them.

★ Two important motives underlie our tendency to conform: the desire to be liked and the desire to be right or accurate. These two motives are reflected in two distinct types of *social influence: normative* and *informational social influence.*

★ The effects of *social influence* are powerful and pervasive but tend to be magnified in situations in which we are uncertain about our own judgments or what is correct.

Resisting Pressures to Conform: Why, Sometimes, We Choose *Not* to "Go Along"

Having read our discussion of normative and informational social influence, you may have the distinct impression that pressures toward conformity are so strong that they are all but impossible to resist. If so, take heart. In many cases, individuals—or groups—*do* resist. This was certainly true in Asch's research, in which most of the participants yielded to social pressure, but *only part of the time.* On many occasions, they stuck to their guns even in the face of a unanimous majority that disagreed with them. If you want other illustrations of resistance to conformity pressures, just look around: You will find that while most persons adhere to social norms most of the time, some do not. And most people do not go along with all social norms; rather, they pick and choose, conforming to most norms but rejecting at least a few. Do you have any friends who hold very unpopular political or social views, and continue to do so despite strong pressure to conform? Conformity pressures are *not* irresistible. What accounts for our ability to resist them? Although many factors appear to be important (e.g., Burger, 1992), two seem to be most important: (1) the need to maintain our individuality and (2) the need to maintain control over our lives. (In Chapter 4, we examined a third factor—our tendency to restore our personal freedom by doing the opposite of what someone else is trying to get us to do [reactance].)

■ The Need to Maintain Individuality, Culture, and Resistance to Conformity

The need to maintain our individuality appears to be a powerful one. Yes, we want to be like others but not, it seems, to the extent that we lose our personal identity. Along with needs to be right and liked, most of us possess a desire for **individuation**—for being distinguishable from others in some respects (e.g., Maslach, Santee, & Wade, 1987). In general, we want to be like others, especially others we like or respect, but we don't want to be *exactly* like them, because that would involve giving up our individuality.

individuation
The need to be distinguishable from others in some respects.

If this is true, then an interesting prediction relating to the impact of culture on conformity—and on the ability to resist it—follows logically: The tendency to conform will be lower in cultures that emphasize individuality (individualistic cultures) than in those that emphasize being part of the group (collectivist cultures). Research by Bond and Smith (1996) examined this hypothesis by comparing conformity in seventeen countries. They examined the results of 133 past studies that used the Asch line-judging task to measure conformity. Among these studies, they identified ones conducted in countries with collectivist cultures (e.g., in Africa and Asia) and in countries with individualistic cultures (e.g., in North America and Western Europe). Then, they compared the amount of conformity shown in these two groups. Results were clear: More conformity did occur in the countries with collectivistic cultures, where the motive to maintain one's individuality was expected to be lower, and this was true regardless of the size of the influencing group. Similar results have been obtained in other studies (e.g., Hamilton & Sanders, 1995), so it appears that the need for individuation varies across different cultures and that these differences influence the tendency to conform.

■ The Desire for Personal Control

Another reason why individuals often choose to resist group pressure involves their desire to maintain control over their lives (e.g., Daubman, 1993). Most people want to believe that they can determine what happens to them, and yielding to social pressure can run counter to this desire. After all, going along with a group implies behaving in ways one might not ordinarily choose, and can be viewed as a restriction of personal freedom. Many study results suggest that the stronger the individuals' need for personal control, the less likely they are to yield to social pressure, so this, too, appears to be important where resisting conformity is concerned.

In sum, two motives—the desire to retain our individuality and the desire to retain control over our lives—serve to counter our desires to be liked and to be accurate, and so reduce conformity. Whether we conform in a given situation, then, depends on the relative strength of these motives and the complex interplay between them. Once again, therefore, we come face to face with the fact that trying to understand the roots of social behavior is often as complex as it is fascinating.

■ People Who Cannot Conform

So far, we have been focusing on people who can conform but choose not to. There are also many who cannot conform for physical, legal, or psychological reasons. Consider persons who are physically challenged. Though they can lead rich, full lives and participate in many activities that able-bodied persons enjoy, they cannot adhere to some social norms because of physical limitations. For instance, some cannot stand when the national anthem is played.

Homosexuals, too, face difficulties in adhering to social norms. Many same-sex couples participate in stable, long-term relationships and would like to adhere to the same social norms as heterosexuals, such as being entitled to marry, share benefits, and have families. Until recently, however, this was not possible in most countries. Even now, marriage between homosexuals is fully legal in only one country—the Netherlands. Marriage

Figure 9.7 ■ When People Can't Obey Social Norms
Sometimes, individuals want to conform to social norms but simply can't. For instance, many homosexual couples want to marry—but cannot because laws in many places restrict marriage to heterosexual couples. Although marriage between people of the same sex is now permitted in some locations, this is still the exception rather than the rule.

licenses are being granted in some places to same-sex couples, and some famous weddings have taken place—for instance, that of media-celebrities (see Figure 9.7) including that of Rosie O'Donnell (February 26, 2004). But stay tuned: Many people object to these changes on religious or moral grounds, so it is not entirely clear what the outcome will be. (Do men and women differ in the tendency to conform? For a discussion of this issue, see the **Making Sense of Common Sense** section.)

The Science of
Social Psychology

MAKING SENSE OF COMMON SENSE

Do Women and Men Differ in the Tendency to Conform?

Consider the following statement by Queen Victoria of England, one of the most powerful rulers in world history: *"We women are not made for governing—and if we are good women, we must dislike these masculine occupations. . . ."* (Letter of February 3, 1852). This and many similar quotations suggest that women do not like to be in charge—they would prefer to follow. And that idea, in turn, suggests that women may be more susceptible to conformity pressures than men. As informal evidence for this view, many people who accept it point to the fact that, in general, women seem to be more likely than men to follow changes in fashion with respect to clothing and personal grooming. But does this mean that they are really more likely to conform than men? Early studies on conformity (e.g., Crutchfield, 1955) seemed to suggest that they are. The results of these experiments indicated that women showed a greater tendency than men to yield to social pressure. More recent research, however, points to very different conclusions.

For instance, Eagly and Carli (1981) conducted a meta-analysis of 145 different studies in which more than twenty thousand people participated. Results indicated the existence of a very small difference between men and women, with women being slightly more accepting of social influence than men. So, if such gender differences existed, they were much smaller than common sense suggested.

But that's not the end of the story. Additional research has further clarified when and why these small differences may exist—if they exist at all. With respect to "when," it appears that both genders are more easily influenced when they are uncertain about how to behave or about the correctness of their judgments. And careful examination of many studies on conformity indicates that the situations and materials used were ones more familiar to men. The result? Men were more certain about how to behave and showed less conformity. Direct evidence for this reasoning was obtained by Sistrunk and McDavid (1971) who found that when males and females were equally familiar with the situations or materials employed, differences between them, in terms of conformity, disappeared.

Turning to "why" any gender differences in conformity might exist, the answer seems to involve differences in status. In the past—and even to some extent today—men tended to hold higher status jobs and positions in many societies than women. And there was a relationship between status and susceptibility to social influence: Lower status led to greater tendencies to conform (Eagly, 1987). So, when and if gender differences in conformity continue to exist, they seem to be linked to social factors such as differences in status and gender roles, not to any basic, "built-in" differences between the two genders.

Contrary to what common sense suggests, women are *not* much more accepting of social influence than men. On the contrary, any differences between the two genders that do exist are very small. And when such factors as confidence in one's judgments (as determined by familiarity with the situation) and social status are considered, these differences totally disappear. Once again, therefore, we see how the careful, scientific methods adopted by social psychologists help us to clarify and refine "common sense" views about important social issues.

Minority Influence: Does the Majority Always Rule?

As noted, individuals can, and often do, resist group pressure. Lone dissenters or small minorities can refuse to go along. Yet there is more going on in such situations than simply resistance; in addition, there are instances in which such persons—*minorities* within their groups—actually turn the tables on the majority and *exert* rather than merely *receive* social influence. History provides many examples of such events. Giants of science, such as Galileo, Pasteur, and Freud, faced virtually unanimous majorities that initially rejected their views. Yet, over time, these famous men overcame such resistance and won widespread acceptance of their theories. More recent examples of minorities influencing majorities are provided by the successes of environmentalists. Initially they were viewed as wild-eyed radicals with strange ideas. Gradually, however, they succeeded in changing the attitudes of the majority so that today, many of their views are widely accepted. And, of course, the framers of the U.S. Constitution were so concerned about protecting the rights of persons holding minority views that they established an indirect mechanism for electing the president—the electoral college.

But when, precisely, do minorities succeed in influencing majorities? Research findings suggest that they are most likely to do so under certain conditions (Moscovici, 1985). First, the members of such groups must be *consistent* in their opposition to majority opinions. If they waver or seem divided, their impact is reduced. Second, members of the minority must avoid appearing rigid and dogmatic (Mugny, 1975). A minority that merely repeats the same position is less persuasive than one that demonstrates a degree of flexibility. Third, the general social context in which a minority operates is important. If a minority argues for a position that is consistent with current social trends (e.g., conservative views at a time of growing conservatism), its chances of influencing the majority are greater than if it argues for a position out of step with such trends.

Of course, even when these conditions are met, minorities face a tough uphill fight. The power of majorities is great, especially in ambiguous or complex social situations in which majorities are viewed as more reliable sources of information about what is true. In this sense, however, the threat posed by majorities to minorities may actually help these minorities. Research findings indicate that because they feel greater concern over being right, minorities tend to overestimate the number of persons who share their views. In other words, they perceive more support for their positions than actually exists (Kenworthy & Miller, 2001). This can be encouraging and can strengthen the resolve of minorities to persevere in the face of daunting odds.

Additional evidence suggests that one positive effect produced by minorities is that they induce the majority to exert increased cognitive effort in order to understand *why* the minority holds its unusual and unpopular views (Nemeth, 1995; Vonk & van Knippenberg, 1995). In other words, deeply committed and vocal minorities can encourage members of the majority to engage in *systematic processing* with respect to information they provide (e.g., Smith, Tindale, & Dugoni, 1996; Wood et al., 1996; see Figure 9.8). Similarly, minority members may engage in more careful (systematic) thought themselves concerning their unpopular views. This, in turn, may lead them to generate stronger arguments with which to influence the majority (Zdaniuk & Levine, 1996). So, even if minorities fail to sway majorities initially, they may initiate processes that ultimately lead to large-scale social change (e.g., Alvaro & Crano, 1996).

Figure 9.8 ■ How Minorities Sometimes Influence Majorities
Minorities can encourage majorities to engage in more systematic processing of social information. This can lead at least some members of the majority to change their views.

KEY POINTS

★ Although pressures toward conformity are strong, many resist them, at least part of the time. This resistance seems to stem from two strong motives: the desire to retain one's individuality and the desire to exert control over one's life.

★ There are some people—for example, ones who are physically challenged and homosexuals who wish to marry—who cannot conform even if they wish to because of physical limitations or legal barriers, respectively.

★ Under some conditions, minorities can induce majorities to change their attitudes or behavior.

★ Because their views are threatened, minorities often overestimate the number of persons who share their beliefs.

★ One positive effect of minorities is that they induce majorities to think more systematically about the issues they raise, which may facilitate large-scale social change.

Compliance: To Ask—Sometimes—Is to Receive

Suppose that you wanted someone to do something for you. How would you go about getting them to agree? If you think about this for a moment, you may realize that you have quite a few tricks up your sleeve for gaining *compliance*. What are these techniques? Which ones work best? These are among the questions we now consider. Before doing so, however, we introduce a basic framework for understanding the nature of these procedures and why they often work.

Compliance: The Underlying Principles

Some years ago, one well-known social psychologist (Robert Cialdini) decided that the best way to find out about compliance was to study what he termed *compliance professionals*—people whose success (financial or otherwise) depends on their ability to get others to say "yes." They include salespeople, advertisers, political lobbyists, fundraisers, politicians, con artists, and professional negotiators, to name a few. Cialdini's technique for learning from these people was simple: He temporarily concealed his true identity and took jobs in various settings in which gaining compliance is a way of life. He worked in advertising, direct sales, fundraising, and other compliance-focused fields. On the basis of these first-hand experiences, he concluded that although techniques for gaining compliance take many forms, they all rest to some degree on six basic principles (Cialdini, 1994):

- *Friendship/Liking:* In general, we are more willing to comply with requests from friends or from people we like than from strangers or people we don't like.

- *Commitment/Consistency:* Once we have committed ourselves to a position or action, we are more willing to comply with requests for behaviors that are consistent with this position or action than with requests that are inconsistent with it.

- *Scarcity:* In general, we value, and try to secure, outcomes or objects that are scarce or decreasing in their availability. As a result, we are more likely to comply with requests that focus on scarcity than ones that make no reference to this issue.

- *Reciprocity:* We are generally more willing to comply with a request from someone who has previously provided a favor or concession to us than from someone who has not.

- *Social Validation:* We are more willing to comply with a request for some action if it is action is consistent with what we believe persons similar to ourselves are doing (or thinking). We want to be correct, and one way to do so is to act and think like others.

- *Authority:* In general, we are more willing to comply with requests from someone who holds legitimate authority—or simply appears to do so.

According to Cialdini (1994), these basic principles underlie many techniques used by professionals—and ourselves—for gaining compliance. We now examine techniques based on these principles, plus a few others.

"Very well put, Harper."

Tactics Based on Friendship or Liking: Ingratiation

We've already considered several techniques for increasing compliance through liking in our discussion of *impression management* (Chapter 3). Although this can be an end in itself, impression management techniques are often used for purposes of **ingratiation**—getting others to like us so that they will be more willing to agree to our requests (Jones, 1964; Liden & Mitchell, 1988).

Which ingratiation techniques work best? A review of existing studies on this topic (Gordon, 1996) suggests that *flattery*—praising others—is one of the best (see Figure 9.9). Other techniques that seem to work are improving one's appearance, emitting many positive nonverbal cues, and doing small favors for the target persons (Gordon, 1996; Wayne & Liden, 1995). We described many of these tactics in Chapter 3. Here, suffice it to say that many of the tactics used for purposes of impression management are also successful for increasing compliance.

Still another means of increasing others' liking for us, and thus raising the chances that they will agree to our requests, involves what has been termed *incidental similarity*—calling attention to small and slightly surprising similarities between them and ourselves. In several studies, Burger and his colleagues (Burger et al., 2004) found that research participants were more likely to agree to a small request (make a donation to charity) from a stranger when this person appeared to have the same first name or birthday as they did than when the requester was not similar to them in these ways. Apparently, these trivial forms of similarity enhance liking or a feeling of affiliation with the requester and so increase the tendency to comply with this person's requests.

ingratiation
A technique for gaining compliance in which requesters first induce target persons to like them and then attempt to change the persons' behavior in some desired manner.

Tactics Based on Commitment or Consistency: The Foot-in-the-Door and the Lowball

When you visit the food court of your local shopping mall, are you ever approached by people offering you free samples of food? If so, why do they do this? The answer is simple: They know that once you have accepted this small free gift, you will be more willing to buy something from them. This is the basic idea behind the **foot-in-the-door technique.** Basically, this involves inducing targets to agree to a small initial request ("Accept this free sample") and then making a larger request—the one desired all along. The results of many studies indicate that this tactic works; it succeeds in inducing increased compliance (e.g., Beaman et al., 1983; Freedman & Fraser, 1966). Why? Because the foot-in-the-door technique rests on the principle of *consistency:* Once we have said "yes" to the small request, we are more likely to say "yes" to subsequent and larger ones, because refusing would be inconsistent with our previous behavior.

The foot-in-the-door technique is not the only compliance tactic based on the consistency/commitment principle. Another is the **lowball procedure.** With this technique, which is often used by automobile salespersons, a very good deal is offered to a customer. After the customer accepts, something happens that makes it necessary for the salesperson to change the deal and

foot-in-the-door technique
A procedure for gaining compliance in which requesters begin with a small request and then, when this is granted, escalate to a larger one (the one they actually desire all along).

lowball procedure
A technique for gaining compliance in which an offer or deal is changed to make it less attractive to the target person after this person has accepted it.

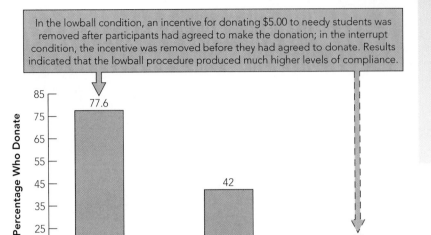

In the lowball condition, an incentive for donating $5.00 to needy students was removed after participants had agreed to make the donation; in the interrupt condition, the incentive was removed before they had agreed to donate. Results indicated that the lowball procedure produced much higher levels of compliance.

Figure 9.10 ■ The Role of Commitment in the Lowball Technique
Results indicated that the lowball procedure generated much higher rates of compliance. These findings underscore the importance of an initial commitment in the lowball technique. (*Source: Based on data from Burger & Cornelius, 2003.*)

make it less advantageous for the customer—for example, the sales manager rejects the deal. The totally rational reaction for customers, of course, is to walk away. Yet, they often agree and accept the less desirable arrangement (Cialdini et al., 1978). In such instances, an initial commitment seems to make it more difficult for individuals to say "no," even though the conditions that led them to say "yes" in the first place have changed.

Clear evidence for the importance of an initial commitment in the success of the lowball technique is provided by research conducted by Burger and Cornelius (2003). These researchers phoned students living in dorms and asked them if they would contribute $5 to a scholarship fund for underprivileged students. In the lowball condition, a researcher indicated that persons who contributed would receive a coupon for a free smoothie at a local juice bar. Then, if participants agreed to make a donation, she told them that she had just run out of coupons and couldn't offer them this incentive. She then asked if they would still contribute. In another condition (the interrupt condition), she made the initial request, but before the participants could answer "yes" or "no," interrupted them and indicated that there were no more coupons for persons who donated. Finally, in a third (control) condition, participants were asked to donate $5 with no mention of any coupons. Results indicated that more persons in the lowball condition agreed to make a donation than in either of the other two conditions (see Figure 9.10).

These results indicate that the lowball procedure does rest on the principles of commitment: Only when individuals are permitted to make an initial public commitment—when they say "yes" to the initial offer—does it work. Having made this initial commitment, they feel compelled to stick with it, even though the conditions that led them to say "yes" in the first place no longer exist. Truly, this is a subtle yet powerful technique for gaining compliance.

Tactics Based on Reciprocity: The Door-in-the-Face and the That's-Not-All Techniques

Reciprocity is a basic rule of social life: We usually "do unto others as they have done unto us." If they have done a favor for us, we feel that we should be willing to do one for them in return. While most view this as fair and just, the principle of reciprocity also serves as the basis for several techniques for gaining compliance. One of these is, on the face of it, the opposite of the foot-in-the-door technique. Instead of beginning with a small request and then escalating, persons seeking compliance sometimes start with a large request and after this is rejected, shift to a smaller request—the one they wanted all along. This tactic is known as the **door-in-the-face technique** (because the first refusal seems to slam the door

door-in-the-face technique
A procedure for gaining compliance in which requesters begin with a large request and then, when this is refused, retreat to a smaller one (the one they actually desire all along).

in the face of the requester), and several studies indicate that it can be quite effective. In one well-known experiment, Cialdini and his colleagues (1975) stopped college students on the street and presented a huge request: Would the students serve as unpaid counselors for juvenile delinquents two hours a week for the next *two years!* As you can predict, no one agreed. When the experimenters scaled down their request to a much smaller one—would the same students take a group of delinquents on a two-hour trip to the zoo—50 percent agreed. In contrast, fewer than 17 percent of those in a control group agreed to this smaller request when it was presented alone.

This same tactic is often used by negotiators, who may begin with a position that is extremely advantageous to themselves but then retreat to a position much closer to the one they hope to obtain. Similarly, sellers often begin with a price they know buyers will reject, and then lower it—but one that is still quite favorable to themselves and close to what they wanted all along.

A related procedure for gaining compliance is known as the **that's-not-all technique.** Here, an initial request is followed, *before the target person can say "yes" or "no,"* by something that sweetens the deal—an extra incentive from the person using this tactic (e.g., a reduction in price, something additional for the same price). For example, television commercials for various products frequently offer something extra to induce viewers to pick up the phone and order. Several studies confirm informal observations suggesting that the that's-not-all technique really works (Burger, 1986). Why is this so? One possibility is because it is based on the principle of reciprocity: Persons on the receiving end view the "extra" thrown in as an added concession, and feel obligated to make a concession themselves. The result: They are more likely to say "yes."

Another possibility is that creating the appearance of a bargain by reducing the price or offering to add something extra causes individuals to think about the situation in an automatic or, as social psychologists sometimes put it, *mindless* way (e.g., Langer, 1984). "This is a bargain," people might reason, and in accordance with this heuristic thinking, become more likely to say "yes" than would be true if they were thinking more systematically. Evidence for this was reported by Pollock and his colleagues (1988). They found that a small price reduction produced the that's-not-all effect for a low-cost item (a $1.25 box of chocolates reduced to $1.00) but did not produce this effect for a more expensive item (a $6.25 box reduced to $5.00). Apparently, individuals thought more about spending $5.00, and this countered their tendency to respond automatically—and favorably—to a small price reduction. Whatever its precise basis, the that's-not-all technique can be an effective means for increasing the likelihood that others will say "yes" to various requests.

that's-not-all technique
A technique for gaining compliance in which requesters offer additional benefits to target persons before these persons have decided whether to comply with or reject specific requests.

Tactics Based on Scarcity: Playing Hard to Get and the Fast-Approaching-Deadline Technique

It's a general rule that things that are scarce, rare, or difficult to obtain are viewed as being more valuable than those that are plentiful. Thus, we are often willing to expend more effort or go to greater expense to obtain items or outcomes that are scarce. This principle serves as the foundation for several techniques for gaining compliance. One of the most common is **playing hard to get.** Many people know that playing hard to get can be an effective tactic in the area of romance. This tactic is not restricted to interpersonal attraction, however; research findings indicate that it is also used by job candidates to increase their attractiveness to potential employers, and hence increase the likelihood that they will offer them a job. Persons using this tactic let the potential employer know that they have other offers and so are a very desirable employee. Research findings indicate that this technique often works (Williams et al., 1993).

A related procedure also based on the what's-scarce-is-valuable principle is one frequently used by department stores. Ads using this **deadline technique** state that a special sale will end on a certain date, implying that after that, the prices will go up. In many cases, the time limit is false: The prices won't go up after the indicated date and may continue to drop if the merchandise remains unsold. Yet many persons reading such ads or seeing signs such as the one

playing hard to get
A technique that can be used for increasing compliance by suggesting that a person or object is scarce and hard to obtain.

deadline technique
A technique for increasing compliance in which target persons are told that they have only limited time to take advantage of some offer or to obtain some item.

plate! That these chilling results are not restricted to a single culture is indicated by the fact that similar findings were reported in several different countries (e.g., Jordan, Germany, Australia) and with children as well as adults (e.g., Kilham & Mann, 1974; Shanab & Yahya, 1977). Thus, Milgram's findings seemed to be alarmingly general in scope.

Destructive Obedience: Why It Occurs

One reason Milgram's results are so disturbing is that they seem to parallel many real-life events involving atrocities against innocent victims. Why does such destructive obedience occur? Social psychologists have identified several factors that seem to play a role, and several of these are related to other aspects of social influence we have already considered.

First, in many situations, the persons in authority relieve those who obey of responsibility for their own actions. "I was only carrying out orders" is the defense many offer after obeying harsh commands. In real-life situations, this transfer of responsibility may be implicit; the person in charge is assumed to have the responsibility for what happens, which seems to be what happened in the tragic events of 2004 when U.S. soldiers—both men and women—were filmed abusing and torturing Iraqi prisoners. Their defense? "I was only following orders . . . I was told to do this, and a good soldier always obeys!" In Milgram's experiments, this transfer of responsibility was explicit. Participants were told at the start that the experimenter, not they, would be responsible for the learner's well-being. In view of this fact, it is not surprising that many obeyed: After all, they were let completely off the hook.

Second, persons in authority often possess visible badges or signs of their status. They wear special uniforms or insignia, have special titles, and so on. These indicators serve to remind many of the social norm "Obey the persons in charge." This norm is powerful, and when confronted with it, most people find it difficult to disobey. After all, we do not want to do the wrong thing, and obeying the commands of those in charge usually helps us avoid such errors. In a sense, then, informational social influence—a key factor in conformity to social norms—may have contributed to Milgram's results (e.g., Bushman, 1988; Darley, 1995).

A third reason for obedience in many situations in which the targets of such influence might otherwise resist involves the gradual escalation of the authority figure's orders. Initial commands may call for relatively mild actions, such as merely arresting people. Only later do orders come to require dangerous or objectionable behavior. For example, police or military personnel may at first be ordered to question or threaten potential victims. Gradually, demands are increased to beat, torture, or even murder unarmed civilians. In a sense, persons in authority use the foot-in-the-door technique, asking for small actions first but ever-larger ones later. In a similar manner, participants in Milgram's research were first required to deliver only mild and harmless shocks. Only as the sessions continued did the intensity of these "punishments" rise to potentially harmful levels.

Finally, events in many situations involving destructive obedience move very quickly: Demonstrations turn into riots, arrests into mass beatings, and so on. The fast pace of such events gives participants little time for reflection or systematic processing: People are ordered to obey and—almost automatically—they do so. Such conditions prevailed in Milgram's research; within a few minutes of entering the laboratory, participants found themselves faced with commands to deliver strong electric shocks to the learner. This fast pace, too, may tend to increase obedience.

Destructive Obedience: Resisting Its Effects

Now that we have considered some of the factors responsible for the strong tendency to obey sources of authority, we turn to a related question: How can this type of social influence be resisted? Several strategies may be helpful.

First, individuals exposed to commands from authority figures can be reminded that they—not the authorities—are responsible for any harm produced. Under these conditions, sharp reductions in the tendency to obey have been observed (e.g., Hamilton, 1978; Kilham & Mann, 1974).

Chapter 9 / Social Influence

Figure 9.14 ■ Resisting Authority: Sometimes, It Can Change the World
When small bands of colonists took a stand against Great Britain—the most powerful nation in the world at that time—they started a process that ultimately changed the world.

Second, individuals can be provided with a clear indication that beyond some point, total submission to destructive commands is inappropriate. One procedure that is highly effective involves exposing individuals to the actions of *disobedient models*—persons who refuse to obey an authority figure's commands. Research findings indicate that such models can reduce unquestioning obedience (e.g., Rochat & Modigliani, 1995). When we see one or more persons refuse to obey the commands of an authority figure, we may be encouraged to do the same, with the ultimate result that the power of those in authority is severely weakened.

Third, individuals may find it easier to resist influence from authority figures if they question their expertise and motives. Are those in authority really in a better position to judge what is and is not appropriate? What motives lie behind their commands: socially beneficial goals or selfish gains? Dictators always claim that their brutal orders reflect their undying concern for their fellow citizens and are in their best interests, but to the extent that large numbers of persons question these motives, the power of such dictators can be eroded and perhaps, ultimately, swept away.

Finally, simply knowing about the power of authority figures to command blind obedience may be helpful. Some research findings (e.g., Sherman, 1980) suggest that when individuals learn about the results of social psychological research, they often recognize these as important (Richard, Bond, & Stokes-Zooter, 2001) and sometimes change their behavior to take account of this new knowledge. With respect to destructive obedience, there is some hope that knowing about this process can enhance individuals' resolve to resist. To the extent that this enlightenment takes place, even exposure to findings as disturbing as Milgram's can have positive social value.

To conclude, the power of authority figures to command obedience is great, but it is not irresistible. Under appropriate conditions, it can be countered or reduced. As in other areas of life, there is a choice. Deciding to resist the commands of persons in authority can be highly dangerous: Persons in authority usually control most of the weapons, the army, and the police. Yet, history is filled with instances in which the authority of powerful and entrenched regimes has been resisted by courageous persons who ultimately triumphed. Indeed, the American Revolution began in just this way: Small bands of poorly armed citizens decided to make a stand against Great Britain, the most powerful country on earth at the time (see Figure 9.14). The success of the colonists in winning their independence became a model for many people all over the world—and changed history. The lesson is clear: Power is never permanent, and, ultimately, victory often goes to those who stand for freedom and decency rather than those who wish to exert total control over the lives of their fellow human beings.

KEY POINTS

★ *Obedience* is a form of social influence in which one person orders one or more persons to do something, and they do so. It is, in a sense, the most direct form of *social influence*.

★ Research by Stanley Milgram indicates that many persons readily obey orders from a relatively powerless source of authority, even if the orders require them to harm an innocent stranger.

★ Such destructive obedience stems from several factors. These include the shifting of responsibility to the authority figure; outward signs of authority on the part of these persons, which serve as reminders of the norm "Obey those *(continued)*

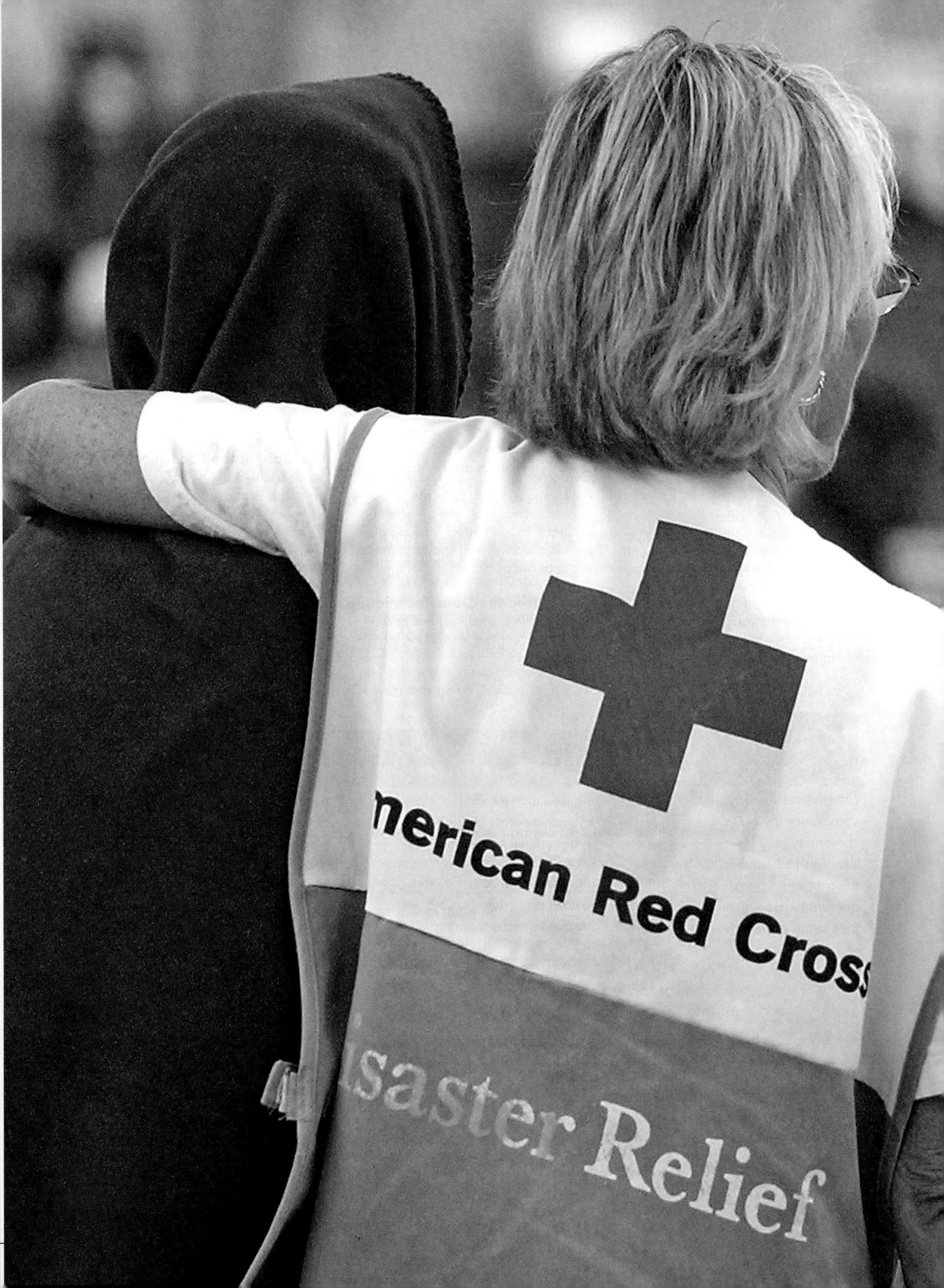

merican Red Cross
isaster Relief

10 PROSOCIAL BEHAVIOR
Helping Others

I (Donn Byrne) traveled to Kansas State University to give a talk in honor of William Griffitt, one of my former students who died suddenly, many years before his time. My daughter, Rebecka, and I flew to Kansas City, rented a car, and drove to Manhattan. The next morning we planned to drive to the psychology department to meet a group for lunch. At the motel desk, I asked for directions. The desk clerks were unsure, but told me where to drive on campus to obtain a parking permit and a map.

As is true of most university campuses, space for cars is limited, and we discovered that the parking area was located some distance from where we needed to go. That would have been OK, but it was raining that morning, and a long walk would have resulted in some damp and messy notes and slides.

So, we returned quickly to the motel and told the ladies at the desk that we needed a taxi. Unlike that other place named Manhattan, the streets of Manhattan, Kansas, are not characterized by fleets of cruising cabs. We were told it would probably be a half hour to forty-five minutes before one could be at the motel. That would have made us late for the luncheon and both my daughter and I must have looked at least mildly distressed and helpless.

The desk clerks conferred and said they would try to locate one of the motel employees who was currently working on a leaking water pipe. They reached his cell phone, and he said he would be glad to drive us to the campus. Not only did he take us exactly where we needed to go, but he was adamant about not accepting a tip—another difference between the two Manhattans.

Our problem was solved, and we were very grateful. Note that we were just strangers in town for a brief period, and our need for help was not in any way the responsibility of the desk clerks or the maintenance man. They spent time and effort solving our little problem, and wanted nothing in return. Why in the world did they help us?

prosocial behavior
A helpful action that benefits other people without necessarily providing any direct benefits to the person performing the act, and that may even involve a risk for the person who helps.

A more general issue, and one that is the subject of this chapter, is the question of why people in need of assistance are sometimes helped by strangers and sometimes ignored. The goal of social psychologists is to understand and predict **prosocial behavior**—any act that benefits others. Generally, the term is applied to acts that do not provide any direct benefit to the persons who perform the acts, and may even involve some degree of risk. The term **altruism** is sometimes used interchangeably with *prosocial behavior*. But altruism specifically means an *unselfish concern* for the welfare of others.

In this chapter, we first describe some of the basic factors that influence whether a person who witnesses an emergency will or will not *respond to an emergency* with a prosocial act. Next, we examine a variety of *situational, emotional, and dispositional influences on helping behavior*. Then, we shift to those who *volunteer* to help others over a long period; the conflict faced by all potential helpers between *self-interest, moral integrity, and moral hypocrisy;* and *how it feels to receive help*. The final topic is a comparison of social psychological and genetic *explanations of prosocial motivation*.

altruism
Behavior that is motivated by an unselfish concern for the welfare of others.

Responding to an Emergency: Will Bystanders Help?

When an emergency arises, you often hear stories of someone providing assistance to a stranger (see Figure 10.1). You also hear stories of people standing by and doing nothing. What explains such dramatic differences in behavior? Before answering, we present a few examples of the extremes that range from heroic actions to apathetic indifference.

When a Stranger Is Distressed: Heroism or Apathy?

The word *heroism* is often used incorrectly to mean anyone who does a difficult job well, and we may speak of a football hero who completed a pass that resulted in the winning touchdown or the person who made a heroic effort by escaping a sinking boat just in time to avoid drowning. As Becker and Eagly (2004) point out, **heroism** actually refers to actions that involve courageous risk taking to obtain a socially valued goal. Both aspects must be involved. Someone who engages in risky behavior for fun is not a hero, and saving one's own life may be valuable but not heroic. Someone who simply does socially valuable work such as nursing is to be congratulated for choosing a prosocial occupation, but not for being a hero. It doesn't matter whether the positive action occurs carefully and deliberately or impulsively and uncontrollably; either way, the behavior receives moral praise (Pizarro, Uhlmann, & Salovey, 2003).

heroism
Actions that involve courageous risk taking to obtain a socially valued goal. An example would be a dangerous act undertaken to save the life of a stranger.

Examples of heroic behavior include winners of the Carnegie Hero Medal each year. The winners are ordinary citizens who have risked their lives in saving or attempting to save another person. Beginning in 1904, winners have typically saved people who were attacked by animals (or criminals), or who were threatened by fires, drowning, electrocution, or other potentially fatal dangers (Wooster, 2000). Equally dramatic was the behavior of many gentiles in Europe during World War II who risked their lives to save Jews from the Nazi threat (United States Holocaust Memorial Museum, 2003). Becker and Eagly (2004) also apply the term *hero* to individuals who take risks in less dangerous and dramatic ways, such as donating a kidney to someone in need of a transplant, joining the Peace Corps, or volunteering to work overseas with Doctors of the World. Reading about the individuals who are willing to take risks to help others suggests that many of our fellow humans are impressively prosocial and unselfish. They can be described as just, brave, and caring (Walker & Hennig, 2004).

Figure 10.1 ■ Responding to an Emergency
The family of this small Iraqi boy was caught in crossfire during a battle in central Iraq; he is being comforted by a U.S. Navy Hospital Corpsman.

Unfortunately, there are also examples of unresponsiveness to emergencies, suggesting selfishness, unconcern, and apathy. Psychological interest in prosocial behavior was initially sparked by an incident in which bystanders *failed* to help a stranger in distress. The event was a murder that took place in the mid-1960s in New York City. Coming home from work as a bar manager, Catherine (Kitty) Genovese was crossing the street to her apartment building when she was approached by a man holding a knife. Ms. Genovese ran, but he chased after her until he was close enough to stab her. She screamed for help, and lights went on in many of the apartments that overlooked the scene. Many residents looked out, trying to determine what was happening. At this point, the attacker started to leave, but when he saw that no one was coming to help the victim, he returned and murdered her. Afterward, investigators found out that the forty-five minute attack was witnessed by thirty-eight residents of the apartment building, but not one of them either ventured out to help or called the police (Rosenthal, 1964). Why not?

Before we describe some of the research designed to answer that question, please read **The Science of Social Psychology: Making Sense of Common Sense,** which deals with one relatively simple explanation.

MAKING SENSE OF COMMON SENSE

Do More Witnesses to an Emergency Mean That More Help Is Given?

Consider the following scenario. You are walking across an icy street, lose your footing as you step up on the curb, and fall, injuring your knee. Because of your pain and the slickness of the ice, you find that you can't get back on your feet. Suppose (1) the block is relatively deserted, and only one person is close enough to witness your accident, or (2) the block is crowded, and a dozen people see what happened. Common sense suggests that the more bystanders that are present, the more likely you are to be helped. In the first situation, you are forced to depend on the helpfulness of just one individual and that person's decision to help or not help. In the second situation, with twelve witnesses, there would seem to be a much greater chance that one of them (and quite possibly more) will be motivated to behave in a prosocial way. Right? Wrong.

The explanation for the fact that multiple bystanders do not translate into multiple helpers was formulated, shortly after the Kitty Genovese murder, by two social psychologists, John Darley and Bibb Latané. Over lunch, they speculated as to why the large number of bystanders did nothing to stop the killer. In the media, there was much speculation about the widespread selfishness and indifference of people in general or at least of people in big cities. If multiple witnesses increase the odds that someone will help, did that mean that the murder was witnessed and ignored by thirty-eight cold and uncaring individuals?

Darley and Latané (1968) proposed a different, and not at all obvious, reason for the unresponsiveness of the bystanders—instead of increasing the odds that prosocial behavior will

occur, having multiple bystanders *decreases* the odds. And, rather than apathy, the large number of witnesses experienced **diffusion of responsibility.** That is, the more bystanders that are present, the less responsibility any one of them feels. If that idea is correct, in a situation with only one bystander, help is very likely to be given because all of the responsibility is centered on one individual. As the number of bystanders increases, each one has a smaller and smaller share of the responsibility, and the less likely anyone is to help. The two psychologists designed an experiment to test their prediction of what has become known as the **bystander effect.**

In their groundbreaking experiment, male college students were deliberately exposed to an "emergency" in which a fellow student apparently had a seizure, began to choke, and was clearly in need of help. The participants interacted by means of an intercom, and it was arranged that some believed they were the only person aware of the emergency, one of two bystanders, or one of five bystanders. Helpfulness was measured in terms of (1) the percentage of participants in each experimental group who attempted to help and (2) the time that passed before the help began.

As summarized in Figure 10.2, the prediction about diffusion of responsibility was correct. The more bystanders, the lower the percentage of students who made a prosocial response and the longer the helpful students waited before responding. In the example we gave, it appears that you would be more likely to be helped if you fell with only one witness present than twelve of them.

Over the years, additional research on prosocial behavior has identified many additional factors that determine how people respond to an emergency, but the bystander effect is clearly an important basic discovery. More recently, the

Five Crucial Steps Determine Helping versus Not Helping

As the study of prosocial behavior expanded beyond the initial concern with the number of bystanders, Latané and Darley (1970) proposed that the likelihood of a person engaging in a prosocial act is determined by a series of decisions that must be made quickly by those who witness an emergency. Any one of us can sit in a comfortable chair and figure out instantly what bystanders should do. The witnesses to the stabbing attack should have called the police immediately or perhaps even intervened by shouting at the attacker or working as a group to halt the attack. On September 11, 2001, the passengers on one of the hijacked planes apparently responded jointly, thus preventing the terrorists from accomplishing their goal of crashing the plane into the U.S. Capitol. When you are suddenly and unexpectedly facing an actual emergency, you have to figure out what is going on and what, if anything, to do about it. At each step in the decision process, as shown in Figure 10.3 on page 278, numerous factors operate to make helping behavior more or less likely to occur.

diffusion of responsibility
The idea that the amount of responsibility assumed by bystanders in an emergency is shared among them.

bystander effect
The fact that the likelihood of a prosocial response to an emergency is affected by the number of bystanders who are present.

implicit bystander effect
The decrease in helping behavior brought about by simply thinking about being in a group.

bystander effect has been extended to include simply thinking about groups. For example, imagining a dinner gathering with a group (versus having dinner with just one person) inhibits prosocial responsiveness (Garcia et al., 2002). Thus, the priming (see Chapter 2) of a social context by inducing people to think about the presence of others results in less helping behavior in a subsequent, unrelated situation. Such findings indicate that diffusion of responsibility can be triggered not only by the presence of others, but also by cognitive processes, thus constituting an **implicit bystander effect.**

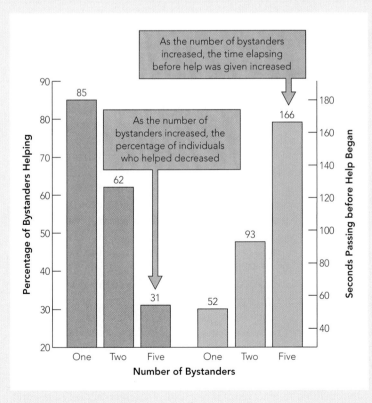

Figure 10.2 ■ The Inhibiting Effect of Multiple Bystanders
In the initial experiment designed to test the proposed *bystander effect,* Darley and Latané (1968) placed college students in a situation in which a fellow student called for help because of what seemed to be a medical emergency. Each participant believed himself to be either the only bystander, one of two bystanders, or one of five. As the number of bystanders increased, the percentage of individuals who tried to help the victim decreased. In addition, among those who did attempt to help, the more bystanders, the greater the delay before help was initiated. This effect is explained in terms of *diffusion of responsibility* among those who could provide help—the more bystanders, the less responsibility for each one. (*Source: Based on data in Darley & Latané, 1968.*)

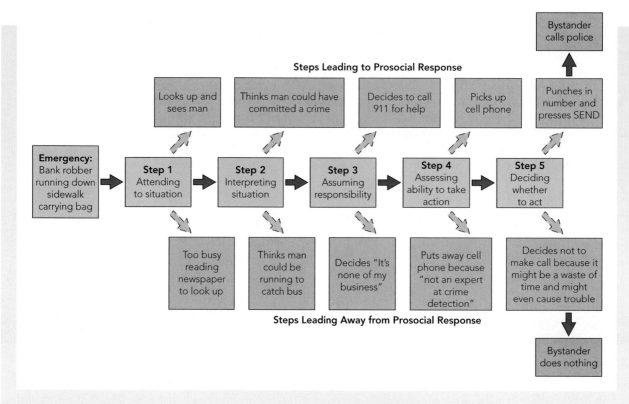

Figure 10.3 ■ **Responding to an Emergency: Five Steps to Prosocial Behavior**
A prosocial response to an emergency has been conceptualized as the end point of a series of five steps or choice points. At each step, an individual either becomes less likely or more likely to engage in a prosocial response. (*Source: Based on material in Latané & Darley, 1970.*)

■ Step 1. Noticing or Failing to Notice That Something Unusual Is Happening

An emergency is obviously something that occurs unexpectedly, and there is no sure way to anticipate that it will occur or to plan how to respond. We are ordinarily doing something else and thinking about other things when we hear a scream outside, observe that a fellow student is coughing and unable to speak, or observe that some of the passengers on our airplane are standing up with box cutters in their hands. If we are asleep, deep in thought, or concentrating on something else, we may simply *fail to notice* that anything unusual is happening.

In everyday life, we ignore many sights and sounds because they are ordinarily not relevant. If we were not able to screen out most aspects of our surroundings, we would be overwhelmed by an overload of information. Darley and Batson (1973) conducted a field study to test the importance of this first step in the decision process. Their research was conducted with students in training for the clergy, individuals who should be especially likely to help a stranger in need. The experimenters instructed each participant to walk to a nearby building on the campus to give a talk. In order to vary the degree of preoccupation, the investigators created three conditions. Some of the seminary students were told that they had plenty of extra time to reach the other building, some were told that they were right on schedule with just enough time to get there, and the third group was told that they were late and needed to hurry. Presumably, during their walk across campus, individuals in the first group would be the least preoccupied by the need to hurry, and those in the third group would be the most preoccupied. Would you guess that the degree of preoccupation influenced whether or not the participants engaged in prosocial behavior? The answer is a resounding "Yes!"

Along the route to the building, an emergency was staged. A stranger (actually a research assistant) was slumped in a doorway, coughing and groaning. Would the students notice this

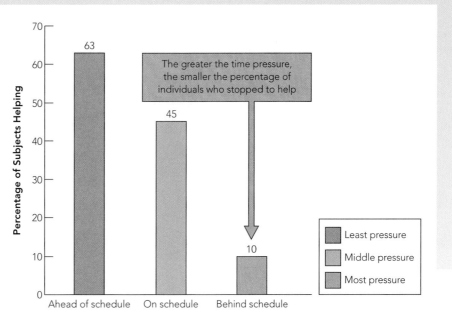

Figure 10.4 ■ In Too Much of a Hurry to Notice an Emergency
When participants were told that they were ahead of schedule in getting to an appointment, most stopped and helped a stranger who was slumped over, coughing and groaning in a doorway. Among those who were told they were on schedule, less than half stopped to help. Among those supposedly late for the appointment, only one out of ten stopped and provided assistance. (*Source: Based on data from Darley & Batson, 1973.*)

The greater the time pressure, the smaller the percentage of individuals who stopped to help

Least pressure
Middle pressure
Most pressure

Percentage of Subjects Helping

Time Pressure Based on Schedule

Ahead of schedule — 63
On schedule — 45
Behind schedule — 10

apparently sick or injured individual? As shown in Figure 10.4, 63 percent of the participants who had time to spare provided help. For the group that was on schedule, 45 percent helped. In the most preoccupied group, only 10 percent responded. Many of the preoccupied students paid little or no attention to the person who was coughing and groaning. They simply stepped over him and continued on their way.

It seems clear that a person who is too busy to pay attention to his or her surroundings is very likely not to notice even an obvious emergency. Under these conditions, little help is given because the potential helper is not aware that an emergency exists.

■ Step 2. Correctly Interpreting an Event as an Emergency

After we pay attention to an event, we have only limited and incomplete information as to what exactly is happening. Most of the time, whatever catches our attention turns out not to be an emergency and need not be a concern of ours. Whenever potential helpers are not completely sure about what is going on, they tend to hold back and wait for further information. It's quite possible that in the early morning when Kitty Genovese was murdered, her neighbors could not clearly see what was happening, even though they heard the screams and knew that a man and a woman seemed to be having a dispute. It could have been a loud argument between a woman and her boyfriend. Or, perhaps the couple had been drinking and were just joking around. Either of these two possibilities is actually more likely to be true than the fact that a stranger was stabbing a woman to death. With ambiguous information as to whether one is witnessing a serious problem or something inconsequential, most people are inclined to accept a comforting, undemanding, and usually accurate interpretation that indicates no need to take action (Wilson & Petrus Ka, 1984).

This suggests that the presence of multiple witnesses may inhibit helping not only because of the diffusion of responsibility, but also because it is embarrassing to misinterpret a situation and to act inappropriately. Making such a serious mistake in front of strangers might lead them to conclude that you are overreacting (see Figure 10.5 on page 280).

When others are present as fellow observers of such events, we rely on social comparisons to test our interpretations (see Chapters 4, 7, and 9). If other people show no sign of alarm about whatever we are witnessing, it is safer to follow their lead. No one wants to look foolish or to lose his or her "cool." The tendency for an individual surrounded by strangers to hesitate and do nothing is based on what is known as **pluralistic ignorance.** That is, because

pluralistic ignorance
The tendency of bystanders in an emergency to rely on what other bystanders do and say, even though none of them is sure about what is happening or what to do about it. Very often, all of the bystanders hold back and behave as if there is no problem. Each individual uses this "information" to justify the failure to act.

"I'M NOT JUMPING . . . THIS IS THE DESIGNATED SMOKING AREA."

©2004 WM. HOEST ENTERPRISES, INC.

Figure 10.5 ■ Misinterpreting a Situation as an Emergency
In order to respond to an emergency, one must interpret the situation correctly. Because people fear making a mistake and looking foolish, they may hesitate before taking action until they are sure. In this cartoon, the man in the window believed he was at the scene of a suicide attempt, but the man on the ledge was only there to smoke a cigarette. (*Source:* © 2004; Reprinted courtesy of Bunny Hoest and Parade Magazine.)

none of the bystanders knows for sure what is happening, each depends on the others to provide cues. Each individual is less likely to respond if the others fail to respond. Latané and Darley (1968) provided a dramatic demonstration of how far people will go to avoid making a possibly inappropriate response to what may or may not be an emergency. The investigators placed students in a room alone or with two others and asked them to fill out questionnaires. After several minutes, the experimenters secretly and quietly pumped smoke into the research room through a vent. When a participant was working there alone, most (75 percent) stopped what they were doing when the smoke appeared and left the room to report the problem. When three people were in the room, however, only 38 percent reacted to the smoke. Even after it became so thick that it was difficult to see, 62 percent continued to work on the questionnaire and failed to make any response to the smoke-filled room. The presence of other people clearly inhibits responsiveness. It is as if risking death is preferable to making a fool of oneself.

This inhibiting effect is much less if the group consists of friends rather than strangers, because friends are likely to communicate with one another (Rutkowski, Gruder, & Romer, 1983). The same is true of people in small towns who are likely to know one another as opposed to big cities where most people are strangers (Levine et al., 1994). Interestingly, any anxiety about the reactions of others and thus the fear of doing the wrong thing is reduced by alcohol. As a result, people who have been drinking show an increased tendency to be helpful (Steele, Critchlow, & Liu, 1985).

■ Step 3. Deciding That It Is Your Responsibility to Provide Help

In many instances, the responsibility is clear (see Figure 10.6). Firefighters are the ones to do something about a blazing building, police officers take charge when cars collide, and medical personnel deal with injuries and illnesses. If responsibility is not clear, people assume that anyone in a leadership role must take responsibility—adults with children, professors with undergraduates, and so on

Figure 10.6 ■ Who Is Responsible for Doing Something?
In many emergency situations, certain individuals are the appropriate ones to take charge—a military officer in response to an armed attack, a police officer in response to an accident or a crime, someone with medical training in response to a injury or illness, and so forth.

(Baumeister et al., 1988). As we pointed out earlier, when there is only *one* bystander, he or she usually takes charge because there is no alternative.

■ Step 4. Deciding That You Have the Necessary Knowledge and/or Skills to Act

Even if a bystander progresses as far as step 3 and assumes responsibility, a prosocial response cannot occur unless the person knows *how* to be helpful. Some emergencies are sufficiently simple that almost everyone has the necessary skills. If someone slips on the ice, almost any bystander is able to help. On the other hand, if you see someone parked on the side of the road, peering under the hood of the car, you can't be of direct help unless you know something about cars. The best you can do is offer to call for assistance.

When emergencies require special skills, usually only a portion of the bystanders are able to help. For example, only good swimmers can assist a person who is drowning. With a medical emergency, a registered nurse is more likely to be helpful than a history professor (Cramer et al., 1988).

■ Step 5. Making the Final Decision to Provide Help

Once a bystander progresses through the first four steps in the decision process, help still does not occur unless he or she makes the ultimate decision to engage in a helpful act. Helping at this final point can be inhibited by fears (often realistic ones) about potential negative consequences. In effect, people are said to engage in "cognitive algebra" as they weigh the positive versus the negative aspects of helping (Fritzsche, Finkelstein, & Penner, 2000). As we will discuss later, the rewards for being helpful are provided primarily by the emotions and beliefs of the helper, but there are a great many kinds of potential costs. For example, if you had intervened in the Kitty Genovese attack, you might have been stabbed yourself. You might slip while helping a person who has fallen on the ice. A person might be asking for assistance simply as a trick that leads to robbery or worse (R. L. Byrne, 2001).

Though it is easy to assume that anyone who fails to provide help must have character flaws, it is not fair to jump to that conclusion. There are some very good reasons why bystanders might avoid a prosocial response.

KEY POINTS

★ When an emergency arises and someone is in need of help, a bystander may or may not respond in a prosocial way. Responses can range from *heroism* to apathy.

★ In part because of *diffusion of responsibility*, the more bystanders present as witnesses to an emergency, the less likely each of them is to provide help and the greater the delay before help occurs (the *bystander effect*).

★ When faced with an emergency, a bystander's tendency to help or not depends, in part, on decisions made at five crucial steps. First, the bystander must pay attention and be aware that an unusual event is occurring. Second, the bystander must correctly interpret the situation as an emergency. Third, the bystander must assume responsibility to provide help. Fourth, the bystander must have the required knowledge and skills to be able to act. Fifth, the bystander must decide to act.

External and Internal Influences on Helping Behavior

As we have seen, interest in prosocial behavior was sparked by the question of why bystanders at an emergency sometimes help and sometimes do nothing. The initial factor to be identified was an external one—number of bystanders. In the five-step process, several internal factors were shown to be important. We now turn to additional aspects of the situation that exert an influence and then to a number of internal factors that also play an important role in prosocial responding.

Situational Factors That Enhance or Inhibit Helping

Among the cues that affect the likelihood of helping are the attributes of the victim that determine *attraction,* details of the situation that indicate whether or not the problem is the *responsibility of the victim,* and exposure to *prosocial models* either in the immediate situation or in the bystander's past experience.

■ Helping Those You Like

Most of the research interest has centered on providing help to strangers, because it is obvious that people are very likely to help their family and friends. If a close friend were being attacked by a killer, or your brother were choking during an experiment, would you be likely to act? Of course, you would.

Consider a less obvious situation. The victim is a stranger but because he or she is similar to you with respect to age and race, would you be more likely to help than if the victim were a great deal older than you and of a different race? The answer is "yes"—a similar victim is more likely to be helped (Hayden, Jackson, & Guydish, 1984; Shaw, Borough, & Fink, 1994). In fact, any characteristic that affects attraction (see Chapter 7) also increases the probability of a prosocial response (Clark et al., 1987). Appearance influences prosocial behavior, and a physically attractive victim receives more help than an unattractive one (Benson, Karabenick, & Lerner, 1976).

Men are very likely to provide help to a woman in distress (Piliavin & Unger, 1985), perhaps because of gender differences in specific skills (e.g., changing a tire), perhaps on the basis of sexual attraction (Przybyla, 1985), and perhaps because women are more willing than men to ask for help (Nadler, 1991).

■ Helping Those Who Mimic Us

mimicry
The automatic tendency to imitate those with whom we interact. Being mimicked increases one's prosocial tendencies.

A seemingly unlikely determinant of prosocial behavior is **mimicry**—the automatic tendency to imitate the behavior of those with whom we interact. Humans are found to mimic the accent, tone of voice, and rate of speech of those around them. They also mimic the postures, mannerisms, and moods of others (Chartrand & Bargh, 1999; van Baaren et al., 2004). This tendency seems to be automatic, unconscious, and innate—and has a positive effect on the person being mimicked. Mimicry increases liking, empathy, and rapport; as a result, it plays a key role in social interactions (Chartrand, Maddux, & Lakin, 2004), much like the role of laughter described in Chapter 7. One of the effects of mimicry is to increase prosocial behavior (van Baaren et al., 2003).

As one example of *deliberate* mimicry, participants interacted for six minutes either with an experimenter who copied their posture, body orientation, and the position of their arms and legs or with a noncopying experimenter. Afterward, the experimenter "accidentally" dropped several pens on the floor. *All* of the participants who had been mimicked helped pick up the pens, while only a third of those who were not mimicked did so. Because mimicry increases attraction, this finding could be an attraction effect and not an indication that mimicry plays a unique role. To investigate this possibility, additional experimental conditions were created.

In these new experiments, students once again were or were not mimicked while interacting with the experimenter. In one condition, a different person entered the room and dropped pens on the floor. In another condition, following the interaction, each student was paid two euros and later given the option of keeping the money or donating some or all of it anonymously to a charity that helps hospitalized children. As can be seen in Figure 10.7, in each of the three experimental conditions, those who had been mimicked were more likely to help than those who had not.

Why should mimicry have this kind of effect? Some investigators suggest that mimicry plays a role in survival and reproductive success because it enhances cohesion and safety among animals in a group (Dijksterhuis, Bargh, & Miedema, 2000) and because imitation is an important aspect of learning and acculturation (de Waal, 2002). In any event, mimicry can be included as *one* of the situational factors influencing helping behavior.

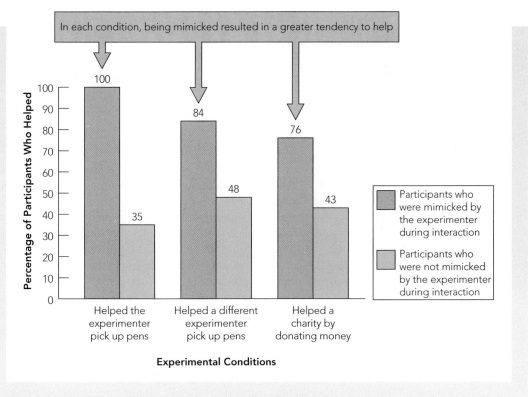

Figure 10.7 ■ Mimicry: An Impetus to Prosocial Behavior
During a six-minute interaction, the experimenter either mimicked or did not mimic each participant. Afterward, helping was greater in the mimicked group with respect to the experimenter, to a different experimenter, and to a charity. In social interactions, mimicry occurs automatically, and evokes a positive response in the person being mimicked. (*Source: Based on data in van Baaren et al., 2004.*)

■ Helping Those Who Are Not Responsible for Their Problem

If you were walking down the sidewalk one morning and passed a man lying unconscious, would you help him? You know that helpfulness would be influenced by all of the factors we have discussed—from the presence of other bystanders to interpersonal attraction. There is an additional consideration. Why is the man lying there? If his clothing is stained and torn and an empty wine bottle is by his side, what would you assume? You might decide that he is a hopeless drunk who passed out. In contrast, what if he is wearing an expensive suit and has a nasty cut on his forehead? These cues might lead you to decide that this was a man who had been brutally mugged. Based on your attributions about the reasons that a person might be lying unconscious on the sidewalk, you would be less likely to help the stranger with the wine bottle than the one with the cut on his head. In general, we are less likely to act if we believe that the victim is to blame for his or her predicament (Higgins & Shaw, 1999; Weiner, 1980).

■ Exposure to Prosocial Models Increases Prosocial Behavior

You are out shopping and come across representatives of a charity organization collecting money. Do you decide to help by making a contribution? An important factor in this decision is whether you observe someone else make a donation. If others give money, you are more likely to do so (Macauley, 1970). Even the presence of coins and bills (presumably contributed earlier in the day) encourages you to respond. The various compliance techniques described in Chapter 9 are directly relevant to this kind of helping behavior. Collecting money for charity involves many of the same psychological processes that are involved in panhandling or in selling a product.

In an emergency, we know that the presence of bystanders who fail to respond inhibits helpfulness. It is equally true, however, that the presence of a helpful bystander provides a

Figure 10.8 ■ **How Likely Are You to Help This Motorist?**
Help is much more likely to be given in such a situation if you have recently witnessed someone else receiving help. Prosocial models facilitate such behavior whether they are members of our family, TV characters, or strangers.

strong *social model,* and the result is an increase in helping behavior among the remaining bystanders. An example is provided by a field experiment in which a young woman (a research assistant) with a flat tire parked her car just off the road (see Figure 10.8). Motorists were much more inclined to stop and help if they had previously driven past a staged scene in which another woman with car trouble could be seen receiving assistance (Bryan & Test, 1967).

Helpful prosocial models in the media also contribute to the creation of a social norm that encourages prosocial behavior. In an investigation of the power of TV, Sprafkin, Liebert, and Poulous (1975) were able to increase the prosocial responsiveness of six-year-olds. Some of the children were shown an episode of *Lassie* in which there was a rescue scene. A second group of children watched a *Lassie* episode that did not focus on a prosocial theme. A third group watched a humorous episode of *The Brady Bunch*—also without prosocial content. After watching the show, the children played a game, with the winner receiving a prize. During the game, it was arranged that each child would encounter a group of whining, hungry puppies. At that point, the child was faced with a choice between pausing to help the pups (and thereby losing the chance to win a prize) and ignoring the puppies in order to continue playing. The children were clearly influenced by which TV show they had watched. Those who had viewed the *Lassie* rescue episode stopped and spent much more time trying to comfort the little animals than did the children who watched either of the other TV shows. As predicted, watching prosocial behavior on television increased the incidence of prosocial behavior in real life.

Additional experiments have confirmed the influence of positive TV models. Preschool children who watch such prosocial shows as *Sesame Street* or *Barney and Friends* are much more apt to respond in a prosocial way than children who do not watch such shows (Forge & Phemister, 1987). Of course, as we will see in Chapter 11, exposure to media can also have negative effects. For example, participants who played violent video games showed a subsequent *decrease* in prosocial behavior (Anderson & Bushman, 2001).

Emotions and Prosocial Behavior

A person's emotional state is determined by internal and external factors. On any given day, one's mood can be happy or sad, angry or loving, as well as many other possibilities. As we discussed in Chapter 7, emotions are often divided into two major categories—positive and negative. It might seem that being in a good mood would increase the tendency to help others, while being in a bad mood would interfere with helping. There is a good deal of evidence supporting that general assumption (Forgas, 1998a). Research indicates, however, that the effects of emotions on prosocial behavior can be more complicated than we might expect (Salovey, Mayer, & Rosenhan, 1991).

■ Positive Emotions and Prosocial Behavior
Children seem quick to pick up the idea that it's better to request something from a parent (or a teacher) when that person is in a good mood. Most often, this is true, and the effect

extends to prosocial acts. Research indicates that people are more willing to help when their mood has been elevated by listening to a comedian (Wilson, 1981), finding a small amount of money (Isen & Levin, 1972), or just spending time outdoors on a pleasant day (Cunningham, 1979).

Under certain specific circumstances, however, a positive mood can *decrease* the probability of responding in a prosocial way (Isen, 1984). A bystander in a very positive mood who encounters an ambiguous emergency tends to interpret the situation as a *nonemergency*. Even if it is clear that an emergency exists, people in a good mood tend to resist helping if that involves doing something difficult and unpleasant (Rosenhan, Salovey, & Hargis, 1981). It seems that a good mood gives us a feeling of independence, and this includes the power to turn our backs on someone in need.

■ Negative Emotions and Prosocial Behavior

Again, it is commonly assumed that someone in a negative mood is less likely to help. And it is true that an unhappy person who is focusing on his or her own problems is less likely to engage in prosocial acts (Amato, 1986). As with positive emotions, however, specific circumstances can reverse this general trend. If the act of helping involves behavior that makes you feel better, a prosocial act is more likely when an individual is in a bad mood than in a neutral one (Cialdini, Kenrick, & Bauman, 1982). A negative emotion most often has a *positive* effect on prosocial behavior if the negative feelings are not too intense, if the emergency is clearcut rather than ambiguous, and if the act of helping is interesting and satisfying rather than dull and unrewarding (Cunningham et al., 1990). The various effects of positive and negative emotions on prosocial behavior are summarized in Figure 10.9.

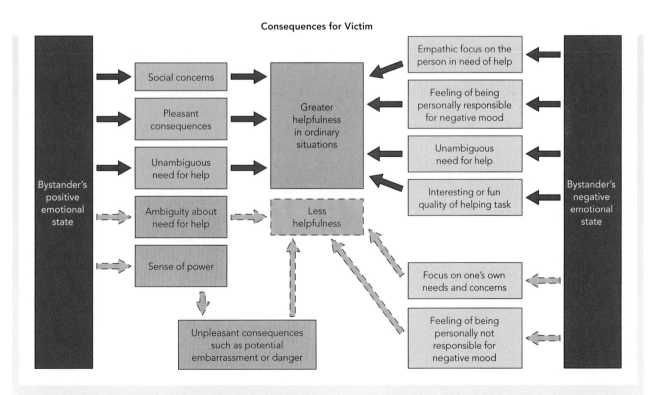

Figure 10.9 ■ Emotional Effects on Prosocial Behavior
Depending on a number of specific factors, a positive emotional state can either increase or decrease the likelihood of a prosocial response—and the same is true of a negative emotional state. This diagram summarizes the primary factors and their effects.

Empathy and Other Personality Dispositions Associated with Helping

We have just described how a variety of situational and emotional factors can affect prosocial behavior, but different people facing the same situation or being in the same emotional state do *not* respond in an identical way. Some are more helpful than others. Such individual differences in behavior are assumed to be based on **personality dispositions**—the characteristic behavioral tendencies of individuals. Personality dispositions are based on differences in genetic composition, learning experiences, or a combination of the two. Such dispositions tend to be relatively consistent over time. For example, children who are prosocial in early childhood behave in a similar way in adolescence (Caprara et al., 2000; Eisenberg et al., 2002).

■ Empathy: A Basic Requirement

Much of the interest in individual differences in helpfulness has concentrated on **empathy** (Clary & Orenstein, 1991; Schlenker & Britt, 2001). Empathy consists of affective and cognitive responses to another's emotional state and includes sympathy, a desire to solve the problem, and taking the other person's perspective (Batson et al., 2003). An empathetic person feels what another person is feeling and understands why that person feels that way (Azar, 1997; Darley, 1993; Duan, 2000).

An affective component is essential to empathy, and children as young as twelve months seem to feel distress in response to the distress of others (Brothers, 1990). This same characteristic is also observed in other primates (Ungerer et al., 1990) and probably among dogs and dolphins as well (Azar, 1997). Evolutionary psychologists suggest that the affective component of empathy includes feeling sympathetic—not only feeling another's pain, but also expressing concern and attempting to relieve the pain. Such findings are consistent with the idea that prosocial behavior has a biological basis.

The cognitive component of empathy appears to be a uniquely human quality that develops after we progress beyond infancy. Such cognitions include the ability to consider the viewpoint of another person, sometimes referred to as *perspective taking*—the ability to "put yourself in someone else's shoes." Social psychologists have identified three different types of perspective taking (Batson, Early, & Salvarani, 1997):

1. You can imagine how the other person perceives an event and how he or she must feel as a result—taking the "imagine other" perspective. Those who take this perspective experience relatively pure empathy, which motivates altruistic behavior.

2. You can imagine how you would feel if you were in that situation—taking the "imagine self" perspective. People who do this also experience empathy, but they tend to be motivated by self-interest, which sometimes interferes with altruism.

3. The third type of perspective taking involves identifying with fictional characters—feeling empathy for someone (or some creature) in a story. In this instance, there is an emotional reaction to the joys, sorrows, and fears of a character. Many children (and adults) may cry when Bambi discovers that his mother has been shot, or cringe in fear when the Wicked Witch of the West threatens Dorothy and "your little dog, too."

■ How Does Empathy Develop?

People differ in how they respond to the emotional distress of others. At one extreme are those willing to risk their lives to help another person. At the other extreme are those who enjoy inflicting pain and humiliation on a helpless victim (see Figure 10.10). As with most dispositional characteristics, the answer seems to lie in a combination of biological differences and differences in experience.

Genetic factors were investigated by Davis, Luce, and Kraus (1994). They examined more than eight hundred sets of identical and nonidentical twins and found that heredity underlies the two affective aspects of empathy (personal distress and sympathetic concern) but not cognitive empathy. Biological differences account for about a third of the variation among people in affective empathy. Presumably, other factors account for differences in cognitive

Figure 10.10 ■ Empathy versus Total Absence of Empathy
Strong feelings of empathy can motivate people to remarkable acts of heroism and tenderness, as with these rescue workers at the World Trade Center on 9-11-01. At the opposite extreme, the absence of empathy can lead to barbarous acts against innocent victims, as with the Chechen separatists who killed several hundred Russian school children, including the 16-year-old girl whose picture is being held up by a relative.

empathy and for two thirds of the variation in affective empathy. Psychologist Janet Strayer (quoted in Azar, 1997) suggests that we are all born with the biological capacity for empathy but that our specific experiences determine whether this innate potential becomes a vital part of our selves or fails to manifest itself. Many children of preschool age are able to differentiate empathic and selfish behavior in others, and those who understand this difference behave in a more prosocial way (Ginsburg et al., 2003).

What kinds of experiences might enhance or inhibit the development of empathy? Having a secure attachment style facilitates an empathic response to the needs of others (Mikulincer et al., 2001). Earlier, we described research indicating the positive effects of brief exposure to prosocial TV models on empathy. It seems likely that *prolonged* exposure to such models would be of added value. Researchers believe that the influence of parents as models is probably much greater than media influence. In his book *The Moral Intelligence of Children,* psychiatrist Robert Coles (1997) emphasizes the importance of mothers and fathers in shaping such behavior. He suggests that the key is to teach children to be "good" and "kind" and to think about other people rather than solely about themselves. *Good* children are not self-centered, and they are more likely to respond to the needs of others. Moral intelligence is not based on memorizing rules and regulations or on learning abstract definitions. Instead, children learn by observing what their parents do and say in their everyday lives. Coles believes that the elementary school years are the crucial time during which a child develops or fails to develop a conscience.

In early adolescence, the positive influence of parents and teachers can be replaced by the negative influence of peers (Ma et al., 2002). Without appropriate models and experiences, children can easily grow into selfish and rude adolescents and then into equally unpleasant adults. Coles states that those who learn to be kind have a strong commitment to helping others rather than hurting them. Empathy is most likely to develop if the child's mother is a warm person, if both parents emphasize how other people are affected by hurtful behavior, and if the family is able to discuss emotions in a supportive atmosphere. Parents who use anger as the major way to control their children inhibit the development of empathy (Azar, 1997; Carpenter, 2001a).

Either because of genetic differences or different socialization experiences, women express higher levels of empathy than men (Trobst, Collins, & Embree, 1994). Consistent with that finding is the fact that women outnumbered men two to one among those in World War II who helped rescue Jews from the Nazis (Anderson, 1993).

External and Internal Influences on Helping Behavior

Figure 10.11 ■ **Massive Disasters Bring Forth Massive Altruism**
As shown here after Hurricane Charley hit Port Charlotte, Florida, whenever there is a human catastrophe, caused either by nature or other human beings, people all over the world express sympathy and often provide assistance in the form of charitable contributions. Empathy tends to be greatest toward victims similar to oneself and in response to a type of catastrophe that one has experienced personally.

A special instance of empathy is the response of people to catastrophes such as a natural disaster or manmade disaster such as the attack on the World Trade Center in 2001 and the train bombing in Madrid in 2004. Most people respond with sympathy and very often with material assistance (see Figure 10.11). Empathy tends to be greater if the victims are similar to yourself and if you have experienced the same kind of catastrophe (Batson, Sager, et al., 1997; den Ouden & Russell, 1997; Sattler, Adams, & Watts, 1995).

■ Additional Personality Variables Associated with Prosocial Behavior

The fact that multiple aspects of the personality are involved in prosocial behavior has led some investigators to propose that a combination of relevant factors constitutes what has been designated as the **altruistic personality.** An altruistic person is high on five dimensions that are found in people who engage in prosocial behavior in an emergency situation (Bierhoff, Klein, & Kramp, 1991). The same five personality characteristics were also found among people who actively helped Jews in Europe in the 1940s. These dispositional factors are as follows:

altruistic personality
A combination of dispositional variables associated with *prosocial behavior*. The components are *empathy*, belief in a just world, acceptance of social responsibility, having an internal locus of control, and not being egocentric.

1. *Empathy.* As you might expect, those who help are found to be higher in empathy. The most altruistic people describe themselves as responsible, socialized, conforming, tolerant, self-controlled, and motivated to make a good impression.

2. *Belief in a just world.* Helpful individuals perceive the world as a fair and predictable place in which good behavior is rewarded and bad behavior is punished. This belief leads to the conclusion that helping those in need is the right thing to do *and also* to the expectation that the person who helps will benefit from doing a good deed.

3. *Social responsibility.* The most helpful individuals express the belief that each person is responsible for doing his or her best to assist anyone who needs help.

4. *Internal locus of control.* A person can choose to behave in ways that maximize good outcomes and minimize bad ones. People who fail to help, tend to have an *external locus of control* and believe that their behavior is irrelevant, because outcomes are controlled by luck, fate, and other uncontrollable factors.

5. *Low egocentrism.* Altruistic people do *not* tend to be self-absorbed and competitive.

Prosocial behavior is found to be influenced in both positive and negative ways by many aspects of the situation, by one's emotional state, as well as by empathy and other personality dispositions that are based, in part, on genetic differences and childhood experiences.

KEY POINTS

★ Positive and negative emotional states can enhance or inhibit *prosocial behavior*, depending on specific factors in the situation and on the nature of the required assistance.

★ Individual differences in altruistic behavior are based, in part, on *empathy,* a complex response that includes both

affective and cognitive components. Responding with empathy depends on a person's hereditary factors and learning experiences.

★ The *altruistic personality* consists of empathy plus belief in a just world, social responsibility, internal locus of control, and low egocentrism.

Long-Term Commitment to Prosocial Action and the Effects of Being Helped

In addition to responding to an emergency situation, prosocial behavior takes many other forms. We have mentioned some of these, including picking up pens, comforting a puppy, protecting victims of persecution, and giving money to charity. A somewhat different type of altruistic behavior is represented by *volunteering* to engage in work for a worthy cause, often over a period of time. With respect to all types of prosocial behavior, moral issues arise in making a choice as to whether to act or not, and the individual must balance *self-interest* with *moral integrity*, while not engaging in *moral hypocrisy*. Still another aspect of prosocial behavior is the *effect of helping* on the person being helped. We deal with each of these issues in the following section.

Volunteering

A special type of prosocial behavior is required when the person in need has a chronic, continuing problem that requires help over a prolonged time period (Williamson & Schulz, 1995). A person who volunteers to provide assistance in this context must commit his or her time and effort over weeks, months, or longer. In the United States, almost one hundred million adults volunteer 20.5 billion hours each year, averaging 4.2 hours of prosocial activity each week (Moore, 1993). Among people age 45 and up, an amazing 87 percent volunteered time or money during 2003. It is reasonable to assume that, around the world, people are spending an enormous amount of time engaged in voluntary acts of helpfulness (see Figure 10.12).

The five steps described earlier required to respond to an emergency also apply to volunteering. In order to help those who are homeless, for example, you must become aware of the problem, interpret the problem accurately, assume personal responsibility to provide help, decide on a course of action that is possible for you, and then actually engage in the behavior.

What motivates people to give up a portion of their lives to help others? One answer is that an individual has to be convinced of the importance of a given need; there are obviously many worthwhile causes, and no one can help all of them. When the people who volunteer time and money are identified by race and ethnic group, different concerns become apparent (What gives?, 2004). In the United States, whites give most to help animals, the environment, and emergency personnel such as police officers and firefighters. African Americans are more likely to assist those who are homeless or hungry, groups fighting for minority rights, and religious institutions. Asian Americans prefer helping museums and other artistic and cultural enterprises. Hispanics provide help to immigrants and people in other countries. It seems that people with different backgrounds are motivated by the specific concerns of their group. Clary and Snyder (1999) identified six basic functions that are served by working as volunteer, summarized in Table 10.1 on page 290.

■ Volunteering because of Mandates, Altruism, or Generativity

One way to generate volunteerism is to mandate it, as when some high schools and colleges require students to spend a specified amount of time in volunteer work in order to graduate. Though this practice does result in a large number of "volunteers," the sense of being

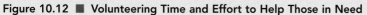

Figure 10.12 ■ Volunteering Time and Effort to Help Those in Need
Volunteerism is a form of prosocial behavior that requires a long-term commitment. Here, former President Jimmy Carter works with Habitat for Humanity to build affordable homes for people who lack adequate housing or enough money to acquire adequate housing.

Table 10.1 ■ Why Do People Volunteer?

Six distinct functions are served by engaging in volunteer activity. Appeals for volunteers are most effective if they recognize that different individuals have different motives. The sample items are taken from a scale developed to measure why people volunteer.

FUNCTION SERVED	DEFINITION	SAMPLE ITEM
Values	To express or act on important values such as humanitarianism	"I feel it is important to help others."
Understanding	To learn more about the world or exercise skills that are often not used	"Volunteering lets me learn through direct, hands-on experience."
Enhancement	To grow and develop psychologically through volunteer activities	"Volunteering makes me feel better about myself."
Career	To gain career-related experiences	"Volunteering can help me to get my foot in the door at a place where I would like to work."
Social	To strengthen social relationships	"People I know share an interest in community service."
Protective	To reduce negative feelings, such as guilt, or to address personal problems	"Volunteering is a good escape from my own problems."

(*Source: Based on information in Clary & Snyder, 1999.*)

forced to engage in such work decreases interest in future volunteer activity for many students (Stukas, Snyder, & Clary, 1999). These programs have been criticized because "if it is required, don't call it volunteering; and if it is volunteering, it should not be required" (Yuval, 2004, p. A22).

Do volunteers exhibit the same dispositional characteristics as those who engage in other altruistic behavior? The answer is "yes," in that volunteers tend to assume internal locus of control (Guagnano, 1995) and to be high in empathy (Penner & Finkelstein, 1998), especially with respect to empathic concern and perspective taking (Unger & Thumuluri, 1997).

A different characteristic of volunteerism has been described by McAdams and his colleagues (1997). They define **generativity** as an adult's interest in and commitment to the well-being of future generations. Those high in generativity show this interest and commitment by becoming parents, teaching young people, and engaging in acts that will have positive effects beyond their own lifetimes.

generativity
An adult's concern for and commitment to the well-being of future generations.

Self-Interest, Moral Integrity, and Moral Hypocrisy

Very few people are consciously apathetic or heartless when confronted by someone who is hurt, frightened, lost, hungry, and so forth. Many people can, however, be nudged in that direction by convincing themselves that there is no reason to provide help (Bersoff, 1999). For example, "It's not my responsibility" and "It's her own fault." With a good enough excuse, we can set aside or disengage moral standards (Bandura, 1999b). We tend to overestimate the frequency of our moral actions and to believe that we are more likely to engage in selfless and kind behavior than most people—a "holier than thou" self-assessment (Epley & Dunning, 2000). In fact, it is fairly easy for otherwise moral people to find a reason not to act morally in situations as varied as a stranger needing help in an emergency, charities needing help, and organizations needing volunteers. We describe some of the motives underlying moral behavior in the following sections.

Chapter 10 / Prosocial Behavior

■ Motivation and Morality

Batson and Thompson (2001) suggest that three major motives are relevant when a person is faced with a moral dilemma such as whether to help someone, donate to a worthy cause, or volunteer time. These motives are *self-interest, moral integrity,* and *moral hypocrisy.* People can be roughly categorized with respect to which motive is primary for them. We examine what is meant by each of these motives.

Most of us are motivated, at least in part, by **self-interest** (sometimes labeled **egoism**). Much of our behavior is based on seeking whatever provides us with the most satisfaction; we seek rewards and try to avoid punishments. People whose primary motive is self-interest are not concerned about questions of right and wrong or fair and unfair—they simply do what is best for themselves.

Other people are strongly motivated by **moral integrity.** They care about questions such as goodness and fairness when they act and frequently agree to sacrifice some self-interest in order to do "the right thing." For a person primarily motivated by morality, the conflict between self-interest and moral integrity is resolved by making the moral choice. This sometimes painful decision has both internal and external support. For example, a moral decision is enhanced by reflecting on one's values or being reminded of those values by others. At times, of course, moral integrity is overwhelmed by self-interest, and the result is questionable behavior and a feeling of guilt.

A third category consists of those who want to *appear* moral while avoiding the costs of actually *being* moral. Their behavior is motivated by **moral hypocrisy.** They are driven by self-interest but are concerned with outward appearances. It is important for them to seem to care about doing the right thing, while they, in fact, act to satisfy their own needs.

To investigate these basic motivations, Batson and his colleagues (Batson, Kobrynowicz, et al., 1997) created a laboratory situation in which undergraduates were faced with a moral dilemma. Each was given the power to assign him- or herself to one of two experimental tasks. The more desirable task included a chance to win raffle tickets. The less desirable task was described as dull and boring (without raffle tickets). Most participants (over 90 percent) agreed that assigning the dull task to oneself was the moral thing to do as well as the polite choice. They accepted the concept that you should "do unto others as you would have them do unto you." Despite these sentiments, most (70 to 80 percent) actually did the opposite. In this simple situation, most people made a choice based on self-interest. Only a minority (20 to 30 percent) behaved in a way they had indicated was the moral thing to do.

self-interest
The motivation to engage in whatever behavior provides the greatest satisfaction for oneself.

egoism
An exclusive concern with one's own personal needs and welfare rather than with the needs and welfare of others.

moral integrity
The motivation to be moral and to actually engage in moral behavior.

moral hypocrisy
The motivation to appear moral while doing one's best to avoid the costs involved in actually being moral.

How Does It Feel to Be Helped?

If you are in need of help, and someone comes along to provide assistance, it seems obvious that you would react positively and with gratitude. Often, however, the reaction is not at all like that.

■ Being Helped Can Be Unpleasant

A person who receives help may react with discomfort and even resentment. For example, someone with a physical impairment may need help, but still feel somewhat depressed when help is given (Newsom, 1999). Requiring help is a reminder of one's physical problem, and receiving help is evidence that someone else is more fortunate because he or she is *not* physically impaired. The person providing assistance needs to be sensitive to the possibility of such reactions.

The general problem is that when you receive help, your self-esteem can suffer. This is especially true when the one who helps is a friend or someone who is similar to you in age, education, or other characteristics (DePaulo et al., 1981; Nadler, Fisher, & Itzhak, 1983). When a young person offers his bus seat to an older person, the offer is likely to be accepted with gratitude. If the offer is made by another older person, however, it may well be refused because the one who offers help can be perceived as expressing a sense of superiority: "I'm in better shape than you, so have a seat." Lowered self-esteem results in negative affect and

Figure 10.13 ■ Being Helped by Strangers: Positive Affect but No Motivation to Change
When help is provided by strangers recipients tend to be grateful and to like those who help, and they are not motivated to behave in such a way as to avoid needing future help. When help is provided by family and friends, recipients tend to feel uncomfortable and to resent those who help. These negative feelings tend to motivate self-help to avoid the need for future help.

dislike (see Chapter 7). In an analogous way, when a member of a stigmatized group (e.g., an African American student) is offered unsolicited help from a member of a nonstigmatized group (e.g., a white student), the response may be negative, because the help is perceived as a patronizing insult (Schneider et al., 1996). For the same reasons, help from a sibling can be unpleasant, especially from a younger brother (Searcy & Eisenberg, 1992), but the same degree of help from someone else tends not to be threatening (Cook & Pelfrey, 1985).

A helper is liked best when the person receiving help believes that the help was offered because of positive feelings toward the individual in need (Ames, Flynn, & Weber, 2004). Such helping evokes the *reciprocity norm,* and the one who was helped is motivated to reciprocate with a kind deed in the future. When the helping is based on the helper's role (e.g., a policeman helping a lost child) or on the helper's cost–benefit analysis (e.g., a helper deciding to help because he would gain more than he would lose from the deed), attraction toward the helper and the desire to reciprocate are less strong.

■ When Help Is Unpleasant, It Can Motivate Self-Help

Whenever a person feels unhappy about receiving help, there is a positive aspect that is not obvious. When being helped is sufficiently unpleasant, he or she is motivated to avoid such a situation in the future by engaging in self-help (Fisher, Nadler, & Whitcher-Alagna, 1982; Lehman et al., 1995). No one wants to be seen as helpless or incompetent, and self-help can reduce feelings of dependence (Daubman, 1995). I (Donn Byrne) have learned many new and marvelous things about the use of my computer over the years because I don't want to depend on my daughters every time I have to copy a file on a disk, search for a website, or add an attachment to an e-mail. In contrast, when I receive help from a stranger who is a computer expert, I am not at all motivated to help myself by trying to gain that person's skills (see Figure 10.13).

KEY POINTS

★ People volunteer on a long-term basis as a function of various "selfish" and "selfless" motives.

★ People can be differentiated in terms of their primary motivation when faced with making a choice that involves relatively moral versus relatively immoral alternatives. The three primary motives are *self-interest, moral integrity,* and *moral hypocrisy.*

★ When the helper and the recipient are similar, the person who is helped tends to react negatively, feel incompetent, experience decreased self-esteem, and resent the helper. These negative reactions also tend to motivate self-help in the future. Help from a dissimilar person elicits a more positive reaction but fails to motivate future self-help.

The Basic Motivation for Engaging in Prosocial Acts

Why do people help? It is obvious that many factors influence whether or not an individual is likely to engage in prosocial behavior. Many aspects of the situation, the bystander's cognitive appraisal of the situation, his or her emotional state, and several dispositional variables all contribute to the probability that helping will or will not occur. We turn now to a different kind of question about prosocial responses: not who will help under what circumstances, but rather *why* anyone would be motivated to engage in a prosocial act. Several theories have been proposed, but most rest on the familiar assumption that people attempt to maximize rewards and minimize punishments. If that assumption is correct, the question becomes "Why is it rewarding to help?"

When asked, people tend to attribute their helpful behavior to unselfish motives such as "It was the right thing to do" or "The Lord put me here for a reason." When asked why someone else engaged in such behavior, the answer is equally split between unselfish motives such as "She was a hero" and selfish ones such as "She just wanted to get her name in the paper" (Doherty, Weigold, & Schlenker, 1990). Even those who spend their lives trying to find solutions to massive problems such as global warming or cancer are often viewed as acting in terms of their own self-interest (J. Baron, 1997). The ultimate example of such attributions is to say that the person engaged in helping others is only doing so because of the prospect of being rewarded by spending eternity in heaven. As a result, it is possible to explain all prosocial behavior as ultimately selfish and self-centered, but it is probably more reasonable to suggest that such behavior is based, in part, on selfish and unselfish motives.

We now turn to three major psychological theories, each of which attempts to explain the reason for prosocial behavior. Figure 10.14 summarizes these formulations. We then discuss a biological perspective on why people help.

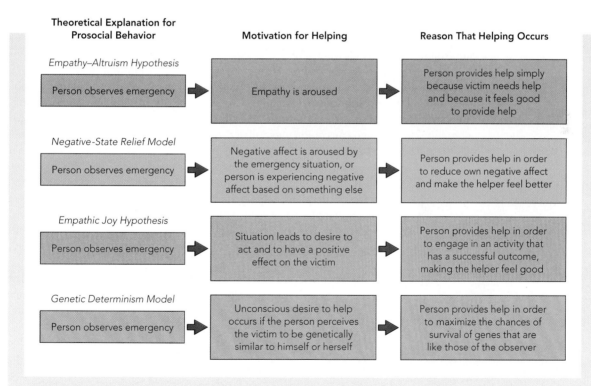

Figure 10.14 ■ Possible Motives for Prosocial Behavior
Four major explanations of the motivation underlying prosocial behavior are outlined here. The first three formulations (*empathy–altruism hypothesis, negative-state relief model,* and *empathic joy hypothesis*) stress the importance of increasing positive affect or decreasing negative affect. The fourth formulation (*genetic determinism model*) rests on the assumption that prosocial behavior is genetically determined.

empathy–altruism hypothesis
The proposal that *prosocial behavior* is motivated solely by the desire to help someone in need and by the fact that it feels good to help.

In some ways, the least selfish and, in some ways, the most selfish explanation of prosocial behavior is that empathetic people help others because "it feels good to do good deeds." As an explanation of why people help, Batson and his colleagues (1981) offered the **empathy–altruism hypothesis.** They suggest that at least some prosocial acts are motivated solely by the desire to help someone in need (Batson & Oleson, 1991). Such motivation can be sufficiently strong that the helper is willing to engage in unpleasant, dangerous, and even life-threatening activity (Batson, Batson, et al., 1995). Compassion for someone in need outweighs all other considerations (Batson, Klein, et al., 1995).

To test this altruistic view of helping behavior, Batson and his colleagues devised an experimental procedure in which they aroused a bystander's empathy by describing a victim as being very similar to himself or herself (see Chapter 7). Other participants were told of the victim's dissimilarity and so did not have their empathy aroused. The bystander was then presented with an opportunity to be helpful (Batson et al., 1983; Toi & Batson, 1982). The participant was given the role of an "observer" who watched a "fellow student" on a TV monitor as she performed a task while (supposedly) receiving electric shocks. The victim was actually a research assistant recorded on videotape. After the task was underway, the assistant said that she was in pain and confided that as a child she had had a traumatic experience with electricity. Though she agreed to continue if necessary, the experimenter asked whether the observer would be willing to trade places with her or whether the experiment should simply be terminated. When empathy was low (victim and participant dissimilar), the participants preferred to end the experiment rather than engage in a painful prosocial act. When empathy was high (victim and participant similar), participants were more likely to take the victim's place, presumably motivated simply by empathic concern for the victim.

Because empathy is strongly motivating, people prefer not to receive information that will arouse empathy (Shaw, Batson, & Todd, 1994). Presented with a victim needing help, participants were willing to learn about empathy-inducing aspects of the victim only if the cost of helping was low. When helping was costly, participants preferred to avoid detailed information about the victim.

Feelings of empathy also complicate matters when there are multiple victims who need help. How do you react when you learn that many people are in need? A mailing from the Feed the Children organization in Oklahoma City states that "over 12 million American children struggle with hunger each month." It is difficult or impossible to feel empathy for 12 million children, and you couldn't help all of them even if you felt intense empathy. Would you be more likely to help if you felt empathy for just one member of the group? That response is encouraged by charitable organizations. With a picture of a single child, and her sad request to help her and her family, you might well respond with **selective altruism,** helping the individual, even though you must neglect the remaining millions (Batson, Ahmed, et al., 1999; Figure 10.15).

Arguing against the empathy–altruism view of prosocial behavior, Cialdini and his colleagues (1997) agreed that empathy leads to altruistic behavior but pointed out that this only occurs when the participant perceives an overlap between self and other. They conducted research to demonstrate that without a feeling of "oneness," helping does not occur. Empathic concern alone does *not* increase helping. Follow-up research by Batson and his colleagues

selective altruism
When a large group of individuals is in need, and only one individual is helped.

Figure 10.15 ■ Selective Altruism
When a large number of people need help, it is difficult or impossible to feel empathy for all of them. Charitable organizations attempt to solve this problem through the use of advertising that evokes empathy and the desire to help one individual or one family. Suppose you received a mailing with this little girl's picture and the message, "Please, can you help? I'm so hungry, and we have no money to buy food." Would you be motivated to help her?

indicated the opposite—"oneness" isn't necessary. Clearly, the issue has not been resolved (Batson et al., 1997).

Negative-State Relief: Helping Makes You Feel Less Bad

Instead of helping because altruism behavior leads to positive emotions, is it possible that perceiving a person in need makes you feel so bad that you help in order to *reduce* your negative emotions? This explanation of prosocial behavior is known as the **negative-state relief model** (Cialdini, Baumann, & Kenrick, 1981). Research designed to test this hypothesis indicates that negative feelings increase the occurrence of helpful behavior. The investigators confirmed that proposal. They also found that it doesn't matter whether the bystander's unhappy state was caused by something unrelated to the emergency or by the emergency itself. You could be upset about receiving a bad grade or about seeing an injured stranger. In either instance, you are likely to engage in a prosocial act primarily as a way to improve your own negative mood (Dietrich & Berkowitz, 1997; Fultz, Schaller, & Cialdini, 1988). Such research suggests that unhappiness leads to prosocial behavior, while empathy is not a necessary component (Cialdini et al., 1987).

negative-state relief model
The proposal that *prosocial behavior* is motivated by the bystander's desire to reduce his or her own uncomfortable negative emotions.

Empathic Joy: Helping as an Accomplishment

It is generally true that it feels good to have a positive effect on other people. It can literally be better to give help than to receive it. Helping can thus be explained on the basis of the **empathic joy hypothesis.** A helper responds to the needs of a victim because he or she wants to accomplish something, and interpersonal accomplishment is rewarding.

An important implication of this proposal is that it is crucial for the person who helps to know that his or her actions had a positive impact. It is argued that if helping were based entirely on empathy, feedback about its effect would be irrelevant. To test that aspect of their empathic joy hypothesis, Smith, Keating, and Stotland (1989) asked participants to watch a videotape in which a female student said she might drop out of college because she felt isolated and distressed. She was described as either similar to the participant (high empathy) or dissimilar (low empathy). After participants watched the tape, they were given the opportunity to offer helpful advice. Some were told they would receive feedback about the effectiveness of their advice, while others were told they would not know what the student eventually decided to do. It was found that empathy alone was not enough to elicit a prosocial response. Rather, participants were helpful only if there was high empathy *and* feedback about the impact of their advice.

empathic joy hypothesis
The proposal that *prosocial behavior* is motivated by the positive emotion a helper anticipates experiencing as the result of having a beneficial impact on the life of someone in need.

Note that in each of these three theoretical models for engaging in prosocial acts, the affective state of the person engaging in an act is crucial. All three formulations rest on the assumption that people engage in helpful behavior because it feels good or it makes make them feel less bad. And, all three formulations are able to predict prosocial behavior under specific conditions. On the basis of other investigations, one could make the case that prosocial behavior can be motivated by self-interest. This includes the expectation of reciprocation from the person being helped, along with various rewards on earth (respect, fame, gratitude, and sometimes, material gain) and in the afterlife. Perhaps there really is no such thing as pure altruism—or at least it is exceedingly rare. Before we return to the question of prosocial behavior as a function of affect and rewards, let's look at a fourth model.

Genetic Determinism: Helping as an Adaptive Response

The **genetic determinism model** is based on a general biological perspective (Pinker, 1998). Presumably, people are no more conscious of being guided by genetic components than are grey geese, and much of what we do is because we are "built that way" (Rushton, 1989b). Genetic roots are well established for most human physical characteristics, and many behavioral characteristics also have a genetic base. Our human characteristics have been "selected" through evolution purely on the basis of their relevance to reproductive success. Therefore, any physical or behavioral characteristic that facilitates reproduction is more likely to be

genetic determinism model
The proposal that behavior is driven by genetic attributes that evolved because they enhanced the probability of transmitting one's genes to subsequent generations.

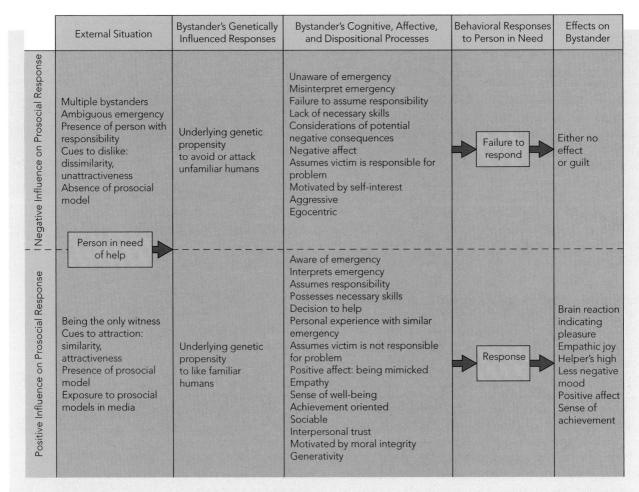

Figure 10.16 ■ Prosocial Behavior: Putting It All Together
Prosocial behavior describes many kinds of specific behaviors, including rescuing someone facing a life-threatening emergency, engaging in acts of kindness, and volunteering hours of charitable work over an extended time. Evolutionary psychologists work to explain both prosocial and antisocial behavior by concentrating on general, adaptive, genetically based tendencies to respond negatively to anyone who is unfamiliar (see Chapter 7) and to cooperate with and help anyone who is familiar. These genetic predispositions to negative or positive interpersonal responses can be enhanced or overridden by the specific situational, cognitive, affective, and dispositional factors on which social psychological research has concentrated. The summary outline here rests on the assumption that both types of explanation are valid and that, together, they provide a useful framework for understanding why and under what circumstances people are likely to behave in ways that benefit other people or fail to engage in such prosocial responses.

inclusive fitness
The concept that natural selection not only applies to individuals, but also involves behaviors that benefit other individuals with whom we share genes. Sometimes referred to as *kin selection*.

represented in future generations than are other characteristics that either interfere with reproductive success or are simply irrelevant to it.

Studies of various species indicate that the greater the genetic similarity between two individual organisms, the more likely it is that one will help the other when help is needed (Ridley & Dawkins, 1981). Evolutionary theorists have coined the term *selfish gene* to describe this phenomenon. The more similar individual A is to individual B, the more genes they probably have in common. If so, when A helps B, some portion of A's genes will be more likely to be represented in future generations because of the genetic overlap of the two individuals (Rushton, Russell, & Wells, 1984). From this perspective, altruism doesn't necessarily benefit the individual who helps, but it is adaptive because adaptation is not limited to the individual and his or her reproductive fitness, but also to **inclusive fitness**—natural selection that favors behaviors that benefit whoever shares our genes (Hamilton, 1964; McAndrew, 2002).

Even though risking one's life to save the life of another doesn't seem adaptive, it is adaptive *if* the person being saved is genetically similar (Burnstein, Crandall, & Kitayama, 1994).

The best person to save is obviously a relative who is still young enough to reproduce, an aspect of inclusive fitness that led to the term **kin selection.** Burnstein and his colleagues conducted a series of studies based on hypothetical decisions about who you would choose to help in an emergency. As predicted on the basis of genetic similarity, participants were more likely to help a close relative than either a distant relative or a nonrelative. And, as predicted on the basis of reproductive ability, help was more likely for young relatives. Given a choice between a female relative young enough to reproduce and a female relative past menopause, help would go to the younger individual.

It seems quite possible that we help one another because that kind of behavior has been sufficiently adaptive over thousands of years that we are programmed to behave this way and to feel good about it. The various social psychological concepts outlined in this chapter are equally valid in identifying the details of the situation and of the cognitive and affective responses of individuals that enhance or inhibit the underlying genetic tendencies (e.g., Maner et al., 2002). Figure 10.16 suggests a way to think about how the diverse research findings relevant to prosocial behavior can be considered as integral elements of a unified explanation of this complex topic.

kin selection
Another term for *inclusive fitness*—the concept that natural selection not only applies to individuals, but also involves behaviors that benefit other individuals with whom we share genes.

KEY POINTS

★ The *empathy–altruism hypothesis* proposes that, because of empathy, we help those in need because it feels good.

★ The *negative-state relief model* proposes that people help others in order to relieve and make their emotional discomfort less negative.

★ The *empathic joy hypothesis* bases helping on the positive feelings of accomplishment that arise when the helper knows that he or she was able to have a beneficial impact on the person in need.

★ The *genetic determinism model* traces prosocial behavior to the general effects of natural selection. Prosocial acts are part of our biological heritage, because both *reciprocal altruism* and *inclusive fitness* are adaptive evolutionary mechanisms.

★ It seems increasingly likely that prosocial behavior can best be conceptualized as an evolved biological predisposition that can be enhanced or inhibited by the situational, cognitive, and affective factors identified by social psychologists.

SUMMARY AND REVIEW OF KEY POINTS

Responding to an Emergency: Will Bystanders Help?

■ When an emergency arises and someone is in need of help, a bystander may or may not respond in a prosocial way. Responses range from *heroism* to apathy.

■ In part because of *diffusion of responsibility*, the more bystanders present as witnesses to an emergency, the less likely each of them is to provide help and the greater the delay before help occurs (the *bystander effect*).

■ When faced with an emergency, a bystander's tendency to help or not depends, in part, on decisions made at five crucial steps.

- First, the bystander must pay attention and be aware that an unusual event is occurring.
- Second, the bystander must correctly interpret the situation as an emergency.
- Third, the bystander must assume responsibility to provide help.
- Fourth, the bystander must have the required knowledge and skills to be able to act.
- Fifth, the bystander must decide to act.

External and Internal Influences on Helping Behavior

■ Positive and negative emotional states can enhance or inhibit *prosocial behavior*, depending on specific factors in the situation and on the nature of the required assistance.

■ Individual differences in altruistic behavior are based, in part, on *empathy*, a complex response that includes both affective and cognitive components. Responding with empathy depends on a person's hereditary factors and learning experiences.

- The *altruistic personality* consists of empathy plus belief in a just world, social responsibility, internal locus of control, and low egocentrism.

Long-Term Commitment to Prosocial Action and the Effects of Being Helped

- People volunteer on a long-term basis as a function of various "selfish" and "selfless" motives.
- People can be differentiated in terms of their primary motivation when faced with making a choice that involves relatively moral versus relatively immoral alternatives. The three primary motives are *self-interest, moral integrity,* and *moral hypocrisy.*
- When the helper and the recipient are similar, the person who is helped tends to react negatively, feel incompetent, experience decreased self-esteem, and resent the helper. These negative responses also tend to motivate self-help in the future. Help from a dissimilar person elicits a more positive reaction but fails to motivate future self-help.

The Basic Motivation for Engaging in Prosocial Acts

- The *empathy–altruism hypothesis* proposes that, because of empathy, we help those in need because it feels good.
- The *negative-state relief model* proposes that people help others in order to relieve and make their emotional discomfort less negative.
- The *empathic joy hypothesis* bases helping on the positive feelings of accomplishment that arise when the helper knows that he or she was able to have a beneficial impact on the person in need.
- The *genetic determinism model* traces prosocial behavior to the general effects of natural selection. Prosocial acts are part of our biological heritage, because both *reciprocal altruism* and *inclusive fitness* are adaptive evolutionary mechanisms.
- It seems increasingly likely that prosocial behavior can best be conceptualized as an evolved biological predisposition that can be enhanced or inhibited by the situational, cognitive, and affective factors identified by social psychologists.

Connections   INTEGRATING SOCIAL PSYCHOLOGY

In this chapter, you read about . . .	In other chapters you will find related discussions of . . .
bystanders' response to nonverbal cues of other bystanders	interpretation of nonverbal cues (Chapter 2)
social comparison processes among the witnesses to an emergency	the importance of social comparison in the study of attitudes (Chapter 4), attraction (Chapter 7), and social influence (Chapter 9)
attributions as to the cause of a victim's problem	attribution theory (Chapter 2)
self-concept as a determinant of helping behavior and the effect of receiving help on self-esteem	research and theory on self-concept and self-esteem (Chapter 5)
similarity of victim and bystander as a determinant of empathy and helping	similarity and attraction (Chapters 7 and 8)
affective state and helping	affect as a factor in attitudes (Chapter 4), prejudice (Chapter 6), attraction (Chapter 7), relationships (Chapter 8), and aggression (Chapter 11)
genetics and helping	genetics as a factor in prejudice (Chapter 6), attraction (Chapter 7), mate selection (Chapter 8), and aggression (Chapter 11)

Thinking about Connections

1. As you are walking out of the building after your social psychology class, you see an elderly man lying face down on the sidewalk. Three students are standing nearby, not speaking but looking at the man. How would you interpret this situation? What might you observe in the facial expressions and bodily gestures of the bystanders (Chapter 2)? As you take a closer look at the man, you may make some guesses as to why he is there. Many different attributions are

possible (Chapter 2). Suggest some of the possibilities that occur to you.

2. Your car won't start, and you are in a hurry. You have plenty of gas, and the battery is almost new. You open the hood but don't see anything obviously wrong. A fellow student comes along and offers to help. She looks under the hood, taps something, and says, "Try it now." You turn the key, and the car starts. How do you feel at that moment? Do you like the student who helped you (Chapter 7)? Does being helped raise or lower your self-esteem (Chapter 5)? Do you think you might be motivated to learn more about automobiles so this won't happen again?

3. On the evening news, you learn about a devastating earthquake in California that has destroyed many homes, leaving families without shelter or food. The announcer gives a telephone number and an address for those who want to contribute money or food. Also, volunteers are needed to help with the cleanup. Do you ignore this information, or do you decide to contribute money, food, or your time? What factors with respect to the disaster itself, where it occurred, and your experiences with such a situation might influence your decision? List the kinds of social psychological processes that could be operating.

Ideas to Take with You—and Use! BEING A RESPONSIBLE BYSTANDER

From time to time, you have probably encountered a number of unexpected situations involving someone who needed your help. Did you help or not? In the future, if you want to be helpful, you might consider the following suggestions.

Pay Attention
In our everyday lives, we often think more about ourselves than about our surroundings. It may be useful to pay more attention to what is going on around us. Remember the students who thought they were late and ignored a man who appeared to have collapsed in a doorway? You may find it worthwhile from time to time to think about other people and their welfare.

Consider Alternate Explanations
When you notice something unusual, think about more than one possible explanation. A child crying in the park may have hurt herself or be lost or simply be tired. The smoke you smell might be burnt toast or a fire in a nearby apartment. The scream you hear outside could be a cry for help or someone responding to a friend's joke. In any such situation, you can simply do nothing because there is probably nothing really wrong. Consider other possibilities, because there may be a serious problem that could be solved with your help.

Think of Yourself as Having as Much Responsibility as Any Other Bystander
If you find yourself in a group of people observing something that could be an emergency, don't just stand around and wait for somebody else to do something. If you see someone lying on the floor in a the-ater lobby, try to find out what is wrong. You know as much as others do and you are as responsible for doing the right thing as any of the other bystanders.

Take the Risk of Making a Fool of Yourself
Sometimes, when others fail to act, and you believe something is wrong, they can be right and you might do something foolish. Being foolish is not the end of the world, and you will probably never see your fellow bystanders again. It is better to make a mistake and offer help to someone who doesn't need it than to make an equally foolish decision to stand back when help is badly needed.

KEY TERMS

altruism (p. 275)

altruistic personality (p. 288)

bystander effect (p. 276)

diffusion of responsibility (p. 276)

egoism (p. 291)

empathic joy hypothesis (p. 295)

empathy (p. 286)

empathy–altruism hypothesis (p. 294)

generativity (p. 290)

genetic determinism model (p. 295)

heroism (p. 275)

implicit bystander effect (p. 277)

inclusive fitness (p. 296)

kin selection (p. 297)

mimicry (p. 282)

moral hypocrisy (p. 291)

moral integrity (p. 291)

negative-state relief model (p. 295)

personality disposition (p. 286)

pluralistic ignorance (p. 279)

prosocial behavior (p. 274)

selective altruism (p. 294)

self-interest (p. 291)

11 AGGRESSION
Its Nature, Causes, and Control

W hen I (Robert Baron) was ten, I had one of my most traumatic childhood experiences. It was a Saturday, and I was just returning home from playing baseball. As I approached the apartment building where I lived, I saw my younger brother Richard, who was about four, standing in some rose bushes, looking at a bee on a flower. On the sidewalk next to him were Nancy Gordon and her friend Evelyn—two girls in my class. Nancy was urging Richard to pick up the bee. "Go ahead," she said, "Pick it up—it won't hurt you! In fact, rub it on your face—it will feel soft!" For some reason, Richard liked insects and had been stung just a few weeks ago when he stepped on a bee and failed to move. Nancy knew this, and was trying to have fun at his expense.

"Hey!" I shouted at her. "Cut it out. Leave him alone!" Nancy was known for her cruel tongue, so I was not surprised when she turned it on me. "Oh, here comes big brother to the rescue," she announced, sarcasm dripping from her lips. "But he's not very big, is he? Go away and let us have fun with your stupid little brother!" That made me mad and I told her so. We exchanged insults and, finally, I must have said something that hit home, because Nancy, who was on roller skates, came up to me and . . . spit in my face! That was it; I saw red. All I can remember is that I pushed her—hard. Because she was on skates, she lost her balance and fell, landing on her right arm. She got up crying and headed for home. Later that evening, I learned that she had broken her wrist. My father and mother wouldn't listen to my explanations—they blamed me entirely. My father made me accompany him to Nancy's home, where I apologized to her and to her parents. But that wasn't the end of it. Nancy wrote "Courtesy of Robert Baron" on her cast and told everyone how I had broken her wrist. I was totally humiliated. To make matters worse, my friends began calling me "Lady Killer." Wow, was I glad when Nancy's cast was removed and the school year ended.

D id I mean to hurt Nancy Gordon? I was certainly angry with her, but I'm sure that I didn't intend to harm her—I just lashed out, without conscious thought. And that is one of the many complexities of human aggression. Intentions are a hidden process we can't observe directly; even the people involved often don't know *why* they behaved as they did or what they wanted to accomplish. So, although social psychologists define **aggression** as

aggression
Behavior directed toward the goal of harming another living being, who is motivated to avoid such treatment.

Chapter 11 / Aggression

Figure 11.1 ■ The Deadly Face of Human Aggression
When the desire to harm others is paired with modern weapons and placed in the hands of terrorists, the results can be both frightening and devastating.

intentional harmdoing, they realize that determining whether some action that caused harm was intentional or unintentional is a difficult task.

Aggression, of course, is not restricted to direct assaults by one person on another (such as my pushing Nancy). On the contrary, it often involves the use of modern weapons that can harm large numbers of persons at once. And in the hands of terrorists, such weapons are aimed not only at soldiers or other armed opponents, but often at innocent civilians—passersby who are seriously harmed or killed without any warning and without any knowledge of who is the cause of these tragic outcomes, or even why they are being attacked (see Figure 11.1).

Given the serious consequences that aggression can produce, it has long been a topic of interest to social psychologists (e.g., Anderson & Bushman, 2002a; Baron & Richardson, 1994). In this chapter, we provide an overview of the intriguing insights their research has produced. First, we describe several *theoretical perspectives* on aggression, contrasting views about its nature and origin. Next, we examine several important determinants of human aggression. These include *social factors* involving the words or deeds of others, either in person or as represented in the mass media (e.g., Anderson et al., 2004); *cultural factors,* such as norms requiring that individuals respond aggressively to insults to their honor; *personal factors*—traits that predispose specific persons toward aggressive outbursts; and *situational factors*—aspects of the external world. Third, we consider two forms of aggression that are especially disturbing because they occur within the context of long-term relationships rather than between total strangers—*bullying* and *workplace aggression.* Finally, to conclude on an optimistic note, we examine various techniques for the *prevention and control* of aggression.

Theoretical Perspectives on Aggression: In Search of the Roots of Violence

Why do humans aggress against others? What makes them turn, with fierce brutality, on their fellow human beings? Thoughtful persons have pondered these questions for centuries and have proposed many contrasting explanations for the paradox of human violence. Here, we examine several explanations that have been especially influential, concluding with the modern answer provided by social psychologists.

The Role of Biological Factors: From Instincts to the Evolutionary Perspective

The oldest and probably best known explanation for human aggression is that humans are somehow "programmed" for violence by their basic nature. Such theories suggest that human violence stems from built-in (i.e., inherited) tendencies. The most famous supporter of this theory was Sigmund Freud, who held that aggression stems mainly from a powerful *death wish* (*thanatos*) possessed by all persons. According to Freud, this instinct is initially aimed at self-destruction but is soon redirected toward others. Similar views were proposed by Konrad Lorenz, a Nobel Prize–winning scientist (Lorenz, 1966, 1974), who suggested that aggression springs mainly from an inherited *fighting instinct,* which assures that only the strongest males will obtain mates and pass their genes on to the next generation.

Until a few years ago, few social psychologists accepted such views. Among the reasons for their objections to the idea that human aggression is genetically programmed were these: (1) Humans aggress against others in different ways—from ignoring others to overt acts of violence. How can such a range of behaviors be determined by genetic factors? (2) The frequency of aggressive actions varies across human societies, so that they are much more likely to occur in some societies than in others (e.g., Fry, 1998). Again, social psychologists asked, "How can aggressive behavior be determined by genetic factors if such differences exist?"

With the advent of the *evolutionary perspective* in psychology, however, this viewpoint has changed considerably. Although most social psychologists continue to reject the view that human aggression stems largely from innate factors, many now accept the possibility that genetic factors may play *some* role in human aggression. Consider the following reasoning, based on an evolutionary perspective (see the discussion of this theory in Chapter 1). In the past (and at present to some extent), males seeking desirable mates found it necessary to compete with other males. One way of eliminating such competition is through successful aggression, which drives rivals away or eliminates them by proving fatal. Because males who were adept at such behavior may have been more successful in securing mates and in transmitting their genes to offspring, this may have led to the development of a genetically influenced tendency for males to aggress against other males. In contrast, males would not be expected to acquire a similar tendency to aggress against females, because females may view males who engage in such behavior as too dangerous, and so may reject these males as potential mates. In contrast, females might aggress equally against males and females, or even more frequently against males than other females. The results of several studies confirm such predictions (e.g., Hilton, Harris, & Rice, 2000). Findings such as these suggest that biological or genetic factors may play some role in human aggression, although in a more complex manner than Freud, Lorenz, and other early theorists suggested.

Drive Theories: The Motive to Harm Others

drive theories (of aggression) Theories suggesting that aggression stems from external conditions that arouse the motive to harm or injure others. The most famous of these is the *frustration–aggression hypothesis.*

frustration–aggression hypothesis The suggestion that frustration is a very powerful determinant of aggression.

When social psychologists rejected the instinct views of aggression proposed by Freud and Lorenz, they countered with an alternative: the view that aggression stems mainly from an externally elicited *drive* to harm others. This approach is reflected in several **drive theories** of aggression (e.g., Berkowitz, 1989; Feshbach, 1984). These theories propose that external conditions—especially *frustration*—arouse a strong motive to harm others. This aggressive drive leads to overt acts of aggression (see Figure 11.2).

The most famous of these theories is the well-known **frustration–aggression hypothesis** (Dollard et al., 1939). According to this view, frustration leads to the arousal of a drive, the primary goal of which is to harm some person or object—primarily the perceived cause of the frustration (Berkowitz, 1989). As we'll see later, the central role assigned to frustration

Figure 11.2 ■ Drive Theories of Aggression: Motivation to Harm Others
Drive theories of aggression suggest that aggressive behavior is pushed from within by drives to harm or injure others. These drives stem from external conditions such as frustration.

by the frustration–aggression hypothesis has turned out to be largely false: Frustration is only one of many causes of aggression, and a fairly weak one at that. Although social psychologists have largely rejected this theory, it still enjoys widespread acceptance outside of the field. In this way, at least, drive theories have continued to have some impact on popular, if not scientific, views of human aggression.

Modern Theories of Aggression: The Social Learning Perspective and the General Aggression Model

Unlike earlier views, modern theories of aggression (e.g., Anderson & Bushman, 2002a; Berkowitz, 1993; Zillmann, 1994) do not focus on a single factor (instincts, drives, frustration) as the primary cause of aggression. Rather, they draw on advances in many fields of psychology to gain added insight into the factors that play a role in the occurrence of such behavior. One such theory, known as the *social learning perspective* (e.g., Bandura, 1997), begins with a very reasonable idea: Humans are not born with a large array of aggressive responses at their disposal. Rather, they must acquire these in much the same way that they acquire other complex forms of social behavior: through direct experience or by observing the behavior of others (i.e., social models—live persons or characters on television, in movies, or even in video games who behave aggressively; Anderson & Bushman, 2001; Bushman & Anderson, 2002). Thus, depending on their experiences and culture, individuals learn (1) various ways of seeking to harm others (see Figure 11.3), (2) which persons or groups are appropriate targets for aggression, (3) what actions by others justify retaliation or vengeance, and (4) what situations or contexts are ones in which aggression is permitted or even approved. In short, the social learning perspective suggests that whether a specific person will aggress in a given situation depends on many factors, including this person's past experience, the current rewards associated with past or present aggression, and attitudes and values that shape this person's thoughts concerning the appropriateness and potential effects of such behavior.

Building on the social learning perspective, a newer framework known as the *general aggression model* (Anderson, 1997; Anderson & Bushman, 2002) provides an even more complete account of the foundations of human aggression. According to this theory, a chain of events that may lead to overt aggression can be initiated by two types of *input variables:* (1) factors relating to the current situation (situational factors) and (2) factors

Figure 11.3 ■ Aggression: A Learned Form of Social Behavior
The social learning perspective suggests that aggression is a learned form of social behavior.

relating to the persons involved (person factors). Variables falling into the first category include frustration, some kind of attack (e.g., an insult), exposure to others behaving aggressively (*aggressive models*) either in person or violent movies or games, and virtually anything that causes individuals to experience discomfort—everything from uncomfortably high temperatures to a dentist's drill or even an extremely dull lecture. Variables in the second category (*individual differences*) include traits that predispose individuals toward aggression (e.g., high irritability), certain attitudes and beliefs about violence (e.g., believing that it is acceptable and appropriate), a tendency to perceive hostile intentions in others' behavior, and specific skills related to aggression (e.g., knowing how to fight or use various weapons).

According to the **general aggression model** (GAM), these situational and individual difference variables can then lead to overt aggression through their impact on three basic processes: *arousal*—they may increase physiological arousal or excitement; *affective states*—they can arouse hostile feelings and outward signs (e.g., angry facial expressions); and *cognitions*—they can induce individuals to think hostile thoughts or bring beliefs and attitudes about aggression to mind. Depending on individuals' interpretations (*appraisals*) of the situation and restraining factors (e.g., the presence of police or the threatening nature of the intended target), they then engage either in thoughtful action, which might involve restraining their anger, or impulsive action, which can lead to overt aggressive actions. (See Figure 11.4 for an overview of this theory.)

Anderson and Bushman (e.g., Bushman & Anderson, 2002) have expanded this theory to explain why individuals who are exposed to high levels of aggression, either directly or in films and video games, may tend to become increasingly aggressive. Repeated exposure to such stimuli serves to strengthen *knowledge structures* relating to aggression—beliefs, attitudes, schemas, and scripts relevant to aggression (refer to Chapter 2). As these knowledge structures grow stronger, it is easier for them to be activated by situational or person variables. The result? The persons in question are truly "primed" for aggression. The GAM is certainly more complex than earlier theories of aggression such as the famous frustration–aggression hypothesis (Dollard et al., 1939). But because the GAM fully reflects recent progress in the field, it seems more likely to provide an accurate view of the nature of human aggression than the earlier theories. And that, of course, is what scientific progress is all about!

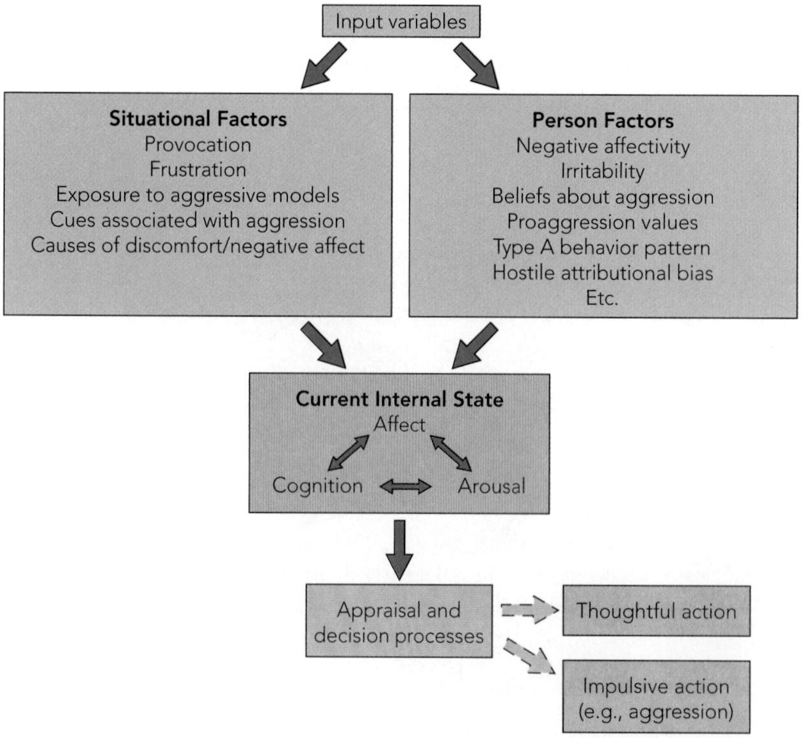

general aggression model
A modern theory of aggression suggesting that aggression is triggered by a wide range of input variables that influence arousal, affective stages, and cognitions.

Figure 11.4 ■ The GAM: A Modern Theory of Human Aggression
The *general aggression model* (GAM) suggests that human aggression stems from many factors. Input variables relating to the situation or person influence cognitions, affect, and arousal, and these internal states plus other factors, such as appraisal and decision mechanisms, determine whether and in what form aggression occurs. (*Source: Based on suggestions by Bushman & Anderson, 2002.*)

KEY POINTS

★ *Aggression* is the intentional infliction of harm on others. Although most social psychologists reject the view that human aggression is strongly determined by genetic factors, many now accept an evolutionary perspective that recognizes the potential role of such factors.

★ *Drive theories* suggest that aggression stems from externally elicited drives to harm or injure others. The *frustration–aggression hypothesis* is the most famous example.

★ Modern theories of aggression, such as the *general aggression model*, recognize the importance of learning, various eliciting input variables, individual differences, affective states, and, especially, cognitive processes in aggression.

Causes of Human Aggression: Social, Cultural, Personal, and Situational

Think back to the last time you lost your temper. What made you blow your cool? Something another person said or did (Harris, 1993), such as a condescending remark or something that made you feel jealous? Something about yourself—are you easily annoyed, do you perceive that others treat you unfairly? Was it something about the situation—had you been drinking, was the weather hot? Research findings indicate that all of these factors can play a role in human aggression. As noted earlier, such behavior appears to stem from a wide range of *social, cultural, personal,* and *situational* variables. We'll now examine the effects of several of these factors.

Social Causes of Aggression: Frustration, Provocation, and Heightened Arousal

Often, individuals aggress because something others have said or done provokes them. But what, precisely, are these *social causes* of aggression? Let's see what research findings have revealed.

■ Frustration: Why Not Getting What You Want (Or What You Expect) Can Sometimes Lead to Aggression

Suppose you asked twenty people you know to name the single most important cause of aggression. What would they say? Chances are good that most would reply *frustration*. And if you asked them to define *frustration,* many would state, "The way I feel when something—or someone—prevents me from getting what I want or expect to get in some situation." This widespread belief in the importance of frustration as a cause of aggression stems, at least in part, from the famous frustration–aggression hypothesis mentioned in our discussion of drive theories of aggression (Dollard et al., 1939). In its original form, this hypothesis made two sweeping assertions: (1) Frustration *always* leads to some form of aggression, and (2) aggression *always* stems from frustration. The theory held that frustrated persons always engage in some type of aggression and that all acts of aggression result from frustration. Bold statements like these are appealing, but this doesn't imply that they are necessarily accurate. Existing evidence suggests that both portions of the frustration–aggression hypothesis assign far too much importance to frustration as a determinant of human aggression. When frustrated, individuals do *not* always respond with aggression. On the contrary, they show many reactions, ranging from sadness, despair, and depression to direct attempts to overcome the source of their frustration. It is equally clear that not all aggression stems from frustration. People aggress for different reasons and in response to many factors. During wars, air force pilots report that flying their planes is a source of pleasure, and they bomb enemy targets while feeling elated or excited, not frustrated.

In view of these facts, few social psychologists accept the idea that frustration is the only, or even the most important, cause of aggression. Instead, most believe that frustration is one of many factors that can lead to aggression. We must add that frustration *can* serve as a powerful determinant of aggression under certain conditions, especially when frustration is viewed as illegitimate or unjustified (e.g., Folger & Baron, 1996). For instance, if an individual believes that she deserves a large raise and then receives a smaller one with no explanation, she may conclude that she has been treated unfairly—that her legitimate needs have been thwarted. The result: She may have hostile thoughts, experience intense anger, and seek revenge against the perceived source of such frustration—her boss or company. As we'll see in a later section, such reactions may play a key role in *workplace aggression* and in the aggressive reactions of some employees who lose their jobs through downsizing (e.g., Catalano, Novaco, & McConnell, 1997, 2002).

■ Direct Provocation: When Aggression Breeds Aggression

Major world religions generally agree in suggesting that when provoked by another person, we should turn the other cheek. In fact, however, research findings indicate that this is easier to say than do, and that physical or verbal **provocation** from others is one of the strongest causes of human aggression. When we are on the receiving end of aggression from others—criticism we consider unfair, sarcastic remarks, or physical assaults—we tend to reciprocate, returning as much aggression as we have received, or perhaps even more, especially if we are certain that the other person *meant* to harm us (Ohbuchi & Kambara, 1985).

What kinds of provocation produce the strongest push toward aggression? Existing evidence suggests that *condescension*—expressions of arrogance or disdain on the part of others—is very powerful (Harris, 1993). Harsh and unjustified criticism, especially that attacks us rather than our behavior, is another powerful form of provocation, and when exposed to it, most people find it difficult to avoid getting angry and retaliating, either immediately or later on (Baron, 1993). Still another form of provocation to which many respond with anger is derogatory statements about their families; even persons who can tolerate attacks on themselves often lose their tempers in the face of an attack on their mothers, fathers, brothers, sisters, or spouse.

■ Heightened Arousal: Emotion, Cognition, and Aggression

Suppose that you are driving to the airport to meet a friend. On the way, another driver cuts you off, and you almost have an accident. Your heart pounds wildly and your blood pressure shoots through the roof; but fortunately, no accident occurs. Now you arrive at the airport. You park and rush inside. When you get to the security check, an elderly man in front of you sets off the buzzer. He becomes confused and can't seem to understand that the security guard wants him to take off his shoes. You are irritated by this delay. In fact, you begin to lose your temper and mutter, "What's wrong with him? Can't he get it?"

Under some conditions, heightened arousal—whatever its source—can enhance aggression in response to provocation, frustration, or other factors. In various experiments, arousal stemming from such varied sources as participation in competitive games (Christy, Gelfand, & Hartmann, 1971), exercise (Zillmann, 1979), and even some types of music (Rogers & Ketcher, 1979) have been found to increase subsequent aggression. Why? A compelling explanation is offered by **excitation transfer theory** (Zillmann, 1983, 1988).

Excitation transfer theory suggests that because physiological arousal tends to dissipate slowly over time, a portion of such arousal may persist as a person moves from one situation to another. When you encounter a minor annoyance, that arousal intensifies your emotional reactions. The result: You become enraged rather than just mildly irritated. Excitation theory suggests further that such effects are most likely to occur when the persons involved are relatively unaware of the presence of residual arousal—a common occurrence, because small elevations in arousal are difficult to notice (Zillmann, 1994). Excitation transfer theory also suggests that such effects are likely to occur when the persons involved recognize their residual arousal but attribute it to events occurring in the present situation

provocation
Actions by others that tend to trigger aggression in the recipient, often because these actions are perceived as stemming from malicious intent.

excitation transfer theory
A theory suggesting that arousal produced in one situation can persist and intensify emotional reactions occurring in later situations.

Chapter 11 / Aggression

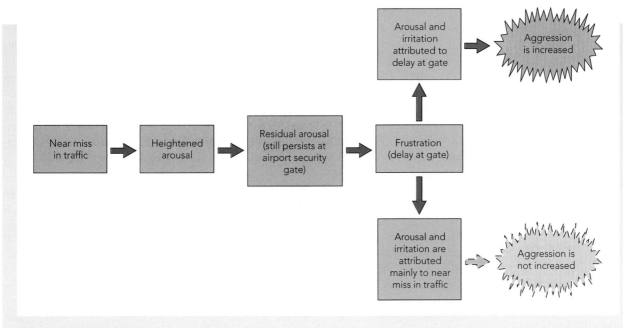

Figure 11.5 ■ Excitation Transfer Theory
Excitation transfer theory suggests that arousal occurring in one situation can persist and intensify emotional reactions in later, unrelated situations. (*Source: Based on suggestions by Zillmann, 1994.*)

(Taylor et al., 1991). In the airport incident, for instance, your anger would be intensified if you recognized your feelings of arousal but attributed them to the elderly man's actions (see Figure 11.5).

Exposure to Media Violence: The Effects of Witnessing Aggression

Think about several films you have seen in recent months. Now, answer the following questions: How much aggression or violence did each contain? How often did the characters hit, shoot at, or otherwise attempt to harm others? Unless you have chosen very carefully, you probably recognize that many of the films you have seen contained violence—much more violence than you are likely to see in real life (Reiss & Roth, 1993; Waters et al., 1993).

This raises an important question that social psychologists have studied for decades: Does exposure to such materials increase aggression among children or adults? Hundreds of studies have been performed to test this possibility, and the results seem clear: Exposure to **media violence** may be one factor contributing to high levels of violence in countries where such materials are viewed by large numbers of persons (e.g., Anderson, 1997; Paik & Comstock, 1994; Wood, Wong, & Cachere, 1991). In a recent summary of findings in this area (Anderson et al., 2004), experts on this topic offered the following conclusions:

media violence
Depictions of violent actions in the mass media.

1. Research on exposure to violent television, movies, video games, and music indicates that such materials significantly increase the likelihood of aggressive and violent behavior by persons exposed to them.

2. Such effects are both short-term and long-term in nature.

3. The magnitude of these effects is large—at least as large as the various medical effects considered to be important by the medical community (e.g., the effect of aspirin on heart attacks).

Social psychology's leading experts on the effects of media violence agree that these effects are real, lasting, and important—effects with important implications for society and for the safety and well-being of millions who are the victims of aggressive actions each year.

What kind of research led these experts to such conclusions? In brief, it was research using every major method known to social psychologists. For example, in *short-term laboratory experiments,* children or adults viewed either violent films and television programs or nonviolent ones; then, their tendency to aggress against others was measured. In general, the results of such experiments revealed higher levels of aggression among participants who viewed the violent programs (e.g., Bandura, Ross, & Ross, 1963; Bushman & Huesmann, 2001).

Other and perhaps even more convincing research employed *longitudinal* procedures, in which the same participants are studied for many years (e.g., Anderson & Bushman, 2002a; Huesmann & Eron, 1984, 1986). Results here, too, are clear: The more violent films or television programs participants watched as children, the higher their levels of aggression as teenagers or adults. Such findings were replicated in different countries—Australia, Finland, Israel, Poland, and South Africa (Botha, 1990). Thus, they appear to hold across different cultures. Further, such effects are not restricted only to actual programs or films: They appear to be produced by violence in news programs, violent lyrics in popular music (e.g., Anderson, Carnagey, & Eubanks, 2003), and violent video games (Anderson et al., 2004). As the group of experts on media violence mentioned, "The cup of research knowledge about violence in the media is relatively full. . . . It . . . supports sustained concern about media violence and sustained efforts to curb its adverse effects" (Anderson et al., 2004, p. 105).

■ The Effects of Media Violence: Why Do They Occur?

By now, you may be wondering: Why does exposure to media violence (of different kinds) increase aggression among persons exposed to it? A compelling answer is provided by Bushman and Anderson (2002), who suggest that the effects of media violence can be readily understood within the context of the GAM. As you may recall, this model suggests that both personal and situational factors influence individuals' internal states—their feelings, thoughts, and arousal—and that these internal states shape individuals' appraisal of a given situation and their decision as to how to behave in it—aggressively (impulsively) or nonaggressively (thoughtfully). Bushman and Anderson suggest that repeated exposure to media violence can strongly affect cognitions relating to aggression, gradually creating a *hostile expectation bias*—a strong expectation that others will behave aggressively. This causes individuals to be more aggressive themselves: After all, they perceive provocations from others, even when the provocations really don't exist!

In one test, Bushman and Anderson (2002) exposed participants to highly aggressive video games (e.g., *Carmageddon, Mortal Kombat*) or nonaggressive video games (*Glider Pro, 3D Pinball*). Then, they asked them to read brief stories in which it is not clear what the characters will do next. After reading the stories, participants described what they thought the main character would do, say, feel, and think as the story continues. In one story, a character has a minor traffic accident after braking quickly for a yellow light. He then approaches the other driver. The researchers predicted that after playing the aggressive video games, participants would expect the story character to act more aggressively, to think more aggressive thoughts, and to feel angrier; as you can see from Figure 11.6, this is what happened.

These findings and the results of related research (e.g., Anderson et al., 2004; Anderson & Bushman, 2001; Bushman & Huesmann, 2001) suggest that exposure to violent media exerts its effects by strengthening beliefs, expectations, and other cognitive processes related to aggression. In other words, as a result of repeated exposure to violent movies, TV programs, or violent video games, individuals develop strong *knowledge structures* relating to aggression—structures reflecting and combining these beliefs, expectations, schemas, and scripts. When these knowledge structures are then activated, such

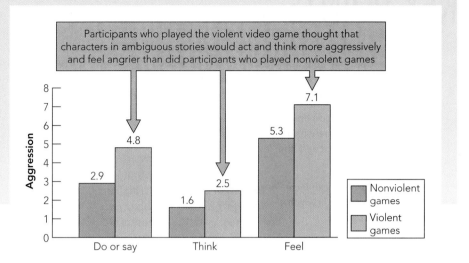

Figure 11.6 ■ Playing Aggressive Video Games: One Source of Aggressive Thoughts, Feelings, and Actions
Participants who played violent video games predicted that characters in ambiguous stories would behave, think, and feel more aggressively than did participants who played nonviolent games. (*Source: Based on data from Bushman & Anderson, 2002.*)

persons feel, think, and act aggressively because this is what, in a sense, they have learned to do.

Whatever the underlying mechanisms, forty years of research suggests that exposure to media violence may have harmful effects on society. So why, then, is there so much of it on television, in movies, and in video games? The answer, sad to relate, is that violence sells. People find it exciting and enjoyable. Moreover, advertisers assume this is true and "put their money where the action is" (Bushman, 1998). This is one more case in which economic motives take precedence.

Violent Pornography: When Sex and Aggression Mix—and Perhaps Explode

Pornographic images are now freely available to virtually everyone, including, unfortunately, children. And, disturbingly, not all of these materials simply show consenting adults engaging in mutually enjoyable sexual activity. Some of it includes violent content, scenes in which victims—usually, but not always, women—are abused, exploited, and harmed in various ways (e.g., Linz, Fuson, & Donnerstein, 1990; Malamuth & Check, 1985).

If exposure to violence in the media can increase aggressive tendencies among persons exposed to such content, it seems possible that exposure to violent pornography might also produce such effects. In fact, because pornography often generates high levels of arousal (both negative and positive emotions), it seems possible that such effects might be stronger than is true for media violence that does not contain sexual content. Although there is currently less evidence on this issue, some findings suggest that violent pornography may indeed have negative effects. Laboratory studies (e.g., Linz, Donnerstein, & Penrod, 1988) suggest that exposure to violent pornography can increase men's willingness to aggress against women. Perhaps even more disturbing, repeated exposure to such materials appears to produce a *desensitizing effect,* in which emotional reactions to mistreatment or harm to sexual victims is gradually reduced. Finally, and most unsettling of all, exposure to violent pornography seems to encourage adoption of callous attitudes toward sexual violence, leading women and men to accept dangerous myths about rape and other forms of sexual violence—for example, the myth that many women unconsciously want to be raped, or that almost all victims of rape are promiscuous and place themselves in situations in which they are likely to be sexually assaulted (Malamuth & Brown, 1994). Not all persons who are exposed to violent pornography become more willing to engage in such behavior, but growing evidence suggests that the mixture of sex and violence such pornography contains can be dangerous and volatile.

temperature *reduced* aggression for both provoked and unprovoked persons. The initial explanation was that the high temperatures were so uncomfortable that participants focused on getting away from them—and this caused them to reduce their aggression. After all, aggression might lead to unfriendly encounters with the victim, and this would prolong their misery.

This explanation seemed reasonable: When people are *very* hot, they seem to become lethargic and concentrate on reducing their discomfort rather than evening the score. However, these early studies suffered from important drawbacks that made it difficult to assess this interpretation. For instance, the exposure to the high temperatures lasted only a few minutes, while, in the real world, such exposure occurs over longer periods. Subsequent studies, therefore, used different methods (e.g., Anderson, 1989; Anderson & Anderson, 1996; Bell, 1992). Specifically, they examined long-term records of temperatures and police records of aggressive crimes to determine whether the frequency of such crimes increased with rising temperatures.

Consider an informative study by Anderson, Bushman, and Groom (1997). These researchers collected average annual temperatures for fifty cities in the United States over a forty-five-year period (1950 to 1995). In addition, they obtained information on the rate of violent crimes (aggravated assault, homicide) and property crimes (burglary, car theft), as well as another crime that has often been viewed as primarily aggressive in nature—rape. They then performed analyses to determine whether temperature were related to these crimes. In general, the results indicated that hotter years produced higher rates of violent crimes but did *not* produce increases in property crimes or rape. This was true even though the effect of other variables that might also influence aggressive crimes (e.g., poverty, age distribution of the population) were eliminated. These findings and those of related studies (e.g., Anderson, Anderson, & Deuser, 1996) suggest that heat is linked to aggression.

Sophisticated as this research was, however, it did not fully resolve one key question: Does this heat–aggression relationship have any limits? In other words, does aggression increase with heat indefinitely, or only up to some point, beyond which aggression actually declines as temperatures continue to rise? As you may recall, that is the pattern obtained in initial laboratory studies on this topic.

Additional studies by Rotton and Cohn (Cohn & Rotton, 1997; Rotton & Cohn, 2000) have addressed this issue. These researchers reasoned that if people try to reduce their discomfort when they are feeling uncomfortable (e.g., when temperatures are very high), the relationship between heat and aggression should be stronger in the evening hours than at midday. Why? Because temperatures fall below their peak in the evening. A finer-grained analysis would reveal a curvilinear relationship between heat and aggression during the day but a linear one at night. This is exactly what they found (see Figure 11.11).

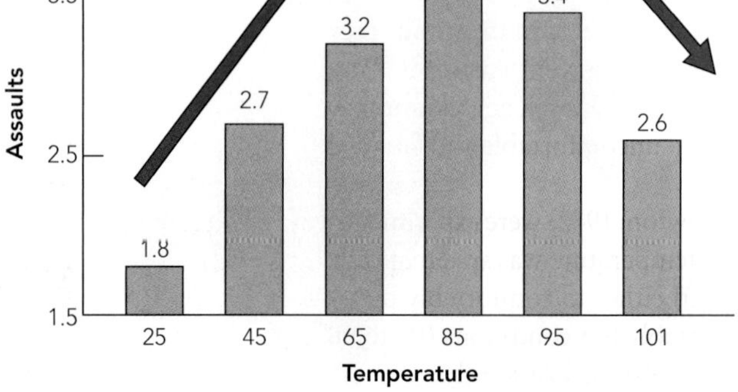

As temperatures rise, assaults increase up to a point; beyond this point, assaults decrease as temperatures continue to rise

Figure 11.11 ■ **Heat and Aggression: Evidence for a Curvilinear Relationship**
In two large U.S. cities, the incidence of violent assaults rose with increasing temperatures but only up to a point; beyond this level, as temperatures continued to rise, the incidence of assaults dropped. These findings suggest that the relationship between heat and aggression may be curvilinear in nature. (*Source: Based on data from Rotton & Cohn, 2000.*)

Chapter 11 / Aggression

■ Alcohol and Aggression: A Potentially Dangerous Mix

It is widely believed that at least some persons become more aggressive when they consume alcohol. This is supported by the fact that bars and nightclubs are frequently the scene of violence. However, though alcohol is certainly consumed in these settings, other factors might be responsible for the fights that often erupt: competition for partners, crowding, and even cigarette smoke, which irritates some people (Zillmann, Baron, & Tamborini, 1981). What does systematic research reveal about a possible link between alcohol and aggression? Interestingly, it tends to confirm the existence of such a link. In several experiments, participants who consumed enough alcohol to make them legally drunk were found to behave more aggressively and respond to provocations more strongly than those who did not consume alcohol (e.g., Bushman & Cooper, 1990; Gustafson, 1990). (Participants in such research are always warned, in advance, that they may be receiving alcoholic beverages, and only those who consent actually take part; e.g., Pihl, Lau, & Assaad, 1997). But *why* does alcohol produce such effects? Findings suggest that the effects of alcohol on aggression may stem from reduced cognitive functioning and what this does to social perception.

Specifically, it has been found that alcohol impairs higher-order cognitive functions such as evaluation of stimuli and memory. This result may make it harder for individuals to evaluate others' intentions (hostile or nonhostile) and to evaluate the effects that various forms of behavior, including aggression, may produce (e.g., Hoaken, Giancola, & Pihl, 1998). Evidence for such effects has been reported by Bartholow et al. (2003) in a study using a social neuroscience approach.

In this research, participants received either a high dose of alcohol, a moderate dose, or no alcohol. Then, they read descriptions of strangers who had either positive or negative traits, and who were described as acting either in a positive or negative manner in a particular situation. Recordings of event-related brain potentials (ERBPs) were made during these procedures. It was predicted that regardless of whether they drank alcohol, participants would show larger late positive potentials (LPPs) in instances in which their expectancies were violated—when a person with positive traits acted in a negative way or when a person with negative traits acted in a positive way. This prediction was confirmed. It was also predicted that if alcohol interferes with the processing of information about others, the size of these LPPs would be reduced. In other words, a participant's ability to handle (try to make sense of) inconsistent information would be reduced. Results indicated that this was *not* the case. Rather, it was found that for individuals who did not consume alcohol, persons with positive traits performing negative behaviors produced the largest LPPs. When participants drank alcohol, however, the opposite was true: Persons with negative traits performing positive behaviors produced the largest LPPs. Alcohol seemed to change the kind of inconsistencies to which individuals directed their attention.

Whatever the precise cognitive processes involved, existing evidence (e.g., Gantner & Taylor, 1992) suggests that alcohol may be one situational factor that contributes to the occurrence of aggression, and that such effects may be especially strong for persons who normally show low levels of aggression (Pihl et al., 1997). In this sense, then, consumption of alcohol may have the release-of-inhibitions effects common sense suggests. (For an overview of the many factors that play a role in human aggression, see the **Ideas to Take with You—and Use!** section at the end of this chapter.)

KEY POINTS

★ High temperatures tend to increase aggression up to a point. Beyond some level, aggression declines as temperatures rise.

★ Consuming alcohol can increase aggression, especially by individuals who normally show low levels of aggression.

★ Alcohol may exert these effects by reducing an individual's capacity to process some kinds of information and by changing their reactions to unexpected behaviors by others.

Aggression in Long-Term Relationships: Bullying and Workplace Violence

Reports of instances in which people are attacked by strangers are disturbing. Even more unsettling, however, are situations in which people are harmed by others they know or with whom they have long-term relationships—family members, spouses or partners, schoolmates, coworkers. Such aggression takes many forms, but we focus on two important topics: *bullying* (e.g., Ireland & Ireland, 2000; Smith & Brain, 2000) and *workplace violence* (Griffin & O'Leary, 2004).

Bullying: Singling Out Others for Repeated Abuse

Almost everyone has either experienced or observed the effects of **bullying**—a form of aggression in which aggression is primarily one way: One person repeatedly assaults one or more others who have little or no power to retaliate (Olweus, 1993). In bullying relationships, one person does the aggressing and the other (or others) are on the receiving end. Although bullying has been studied primarily as something that occurs among children and teenagers (see Figure 11.12), it is also common in workplaces and prisons (e.g., Ireland & Archer, 2002). Research findings indicate that 50 percent of prisoners are exposed to one or more episodes of bullying each week (Ireland & Ireland, 2000). In this discussion, therefore, we consider research on bullying in different contexts.

■ Why Do People Engage in Bullying?

A basic question about bullying, of course, is why does it occur? Why do some individuals choose targets they then repeatedly terrorize? There is no simple answer, but two motives appear to play a key role: the motive to hold power over others and the motive to be part of a group that is "tough" and so confers status on its members (e.g., Olweus, 1999). These motives are clearly visible in research conducted by Roland (2002). In this study, more than two thousand children in Norway answered questions designed to measure their desire to exercise power over others, their desire to be part of powerful groups, and their tendency to be unhappy or depressed. (Previous research had suggested that feeling depressed might be another reason why individuals engage in **bullying**—it makes them feel better!) A measure of bullying was obtained by asking the children to indicate how often they had bullied other children (never, now and then, weekly, daily). Such self-reports of bullying have generally been found to be accurate when compared with teachers' ratings.

Results revealed some interesting gender differences. Among boys, the desire both to gain power and to be part of powerful groups was significantly related to bullying, while feeling depressed was not. For girls, all three motives were related to bullying. This suggests that for girls, at least, aggressing against someone who can't retaliate is one technique for countering the negative feelings of depression. Again, we should note that other factors, too, play a role in the occurrence of bullying. The motives identified here, however, were found to play a role in bullying in many contexts, so they seem to be among the most important causes of bullying.

bullying
A pattern of behavior in which one individual is chosen as the target of repeated aggression by one or more others; the target person (the victim) generally has less power than those who engage in aggression (the bullies).

Figure 11.12 ■ Bullying: One-Way Aggression
In *bullying,* one person repeatedly assaults one or more others who have no ability to defend themselves or retaliate. Such behavior occurs among children, as shown here, but also among adults.

■ The Characteristics of Bullies and Victims

Are bullies always bullies and victims always victims? Although common sense suggests that these roles would tend to be relatively fixed, research indicates that they are not. Many persons who are bullies become victims in other situations, and vice versa. So, there appear to be pure bullies (people who are always bullies), pure victims (people who are always victims), and bully-victims (people who switch back and forth).

But what, aside from the motives for power and belonging, makes some people become bullies? Findings of careful research on bullying point to the following factors. Bullies tend to believe that others act the way they do intentionally or because of lasting characteristics (Smorti & Ciucci, 2000). In contrast, victims tend to perceive others as acting as they do at least in part because they are responding to external conditions, including how others have treated *them*. In other words, bullies are more subject to the hostile attributional bias described earlier in this chapter. In a sense, they attack others because they perceive them to be potentially dangerous and wish to get in the first blows!

Another difference is that bullies (and also bully-victims) tend to be lower in self-esteem. As a result, they often attack to build up their own self-images. In addition, they tend to adopt a ruthless, manipulative approach to life and to dealing with other persons (e.g., Mynard & Joseph, 1997; Andreou, 2000). They believe that others are not to be trusted, so they feel it is justified to take unfair advantage of others.

Finally, bullies and bully-victims believe that the best way to respond to bullying is with aggression. They believe, more than others, that aggressing against others who provoke them will bring respect from others and make them feel better (Ireland & Archer, 2002). The result? They choose to respond to slight provocations with strong aggression, and so start the process of becoming a bully.

■ Reducing the Occurrence of Bullying: Some Positive Steps

Bullying can have devastating effects on its victims. In fact, there have been several cases in which children who have been bullied repeatedly and brutally by their classmates have committed suicide (O'Moore, 2000), and similar results often occur in prisons, in which persons who are brutalized by their fellow inmates see death as the only way out. These distressing facts lead to the following question: What can be done to reduce or eliminate bullying? Many research projects—some involving the entire school systems or prison systems of several countries—have been conducted, and the results have been moderately encouraging. Here is an overview of the main findings:

• First, bullying must be seen to be a problem by all involved parties—teachers, parents, students, prisoners, guards, fellow employees, and supervisors (if bullying occurs in work settings).

• If bullying occurs, persons in authority (teachers, prison guards, supervisors) must draw attention to it and take an unequivocal stand against it.

• Potential victims must be provided with direct means for dealing with bullying—they must be told precisely what to do and whom to see when bullying occurs.

• Outside help is often useful in identifying the cause of bullying and in devising programs to reduce it.

Programs that have emphasized these points have produced encouraging results. There appear to be grounds for optimism—provided bullying is recognized as the serious problem it is, and organizations (schools, prisons, businesses) take vigorous steps to deal with it.

Workplace Violence: Aggression on the Job

Dr. carves initials on woman—Obstetrician is being sued for using scalpel to etch letters on abdomen after Cesarean section (Albany, NY, January 22, 2000).

Portland, Oregon—A man accused of shooting two people and taking four others hostage in an office tower appeared in court Friday. . . . Police initially said Rancor

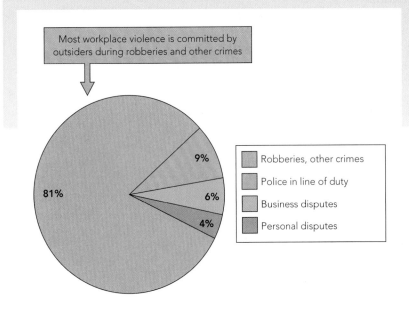

Most workplace violence is committed by outsiders during robberies and other crimes

9%
81%
6%
4%

Robberies, other crimes
Police in line of duty
Business disputes
Personal disputes

Figure 11.13 ■ Workplace Violence: A Closer Look
Most instances of workplace violence are performed by outsiders during robberies and other crimes. Very few instances involve one employee physically attacking another. (*Source: Baron & Neuman, 1996.*)

intended to shoot female office workers for having him fired from his job. . . . (Associated Press, 1996).

Reports of incidents such as these have appeared with alarming frequency and seem to reflect a rising tide of workplace violence. More than eight hundred people are murdered at work each year in the United States (National Institute for Occupational Safety and Health, 1993). While these statistics seem to suggest that workplaces are becoming dangerous locations where disgruntled employees frequently attack or even shoot one another, two facts must be noted: (1) A large majority of violence occurring in work settings is performed by "outsiders"—people who do not work there but enter a workplace to commit crimes (see Figure 11.13), and (2) recent surveys indicate that threats of physical harm or actual harm in work settings are rare—the chances of being killed at work (by outsiders or coworkers combined) are 1 in 450,000 (although this is considerably higher in some "high-risk occupations" such as taxi driver or police; LeBlanc & Barling, 2004).

Growing evidence suggests that while workplace *violence* is an important topic worthy of careful study, it is rare and is only the dramatic tip of the much larger problem of **workplace aggression**—any form of behavior through which individuals seek to harm others in their places of work (Griffin & O'Leary, 2004; Neuman & Baron, 2004). What is such aggression like? Evidence suggests that it is largely *covert* rather than *overt* in nature. That is, it is relatively subtle and allows aggressors to harm others while simultaneously preventing the victims from identifying them as the source. This type of aggression is strongly preferred in workplaces, because aggressors expect to interact with their intended victims frequently in the future. Using covert forms of aggression reduces the likelihood that their victims will retaliate.

What specific forms of aggression do individuals use in workplaces? Evidence on this issue is provided by research conducted by Baron, Neuman, and Geddes (1999). These researchers asked almost five hundred employed persons to rate the frequency with which they had experienced a wide range of aggressive behaviors at work. Careful analysis of their responses indicated that most aggression occurring in workplaces falls into three major categories:

- *Expressions of hostility:* Behaviors that are primarily verbal or symbolic in nature (e.g., belittling others' opinions, talking behind their backs)

- *Obstructionism:* Behaviors designed to obstruct or impede the target's performance (e.g., failure to return phone calls or respond to memos, failure to transmit needed information, interfering with activities important to the target)

- *Overt aggression:* Behaviors that have typically been included under the heading "workplace violence" (e.g., physical assault, theft or destruction of property, threats of physical violence)

workplace aggression
Any form of behavior through which individuals seek to harm others in their workplace.

How common are these forms of behavior? Research on what is known as **abusive supervision**—behavior in which supervisors direct frequent hostile verbal and nonverbal behavior toward their subordinates (Tepper, 2000)—suggests that the answer is, "More common than you might guess." It occurs not just between coworkers but also among supervisors and employees as well. Abusive supervision, one form of workplace aggression, includes actions such as public and private ridicule, exclusion from important activities, invasion of personal space, rude and discourteous behavior, lying, and taking credit for a subordinate's work; all seem to occur with high frequency. Although workplace violence involving physical assaults is relatively rare, workplace aggression is much more common. In many workplaces, aggression is an everyday occurrence.

abusive supervision
Behavior in which supervisors direct frequent hostile verbal and nonverbal behavior toward their subordinates.

What are the causes of workplace aggression? As is true of aggression in any context, many factors seem to play a role. However, one that has emerged again and again in research is *perceived unfairness* (e.g., Skarlicki & Folger, 1997). When individuals feel that they have been treated unfairly by others in their organization—or by the organization itself—they experience intense feelings of anger and resentment and often seek to even the score by harming the people they hold responsible. In addition, aggression in work settings seems to be influenced by general societal norms concerning the acceptability of such behavior. One recent study (Dietz et al., 2003) found that the greater the incidence of violence in communities surrounding U.S. Post Offices, the higher the rates of aggression within these offices. It was as if acceptance of violence in the surrounding communities paved the way for similar behavior inside this organization.

Other factors that seem to play a role in workplace aggression relate to changes that have occurred recently in many workplaces: downsizing, layoffs, and increased use of part-time employees, to name a few. Several studies indicate that the greater the extent to which such changes have occurred, the greater the aggression (e.g., Andersson & Pearson, 1999; Neuman & Baron, 1998). Such findings are only correlational in nature, but because downsizing, layoffs, and other changes have been found to produce negative feelings among employees, it seems possible that these changes may well contribute, through such reactions, to increased aggression. One final point: Because such changes have occurred with increasing frequency, it seems possible that the incidence of workplace aggression, too, may be increasing for this reason.

KEY POINTS

★ *Bullying* involves repeated aggression against individuals who, for various reasons, are unable to defend themselves. Bullying occurs in many contexts, including schools, workplaces, and prisons. Few persons are solely bullies or victims; more play both roles. Bullies and bully-victims appear to have lower self-esteem than do people who are not involved in bullying.

★ *Workplace aggression* takes different forms but is usually covert in nature. It stems from a range of factors, including perceptions of having been treated unfairly and many disturbing changes that have occurred in workplaces recently.

The Prevention and Control of Aggression: Some Useful Techniques

If there is one idea in this chapter we hope you remember, it is this: Aggression is *not* an inevitable or unchangeable form of behavior. On the contrary, because it stems from a complex interplay between external events, cognitions, and personal characteristics, it *can* be prevented or reduced. In this section, we consider several procedures that can be effective in reducing the frequency or intensity of human aggression.

Punishment: Just Desserts versus Deterrence

In most societies, **punishment**—delivery of aversive consequences—is a major technique for reducing aggression. Persons who engage in such behavior receive large fines, are put in prison, and, in some countries, are placed in solitary confinement or receive physical punishment. In the most extreme cases, they receive *capital punishment* and are executed in various ways by legal authorities (see Figure 11.14). This raises two important questions: Why is punishment used so frequently to reduce human aggression, and does punishment really work? These are complex questions that we can't hope to resolve here, but we can describe what research on these important issues has revealed.

Turning to the first question, there are two major grounds for punishing persons who commit aggressive actions (e.g., Darley, Carlsmith, & Robinson, 2000). The first involves the belief that when individuals engage in acts of aggression that are viewed as inappropriate, they *deserve* to be punished to make amends for the harm they have caused. This perspective suggests that the amount of punishment people receive should be matched to the magnitude of harm they have caused (e.g., breaking someone's arm deserves less punishment than permanently harming or killing someone). In addition, the magnitude of punishment should take account of extenuating circumstances. For instance, was there some "good" motive for the aggressive action, such as self-defense or defense of one's family?

The second reason for punishing persons who commit aggressive actions is to *deter* them (or others) from engaging in such behavior in the future. This basis for punishment implies that ease of detection of the crime should be given careful attention: If aggressive actions are hard to detect (e.g., they involve hidden forms of harming others), they should be strongly punished. Similarly, public punishment would be expected to be more effective in deterring future crimes than would private punishment.

Which of these two perspectives are most important in terms of the magnitude of punishment people feel is justified for aggressive acts or other offenses? Research by Carlsmith, Darley, and Robinson (2002) suggests that, in general, the first perspective—punishing people to make amends for the harm they have done—is more important. These researchers asked participants to read brief descriptions of crimes that varied in the extent to which the crimes seemed to deserve punishment (i.e., how much harm they had caused), and also varied in terms of the ease with which these crimes could be detected. An example of a crime that produced relatively little harm and might deserve low punishment was an employee embezzling money, while a crime that seemed to deserve high punishment was dumping toxic waste to increase profits. Participants also learned that the ease of detecting these crimes was either low or high. After reading, participants rated the extent to which the perpetrator should be punished. Results offered strong support for the view that in deciding how much punishment to deliver, we seem to be strongly influenced by how much punishment is *deserved*: Participants in the study assigned much harsher punishment for the dumping of toxic waste, which produced much harm, than to embezzling funds, which produced less harm. In contrast, the punishments they recommended were *not* significantly influenced by the ease of detecting various crimes. Using punishment as a deterrent to future crimes seemed to be much less important.

Does this mean that we don't consider the deterrence value of punishment? Carlsmith, Darley, and Robinson (2002) do not believe this is so. Other results they obtained suggest that when thinking about punishment for a particular person, we

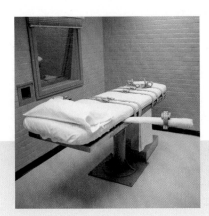

Figure 11.14 ■ Punishment: Its Most Extreme Form
Most societies use *punishment*—delivery of aversive consequences—as a means of reducing aggression. In its most extreme form, capital punishment, individuals judged to be a danger to their society are executed in a way prescribed by law.

Chapter 11 / Aggression

tend to focus mainly on how much punishment she or he deserves. However, when thinking more generally, about the good of society, we *do* consider deterrence important. Overall it appears that both motives lie behind the use of punishment as a means of dealing with aggression.

At this point, we must note that there is still one other rationale for using punishment to reduce aggressive behavior: It removes dangerous people from society (e.g., by placing them in prison), and in this way protects future victims. Statistics indicate that once people engage in violent crimes, they are likely to do so again, so removing them from society can help prevent additional acts of aggression. This basis for giving convicted persons long prison sentences is not stated very often, but logically, it appears to make some sense.

Now for the next questions: Does punishment work? Can it reduce the tendency of specific persons to engage in harmful acts of aggression? Here, evidence is relatively clear: Punishment *can* reduce aggression but only if it meets four basic requirements: (1) It must be *prompt*—it must follow aggressive actions as quickly as possible; (2) it must be *certain to occur*—the probability that it will follow aggression must be very high; (3) it must be *strong*—strong enough to be highly unpleasant to potential recipients; and (4) it must be perceived by recipients as *justified* or deserved.

Unfortunately, these conditions are often *not* present in the criminal justice systems of many nations. In most societies, the delivery of punishment for aggressive actions is delayed. Similarly, many criminals avoid arrest and conviction, so the certainty of punishment is low. The magnitude of punishment itself varies from one city, state, or even courtroom to another. And, often, punishment does not seem to fit the crime—it does not seem to be justified or deserved. In such cases, the persons who receive punishment may view it as aggression against *them*—as a kind of provocation. And as we saw earlier, provocation is a very powerful trigger for aggression. In view of these facts, it is hardly surprising that the threat of punishment—even the most severe punishment (execution)—does not seem to be effective in deterring violent crime. The conditions necessary for it to be effective are simply not present. This raises an intriguing question: Could punishment prove effective as a deterrent to violence if it were used more effectively? We can't say for sure, but existing evidence suggests that it could exert such effects *if* it were used in accordance with the principles described above. But instituting such conditions would raise complex issues relating to ethical and religious beliefs, so scientific data are clearly only one consideration, and for that reason, we cannot offer a clear position here. Rather, this is a matter each person must decide for her- or himself. (For information on another potential means of reducing aggression—one that is widely viewed as highly effective—see the **Science of Social Psychology: Making Sense of Common Sense** section.)

Cognitive Interventions: Apologies and Overcoming Cognitive Deficits

Do you find it easy or hard to apologize? If your answer is "hard," you should work on this particular social skill, because research findings agree with what common sense suggests: *apologies*—admissions of wrongdoing that include a request for forgiveness—often go a long way toward defusing aggression (e.g., Ohbuchi, Kameda, & Agarie, 1989). Similarly, good excuses—ones that make reference to factors beyond the excuse-giver's control—can also be effective in reducing anger and overt aggression by persons who have previously been provoked in some manner (e.g., Baron, 1989a; Weiner et al., 1987). So, if you feel that you are making another person angry, apologize without delay: The trouble you save makes it quite worthwhile to say, "I'm sorry."

When we are very angry, our ability to think clearly may be sharply reduced. When this occurs, restraints that normally hold aggression in check (e.g., fear of retaliation) may diminish. As noted by Lieberman and Greenberg (1999), when we are emotionally aroused, we may adopt modes of thoughts in which we process information in a quick and impetuous manner. This may increase the chances that we will lash out against someone else, including

In this chapter, you read about . . .	In other chapters, you will find related discussions of . . .
the role of cognitive and affective variables in aggression	the role of these factors in many other forms of social behavior . . . attitude change (Chapter 4) prejudice (Chapter 6) helping (Chapter 10)
social factors that play a role in aggression	the effects of these factors on other forms of social behavior . . . attributions (Chapter 2) arousal (Chapter 7) social models (Chapter 10)
personal characteristics that influence aggression	the role of these factors in several other forms of social behavior . . . social perception (Chapter 3) obedience (Chapter 9) helping behavior (Chapter 10)

Thinking about connections

1. Attorneys sometimes defend individuals who commit violent acts by suggesting that these persons were "overwhelmed" by emotions beyond their control. In view of our discussions in other chapters (e.g., Chapters 2, 10) of the effects of emotions on social thought and behavior, what are your reactions to such defenses?

2. There seems to be overwhelming evidence that exposure to media violence can increase aggression. Yet, "violence sells": Television programs and films containing graphic violence are often very popular. In view of this, do you think anything can be done to reduce this potential cause of increased aggression? If so, what do you recommend?

3. Violence and other forms of aggression appear to be increasing in many workplaces. Do you think

it is possible to screen potential employees, so as to reject those who have a high propensity for engaging in such behavior? If so, what aspects of their self-concept (Chapter 5), attitudes (see Chapter 4), or past behavior (e.g., the kind of relationships they have had with others; see Chapter 8) might be useful predictors of the likelihood that they would engage in workplace aggression if hired?

Ideas to Take with You—and Use! CAUSES OF AGGRESSION

Research indicates that aggression stems from a range of variables—social factors, personal characteristics, and situational factors. Here is an overview of the most important factors identified by systematic research.

Social Determinants of Aggression

Frustration
Direct Provocation
Exposure to Media Violence
Heightened Arousal
→ Aggression

Personal Determinants of Aggression

Type A Behavior Pattern
Hostile Attributional Bias
Gender
Narcissism
Sensation Seeking
→ Aggression

Situational Determinants of Aggression

High Temperatures
Alcohol
Cultural Beliefs, Values
→ Aggression

KEY TERMS

abusive supervision (p. 323)
aggression (p. 302)
bullying (p. 320)
catharsis hypothesis (p. 326)
cultures of honor (p. 312)
displaced aggression (p. 326)
drive theories (of aggression) (p. 304)

excitation transfer theory (p. 308)
forgiveness (p. 327)
frustration–aggression hypothesis (p. 304)
general aggression model (p. 306)
hostile aggression (p. 315)
hostile attributional bias (p. 315)

instrumental aggression (p. 315)
media violence (p. 309)
provocation (p. 308)
punishment (p. 324)
Type A behavior pattern (p. 314)
Type B behavior pattern (p. 315)
workplace aggression (p. 322)

12 GROUPS AND INDIVIDUALS
The Consequences of Belonging

When I (Robert Baron) was fifteen, I needed a summer job. Very few jobs were open to someone my age, but one that was available was for a company that supplied umbrellas and folding chairs to beach visitors. The job involved carrying these items—which were really heavy!—and setting them up for customers. It didn't pay much, but it was close to where I lived, so I wanted it. The day I applied, there must have been fifty of us waiting to hear what the owner had to say. His remarks were ones I'll never forget: "OK, you guys, we need help for the summer and even though you are the most pitiful bunch I've ever seen, you'll have to do. But here's the deal: The government just raised the minimum wage, and I can't afford to pay it. So to make up the difference, you'll have to turn in your tips at the end of every day." "Turn in our tips?" I remember thinking. "Tips make this crummy job worthwhile!" One young man spoke up: "But the tips are ours," he said. "Why should we give them to you?" The owner walked up to him and said: "A wise guy, eh? Get lost; I don't need you. Go find another job." After that, the rest of us kept quiet: We needed the job, so we didn't protest. But later, most of us got together about a block away and discussed this arrangement. Our conclusion? It wasn't fair and we would resist—not immediately and not openly, but we would work on it!

Over the next few weeks, small groups of us met to exchange ideas for keeping at least part of our tips. One solution was to have friends meet us late in the day; we'd give them our tips to hold until later. Another was to find hiding places so we could retrieve them later.

The best thing that came out of our meetings—and the one that made the difference—was this: One of us had an attorney for an uncle, and he asked him if the owner could legally take our tips. We soon learned that he could not. In fact, the attorney was furious and wrote a letter threatening legal action if the owner continued this policy. Faced with this risk, he shouted at us and called us a bunch of troublemakers, but grudgingly told us we could keep our tips. We did a lot of celebrating *that* night!

These events took place many years ago in a world very different from the one faced by teenaged workers today. But the points they illustrate are still valid. First, we all join *groups;* some are temporary and come into existence to accomplish a specific purpose, like

Figure 12.1 ■ Groups: Often, They Provide Us with Important Benefits
People join groups for many reasons, but an important factor is the benefits they confer.

the group my fellow workers and I formed to resist the owner's "give me your tips" policy. Other groups are much more lasting in nature and focus on different issues and activities (e.g., professional organizations; religious or political groups; fraternities and sororities). Second, the groups we join often provide us with important benefits; that's why we join them! (See Figure 12.1.) Third, all groups have to make decisions (e.g., "How should we resist the owner's policy?"), and, fourth, all seek to maximize *cooperation*—working together to reach various goals, and to minimize or at least manage *conflict* between members. Finally, most, if not all groups, must deal with the issue of *fairness*—both within the group and outside it.

We examine these questions—plus several others—in this chapter. We begin by examining the basic nature of groups and the central question of why we join them and why, sometimes, we choose to quit. Next, we examine the impact of what is, in some ways, the most basic group effect: the mere presence of others. The presence of others, even if we are not in a formal group, can affect our performance on many tasks and other aspects of our behavior. Third, we briefly examine the nature of cooperation and conflict in groups—why these contrasting patterns emerge and the effects they produce. After that, we consider the closely related question of perceived *fairness* in groups—the central process at work in the salary incident described earlier. Finally, we turn to *decision making* in groups and the unexpected dangers this process sometimes poses.

Groups: Why We Join ... and Why We Leave

Look at the photos in Figure 12.2. Which shows a group? Probably you would identify the one on the right as a group, but the one on the left as a collection of persons. Why? Because implicitly, you already accept a definition of the term **group** close to the one adopted by

group
A collection of persons who are perceived to be bonded together in a coherent unit to some degree.

Figure 12.2 ■ What Makes a Group a Group?
The photo on the left shows a collection of persons who happen to be in the same place at the same time; they are not part of a *group*. The photo on the right shows a true group: The people in this group interact with one another and have shared goals and outcomes. Moreover, they feel that they are, in fact, part of a group.

social psychologists: a collection of persons who are perceived to be bonded together in a coherent unit to some degree (e.g., Dasgupta, Banji, & Abelson, 1999; Lickel et al., 2000). Social psychologists refer to this property of groups as **entiativity**—the extent to which a group is perceived as being a coherent entity (Campbell, 1958). Entiativity varies greatly, ranging from mere collections of people who happen to be in the same place at the same time but have little or no connection with one another, to highly intimate groups such as our families or persons with whom we have romantic relationships. So, clearly, some groups are much closer to our conception of what a group is like than others. But what determines whether, and to what extent, we perceive several persons as forming a coherent group? This question has received growing attention from researchers, and a clear answer has begun to emerge (Lickel et al., 2000). In particular, it appears that true groups—ones high in entiativity—show the following characteristics: (1) Members interact with one another often, (2) the group is important to its members, (3) members share common goals and outcomes, and (4) members are similar to one another in important ways. The higher groups are on these dimensions, the more they are seen by their members as forming coherent entities—real groups to which they choose to belong.

Groups: Some Basic Aspects

Before turning to the specific ways in which groups affect various aspects of our behavior and thought, it is useful to first describe several basic features of groups—ones that are present in virtually every group deserving of this label. These features are *roles*, *status*, *norms*, and *cohesiveness*.

■ Roles: Differentiation of Functions within Groups

Think of a group to which you belong or have belonged—anything from the scouts to a professional association. Now consider this question: Did everyone in the group act in the same way or perform the same functions? Your answer is probably "no." Different persons performed different tasks and were expected to accomplish different things for the group. In short, they played different **roles.** Sometimes roles are assigned; for instance, a group may select different individuals to serve as its leader, treasurer, and secretary. In other cases, individuals gradually acquire certain roles without being formally assigned to them. Regardless of how roles are acquired, people often *internalize* them; they link their roles to key aspects of their self-concept (see Chapter 5). When this happens, a role may exert profound effects on a person's behavior, even when she or he is not in the group. A very dramatic illustration of the powerful effects roles can exert on us was provided by Zimbardo and his colleagues (Haney, Banks, & Zimbardo, 1973). In this study, male college students who had volunteered for a study of prison life were "arrested" and confined to a simulated prison in the basement of the Stanford University psychology building. The prison "guards" were also paid volunteers, and assignment to these two roles—prisoner and guard—was completely random.

The major purpose of the study was to determine whether, as a result of the roles they played, the participants would come to behave like real guards and prisoners. The answer was quick to appear: Absolutely! So dramatic were the changes in the behavior of both the prisoners and the guards that it was necessary to stop the study after only six days. The prisoners, who at first were rebellious, became increasingly passive and depressed, while the guards became increasingly brutal. They harassed the prisoners constantly, forcing them to derogate one another and assigning them to tedious, senseless tasks. Participants started to act more and more like actual prisoners and actual guards in real prisons. The roles they played exerted powerful—and chilling—effects on their behavior, and are indicative of the powerful impact that roles often exert on us in different groups.

■ Status: Hierarchies in Groups

When the president of my (Robert Baron's) university enters the room, everyone stands, and no one sits down until she has taken a seat. Why? One answer involves an important

Figure 12.3 ■ Does Height Confer Status?
Research findings indicate the existence of a relationship between height and status, at least for men. Presidents, heads of major corporations, and military leaders all tend to be taller than average.

aspect of groups or, rather, positions within them: **status**—position or rank within a group. Different roles or positions in a group are often associated with different levels of status, and our president is clearly very high on this dimension. People are often extremely sensitive to status because it is linked to a wide range of desirable outcomes—everything from salary and "perks" to first choice among potential romantic partners (Buss, 1991). For this reason, groups often use status as a means of influencing the behavior of their members: Only "good" members—ones who follow the group's rules—receive it.

status
An individual's position or rank in a group.

Evolutionary psychologists attach considerable importance to status, noting that in many species, including ours, high status confers important advantages on those who possess it. Specifically, high-status persons have greater access than lower-status persons to key resources relating to survival and reproduction, such as food and access to mates (e.g., Buss, 1999). But how, precisely, do people acquire high status? Height may play some role—taller men have an edge (see Figure 12.3). For instance, presidents and heads of large corporations tend to be taller than average (e.g., Gillis, 1982). Whether the advantage of being tall will fade as women move increasingly into high-status positions remains to be seen, but at least for men, "bigger" does seem to be "better" where status is concerned.

Factors relating to individuals' behavior also play a role in acquiring status. Research by Tiedens (2001), for instance, suggests that people can sometimes boost their status through *intimidation*—by appearing angry and threatening. Whatever its basis, however, there can be little doubt that differences in status are an important fact of life in most groups.

■ Norms: The Rules of the Game

A third factor responsible for the powerful impact of groups on their members is **norms**—rules established by groups that tell members how they are supposed to behave. We discussed norms in detail in Chapter 9, so here we simply note again that they often exert powerful effects on behavior. Moreover, adherence to such norms is often a necessary condition for gaining status and other rewards controlled by groups.

norms
Rules within a group indicating how its members should (or should not) behave.

■ Cohesiveness: The Forces that Bind

Consider two groups. In the first, members like one another, strongly desire the goals their group is seeking, and feel that they could not possibly find another group that would better satisfy their needs. In the second, the opposite is true: Members don't like one another very much, don't share common goals, and are actively seeking other groups. Which group would exert stronger effects on the behavior of its members? The answer is obvious: the first. The reason for this difference involves a concept we discussed in Chapter 9, **cohesiveness**—all the factors that bind members together and cause them to want to remain in the group, such as liking for the other members, similarity between members, and the desire to gain status by belonging to the "right" groups (Festinger, Schachter, & Back, 1950). Cohesiveness can be a powerful force; in fact, findings suggest that to the extent members identify with a group (the greater their *social identity* with it), the less likely they are to leave it, even if desirable options exist (e.g., leaving to join some other, more attractive group; Van Vugt & Hart, 2004).

cohesiveness
All forces (factors) that cause group members to remain in the group.

Several factors influence cohesiveness, including (1) status within the group (Cota et al., 1995)—cohesiveness is often higher for high- than low-status members; (2) the effort required to gain entry into the group—the greater these costs, the higher the cohesiveness (see Chapter 4); (3) the existence of external threats or severe competition—such threats increase members' attraction and commitment to the group; and (4) size—small groups tend to be more cohesive than large ones.

KEY POINTS

★ *Groups* are collections of persons perceived to form a coherent unit to some degree. The extent to which the group is perceived to form a coherent entity is known as *entiativity*.

★ Basic aspects of groups involve *roles, status, norms,* and *cohesiveness.* The effects of roles on our behavior are often powerful, causing us to act in ways that we might not otherwise.

★ People gain status in a group for many reasons, ranging from physical characteristics (e.g., height) to various aspects of their behavior.

★ Another important feature of groups is their level of *cohesiveness*—the sum of all the factors that cause people to want to remain members.

The Benefits—and Costs—of Joining

Think for a moment: To how many different groups do you belong? If you give this careful thought, you may be surprised at the length of the list. Though some individuals belong to more groups than others, it's clear that, in general, we are "joiners"—members of many groups. Why? What do we gain from group membership? And why, if these benefits are so great, do we sometimes choose to leave—to withdraw from a group to which we have belonged for months, years, or even decades? Here's a summary of what social psychologists have found out about these issues.

■ The Benefits of Joining: What Groups Do for Us

That people sometimes go through a lot to join specific groups is clear: Membership in many groups is by invitation only, and winning that invitation can be difficult! Perhaps even more surprising, once they gain admission, many stick with a group, even when it experiences hard times and falls from favor. For instance, consider sports fans and how they remain loyal to their teams, even when the teams have a miserable season. What accounts for this strong desire to join—and remain in—many social groups? The answer, it appears, is many different factors.

First, we often gain *self-knowledge* from belonging to various groups. Our membership in them tells us what kinds of persons we are—or perhaps, would like to be—so group membership becomes central to our self-concept (recall our discussion in Chapter 5). The result? We want "in," and once we belong, we find it hard to imagine life outside this group, because being a member partly defines who we are!

As noted earlier, groups often provide a boost to our status. When individuals are accepted into prestigious groups—a highly selective school, an exclusive social club, a varsity sports team—their status and self-esteem often rise significantly. This is another important reason why individuals join specific groups. Just how important is this status-boost to joining and identifying with groups? Research findings suggest that this depends, to an important extent, on the degree to which the persons involved are seeking *self-enhancement*—boosting their own public image and feeling that they are somehow superior to others—or, alternatively, are seeking *self-transcendence*—the desire to help others, regardless of their status, and to seek such goals as increased understanding of others and social justice (e.g., Brown, 2000; Schwartz & Bardi, 2001). As you can probably guess, the greater the degree to which individuals are seeking self-enhancement, the more important a group's status will be to them and the more strongly they will identify with it. In contrast, the greater the degree to which they are seeking self-transcendence, the less important a group's status will be. This is precisely

Figure 12.4 ■ Producing Social Change: One Reason Why People Join Groups One potential benefit individuals obtain from groups is social change. By joining together, members of oppressed groups can often improve their standing in, and treatment by, society.

what was found in research by Roccas (2003). She obtained measures of business students' desires for self-enhancement and self-transcendence, the perceived status of a group to which they belonged (their school), and their identification with this group. Results indicated that the stronger their desire for self-enhancement, the stronger the link between the group's status and students' identification with it, while the stronger their desire for self-transcendence, the weaker was this link.

Still another benefit of joining groups is that doing so often helps us to accomplish social change. How can members of minority groups, women, gays, or other groups that have been the target of oppression gain their full rights? As we saw in Chapter 6, one way of doing so is to join groups committed to working toward these goals (see Figure 12.4). By joining together, victims of prejudice can gain "social clout" and can often succeed in changing their societies—and so win better treatment for themselves and other minorities (Klandermans, 1997). Indeed, research suggests that identification with such groups is a strong predictor of participation in public marches and parades, initiating and signing petitions, boycotts against businesses that discriminate against various minorities, and so on (Sturmer & Simon, 2004).

Clearly, then, we derive many benefits from belonging to various groups. It is apparent that we really can't meet many of our most basic needs—social and otherwise—outside of groups.

■ The Costs of Membership: Why Groups Sometimes Splinter

Unfortunately, there are few, if any, unmixed blessings in life. Almost everything—no matter how beneficial—has a downside. And this is certainly true of group membership. Although groups help us to reach the goals we seek, and can help to boost our status along the way, they also impose certain costs. We cover many of these in later sections (e.g., the harmful effects of groups on decision making; the increased tendency toward strong adherence to group norms that often occurs in large crowds). Here, though, we call your attention to several more general costs.

First, group membership often restricts personal freedom. Members of various groups are expected to behave in certain ways—to follow the group's norms or to comply with requirements of their roles in the groups. If they don't, the groups often impose strong sanctions on them or may, ultimately, expel them. In the United States, it is considered inappropriate for military officers to make public statements about politics. Thus, even a high-ranking general who engages in such actions may be strongly reprimanded.

Similarly, groups often make demands on members' time, energy, and resources, and they must meet these demands or surrender their membership. Some churches, for instance, require that their members donate 10 percent of their income to the church. Persons wishing to remain in these groups must comply—or face expulsion. Finally, groups sometimes adopt positions or policies of which some members disapprove. Again, the dissenting members must either remain silent, speak out and run the risk of strong sanctions, or withdraw.

Withdrawing from a group can be a major and costly step, and so raises an intriguing question: Why, specifically, do individuals take this ultimate action? One answer provided by

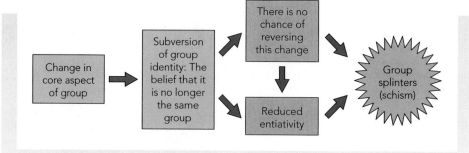

Figure 12.5 ■ Why Groups Splinter: One View
Research findings indicate that groups splinter when current members perceive that the group has changed so much (subversion) that it is no longer the same entity (group) they originally joined, and when they conclude that no one will listen to their protests over this change. (*Source: Based on suggestions by Sani & Todman, 2002.*)

research (e.g., Sani & Reicher, 2000) is based on the fact that when individuals identify with a social group, they often redraw the boundaries of their self-concept to include other group members (Aron & McLaughlin-Volpe, 2001). To the extent that this is true, then an explanation for why specific members sometimes withdraw from groups or why groups themselves splinter follows logically. Perhaps individuals decide to leave a group and form a new subgroup when they conclude that other members have changed sufficiently that they can no longer be viewed as "we"—as falling within the boundaries of their extended self-concept.

Evidence for this process was reported by Sani and Todman (2002). These researchers studied the Church of England, which, in 1992, adopted the policy of making women priests within the church. In 1994, the first women were ordained as priests, and, as a result, hundreds of clergy decided to leave the church. Why did they feel this drastic action was necessary? To find out, the researchers asked priests and deacons in the Church of England to express their views about the new policy of ordaining women as priests, the extent to which they felt this had changed the church, and the degree to which they felt their views (if they were opposed to this policy) would be heard. Results indicated that clergy who left the Church did not do so because they were hard-core sexists, against equal rights for women. Rather, they left because they felt it had changed so much that it was no longer the same organization as the one they originally joined and no longer represented their views. Further, they felt strongly that no one would pay attention to their dissenting opinions and that this left them no choice but to withdraw (see Figure 12.5).

Sani and Todman (2002) suggest that this process is not restricted to religious groups. They note that similar splits have occurred in many other groups—political parties, social movements, and any group based on shared beliefs and values. Groups change, and when they do so to the extent that members feel that they can no longer identify with the group, the final outcome is inevitable: Members withdraw from groups that, they believe, no longer possess the *entiativity* we described at the start of this chapter.

KEY POINTS

★ Joining groups confers important benefits on members, including increased self-knowledge, progress toward important goals, enhanced status, and attaining social change.

★ However, group membership also exacts important costs, such as loss of personal freedom and heavy demands on time, energy, and resources.

★ Individuals often withdraw from groups when they feel that the group has changed so much that it no longer reflects their basic values or beliefs.

Effects of the Presence of Others: From Task Performance to Behavior in Crowds

The fact that our behavior is often affected by the groups to which we belong is far from surprising; after all, in these groups we have specific roles and status, and the groups usually have well-established norms that tell us how we are expected to behave. Perhaps more surprising is that, often, we are strongly affected by the *mere presence of others,* even if we, and they, do not belong to formal groups. You already know about such effects from your experiences. For instance, suppose you are sitting alone in a room, studying. When you itch, you will probably scratch, and you may sit in any way you find comfortable. But if a stranger enters the room, all of this may change. You will probably refrain from doing some things you might have done when alone, and you may change other aspects of your behavior, even though you don't know this person and are not interacting with her or him. So, clearly, we are often affected by the mere physical presence of others. Although such effects take different forms, we focus here on two that are especially important: the effects of the presence of others on our performance of various tasks, and the effects of being in a large crowd.

Sometimes, when we perform a task, we work alone; for instance, you might study alone in your room, and as I write these words, I am alone in my office. In other cases, even if we are working on a task by ourselves, other people *are* present—you might study in a crowded library or in your room while your roommate sleeps. In other situations, we work on tasks together with others as part of a task-performing group. What are the effects of the presence of others on our performance? Let's see what research findings suggest.

Social Facilitation: Performing in the Presence of Others

Imagine that you are a young singer preparing for your first important concert. You practice your routines alone for several hours each day, month after month. Finally, the big day arrives and you walk onto the stage to find a huge audience seated in a beautiful concert hall (see Figure 12.6). How will you do? Better or worse than when you practiced alone?

This was one of the first topics studied by social psychologists, and early results (e.g., Allport, 1920) suggested that performance was better when people worked in the presence of others than when they worked alone. In one study, Allport (1920) asked participants to write down as many associations as they could think of to words printed at the top of an otherwise blank sheet of paper (e.g., *building, laboratory*). They were allowed to work for three one-minute periods, and performed this task both alone and in the presence of two others. Results were clear: Ninety-three percent produced more associations when working in the presence of others. On the basis of such findings, Allport and other researchers referred to the effects on performance of the presence of other persons as **social facilitation,** because it appeared that when others were present, performance was enhanced. But other research soon reported opposite results: performance was *worse* in the presence of an audience or other people performing the same task (coactors) than it was when individuals performed alone (Pessin, 1933). Why? How could the presence of others sometimes enhance and sometimes reduce performance? One elegant answer to this mystery was offered by Robert Zajonc.

social facilitation
Effects on performance resulting from the presence of others.

Figure 12.6 ■ The Presence of an Audience: How Does It Affect Our Performance?
What happens when people perform in front of an audience—do they do better or worse than when performing the same tasks alone?

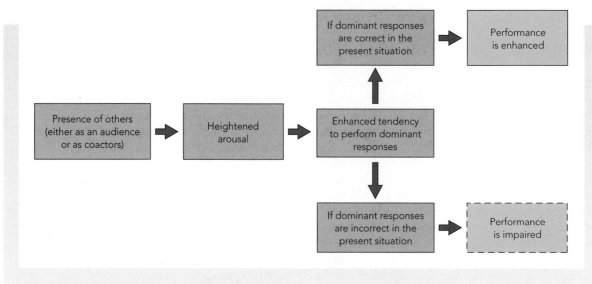

Figure 12.7 ■ The Drive Theory of Social Facilitation
According to the *drive theory of social facilitation* (Zajonc, 1965), the presence of others, either as an audience or coactors, increases arousal, and this strengthens the tendency to perform dominant responses. If these responses are correct, performance is enhanced; if they are incorrect, performance is impaired.

■ Zajonc's Drive Theory of Social Facilitation: Other Persons as a Source of Arousal

Imagine that you are performing some task alone. Then, several people arrive on the scene and begin to watch you intently. Will your pulse beat quicker because of this audience? Informal experience suggests that it may—that the presence of others in the form of an interested audience can increase our activation or arousal. Taking note of this fact, Zajonc suggested that this might provide the solution to the puzzle of social facilitation.

When arousal increases, our tendency to perform *dominant responses*—the ones that are most likely to occur in a given situation—rises. Such dominant responses can be correct or incorrect. If this is so, then it follows logically that if the presence of an audience increases arousal, this factor will *improve* performance when dominant responses are correct ones, but may *impair* performance when such responses are incorrect (see Figure 12.7).

Another implication of Zajonc's reasoning—known as the **drive theory of social facilitation** because it focuses on arousal or drive—is this: The presence of others will improve individuals' performance when they are highly skilled at the task (in this case, their dominant responses would tend to be correct), but will interfere with performance when they are not highly skilled—for instance, when they are learning to perform it. (Under these conditions, their dominant responses would *not* be correct.)

Many studies soon provided support for Zajonc's theory. Individuals were more likely to perform dominant responses in the presence of others and their performance on various tasks was either enhanced or impaired, depending on whether these responses were correct or incorrect in each situation (e.g., Geen, 1989; Zajonc & Sales, 1966).

But the story does not end there: Additional research raised an important question: Does social facilitation stem from the *mere physical presence of others*? Or do additional factors, such as concern about others' evaluations of us, also play a role? If that is so, then, *type of audience* should matter. Several studies found that this is the case: For instance, social facilitation effects did *not* occur if the audience was blindfolded or showed no interest in watching the person (Cottrell et al., 1968). Such findings indicate that there is more to social facilitation than just increased drive; concern over being evaluated also plays a role.

As reasonable as these conclusions seem, however, they didn't appear to apply in all cases; studies conducted with animals found that performance of simple tasks was facilitated

drive theory of social facilitation
A theory suggesting that the mere presence of others is arousing and increases the tendency to perform dominant responses.

by the presence of an audience. For instance, Zajonc, Heingartner, and Herman (1969) found that cockroaches would run faster through a maze when other roaches were present (in clear plastic boxes next to the maze). Clearly, it makes little sense to suggest that insects are concerned about the impressions they make on others, so these findings suggest that social facilitation does not stem entirely from **evaluation apprehension.** So what's the answer?

evaluation apprehension
Concern over being evaluated by others. Such concern can increase arousal and so contribute to social facilitation.

One researcher, Robert S. Baron (*not* the author of this text!) suggests that it may involve shifts in attention and the effects these produce. Baron (1986) argues that presence of others, either as an audience or coactors, can be distracting, and therefore, it can threaten the organism performing a task with cognitive overload (e.g., Baron, 1986). Specifically, task performers must divide their attention between the task and the audience, and this generates increased arousal *and* the possibility of cognitive overload. Cognitive overloads can lead to a tendency to restrict one's attention so as to focus only on essential cues or stimuli while "screening out" nonessential ones.

Several findings offer support for this view, known as **distraction–conflict theory** (Baron, 1986). For example, audiences produce social facilitation effects only when directing attention to them conflicts in some way with task demands (Groff, Baron, & Moore, 1983). Similarly, individuals experience greater distraction when they perform various tasks in front of an audience than when they perform them alone (Baron, Moore, & Sanders, 1978).

distraction–conflict theory
A theory suggesting that *social facilitation* stems from the conflict produced when individuals attempt, simultaneously, to pay attention to other persons and to the task being performed.

But a key question remains: Which is more important—increased drive or this tendency toward a narrowed attentional focus? According to Baron (1986), the two theories (drive theory and distraction–conflict theory) make contrasting predictions with respect to one type of task: a poorly learned task that involves only a few key stimuli. Drive theory predicts that the presence of others will facilitate dominant responses, which, on a poorly learned task, are errors. Thus, performance will be reduced by the presence of an audience. In contrast, the distraction–conflict theory, with its emphasis on attentional focus, predicts that the presence of others will cause individuals to focus more closely on the important task-relevant cues, with the result that performance will be *improved.*

Research findings have confirmed these predictions (e.g., Huguet et al., 1999), so it appears that social facilitation stems from cognitive factors—not just heightened arousal, as Zajonc (1965) proposed. Yes, the presence of others generates increased arousal, but it may do so because of the cognitive demands of paying attention both to an audience and to the task being performed rather than as a result of their mere physical presence; and it may influence task performance by inducing a narrowed attention focus. One advantage of this cognitive perspective is that it helps explain why animals as well as people are affected by an audience. After all, animals, too (even cockroaches), can experience conflicting tendencies to work on a task *and* pay attention to an audience. A theory that can explain similar patterns of behavior among organisms ranging from cockroaches to humans is powerful indeed and seems to provide a compelling explanation for the effects of an audience or coactors on performance.

KEY POINTS

★ The mere presence of others either as an audience or coactors can influence our performance. Such effects are known as *social facilitation* (or as social facilitation–inhibition effects).

★ The *drive theory of social facilitation* suggests that the presence of others is arousing and can either increase or reduce performance, depending on whether dominant responses in a given situation are correct or incorrect.

★ The *distraction–conflict theory* suggests that the presence of others induces conflicting tendencies to focus on the task being performed and on an audience or coactors. This can result in increased arousal and narrowed attentional focus.

★ Recent findings offer support for the view that several kinds of audiences produce narrowed attentional focus among persons performing a task. This cognitive view of social facilitation helps explain why it occurs among animals as well as people.

Social Loafing: Letting Others Do the Work

Suppose that you and several other people are helping to push a stalled SUV. Because it is a large vehicle, you all pitch in to get it moving. Question: Will all of the people helping exert equal effort? Probably not. Some will push as hard as they can, others will push moderately, and some may simply hang on and pretend to push.

This pattern is common in situations in which groups perform what are known as **additive tasks**—ones in which the contributions of each member are combined into a single group output. On such tasks, some persons work hard while others goof off, doing less than their share and less than they might do if working alone. Social psychologists refer to such effects as **social loafing**—reductions in motivation and effort that occur when individuals work collectively in a group compared with when they work individually as independent coactors (Karau & Williams, 1993).

Social loafing has been demonstrated in many experiments. In one of the first, Latané, Williams, and Harkins (1979) asked groups of male students to clap or cheer as loudly as possible at specific times, supposedly so the experimenter could determine how much noise people make in social settings. Participants performed these tasks in groups of two, four, or six. Results indicated that although the total amount of noise rose as group size increased, the amount produced *by each participant* dropped. Such effects are not restricted to simple and seemingly meaningless situations like this; on the contrary, they appear to be quite general in scope, and occur with respect to many different tasks—cognitive ones as well as physical ones (Weldon & Mustari, 1988; Williams & Karau, 1991). Moreover, these effects appear among both genders and among children as well as adults, although this tendency may be slightly stronger in men than in women (Karau & Williams, 1993). There appear to be only two exceptions to the generality of social loafing. First, as just noted, women may be slightly less likely to show this effect than men (Karau & Williams, 1993), perhaps because they tend to be higher in concern for others' welfare. Second, social loafing effects don't seem to occur in *collectivistic* cultures, such as those in many Asian countries—cultures in which the collective good is more highly valued than individual accomplishment or achievement (Earley, 1993). In such cultures, people seem to work *harder* when in groups than when alone. So, as we've noted repeatedly, cultural factors sometimes play an important role in social behavior.

Aside from this important exception, however, social loafing appears to be a pervasive fact of social life. Because that's true, the next question is obvious: What can be done to reduce it?

The first and most obvious way of reducing social loafing involves making the output or effort of each participant readily identifiable (e.g., Williams, Harkins, & Latané, 1981). Under these conditions, people can't sit back and let others do their work, so social loafing is reduced. Second, groups can reduce social loafing by increasing group members' commitment to successful task performance (Brickner, Harkins, & Ostrom, 1986). Pressures toward working hard will then serve to offset temptations to engage in social loafing. Third, social loafing can be reduced by increasing the apparent importance or value of a task (Karau & Williams, 1993). Fourth, social loafing is reduced when individuals view their contributions to the task as unique rather than as merely redundant with those of others (Weldon & Mustari, 1988). Together, these steps can sharply reduce social loafing—and the temptation to "goof off" at the expense of others. (Please see the **Ideas to Take with You—and Use!** section at the end of this chapter for some practical suggestions on how you can benefit from social facilitation and protect yourself against social loafing by others.)

Deindividuation: Submerged in the Crowd

Have you attended a football or basketball game at which the crowd shouted obscenities, threw things at the referees, or engaged in other behavior they would probably never

---

additive tasks
Tasks for which the group product is the sum or combination of the efforts of individual members.

social loafing
Reductions in motivation and effort when individuals work collectively in a group, compared with when they work individually or as independent coactors.

Figure 12.8 ■ Unrestrained Behavior by Crowds: A Dramatic Example of the Effects of the Presence of Others
Crowds often engage in actions individual members would never dream of performing if they were alone. This is a dramatic illustration of how the mere presence of others can strongly affect our behavior.

show in other settings? (See Figure 12.8) If so, you already have first-hand experience with another potential effect of the presence of others—in this case, many others—on our behavior. These effects, a drift toward wild, unrestrained behavior, are termed **deindividuation** by social psychologists because they seem to stem from the fact that when we are in a large crowd, we tend to submerge our identity in the crowd—to lose our individuality. And when we do, the restraints that usually hold many kinds of objectionable or dangerous behavior in check seem to melt away. In fact, the larger the crowd, the more likely such effects are to occur, and the more extreme and savage the behavior that follows (Mullen, 1986). More formally, the term *deindividuation* refers to a psychological state characterized by reduced self-awareness and social identity brought on by external conditions such as being an anonymous member of a large crowd.

Initial research on deindividuation (Zimbardo, 1976) seemed to suggest that being an anonymous member of a crowd makes people feel less responsible or accountable for their actions and that this encourages wild, antisocial actions. More recent evidence, though, indicates that another factor may be more important. When we are part of a large crowd, it seems we are more likely to obey the norms of this group and less likely to act in accordance with other norms (Postmes & Spears, 1998).

But what, exactly, happens to people when they feel anonymous? Research by Mullen, Migdal, and Rozell (2003) suggests that when individuals feel anonymous, they experience a reduction in self-awareness *and,* simultaneously, a reduction in their social identity (awareness of the fact that they belong to specific social or ethnic groups). Such effects are fully consistent with the idea that when we are part of a large crowd, we are more likely to follow the norms operating in that situation: After all, we feel less connected to other groups that may have different norms. Mullen, Migdal, and Rozell (2003) reached these conclusions on the basis of research in which individuals completed questionnaires designed to measure their degree of self-awareness *and* their degree of social identity. They completed these measures while either sitting in front of a mirror (a procedure known, from earlier research, to increase self-awareness), while wearing a mask (a procedure known to induce feelings of anonymity and deindividuation), or after filling out a small family tree, in which they entered the names of their fathers, mothers, and themselves in empty boxes (this procedure was designed to increase social identity). Results indicated that the mirror increased self-awareness and reduced social identity, while completing a family tree increased social identity but reduced self-awareness. Most relevant to the present discussion, wearing a mask reduced both self-awareness *and* social identity. In this condition, participants felt less aware of themselves as individuals and less aware of their social ties to others (in this case, their families). These findings, and those of several related studies (e.g., Postmes & Spears, 1998), suggest that being part of a large, anonymous crowd casts individuals adrift from their usual social ties: Not only do they experience reduced awareness of themselves and their behavior, they also often experience a temporary weakening of ties to the social groups to which they ordinarily belong. Given these effects, it is not surprising that large crowds often demonstrate behavior that the persons of whom they are composed would never, under other conditions, perform themselves.

deindividuation
A psychological state characterized by reduced self-awareness and reduced social identity, brought on by external conditions, such as being an anonymous member of a large crowd.

Effects of the Presence of Others

KEY POINTS

★ When individuals work together on a task, *social loafing*—reduced output by each group member—sometimes occurs.

★ Social loafing can be reduced in several ways: by making outputs individually identifiable, by increasing commitment to the task and task importance, and by assuring that each member's contributions to the task are unique.

★ When we are part of a large crowd, we experience reductions in both our self-awareness and our social identity. This causes us to adopt the norms operating in the current situation—norms that often sanction impulsive, unrestrained behavior.

Coordination in Groups: Cooperation or Conflict?

cooperation
Behavior in which groups work together to attain shared goals.

In Chapter 10, we noted that individuals often engage in *prosocial behavior*—actions that benefit others but have no obvious or immediate benefits for the persons who perform them. Although such behavior is far from rare, another pattern—one in which helping is mutual and both sides benefit—is more common. This pattern is known as **cooperation** and involves groups working together to attain shared goals. Cooperation can be highly beneficial; indeed, through this process, groups of persons can attain goals they could never hope to reach by themselves. Surprisingly, though, cooperation does not always develop. Frequently, group members try to coordinate their efforts but somehow fail. Even worse, they may perceive their personal interests as incompatible, with the result that instead of working together and coordinating their efforts, they work *against* each other. This is known as **conflict,** defined as a process in which individuals or groups perceive that others have taken or will take actions that are incompatible with their own interests. Conflict is a process, for as you probably know from your own experience, it has a nasty way of escalating, starting, perhaps, with simple mistrust and moving through a spiral of anger, resentment, and actions designed to harm the other side. When carried to extremes, the ultimate effects can be very harmful to both sides.

conflict
A process in which individuals or groups perceive that others have taken or will soon take actions incompatible with their own interests.

Cooperation: Working with Others to Achieve Shared Goals

Cooperation is often highly beneficial. A key question, then, is this: Why don't group members always coordinate their activities? One answer is straightforward: They don't cooperate because some goals that people seek simply can't be shared. Several people seeking the same job, promotion, or romantic partner can't combine forces: The rewards can go to only one. In such cases, cooperation is not possible, and *conflict* may develop quickly, as each person (or group) attempts to maximize its outcomes (Tjosvold, 1993).

In other situations, however, cooperation *could* develop but does not. This is precisely the kind of situation that has been of most interest to social psychologists, who have tried to identify the factors that tip the balance either toward or away from cooperation. We now consider some of the most important of these factors.

■ Social Dilemmas: Situations in Which Cooperation Could Occur But Often Doesn't

social dilemmas
Situations in which each person can increase his or her individual gains by acting in one way; but if all (or most) persons do the same thing, the outcomes experienced by all are reduced.

Many situations in which cooperation could potentially develop but does not can be described as ones involving **social dilemmas**—situations in which each person can increase his or her individual gains by acting in a purely selfish manner, but if all (or most) persons do the same thing, the outcomes experienced by all are reduced (Komorita & Parks, 1994). As a result, these persons must deal with *mixed motives:* There are reasons to cooperate (avoid negative outcomes for all), but also reasons to *defect* (to do what is best for oneself), because if only one or a few engage in such behavior, they will benefit and the others will

Figure 12.9 ■ The Prisoner's Dilemma: To Cooperate or to Compete—That Is the Question!
In the prisoner's dilemma, two persons can choose to cooperate or compete with one another. If both choose to cooperate, each receives favorable outcomes. If both choose to compete, each receives negative outcomes. If one chooses to compete while the other chooses to cooperate, the first person receives a much better outcome than the second. Findings indicate that many factors influence the choices people make in this kind of mixed-motive situation.

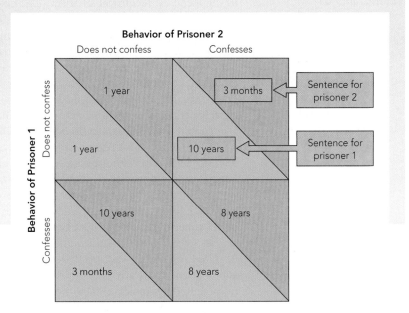

not. A classic illustration of this kind of situation, and one in which it is reduced to its simplest form, is known as the *prisoner's dilemma* (see Figure 12.9). Here, there are two persons, and each can choose to cooperate or compete. If both cooperate, they both experience large gains. If both compete, each person experiences much smaller gains, or actual losses. The most interesting pattern occurs if one chooses to compete, but the other chooses to cooperate. In this case, the first person experiences much larger gains than the second. This situation is called the prisoner's dilemma because it reflects a dilemma faced by two suspects who have been caught by police. Assume that the police do not have enough evidence to convict either person. If both stick to their stories (they both cooperate), they will be set free or receive a very short sentence for a minor crime. If both confess, they will both be convicted and receive a stiff sentence. If one confesses (turns states' evidence) but the other does not, the police will have enough evidence to convict both, but the person who confesses will receive a lighter sentence because of the help she or he has given. As you can see, this situation captures the essence of many social dilemmas: Each suspect experiences pressures to cooperate and to compete. Social psychologists have used this type of situation, or ones very much like it (simulated, of course!), to examine the factors that tip the balance toward trust and cooperation or mistrust and competition (e.g., Insko et al., 2001). The findings of such research indicate that many factors play a role in whether cooperation or competition develops.

■ Factors Influencing Cooperation: Reciprocity, Personal Orientations, and Communication

Though many different factors determine whether individuals will choose to cooperate in situations involving the mixed motives generated by social dilemmas, three appear to be most important: tendencies toward *reciprocity, personal orientations* concerning cooperation, and *communication*.

Reciprocity is probably the most obvious. Throughout life, we tend to follow this principle, treating others much as they have treated us (e.g., Pruitt & Carnevale, 1993). In choosing between cooperation and competition, too, we seem to adopt this general rule. When others cooperate with us and put their selfish interests aside, we usually respond in kind. In contrast, if they defect and pursue their own interests, we generally do the same (Kerr & Kaufman-Gililland, 1994).

Evolutionary psychologists have noted that this tendency to adopt reciprocity where cooperation is concerned is not restricted to humans; it has been observed among other species (e.g., bats, chimpanzees; Buss, 1999). This raises an intriguing question: Because "cheaters" (those who do not return cooperation after receiving it) often gain an advantage, how could a strong tendency toward reciprocity have evolved? One possible answer is provided

reciprocity
A basic rule of social life, suggesting that individuals should treat others as these persons have treated them.

reciprocal altruism
A theory suggesting that by sharing resources such as food, organisms increase their chances of survival, and thus the likelihood that they will pass their genes on to the next generation.

by the theory of **reciprocal altruism** (e.g., Cosmides & Tooby, 1992). This theory suggests that by sharing resources such as food, organisms increase their chances of survival, and thus the likelihood that they will pass their genes on to the next generation. Further, they tend to share in such a way that the benefits are relatively great for the recipients of such cooperation while the costs are relatively minimal to the provider. If one hunter has more meat than he and his family can eat while another is starving, the costs to the first for sharing are minimal, while the gains to the second are great. When the situation is reversed, cooperation will again benefit both parties and increase their chances of survival. In contrast, organisms who act in a purely selfish manner do not gain such benefits.

A second factor that exerts strong effects on cooperation is *personal orientation* toward such behavior. Think about the people you have known in your life. Can you remember ones who strongly preferred cooperation? In contrast, can you remember others who usually preferred to pursue their own selfish interests and could *not* be relied on to cooperate, who seem to turn every social encounter into competition? You probably have little difficulty bringing examples of both types to mind, for large individual differences in the tendencies to cooperate exist. Such differences seem to reflect contrasting perspectives toward working with others—perspectives that individuals carry with them from situation to situation, even over relatively long periods of time (e.g., Knight & Dubro, 1984). Specifically, research findings indicate that individuals can possess any one of three distinct orientations toward situations involving social dilemmas: (1) a *cooperative* orientation, in which they prefer to maximize the joint outcomes received by all the persons involved; (2) an *individualistic* orientation, in which they focus primarily on maximizing their own outcomes; or (3) a *competitive* orientation, in which they focus primarily on defeating others—on obtaining better outcomes than others (DeDreu and McCusker, 1997; Van Lange & Kuhlman, 1994). These orientations exert strong effects on how people behave, so they are an important factor in whether cooperation does or does not develop.

A third factor that influences the choice between cooperation and competition is *communication*. Common sense suggests that if individuals can discuss the situation with others, they may soon conclude that the best option is for everyone to cooperate; after all, this will result in gains for all. Surprisingly, though, early research produced mixed results. In many situations, the opportunity for group members to communicate with each other about what they should do in the situation did *not* increase cooperation. On the contrary, group members seemed to use this opportunity primarily to *threaten* one another, with the result that cooperation did not occur (e.g., Deutsch & Krauss, 1960; Stech & McClintock, 1981). Is this always the case? Fortunately, research findings point to more optimistic conclusions: Apparently, communication between group members *can* lead to increased cooperation, provided certain conditions are met (e.g., Kerr & Kaufman-Gilliland, 1994; Sally, 1998). Specifically, beneficial effects can, and do, occur if group members make personal commitments to cooperate with one another, and if these commitments are backed up by strong, personal norms to honor them (see Chapter 9 for a discussion of the nature and impact of social norms; e.g., Kerr et al., 1997).

KEY POINTS

★ *Cooperation*—working together with others to obtain shared goals—is a common aspect of social life.

★ Cooperation does not develop in many situations in which it is possible, partly because such situations involve *social dilemmas*, in which individuals can increase their own gains by defection.

★ Several factors influence whether cooperation occurs in such situations. These include strong tendencies toward *reciprocity, personal orientation* toward cooperation, and *communication*.

★ Evolutionary psychologists suggest that our tendency to reciprocate may result from the fact that organisms that cooperate are more likely to survive and reproduce.

Chapter 12 / Groups and Individuals

Conflict: Its Nature, Causes, and Effects

If prosocial behavior (see Chapter 10) and cooperation constitute one end of a dimension describing how individuals and groups work together, then *conflict* lies at or near the other end. As noted earlier, conflict refers to a process in which one individual or group perceives that others have taken or will take actions that are incompatible with their interests. The key elements in conflict seem to include (1) opposing interests between individuals or groups, (2) recognition of such opposition, (3) the belief by each side that the other will act to interfere with these interests, and (4) actions that produce such interference.

Unfortunately, conflict is an all-too-common part of social life and can be extremely costly to both sides. What factors cause such seemingly irrational behavior? And what can be done to reduce it? These are the key questions that social psychologists have addressed.

■ Major Causes of Conflict

Our definition of *conflict* emphasizes the existence of incompatible interests and recognition of this fact by the parties involved. Indeed, this is *the* defining feature of conflicts. Interestingly, though, conflicts sometimes fail to develop, even though both sides have incompatible interests; and in other cases, conflicts occur when the two sides don't really have opposing interests—they may simply *believe* that these exist (e.g., De Dreu & Van Lange, 1995; Tjosvold & DeDreu, 1997). In short, conflict involves much more than opposing interests. A growing body of evidence suggests that *social* factors may play as strong a role in initiating conflicts as incompatible interests.

One social factor that plays a role is what have been termed *faulty attributions*—errors concerning the causes behind others' behavior (e.g., Baron, 1989a). When individuals find that their interests have been thwarted, they generally try to determine *why* this occurred. Was it bad luck? A lack of planning on their part? A lack of needed resources? Or was it due to intentional interference by another person or group? If they conclude that the latter is true, then the seeds for an intense conflict may be planted—even if others actually had nothing to do with the situation!

Another social factor that seems to play an important role in conflict is what might be termed *faulty communication*—the fact that individuals sometimes communicate with others in a way that angers or annoys them, even though it is *not* their intention to do so. Have you been on the receiving end of harsh criticism—criticism you felt was unfair, insensitive, and not helpful? The results of several studies indicate that feedback of this type, known as *destructive* criticism, can leave the recipient hungry for revenge, and set the stage for conflicts that, again, do not necessarily stem from incompatible interests (see Figure 12.10; e.g., Baron, 1990; Cropanzano, 1993).

A third social cause of conflict involves the tendency to perceive our views as objective and reflecting reality, but those of others as biased by their ideology (e.g., Keltner & Robinson, 1997; Robinson et al., 1995). As a result, we tend to magnify differences between our views and those of others, and to exaggerate conflicts of interest. Research indicates that this tendency is stronger for groups or individuals who currently hold a dominant or powerful position (Keltner & Robinson, 1997). This often leads to what is known as the *status quo bias*—a tendency for powerful groups defending the current status quo to be less accurate at intergroup perception than the groups that are challenging them. For instance, they perceive their position as much more reasonable or objective than it is.

Figure 12.10 ■ Destructive Criticism: One Social Cause of Conflict
When one person criticizes another harshly and without clear justification, the recipient may react with anger and a desire for revenge. The result? The seeds for bitter and lasting conflict between them may be planted—a conflict that does not stem from incompatible interests.

Personal traits or characteristics, too, play a role in conflict. For example, *Type A* individuals—ones who are highly competitive, always in a hurry, and quite irritable—tend to become involved in conflicts more often than calmer and less irritable Type B persons (Baron, 1989b).

Finally, Peterson and Behfar (2003) indicate that conflict within a group may stem from poor initial performance by the group. Poor performance, and negative feedback about this performance, may be threatening to group members, and this can lead them to blame each other (not themselves!) for these poor results (recall our discussion of the self-serving bias in Chapter 3). The overall result may be increased conflict among group members. To test these predictions, Peterson and Behfar (2003) asked groups of MBA students to complete questionnaires designed to measure the amount of conflict they experienced at two different times during one semester. Course instructors provided information on the grades received by each team on class projects—this was the measure of performance feedback to the teams. Results indicated that, as the researchers expected, the more negative the initial feedback groups received, the greater the conflict they reported after receiving this information. In addition, and not surprisingly, the more conflict the groups reported initially, before receiving the feedback, the more they reported later. Conflict has a nasty way of persisting unless active steps are taken to reduce it.

So where does all of this leave us? With the conclusion that conflict does *not* stem solely from opposing interests. On the contrary, it often derives from social factors—long-standing grudges or resentment, the desire for revenge, inaccurate social perceptions, poor communication, and similar factors.

Resolving Conflicts: Some Useful Techniques

Because conflicts are often costly, the persons involved usually want to resolve them as quickly as possible. What steps are most useful for reaching this goal? Although many may succeed, two seem especially useful: *bargaining* and *superordinate goals*.

■ Bargaining: The Universal Process

bargaining (negotiation)
A process in which opposing sides exchange offers, counteroffers, and concessions, either directly or through representatives.

By far the most common strategy for resolving conflicts is **bargaining** or *negotiation* (e.g., Pruitt & Carnevale, 1993). In this process, opposing sides exchange offers, counteroffers, and concessions, either directly or through representatives. If the process is successful, an acceptable solution is attained and the conflict is resolved. If bargaining is unsuccessful, costly deadlock may result and the conflict will intensify. What factors determine these outcomes? As you can probably guess, many play a role.

First, and perhaps most obviously, the outcome of bargaining is determined, in part, by the specific tactics adopted by the bargainers. Many of these are designed to accomplish a key goal: reduce the opponent's *aspirations* (i.e., hopes or goals) so that this person or group becomes convinced that it cannot get what it wants and should settle for something favorable to the other side. Tactics for accomplishing this goal include (1) beginning with an extreme initial offer—one that is very favorable to the side proposing it; (2) the "big-lie" technique—convincing the other side that one's break-even point is much higher than it is so that they offer more than would otherwise be the case; and (3) convincing the other side that you have an "out"—if they won't make a deal with you, you can go elsewhere and get even better terms (Thompson, 1998).

Do these tactics seem ethical? This is a complex question on which individuals may well differ, but social psychologists who have conducted research on this question (Robinson, Lewicki, & Donahue, 1998) have found that there is general agreement that four types of tactics are questionable from an ethical standpoint: (1) *attacking an opponent's network*—manipulating or interfering with an opponent's network of support and information; (2) *false promises*—offering false commitments or lying about future intentions; (3) *misrepresentation*—providing misleading or false information to an opponent; and (4) *inappropriate information gathering*—collecting information in an unethical manner (e.g., through theft, spying, etc.). These tactics are measured by a questionnaire known as the Self-Reported Inappropriate Negotiation Strategies Scale (or SINS for short).

A second and very important determinant of the outcome of bargaining involves the overall orientation of the bargainers to the process (Pruitt & Carnevale, 1993). People taking part in negotiations can approach such discussions from either of two distinct perspectives. In one, they can view the negotiations as win–lose situations, in which gains by one side are necessarily linked with losses for the other. In the other, they can approach negotiations as potential win–win situations, in which the interests of the two sides are not necessarily incompatible and in which the potential gains of both sides can be maximized.

Not all situations offer the potential for such agreements, but many provide such possibilities. If participants are willing to explore all options, they can sometimes attain what are known as *integrative agreements*—ones that offer greater joint benefits than simple compromise—splitting all differences down the middle. Here's an example: Suppose that two cooks are preparing recipes that call for an entire orange, and they have only one. What should they do? One possibility is to divide the orange in half. That leaves both with less than they need. Suppose, however, that one cook needs all the juice while the other needs all the peel. Here, a much better solution is possible: They can share the orange, each using the part she or he needs. Many techniques for attaining such integrative solutions exist; a few of these are summarized in Table 12.1.

■ Superordinate Goals: "We're All in This Together"

As we saw in Chapter 6, individuals often divide the world into two opposing camps—"us" and "them." They perceive members of their own group (us) as quite different from, and usually better than, people belonging to other groups (them). These tendencies to magnify differences between one's own group and others and to disparage outsiders are very powerful and often play a role in the occurrence and persistence of conflicts. Fortunately, such tendencies can be countered through the induction of **superordinate goals**—goals that both sides seek and that tie their interests together rather than drive them apart (e.g., Sherif et al., 1961; Tjosvold, 1993). When opposing sides can be made to see that they share overarching goals, conflict is often reduced and may be replaced by overt cooperation.

superordinate goals
Goals that both sides of a conflict seek and that tie their interests together rather than drive them apart.

Table 12.1 ■ Tactics for Reaching Integrative Agreements

Many strategies can be useful in attaining integrative agreements—ones that offer better outcomes than simple compromise. Several of these strategies are summarized here.

TACTIC	DESCRIPTION
Broadening the pie	Available resources are increased so that both sides can obtain their major goals
Nonspecific compensation	One side gets what it wants; the other is compensated on an unrelated issue.
Logrolling	Each party makes concessions on low-priority issues in exchange for concessions on issues it values more highly.
Bridging	Neither party gets its initial demands, but a new option that satisfies the major interests of both sides is developed.
Cost cutting	One party gets what it desires, and the costs to the other party are reduced in some manner.

★ *Conflict* is a process that begins when individuals or groups perceive that others' interests are incompatible with theirs.

★ Conflict also can stem from social factors such as faulty attributions, poor communication, the tendency to perceive our own views as objective, and personal traits.

★ Conflict can be reduced in many ways, but *bargaining* and the induction of *superordinate goals* seem to be most effective.

Perceived Fairness in Groups: Its Nature and Effects

Have you been in a situation in which you felt that you were getting less than you deserved from some group to which you belonged—less status, less approval, less pay? If so, you probably remember that your reactions to such *perceived unfairness* were probably strong and not pleasant. Perhaps you experienced anger, resentment, and powerful feelings of injustice (e.g., Cropanzano, 1993; Scher, 1997). And if you did, you probably did not sit around waiting for the situation to improve; on the contrary, you may have taken some concrete action to rectify it and get whatever it was you felt you deserved—as I and my fellow coworkers did in the "give me your tips" incident described at the start of this chapter. Whatever you did may well have affected the functioning of the group. Social psychologists have recognized such effects for many years, and have conducted many studies to understand (1) the factors that lead individuals to decide they have been treated fairly or unfairly, and (2) what they do about it—their efforts to deal with perceived unfairness (e.g., Adams, 1965). We now consider both questions.

Basic Rules for Judging Fairness: Distributive, Procedural, and Transactional Justice

Deciding whether we have been treated fairly in our relations with others is a complex and tricky task. First, we rarely have all the information needed to make such a judgment accurately (e.g., Van den Bos & Lind, 2002). Second, even if we did have enough information, perceived fairness is very much in the eye of the beholder, so it is subject to many of the kinds of bias and distortion we have described throughout this book. For instance, it is always tempting to conclude that *we* deserve more than others, even if this is not really true (the self-serving bias in action). Despite such complexities, though, research on perceived fairness in group settings indicates that, in general, we make these judgments on the basis of three distinct rules.

distributive justice (equity) Refers to individuals' judgments about whether they are receiving a fair share of available rewards—a share proportionate to their contributions to the group or any social relationship.

The first, known as **distributive justice** (or *equity*; Adams, 1965), involves the outcomes we and others receive. According to this rule, available rewards should be distributed among group members in accordance with their contributions: The more they provide in terms of effort, experience, skills, and other contributions to the group, the more they should receive. We often judge fairness in terms of the ratio between the contributions group members have provided and the rewards they receive. We expect this ratio to be approximately the *same* for all members, and to the extent it is not, we perceive that distributive justice has been violated and that unfairness exists (e.g., Brockner & Wiesenfeld, 1996; Greenberg, 1993).

Although we are certainly concerned with the outcomes we and others receive, this is far from the entire story where judgments of fairness are concerned. In addition, we are also often interested in the fairness of the *procedures* through which rewards have been distributed. This is known as **procedural justice** (e.g., Folger & Baron, 1996), and we base our judgments about it on factors such as these: (1) the consistency of procedures—the extent to which they are applied in the same manner to all persons; (2) accuracy—the extent to

procedural justice Judgments concerning the fairness of the procedures used to distribute available rewards among group members.

which procedures are based on accurate information about the relative contributions of all group members; (3) opportunity for corrections—the extent to which any errors in distributions that are made can be adjusted; (4) bias suppression—the extent to which decision makers avoid being influenced by their own self-interest; and (5) ethicality—the extent to which decisions are made in a manner compatible with ethical and moral values held by the people affected.

Evidence that such factors really do influence our judgments concerning procedural justice has been obtained in many studies (e.g., Brockner et al., 1994; Leventhal, Karuza, & Fry, 1980). For instance, in one investigation, Magner et al. (2000) asked property owners in a medium-sized city to rate the extent to which their taxes were determined through fair procedures. Results indicated that ethicality, accuracy, and bias suppression were important factors in taxpayers' decisions about procedural justice: The more these factors were present, the more they perceived the process of setting each person's taxes to be fair.

Finally, we also judge fairness in terms of the way in which information about outcomes and procedures is given to us. This is known as **transactional justice** (or sometimes, interactional justice), and two factors seem to play a key role in our judgments about it: the extent to which we are given clear and rational reasons for *why* rewards were divided as they were (Bies, Shapiro, & Cummings, 1988), and the courtesy and sensitivity with which we are informed about these divisions (e.g., Greenberg, 1993a). Here's an illustration: Suppose you receive a term paper from one of your professors. On the top is the grade "C–." You expected at least a B, so you are quite disappointed. Reading on, though, you see a detailed explanation of why you received the grade you did, and, after reading it, you have to admit that it is clear and reasonable. In addition, the professor inserts the following comment: "I know you'll be disappointed with this grade, but I feel you are capable of much better work and would be glad to work with you to help you improve your grade." How would you react? Probably by concluding that the grade is low but the professor treated you fairly. In contrast, imagine how you'd react if there were no explanation for the grade, and the professor wrote the following comment: "Very poor work; you simply haven't met my standards. And don't bother to try to see me: I never change grades." In this case, you are more likely to experience feelings of anger and resentment, and to view your treatment as unfair.

transactional (interactional) justice
Refers to the extent to which persons who distribute rewards explain or justify their decisions and show considerateness and courtesy to those who receive the rewards.

Reactions to Perceived Unfairness: Tactics for Dealing with Injustice

What do people do when they feel that they have been treated unfairly? As you probably know from your own experience, many different things. First, if unfairness centers around rewards (distributive justice), people may focus on changing the balance between their contributions and outcomes. For example, they may reduce contributions or demand larger rewards. If these are not delivered, they may take more drastic actions, such as leaving the group altogether. All these reactions are readily visible in workplaces—one setting in which judgments concerning fairness play a key role. Employees who feel that they are being underpaid may come in late, leave early, do less on the job, and request more benefits— higher pay, more vacation, and so on. If these tactics fail, they may protest, join a union and go out on strike, or, ultimately, quit and look for another job.

When unfairness centers around procedures (procedural justice) or a lack of courteous treatment by the persons who determine reward divisions (transactional justice) rather than on rewards themselves (distributive justice), individuals may adopt somewhat different tactics. Procedures are often harder to change than specific outcomes because they go on behind "closed doors" and may depart from announced policies in many ways. Similarly, changing the negative attitudes or personality traits that lie behind insensitive treatment by bosses, professors, or others who allocate rewards is a difficult task. As a result, individuals who feel that they have been treated unfairly in these ways often turn to more covert techniques for "evening the score." A growing body of evidence suggests that such

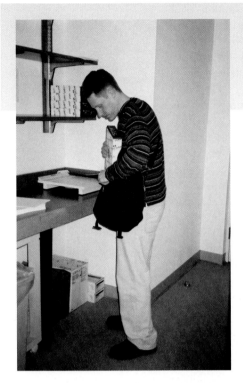

Figure 12.11 ■ Employee Theft: One Tactic for Dealing with Perceived Unfairness
When employees feel that they have been treated unfairly by management and have no legitimate means for correcting this situation, they may engage in employee theft or sabotage. In this way, they seek to "even the score" with their employers.

feelings of unfairness lie behind many instances of employee theft and sabotage (e.g., Greenberg, 1997; see Figure 12.11). As noted in Chapter 11, feelings of unfairness also play a major role in many forms of workplace aggression—especially in subtle, hidden actions individuals perform to get even with others who, they believe, have treated them unfairly.

Finally, individuals who feel that they have been treated unfairly and conclude that there is little they can do about this may cope by changing their perceptions. They can conclude, for instance, that other persons who receive larger rewards than they do *deserve* this special treatment because they possess something "special"—extra talent, greater experience, a bigger reputation, or some other special qualities. In such cases, individuals who feel that they cannot eliminate unfairness can at least cope with it and reduce the discomfort it produces, even though they continue to be treated unfairly by others.

KEY POINTS

★ Individuals wish to be treated fairly by the groups to which they belong. Fairness can be judged in terms of outcomes (*distributive justice*), in terms of procedures (*procedural justice*), or in terms of courteous treatment (*transactional justice*).

★ When individuals feel that they have been treated unfairly, they often take steps to restore fairness.

★ These steps range from overt actions (reducing or protesting their contributions), covert actions (employee theft or sabotage), or changes in perception.

Decision Making by Groups: How It Occurs and the Pitfalls It Faces

decision making
Processes involved in combining and integrating available information in order to choose one out of several possible courses of action.

Groups are called on to perform tasks—everything from playing music to performing surgical operations. One of the most important activities they perform, however, is **decision making**—combining and integrating available information in order to choose one out of several possible courses of action. Governments, large corporations, military units, sports teams—these and many other organizations entrust key decisions to groups. Why? Although many factors play a role, the most important seems to be this: Most people believe that groups usually reach better decisions than individuals. After all, groups can pool the expertise of their members and avoid extreme decisions.

Are such beliefs accurate? Do groups really make better or more accurate decisions? In their efforts to answer this question, social psychologists have focused on three major topics: (1) How do groups actually make their decisions and reach consensus? (2) Do decisions reached by groups differ from those reached by individuals? (3) What accounts for the fact that groups sometimes make truly disastrous decisions—ones so bad it is hard to believe they were actually reached?

The Decision-Making Process: How Groups Attain Consensus

When groups first begin to discuss any issue, their members rarely voice unanimous agreement. Rather, they come to the decision-making task with different information, and so support a wide range of views (e.g., Larson, Foster-Fishman, & Franz, 1998; Gigone & Hastie, 1997). After some discussion, however, groups usually reach a decision. This does not always happen: Juries become "hung," and other decision-making groups sometimes deadlock. But, in general, some decision is reached. How is this accomplished, and can the final outcome be predicted from the views initially held by a group's members? Here is what research findings suggest.

■ Social Decision Schemes: Blueprints for Decisions

Let's begin with the question of whether a group's decisions can be predicted from the views held by its members at the start. Here, the answer itself is quite straightforward, even though the processes involved are more complex: "Yes." The final decisions reached by groups can often be predicted by relatively simple rules known as **social decision schemes.** These rules relate the initial distribution of members' views or preferences to the group's final decisions. For example, one scheme—the *majority-wins rule*—suggests that, in many cases, the group will opt for whatever position is initially supported by most of its members (e.g., Nemeth et al., 2001). According to this rule, discussion serves mainly to confirm or strengthen the most popular initial view; it is generally accepted no matter how passionately the minority argues for a different position. A second decision scheme is the *truth-wins rule.* This indicates that the correct solution or decision will ultimately be accepted as its correctness is recognized by more and more members. A third decision rule is known as the *first-shift rule.* Groups tend to adopt a decision consistent with the direction of the first shift in opinion shown by any member. Still another rule—*unanimity*—is often imposed by the legal system, which requires that juries reach unanimous verdicts.

Surprising as it may seem, the results of many studies indicate that these simple rules are quite successful in predicting even complex group decisions. They have been found to be accurate up to 80 percent of the time (e.g., Stasser, Taylor, & Hanna, 1989), although members holding extreme views—outliers—can sometimes exert strong influence and shift groups away from reaching decisions predicted by these basic rules (e.g., Ohtsubo et al., 2004). Thus, social decision schemes seem to provide important insights into how groups move toward consensus. (That groups do reach decisions is clear; but what about the *quality* of these decisions—are they better or worse than the decisions individuals would make? More balanced and conservative? For a discussion of this issue, please see the **Making Sense of Common Sense** section.)

social decision schemes
Rules relating the initial distribution of member views to final group decisions.

The Science of Social Psychology

MAKING SENSE OF COMMON SENSE

Are Groups Really Less Likely Than Individuals to "Go over the Edge"?

Truly important decisions are rarely left to individuals. Instead, they are usually assigned to groups—preferably, highly qualified groups. For instance, medical decisions are made by teams of physicians, and government policies are set, or at least recommended, by groups of experts. Why? One answer involves the widespread belief that groups are less likely than individuals to make risky and hazardous decisions—to rush blindly over the edge. Is common sense correct in this respect? Research findings offer a straightforward answer: "Not really!" A large body of evidence indicates that groups are actually *more* likely to adopt extreme positions than individuals making decisions alone. In fact, across many decisions and contexts, groups show a pronounced tendency to shift toward views more extreme than the ones with which they initially began (Burnstein, 1983;

Hilton, 1998; Lamm & Myers, 1978). This is known as **group polarization,** and its major effects can be summarized as follows: Whatever the initial leaning or preference of a group prior to its discussions, this preference is strengthened during the group's deliberations. As result, not only does the *group* shift toward more extreme views, individual members often show such a shift (see Figure 12.12). Initial research on this topic (e.g., Kogan & Wallach, 1964) suggested that groups move toward riskier alternatives as they discuss important issues—a change described as the *risky shift*. But additional research indicated that the shift was not always one toward risk—that happened only in situations in which the initial preference of the group leaned in this direction. The shift could be in the opposite direction—toward increased caution—if *this* was the group's initial preference. So, do groups tend to make more conservative and therefore better decisions than individuals? The findings of careful research suggest this answer: "Not at all."

But why do groups tend to move, over the course of their discussions, toward increasingly extreme views and decisions? Two major factors seem to be involved. First, it appears that *social comparison* plays an important role. Everyone wants to be "above average," and where opinions are concerned, this implies holding views that are "better" than those of other members. What does *better* mean? In this context, *better* implies holding views in line with the group's overall preference, but even more so. For example, in a group of liberals, *better* would mean "more liberal." Among a group of conservatives, it would mean "more conservative." And among a group of racists, it would mean "even more bigoted." People who voice opinions even stronger than those of the group are admired, and so tend to become influential.

Another aspect of this process involves the fact that during group discussions, at least some members discover—often to their surprise—that their views are *not* better than those of most other members. The result: After comparing themselves with these persons, they shift to even more extreme views, and the group polarization effect is off and running (Goethals & Zanna, 1979).

A second factor involves the fact that during group discussion, most arguments presented are ones favoring the group's initial preference. As a result of hearing such arguments, persuasion occurs (presumably through the *central route* described in Chapter 4), and members shift toward the majority view. As a result of these shifts, the proportion of arguments favoring the group's initial preference increases, so that members convince themselves that this must be the "right" view. Group polarization results from this process (Vinokur & Burnstein, 1974).

Regardless of the precise basis for group polarization, it has important implications. The occurrence of polarization may lead many decision-making groups to adopt positions that are increasingly extreme, and therefore dangerous. In this context, it is chilling to speculate about the potential role of such shifts in disastrous decisions by political, military, or business groups, which should, by all accounts, have known better—for example, the decision by the "hard-liners" in the now-vanished Soviet Union to stage a coup to restore firm communist rule, or the decision by Apple computer *not* to license its software to other manufacturers—a decision that ultimately assured the success of its competitors. Did group polarization influence these and other disastrous decisions? It is impossible to say for sure, but research suggests that this is a real possibility.

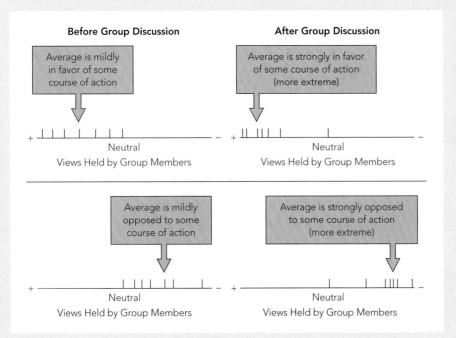

Before Group Discussion

Average is mildly in favor of some course of action

Neutral
Views Held by Group Members

Average is mildly opposed to some course of action

Neutral
Views Held by Group Members

After Group Discussion

Average is strongly in favor of some course of action (more extreme)

Neutral
Views Held by Group Members

Average is strongly opposed to some course of action (more extreme)

Neutral
Views Held by Group Members

Figure 12.12 ■ Group Polarization: How It Works
Group polarization involves the tendency for decision-making groups to shift toward views that are more extreme than the ones with which they began, but in the same general direction. Thus, if groups start out slightly in favor of one view or position, they often end up holding this view more strongly after discussions of it. This shift toward extremity can be quite dangerous in many settings.

Potential Dangers of Group Decision Making: Groupthink, Biased Processing, and Restricted Sharing of Information

The drift of many decision-making groups toward polarization is a serious problem—one that can interfere with their ability to make accurate decisions. Unfortunately, this is not the only process that can exert such negative effects. Several others emerge during group discussions and can lead groups to make costly, even disastrous, decisions (Hinsz, 1995). Among the most important are (1) *groupthink,* (2) biased processing of information by group members, and (3) groups' seeming inability to share and use information held by some, but not all, of their members.

■ Groupthink: When Too Much Cohesiveness Is a Dangerous Thing

Earlier, we noted that high levels of cohesiveness in groups can be a good thing: It increases motivation and morale and makes groups more pleasant. But like anything else, there can be "too much of a good thing" where group cohesiveness is concerned. When cohesiveness reaches very high levels, it appears **groupthink** may develop. This is a strong tendency for decision-making groups to "close ranks," cognitively, around a decision, assuming that the group *can't* be wrong, that all members must support the decision strongly, and that any information contrary to it should be rejected (Janis, 1972, 1982). Once this collective state of mind develops, it has been suggested, groups become unwilling—and perhaps *unable*—to change their decisions, even if external events suggest that these decisions are poor. Consider the repeated decisions by three U.S. presidents (Kennedy, Johnson, and Nixon) to escalate the war in Vietnam. Each escalation brought increased American casualties and no visible progress toward the goal of assuring the survival of South Vietnam as an independent country; yet, the cabinets of each president continued to recommend escalation. According to Janis (1982), the social psychologist who originated the concept of *groupthink,* this process—and the increasing unwillingness to consider alternative courses of action that it encourages among group members—may well have contributed to this tragic chain of events.

Why does groupthink occur? Research findings (e.g., Tetlock et al., 1992; Kameda & Sugimori, 1993) suggest that two factors may be crucial. One of these is a very high level of *cohesiveness* among group members. The second is *emergent group norms*—norms suggesting that the group is infallible, morally superior, and that because of these factors, there should be no further discussion of the issues at hand: The decision has been made, and the only task now is to support it as strongly as possible.

Closely related to these effects is a tendency to reject any criticism by outside sources—persons who are not members of the group. Criticism from outsiders is viewed with suspicion and attributed to negative motives rather than to a genuine desire to help. The result? It is largely ignored, and may even tend to strengthen the group's cohesiveness as members rally to defend the group against assaults by outsiders! Precisely such effects have recently been reported by Hornsey and Imani (2004). These researchers asked Australian college students to read comments about Australia supposedly made during an interview by a stranger. These comments were either positive ("When I think of Australians, I think of them as being fairly friendly and warm people") or negative ("When I think of Australians, I think of them as being fairly racist"). Moreover, they were attributed either to another Australian (an in-group member), a person from another country who had never lived in Australia (out-group—inexperienced), or to a person from another country who had once lived in Australia (out-group—experienced). Participants then rated the source of the comments in terms of personal traits (e.g., intelligence, friendliness, openmindedness) and the extent to which this person's comments were designed to be constructive. Hornsey and Imani (2004) reasoned that when the comments made by the stranger were negative, both the stranger and the comments would receive lower ratings when this person was an out-group member than when he or she was an in-group member. Further, they reasoned that experience with the in-group (having lived in Australia) would not make any difference because this person was still not a member of the in-group. When the comments were positive, such effects were not expected to occur; after all, praise is acceptable,

group polarization
The tendency of group members to shift toward more extreme positions than those they initially held as a result of group discussion.

groupthink
The tendency of the members of highly cohesive groups to assume that their decisions can't be wrong, that all members must support the groups' decisions strongly, and that information contrary to these decisions should be ignored.

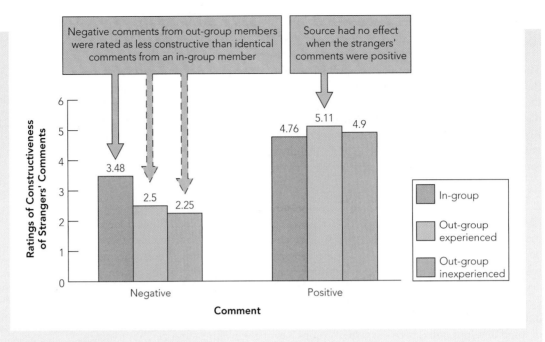

Figure 12.13 ■ Rejection of Criticism from Out-Group Members: One Reason Why Groups Sometimes Make Bad Decisions
When a stranger made critical comments about research participant's in-group (Australians), these comments were viewed more negatively when the stranger was supposedly from another country (an out-group member) than when the stranger was a member of the in-group (another Australian). Moreover, this was true even if the person had lived in Australia for several years. These findings suggest that groups' tendency to reject criticism from outsiders may be one reason why they often make very bad decisions. (*Source: Based on data from Hornsey & Imani, 2004.*)

no matter what its source! As you can see from Figure 12.13, this is precisely what happened. When the stranger's comments were positive, whether this person was an Australian or someone from another country made no difference. But when this person made negative comments, both the stranger and the comments were viewed more negatively when this person was from an out-group than when this person was an Australian (a member of the in-group.) These findings are consistent with Janis's (1982) description of groupthink and suggest that it may be increasingly difficult for members of highly cohesive groups to accept criticism from outsiders.

One final comment: Although several of the processes included under the heading *groupthink* do appear to be real, more recent research has raised questions about whether groupthink unfolds in the manner described by Janis (1982). For instance, careful study of recently declassified government documents in the United States found little support for the processes suggested by Janis in decision-making groups. Similarly, groupthink does not seem to operate as Janis described in decision-making groups in large companies (Turner, Pratkanis, & Samuels, 2003). It is best to view *groupthink* as a summary term for processes that may lead decision-making groups to disastrous choices rather than as a fully tested or validated theory. However, a key fact remains: Groups sometimes do become impervious to outside criticism or influence, and when they do, they may be on the road to making potentially disastrous decisions.

■ Biased Processing of Information in Groups

Although groupthink is a dramatic process, other more subtle but equally costly sources of bias exist in decision-making groups. One of the most important is the tendency for such groups to process available information in a biased manner. Groups, like individuals, are not always motivated to maximize accuracy; on the contrary, they are often motivated to find support for the views they initially favor. In other words, they act more like "intuitive lawyers," searching for evidence that supports their case (initial preferences) than as "intuitive scientists," seeking truth and accuracy (e.g., Baumeister & Newman, 1994). Such tendencies do not always stem from the selfish pursuit of self-interest; rather, they may derive from adherence to values or principles that are generally accepted in society and viewed in a positive light. Research findings (Sommer, Horowitz, & Bourgeois, 2001) indicate that jurors in civil suits, in which one side seeks damages from the other, often process information in a way that allows them to adhere to the rule of *comparative negligence,* a rule suggesting that damages should be awarded to the injured party only to the extent that this person was *not* responsible for the harm she or he experienced. Moreover—and this is the key point—jurors often do this even if they are instructed by judges to follow others rules: for instance, *contributory negligence*—award the plaintiff *no damages* if she or he were negligent to any extent—or *strict liability*—award *full damages* to the plaintiff if the defendant were negligent.

These findings and those of related research (e.g., Frey, Schulz-Hardt, & Stahlberg, 1996) indicate that juries and other decision-making groups often engage in biased processing. They process available information in ways that allow them to reach the decisions they want. Certainly, this is not the outcome desired when important decisions are turned over to groups.

■ The Failure to Share Information Unique to Each Member

A third potential source of bias for decision-making groups involves the fact that, contrary to what common sense suggests, groups do not always pool their resources—share information and ideas unique to each member. Research on this issue (Gigone & Hastie, 1993, 1997; Stasser, 1992) indicates that such pooling of resources or information may be the exception rather than the rule. When groups discuss a given issue and try to reach a decision, they tend to discuss information shared by most, if not all members, rather than information that is known to only a few. The result: The decisions they make tend to reflect the shared information (e.g., Gigione & Hastie, 1993). This is not a problem if such information points to the best decision, but consider what happens when information pointing to the best decision is *not* shared by most members. In such cases, the tendency of members to discuss mainly the information they all already possess may prevent them from reaching the best decision.

Disturbingly, recent findings suggest that this tendency is strong. For instance, even with respect to a medical diagnosis, which can involve life-and-death decisions, teams of interns and medical students discuss more shared than unshared information during diagnostic conferences. Further, the more they pooled *unshared* information (information known initially to only some members), the more accurate were the groups' diagnoses (e.g., Larson et al., 1998; Winquist & Larson, 1998).

■ Improving Group Decisions

Groupthink, biased processing, failing to share information unique to each member—these are discouraging barriers to effective decision making by groups. Can these potential pitfalls be overcome? Many studies have addressed this issue, and together they point to some promising techniques. Several of these involve encouraging dissent because doing so may slow the rapid movement of groups toward consensus. One such approach is the **devil's advocate technique** (e.g., Hirt & Markman, 1995), in which one group member is assigned the task of disagreeing with and criticizing whatever plan or decision is under consideration. This tactic often works because it induces members to think carefully about the decision toward which they are moving (see Figure 12.14). Another approach is building **authentic dissent** into groups by ensuring that persons assigned to such groups hold different initial opinions. Research findings indicate that this technique may be considerably more effective in inducing groups to examine all available

devil's advocate technique
A technique for improving the quality of group decisions in which one group member is assigned the task of disagreeing with and criticizing whatever plan or decision is under consideration.

authentic dissent
A technique for improving the quality of group decisions in which one or more group members actively disagree with the group's initial preference without being assigned this role.

"That makes four 'Yes'es and one 'No, no, a thousand times no.'"

Figure 12.14 ■ The Devil's Advocate Technique in Operation
In the *devil's advocate technique,* one member of a group is assigned the task of disagreeing with and criticizing whatever decision or action is favored by the majority. This can improve decision making by forcing other members to think more carefully about the issues they are considering. Although the example shown here is extreme, it is clear that the member voting no so strongly will stimulate further discussion in the group. (*Source:* © The New Yorker Collection 1982 Dean Vietor from cartoonbank.com. All Rights Reserved.)

information than the devil's advocate approach (Nemeth et al., 2001; Schulz-Hardt, Jochims, & Frey, 2002).

Decision making by groups *can* be improved; however, active steps must be taken to achieve this goal. Left to their own devices, and without outside intervention, groups often slip into the "mental traps" outlined here—often with devastating results.

KEY POINTS

★ It is widely believed that groups make better decisions than individuals. However, research findings indicate that groups are often subject to *group polarization* effects, which lead them to make more extreme decisions than individuals.

★ In addition, groups often suffer from *groupthink*—a tendency to assume that they can't be wrong and that information contrary to the groups' views should be rejected.

★ Although not all aspects of groupthink have been verified in research, recent findings indicate that groups tend to reject criticism from out-group members relative to identical criticism from in-group members.

★ Groups often engage in biased processing of information to reach the decisions they initially prefer, or to adhere to general values, such as the principle of *distributive justice.*

★ Group decision making can be improved in several ways, such as the *devil's advocate technique* and building *authentic dissent* into groups when they are formed.

Groups: Why We Join Them ... and Why We Leave

■ *Groups* are collections of persons perceived to form a coherent unit to some degree. The extent to which the group is perceived to form a coherent entity is known as *entiativity*.

■ Basic aspects of groups involve *roles, status, norms,* and *cohesiveness*. The effects of roles on our behavior are often powerful, causing us to act in ways that we might not otherwise.

■ People gain status in a group for many reasons, ranging from physical characteristics (e.g., height) to various aspects of their behavior.

■ Another important feature of groups is their level of *cohesiveness*—the sum of all the factors that cause people to want to remain members.

■ Joining groups confers important benefits on members, including increased self-knowledge, progress toward important goals, enhanced status, and attaining social change.

■ However, group membership also exacts important costs, such as loss of personal freedom and heavy demands on time, energy, and resources.

■ Individuals often withdraw from groups when they feel that the group has changed so much that it no longer reflects their basic values or beliefs.

Effects of the Presence of Others: From Task Performance to Behavior in Crowds

■ The mere presence of others either as an audience or coactors can influence our performance. Such effects are known as *social facilitation* (or as social facilitation–inhibition effects).

■ The *drive theory of social facilitation* suggests that the presence of others is arousing and can either increase or reduce performance, depending on whether dominant responses in a given situation are correct or incorrect.

■ The *distraction–conflict theory* suggests that the presence of others induces conflicting tendencies to focus on the task being performed and on an audience or coactors. This can result in increased arousal and narrowed attentional focus.

■ Recent findings offer support for the view that several kinds of audiences produce narrowed attentional focus among persons performing a task. This cognitive view of social facilitation helps explain why social facilitation occurs among animals as well as people.

■ When individuals work together on a task, *social loafing*—reduced output by each group member—sometimes occurs.

■ Social loafing can be reduced in several ways: by making outputs individually identifiable, by increasing commitment to the task and task importance, and by assuring that each member's contributions to the task are unique.

■ When we are part of a large crowd, we experience reductions in both our self-awareness and our social identity. This causes us to adopt the norms operating in the current situation—norms that often sanction impulsive, unrestrained behavior.

Coordination in Groups: Cooperation or Conflict?

■ *Cooperation*—working together with others to obtain shared goals—is a common aspect of social life.

■ Cooperation does not develop in many situations in which it is possible, partly because such situations involve *social dilemmas,* in which individuals can increase their own gains by defection.

■ Several factors influence whether cooperation occurs in such situations. These include strong tendencies toward *reciprocity, personal orientation* toward cooperation, and *communication*.

■ Evolutionary psychologists suggest that our tendency to reciprocate may result from the fact that organisms that cooperate are more likely to survive and reproduce.

■ *Conflict* is a process that begins when individuals or groups perceive that others' interests are incompatible with theirs.

■ Conflict can also stem from social factors such as faulty attributions, poor communication, the tendency to perceive our own views as objective, and personal traits.

■ Conflict can be reduced in many ways, but *bargaining* and the induction of *superordinate goals* seem to be most effective.

Perceived Fairness in Groups: Its Nature and Effects

■ Individuals wish to be treated fairly by the groups to which they belong. Fairness can be judged in terms of outcomes (*distributive justice*), in terms of procedures (*procedural justice*), or in terms of courteous treatment (*transactional justice*).

■ When individuals feel that they have been treated unfairly, they often take steps to restore fairness.

■ These steps range from overt actions (reducing or protesting their contributions), covert actions (employee theft or sabotage), or changes in perception.

Decision Making by Groups: How It Occurs and the Pitfalls It Faces

■ It is widely believed that groups make better decisions than individuals. However, research findings indicate that groups are often subject to *group polarization* effects, which lead them to make more extreme decisions than individuals.

- In addition, groups often suffer from *groupthink*—a tendency to assume that they can't be wrong and that information contrary to the groups' views should be rejected.
- Although not all aspects of groupthink have been verified in research, recent findings indicate that groups tend to reject criticism from out-group members relative to identical criticism from in-group members.
- Groups often engage in biased processing of information to reach the decisions they initially prefer, or to adhere to general values, such as the principle of *distributive justice*.
- Group decision making can be improved in several ways, such as the *devil's advocate technique* and building *authentic dissent* into groups when they are formed.

Connections INTEGRATING SOCIAL PSYCHOLOGY

In this chapter, you read about . . .	In other chapters, you will find related discussions of . . .
the role of norms in the functioning of groups	the nature of norms and their role in social influence (Chapter 9) and aggression (Chapter 11)
the nature of cooperation and conflict and factors that affect their occurrence	other forms of behavior that either assist or harm others: discrimination (Chapter 6) helping behavior (Chapter 10) aggression (Chapter 11)
individuals' concern with others' evaluations of their performance	the effects of others' evaluations on our self-concept (Chapter 5) and on our liking for others (Chapter 7)
perceived fairness	the effects of perceived fairness on many other forms of social behavior, such as helping (Chapter 10) and aggression (Chapter 11), and the role of fairness in close relationships (Chapter 8)
the role of persuasion and other forms of social influence in group decision making	the nature of persuasion (Chapter 4), and various forms of social influence (Chapter 9)

Thinking about Connections

1. Do you see any connection between social loafing and perceived fairness? (Hint: If you have been in a group in which you suspected that other people were engaging in "social loafing," what did you do about it? And if you did take action, why?)

2. Suppose you had to give an important speech to a large audience. According to research on social facilitation, what would be the best way to prepare?

3. Many situations involve social dilemmas: If we cooperate with others, everyone gains, but it is tempting to pursue our own self-interests, because, in the short-run, it is easier and offers immediate gains. Can you think of such a situation in your life? What did you do when you found yourself in it—the "right" thing or the "easy" thing? Do you think that after reading this chapter, you might behave differently in such situations than you have in the past?

4. If groups are more likely to make extreme decisions, to reject input from outsiders, and to engage in biased processing of available information, why are so many important decisions still entrusted to groups? Do groups offer any advantages not discussed in this chapter?

Social facilitation effects seem to occur because the presence of others is arousing. This increases our tendency to perform dominant responses. If these dominant responses are correct, performance is improved; if they are incorrect, performance is impaired. This leads to two practical suggestions:

■ Study alone but take tests in the presence of others: If you study alone, you'll avoid the distraction caused by others and so will learn new materials more efficiently. If you have studied hard, your domi-nant responses will probably be correct, so the increased arousal generated by other persons will improve your performance.

■ Work on simple tasks (e.g., ones requiring pure physical effort) in front of an audience: The presence of an audience will increase your arousal and your ability to put out physical effort on such tasks.

Social loafing occurs when persons working together put out less effort than if they were alone. This can be costly to you if *you* work hard but others goof off. Here's how you can avoid such an outcome:

■ Make sure that the contribution of each member of the group can be assessed individually—don't let social loafers hide!

■ Try to work only with people who are committed to the group's goals.

■ Make sure that each person's contribution is unique, not redun-dant with others. In that way, each person can be personally responsible for what she or he produces.

KEY TERMS

additive tasks (p. 344)

authentic dissent (p. 359)

bargaining (negotiation) (p. 350)

cohesiveness (p. 337)

conflict (p. 346)

cooperation (p. 346)

decision making (p. 354)

deindividuation (p. 345)

devil's advocate technique (p. 359)

distraction–conflict theory (p. 343)

distributive justice (fairness) (p. 352)

drive theory of social facilitation (p. 342)

entiativity (p. 336)

evaluation apprehension (p. 343)

group (p. 335)

group polarization (p. 356)

groupthink (p. 357)

norms (p. 337)

procedural justice (p. 352)

reciprocal altruism (p. 348)

reciprocity (p. 347)

roles (p. 336)

social decision schemes (p. 355)

social dilemmas (p. 346)

social facilitation (p. 341)

social loafing (p. 344)

status (p. 337)

superordinate goals (p. 351)

transactional (interpersonal) justice (p. 353)

GLOSSARY

above-average effect The tendency for people to rate themselves as above the average on most positive social attributes.

abusive supervision Behavior in which supervisors direct frequent hostile verbal and nonverbal behavior toward their subordinates.

actor–observer effect The tendency to attribute our own behavior mainly to situational causes but the behavior of others mainly to internal (dispositional) causes.

adaptive response Any physical characteristic or behavioral tendency that enhances the odds of reproductive success for an individual or for other individuals with similar genes.

affect A person's emotional state—positive and negative feelings and moods; our current feelings and moods.

affect-centered model of attraction A conceptual framework in which attraction is assumed to be based on positive and negative emotions. These emotions can be aroused directly by another person or simply associated with that person. The emotional arousal can also be enhanced or mitigated by cognitive processes.

aggression Behavior directed toward the goal of harming another living being, who is motivated to avoid such treatment.

altruism Behavior that is motivated by an unselfish concern for the welfare of others.

altruistic personality A combination of dispositional variables associated with *prosocial behavior*. The components are *empathy*, belief in a just world, acceptance of social responsibility, having an internal locus of control, and not being egocentric.

anchoring and adjustment heuristic A heuristic that involves the tendency to use a number or value as a starting point, to which we then make adjustments.

appearance anxiety Apprehension or worry about whether one's physical appearance is adequate and about the possible negative reactions of other people.

assumed similarity The extent to which two people believe they are similar with respect to specific attitudes, beliefs, values, and so forth, as opposed to the extent to which they are actually similar.

attachment style The degree of security experienced in interpersonal relationships. Differential styles initially develop in the interactions between infant and caregiver when the infant acquires basic attitudes about self-worth and *interpersonal trust*.

attitude accessibility The ease with which specific attitudes can be remembered and brought into consciousness.

attitude similarity The extent to which two individuals share the same attitudes about a range of topics. In practice, the term also includes similarity of beliefs, values, and interests—as well as attitudes.

attitude Evaluation of various aspects of the social world.

attitude-to-behavior process model A model of how attitudes guide behavior that emphasizes the influence of attitudes and stored knowledge of what is appropriate in a given situation on an individual's definition of the present situation. This definition, in turn, influences overt behavior.

attribution The process through which we seek to identify the causes of others' behavior and so gain knowledge of their stable traits and dispositions.

augmenting principle The tendency to attach greater importance to a potential cause of behavior if the behavior occurs despite the presence of other, inhibitory causes.

authentic dissent A technique for improving the quality of group decisions in which one or more group members actively disagree with the group's initial preference without being assigned this role.

automatic processing After extensive experience with a task or type of information, the stage at which we can perform the task or process the information in a seemingly effortless, automatic, and nonconscious manner.

availability heuristic A strategy for making judgments on the basis of how easily specific kinds of information can be brought to mind.

balance theory The formulations of Heider and of Newcomb that specify the relationships among (1) an individual's liking for another person, (2) his or her attitude about a given topic, and (3) the other person's attitude about the same topic. Balance (liking plus agreement) results in a positive emotional state. Imbalance (liking plus disagreement) results in a negative state and a desire to restore balance. Nonbalance (disliking plus either agreement or disagreement) leads to indifference.

bargaining (negotiation) A process in which opposing sides exchange offers, counteroffers, and concessions, either directly or through representatives.

benevolent sexism Views suggesting that women are superior to men in various ways and are truly necessary for men's happiness.

bilateral symmetry The alikeness of the left and the right sides of the body (or parts of the body).

black sheep effect When a member of the ingroup behaves in a way that threatens the value of the group identity and is intensely derogated as a means of protecting the group identity.

body language Cues provided by the position, posture, and movement of others' bodies or body parts.

bona fide pipeline A technique that uses *priming* to measure implicit racial attitudes.

bullying A pattern of behavior in which one individual is chosen as the target of repeated aggression by one or more others; the target person (the victim) generally has less power than those who engage in aggression (the bullies).

bystander effect The fact that the likelihood of a prosocial response to an emergency is affected by the number of bystanders who are present.

catharsis hypothesis The view that providing angry persons with an opportunity to express their aggressive impulses in relatively safe ways will reduce their tendencies to engage in more harmful forms of aggression.

central route (to persuasion) Attitude change resulting from systematic processing of information presented in persuasive messages.

classical conditioning A basic form of learning in which one stimulus, initially neutral, acquires the capacity to evoke reactions through repeated pairing with another stimulus. In a

that's-not-all technique   A technique for gaining compliance in which requesters offer additional benefits to target persons before these persons have decided whether to comply with or reject specific requests.

theories   Efforts by scientists in any field to answer the question "why?" Theories involve attempts to understand why certain events or processes occur as they do.

theory of planned behavior   An extension of the *theory of reasoned action*, suggesting that in addition to attitudes toward a given behavior and subjective norms about it, individuals also consider their ability to perform the behavior.

theory of reasoned action   A theory suggesting that the decision to engage in a particular behavior is the result of a rational process in which behavioral options are considered, consequences or outcomes of each are evaluated, and a decision is reached to act or not to act. That decision is then reflected in behavioral intentions, which strongly influence overt behavior.

third-person effect   Effect that occurs when the impact of media exposure on others' attitudes and behaviors is overestimated and the impact on the self is underestimated.

thought suppression   Efforts to prevent certain thoughts from entering consciousness.

threat   Threat can take different forms, but it primarily concerns fear that one's group interests will be undermined or that one's self-esteem is in jeopardy.

tokenism   Tokenism can refer to hiring based on group membership. It also can concern instances in which individuals perform trivial positive actions for members of out-groups that are later used as an excuse for refusing more meaningful beneficial actions for members of these groups.

transactional (interpersonal) justice   Refers to the extent to which persons who distribute rewards explain or justify their decisions and show considerateness and courtesy to those who receive the rewards.

triangular model of love   Sternberg's conceptualization of love relationships consisting of three basic components: *intimacy*, *passion*, and *decision/commitment*.

trivialization   A technique for reducing dissonance in which the importance of attitudes or behaviors that are inconsistent with each other is cognitively reduced.

Type A behavior pattern   A pattern consisting primarily of high levels of competitiveness, time urgency, and hostility.

Type B behavior pattern   A pattern consisting of the absence of characteristics associated with the Type A behavior pattern.

ultimate attribution error   The tendency to make more favorable and flattering attributions about members of one's own group than about members of other groups. In effect, it is the self-serving attributional bias at the group level.

unrequited love   *Love* felt by one person for another who does not feel love in return.

upward social comparison   A comparison with someone who does better than the self.

within-group comparisons   Comparisons made between a target and other members of that same category only.

workplace aggression   Any form of behavior through which individuals seek to harm others in their workplace.

REFERENCES

Aarts, H., & Dijksterhuis, A. (2003). The silence of the library: Environment, situational norms, and social behavior. *Journal of Personality and Social Psychology, 84*, 18–24.

Adams, J. S. (1965). Inequity in social exchange. In L. Berkowitz (Ed.), *Advances in experimental social psychology* (Vol. 2, pp. 267–299). New York: Academic Press.

Ahrons, C. (2004). *We're still family: What grown children have to say about their parents' divorce.* New York: Harper Collins.

Ajzen, I. (1987). Attitudes, traits, and actions: Dispositional prediction of behavior in personality and social psychology. In L. Berkowitz (Ed.), *Advances in experimental social psychology* (Vol. 20). San Diego, CA: Academic Press.

Ajzen, I. (1991). The theory of planned behavior: Special issue: Theories of cognitive self-regulation. *Organizational Behavior and Human Decision Processes, 50*, 179–211.

Ajzen, I. (2001). Nature and operation of attitudes. *Annual Review of Psychology, 52*, 27–58.

Ajzen, I., & Fishbein, M. (1980). *Understanding attitudes and predicting social behavior.* Englewood Cliffs, NJ: Prentice-Hall.

Alagna, F. J., Whitcher, S. J., & Fisher, J. D. (1979). Evaluative reactions to interpersonal touch in a counseling interview. *Journal of Counseling Psychology, 26*, 465–472.

Alexander, M. J., & Higgins, E. T. (1993). Emotional trade-offs of becoming a parent: How social roles influence self-discrepancy effects. *Journal of Personality and Social Psychology, 65*, 1259–1269.

Alexander, R., Feeney, J., Hohaus, L., & Noller, P. (2001). Attachment style and coping resources as predictors of coping strategies in the transition to parenthood. *Personal Relationships, 8*, 137–152.

Alicke, M. D., Vredenburg, D. S., Hiatt, M., & Govorun, O. (2001). The better than myself effect. *Motivation and Emotion, 25*, 7–22.

Allgeier, E. R., & Wiederman, M. W. (1994). How useful is evolutionary psychology for understanding contemporary human sexual behavior? *Annual Review of Sex Research, 5*, 218–256.

Allport, F. H. (1920). The influence of the group upon association and thought. *Journal of Experimental Psychology, 3*, 159–182.

Allport, F. H. (1924). *Social psychology.* Boston: Houghton Mifflin.

Allyn, J., & Festinger, L. (1961). The effectiveness of unanticipated persuasive communications. *Journal of Abnormal and Social Psychology, 62*, 35–40.

Alvaro, E. M., & Crano, W. D. (1996). Cognitive responses to minority- or majority-based communications: Factors that underlie minority influence. *British Journal of Social Psychology, 34*, 105–121.

Amato, P. R. (1986). Emotional arousal and helping behavior in a real-life emergency. *Journal of Applied Social Psychology, 16*, 633–641.

Amato, P. R., & Booth, A. (2001). The legacy of parents' marital discord: Consequences for children's marital quality. *Journal of Personality and Social Psychology, 81*, 627–638.

American Psychiatric Association. (1994). *Diagnostic and statistical manual of mental disorders* (4th ed.). Washington, DC: American Psychiatric Association.

Ames, D. R., Flynn, F. J., & Weber, E. U. (2004). It's the thought that counts: On perceiving how helpers decide to lend a hand. *Personality and Social Psychology Bulletin, 30*, 461–474.

Andersen, S. M., & Baum, A. (1994). Transference in interpersonal relations: Inferences and affect based on significant-other representations. *Journal of Personality, 62*, 459–497.

Anderson, C. A. (1989). Temperature and aggression: Effects on quarterly, yearly, and city rates of violent and nonviolent crime. *Journal of Personality and Social Psychology, 52*, 1161–1173.

Anderson, C. A. (1997). Effects of violent movies and trait hostility on hostile feelings and aggressive thoughts. *Aggressive Behavior, 23*, 161–178.

Anderson, C. A., & Anderson, K. B. (1996). Violent crime rate studies in philosophical context: A destructive testing approach to heat and Southern culture of violence effects. *Journal of Personality and Social Psychology, 70*, 740–756.

Anderson, C. A., Anderson, K. B., & Deuser, W. E. (1996). Examining an affective aggression framework: Weapon and temperature effects on aggressive thoughts, affect, and attitudes. *Personality and Social Psychology Bulletin, 22*, 366–376.

Anderson, C. A., & Bushman, B. J. (2001). Effects of violent video games on aggressive behavior, aggressive cognition, aggressive affect, physiological arousal, and prosocial behavior: A meta-analytic review of the scientific literature. *Psychological Science, 12*, 353–359.

Anderson, C. A., & Bushman, B. J. (2002a). Media violence and the American public revisited. *American Psychologist, 57*, 448–450.

Anderson, C. A., Bushman, B. J., & Groom, R. W. (1997). Hot years and serious and deadly assault: Empirical tests of the heat hypothesis. *Journal of Personality and Social Psychology, 73*, 1213–1223.

Anderson, C. A., Carnagey, N. L., & Eubanks, J. (2003). Exposure to violent media: The effects of songs with violent lyrics on aggressive thoughts and feelings. *Journal of Personality and Social Psychology, 84*, 960–971.

Anderson, C. A., Miller, R. S., Riger, A. L., Dill, J. C., & Sedikides, C. (1994). Behavioral and characterological attributional styles as predictors of depression and loneliness: Review, refinement, and test. *Journal of Personality and Social Psychology, 66*, 549–558.

Anderson, C. A., Berkowitz, L., Donnerstein, E., Huesmann, L. R., Johnson, J. D., Linz, D., Malamuth, N. M., & Wartella, E. (2004). The influence of media violence on youth. *Psychology in the Public Interest, 4*, 81–110.

Anderson, N. H. (1965). Averaging versus adding as a stimulus combination rule in impression formation. *Journal of Experimental Social Psychology, 70*, 394–400.

Anderson, N. H. (1968). Application of a linear-serial model to a personality impression task. Using serial presentation. *Journal of Personality and Social Psychology, 10*, 354–362.

Anderson, N. H. (1973). Cognitive algebra: Integration theory applied to social attribution. In L. Berkowitz (Ed.), *Advances in experimental social psychology.* New York: Academic Press.

Anderson, V. L. (1993). Gender differences in altruism among holocaust rescuers. *Journal of Social Behavior and Personality, 8*, 43–58.

Andersson, L. M., & Pearson, C. M. (1999). Tit-for-tat? The spiraling effect of incivility in the workplace. *Academy of Management Review, 24*, 452–471.

Andreoletti, C., Zebrowitz, L. A., & Lachman, M. E. (2001). *Personality and Social Psychology Bulletin, 27*, 969–981.

Andreou, E. (2000). Bully/victim problems and their association with psychological constructs in 8- to 12-year-old Greek school-children. *Aggressive Behavior, 26*, 49–58.

Angier, N. (1998a, September 1). Nothing becomes a man more than a woman's face. *New York Times*, p. F3.

Angier, N. (2003, July 8). Opposites attract? Not in real life. *The New York Times*, F1, F6.

Apanovitch, A. M., Hobfoll, S. E., & Salovey, P. (2002). The effects of social influence on perceptual and affective reactions to scenes of sexual violence. *Journal of Applied Social Psychology, 32*, 443–464.

Archibald, F. S., Bartholomew, K., & Marx, R. (1995). Loneliness in early adolescence: A test of the cognitive discrepancy model of loneliness. *Personality and Social Psychology Bulletin, 21*, 296–301.

Aristotle. (1932). *The rhetoric* (L. Cooper, Trans.). New York: Appleton-Century-Crofts. (Original work published c. 330 B.C.)

Armitage, C. J., & Conner, M. (2000). Attitudinal ambivalence: A test of three key hypotheses.

swimsuit becomes you: Sex differences in self-objectification, restrained eating, and math performance. *Journal of Personality and Social Psychology, 75,* 269–284.

Freedman, J. L., & Fraser, S. C. (1966). Compliance without pressure: The foot-in-the-door technique. *Journal of Personality and Social Psychology, 4,* 195–202.

Frey, D., Schulz-Hardt, S., & Stahlberg, D. (1996). Information seeking among individuals and groups and possible consequences for decision making in business and politics. In E. Witte & J. H. Davis (Eds.), *Understanding group behavior: Small group processes and interpersonal relation* (Vol. 2, pp. 211–225). Mahwah, NJ: Erlbaum.

Fried, C. B., & Aronson, E. (1995). Hypocrisy, misattribution, and dissonance reduction. *Personality and Social Psychology Bulletin, 21,* 925–933.

Friedman, H. S., Riggio, R. E., & Casella, D. F. (1988). Nonverbal skill, personal charisma, and initial attraction. *Personality and Social Psychology Bulletin, 14,* 203–211.

Friedman, H. S., Tucker, J. S., Schwartz, J. E., Martin, L. R., Tomlinson-Keasey, C., Wingard, D. L., & Criqui, M. H. (1995). Childhood conscientiousness and longevity: Health behaviors and cause of death. *Journal of Personality and Social Psychology, 68,* 696–703.

Fries, J. H. (2001). Reports of anti-Arab hate crimes dip, but concerns linger. *The New York Times,* December 22.

Fritzsche, B. A., Finkelstein, M. A., & Penner, L. A. (2000). To help or not to help: Capturing individuals' decision policies. *Social Behavior and Personality, 28,* 561–578.

Fry, D. P. (1998). Anthropological perspectives on aggression: Sex differences and cultural variation. *Aggressive Behavior, 24,* 81–95.

Fuegen, K., & Biernat, M. (2002). Reexamining the effects of solo status for women and men. *Personality and Social Psychology Bulletin, 28,* 913–925.

Fuegen, K., & Brehm, J. W. (2004). The intensity of affect and resistance to social influence. In E. S. Knowles & J. A. Linn (Eds.), *Resistance and persuasion* (pp. 39–63). Mahwah, NJ: Erlbaum.

Fultz, J., Shaller, M., & Cialdini, R. B. (1988). Empathy, sadness, and distress: Three related but distant vicarious affective responses to another's suffering. *Personality and Social Psychology Bulletin, 14,* 312–325.

Furman, W. (2002). The emerging field of adolescent romantic relationships. *Current Directions in Psychological Science, 11,* 177–180.

Gable, S. L., Reis, H. T., & Elliot, A. J. (2000). Behavioral activation and inhibition in everyday life. *Journal of Personality and Social Psychology, 78,* 1135–1149.

Gabriel, M. T., Critelli, J. W., & Ee, J. S. (1994). Narcissistic illusions in self-evaluations of intelligence and attractiveness. *Journal of Personality, 62,* 143–155.

Gaertner, S. L., Rust, M. C., Dovidio, J. F., Bachman, B. A., & Anastasio, P. A. (1994). The contact hypothesis: The role of common ingroup identity on reducing intergroup bias. *Small Group Research, 25,* 224–249.

Gaertner, S. L., Mann, J., Murrell, A., & Dovidio, J. F. (1989). Reducing intergroup bias: The benefits of recategorization. *Journal of Personality and Social Psychology, 57,* 239–249.

Gaertner, S. L., Mann, J. A., Dovidio, J. F., Murrell, A. J., & Pomare, M. (1990). How does cooperation reduce intergroup bias? *Journal of Personality and Social Psychology, 59,* 692–704.

Gagne, F. M., & Lydon, J. E. (2003). Identification and the commitment shift: Accounting for gender differences in relationship illusions. *Personality and Social Psychology Bulletin, 29,* 907–919.

Gallucci, G. (2003). I sell seashells by the seashore and my name is Jack: Comment on Pelham, Mirenberg, and Jones (2002). *Journal of Personality and Social Psychology, 85,* 789–799.

Gallup, G. G. (1994). Monkeys, mirrors, and minds. *Behavioral and Brain Sciences, 17,* 572–573.

Galton, F. (1952). *Hereditary genius: An inquiry into its laws and consequences.* New York: Horizon. (Original work published 1870.)

Gantner, A. B., & Taylor, S. P. (1992). Human physical aggression as a function of alcohol and threat of harm. *Aggressive Behavior, 18,* 29–36.

Garcia, D. M., Desmarais, S., Branscombe, N. R., & Gee, S. S. (in press). Opposition to redistributive employment policies for women: The role of policy experience and group interest. *British Journal of Social Psychology.*

Garcia, M., & Shaw, D. (2000). Destructive sibling conflict and the development of conduct problems in young boys. *Developmental Psychology, 36,* 44–53.

Garcia, S. M., Weaver, K., Moskowitz, G. B., & Darley, J. M. (2002). Crowded minds: The implicit bystander effect. *Journal of Personality and Social Psychology, 83,* 843–853.

Garcia-Marques, T., Mackie, D. M., Claypool, H. M., & Garcia-Marques, L. (2004). Positivity can cue familiarity. *Personality and Social Psychology Bulletin, 30,* 585–593.

Gardner, R. M., & Tockerman, Y. R. (1994). A computer–TV methodology for investigating the influence of somatotype on perceived personality traits. *Journal of Social Behavior and Personality, 9,* 555–563.

Gardner, W. L., Pickett, C. L., & Brewer, M. B. (2000). Social exclusion and selective memory: How the need to belong influences memory for social events. *Personality and Social Psychology Bulletin, 26,* 486–496.

Gawronski, G. (2003). Implicational schemata and the correspondence bias: On the diagnostic value of situationally constrained behavior. *Journal of Personality and Social Psychology 84,* 1154–1171.

Geary, D. C., Vigil, J., & Byrd-Craven, J. (2004). Evolution of human mate choice. *Journal of Sex Research, 41,* 27–42.

Geen, R. G. (1989). Alternative conceptions of social facilitation. In P. B. Paulus (Ed.), *Psychology of group influence* (2nd ed., pp. 16–31). New York: Academic Press.

Geis, F. L. (1993). Self-fulfilling prophecies: A social psychological view of gender. In A. E. Beall & R. J. Sternberg (Eds.), *The psychology of gender* (pp. 9–54). New York: Guilford Press.

George, M. S., Ketter, T. A., Parekh-Priti, I., Horwitz, B., et al. (1995). Brain activity during transient sadness and happiness in healthy women. *American Journal of Psychiatry, 152,* 341–351.

Gerard, H. B., Wilhelmy, R. A., & Conolley, E. S. (1968). Conformity and group size. *Journal of Personality and Social Psychology, 8,* 79–82.

Gerstenfeld, P. B. (2002). A time to hate: Situational antecedents of intergroup bias. *Analyses of Social Issues and Public Policy, 2,* 61–67.

Gibbons, F. X., Eggleston, T. J., & Benthin, A. C. (1997). Cognitive reactions to smoking relapse: The reciprocal relation between dissonance and self-esteem. *Journal of Personality and Social Psychology, 72,* 184–195.

Gigone, D., & Hastie, R. (1993). The common knowledge effect: Information sharing and group judgment. *Journal of Personality and Social Psychology, 65,* 959–974.

Gigone, D., & Hastie, R. (1997). The impact of information on small group choice. *Journal of Personality and Social Psychology, 72,* 132–140.

Gilbert, D. T. (2002). Inferential correction. In T. Gilovich, D. W. Griffin, & D. Kahneman (Eds.), *Heuristics and biases: The psychology of intuitive judgment* (pp. 167–184) New York: Cambridge University Press.

Gilbert, D. T., & Malone, P. S. (1995). The correspondence bias. *Psychological Bulletin, 117,* 21–38.

Gilbert, D. T., & Wilson, T. D. (2000). Miswanting: Some problems in the forecasting of future affective states. In J. Forgas (Ed.), *Feeling and thinking: The role of affect in social cognition.* New York: Cambridge University Press.

Gilbert, L. A. (1993). *Two careers/one family.* Newbury Park, CA: Sage.

Gillis, J. S. (1982). *Too small, too tall.* Champaign, IL: Institute for Personality and Ability Testing.

Gilovich, T., Medvec, V. H., & Savitsky, K. (2000). The spotlight effect in social judgment: An egocentric bias in estimates of the salience of one's own actions and appearance. *Journal of Personality and Social Psychology, 78,* 211–222.

Giner-Sorolla, R., & Chaiken, S. (1994). The causes of hostile media effects. *Journal of Experimental Social Psychology, 30,* 165–180.

Giner-Sorolla, R., & Chaiken, S. (1997). Selective use of heuristic and systematic processing under defense motivation. *Personality and Social Psychology Bulletin, 23,* 84–97.

Ginsburg, H. J., Ogletree, S. M., Silakowski, T. D., Bartels, R. D., Burk, S. L., & Turner, G. M. (2003). Young children's theories of mind about empathic and selfish motives. *Social Behavior and Personality, 31,* 237–244.

Gladue, B. A., & Delaney, H. J. (1990). Gender differences in perception of attractiveness of men and women in bars. *Personality and Social Psychology Bulletin, 16,* 378–391.

Glass Ceiling Commission. (1995). *Good for business: Making full use of the nation's human capital.* Washington, DC: Glass Ceiling Commission.

Glass, D. C. (1977). *Behavior patterns, stress, and coronary disease.* Hillsdale, NJ: Erlbaum.

Gleicher, F., Boninger, D., Strathman, A., Armor, D., Hetts, J., & Ahn, M. (1995). With an eye toward the future: Impact of counterfactual thinking on affect, attitudes, and behavior. In N. J. Roses & J. M. Olson (Eds.), *What might have been: the social psychology of counterfactual thinking* (pp. 283–304). Mahwah, NJ: Erlbaum.

Glick, P. (2002). Sacrificial lambs dressed in wolves' clothing: Envious prejudice, ideology, and the scapegoating of Jews. In *Understanding genocide: The social psychology of the Holocaust* (pp. 113–142). New York: Oxford University Press.

Glick, P., Fiske, S. T., et al. (2000). Beyond prejudice as simple antipathy: Hostile and benevolent sexism across cultures. *Journal of Personality and Social Psychology, 79,* 763–775.

Goethals, G. R., & Darley, J. (1977). Social comparison theory: An attributional approach. In J. M. Suls & R. L. Miller (Eds.), *Social comparison processes: Theoretical and empirical perspectives* (pp. 259–278). Washington, DC: Hemisphere.

Goethals, G. R., & Zanna, M. P. (1979). The role of social comparison in choice shifts. *Journal of Personality and Social Psychology, 37,* 1469–1476.

Gold, J. A., Ryckman, R. M., & Mosley, N. R. (1984). Romantic mood induction and attraction to a dissimilar other: Is love blind? *Personality and Social Psychology Bulletin, 10,* 358–368.

Goldberg, J. L., Pyszczynski, T., Greenberg, J., McCoy, S. K., & Solomon, S. (1999). Death, sex, love, and neuroticism: Why is sex such a problem? *Journal of Personality and Social Psychology, 77,* 1173–1187.

Goldinger, S. D., Kleider, H. M., Tamiko, Azuma, & Beike, D. R. (2003). Blaming the victim under memory load. *Psychological Science, 14,* 81–85.

Gonnerman, M. E., Jr., Parker, C. P., Lavine, H., & Huff, J. (2000). The relationship between self-discrepancies and affective states: The moderating roles of self-monitoring and standpoints on the self. *Personality and Social Psychology Bulletin, 26,* 810–819.

Goodwin, R., Cook, O., & Yung, Y. (2001). Loneliness and life satisfaction among three cultural groups. *Personal Relationships, 8,* 225–230.

Goodwin, S. A., Gubin, A., Fiske, S. T., & Yzerbyt, V. (2000). Power can bias impression processes: Stereotyping subordinates by default and by design. *Group Processes and Intergroup Relations, 3,* 227–256.

Gootman, E. (2004, June 15). The killer gown is essential, but the prom date? Not so much. *The New York Times,* B1, B4.

Gordon, R. A. (1996). Impact of ingratiation in judgments and evaluations: A meta-analytic investigation. *Journal of Personality and Social Psychology, 71,* 54–70.

Gould, S. J. (1996, September). The Diet of Worms and the defenestration of Prague. *Natural History,* 18–24, 64, 66–67.

Graham, S., & Folkes, V. (Eds.). (1990). *Attribution theory: Applications to achievement, mental health, and interpersonal conflict.* Hillsdale, NJ: Erlbaum.

Graham, S., Weiner, B., & Zucker, G. S. (1997). An attributional analysis of punishment goals and public reactions to O. J. Simpson. *Personality and Social Psychology Bulletin, 23,* 331–346.

Gray, H. M., Ambady, N., Lowenthal, W. T., & Deldin, P. (2004). P300 as an index of attention to self-relevant stimuli. *Journal of Experimental Social Psychology, 40,* 216–224.

Graziano, W. G., Jensen-Campbell, L. A., & Hair, E. C. (1996). Perceiving interpersonal conflict and reacting to it: The case for agreeableness. *Journal of Personality and Social Psychology, 70,* 820–835.

Green, J. D., & Campbell, W. K. (2000). Attachment and exploration in adults: Chronic and contextual accessibility. *Personality and Social Psychology Bulletin, 26,* 452–461.

Green, L. R., Richardson, D. R., & Lago, T. (1996). How do friendship, indirect, and direct aggression relate? *Aggressive Behavior, 22,* 81–86.

Greenbaum, P., & Rosenfield, H. W. (1978). Patterns of avoidance in responses to interpersonal staring and proximity: Effects of bystanders on drivers at a traffic intersection. *Journal of Personality and Social Psychology, 36,* 575–587.

Greenberg, J. (1993). The social side of fairness: Interpersonal and informational classes of organizational justice. In R. Cropanzano (Ed.), *Justice in the workplace: Approaching fairness in human resources management.* Hillsdale, NJ: Erlbaum.

Greenberg, J. (1997). A social influence model of employee theft: Beyond the fraud triangle. In R. J. Lewicki, R. J. Bies, & B. H. Sheppard (Eds.), *Research on negotiation in organizations* (Vol. 6, pp. 29–52). Greenwich, CT: JAI Press.

Greenberg, J., & Baron, R. A. (2002). *Behavior in organizations* (8th ed.). Upper Saddle River, NJ: Prentice-Hall.

Greenberg, J., Pyszczynski, T., & Solomon, S. (1982). The self-serving attributional bias: Beyond self-presentation. *Journal of Experimental Social Psychology, 18,* 56–67.

Greenberg, J., Solomon, S., Pyszczynski, T., Rosenblatt, A., Burling, J., Lyon, D., Simon, L., & Pinel, E. (1992). Why do people need self-esteem? Converging evidence that self-esteem serves an anxiety-buffering function. *Journal of Personality and Social Psychology, 63,* 913–922.

Greenhaus, J. H., & Parasuraman, S. (1993). Job performance attributions and career advancement prospects: An examination of gender and race effects. *Organizational Behavior and Human Decision Processes, 55,* 273–297.

Greenwald, A. G. (2002). Constructs in student ratings of instructors. In H. I. Braun & D. N. Douglas (Eds.), *The role of constructs in psychological and educational measurement* (pp. 277–297). Mahwah, NJ: Erlbaum.

Greenwald, A. G., & Banaji, M. R. (1995). Implicit social cognition: Attitudes, self-esteem, and stereotypes. *Psychological Review, 102,* 4–27.

Greenwald, A. G., McGhee, D. E., & Schwartz, J. L. K. (1998). Measuring individual differences in implicit cognition: The implicit association test. *Journal of Personality and Social Psychology, 74,* 1464–1480.

Griffin, R. W., & O'Leary-Kelly, V. (Eds.). (2004). *The dark side of organizational behavior.* San Francisco: Jossey-Bass.

Groff, D. B., Baron, R. S., & Moore, D. L. (1983). Distraction, attentional conflict, and drive-like behavior. *Journal of Experimental Social Psychology, 19,* 359–380.

Grote, N. K., & Clark, M. S. (2001). Perceiving unfairness in the family: Cause of consequence of marital distress? *Journal of Personality and Social Psychology, 80,* 281–289.

Grote, N. K., Frieze, I. H., & Stone, C. A. (1996). Children, traditionalism in the division of family work, and marital satisfaction: "What's love got to do with it?" *Personal Relationships, 3,* 211–228.

Guagnano, G. A. (1995). Locus of control, altruism and agentic disposition. *Population and Environment, 17,* 63–77.

Guimond, S. (2000). Group socialization and prejudice: The social transmission of intergroup attitudes and beliefs. *European Journal of Social Psychology, 30,* 335–354.

Gump, B. B., & Kulik, J. A. (1997). Stress, affiliation, and emotional contagion. *Journal of Personality and Social Psychology, 72,* 305–319.

Gunther, A. (1995). Overrating the X-rating: The third-person perception and support for censorship of pornography. *Journal of Communication, 45,* 27–38.

Gustafson, R. (1990). Wine and male physical aggression. *Journal of Drug Issues, 20,* 75–86.

Hackel, L. S., & Ruble, D. N. (1992). Changes in the marital relationship after the first baby is born: Predicting the impact of expectancy disconfirmation. *Journal of Personality and Social Psychology, 62,* 944–957.

Hahn, J., & Blass, T. (1997). Dating partner preferences: A function of similarity of love styles. *Journal of Social Behavior and Personality, 12,* 595–610.

Halberstadt, J., & Rhodes, G. (2000). The attractiveness of nonface averages: Implications for an evolutionary explanation of the attractiveness of average faces. *Psychological Science, 11,* 285–289.

Jetten, J., & Spears, R. (2003). The divisive potential of differences and similarities: The role of intergroup distinctiveness in intergroup differentiation. *European Review of Social Psychology, 14,* 203–241.

Jetten, J., Spears, R., & Manstead, A. S. R. (1997). Strength of identification and intergroup differentiation: The influence of group norms. *European Journal of Social Psychology, 27,* 603–609.

Jetten, J., Branscombe, N. R., Schmitt, M. T., & Spears, R. (2001). Rebels with a cause: Group identification as a response to perceived discrimination from the mainstream. *Personality and Social Psychology Bulletin, 27,* 1204–1213.

Johnson, B. T. (1994). Effects of outcome-relevant involvement and prior information on persuasion. *Journal of Experimental Social Psychology, 30,* 556–579.

Johnson, C., & Mullen, B. (1994). Evidence for the accessibility of paired distinctiveness in the distinctiveness-based illusory correlation in stereotyping. *Personality and Social Psychology Bulletin, 20,* 65–70.

Johnson, J. C., Poteat, G. M., & Ironsmith, M. (1991). Structural vs. marginal effects: A note on the importance of structure in determining sociometric status. *Journal of Social Behavior and Personality, 6,* 489–508.

Johnson, M. K., & Sherman, S. J. (1990). Constructing and reconstructing the past and the future in the present. In E. T. Higgins & R. M. Sorrentino (Eds.), *Handbook of motivation and social cognition: Foundations of social behavior* (pp. 482–526). New York: Guilford.

Johnson, S. (2003, April). Laughter. *Discover,* 62–68.

Johnston, V. S., & Oliver-Rodriguez, J. C. (1997). Facial beauty and the late positive component of event-related potentials. *Journal of Sex Research, 34,* 188–198.

Johnstone, B., Frame, C. L., & Bouman, D. (1992). Physical attractiveness and athletic and academic ability in controversial–aggressive and rejected–aggressive children. *Journal of Social and Clinical Psychology, 11,* 71–79.

Joireman, J., Anderson, J., & Strathman, A. (2003). The aggression paradox: Understanding links among aggression, sensation seeking, and the consideration of future consequences. *Journal of Personality and Social Psychology, 84,* 1287–1302.

Jones, E. E. (1964). *Ingratiation: A social psychology analysis.* New York: Appleton-Century-Crofts.

Jones, E. E. (1979). The rocky road from acts to dispositions. *American Psychologist, 34,* 107–117.

Jones, E. E., & Davis, K. E. (1965). From acts to disposition: The attribution process in person perception. In L. Berkowitz (Ed.), *Advances in experimental social psychology* (Vol. 2, pp. 219–266). New York: Academic Press.

Jones, E. E., & Harris, V. A. (1967). The attribution of attitudes. *Journal of Experimental Social Psychology, 3,* 1–24.

Jones, E. E., & McGillis, D. (1976). Corresponding inferences and attribution cube: A comparative reappraisal. In J. H. Har, W. J. Ickes, & R. F. Kidd (Eds.), *New directions in attribution research* (Vol. 1). Morristown, NJ: Erlbaum.

Jones, E. E., & Nisbett, R. E. (1971). *The actor and the observer: Divergent perceptions of the causes of behavior.* Morristown, NJ: General Learning Press.

Jones, J. H. (1997, August 25 and September 1). Dr. Yes. *New Yorker,* 98–110, 112–113.

Judd, C. M., Ryan, C. S., & Parke, B. (1991). Accuracy in the judgment of in-group and out-group variability. *Journal of Personality and Social Psychology, 61,* 366–379.

Kahneman, D., & Miller, D. T. (1986). Norm theory: Comparing reality to its alternatives. *Psychological Review, 93,* 136–153.

Kallgren, C. A., Reno, R. R., & Cialdini, R. B. (2000). A focus theory of normative conduct: When norms do and do not affect behavior. *Personality and Social Psychology Bulletin, 26,* 1002–1012.

Kameda, T., & Sugimori, S. (1993). Psychological entrapment in group decision making: An assigned decision rule and a groupthink phenomenon. *Journal of Personality and Social Psychology, 65,* 282–292.

Kandel, D. B. (1978). Similarity in real-life adolescent friendship pairs. *Journal of Personality and Social Psychology, 36,* 306–312.

Kanagawa, C., Cross, S. E., & Markus, H. R. (2001). "Who am I?" The cultural psychology of the conceptual self. *Personality and Social Psychology Bulletin, 27,* 90–103.

Karau, S. J., & Williams, K. D. (1993). Social loafing: A meta-analytic review and theoretical integration. *Journal of Personality and Social Psychology, 65,* 681–706.

Karraker, K. H., & Stern, M. (1990). Infant physical attractiveness and facial expression: Effects on adult perceptions. *Basic and Applied Social Psychology, 11,* 371–385.

Karremans, J. C., Van Lange, P. A. M., Ouwerkerk, J. W., & Kluwer, E. S. (2003). When forgiving enhances psychological well-being: The role of interpersonal commitment. *Journal of Personality and Social Psychology, 84,* 1011–1026.

Katz, D. (1960). The functional approach to the study of attitudes. *Journal of Abnormal and Social Psychology, 70,* 1037–1051.

Katz, J., & Beach, S. R. H. (2000). Looking for love? Self-verification and self-enhancement effects on initial romantic attraction. *Personality and Social Psychology Bulletin, 26,* 1526–1539.

Kawakami K., & Dovidio, J. F. (2001). The reliability of implicit stereotyping. *Personality and Social Psychology Bulletin, 27,* 212–225.

Kawakami, K., Dion, K. L., & Dovidio, J. F. (1998). Racial prejudice and stereotype activation. *Personality and Social Psychology Bulletin, 24,* 407–416.

Kawakami K., Dovidio, J. F., Moll, J., Hermsen, S., & Russn, A. (2000). Just say no (to stereotyping): Effects of training in the negation of stereotypic associations on stereotype activation. *Journal and Personality and Social Psychology, 78,* 871–888.

Kellerman, J., Lewis, J., & Laird, J. D. (1989). Looking and loving: The effects of mutual gaze on feelings of romantic love. *Journal of Research in Personality, 23,* 145–161.

Kelley, H. H. (1972). Attribution in social interaction. In E. E. Jones et al. (Eds.), *Attribution: Perceiving the causes of behavior.* Morristown, NJ: General Learning Press.

Kelley, H. H., & Michela, J. L. (1980). Attribution theory and research. *Annual Review of Psychology, 31,* 57–501.

Kelly, A. E., & Kahn, J. H. (1994). Effects of suppression of personal intrusive thoughts. *Journal of Personality and Social Psychology, 66,* 998–1026.

Kelman, H. C. (1967). Human use of human subjects: The problem of deception in social psychological experiments. *Psychological Bulletin, 67,* 1–11.

Keltner, D., & Robinson, R. J. (1997). Defending the status quo: Power and bias in social conflict. *Personality and Social Psychology Bulletin, 23,* 1066–1077.

Keltner, D., Young, R. C., Heerey, E. A., Oemig, C., & Monarch, N. D. (1998). Teasing in hierarchical and intimate relations. *Journal of Personality and Social Psychology, 75,* 1231–1247.

Kenealy, P., Gleeson, K., Frude, N., & Shaw, W. (1991). The importance of the individual in the 'causal' relationship between attractiveness and self-esteem. *Journal of Community and Applied Social Psychology, 1,* 45–56.

Kenrick, D. T., & Gutierres, S. E. (1980). Contrast effects and judgments of physical attractiveness: When beauty becomes a social problem. *Journal of Personality and Social Psychology, 38,* 131–140.

Kenrick, D. T., Montello, D. R., Gutierres, S. E., & Trost, M. R. (1993). Effects of physical attractiveness on affect and perceptual judgments: When social comparison overrides social reinforcement. *Personality and Social Psychology Bulletin, 19,* 195–199.

Kenrick, D. T., Neuberg, S. L., Zierk, K. L., & Krones, J. M. (1994). Evolution and social cognition: Contrast effects as a function of sex, dominance, and physical attractiveness. *Personality and Social Psychology Bulletin, 20,* 210–217.

Kenrick, D. T., Sundie, J. M., Nicastle, L. D., & Stone, G. O. (2001). Can one ever be too wealthy or too chaste? Searching for non-linearities in mate judgement. *Journal of Personality and Social Psychology, 80,* 462–471.

Kenworthy, J. B., & Miller, N. (2001). Perceptual asymmetry in consensus estimates of majority and minority members. *Journal of Personality and Social Psychology, 80,* 597–612.

Kernis, M. H., Cornell, D. P., Sun, C. R., Berry, A. J., & Harlow, T. (1993). There's more to self-esteem than whether it is high or low: The importance of stability of self-esteem. *Journal of Personality and Social Psychology, 65,* 1190–1204.

Kerr, N. L., & Kaufman-Gilliland, C. M. (1994). Communication, commitment, and cooperation in social dilemmas. *Journal of Personality and Social Psychology, 66,* 513–529.

Kerr, N. L., Garst, J., Lewandowski, D. A., & Harris, S. E. (1997). That still, small voice: Commitment to cooperate as an internalized versus a social norm. *Personality and Social Psychology Bulletin, 23,* 1300–1311.

Kilduff, M., & Day, D. V. (1994). Do chameleons get ahead? The effects of self-monitoring on managerial careers. *Academy of Management Journal, 37,* 1047–1060.

Kilham, W., & Mann, L. (1974). Level of destructive obedience as a function of transmitter and executant roles in the Milgram obedience paradigm. *Journal of Personality and Social Psychology, 29,* 696–702.

Killeya, L. A., & Johnson, B. T. (1998). Experimental induction of biased systematic processing: The directed through technique. *Personality and Social Psychology Bulletin, 24,* 17–33.

Kilmartin, C. T. (1994). *The masculine self.* New York: Macmillan.

Kim, H., & Markus, H. R. (1999). Deviance or uniqueness, harmony or conformity? A cultural analysis. *Journal of Personality and Social Psychology, 77,* 785–800.

Kisner, R. D. (2004, April 12). A European marriage. *The New Yorker,* 7.

Kitzmann, K. M., Cohen, R., & Lockwood, R. L. (2002). Are only children missing out? Comparison of the peer-related social competence of only children and siblings. *Journal of Social and Personal Relationships, 19,* 299–316.

Klagsbrun, F. (1992). *Mixed feelings: Love, hate, rivalry, and reconciliation among brothers and sisters.* New York: Bantam.

Klandermans, B. (1997). *The social psychology of protest.* Oxford, UK: Basil Blackwell.

Klar, Y. (2002). Way beyond compare: The non-selective superiority and inferiority biases in judging randomly assigned group members relative to their peers. *Journal of Experimental Social Psychology, 38,* 331–351.

Klein, S. B., & Loftus, J. (1993). Behavioral experience and trait judgments about the self. *Personality and Social Psychology Bulletin, 16,* 740–745.

Klein, S. B., Loftus, J., & Plog, A. E. (1992). Trait judgments about the self: Evidence from the encoding specificity paradigm. *Personality and Social Psychology Bulletin, 18,* 730–735.

Klein, S. B., Loftus, J., Trafton, J. G., & Fuhrman, R. W. (1992). Use of exemplars and abstractions in trait judgments: A model of trait knowledge about the self and others. *Journal of Personality and Social Psychology, 63,* 739–753.

Kleinke, C. L. (1986). Gaze and eye contact: A research review. *Psychological Bulletin, 100,* 78–100.

Kling, K. C., Ryff, C. D., & Essex, M. J. (1997). Adaptive changes in the self-concept during a life transition. *Personality and Social Psychology Bulletin, 23,* 981–990.

Klohnen, E. C., & Bera, S. (1998). Behavioral and experiential patterns of avoidantly and securely attached women across adulthood: A 31-year longitudinal perspective. *Journal of Personality and Social Psychology, 74,* 211–223.

Klohnen, E. C., & Luo, S. (2003). Interpersonal attraction and personality: What is attractive—self similarity, ideal similarity, complementarity, or attachment security? *Journal of Personality and Social Psychology, 85,* 709–722.

Knee, C. R. (1998). Implicit theories of relationships: Assessment and prediction of romantic relationship initiation, coping, and longevity. *Journal of Personality and Social Psychology, 74,* 360–370.

Knight, G. P., & Dubro, A. (1984). Cooperative, competitive, and individualistic social values: An individualized regression and clustering approach. *Journal of Personality and Social Psychology, 46,* 98–105.

Koch, W. (1996, March 10). Marriage, divorce rates indicate Americans are hopelessly in love. *Albany Times Union,* p. A11.

Kochanska, G., Friesenborg, A. F., Lange, L. A., & Martel, M. M. (2004). Parents' personality and infants' temperament as contributors to their emerging relationship. *Journal of Personality and Social Psychology, 86,* 744–759.

Koehler, J. J. (1993). The base rate fallacy myth. *Psychology, 4.*

Koestner, R., Bernieri, F., & Zuckerman, M. (1992). Self-regulation and consistency between attitudes, traits, and behaviors. *Personality and Social Psychology Bulletin, 18,* 52–59.

Kogan, N., & Wallach, M. A. (1964). *Risk-taking: A study in cognition and personality.* New York: Henry Holt.

Komorita, M., & Parks, G. (1994). Interpersonal relations: Mixed-motive interaction. *Annual Review of Psychology, 46,* 183–207.

Kowalski, R. M. (1993). Interpreting behaviors in mixed-gender encounters: Effects of social anxiety and gender. *Journal of Social and Clinical Psychology, 12,* 239–247.

Kowalski, R. M., Walker, S., Wilkinson, R., Queen, A., & Sharpe, B. (2003). Lying, cheating, complaining, and other aversive interpersonal behaviors: A narrative examination of the darker side of relationships. *Journal of Social and Personal Relationships, 20,* 471–490.

Krosnick, J. A. (1988). The role of attitude importance in social evaluation: A study of political preferences, presidential candidate evaluations, and voting behavior. *Journal of Personality and Social Psychology, 55,* 196–210.

Krosnick, J. A. (1989). Attitude importance and attitude accessibility. *Personality and Social Psychology Bulletin, 15,* 297–308.

Krosnick, J. A., Betz, A. L., Jussim, L. J., & Lynn, A. R. (1992). Subliminal conditioning of attitudes. *Personality and Social Psychology Bulletin, 18,* 152–162.

Kulik, J. A., Mahler, H. I. M., & Moore, P. J. (1996). Social comparison and affiliation under threat: Effects on recovery from major surgery. *Journal of Personality and Social Psychology, 71,* 967–979.

Kunda, Z. (1999). *Social cognition: Making sense of people.* Cambridge, MA: MIT Press.

Kunda, Z., & Oleson, K. C. (1995). Maintaining stereotypes in the face of disconfirmation: Constructing grounds for subtyping deviants. *Journal of Personality and Social Psychology, 68,* 565–579.

Kurdek, L. A. (1993). The allocation of household labor in gay, lesbian, and heterosexual married couples. *Journal of Social Issues, 49*(3), 127–139.

Kurdek, L. A. (1996). The deterioration of relationship quality for gay and lesbian cohabiting couples: A five-year prospective longitudinal study. *Personal Relationships, 3,* 417–442.

Kurdek, L. A. (1997). Adjustment to relationship dissolution in gay, lesbian, and heterosexual partners. *Personal Relationships, 4,* 145–161.

Kurdek, L. A. (1999). The nature and predictors of the trajectory of change in marital quality for husbands and wives over the first 10 years of marriage: Predicting the seven-year itch. *Journal of Developmental Psychology, 35,* 1283–1296.

Kurdek, L. A. (2003). Differences between gay and lesbian cohabiting couples. *Journal of Social and Personal Relationships, 20,* 411–436.

Kwon, Y.-H. (1994). Feeling toward one's clothing and self-perception of emotion, sociability, and work competency. *Journal of Social Behavior and Personality, 9,* 129–139.

Lalonde, R. N., & Silverman, R. A. (1994). Behavioral preferences in response to social injustice: The effects of group permeability and social identity salience. *Journal of Personality and Social Psychology, 66,* 78–85.

LaMastro, V. (2001). Childless by choice? Attributions and attitudes concerning family size. *Social Behavior and Personality, 29,* 231–244.

Lambert, A. J. (1995). Stereotypes and social judgment: The consequences of group variability. *Journal of Personality and Social Psychology, 68,* 388–403.

Lambert, T. A., Kahn, A. S., & Apple, K. J. (2003). Pluralistic ignorance and hooking up. *Journal of Sex Research, 40,* 129–133.

Lamm, H., & Myers, D. G. (1978). Group-induced polarization of attitudes and behavior. In L. Berkowitz (Ed.), *Advances in experimental social psychology.* New York: Academic Press.

Langer, E. (1984). *The psychology of control.* Beverly Hills, CA: Sage.

Langlois, J. H., & Roggman, L. A. (1990). Attractive faces are only average. *Psychological Science, 1,* 115–121.

Langlois, J. H., Kalakanis, L., Rubinstein, A. J., Larson, A. I., Hallam, M., & Smoot, M. (2000). Maxims or myths of beauty: A meta-analytic and theoretical review. *Psychological Bulletin, 126,* 390–423.

Lapham, L. H. (1996, September). Back to school. *Harper's Magazine,* 10–11.

LaPiere, R. T. (1934). Attitude and actions. *Social Forces, 13,* 230–237.

Larson, J. R., Jr., Christensen, C., Franz, T. M., & Abbott, A. S. (1998). Diagnosing groups: The pooling, management, and impact of shared and unshared case information in team-based medical decision making. *Jounral of Personality and Social Psychology, 75,* 93–108.

Larson, J. R., Jr., Foster-Fishman, P. G., & Franz, T. M. (1998). Leadership style and the discussion of shared and unshared information in decision-making groups. *Personality and Social Psychology Bulletin, 24,* 482–495.

Latané, B., & Darley, J. M. (1968). Group inhibition of bystander intervention in emergencies. *Journal of Personality and Social Psychology, 10,* 215–221.

Latané, B., & Darley, J. M. (1970). *The unresponsive bystander: Why doesn't he help?* New York: Appleton-Century-Crofts.

Latané, B., & L'Herrou, T. (1996). Spatial clustering in the conformity game: Dynamic social impact in electronic groups. *Journal of Personality and Social Psychology, 70,* 1218–1230.

Latané, B., Williams, K., & Harkins, S. (1979). Many hands make light the work: The causes and consequences of social loafing. *Journal of Personality and Social Psychology, 37,* 822–832.

Lau, S., & Gruen, G. E. (1992). The social stigma of loneliness: Effect of target person's and perceiver's sex. *Personality and Social Psychology Bulletin, 18,* 182–189.

Laurenceau, J.-P., Barrett, L. F., & Pietromonaco, P. R. (1998). Intimacy as an interpersonal process: The importance of self-disclosure, partner disclosure, and perceived partner responsiveness in interpersonal exchanges. *Journal of Personality and Social Psychology, 74,* 1238–1251.

Leary, M. R. (1999). Making sense of self-esteem. *Current Directions in Psychological Science, 8,* 32–35.

Leary, M. R., Tambor, E. S., Terdal, S. K., & Downs, D. L. (1995). Self-esteem as an interpersonal monitor: The sociometer hypothesis. *Journal of Personality and Social Psychology, 68,* 518–530.

LeBlanc, M. M., & Barling, J. (2004). Workplace aggression. *Current Directions in Psychological Science, 13,* 9–12.

Lee, A. Y. (2001). The mere exposure effect: An uncertainty reduction explanation revisited. *Personality and Social Psychology Bulletin, 27,* 1255–1266.

Lee, Y. T., & Seligman, M. E. P. (1997). Are Americans more optimistic than the Chinese? *Personality and Social Psychology Bulletin, 23,* 32–40.

Lehman, T. C., Daubman, K. A., Guarna, J., Jordan, J., & Cirafesi, C. (1995, April). *Gender differences in the motivational consequences of receiving help.* Paper presented at the meeting of the Eastern Psychological Association, Boston.

Leippe, M. R., & Eisenstadt, D. (1994). Generalization of dissonance reduction: Decreasing prejudice through induced compliance. *Journal of Personality and Social Psychology, 67,* 395–413.

Lemley, B. (2000, February). Isn't she lovely? *Discover,* 42–49.

Lemonick, M. D., & Dorfman, A. (2001, July 23). One giant step for mankind. *Time,* 54–61.

Levenson, R. W., Carstensen, L. L., & Gottman, J. M. (1994). The influence of age and gender on affect, physiology, and their interrelations: A study of long-term marriages. *Journal of Personality and Social Psychology, 67,* 56–68.

Leventhal, G. S., Karuza, J., & Fry, W. R. (1980). Beyond fairness: A theory of allocation preferences. In G. Mikula (Ed.), *Justice and social interaction* (pp. 167–218). New York: Springer-Verlag.

Levine, R. V., Martinez, T. S., Brase, G., & Sorenson, K. (1994). Helping in 36 U.S. cities. *Journal of Personality and Social Psychology, 67,* 69–82.

Levy, K. N., & Kelly, K. (2002; July/August). Sex differences in jealousy: Evolutionary style or attachment style? *American Psychological Society,* 25–49.

Lewis, M. (1992). Will the real self or selves please stand up? *Psychological Inquiry, 3,* 123–124.

Leyens, J.-P., Desert, M., Croizet, J.-C., & Darcis, C. (2000). Stereotype threat: Are lower status and history of stigmatization preconditions of stereotype threat? *Personality and Social Psychology Bulletin, 26,* 1189–1199.

Li, N. P., Bailey, J. M., Kenrick, D. T., & Linsenmeier, J. A. W. (2002). The necessities and luxuries of male preferences: Testing the tradeoffs. *Journal of Personality and Social Psychology, 82,* 947–955.

Liberman, A., & Chaiken, S. (1992). Defensive processing of personally relevant health messages. *Personality and Social Psychology Bulletin, 18,* 669–679.

Lickel, B., Hamilton, D. L., & Sherman, S. J. (2001). Elements of a lay theory of groups: Types of groups, relational styles, and the perception of group entitativity. *Personality and Social Psychology Review, 5,* 129–140.

Lickel, B., Hamilton, D. L., Wieczorkowski, G., Lewis, A., Sherman, S. J., & Uhles, A. N. (2000). Varieties of groups and the perception of group entiativity. *Journal of Personality and Social Psychology, 78,* 223–246.

Liden, R. C., & Mitchell, T. R. (1988). Ingratiatory behaviors in organizational settings. *Academy of Management Review, 13,* 572–587.

Lieberman, J. D., & Greenberg, J. (1999). Cognitive-experiential self-theory and displaced aggression. *Journal of Personality and Social Psychology,* in press.

Linden, E. (1992). Chimpanzees with a difference: Bonobos. *National Geographic, 18*(3), 46–53.

Linville, P. W. (1987). Self-complexity as a cognitive buffer against stress-related illness and depression. *Journal of Personality and Social Psychology, 52,* 663–676.

Linville, P. W., Fischer, G. W., & Salovey, P. (1989). Perceived distributions of the characteristics of in-group and out-group members: Empirical evidence and a computer simulation. *Journal of Personality and Social Psychology, 57,* 165–188.

Linz, D., Donnerstein, E., & Penrod, S. (1988). Effects of long-term exposure to violent and sexually degrading depictions of women. *Journal of Personality and Social Psychology, 55,* 758–768.

Linz, D., Fuson, I. A., & Donnerstein, E. (1990). Mitigating the negative effects of sexually violent mass communications through pre-exposure briefings. *Communication Research, 17,* 641–674.

Lipkus, I. M., Green, J. D., Feaganes, J. R., & Sedikides, C. (2001). The relationships between attitudinal ambivalence and desire to quite smoking among college smokers. *Journal of Applied Social Psychology, 31,* 113–133.

Lippa, R., & Donaldson, S. I. (1990). Self-monitoring and idiographic measures of behavioral variability across interpersonal relationships. *Journal of Personality, 58,* 465–479.

Locke, V., & Johnston, L. (2001). Stereotyping and prejudice: A social cognitive approach. In M. Augoustinos & K. J. Reynolds (Eds.), *Understanding prejudice, racism, and social conflict* (pp. 107–125). London: Sage.

Locke, V., & Walker, I. (1999). Stereotyping, processing goals, and social identity: Inveterate and fugacious characteristics of stereotypes. In D. Abrams & M. A. Hogg (Eds.), *Social identity and social cognition* (pp. 164–182). Oxford: Blackwell.

Lockwood, P., & Kunda, Z. (1999). Increasing the salience of one's best selves can undermine inspiration by outstanding role models. *Journal of Personality and Social Psychology, 76,* 214–228.

Long, C. R., Seburn, M., Averill, J. R., & More, T. A. (2003). Solitude experiences: Varieties, settings, and individual differences. *Personality and Social Psychology Bulletin, 29,* 578–583.

Lopez, F. G., Gover, M. R., Leskela, J., Sauer, E. M., Schirmer, L., & Wyssmann, J. (1997). Attachment styles, shame, guilt, and collaborative problem-solving orientations. *Personal Relationships, 4,* 187–199.

Lord, C. G., & Saenz, D. S. (1985). Memory deficits and memory surfeits: Differential cognitive consequences of tokenism for tokens and observers. *Journal of Personality and Social Psychology, 49,* 918–926.

Lorenz, K. (1966). *On aggression.* New York: Harcourt, Brace, & World.

Lorenz, K. (1974). *Civilized man's eight deadly sins.* New York: Harcourt, Brace, Jovanovich.

Losch, M., & Cacioppo, J. (1990). Cognitive dissonance may enhance sympathetic tonis, but attitudes are changed to reduce negative affect rather than arousal. *Journal of Experimental Social Psychology, 26,* 289–304.

Luczak, S. E. (2001). Binge drinking in Chinese, Korean, and White college students: Genetic and ethnic group differences. *Psychology of Addictive Behaviors, 15,* 306–309.

Lundberg, J. K., & Sheehan, E. P. (1994). The effects of glasses and weight on perceptions of attractiveness and intelligence. *Journal of Social Behavior and Personality, 9,* 753–760.

Lyness, K. S., & Thompson, D. E. (1997). Above the glass ceiling? A comparison of matched samples of female and male executives. *Journal of Applied Psychology, 82,* 359–375.

Lyness, K. S., & Thompson, D. E. (2000). Climbing the corporate ladder: Do female and male executives follow the same route? *Journal of Applied Psychology, 85,* 86–101.

Ma, H. K., Shek, D. T. L., Cheung, P. C., & Tam, K. K. (2002). A longitudinal study of peer and teacher influences on prosocial and antisocial behavior of Hong Kong Chinese adolescents. *Social Behavior and Personality, 30,* 157–168.

Maass, A., & Clark, R. D. III (1984). Hidden impact of minorities: Fifteen years of minority influence research. *Psychological Bulletin, 95,* 233–243.

Macaulay, J. (1970). A shill for charity. In J. Macaulay & L. Berkowitz (Eds.), *Altruism and helping behavior* (pp. 43–59). New York: Academic Press.

Mack, D., & Rainey, D. (1990). Female applicants' grooming and personnel selection. *Journal of Social Behavior and Personality, 5,* 399–407.

Mackie, D. M., & Smith, E. R. (2002). Beyond prejudice: Moving from positive and negative evaluations to differentiated reactions to social groups. In D. M. Mackie & E. R. Smith (Eds.), *From prejudice to intergroup emotions: Differentiated reactions to social groups* (pp. 1–12). New York: Psychology Press.

Mackie, D. M., & Worth, L. T. (1989). Cognitive deficits and the mediation of positive affect in persuasion. *Journal of Personality and Social Psychology, 57,* 27–40.

Macrae, C. N., Milne, A. B., & Bodenhausen, G. V. (1994). Stereotypes as energy-saving devices: A peek inside the cognitive toolbox. *Journal of Personality and Social Psychology, 66,* 37–47.

Macrae, C. N., Mitchell, J. P., & Pendry, L. F. (2002). What's in a forename? Cue familiarity and stereotypical thinking. *Journal of Experimental Social Psychology, 38,* 186–193.

Macrae, C. N., Bodenhausen, G. V., Milne, A. B., & Ford, R. (1997). On the regulation of recollection: The intentional forgetting of

steretypical memories. *Journal of Personality and Social Psychology, 72,* 709–719.

Maeda, E., & Ritchie, L. D. (2003). The concept of *shinyuu* in Japan: A replication of and comparison to Cole and Bradac's study on U.S. friendship. *Journal of Social and Personal Relationships, 20,* 579–598.

Maestripieri, D. (2001). Biological bases of maternal attachment. *Current Directions in Psychological Science, 10,* 79–82.

Magner, N. R., Johnson, G. G., Sobery, J. S., & Welker, R. B. (2000). Enhancing procedural justice in local government budget and tax decision making. *Journal of Applied Social Psychology, 30,* 798–815.

Maheswaran, D., & Chaiken, S. (1991). Promoting systematic processing in low-motivation settings: Effect of incongruent information on processing and judgment. *Journal of Personality and Social Psychology, 61,* 13–25.

Mahoney, S. (2003, November & December). Seeking love. *AARP Magazine,* 66–67.

Maio, G. R., Esses, V. M., & Bell, D. W. (1994). The formation of attitudes toward new immigrant groups. *Journal of Applied Social Psychology, 24,* 1762–1776.

Maisonneuve, J., Palmade, G., & Fourment, C. (1952). Selective choices and propinquity. *Sociometry, 15,* 135–140.

Major, B. (1994). From social inequality to personal entitlement: The role of social comparisons, legitimacy appraisals, and group membership. In M. P. Zanna (Ed.), *Advances in experimental social psychology* (Vol. 26, pp. 293–348). San Diego, CA: Academic Press.

Major, B., Kaiser, D. R., & McCoy, S. K. (2003). It's not my fault; When and why attributions to prejudice protect self-esteem. *Personality and Social Psychology Bulletin, 29,* 772–781.

Major, B., Barr, L., Zubek, J., & Babey, S. H. (1999). Gender and self-esteem: A meta-analysis. In W. B. Swann, J. H. Langlois, & L. A. Gilbert (Eds.), *Sexism and stereotypes in modern society* (pp. 223–253). Washington, DC: American Psychological Association.

Malamuth, N. M., & Brown, L. M. (1994). Sexually aggressive men's perceptions of women's communications: testing three explanations. *Journal of Personality and Social Psychology, 67,* 699–712.

Malamuth, N. M., & Check, J. V. P. (1985). The effects of aggressive pornography on beliefs in rape myths: Individual differences. *Journal of Research in Personality, 19,* 299–320.

Malone, B. E., & DePaulo, B. M. (2003). Measuring sensitivity to deception. In J. A. Hall & F. J. Bernieri (Eds.), *Interpersonal sensitivity: Theory and measurement* (pp. 103–124). Mahwah, NJ: Lawrence Erlbaum.

Maner, J. K., Luce, E. L., Neuberg, S. L., Ciaddini, R. B., Brown, S., & Sagarin, B. J. (2002). The effects of perspective taking on motivations for helping: Still no evidence for altruism. *Personality and Social Psychology Bulletin, 28,* 1601–1610.

Manning, J. T., Koukourakis, K., & Brodie, D. A. (1997). Fluctuating asymmetry, metabolic

rate and sexual selection in human males. *Evolution and Human Behavior, 18,* 15–21.

Manstead, A. S. R. (2000). The role of moral norm in the attitude-behavior relation. In D. J. Terry & M. A. Hogg (Eds.), *Attitudes, behavior, and social context* (pp. 11–30). Mahwah, NJ: Erlbaum.

Marcus, D. K., & Miller, R. S. (2003). Sex differences in judgments of physical attractiveness: A social relations analysis. *Personality and Social Psychology Bulletin, 29,* 325–335.

Markey, P. M., Funder, D. C., & Ozer, D. J. (2003). Complementarity of interpersonal behaviors in dyadic interactions. *Personality and Social Psychology Bulletin, 29,* 1082–1090.

Markman, G. D., Balkin, D. B., & Baron R. A. (2002). Inventors and new venture formation: The effects of general self-efficacy and regretful thinking. *Entrepreneurship Theory & Practice, 27,* 149–165.

Markus, H., & Kitayama, S. (1991). Culture and the self: Implications for cognition, emotion, and motivation. *Psychological Review, 98,* 224–253.

Markus, H., & Nurius, P. (1986). Possible selves. *American Psychologist, 41,* 954–969.

Marques, J., & Paez, D. (1994). The "black sheep effect": Social categorization, rejection of ingroup deviates, and perception of group variability. *European Review of Social Psychology, 5,* 37–68.

Martin, C. L., & Parker, S. (1995). Folk theories about sex and race differences. *Personality and Social Psychology Bulletin, 21,* 45–57.

Martin, R. (1997). "Girls don't talk about garages!": Perceptions of conversation in same- and cross-sex friendships. *Personal Relationships, 4,* 115–130.

Martz, J. M., Verette, J., Arriaga, X. B., Slovik, L. F., Cox, C. L., & Rusbult, C. E. (1998). Positive illusion in close relationships. *Personal Relationships, 5,* 159–181.

Maslach, C., Santee, R. T., & Wade, C. (1987). Individuation, gender role, and dissent: Personality mediators of situational forces. *Journal of Personality and Social Psychology, 53,* 1088–1094.

Mastekaasa, A. (1995). Age variation in the suicide rates and self-reported subjective well-being of married and never married persons. *Journal of Community and Applied Social Psychology, 5,* 21–39.

Maticka-Tyndale, E., Herold, E. S., & Oppermann, M. (2003). Casual sex among Australian schoolies. *Journal of Sex Research, 40,* 158–169.

Matsushima, R., & Shiomi, K. (2001). Self-disclosure and friendship in junior high school students. *Social Behavior and Personality, 30,* 515–526.

May, J. L., & Hamilton, P. A. (1980). Effects of musically evoked affect on women's interpersonal attraction and perceptual judgments of physical attractiveness of men. *Motivation and Emotion, 4,* 217–228.

Mayer, J. D., & Hanson, E. (1995). Mood-congruent judgment over time. *Personality and Social Psychology Bulletin, 21,* 237–244.

Mayo, C., & Henley, N. M. (Eds.). (1981). *Gender and nonverbal behavior.* Seacaucus, NJ: Springer-Verlag.

McAndrew, F. T. (2002). New evolutionary perspectives on altruism: Multilevel-selection and costly-signaling theories. *Current Directions in Psychological Science, 11,* 79–82.

McArthur, L. Z., & Friedman, S. A. (1980). Illusory correlation in impression formation: Variations in the shared distinctiveness effect as a function of the distinctive person's age, race, and sex. *Journal of Personality and Social Psychology, 39,* 615–624.

McCall, M. (1997). Physical attractiveness and access to alcohol: What is beautiful does not get carded. *Journal of Applied Social Psychology, 23,* 453–562.

McClure, J. (1998). Discounting causes of behavior: Are two reasons better than one? *Journal of Personality and Social Psychology, 74,* 7–20.

McConahay, J. B. (1986). Modern racism, ambivalence, and the Modern Racism Scale. In J. F. Dovidio & S. L. Gaertner (Eds.), *Prejudice, discrimination, and racism* (pp. 91–125). New York: Academic Press.

McConnell, A. R., Sherman, S. J., & Hamilton, D. L. (1994). Illusory correlation in the perception of groups: An extension of the distinctiveness-based account. *Journal of Personality and Social Psychology, 67,* 414–429.

McCullough, M. E., Fincham, F. D., & Tsang, J. A. (2003). Forgiveness, forbearance, and time: The temporal unfolding of transgression-related interpersonal motivations. *Journal of Personality and Social Psychology, 84,* 540–557.

McCullough, M. E., Bellah, C. G., Kilpatrick, S. D, & Johnson, S. L. (2001). Vengefulness: Relationships with forgiveness, rumination, well-being, and the Bit Five. *Personality and Social Psychology Bulletin, 27,* 601–610.

McCullough, M. E., Emmons, R. A., Kilpatrick S. D., & Mooney, C. N. (2003). Narcissists as "Victims": The role of narcissism in the perception of transgressions. *Personality and Social Psychology Bulletin, 29,* 885–893.

McDonald, F. (2001). *States' rights and the union: Imperium in imperio, 1776–1876.* Lawrence: University of Kansas Press.

McDonald, H. E., & Hirt, E. R. (1997). When expectancy meets desire: Motivational effects in reconstructive memory. *Journal of Personality and Social Psychology, 72,* 5–23.

McDonald, R. D. (1962). *The effect of reward–punishment and affiliation need on interpersonal attraction.* Unpublished doctoral dissertation, University of Texas.

McGuire, S., & Clifford, J. (2000). Genetic and environmental contributions to loneliness in children. *Psychological Science, 11,* 487–491.

McGuire, S., McHale, S. M., & Updegraff, K. A. (1996). Children's perceptions of the sibling relationship in middle childhood: Connections within and between family relationships. *Personal Relationships, 3,* 229–239.

McGuire, W. J. (1961). Resistance to persuasion confirmed by active and passive prior refutation of the same and alternate counterarguments. *Journal of Abnormal and Social Psychology, 63,* 326–332.

McGuire, W. J., & McGuire, C. V. (1996). Enhancing self-esteem by directed-thinking tasks: Cognitive and affective positivity asymmetries. *Journal of Personality and Social Psychology, 70,* 1117–1125.

McGuire, W. J., & Papageorgis, D. (1961). The relative efficacy of various types of prior belief-defense in producing immunity against persuasion. *Journal of Abnormal and Social Psychology, 62,* 327–337.

McKelvie, S. J. (1993a). Perceived cuteness, activity level, and gender in schematic babyfaces. *Journal of Social Behavior and Personality, 8,* 297–310.

McKelvie, S. J. (1993b). Stereotyping in perception of attractiveness, age, and gender in schematic faces. *Social Behavior and Personality, 21,* 121–128.

McLaughlin, L. (2001a, April 30). Happy together. *Time,* 82.

McNulty, J. K., & Karney, B. R. (2004). Positive expectations in the early years of marriage: Should couples expect the best or brace for the worst? *Journal of Personality and Social Psychology, 86,* 729–743.

Mead, G. H. (1934). *Mind, self, and society.* Chicago: University of Chicago Press.

Medvec, V. H., Madey, S. F., & Gilovich, T. (1995). When less is more: Counterfactual thinking and satisfaction among Olympic athletes. *Journal of Personality and Social Psychology, 69,* 603–610.

Mehrabian, A., & Piercy, M. (1993). Affective and personality characteristics inferred from length of first names. *Personality and Social Psychology Bulletin, 19,* 755–758.

Meier, B. P., Robinson, M. D., & Clore, G. L. (2004). Why good guys wear white. Automatic interferences about stimulus valence based on brightness. *Psychological Science, 15,* 82–87.

Mendoza-Denton, R., Ayduk, O., Mischel, W., Shoda, Y., & Testa, A. (2001). Person X situation interactionism in self-encoding (*I am . . . When . . .*): Implications for affect regulation and social information processing. *Journal of Personality and Social Psychology, 80,* 533–544.

Meyers, S. A., & Berscheid, E. (1997). The language of love: The difference a preposition makes. *Personality and Social Psychology Bulletin, 23,* 347–362.

Miall, D., & Dissanayake, E. (2004). The poetics of babytalk. *Human Nature, 14,* 337–364.

Michael, R. T., Gagnon, J. H., Laumann, E. O., & Kolata, G. (1994). *Sex in America: A definitive survey.* Boston: Little, Brown.

Mikulincer, M. (1998a). Adult attachment style and individual differences in functional versus dysfunctional experiences of anger. *Journal of Personality and Social Psychology, 74,* 513–524.

Mikulincer, M., Gillath, O., Halevy, V., Avihou, N., Avidan, S., & Eshkoli, N. (2001). Attachment theory and reactions to others' needs: Evidence that activation of the sense of attachment security promotes empathic responses. *Journal of Personality and Social Psychology, 81,* 1205–1224.

Milanese, M. (2002, May/June). Hooking up, hanging out, making up, moving on. *Stanford,* 62–65.

Miles, S. M., & Carey, G. (1997). Genetic and environmental architecture of human aggression. *Journal of Personality and Social Psychology, 72,* 207–217.

Milgram, S. (1963). Behavior study of obedience. *Journal of Abnormal and Social Psychology, 67,* 371–378.

Milgram, S. (1965a). Liberating effects of group pressure. *Journal of Personality and Social Psychology, 1,* 127–134.

Milgram, S. (1965b). Some conditions of obedience and disobedience to authority. *Human Relations, 18,* 57–76.

Milgram, S. (1974). *Obedience to authority.* New York: Harper.

Miller, D. A., Smith, E. R., & Mackie, D. M. (2004). Effects of intergroup contact and political predispositions on prejudice: Role of intergroup emotions. *Group Processes and Intergroup Relations, 7,* 221–237.

Miller, D. T., & Prentice, D. A. (1996). The construction of social norms and standards. In E. T. Higgins & A. W. Kruglanski (Eds.), *Social psychology: Handbook of basic principles* (pp. 799–829). New York: Guilford Press.

Miller, D. T., Monin, B., & Prentice, D. A. (2000). Pluralistic ignorance and inconsistency between private attitudes and public behaviors. In D. J. Terry & M. A. Hogg (Eds.), *Attitudes, behavior, and social context* (pp. 95–113). Mahwah, NJ: Erlbaum.

Miller, L. C., Putcha-Bhagavatula, A., & Pedersen, W. C. (2002, June). Men's and women's mating preferences: Distinct evolutionary mechanisms? *Current Directions in Psychological Science, 11,* 88–93.

Miller, N., Maruayama, G., Beaber, R. J., & Valone, K. (1976). Speed of speech and persuasion. *Journal of Personality and Social Psychology, 34,* 615–624.

Miller, P. J. E., & Rempel, J. K. (2004). Trust and partner-enhancing attributions in close relationships. *Personality and Social Psychology Bulletin, 30,* 695–705.

Mills, J., Clark, M. S., Ford, T. E., & Johnson, M. (2004). Measurement of communal strength. *Personal Relationships, 11,* 213–230.

MIT-report: A study on the status of women faculty in science at MIT. (1999). Cambridge, MA: Massachusetts Institute of Technology.

Monahan, J. L., Murphy, S. T., & Zajonc, R. B. (2000). Subliminal mere exposure: Specific, general, and diffuse effects. *Psychological Science, 11,* 462–466.

Mondloch, C. J., Lewis, T. L., Budreau, D. R., Maurer, D., Dannemiller, J. L., Stephens, B. R., & Kleiner-Gathercoal, K. A. (1999). Face perception during early infancy. *Psychological Science, 10,* 419–422.

Monin, B. (2003). The warm glow heuristic: When liking leads to familiarity. *Journal* of *Personality and Social Psychology, 85,* 1035–1048.

Montepare, J. M., & Zebrowitz-McArthur, L. (1988). Impressions of people created by age-related qualities of their gates. *Journal of Personality and Social Psychology, 55,* 547–556.

Montgomery, R. (2004, February 20). Trip down aisle a road less traveled. Knight Ridder. Albany *Times Union,* pp. A1, A6.

Montoya, R. M., & Horton, R. S. (2004). On the importance of cognitive evaluation as a determinant of interpersonal attraction. *Journal of Personality and Social Psychology, 86,* 696–712.

Moore, T. (1993, August 16). Millions of volunteers counter image of a selfish society. *Albany Times Union,* p. A-2.

Moreland, R. L., & Beach, S. R. (1992). Exposure effects in the classroom: The development of affinity among students. *Journal of Experimental Social Psychology, 28,* 255–276.

Morey, N., & Gerber, G. L. (1995). Two types of competitiveness: Their impact on the perceived interpersonal attractiveness of women and men. *Journal of Applied Social Psychology, 25,* 210–222.

Morris, M. W., & Larrick, R. P. (1995). When one cause casts doubt on another: A normative analysis of discounting in causal attribution. *Psychological Review, 102,* 331–335.

Morrison, E. W., & Bies, R. J. (1991). Impression management in the feedback-seeking process: A literature review and research agenda. *Academy of Management Review, 16,* 322–341.

Moscovici, S. (1985). Social influence and conformity. In G. Lindzey & E. Aronson (Eds.), *Handbook of social psychology* (3rd ed.). New York: Random House.

Mugny, G. (1975). Negotiations, image of the other and the process of minority influence. *European Journal of Social Psychology, 5,* 209–229.

Mullen, B. (1986). Stuttering, audience size, and the other-total ratio: A self-attention perspective. *Journal of Applied Social Psychology, 16,* 141–151.

Mullen, B., Migdal, M. J., & Rozell, D. (2003). Self-awareness, deindividuation, and social identity: Unraveling theoretical paradoxes by filling empirical lacunae. *Personality and Social Psychology Bulletin, 29,* 1071–1081.

Mummendey, A., & Schreiber, H. J. (1984). "Different" just means "better": Some obvious and some hidden pathways to ingroup favoritism. *British Journal of Social Psychology, 23,* 363–368.

Munro, G. D., & Ditto, P. H. (1997). Biased assimilation, attitude polarization, and affect in reactions to stereotype-relevant scientific information. *Personality and Social Psychology Bulletin, 23,* 636–653.

Murray, L., & Trevarthen, C. (1986). The infant's role in mother-infant communications. *Journal of Child Language, 13,* 15–29.

Murray, S. L., & Holmes, J. G. (1997). A leap of faith? Positive illusions in romantic relationships. *Personality and Social Psychology Bulletin, 23,* 586–604.

Murray, S. L., & Holmes, J. G. (1999). The (mental) ties that bind: Cognitive structures that predict relationship resilience. *Journal of Personality and Social Psychology, 77,* 1228–1244.

Murray, S. L., Holmes, J. G., Griffin, D. W., Bellavia, G., & Rose, P. (2001). The mismeasure of love: How self-doubt contaminates relationship beliefs. *Personality and Social Psychology Bulletin, 27,* 423–436.

Mussweiler, T., Gabriel, S., & Bodenhausen, G. V. (2000). Shifting social identities as a strategy for deflecting threatening social comparisons. *Journal of Personality and Social Psychology, 79,* 398–409.

Mynard, H., & Joseph, S. (1997). Bully victim problems and their association with Eysenck's personality dimensions in 8 to 13 year olds. *British Journal of Educational Psychology, 67,* 51–54.

Nadler, A. (1991). Help-seeking behavior: Psychological costs and instrumental benefits. In M. S. Clark (Ed.), *Prosocial behavior* (pp. 290–311). Newbury Park, CA: Sage.

Nadler, A., Fisher, J. D., & Itzhak, S. B. (1983). With a little help from my friend: Effect of a single or multiple acts of aid as a function of donor and task characteristics. *Journal of Personality and Social Psychology, 44,* 310–321.

National Institute for Occupational Safety and Health, Center for Disease Control and Prevention. "Homicide in the workplace." Document #705003, December 5, 1993.

Nemeth, C. J. (1995). Dissent as driving cognition, attitudes, and judgments. *Social Cognition, 13,* 273–291.

Nemeth, C. J., Connell, J. B., Rogers, J. D., & Brown, K. S. (2001). Improving decision making by means of dissent. *Journal of Applied Social Psychology, 31,* 45–58.

Neto, F., & Barrios, J. (2001). Predictors of loneliness among adolescents from Portuguese immigrant families in Switzerland. *Social Behavior and Personality, 28,* 193–206.

Neuberg, S. L., & Cottrell, C. A. (2002). Intergroup emotions: A biocultural approach. In D. M. Mackie & E. R. Smith (Eds.), *From prejudice to intergroup emotions: Differentiated reactions to social groups* (pp. 265–283). Philadelphia: Psychology Press.

Neuberg, S. L., & Newsom, J. T. (1993). Personal need for structure: Individual differences in the desire for simple structure. *Journal of Personality and Social Psychology, 65,* 113–131.

Neuman, J. H., & Baron, R. A. (1998). Workplace violence and workplace aggression: Evidence concerning specific forms, potential causes, and preferred targets. *Journal of Management, 24,* 391–420.

Neuman, J. H., & Baron, R. A. (2004). Aggression in the workplace: A social-psychological perspective. In S. Fox, & P. E. Spector (Eds.), *Counterproductive workplace behavior: An integration of both actor and recipient perspectives on causes and consequences.* Washington, DC: American Psychological Association.

Neumann, R., & Strack, F. (2000). "Mood contagion": The automatic transfer of mood between persons. *Journal of Personality and Social Psychology, 79,* 211–223.

Newcomb, T. M. (1956). The prediction of interpersonal attraction. *Psychological Review, 60,* 393–404.

Newcomb, T. M. (1961). *The acquaintance process.* New York: Holt, Rinehart and Winston.

Newman, M. L., Pennebaker, H. W., Berry, D. S., & Richards, J. M. (2003). Lying words: Predicting deception from linguistic styles. *Personality and Social Psychology Bulletin, 29,* 665–675.

Newsom, J. T. (1999). Another side to caregiving: Negative reactions to being helped. *Current Directions in Psychological Science, 8,* 183–187.

Newsweek Poll (May 24, 2004). The "Will and Grace" effect.

Newton, T. L., Kiecolt-Glaser, J. K., Glaser, R., & Malarkey, W. B. (1995). Conflict and withdrawal during marital interaction: The roles of hostility and defensiveness. *Personality and Social Psychology Bulletin, 21,* 512–524.

Neyer, F. J. (2002). Twin relationships in old age: A developmental perspective. *Journal of Social and Personal Relationships, 19,* 155–177.

Nida, S. A., & Koon, J. (1983). They get better looking at closing time around here, too. *Psychological Reports, 52,* 657–658.

Nienhuis, A. E., Manstead, A. S. R., & Spears, R. (2001). Multiple motives and persuasive communication: Creative elaboration as a result of impression motivation and accuracy motivation. *Personality and Social Psychology Bulletin, 27,* 118–132.

Nisbett, R. E. (1990). Evolutionary psychology, biology, and cultural evolution. *Motivation and Emotion, 14,* 255–264.

Nisbett, R. E., & Cohen, D. (1996). *Culture of honor: The psychology of violence in the South.* Boulder, CO: Westview Press.

Nisbett, R. E., & Wilson, T. D. (1977). Telling more than we can know: Verbal reports on mental processes. *Psychological Review, 84,* 231–259.

Noel, J. G., Wann, D. L., & Branscombe, N. R. (1995). Peripheral ingroup membership status and public negativity toward outgroups. *Journal of Personality and Social Psychology, 68,* 127–137.

Nolen-Hoeksema, S. (1987). Sex differences in unipolar depression: Evidence and theory. *Psychological Bulletin, 101,* 259–282.

Nunn, J. S., & Thomas, S. L. (1999). The angry male and the passive female: The role of gender and self-esteem in anger expression. *Social Behavior and Personality, 27,* 145–154.

Nussbaum, S., Trope, Y., & Liberman, N. (2003). Creeping dispositionism: The temporal dynamics of behavior prediction. *Journal of Personality and Social Psychology 84,* 485–497.

Nyman, L. (1995). The identification of birth order personality attributes. *The Journal of Psychology, 129,* 51–59.

O'Brien, M., & Bahadur, M. A. (1998). Marital aggression, mother's problem-solving behavior with children, and children's emotional and behavioral problems. *Journal of Social and Clinical Psychology, 17,* 249–272.

O'Connor, S. C., & Rosenblood, L. K. (1996). Affiliation motivation in everyday experience: A theoretical comparison. *Journal of Personality and Social Psychology, 70,* 513–522.

O'Donohue, W. (1997). *Sexual harassment: Theory, research, and treatment.* Boston: Allyn & Bacon.

O'Leary, S. G. (1995). Parental discipline mistakes. *Current Directions in Psychological Science, 4,* 11–13.

O'Moore, M. N. (2000). Critical issues for teacher training to counter bullying and victimization in Ireland. *Aggressive Behavior, 26,* 99–112.

O'Sullivan, C. S., & Durso, F. T. (1984). Effects of schema-incongruent information on memory for stereotypical attributes. *Journal of Personality and Social Psychology, 47,* 55–70.

O'Sullivan, M. (2003). The fundamental attribution error in detecting deception: The boy-who-cried-wolf effect. *Personality and Social Psychology Bulletin, 29,* 1316–1327.

Oakes, P. J., & Reynolds, K. J. (1997). Asking the accuracy question: Is measurement the answer? In R. Spears, P. J. Oakes, N. Ellemers, & S. A. Haslam (Eds.), *The social psychology of stereotyping and group life* (pp. 51–71). Oxford: Blackwell.

Oakes, P. J., Haslam, S. A., & Turner, J. C. (1994). *Stereotyping and social reality.* Oxford: Blackwell.

Oberlander, E. (2003, August). Cross-disciplinary perspectives on attachment processes. *American Psychological Society, 16,* 23, 35.

Oettingen, G. (1995). Explanatory style in the context of culture. In G. M. Buchanan & M. E. P. Seligman (Eds.)., *Explanatory style.* Hillsdale, NJ: Erlbaum.

Oettingen, G., & Seligman, M. E. P. (1990). Pessimism and behavioral signs of depression in East versus West Berlin. *European Journal of Social Psychology, 201,* 207–220.

Ohbuchi, K., & Kambara, T. (1985). Attacker's intent and awareness of outcome, impression management, and retaliation. *Journal of Experimental Social Psychology, 21,* 321–330.

Ohbuchi, K., Kameda, M., & Agarie, N. (1989). Apology as aggression control: Its role in mediating appraisal of and response to harm. *Journal of Personality and Social Psychology, 56,* 219–227.

Ohman, A., Lundqvist, D., & Esteves, F. (2001). The face in the crowd revisited: Threat advantage with schematic stimuli. *Journal of Personality and Social Psychology, 80,* 381–396.

Ohtsubo, Y., Miller, C. E., Hayashi, N., & Masuchi, A. (2004). Effects of group decision rules on decisions involving continuous alternatives: the unanimity rule and extreme decisions in mock civil juries. *Journal of Experimental Social Psychology, 40,* 320–331.

Olson, J. M., & Maio, G. R. (2003). Attitudes in social behavior. In T. Millon & M. J. Lerner (Eds.), *Handbook of psychology: Personality and social psychology* (Vol. 5., pp. 299–325). New York: Wiley.

Olson, M. A., & Fazio, R. H. (2001). Implicit attitude formation through classical conditioning. *Psychological Science, 12,* 413–417.

Olweus, D. (1993). *Bullying at school: What we know and what we can do.* Oxford: Blackwell.

Olweus, D. (1999). Sweden. In P. K. Smith, Y. Morita, J. Junger-Tas, D. Olweus, R. F. Catalano, & P. Slee (Eds.), *The nature of school bullying: A cross-national perspective* (pp. 7–27). New York: Routledge.

Onishi, M., Gjerde, P. F., & Block, J. (2001). Personality implications of romantic attachment patterns in young adults: A multi-method, multi-informant study. *Personality and Social Psychology Bulletin, 27,* 1097–1110.

Orbell, S., Blair, C., Sherlock, K., & Conner, M. (2001). The theory of planned behavior and ecstasy use: Roles for habit and perceived control over taking versus obtaining substances. *Journal of Applied Social Psychology, 31,* 31–47.

Orpen, C. (1996). The effects of ingratiation and self promotion tactics on employee career success. *Social Behavior and Personality, 24,* 213–214.

Osborne, J. W. (2001). Testing stereotype threat: Does anxiety explain race and sex differences in achievement? *Contemporary Educational Psychology, 26,* 291–310.

Österman, K., Björkqvist, K., Lagerspetz, K. M. J., Kaukiainen, A., Landua, S. F., Fraczek, A., & Caprara, G. V. (1998). Cross-cultural evidence of female indirect aggression. *Aggressive Behavior, 24,* 1–8.

Owens, L., Shute, R., & Slee, P. (2000). "Guess what I just heard!": Indirect aggression among teenage girls in Australia. *Aggressive Behavior, 26,* 57–66.

Packer, G. (2004). Caught in the crossfire. *The New Yorker,* May 17, 63–68, 70–73.

Paik, H., & Comstock, G. (1994). The effects of television violence on antisocial behavior: A meta-analysis. *Communication Research, 21,* 516–546.

Palmer, J., & Byrne, D. (1970). Attraction toward dominant and submissive strangers: Similarity versus complementarity. *Journal of Experimental Research in Personality, 4,* 108–115.

Paolini, S., Hewstone, M., Cairns, E., & Voci, A. (2004). Effects of direct and indirect cross-group friendships on judgments of Catholics and Protestants in Northern Ireland: The mediating role of an anxiety-reduction mechanism. *Personality and Social Psychology Bulletin, 30,* 770–786.

Park, J., & Banaji, M. R. (2000). Mood and heuristics: The influence of happy and sad states on sensitivity and bias in stereotyping. *Journal of Personality and Social Psychology, 78,* 1005–1023.

Patrick, H., Neighbors, C., & Knee, C. R. (2004). Appearance-related social comparisons: The role of contingent self-esteem and self-perceptions of attractiveness. *Personality and Social Psychology Bulletin, 30,* 501–514.

Paul, E. L., & Hayes, K. A. (2002). The casualties of "casual" sex: A qualitative exploration of the phenomenology of college students' hookups. *Journal of Social and Personal Relationships, 19,* 639–661.

Paulhus, D. L., Bruce, M. N., & Trapnell, P. D. (1995). Effects of self-presentation strategies on personality profiles and their structure. *Personality and Social Psychology Bulletin, 21,* 100–108.

Pavalko, E. K., Mossakowski, K. N., & Hamilton, V. J. (2003). Does perceived discrimination affect health? Longitudinal relationships between work discrimination and women's physical and emotional health. *Journal of Health and Social Behavior, 43,* 18–33.

Pearson, K., & Lee, A. (1903). On the laws of inheritance in man: I. Inheritance of physical characters. *Biometrika, 2,* 357–462.

Pederson, W. C., Gonzales, C., & Miller, N. (2000). The moderating effect of trivial triggering provocation on displaced aggression. *Journal of Personality and Social Psychology, 78,* 913–947.

Pelham, B. W., Mirenberg, M. C., & Jones, J. T. (2002). Why Susie sells seashells by the seashore: Implicit egotism and major life decisions. *Journal of Personality and Social Psychology, 82,* 469–487.

Pelham, B. W., Carvallo, M., DeHart, T., & Jones, T. J. (2003). Assessing the validity of implicit egotism: A reply to Gallucci (2003). *Journal of Personality and Social Psychology, 85,* 800–807.

Pennebaker, J. W., Dyer, M. A., Caulkins, R. S., Litowicz, D. L., Ackerman, P. L., & Anderson, D. B. (1979). Don't the girls all get prettier at closing time: A country and western application to psychology. *Personality and Social Psychology Bulletin, 5,* 122–125.

Penner, L. A., & Finkelstein, M. A. (1998). Dispositional and structural determinants of volunteerism. *Journal of Personality and Social Psychology, 74,* 525–537.

People. (2001, August 6). *U.S. News & World Report,* 14.

Perrett, D. I., May, K. A., & Yoshikawa, S. (1994). Facial shape and judgements of female attractiveness. *Nature, 368,* 239–242.

Perrewe, P. L., & Hochwarter, W. A. (2001). Can we really have it all? The attainment of work and family values. *Current Directions in Psychological Science, 10,* 29–32.

Pessin, J. (1933). The comparative effects of social and mechanical stimulation on memorizing. *American Journal of Psychology, 45,* 263–270.

Peterson, R. S., & Behfar, K. J. (2003). The dynamic relationship between performance feedback, trust, and conflict in groups: A longitudinal study. *Organizational Behavior and Human Decision Processes, 92,* 102–112.

Peterson, V. S., & Runyan, A. S. (1993). *Global gender issues.* Boulder, CO: Westview Press.

Pettigrew, T. F. (1969). Racially separate or together? *Journal of Social Issues, 24,* 43–69.

Pettigrew, T. F. (1979). The ultimate attribution error: Extending Allport's cognitive analysis of prejudice. *Personality and Social Psychology Bulletin, 5,* 461–476.

Pettigrew, T. F. (1981). Extending the stereotype concept. In D. L. Hamilton (Ed.), *Cognitive processes in stereotyping and intergroup behavior* (pp. 303–331). Hillsdale, NJ: Erlbaum.

Pettigrew, T. F. (1997). Generalized intergroup contact effects on prejudice. *Personality and Social Psychology Bulletin, 23,* 173–185.

Pettigrew, T. F. (2004). Justice deferred: A half-century after Brown v. Board of Education. *American Psychologist, 59,* 1–9.

Pettijohn, T. E. F., II, & Jungeberg, B. J. (2004). Playboy playmate curves: Changes in facial and body feature preferences across social and economic conditions. *Personality and Social Psychology Bulletin, 30,* 1186–1197.

Petty, R. E., & Cacioppo, J. T. (1986). The elaboration likelihood model of persuasion. In L. Berkowitz (Ed.), *Advances in experimental social psychology* (Vol. 19, pp. 123–205). New York: Academic Press.

Petty, R. E., & Cacioppo, J. T. (1990). Involvement and persuasion: Tradition versus integration. *Psychological Bulletin, 107,* 367–374.

Petty, R. E., Wheeler, C., & Tormala, Z. L. (2003). Persuasion and attitude change. In T. Millon & M. J. Lerner (Eds.), *Handbook of psychology: Personality and social psychology* (Vol. 5, pp. 353–382). New York: Wiley.

Petty, R. J., & Krosnick, J. A. (Eds.). (1995). *Attitude strength: Antecedents and consequences* (Vol. 4). Hillsdale, NJ: Erlbaum.

Phelps, E. A., O'Connor, K. J., Gatenby, J. C., Gore, J. C., Grillon, C., & Davis, M. (2001). Activation of the left amygdala to a cognitive representation of fear. *Nature Neuroscience, 4,* 437–441.

Pickett, C. L., Gardner, W. L., & Knowles, M. (2004). Getting a cue: The need to belong and enhanced sensitivity to social cues. *Personality and Social Psychology Bulletin, 30,* 1095–1107.

Pihl, R. O., Lau, M. L., & Assad, J. M. (1997). Aggressive disposition, alcohol, and aggression. *Aggressive Behavior, 23,* 11–18.

Piliavin, J. A., & Unger, R. K. (1985). *The helpful but helpless female: Myth or reality?* In V. E. O'Leary, R. K. Unger, & B. S. Wallston (Eds.), *Women, gender, and social psychology* (pp. 149–189). Hillsdale, NJ: Erlbaum.

Pines, A. (1997). Fatal attractions or wise unconscious choices: The relationship between causes for entering and breaking intimate relationships. *Personal Relationship Issues, 4,* 1–6.

Pinker, S. (1998). *How the mind works.* New York: Norton.

Pittman, T. S. (1993). Control motivation and attitude change. In G. Weary, F. Gleicher, & K. L. Marsh (Eds.), *Control motivation and social cognition* (pp. 157–175). New York: Springer-Verlag.

Pizarro, D., Uhlmann, E., & Salovey, P. (2003). Asymmetry in judgments of moral blame and praise: The role of perceived metadesires. *Psychological Science, 14,* 267–272.

Plant, E. A., Hyde, J. S., Keltner, D., & Devine, P. G. (2000). The gender stereotyping of emotions. *Psychology Women Quarterly, 24,* 81–92.

Pleban, R., & Tesser, A. (1981). The effects of relevance and quality of another's performance on interpersonal closeness. *Social Psychology Quarterly, 44,* 278–285.

Polivy, J., & Herman, C. P. (2000). The false-hope syndrome: Unfulfilled expectations of self-change. *Current Directions in Psychological Science, 9,* 128–131.

Pollak, K. I., & Niemann, Y. F. (1998). Black and white tokens in academia: A difference in chronic versus acute distinctiveness. *Journal of Applied Social Psychology, 28,* 954–972.

Pollock, C. L., Smith, S. D., Knowles, E. S., & Bruce, H. J. (1998). Mindfulness limits compliance with the that's-not-all technique. *Personality and Social Psychology Bulletin, 24,* 1153–1157.

Pontari, B. A., & Schlenker, B. R. (2000). The influence of cognitive load on self-presentation: Can cognitive busyness help as well as harm social performance? *Journal of Personality and Social Psychology, 78,* 1092–1108.

Ponzetti, J. J., Jr., & James, C. M. (1997). Loneliness and sibling relationships. *Journal of Social Behavior and Personality, 12,* 103–112.

Postmes, T., & Branscombe, N. R. (2002). Influence of long-term racial environmental composition on subjective well-being in African Americans. *Journal of Personality and Social Psychology, 83,* 735–751.

Postmes, T., & Spears, R. (1998). Deindividuation and antinormative behavior: A meta-analysis. *Psychological Bulletin, 123,* 238–259.

Pratto, F., & Bargh, J. A. (1991). Stereotyping based on apparently individuating information: Trait and global components of sex stereotypes under attentional overload. *Journal of Experimental Social Psychology, 27,* 26–47.

Previti, D., & Amato, P. R. (2004). Is infidelity a cause or a consequence of poor marital quality? *Journal of Social and Personal Relationships, 21,* 217–230.

Priester, J. R., & Petty, R. E. (2001). Extending the bases of subjective attitudinal ambivalence: Interpersonal and intrapersonal antecedents of evaluative tension. *Journal of Personality and Social Psychology, 80,* 19–34.

Pronin, E., Steele, C. M., & Ross, L. (2004). Identity bifurcation in response to stereotype threat: Women and mathematics. *Journal of Experimental Social Psychology, 40,* 152–168.

Pruitt, D. G., & Carnevale, P. J. (1993). *Negotiation in social conflict.* Pacific Grove, CA: Brooks/Cole.

Przybyla, D. P. J. (1985). *The facilitating effect of exposure to erotica on male prosocial behavior.* Unpublished doctoral dissertation, University at Albany, State University of New York.

Puente, S., & Cohen, D. (2003). Jealousy and the meaning (or nonmeaning) of violence. *Personality and Social Psychology Bulletin, 29,* 449–460.

Pyszczynski, T., & Greenberg, J. (1987). Toward an integration of cognitive and motivational perspectives on social inference: A biased hypothesis-testing model. *Advances in experimental social psychology, 20,* 297–341.

Pyszczynski, T., Greenberg, J., Solomon, S., Arndt, J., & Schimel, J. (2004). Why do people need self-esteem? A theoretical and empirical review. *Psychological Bulletin, 130,* 435–468.

Queller, S., & Smith, E. R. (2002). Subtyping versus bookkeeping in stereotype learning and change: Connectionist simulations and empirical findings. *Journal of Personality and Social Psychology, 82,* 300–313.

Quinn, J. M., & Wood, W. (2004). Forewarnings of influence appeals: Inducing resistance and acceptance. In E. S. Knowles & J. A. Linn (Eds.), *Resistance and persuasion* (pp. 193–213). Mahwah, NJ: Erlbaum.

Ray, G. E., Cohen, R., Secrist, M. E., & Duncan, M. K. (1997). Relating aggressive victimization behaviors to children's sociometric status and friendships. *Journal of Social and Personal Relationships, 14,* 95–108.

Read, S. J., & Miller, L. C. (1998). *Connectionist and PDP models of social reasoning and social behavior.* Mahwah, NJ: Erlbaum.

Redersdorff, S., Martinot, D., & Branscombe, N. R. (2004). The impact of thinking about group-based disadvantages or advantages on women's well-being: An experimental test of the rejection-identification model. *Current Psychology of Cognition, 22,* 203–222.

Regan, P. C. (1998). Of lust and love: Beliefs about the role of sexual desire in romantic relationships. *Personal Relationships, 5,* 139–157.

Regan, P. C. (2000). The role of sexual desire and sexual activity in dating relationships. *Social Behavior and Personality, 28,* 51–60.

Regan, P. C., Lyle, J. L., Otto, A. L., & Joshi, A. (2003). Pregnancy and changes in female sexual desire: A review. *Social Behavior and Personality, 31,* 603–612.

Reisman, J. M. (1984). Friendliness and its correlates. *Journal of Social and Clinical Psychology, 2,* 143–155.

Reiss, A. J., & Roth, J. A. (Eds.). (1993). *Understanding and preventing violence.* Washington, DC: National Academy Press.

Reno, R. R., Cialdini, R. B., & Kallgren, C. A. (1993). The transsituational influence of social norms. *Journal of Personality and Social Psychology, 64,* 104–112.

Rensberger, B. (1993, November 9). Certain chemistry between vole pairs. *Albany Times Union,* pp. C-1, C-3.

Rentsch, J. R., & Heffner, T. S. (1994). Assessing self-concept: Analysis of Gordon's coding scheme using "Who am I?" responses. *Journal of Social Behavior and Personality, 9,* 283–300.

Reskin, B., & Padavic, I. (1994). *Women and men at work.* Thousand Oaks, CA: Pine Forge Press.

Rhodes, G., & Tremewan, T. (1996). Averageness, exaggeration, and facial attractiveness. *Psychological Science, 7,* 105–110.

Rhodewalt, F., & Davison, J., Jr. (1983). Reactance and the coronary-prone behavior pattern: The role of self-attribution in response to reduced behavioral freedom. *Journal of Personality and Social Psychology, 44,* 220–228.

Richard, F. D., Bond, C. F., Jr., & Stokes-Zoota, J. J. (2001). "That's completely obvious . . . and important." Lay judgments of social psychological findings. *Personality and Social Psychology Bulletin, 27,* 497–505.

Richards, Z., & Hewstone, M. (2001). Subtyping and subgrouping: Processes for the prevention and promotion of stereotype change. *Personality and Social Psychology Review, 5,* 52–73.

Ridgeway, C. L. (2001). Social status and group structure. In M. A. Hogg & R. S. Tindale (Eds.), *Blackwell handbook of social psychology: Group processes* (pp. 352–375). Oxford: Blackwell.

Ridley, M., & Dawkins, R. (1981). The natural selection of altruism. In J. P. Rushton & R. M. Sorrentino (Eds.), *Altruism and helping behavior.* Hillsdale, NJ: Erlbaum.

Riess, M., & Schlenker, B. R. (1977). Attitude change and responsibility avoidance as modes of dilemma resolution in forced-compliance situations. *Journal of Personality and Social Psychology, 35,* 21–30.

Riggio, H. R. (2004). Parental marital conflict and divorce, parent-child relationships, social support, and relationship anxiety in young adulthood. *Personal Relationships, 11,* 99–114.

Ro, T., Russell, C., & Lavie, N. (2001). Changing faces: A detection advantage in the flicker paradigm. *Psychological Science, 12,* 94–99.

Robbins, T. L., & DeNisi, A. S. (1994). A closer look at interpersonal affect as a distinct influence on cognitive processing in performance evaluations. *Journal of Applied Psychology, 79,* 341–353.

Robins, R. W., Caspi, A., & Moffitt, T. E. (2000). Two personalities, one relationship: Both partners' personality traits shape the quality of their relationship. *Journal of Personality and Social Psychology, 79,* 251–259.

Robins, R. W., Hendin, H. M., & Trzesniewski, K. H. (2001). *Personality and Social Psychology Bulletin, 27,* 151–161.

Robins, R. W., Spranca, M. D., & Mendelsohn, G. A. (1996). The actor–observer effect revisited: Effects of individual differences and repeated social interactions on actor and observer attribution. *Journal of Personality and Social Psychology, 71,* 375–389.

Robinson, L. A., Berman, J. S., & Neimeyer, R. A. (1990). Psychotherapy for the treatment of depression: A comprehensive review of controlled outcome research. *Psychological Bulletin, 108,* 30–49.

Robinson, R., Keltner, D., Ward, A., & Ross, L. (1995). Actual versus assumed differences in construal: "Naïve realism" in intergroup perception and conflict. *Journal of Personality and Social Psychology, 68,* 404–417.

Robinson, R. J., Lewicki, R. J., & Donahue, C. M. (1998). A five factor model of unethical tactics: The SINS scale. *Australian Industrial and Organizational Psychology Best Paper Proceeding, 131*–137.

Roccas, S. (2003). Identification and status revisited: the moderating role of self-enhancement and self-transcendence values. *Personality and Social Psychology Bulletin, 29,* 726–736.

Roccas, S., & Brewer, M. B. (2002). Social identity complexity. *Personality and Social Psychology Review, 6,* 88–106.

Rochat, F., & Modigliani, A. (1995). The ordinary quality of resistance: From Milgram's laboratory to the village of Le Chambon. *Journal of Social Issues, 5,* 195–210.

Rogers, R. W., & Ketcher, C. M. (1979). Effects of anonymity and arousal on aggression. *Journal of Psychology, 102,* 13–19.

Rokach, A., & Bacanli, H. (2001). Perceived causes of loneliness: A cross-cultural comparison. *Social Behavior and Personality, 29,* 169–182.

Rokach, A., & Neto, F. (2000). Coping with loneliness in adolescence: A cross-cultural study. *Social Behavior and Personality, 28,* 329–342.

Rokach, A., Moya, M. C., Orzeck, T., & Exposito, F. (2001). Loneliness in North America and Spain. *Social Behavior and Personality, 29,* 477–490.

Roland, E. (2002). Aggression, depression, and bullying others. *Aggressive Behavior, 28,* 198–206.

Rosenbaum, M. E. (1986). The repulsion hypothesis: On the nondevelopment of relationships. *Journal of Personality and Social Psychology, 51,* 1156–1166.

Rosenberg, E. L., & Ekman, P. (1995). Conceptual and methodological issues in the judgment of facial expressions of emotion. *Motivation and Emotion, 19,* 111–138.

Rosenberg, M. (1965). *Society and the adolescent self-image.* Princeton, NJ: Princeton University Press.

Rosenhan, D. L., Salovey, P., & Hargis, K. (1981). The joys of helping: Focus of attention mediates the impact of positive affect on altruism. *Journal of Personality and Social Psychology, 40,* 899–905.

Rosenthal, A. M. (1964). *Thirty-eight witnesses.* New York: McGraw-Hill.

Rosenthal, E. (1992, August 18). Troubled marriage? Sibling relations may be at fault. *New York Times,* pp. C1, C9.

Rosenthal, R. (1994). Interpersonal expectancy effects: A thirty year perspective. *Current Direction in Psychological Science, 3,* 176–179.

Rosenthal, R., & DePaulo, B. M. (1979). Sex differences in accommodation in nonverbal communication. In R. Rosenthal (Ed.), *Skill in nonverbal communication: Individual differences* (pp. 68–103). Cambridge, MA: Oelgeschlager, Gunn & Hain.

Rosenthal, R., & Jacobson, L. (1968). *Pygmalion in the classroom: Teacher expectation and student intellectual development.* New York: Holt, Rinehart, & Winston.

Ross, L. (1977). The intuitive scientist and his shortcoming. In L. Berkowitz (Ed.), *Advances in experimental social psychology* (Vol. 10, pp. 174–221). New York: Academic Press.

Rotenberg, K. J. (1997). Loneliness and the perception of the exchange of disclosures. *Journal of Social and Clinical Psychology, 16,* 259–276.

Rotenberg, K. J., & Kmill, J. (1992). Perception of lonely and non-lonely persons as a function of individual differences in loneliness. *Journal of Social and Personal Relationships, 9,* 325–330.

Rothgerber, H. (1997). External intergroup threat as an antecedent to perceptions of ingroup and out-group homogeneity. *Journal of Personality and Social Psychology, 73,* 1206–1212.

Rothman, A. J., & Hardin, C. D. (1997). Differential use of the availability heuristic in social judgment. *Personality and Social Psychology Bulletin, 23,* 123–138.

Rotton, J., & Cohn, E. G. (2000). Violence is a curvilinear function of temperature in Dallas: A replication. *Journal of Personality and Social Psychology, 78,* 1074–1081.

Rowatt, W. C., Cunningham, M. R., & Druen, P. B. (1998). Deception to get a date. *Personality and Social Psychology Bulletin, 24,* 1228–1242.

Rowe, P. M. (1996, September). On the neurobiological basis of affiliation. *APS Observer,* 17–18.

Roy, M. M., & Christenfeld, N. J. S. (2004). Do dogs resemble their owners? *Psychological Science, 15,* 361–363.

Rozin, P., & Nemeroff, C. (1990). The laws of sympathetic magic: A psychological analysis of similarity and contagion. In W. Stigler, R. A. Shweder, & G. Herdt (Eds.), *Cultural psychology: Essays in comparative human development* (pp. 205–232). Cambridge, England: Cambridge University Press.

Rozin, P., Lowery, L., & Ebert, R. (1994). Varieties of disgust faces and the structure of disgust. *Journal of Personality and Social Psychology, 66,* 870–881.

Rubin, J. Z. (1985). Deceiving ourselves about deception: Comment on Smith and Richardson's "Amelioration of deception and harm in psychological research." *Journal of Personality and Social Psychology, 48,* 252–253.

Rubin, Z. (1970). Measurement of romantic love. *Journal of Personality and Social Psychology, 16,* 265–273.

Ruder, M., & Bless, H. (2003). Mood and the reliance on the ease of retrieval heuristic. *Journal of Personality and Social Psychology, 85,* 20–32.

Rudman, L. A., & Fairchild, K. (2004). Reactions to counterstereotypic behavior: The role of backlash in cultural stereotype maintenance. *Journal of Personality and Social Psychology, 87,* 157–176.

Rusbult, C. E., & Zembrodt, I. M. (1983). Responses to dissatisfaction in romantic involvements: A multidimensional scaling analysis. *Journal of Experimental Social Psychology, 19,* 274–293.

Rusbult, C. E., Martz, J. M., & Agnew, C. R. (1998). The Investment Model Scale: Measuring commitment level, satisfaction level, quality of alternatives, and investment size. *Personal Relationships, 5,* 467–484.

Rusbult, C. E., Morrow, G. D., & Johnson, D. J. (1990). Self-esteem and problem-solving behavior in close relationships. *British Journal of Social Psychology,*

Ruscher, J. B., & Hammer, E. D. (1994). Revising disrupted impressions through conversation. *Journal of Personality and Social Psychology, 66,* 530–541.

Rushton, J. P. (1989b). Genetic similarity, human altruism, and group selection. *Behavioral and Brain Sciences, 12,* 503–559.

Rushton, J. P., Russell, R. J. H., & Wells, P. A. (1984). Genetic similarity theory: Beyond kin selection. *Behavior Genetics, 14,* 179–193.

Russell, J. A. (1994). Is there universal recognition of emotion from facial expressions? A review of cross-cultural studies. *Psychological Bulletin, 115,* 102–141.

Rutkowski, G. K., Gruder, C. L., & Romer, D. (1983). Group cohesiveness, social norms, and bystander intervention. *Journal of Personality and Social Psychology, 44,* 542–552.

Ruvolo, A. P., Fabin, L. A., & Ruvolo, C. M. (2001). Relationship experiences and change in attachment characteristics of young adults: The role of relationship breakups and conflict avoidance. *Personal Relationships, 8,* 265–281.

Ryan, M. K., David, B., & Reynolds, K. J. (2004). Who cares? The effect of gender and context on the self and moral reasoning. *Psychology of Women Quarterly, 28,* 246–255.

Ryckman, R. M., Robbins, M. A., Kaczor, L. M., & Gold, J. A. (1989). Male and female raters' stereotyping of male and female physiques. *Personality and Social Psychology Bulletin, 15,* 244–251.

Ryff, C. D., & Singer, B. (2000). Interpersonal flourishing: A positive health agenda for the new millennium. *Personality and Social Psychology Review, 4,* 30–44.

Sadler, P., & Woody, E. (2003). Is who you are who you're talking to? Interpersonal style and complementarity in mixed-sex interactions. *Journal of Personality and Social Psychology, 84,* 80–96.

Sally, D. (1998). Conversation and cooperation in social dilemmas: A meta-analysis of experiments from 1958–1992. *Rationality and Society.*

Salmela-Aro, K., & Nurmi, J.-E. (1996). Uncertainty and confidence in interpersonal projects: Consequences for social relationships and well-being. *Journal of Social and Personal Relationships, 13,* 109–122.

Salovey, P., Mayer, J. D., & Rosenhan, D. L. (1991). Mood and helping: Mood as a motivator of helping and helping as a regulator of mood. In M. S. Clark (Ed.), *Prosocial behavior* (pp. 215–237). Newbury Park, CA: Sage.

Sangrador, J. L., & Yela, C. (2000). 'What is beautiful is loved': Physical attractiveness in love relationships in a representative sample. *Social Behavior and Personality, 28,* 207–218.

Sani, F., & Reicher, S. (2000). Contested identities and schisms in groups: Opposing the ordination of women as priests in the Church of England. *British Journal of Social Psychology, 39,* 95–112.

Sani, F., & Todman, J. (2002). Should we stay or should we go? A social psychological model of schisms in groups. *Personality and Social Psychology Bulletin, 28,* 1647–1655.

Sanitioso, R. B., & Wlodarski, R. (2004). In search of information that confirms a desired self-perception: Motivated processing of social feedback and choice of social interactions. *Personality and Social Psychology Bulletin, 30,* 412–422.

Sanitioso, R. B., Kunda, Z., & Fong, G. T. (1990). Motivated recruitment of autobiographical memories. *Journal of Personality and Social Psychology, 59,* 229–241.

Sanna, L. J. (1997). Self-efficacy and counterfactual thinking: Up a creek with and without a paddle. *Personality and Social Psychology Bulletin, 23,* 654–666.

Sanna, L. J., & Pusecker, P. A. (1994). Self-efficacy, valence of self-evaluation, and performance. *Personality and Social Psychology Bulletin, 20,* 82–92.

Sattler, D. N., Adams, M. G., & Watts, B. (1995). Effects of personal experience on judgments about natural disasters. *Journal of Social Behavior and Personality, 10,* 891–898.

Schachter, S. (1951). Deviation, rejection, and communication. *Journal of Abnormal and Social Psychology, 46,* 190–207.

Schachter, S. (1959). *The psychology of affiliation.* Stanford, CA: Stanford University Press.

Schachter, S. (1964). The interaction of cognitive and physiological determinants of emotional state. In L. Berkowitz (Ed.), *Advances in experimental social psychology* (Vol. 1, pp. 48–81). New York: Academic Press.

Schaller, M., & Maass, A. (1989). Illusory correlation and social categorization: Toward an integration of motivational and cognitive factors in stereotype formation. *Journal of Personality and Social Psychology, 56,* 709–721.

Schein, V. E. (2001). A global look at psychological barriers to women's progress in management. *Journal of Social Issues, 57,* 675–688.

Scher, S. J. (1997). Measuring the consequences of injustice. *Personality and Social Psychology Bulletin, 23,* 482–497.

Schimel, J., Pyszczynski, T., Greenberg, J., O'Mahen, H., & Arndt, J. (2000). Running from the shadow: Psychological distancing from others to deny characteristics people fear in themselves. *Journal of Personality and Social Psychology, 78,* 446–462.

Schlenker, B. R., & Britt, T. W. (2001). Strategically controlling information to help friends: Effects of empathy and friendship strength on beneficial impression management. *Journal of Experimental Social Psychology, 37,* 357–372.

Schlenker, B. R., & Pontari, B. A. (2000). The strategic control of information: Impression management and self-presentation in daily life. In A. Tesser, R. Felson, & J. Suls (Eds.), *Perspectives on self and identity.* Washington, DC: American Psychological Association.

Schlenker, B. R., Weigold, M. F., & Hallam, J. R. (1990). Self-serving attributions in social context: Effects of self-esteem and social pressure. *Journal of Personality and Social Psychology, 58,* 855–863.

Schmid, R. E. (2001, April 18). Teen pregnancy drops to record low. Associated Press.

Schmitt, D. P. (2003b). Universal sex differences in the desire for sexual variety: Tests from 52 nations, 6 continents, and 13 islands. *Journal of Personality and Social Psychology, 85,* 85–104.

Schmitt, D. P. (2004). Patterns and universals of mate poaching across 53 nations: The effects of sex, culture, and personality on romantically attracting another person's partner. *Journal of Personality and Social Psychology, 86,* 560–584.

Schmitt, D. P., & Buss, D. M. (2001). Human mate poaching: Tactics and temptations for infiltrating existing mateships. *Journal of Personality and Social Psychology, 80,* 894–917.

Schmitt, D. P., & Schackelford, T. K. (2003). Nifty ways to leave your lover: The tactics people use to entice and disguise the process of human mate poaching. *Personality and Social Psychology Bulletin, 29,* 1018–1035.

Schmitt, E. (2001, May 15). In census, families changing. *New York Times.*

Schmitt, M. T., & Branscombe, N. R. (2002a). The meaning and consequences of perceived discrimination in disadvantaged and privileged social groups. *European Review of Social Psychology, 12,* 167–199.

Schmitt, M. T., & Branscombe, N. R. (2002b). The causal loci of attributions to prejudice. *Personality and Social Psychology Bulletin, 28,* 484–492.

Schmitt, M. T., Branscombe, N. R., & Postmes, T. (2003). Women's emotional responses to the pervasiveness of gender discrimination. *European Journal of Social Psychology, 33,* 297–312.

Schmitt, M. T., Ellemers, N., & Branscombe, N. R. (2003). Perceiving and responding to gender discrimination at work. In S. A. Haslam, D. van Knippenberg, M. Platow, & N. Ellemers (Eds.), *Social identity at work: Developing theory for organizational practice* (pp. 277–292). Philadelphia, PA: Psychology Press.

Schmitt, M. T., Silvia, P. J., & Branscombe, N. R. (2000). The intersection of self-evaluation maintenance and social identity theories: Intragroup judgment in interpersonal and intergroup contexts. *Personality and Social Psychology Bulletin, 26*, 1598–1606.

Schneider, M. E., Major, B., Luhtanen, R., & Crocker, J. (1996). Social stigma and the potential costs of assumptive help. *Personality and Social Psychology Bulletin, 22*, 201–209.

Schubert, T. W. (2004). The power in your hand: Gender differences in bodily feedback from making a fist. *Personality and Social Psychology Bulletin, 30*, 757–769.

Schul, Y., & Vinokur, A. D. (2000). Projection in person perception among spouses as a function of the similarity in their shared experiences. *Personality and Social Psychology Bulletin, 26*, 987–1001.

Schulz-Hardt, S., Jochims, M., & Frey, D. (2002). Productive conflict in group decision making: Genuine and contrived dissent as strategies to counteract biased information seeking. *Organizational Behavior and Human Decision Processes, 88*, 563–586.

Schumacher, M., Corrigan, P. W., & Dejong, T. (2003). Examining cues that signal mental illness stigma. *Journal of Social and Clinical Psychology, 22*, 467–476.

Schusterman, R. J., Reichmuth, C. J., & Kastak, D. (2000). How animals classify friends and foes. *Current Directions in Psychological Science, 9*, 1–6.

Schwarz, N., & Bohner, G. (2001). The construction of attitudes. In A. Tesser & N. Schwarz (Eds.), *Blackwell handbook of social psychology: Intrapersonal processes* (pp. 436–457). Oxford, UK: Blackwell.

Schwarz, N., Bless, H., Strack, F., Klumpp, G., Rittenauer-Schatka, G., & Simons, A. (1991). Ease of retrieval as information: Another look at the availability heuristic. *Journal of Personality and Social Psychology, 61*, 195–202.

Schwarz, S. H., & Bardi, A. (2001). Value hierarchies across cultures: Taking a similarities perspective. *Journal of Cross Cultural Psychology, 32*, 268–290.

Schwarzer, R. (1994). Optimism, vulnerability, and self-beliefs as health-related cognitions: A sytematic overview. *Psychology and Health, 9*, 161–180.

Scutt, D., Manning, J. T., Whitehouse, G. H., Leinster, S. J., & Massey, C. P. (1997). The relationship between breast symmetry, breast size and occurrence of breast cancer. *British Journal of Radiology, 70*, 1017–1021.

Searcy, E., & Eisenberg, N. (1992). Defensiveness in response to aid from a sibling. *Journal of Personality and Social Psychology, 62*, 422–433.

Sears, D. O. (1986). College sophomores in the laboratory: Influences of a narrow data base on social psychology's view of human nature. *Journal of Personality and Social Psychology, 51(3)*, 515–530.

Sears, D. O. (1988). Symbolic racism. In P. A. Katz & D. A. Taylor (Eds.), *Eliminating racism: Profiles in controversy* (pp. 53–84). New York: Plenum.

Sedikides, C., & Anderson, C. A. (1994). Causal perception of intertrait relations: the glue that holds person types together. *Personality and Social Psychology Bulletin, 21*, 294–302.

Sedikides, C., & Gregg, A. P. (2003). Portraits of the self. In M. A. Hogg & J. Cooper (Eds.), *The Sage handbook of social psychology* (pp. 110–138). Thousand Oaks, CA: Sage.

Sedikides, C., & Skowronski, J. J. (1997). The symbolic self in evolutionary context. *Personality and Social Psychology Review, 1*, 80–102.

Seery, M. D., Blascovich, J., Weisbuch, M., & Vick, B. (2004). The relationship between self-esteem level, self-esteem stability, and cardiovascular reactions to performance feedback. *Journal of Personality and Social Psychology, 87*, 133–145.

Segal, M. M. (1974). Alphabet and attraction: An unobtrusive measure of the effect of propinquity in a field setting. *Journal of Personality and Social Psychology, 30*, 654–657.

Selim, J. (2003, April). Anatomy of a belly laugh. *Discover*, 65.

Selim, J. (2004, May). Who's a little bitty artist? Yes, you are! *Discover*, 16.

Senecal, C., Vallerand, R. J., & Guay, F. (2001). Antecedents and outcomes of work-family conflict: Toward a motivational model. *Personality and Social Psychology Bulletin, 27*, 176–186.

Seta, C. E., Hayes, N. S., & Seta, J. J. (1994). Mood, memory, and vigilance: The influence of distraction on recall and impression formation. *Personality and Social Psychology Bulletin, 20*, 170–177.

Settles, I. H. (2004). When multiple identities interfere: The role of identity centrality. *Personality and Social Psychology Bulletin, 30*, 487–500.

Shah, J. (2003). Automatic for the people; How representations of significant others implicitly affect goal pursuit. *Journal of Personality and Social Psychology, 84*, 661–681.

Shams, M. (2001). Social support, loneliness and friendship preference among British Asian and non-Asian adolescents. *Social Behavior and Personality, 29*, 399–404.

Shanab, M. E., & Yahya, K. A. (1977). A behavioral study of obedience in children. *Journal of Personality and Social Psychology, 35*, 530–536.

Shannon, M. L., & Stark, C. P. (2003). The influence of physical appearance on personnel selection. *Social Behavior and Personality, 31*, 613–624.

Shapiro, A., & Gottman, J. (2000). The baby and the marriage: Identifying factors that buffer against decline in marital satisfaction after the first baby arrives. *Journal of Family Psychology, 14*, 59–70.

Shapiro, J. P., Baumeister, R. F., & Kessler, J. W. (1991). A three-component model of children's teasing: Aggression, humor, and ambiguity. *Journal of Social and Clinical Psychology, 10*, 459–472.

Sharp, M. J., & Getz, J. G. (1996). Substance use as impression management. *Personality and Social Psychology Bulletin, 22*, 60–67.

Shaver, P. R., & Brennan, K. A. (1992). Attachment styles and the "big five" personality traits: Their connections with each other and with romantic relationship outcomes. *Personality and Social Psychology Bulletin, 18*, 536–545.

Shaver, P. R., Morgan, H. J., & Wu, S. (1996). Is love a "basic" emotion? *Personal Relationships, 3*, 81–96.

Shavitt, S. (1990). The role of attitude objects in attitude functions. *Journal of Experimental Social Psychology, 26*, 124–148.

Shaw, J. I., Borough, H. W., & Fink, M. I. (1994). Perceived sexual orientation and helping behavior by males and females: The wrong number technique. *Journal of Psychology and Human Sexuality, 6*, 73–81.

Shaw, L. L., Batson, C. D., & Todd, R. M. (1994). Empathy avoidance: Forestalling feeling for another in order to escape the motivational consequences. *Journal of Personality and Social Psychology, 67*, 879–887.

Sheeran, P., & Abraham, C. (1994). Unemployment and self-conception: A symbolic interactionist analysis. *Journal of Community & Applied Social Psychology, 4*, 115–129.

Sheldon, W. H., Stevens, S. S., & Tucker, W. B. (1940). *The varieties of human physique.* New York: Harper.

Shepperd, J. A., & McNulty, J. K. (2002). The affective consequences of expected and unexpected outcomes. *Psychological Science, 13*, 84–87.

Shepperd, J. A., Findley-Klein, C., Kwavnick, K., Walker, D., & Perez, S. (2000). Bracing for loss. *Journal of Personality and Social Psychology, 78*, 620–634.

Sherif, M. (1966). *In common predicament: Social psychology of intergroup conflict and cooperation.* Boston, MA: Houghton-Mifflin.

Sherif, M., Harvey, D. J., White, B. J., Hood, W. R., & Sherif, C. W. (1961). *The Robbers' cave experiment.* Norman, OK: Institute of Group Relations.

Sherman, J. W., & Klein, S. B. (1994). Development and representation of personality impressions. *Journal of Personality and Social Psychology, 67*, 972–983.

Sherman, M. D., & Thelen, M. H. (1996). Fear of intimacy scale: Validation and extension with adolescents. *Journal of Social and Personal Relationships, 13*, 507–521.

Sherman, S. S. (1980). On the self-erasing nature of errors of prediction. *Journal of Personality and Social Psychology, 16*, 388–403.

Sidanius, J., & Pratto, F. (1999). *Social dominance.* New York: Cambridge University Press.

Sigall, H. (1997). Ethical considerations in social psychological research: Is the bogus pipeline a special case? *Journal of Applied Social Psychology, 27,* 574–581.

Sigelman, C. K., Thomas, D. B., Sigelman, L., & Robich, F. D. (1986). Gender, physical attractiveness, and electability: An experimental investigation of voter biases. *Journal of Applied Social Psychology, 16,* 229–248.

Sillars, A. L., Folwell, A. L., Hill, K. C., Maki, B. K., Hurst, A. P., & Casano, R. A. (1994). *Journal of Social and Personal Relationships, 11,* 611–617.

Silverstein, R. (1994). Chronic identity diffusion in traumatized combat veterans. *Social Behavior and Personality, 22,* 69–80.

Simon, B. (1992). The perception of ingroup and outgroup homogeneity: Reintroducing the social context. In W. Stroebe & M. Hewstone (Eds.), *European Review of Social Psychology* (Vol. 3, pp. 1–30). Chichester: Wiley.

Simon, B. (1998). The self in minority-majority contexts. In W. Stroebe & M. Hewstone (Eds.), *European Review of Social Psychology* (Vol. 9, pp. 1–31). Chichester: Wiley.

Simon, B. (2004). *Identity in modern society: A social psychological perspective.* Oxford: Blackwell.

Simon, B., & Klandermans, B. (2001). Politicized collective identity: A social psychological analysis. *American Psychologist, 56,* 319–331.

Simon, B., & Pettigrew, T. F. (1990). Social identity and perceived group homogeneity: Evidence for the ingroup homogeneity effect. *European Journal of Social Psychology, 20,* 269–286.

Simon, B., Glassner-Bayerl, B., & Stratenwerth, I. (1991). Stereotyping and self-stereotyping in a natural intergroup context: The case of heterosexual and homosexual men. *Social Psychology Quarterly, 54,* 252–266.

Simon, L., & Greenberg, J. (1996). Further progress in understanding the effects of derogatory ethnic labels: The role of pre-existing attitudes toward the targeted group. *Personality and Social Psychology Bulletin, 22,* 1195–1204.

Simon, L., Greenberg, J., & Brehm, J. (1995). Trivialization: The forgotten mode of dissonance reduction. *Journal of Personality and Social Psychology, 68,* 247–260.

Simpson, J. A., & Gangestad, S. W. (1992). Sociosexuality and romantic partner choice. *Journal of Personality, 60,* 31–51.

Simpson, J. A., Ickes, W., & Blackstone, T. (1995). When the head protects the heart: Empathic accuracy in dating relationships. *Journal of Personality and Social Psychology, 69,* 629–641.

Sinclair, L., & Kunda, Z. (1999). Reactions to a black professional: Motivated inhibition and activation of conflicting stereotypes. *Journal of Personality and Social Psychology, 77,* 885–904.

Singh, R., & Ho, S. Y. (2000). Attitudes and attraction: A new test of the attraction, repulsion and similarity–dissimilarity asymmetry hypotheses. *British Journal of Social Psychology, 39,* 197–211.

Singh, R., Choo, W. M., & Poh, L. L. (1998). Ingroup bias and fair-mindedness as strategies of self-presentation in intergroup perception. *Personality and Social Psychology Bulletin, 24,* 147–162.

Sistrunk, F., & McDavid, J. W. (1971). Sex variable in conforming behavior. *Journal of Personality and Social Psychology, 17,* 200–207.

Sivacek, J., & Crano, W. D. (1982). Vested interest as a moderator of attitude-behavior consistency. *Journal of Personality and Social Psychology, 43,* 210–221.

Skarlicki, D. P., & Folger, R. (1997). Retaliation in the workplace: The roles of distributive, procedural, and interactional justice. *Journal of Applied Psychology, 821,* 434–443.

Smeaton, G., Byrne, D., & Murnen, S. K. (1989). The repulsion hypothesis revisited: Similarity irrelevance or dissimilarity bias? *Journal of Personality and Social Psychology, 56,* 54–59.

Smirles, K. E. (2004). Attributions of responsibility in cases of sexual harassment: The person and the situation. *Journal of Applied Social Psychology, 34,* 342–365.

Smith, C. M., Tindale, R. S., & Dugoni, B. L. (1996). Minority and majority influence in freely interacting groups: Qualitative versus quantitative differences. *British Journal of Social Psychology, 35,* 137–149.

Smith, D. E., Gier, J. A., & Willis, F. N. (1982). Interpersonal touch and compliance with a marketing request. *Basic and Applied Social Psychology, 3,* 35–38.

Smith, E. R., & Zarate, M. A. (1992). Exemplar-based model of social judgment. *Psychological Review, 99,* 3–21.

Smith, E. R., Byrne, D., Becker, M. A., & Przybyla, D. P. J. (1993). Sexual attitudes of males and females as predictors of interpersonal attraction and marital compatibility. *Journal of Applied Social Psychology, 23,* 1011–1034.

Smith, K. D., Keating, J. P., & Stotland, E. (1989). Altruism reconsidered: The effect of denying feedback on a victim's status to empathetic witnesses. *Journal of Personality and Social Psychology, 57,* 641–650.

Smith, P. B., & Bond, M. H. (1993). *Social psychology across cultures.* Boston: Allyn & Bacon.

Smith, P. K., & Brain, P. (2000). Bullying in schools; lessons from two decades of research. *Aggressive Behavior, 26,* 1–9.

Smith, S. S., & Richardson, D. (1985). On deceiving ourselves about deception: Reply to Rubin. *Journal of Personality and Social Psychology, 48,* 254–255.

Smorti, A., & Ciucci, E. (2000). Narrative strategies in bullies and victims in Italian school-children. *Aggressive Behavior, 26,* 33–48.

Smuts, B. (2001/2002, December/January). Common ground. *Natural History,* 78–83.

Snyder, M., & Ickes, W. (1985). Personality and social behavior. In G. Lindzey & E. Aronson (Eds.), *Handbook of social psychology* (3rd ed., Vol. 2, pp. 883–947). New York: Random House.

Sommer, K. L., Horowitz, I. A., & Bourgeois, M. J. (2001). When juries fail to comply with the law: Biased evidence processing in individual and group decision making. *Personality and Social Psychology Bulletin, 27,* 309–320.

Spears, R., Doosje, B., & Ellemers, N. (1999). Commitment and the context of social perception. In N. Ellemers, R. Spears, & B. Doosje (Eds.), *Social identity: Context, commitment, content* (pp. 59–83). Oxford: Blackwell.

Spears, R., Jetten, J., & Doosje, B. (2001). The (il)legitimacy of ingroup bias: From social reality to social resistance. In J. T. Jost & B. Major (Eds.), *The psychology of legitimacy* (pp. 332–362). New York: Cambridge University Press.

Spencer, S. J., Steele, C. M., & Quinn, D. M. (1999). Stereotype threat and women's math performance. *Journal of Experimental Social Psychology, 35,* 4–28.

Sprafkin, J. N., Liebert, R. M., & Poulous, R. W. (1975). Effects of a prosocial televised example on children's helping. *Journal of Personality and Social Psychology, 48,* 35–46.

Sprecher, S. (2002). Sexual satisfaction in premarital relationships: Associations with satisfaction, love, commitment, and stability. *Journal of Sex Research, 39,* 190–196.

Sprecher, S., & Regan, P. C. (2002). Liking some things (in some people) more than others: Partner preferences in romantic relationships and friendships. *Journal of Social and Personal Relationships, 19,* 463–481.

Stacey, J., & Biblarz, T. (2001). Does the sexual orientation of parents matter? *American Sociological Review, 66,* 159–183.

Stafford, L., Kline, S. L., & Rankin, C. T. (2004). Married individuals, cohabiters, and cohabiters who marry: A longitudinal study of relational and individual well-being. *Journal of Social and Personal Relationships, 21,* 231–248.

Stangor, C., & McMillan, D. (1992). Memory for expectancy-congruent and expectancy-incongruent information: A review of the social and social developmental literatures. *Psychological Bulletin, 111,* 42–61.

Stangor, C., Sechrist, G. B., & Jost, T. J. (2001). Changing racial beliefs by providing consensus information. *Personality and Social Psychology Bulletin, 27,* 486–496.

Stasser, G. (1992). Pooling of unshared information during group discussion. In S. Worchel, W. Wood, & J. H. Simpson (Eds.), *Group process and productivity* (pp. 48–67). Newbury Park, CA: Sage.

Stasser, G., Taylor, L. A., & Hanna, C. (1989). Information sampling in structured and unstructured discussions of three- and six-person groups. *Journal of Personality and Social Psychology, 57,* 67–78.

Staub, E. (1999). The roots of evil: Social conditions, culture, personality, and basic human needs. *Personality and Social Psychology Review, 3,* 179–192.

Stech, F., & McClintock, C. G. (1981). Effects of communication timing on duopoly bargaining outcomes. *Journal of Personality and Social Psychology, 40,* 664–674.

Steele, C. M. (1988). The psychology of self-affirmation: Sustaining the integrity of the self. In L. Berkowitz (Ed.), *Advances in experimental social psychology* (pp. 261–302). Hillsdale, NJ: Erlbaum.

Steele, C. M. (1997). A threat in the air: How stereotypes shape the intellectual identities and performance of women and African-Americans. *American Psychologist, 52,* 613–629.

Steele, C. M., & Aronson, J. (1995). Stereotype threat and the intellectual test performance of African Americans. *Journal of Personality and Social Psychology, 69,* 797–811.

Steele, C. M., & Lui, T. J. (1983). Dissonance processes as self-affirmation. *Journal of Personality and Social Psychology, 45,* 5–19.

Steele, C. M., Critchlow, B., & Liu, T. J. (1985). Alcohol and social behavior II: The helpful drunkard. *Journal of Personality and Social Psychology, 48,* 35–46.

Steele, C. M., Southwick, L., & Critchlow, B. (1981). Dissonance and alcohol: Drinking your troubles away. *Journal of Personality and Social Psychology, 41,* 831–846.

Steele, C. M., Spencer, S. J., & Aronson, J. (2002). Contending with group image: The psychology of stereotype and social identity threat. *Advances in Experimental Social Psychology, 34,* 379–439.

Steele, C. M., Spencer, S. J., & Lynch, M. (1993). Self-image resilience and dissonance: The role of affirmational resources. *Journal of Personality and Social Psychology, 64,* 885–896.

Stein, R. I., & Nemeroff, C. J. (1995). Moral overtones of food: Judgments of others based on what they eat. *Personality and Social Psychology Bulletin, 21,* 480–490.

Steinhauer, J. (1995, April 10). Big benefits in marriage, studies say. *New York Times,* p. A10.

Stephan, W. G. (1985). Intergroup relations. In G. Lindzey & E. Aronson (Eds.), *Handbook of social psychology* (Vol. 3, pp. 599–658). New York: Addison-Wesley.

Stephan, W. G., & Stephan, C. W. (2000). An integrated threat theory of prejudice. In S. Oskamp (Ed.), *Reducing prejudice and discrimination* (pp. 23–45). Mahwah, NJ: Erlbaum.

Sternberg, R. J. (1986). A triangular theory of love. *Psychological Review, 93*(2), 119–135.

Sternberg, R. J. (1996). Love stories. *Personal Relationships, 3,* 59–79.

Sternberg, R. J., & Hojjat, M. (Eds.). (1997). *Satisfaction in close relationships.* New York: Guilford.

Stevens, C. K., & Kristof, A. L. (1995). Making the right impression: A field study of applicant impression management during job interviews. *Journal of Applied Psychology, 80,* 587–606.

Stevens, L. E., & Fiske, S. T. (2000). Motivated impressions of a powerholder: Accuracy under task dependency and misperception under evaluation dependency. *Personality and Social Psychology Bulletin, 26,* 907–922.

Stewart, R. B., Verbrugge, K. M., & Beilfuss, M. C. (1998). Sibling relationships in early adulthood: A typology. *Personal Relationships, 5,* 59–74.

Stewart, T. L., Vassar, P. M., Sanchez, D. T., & David, S. E. (2000). Attitudes toward women's societal roles moderates the effect of gender cues on target individuation. *Journal of Personality and Social Psychology, 79,* 143–157.

Stone, A. A., Neale, J. M., Cox, D. S., Napoli, A., Valdimarsdottir, H., & Kennedy-Moore, E. (1994). Daily events are associated with a secretory immune response to an oral antigen in men. *Health Psychology, 13,* 440–446.

Stone, J., Lynch, C. I., Sjomeling, M., & Darley, J. M. (1999). Stereotype threat effects on Black and White athletic performance. *Journal of Personality and Social Psychology, 77,* 1213–1227.

Stone, J., Wiegand, A. W., Cooper, J., & Aronson, E. (1997). When exemplification fails: Hypocrisy and the motives for self-integrity. *Journal of Personality and Social Psychology, 72,* 54–65.

Stowers, L., Holy, T. E., Meister, M., Dulac, C., & Loentges, G. (2002). Loss of sex discrimination and male-male aggression in mice deficient for TRP2. *Science, 295,* 1493–1500.

Stroebe, M., Gergen, M. M., Gergen, K. J., & Stroebe, W. (1995). Broken hearts or broken bonds: Love and death in historical perspective. In L. A. DeSpelder & A. L. Strickland (Eds.), *The path ahead: Readings in death and dying* (pp. 231–241). Mountain View, CA: Mayfield.

Stroessner, S. J., Hamilton, D. L., & Mackie, D. M. (1992). Affect and stereotyping: the effect of induced mood on distinctiveness-based illusory correlations. *Journal of Personality and Social Psychology, 62,* 564–576.

Stroh, L. K., Langlands, C. L., & Simpson, P. A. (2004). Shattering the glass ceiling in the new millenium. In M. S. Stockdale and F. J. Crosby (Eds.), *The psychology and management of workplace diversity* (pp. 147–167). Malden, MA: Blackwell.

Strube, M. J. (1989). Evidence for the Type in Type A behavior: A taxonometric analysis. *Journal of Personality and Social Pychology, 56,* 972–987.

Strube, M., Turner, C. W., Cerro, D., Stevens, J., & Hinchey, F. (1984). Interpersonal aggression and the Type A coronary-prone behavior pattern: A theoretical distinction and practical implications. *Journal of Personality and Social Psychology, 47,* 839–847.

Stukas, A. A., Snyder, M., & Clary, E. G. (1999). The effects of "mandatory volunteerism" on intentions to volunteer. *Psychological Science, 10,* 59–64.

Sturmer, S., & Simon, B. (2004). The role of collective identification in social movement participation: A panel study in the context of the German gay movement. *Personality and Social Psychology Bulletin, 30,* 263–277.

Suls, J., & Rosnow, J. (1988). Concerns about artifacts in behavioral research. In M. Morawski (Ed.), *The rise of experimentation in American psychology* (pp. 163–187). New Haven, CT: Yale University Press.

Swann, W. B. (1990). To be adored or to be known? The interplay of self-enhancement and self-verification. In E. T. Higgins & R. M. Sorrentino (Eds.), *Handbook of motivation and cognition: Foundations of social behavior* (pp. 408–448). New York: Guilford Press.

Swann, W. B., Jr., & Gill, M. J. (1997). Confidence and accuracy in person perception: Do we know what we think we know about our relationship partners? *Journal of Personality and Social Psychology, 73,* 747–757.

Swann, W. B., Jr., De La Ronde, C., & Hixon, J. G. (1994). Authenticity and positivity strivings in marriage and courtship. *Journal of Personality and Social Psychology, 66,* 857–869.

Swann, W. B., Jr., Rentfrow, P. J., & Gosling, S. D. (2003). The precarious couple effect: verbally inhibited men + critical, disinhibited women = bad chemistry. *Journal of Personality and Social Psychology, 85,* 1095–1106.

Swap, W. C. (1977). Interpersonal attraction and repeated exposure to rewarders and punishers. *Personality and Social Psychology Bulletin, 3,* 248–251.

Swim, J. K. (1994). Perceived versus meta-analytic effect sizes: An assessment of the accuracy of gender stereotypes. *Journal of Personality and Social Psychology, 66,* 21–36.

Swim, J. K., & Campbell, B. (2001). Sexism: Attitudes, beliefs, and behaviors. In R. Brown & S. Gaertner (Eds.), *Blackwell Handbook of Social Psychology: Intergroup Processes* (pp. 218–237). Oxford, UK: Blackwell.

Swim, J. K., Aikin, K. J., Hall, W. S., & Hunter, B. A. (2001). Sexism and racism: Old-fashioned and modern prejudices. *Journal of Personality and Social Psychology, 68,* 199–214.

Tajfel, H. (1978). *The social psychology of the minority.* New York: Minority Rights Group.

Tajfel, H. (1981). Social stereotypes and social groups. In J. C. Turner & H. Giles (Eds.), *Intergroup behavior* (pp. 144–167). Chicago, IL: University of Chicago Press.

Tajfel, H. (1982). *Social identity and intergroup relations.* Cambridge, England: Cambridge University Press.

Tajfel, H., & Turner, J. C. (1986). The social identity theory of intergroup behavior. In S. Worchel & W. G. Austin (Eds.), *The social psychology of intergroup relations* (2nd ed., pp. 7–24). Monterey, CA: Brooks-Cole.

Takata, T., & Hashimoto, H. (1973). Effects of insufficient justification upon the arousal of cognitive dissonance: Timing of justification and evaluation of task. *Japanese Journal of Experimental Social Psychology, 13,* 77–85.

Tan, D. T. Y., & Singh, R. (1995). Attitudes and attraction: A developmental study of the similarity–attraction and dissimilarity–repulsion hypotheses. *Personality and Social Psychology Bulletin, 21* 975–986.

Taylor, K. M., & Shepperd, J. A. (1998). Bracing for the worst: Severity, testing, and feedback timing as moderators of the optimistic bias. *Personality and Social Psychology Bulletin, 24,* 915–926.

Taylor, S. E., & Brown, J. D. (1988). Illusion and well-being: A social psychological perspective on mental health. *Psychological Bulletin, 103,* 193–210.

Taylor, S. E., Buunk, B. P., & Aspinwall, L. G. (1990). Social comparison, stress, and coping. *Personality and Social Psychology Bulletin, 16,* 74–89.

Taylor, S. E., Helgeson, V. S., Reed, G. M., & Skokan, L. A. (1991). Self-generated feelings of control and adjustment to physical illness. *Journal of Social Issues, 47,* 91–109.

Taylor, S. E., Lerner, J. S., Sherman, D. K., Sage, R. M., & McDowell, N. K. (2003). Are self-enhancing cognitions associated with healthy or unhealthy biological profiles? *Journal of Personality and Social Psychology, 85,* 605–615.

Tepper, B. J. (2000). Consequences of abusive supervision. *Academy of Management Journal, 43,* 178–190.

Terman, L. M., & Buttenwieser, P. (1935a). Personality factors in marital compatibility: I. *Journal of Social Psychology, 6,* 143–171.

Terman, L. M., & Buttenwieser, P. (1935b). Personality factors in marital compatibility: II. *Journal of Social Psychology, 6,* 267–289.

Terry, D. J., Hogg, M. A., & Duck, J. M. (1999). Group membership, social identity, and attitudes. In D. Abrams & M. A. Hogg (Eds.), *Social identity and social cognition* (pp. 280–314). Oxford: Blackwell.

Terry, R. L., & Krantz, J. H. (1993). Dimensions of trait attributions associated with eyeglasses, men's facial hair, and women's hair length. *Journal of Applied Social Psychology, 23,* 1757–1769.

Tesser, A. (1988). Toward a self-evaluation maintenance model of social behavior. *Advances in Experimental Social Psychology, 21,* 181–227.

Tesser, A., & Martin, L. (1996). The psychology of evaluation. In E. T. Higgins & A. W. Kruglanski (Eds.), *Social psychology: Handbook of basic principles* (pp. 400–423). New York: Guilford Press.

Tesser, A., Martin, L. L., & Cornell, D. P. (1996). On the substitutability of the self-protecting mechanisms. In P. Gollwitzer & J. Bargh (Eds.), *The psychology of action* (pp. 48–68). New York: Guilford.

Tetlock, P. E., Peterson, R. S., McGuire, C., Change, S., & Feld, P. (1992). Assessing political group dynamics: A test of the groupthink model. *Journal of Personality and Social Psychology, 63,* 403–425.

Thompson, J. M., Whiffen, V. E., & Blain, M. D. (1995). Depressive symptoms, sex and perceptions of intimate relationships. *Journal of Social and Personal Relationships, 12,* 49–66.

Thompson, L. (1998). *The mind and heart of the negotiator.* Upper Saddle River, NJ: Prentice-Hall.

Tice, D. M., Bratslavsky, E., & Baumeister, R. F. (2000). Emotional distress regulation takes precedence over impulse control: If you feel bad, do it! *Journal of Personality and Social Psychology, 80,* 53–67.

Tice, D. M., Butler, J. L., Muraven, M. B., & Stillwell, A. M. (1995). When modesty prevails: Differential favorability of self-presentation to friends and strangers. *Journal of Personality and Social Psychology, 69,* 1120–1138.

Tidwell, M.-C. O., Reis, H. T., & Shaver, P. R. (1996). Attachment, attractiveness, and social interaction: A diary study. *Journal of Personality and Social Psychology, 71,* 729–745.

Tiedens, L. Z. (2001). Anger and advancement versus sadness and subjugation: The effect of negative emotion expressions on social status control. *Journal of Personality and Social Psychology, 80,* 86–94.

Tiedens, L. Z., & Fragale, A. R. (2003). Power moves: Complementarity in dominant and submissive nonverbal behavior. *Journal of Personality and Social Psychology, 84,* 558–568.

Tjosvold, D. (1993). *Learning to manage conflict: Getting people to work together productively.* New York: Lexington.

Tjosvold, D., & DeDreu, C. (1997). Managing conflict in Dutch organizations: A test of the relevance of Deutsch's cooperation theory. *Journal of Applied Social Psychology, 27,* 2213–2227.

Toi, M., & Batson, C. D. (1982). More evidence that empathy is a source of altruistic motivation. *Journal of Personality and Social Psychology, 43,* 281–292.

Tormala, Z. L., Petty, R. E., & Brunol, P. (2002). Ease of retrieval effects in persuasion: A self validation analysis. *Personality and Social Psychology Bulletin.*

Towles-Schwen, T., & Fazio, R. H. (2001). On the origins of racial attitudes: Correlates of childhood experiences. *Personality and Social Psychology Bulletin, 27,* 162–175.

Townsend, J. M. (1995). Sex without emotional involvement: An evolutionary interpretation of sex differences. *Archives of Sexual Behavior, 24,* 173–206.

Trafimow, D., Silverman, E., Fan, R., & Law, J. (1997). The effects of language and priming on the relative accessibility of the private self and collective self. *Journal of Cross-Cultural Psychology, 28,* 107–123.

Trevarthen, C. (1993). The function of emotions in early infant communication and development. In J. Nadel & L. Camaioni (Eds.), *New perspectives in early communication development* (pp. 48–81). London: Routledge.

Triandis, H. C. (1990). Cross-cultural studies of individualism and collectivism. In J. J. Berman (Ed.), *Nebraska symposium on motivation, 1989* (pp. 41–133). Lincoln: University of Nebraska Press.

Trobst, K. K., Collins, R. L., & Embree, J. M. (1994). The role of emotion in social support provision: Gender, empathy, and expressions of distress. *Journal of Social and Personal Relationships, 11,* 45–62.

Trope, Y., & Liberman, A. (1996). Social hypothesis testing: Cognitive and motivational mechanisms. In E. T. Higgins & A. W. Kruglanski (Eds.), *Social psychology: Handbook of basic principles* (pp. 239–270). New York: Guilford.

Tucker, J. S., Friedman, H. S., Schwartz, J. E., Criqui, M. H., Tomlinson-Keasey, C., Wingard, D. L., & Martin, L. R. (1997). Parental divorce: Effects on individual behavior and longevity. *Journal of Personality and Social Psychology, 73,* 381–391.

Tucker, P., & Aron, A. (1993). Passionate love and marital satisfaction at key transition points in the family life cycle. *Journal of Social and Clinical Psychology, 12,* 135–147.

Turner, J. C. (1985). Social categorization and the self-concept: A social cognitive theory of group behavior. In E. J. Lawler (Ed.), *Advances in group processes* (Vol. 2, pp. 77–122). Greenwich, CT: JAI Press.

Turner, J. C. (1991). *Social influence.* Pacific Grove, CA: Brooks/Cole.

Turner, J. C., & Onorato, R. S. (1999). Social identity, personality, and the self-concept: A self-categorization perspective. In T. R. Tyler, R. M. Kramer & O. P. John (Eds.), *The psychology of the social self* (pp. 11–46). Mahwah, NJ: Erlbaum.

Turner, J. C., Hogg, M. A., Oakes, P. J., Reicher, S. D., & Wetherell, M. S. (1987). *Rediscovering the social group: A self-categorization theory.* Oxford, UK: Blackwell.

Turner, M. E., Pratkanis, A. R., & Samuels, S. (2003). In S. A. Haslam, D. Van Knippenberg, M. J. Platow, and N. Ellemers (Eds.), *Social Identity at work: Developing theory for organizational practice.* New York: Psychology Press.

Tversky, A., & Kahneman, D. (1973). Availability: A heuristic for judging frequency and probability. *Cognitive Psychology, 5,* 207–232.

Tversky, A., & Kahneman, D. (1982). Judgment under uncertainty: Heuristics and biases. In D. Kahneman, P. Slovic, & A. Tversky (Eds.), *Judgment under uncertainty* (pp. 3–20). New York: Cambridge University Press.

Twenge, J. M. (1999). Mapping gender: The multifactorial approach and the organization of gender-related attributes. *Psychology of Women Quarterly, 23,* 485–502.

Twenge, J. M., & Crocker, J. (2002). Race and self-esteem: Meta-analyses comparing Whites, Blacks, Hispanics, Asians, and American Indians. *Psychological Bulletin, 128,* 371–408.

Twenge, J. M., & Manis, M. M. (1998). First-name desirability and adjustment: Self-satisfaction, others' ratings, and family background. *Journal of Applied Social Psychology, 24,* 41–51.

Twenge, J. M., Catanese, K. R., & Baumeister, R. F. (2003). Social exclusion and the deconstructed state: Time perception, meaninglessness, lethargy, lack of emotion, and self-awareness. *Journal of Personality and Social Psychology, 85,* 409–423.

Tykocinski, O. E. (2001). I never had a chance: Using hindsight tactics to mitigate disappointments. *Personality and Social Psychology Bulletin, 27,* 376–382.

Tyler, T. R., & Blader, S. (2000). *Cooperation in groups: Procedural justice, social identity and behavioral engagement.* Philadelphia, PA: Psychology Press.

U.S. Department of Justice. (1994). *Criminal victimization in the United States, 1992.* Washington, DC: Office of Justice Programs, Bureau of Justice Statistics.

U.S. Department of Labor. (1992). *Employment and earnings* (Vol. 39, No. 5: Table A-22). Washington, DC: U.S. Department of Labor.

Udry, J. R. (1980). Changes in the frequency of marital intercourse from panel data. *Archives of Sexual Behavior, 9,* 319–325.

Unger, L. S., & Thumuluri, L. K. (1997). Trait empathy and continuous helping: The case of volunteerism. *Journal of Social Behavior and Personality, 12,* 785–800.

Ungerer, J. A., Dolby, R., Waters, B., Barnett, B., Kelk, N., & Lewin, V. (1990). The early development of empathy: Self-regulation and individual differences in the first year. *Motivation and Emotion, 14,* 93–106.

United States Holocaust Memorial Museum. (2003). *Index to Righteous Gentile registry of Yad Vashem.* Washington, DC: Author.

Urbanski, L. (1992, May 21). Study uncovers traits people seek in friends. *The Evangelist,* 4.

Vallone, R., Ross, L., & Lepper, M. (1985). Social status, cognitive alternatives, and intergroup relations. In H. Tajfel (Ed.), *Differentiation between social groups* (pp. 201–226). London: Academic Press.

van Baaren, R. B., Holland, R. W., Kawakami, K., & van Knippenberg, A. (2004). Mimicry and prosocial behavior. *Psychological Science, 15,* 71–74.

van Baaren, R. B., Holland, R. W., Steenaert, B., & van Knippenberg, A. (2003). A mimicry for money: Behavioral consequences of imitation. *Journal of Experimental Social Psychology, 39,* 393–398.

Van Boven, L., White, K., Kamada, A., & Gilovich, T. (2003). Intuitions about situational correction in self and others. *Journal of Personality and Social Psychology, 85,* 249–258.

Van den Bos, K., & Lind, E. W. (2002). Uncertainty management by means of fairness judgments. In M. P. Zanna (Ed.), *Advances in experimental social psychology* (Vol. 34, pp. 1–60). San Diego, CA: Academic Press.

Van Dick, R., Wagner, U., Pettigrew, T. F., Christ, O., Wolf, C., Petzel, T., Castro, V. S., & Jackson, J. S. (2004). Role of perceived importance in intergroup contact. *Journal of Personality and Social Psychology, 87,* 211–227.

Van Lange, P. A. M., & Kuhlman, M. D. (1994). Social value orientation and impressions of partner's honesty and intelligence: A test of

the might versus morality effect. *Journal of Personality and Social Psychology, 67,* 126–141.

Van Overwalle, F. (1997). Dispositional attributions require the joint application of the methods of difference and agreement. *Personality and Social Psychology Bulletin, 23,* 974–980.

Van Overwalle, F. (1998). Causal explanation as constraint satisfaction: A critique and a feedforward connectionist alternative. *Journal of Personality and Social Psychology, 74,* 312–328.

Van Vugt, M., & Hart, C. M. (2004). Social identity as social glue: The origins of group loyalty. *Journal of Personality and Social Psychology, 86,* 585–598.

Vandello, J. A., & Cohen, D. (1999). Patterns of individualism and collectivism in the United States. *Journal of Personality and Social Psychology, 77,* 279–292.

Vandello, J. A., & Cohen, D. (2003). Male honor and female fidelity: Implicit cultural scripts that perpetuate domestic violence. *Journal of Personality and Social Psychology, 84,* 997–1010.

Vanderbilt, A. (1957). *Amy Vanderbilt's complete book of etiquette.* Garden City, NY: Doubleday.

Vanman, E. J., Paul, B. Y., Ito, T. A., & Miller, N. (1997). The modern face of prejudice and structure features that moderate the effect of cooperation on affect. *Journal of Personality and Social Psychology, 73,* 941–959.

Vasquez, K., Durik, A. M., & Hyde, J. S. (2002). Family and work: Implications of adult attachment styles. *Personality and Social Psychology Bulletin, 28,* 874–886.

Vasquez, M. J. T. (2001). Leveling the playing field—Toward the emancipation of women. *Psychology of Women Quarterly, 25,* 89–97.

Vertue, F. M. (2003). From adaptive emotion to dysfunction: An attachment perspective on social anxiety disorder. *Personality and Social Psychology Review, 7,* 170–191.

Vinokur, A., & Burnstein, E. (1974). Effects of partially shared persuasive arguments on group-induced shifts: A group problem-solving approach. *Journal of Personality and Social Psychology, 29,* 305–315.

Vinokur, A. D., & Schul, Y. (2000). Projection in person perception among spouses as a function of the similarity in their shared experiences. *Personality and Social Psychology Bulletin, 26,* 987–1001.

Vobejda, B. (1997, June 3). Pain of divorce follows children. *Washington Post.*

Volpe, K. (2002, July/August). Measuring emotion. *American Psychological Society, 15,* 7–8.

Vonk, R. (1998). The slime effect: Suspicion and dislike of likeable behavior toward superiors. *Journal of Personality and Social Psychology, 74,* 849–864.

Vonk, R. (1999). Differential evaluations of likeable and dislikeable behaviours enacted towards superiors and subordinates. *European Journal of Social Psychology, 29,* 139–146.

Vonk, R. (2002). Self-serving interpretations of flattery: Why ingratiation works. *Journal*

of Personality and Social Psychology, 82, 515–526.

Vonk, R., & van Knippenberg, A. (1995). Processing attitude statements from in-group and out-group members: Effects of within-group and within-person inconsistencies on reading times. *Journal of Personality and Social Psychology, 68,* 215–227.

Vriz, A., Edward, K., & Bull, R. (2001). Police officers' ability to detect deceit: The benefit of indirect deception detection measures. *Legal and Criminological Psychology 81,* 365–376.

Wade, N. (2002, February 26). Fight or woo? Sex scents for a male mouse. *New York Times,* F3.

Wade, N. (2003, November 25). A course in evolution taught by chimps. *New York Times,* F1, F4.

Walker, L. J., & Hennig, K. H. (2004). Differing conceptions of moral exemplarity: Just, brace, and caring. *Journal of Personality and Social Psychology, 86,* 629–647.

Walker, S., Richardson, D. S., & Green, L. R. (2000). Aggression among older adults: The relationship of interaction networks and gender role to direct and indirect responses. *Aggressive Behavior, 26,* 145–154.

Walster, E., & Festinger, L. (1962). The effectiveness of "overheard" persuasive communication. *Journal of Abnormal and Social Psychology, 65,* 395–402.

Wann, D. L., & Branscombe, N. R. (1993). Sports fans: Measuring degree of identification with their team. *International Journal of Sport Psychology, 24,* 1–17.

Waters, H. F., Block, D., Friday, C., & Gordon, J. (1993, July 12). Networks under the gun. *Newsweek,* 64–66.

Watson, C. B., Chemers, M. M., & Preiser, N. (2001). Collective efficacy: A multilevel analysis. *Personality and Social Psychology Bulletin, 27,* 1057–1068.

Watson, D., Hubbard, B., & Wiese, D. (2000). Self–other agreement in personality and affectivity: The role of acquaintanceship, trait visibility, and assumed similarity. *Journal of Personality and Social Psychology, 78,* 546–558.

Watts, B. L. (1982). Individual differences in circadian activity rhythms and their effects on roommate relationships. *Journal of Personality, 50,* 374–384.

Wayne, J. H., Riordan, C. M., & Thomas, K. M. (2001). Is all sexual harassment viewed the same? Mock juror decisions in same- and cross-gender cases. *Journal of Applied Social Psychology, 86,* 179–187.

Wayne, S. J., & Ferris, G. R. (1990). Influence tactics, and exchange quality in supervisor–subordinate interactions: A laboratory experiment and field study. *Journal of Applied Psychology, 75,* 487–499.

Wayne, S. J., & Kacmar, K. M. (1991). The effects of impression management on the performance appraisal process. *Organizational Behavior and Human Decision Processes, 48,* 70–88.

Wayne, S. J., & Liden, R. C. (1995). Effects of impression management on performance ratings: A longitudinal study. *Academy of Management Journal, 38,* 232–260.

Wayne, S. J., Liden, R. C., Graf, I. K., & Ferris, G. R. (1997). The role of upward influence tactics in human resource decisions. *Personnel Psychology, 50,* 979–1006.

Weaver, S. E., & Ganong, L. H. (2004). The factor structure of the Romantic Beliefs Scale for African Americans and European Americans. *Journal of Social and Personal Relationships, 21,* 171–185.

Wegener, D. T., Petty, R. E., Smoak, N. D., & Fabrigar, L. R. (2004). Multiple routes to resisting attitude change. In E. S. Knowles & J. A. Linn (Eds.), *Resistance and persuasion* (pp. 13–38). Mahwah, NJ: Erlbaum.

Wegner, D. M. (1992a). The premature demise of the solo experiment. *Personality and Social Psychology Bulletin, 18,* 504–508.

Wegner, D. M. (1992b). You can't always think what you want: Problems in the suppression of unwanted thoughts. In M. Zanna (Ed.), *Advances in experimental social psychology* (Vol. 25, pp. 193–225). San Diego, CA: Academic Press.

Wegner, D. M., & Bargh, J. A. (1998). Control and automaticity in social life. In D. T. Gilbert, S. T. Fiske, & G. Lindsey (Eds.), *Handbook of social psychology* (4th ed.). New York: McGraw-Hill.

Wegner, D. M., & Zanakos, S. (1994). Chronic thought suppression. *Journal of Personality, 62,* 615–640.

Wegner, D. T., & Petty, R. E. (1994). Mood management across affective states: The hedonic contingency hypothesis. *Journal of Personality and Social Psychology, 66,* 1034–1048.

Weigel, D. J., & Ballard-Reisch, D. S. (2002). Investigating the behavioral indicators of relational commitment. *Journal of Social and Personal Relationships 19,* 403–423.

Weinberg, M. S., Lottes, I. L., & Shaver, F. M. (1995). Swedish or American heterosexual college youth: Who is more permissive? *Archives of Sexual Behavior, 24,* 409–437.

Weiner, B. (1980). A cognitive (attribution) emotion–action model of motivated behavior: An analysis of judgments of help-giving. *Journal of Personality and Social Psychology, 39,* 186–200.

Weiner, B. (1985). An attributional theory of achievement motivation and emotion. *Psychological Review, 92,* 548–573.

Weiner, B. (1993). On sin versus sickness: A theory of perceived responsibility and social motivation. *American Psychologist, 48,* 957–965.

Weiner, B. (1995). *Judgments of responsibility: A foundation for a theory of social conduct.* New York: Guilford.

Weiner, B., Amirkhan, J., Folkes, V. S., & Verette, J. A. (1987). An attributional analysis of excuse giving: Studies of a naive theory of emotion. *Journal of Personality and Social Psychology, 52,* 316–324.

Weldon, E., & Mustari, L. (1988). Felt dispensability in groups of coactors: The effects of shared responsibility and explicit anonymity

on cognitive effort. *Organizational Behavior and Human Decision Processes, 41,* 330–351.

Wentura, D., Rothermund, K., & Bak, P. (2000). Automatic vigilance: The attention-grabbing power of approach- and avoidance-related social information. *Journal of Personality and Social Psychology, 78,* 1024–1037.

What gives? (2004, January/February) *AARP, 78.*

Wheeler, L., & Kim, Y. (1997). What is beautiful is culturally good: The physical attractiveness stereotype has different content in collectivistic cultures. *Personality and Social Psychology Bulletin, 23,* 795–800.

Whiffen, V. E., Aube, J. A., Thompson, J. M., & Campbell, T. L. (2000). Attachment beliefs and interpersonal contexts associated with dependency and self-criticism. *Journal of Social and Clinical Psychology, 19,* 184–205.

White, R. K. (1977). Misperception in the Arab-Israeli conflict. *Journal of Social Issues, 33,* 190–221.

Whitelaw, K. (2003, July 21). In death's shadow. *U.S. News & World Report,* 17–21.

Wiederman, M. W., & Allgeier, E. R. (1996). Expectations and attributions regarding extramarital sex among young married individuals. *Journal of Psychology & Human Sexuality, 8,* 21–35.

Williams, C. L. (1992). The glass escalator: Hidden advantages for men in the "female" professions. *Social Problems, 39,* 253–267.

Williams, J. E., & Best, D. L. (1990). *Sex and psyche: Gender and self viewed cross-culturally.* Newbury Park, CA: Sage.

Williams, K. B., Radefeld, P. A., Binning, J. F., & Suadk, J. R. (1993). When job candidates are "hard-" versus "easy-to-get": Effects of candidate availability on employment decisions. *Journal of Applied Social Psychology, 23,* 169–198.

Williams, K. D. (2001). *Ostracism: The power of silence.* New York: Guilford Press.

Williams, K. D., & Karau, S. J. (1991). Social loafing and social compensation: The effects of expectations of co-worker performance. *Journal of Personality and Social Psychology, 61,* 570–581.

Williams, K. D., Cheung, C. K. T., & Choi, W. (2000). Cyberostracism: Effects of being ignored over the Internet. *Journal of Personality and Social Psychology, 79,* 748–762.

Williams, K. D., Harkins, S., & Latané, B. (1981). Identifiability as a deterrent to social loafing: Two cheering experiments. *Journal of Personality and Social Psychology, 40,* 303–311.

Williamson, G. M., & Schulz, R. (1995). Caring for a family member with cancer: Past communal behavior and affective reactions. *Journal of Applied Social Psychology, 25,* 93–116.

Willingham, D. T., & Dunn, E. W. (2003). What neuroimaging and brain localization can do, cannot, and should not do for social psychology. *Journal of Personality and Social Psychology, 85,* 662–671.

Wilson, A. E., & Ross, M. (2000). The frequency of temporal-self and social comparisons in

people's personal appraisals. *Journal of Personality and Social Psychology, 78,* 928–942.

Wilson, D. W. (1981). Is helping a laughing matter? *Psychology, 18,* 6–9.

Wilson, J. P., & Petruska, R. (1984). Motivation, model attributes, and prosocial behavior. *Journal of Personality and Social Psychology, 46,* 458–468.

Wilson, M. L., & Wrangham, R. W. (2003). Intergroup relations in chimpanzees. *The Annual Review of Anthropology, 32,* 363–392.

Wilson, T. D., & Kraft, D. (1993). Why do I love thee?: Effects of repeated introspections about a dating relationship on attitudes toward the relationship. *Personality and Social Psychology Bulletin, 19,* 409–418.

Winograd, E., Goldstein, F. C., Monarch, E. S., Peluso, J. P., & Goldman, W. P. (1999). The mere exposure effect in patients with Alzheimer's disease. *Neuropsychology, 13,* 41–46.

Winquist, J. R., & Larson, J. R., Jr. (1998). Information pooling: When it impacts group decision making. *Journal of Personality and Social Psychology, 74,* 317–377.

Wiseman, H. (1997). Far away from home: The loneliness experience of overseas students. *Journal of Social and Clinical Psychology, 16,* 277–298.

Wisman, A., & Koole, S. L. (2003). Hiding in the crowd: Can mortality salience promote affiliation with others who oppose one's world view? *Journal of Personality and Social Psychology, 84,* 511–526.

Witt, L. A., & Ferris, G. B. (2003). Social skill as moderator of the conscientiousness-performance relationship: Convergent results across four studies. *Journal of Applied Psychology, 88,* 808–820.

Wohl, M. J. A., & Branscombe, N. R. (2005). Forgiveness and collective guilt assignment to historical perpetrator groups depend on level of social category inclusiveness. *Journal of Personality and Social Psychology, 88.*

Wood, G. S. (2004, April 12 & 19). Pursuits of happiness. *The New Republic,* 38–42.

Wood, J. V. (1989). Theory and research concerning social comparisons of personal attributes. *Psychological Bulletin, 106,* 231–248.

Wood, J. V., & Wilson, A. E. (2003). How important is social comparison? In M. R. Leary & J. P. Tangney (Eds.), *Handbook of self and identity* (pp. 344–366). New York: Guilford Press.

Wood, W., & Quinn, J. M. (2003). Forewarned and forearmed? Two meta-analytic syntheses of forewarning of influence appeals. *Psychological Bulletin, 129,* 119–138.

Wood, W., Wong, F. Y., & Cachere, J. G. (1991). Effects of media violence on viewers' aggression in unconstrained social interaction. *Psychological Bulletin, 109,* 371–383.

Wood, W., Pool, G. J., Leck, K., & Purvis, D. (1996). Self-definition, defensive processing, and influence: The normative impact of majority and minority groups. *Journal of Personality and Social Psychology, 71,* 1181–1193.

Wooster, M. M. (2000, September). Ordinary people, extraordinary rescues. *American Enterprise, 11,* 18–21.

Wright, S. C. (2001). Strategic collective action: Social psychology and social change. In R. Brown & S. Gaertner (Eds.), *Blackwell handbook of social psychology: Intergroup processes* (pp. 409–430). Oxford: Blackwell.

Wright, S. C., Taylor, D. M., & Moghaddam, F. M. (1990). Responding to membership in a disadvantaged group: From acceptance to collective protest. *Journal of Personality and Social Psychology, 58,* 994–1003.

Wright, S. C., Aron, A., McLaughlin-Volpe, T., & Ropp, S. A. (1997). The extended contact effect: Knowledge of cross-group friendships and prejudice. *Journal of Personality and Social Psychology, 73,* 73–90.

Wyer, R. S., Jr., & Srull, T. K. (Eds.). (1994). *Handbook of social cognition* (2nd ed., Vol. 1). Hillsdale, NJ: Erlbaum.

Wyer, R. S., Jr., Budesheim, T. L., Lambert, A. J., & Swan, S. (1994). Person memory judgment: Pragmatic influences on impressions formed in a social context. *Journal of Personality and Social Psychology, 66,* 254–267.

Yoder, J. D., & Berendsen, L. L. (2001). "outsider within" the firehouse: African American and white women firefighters. *Psychology of Women Quarterly, 25,* 27–36.

Yoshida, T. (1977). Effects of cognitive dissonance on task evaluation and task performance. *Japanese Journal of Psychology, 48,* 216–223.

Yovetich, N. A., & Rusbult, C. E. (1994). Accommodative behavior in close relationships: Exploring transformation of motivation. *Journal of Experimental Social Psychology, 30,* 138–164.

Yu, W. (1996, May 12). Many husbands fail to share housework. *Albany Times Union,* pp. A1, A7.

Yukl, G., & Falbe, C. M. (1991). Importance of different power sources in downward and lateral relations. *Journal of Applied Psychology, 76,* 416–423.

Yukl, G., & Tracey, J. B. (1992). Consequences of influence tactics used with subordinates, peers, and the boss. *Journal of Applied Psychology 77,* 525–535.

Yukl, G., Falbe, C. M., & Young, J. Y. (1993). Patterns of influence behavior for managers. *Group & Organizational Management, 18,* 5–28.

Yukl, G., Kim, H., & Chavez, C. (1999). Task importance, feasibility, and agent influence behavior as determinants of target commitment. *Journal of Applied Psychology, 84,* 137–143.

Yuval, G. (2004, June 15). Volunteers in college. *The New York Times,* p. A22.

Yzerbyt, V., Rocher, S., & Schradron, G. (1997). Stereotypes as explanations: A subjective essentialist view of group perception. In R. Spears, P. J. Oakes, N. Ellemers, & S. A. Haslam (Eds.), *The social psychology of stereotyping and group life* (pp. 20–50). Oxford: Blackwell.

Zajonc, R. B. (1965). Social facilitation. *Science, 149,* 269–274.

Zajonc, R. B. (1968). Attitudinal effects of mere exposure [monograph]. *Journal of Personality and Social Psychology, 9,* 1–27.

Zajonc, R. B. (2001). Mere exposure: A gateway to the subliminal. *Current Directions in Psychological Science, 10,* 224–228.

Zajonc, R. B., & Sales, S. M. (1966). Social facilitation of dominant and subordinate responses. *Journal of Experimental Social Psychology, 2,* 160–168.

Zajonc, R. B., Heingartner, A., & Herman, E. M. (1969). Social enhancement and impairment of performance in the cockroach. *Journal of Personality and Social Psychology, 13,* 83–92.

Zajonc, R. B., Adelmann, P. K., Murphy, S. T., & Niedenthal, P. M. (1987). Convergence in the physical appearance of spouses. *Motivation and Emotion, 11,* 335–346.

Zarate, M. A., Garcia, B., Garza, A. A., & Hitlan, R. T. (2004). Cultural threat and perceived realistic conflict as dual predictors of prejudice. *Journal of Experimental Social Psychology, 40,* 99–105.

Zdaniuk, B., & Levine, J. M. (1996). Anticipated interaction and thought generation: The role of faction size. *British Journal of Social Psychology, 35,* 201–218.

Zebrowitz, L. A. (1997). *Reading faces.* Boulder, CO: Westview Press.

Zebrowitz, L. A., Collins, M. A., & Dutta, R. (1998). The relationship between appearance and personality across the life span. *Personality and Social Psychology Bulletin, 24,* 736–749.

Zillmann, D. (1979). *Hostility and aggression.* Hillsdale, NJ: Erlbaum.

Zillmann, D. (1983). Transfer of excitation in emotional behavior. In J. T. Cacioppo & R. E. Petty (Eds.), *Social psychophysiology: A sourcebook* (pp. 215–240). New York: Guilford Press.

Zillmann, D. (1988). Cognition–excitation interdependencies in aggressive behavior. *Aggressive Behavior, 14,* 51–64.

Zillmann, D. (1993). Mental control of angry aggression. In D. M. Wegner & J. W. Pennebaker (Eds.), *Handbook of mental control.* Englewood Cliffs, NJ: Prentice-Hall.

Zillmann, D. (1994). Cognition–excitation interdependencies in the escalation of anger and angry aggression. In M. Potegal & J. F. Knutson (Eds.), *The dynamics of aggression.* Hillsdale, NJ: Erlbaum.

Zillmann, D., Baron, R. A., & Tamborini, R. (1981). The social costs of smoking: Effects of tobacco smoke on hostile behavior. *Journal of Applied Social Psychology, 11,* 548–561.

Zimbardo, P. G. (1976). The human choice: Individuation, reason, and order versus deindividuation, impulse, and chaos. *Nebraska Symposium on Motivation, 17,* 237–307.

Zimbardo, P. G. (1977). *Shyness: What it is and what you can do about it.* Reading, MA: Addison-Wesley.

Zoglin, R. (1993). The shock of the blue. *Time, 142*(17), 71–72.

Zukerman, M. (1994). Behavioral expressions and biosocial bases of sensation seeking. New York: Cambridge University Press.

NAME INDEX

Aarts, H., 251, 252
Abelson, R. P., 336
Abraham, C., 134
Abrams, D., 156
Adams, J. M., 238
Adams, J. S., 352
Adams, M. G., 288
Agarie, N., 325
Agnew, C. R., 239
Ahmed, N., 294
Ahrons, C., 239
Ajzen, I., 93, 105
Alagna, F. J., 64
Alexander, M. J., 235
Alexander, R., 235
Algom, D., 35
Alicke, M. D., 136
Allen, J., 229
Allen, J. J. B., 197
Allgeier, E. R., 229, 230
Allport, F. H., 94, 341
Allyn, J., 110
Alvaro, E. M., 257
Amato, P. R., 238, 239, 285
American Psychiatric Association, 233
Ames, D. R., 292
Amsel, R., 201
Andersen, S. M., 197
Anderson, C. A., 9, 81, 220, 284, 303, 305,
    306, 309, 310, 311, 318, 326, 327
Anderson, J., 316
Anderson, K. B., 318
Anderson, N. H., 83
Anderson, V. L., 287
Andersson, L. M., 323
Andreoletti, C., 197
Andreou, E., 321
Angier, N., 200, 204
Antill, J. K., 232
Apanovitch, A. M., 253, 254
Apple, K. J., 226
Archer, J., 320, 321
Archibald, F. S., 220
Armitage, C. J., 93
Arms, R. L., 315
Aron, A., 194, 228, 229, 231, 234, 235, 340
Aron, E. N., 228, 229
Aronoff, J., 63
Aronson, E., 116
Aronson, J., 117, 147
Aronson, L., 148
Arriaga, X. B., 238
Asakawa, K., 15
Asch, S. E., 80, 248, 249, 250
Aseltine, R. H. Jr., 239
Asendorpf, J. B., 222
Asher, S. R., 220
Ashmore, R. D., 132, 199

Aspinwall, L. G., 134
Assaad, J. M., 319
Aune, K. S., 224
Averill, J. R., 229
Azar, B., 286, 287

Bacanli, H., 220
Baccman, C., 223
Bachorowski, J., 194
Back, K., 196, 337
Bahadur, M. A., 239
Bak, P., 207
Baker, N. V., 312
Baldwin, D. A., 190
Baldwin, M. W., 262
Balkin, D. B., 134
Ballard-Reisch, D. S., 238
Banaji, M., 169, 177
Banaji, M. R., 39, 52, 177, 336
Bandura, A., 97, 132, 207, 290, 305, 310
Banks, J. S., 205
Banks, W., 336
Banse, R., 234
Barak, A., 231
Barash, D. P., 10
Bardi, A., 338
Bargh, J. A., 31, 34, 37, 38, 39, 45, 99, 107,
    161, 207, 247, 262, 263, 282
Barling, J., 322
Baron, J., 293
Baron, R. A., 9, 50, 51, 72, 78, 134, 303,
    308, 315, 317, 319, 322, 323, 325, 349,
    350, 352
Baron, R. S., 249, 253, 343
Barrett, L. F., 219
Barrios, J., 220
Bar-Tal, D., 171
Bartholomew, K., 217
Bartholow, B. D., 14, 319
Bartsch, R. A., 197
Baskett, G. D., 208
Bassili, J. N., 23
Batholomew, K., 220
Batson, C. D., 120, 278, 279, 286, 288,
    291, 294
Batson, J. G., 294
Baum, A., 197
Baumann, D. J., 285, 295
Baumeister, R., 281
Baumeister, R. F., 33, 54, 137, 139, 190,
    191, 192, 222, 229, 315, 326, 359
Beach, S. R., 196
Beach, S. R. H., 224
Beall, A. E., 228
Beaman, A. I., 259
Becker, S. W., 275
Behfar, K. J., 350
Beilfuss, M. C., 218

Bell, B., 220
Bell, B. E., 202
Bell, D. C., 235
Bell, D. W., 98
Bell, P. A., 318
Bell, R. A., 220, 222
Benjamin, E., 191
Ben-Porath, D. D., 192
Benson, P. L., 282
Benthin, A. C., 120
Ben-Zeev, T., 147
Bera, S., 217
Berant, E., 235
Berendsen, L. L., 131, 159
Berg, J. H., 220
Berkowitz, L., 295, 304, 305
Bernieri, F., 141
Bernieri, F. J., 202
Berntson, G. C., 192
Berry, D. S., 191, 193
Berry, J. W., 328
Berscheid, E., 198, 215, 228, 229, 237
Bersoff, D. M., 290
Best, D. L., 137
Bettencourt, B. A., 161, 316
Biblarz, T., 236
Bierhoff, H. W., 288
Biernat, M., 131, 139, 156, 159, 162, 163
Bies, R. J., 85, 353
Binney, V., 218
Bjørklund, D. F., 235
Bjørkqvist, K., 316, 317
Blackstone, T., 147, 224
Blader, S., 141
Blain, M. D., 238
Blair, I. V., 155
Blaney, P. H., 50
Blanton, H., 117
Blascovich, J., 167
Blass, T., 230
Blaylock, B., 233
Blazer, D. G., 77
Bleske-Rechek, A. L., 220
Bless, H., 15, 36, 52
Blickle, G., 269
Block, C. J., 159
Block, J., 217
Bobo, L., 171
Boden, J., 137
Bodenhausen, G. F., 162
Bodenhausen, G. V., 140, 162, 167
Bodenmann, G., 238
Boer, F., 218
Bogard, M., 316
Bohner, G., 101
Bombardieri, M., 226, 227
Bond, C. F. Jr., 267

Hochwarter, W. A., 235
Hodges, L. A., 208
Hogg, M. A., 98, 131, 156, 174, 175
Hojjat, M., 215
Holmes, J. G., 215, 224
Holt, C. S., 222
Hope, D. A., 222
Hopkins, A. B., 158
Horney, K., 206
Hornsey, M. J., 174, 175, 357, 358
Horowitz, I. A., 359
Horowitz, L. M., 217
Horton, R. S., 207
Hovland, C. I., 109, 110
Hoyer, W. D., 110
Huang, I.-C., 132
Hubbard, B., 233
Huesmann, L. R., 310
Huff, C., 25
Hugenberg, K., 167
Hughes, J., 226, 228
Hughes, S. M., 225
Huguet, P., 343
Hummert, M. L., 206
Hunt, A., 203
Hyde, J. S., 235
Hyman, L. M., 63

Ickes, W., 141, 224
Imani, A., 357, 358
Insko, C. A., 12, 206, 252, 347
Inzlicht, M., 147
Ireland, C. A., 320
Ireland, J. L., 320, 321
Ironsmith, M., 221
Irvine, M., 236
Isen, A. M., 50, 51, 285
Istvan, J., 229
Ito, T. A., 13, 42, 93, 99
Izard, C., 62

Jackman, M. R., 156
Jackson, L. M., 161
Jackson, T., 220, 221
Jackson, T. T., 282
Jacobi, L., 225
Jacobs, J. A., 156
Jacobson, L., 34
James, C. M., 221
Janis, I. L., 109, 357, 358
Jarrell, A., 201
Jellison, J. M., 74
Jensen-Campbell, L. A., 202, 238
Jetten, J., 131, 160, 166, 167
Jochims, M., 360
Johnson, B. T., 9, 113, 120
Johnson, C., 164
Johnson, D. J., 238
Johnson, J. C., 221
Johnson, J. D., 166
Johnson, M. K., 43
Johnson, S., 194
Johnston, L., 164

Johnston, V. S., 199
Johnstone, B., 199
Joireman, J., 316
Jones, C. R., 37
Jones, E. E., 68, 69, 73, 75, 82, 259
Jones, J. H., 231
Jones, J. T., 14, 15
Jones, W. H., 238
Joseph, S., 321
Jost, T. J., 182
Judd, C. M., 163, 167
Jungeberg, B. J., 11

Kacmar, K. M., 85
Kahn, A. S., 226
Kahn, J. H., 47
Kahneman, D., 36, 138
Kaiser, D. R., 145, 146
Kallgren, C. A., 247, 250, 251
Kambara, T., 308
Kameda, T., 325, 357
Kanagawa, C., 141
Kandel, D. B., 205
Karabenick, S. A., 282
Karau, S. J., 66, 157, 344
Karney, B. R., 44, 236, 238
Karraker, K. H., 198
Karremans, J. C., 327
Karuza, J., 353
Kashy, D. A., 219
Kastak, D., 197
Katz, D., 100
Katz, J., 224
Kaufman-Gililland, C. M., 347, 348
Kaukiainen, A., 317
Kawakami, K., 169, 177, 181
Kay, A. C., 219
Keating, J. P., 295
Keelan, J. P., 199
Kellerman, J., 229
Kelley, H. H., 70, 109
Kelly, A. E., 47
Kelly, K., 237
Kelman, H. C., 25
Keltner, D., 222, 349
Kemper, S., 206
Kenealy, P., 199
Kenrick, D. T., 201, 205, 225, 285, 295
Kenworthy, J. B., 257
Kernis, M. H., 137
Kerr, N. L., 347, 348
Kessler, J. W., 192
Ketcher, C. M., 308
Khulman, M. D., 348
Kilduff, M., 85
Kilham, W., 266
Killeya, L. A., 9
Kilmartin, C. T., 170
Kim, H., 128, 247, 269
Kim, Y., 81, 199
King, G., 37
Kisner, R. D., 232
Kitayama, S., 128, 296

Kite, M. E., 157
Kitzmann, K. M., 218
Klagsbrun, F., 218
Klandermans, B., 134, 339
Klar, Y., 136
Klein, R., 288
Klein, S. B., 83, 84
Klein, T. R., 294
Kleinke, C. L., 63, 229
Kline, S. L., 232, 234
Kling, K. C., 134
Klohnen, E. C., 205, 217, 223
Klonsky, B. G., 157
Kmill, J., 220
Knee, C. R., 128, 199
Knight, G. P., 348
Knowles, M., 65
Koch, W., 239
Kochanska, G., 216
Koehler, J. J., 36
Koestner, R., 141, 190
Kogan, N., 356
Komorita, M., 346
Koole, S. L., 191
Koon, J., 201
Koukourakis, K., 225
Kowalski, R. M., 221, 222, 238
Kraft, D., 143
Kramp, P., 288
Krantz, J. H., 85
Kraus, R. M., 348
Kraus, S. J., 286
Kristoff, A. L., 85
Krosnick, J. A., 93, 95, 103, 104, 109, 114, 193
Kulik, J. A., 191
Kunda, Z., 31, 33, 41, 132, 136, 163, 170
Kurdek, L. A., 223, 234, 235, 238
Kus, L. A., 221
Kwon, Y.-H., 135

Lachman, M. E., 197
LaFrance, M., 156
Lago, T., 317
Laird, J. D., 229
Lakin, J. L., 282
Lalonde, R. N., 159
LaMastro, V., 235
Lambert, A. J., 173
Lambert, T. A., 226
Lamm, H., 356
Langer, E., 261
Langerspetz, K. M., 317
Langlands, C. L., 157
Langlois, J. H., 15, 199, 200
Lapham, L. H., 208
LaPiere, R. T., 102
Larrick, R. P., 71
Larson, J. R. Jr., 355, 359
Latané, B., 250, 276, 277, 278, 280, 344
Lau, M. L., 319
Lau, S., 220
Laurenceau, J.-P., 219

Lavie, N., 190
Lawton, S. F., 317
Leary, M. R., 135, 142, 190, 191
LeBlanc, M. M., 322
Lecci, L., 166
Ledbetter, J. E., 103
Lee, A., 233
Lee, A. Y., 197
Lee, Y. T., 76
Lehman, D. R., 118, 224
Lehman, T. C., 292
Leippe, M., 117
Leippe, M. R., 119, 135
Lemley, B., 200
Lemonick, M. D., 229
Lepper, M., 42
Lerner, R. M., 282
Letchford, J., 221
Levenson, R. W., 238
Leventhal, G. S., 353
Levin, P. A., 51, 285
Levine, J. M., 257
Levine, R. V., 280
Levy, K. N., 237
Lewicki, R. J., 350
Lewin, K., 77
Lewis, J., 229
Lewis, M., 132, 196
Leyens, J.-P., 148
L'Herrou, T., 250
Li, N. P., 225
Liberman, A., 71, 108, 111
Liberman, N., 73
Lickel, B., 131, 336
Liden, R. C., 84, 259
Lieberman, J. D., 325
Liebert, R. M., 284
Lin, M. H., 79, 82, 84
Lind, E. W., 352
Linden, E., 17
Linville, P. W., 129, 165
Linz, D., 311
Lipkus, I. M., 116
Lippa, R., 142
Lipton, J. E., 10
Liu, T. J., 280
Locke, V., 163
Lockwood, P., 132
Lockwood, R. L., 218
Loftus, J., 83, 84
Long, C. R., 220
Longo, L. C., 199
Lopez, D. F., 262
Lopez, F. G., 217
Lord, C. G., 147
Lorenz, K., 304
Losch, M., 117
Lottes, I. L., 231
Louis-Dreyfus, E., 50
Lowery, L., 62
Lucas, J. A., 159
Luce, C., 286
Luczak, S. E., 15

Lui, T. J., 116
Lundberg, J. K., 201
Lundqvist, D., 42
Luo, S., 205, 223
Lydon, J. E., 224
Lynch, M., 117
Lyness, K. S., 158

Ma, H. K., 287
Maass, A., 164, 249
Macauley, J., 283
MacDonald, H., 43
Mack, D., 201
Mackie, D. M., 52, 165, 167
Macrae, C. N., 162, 163, 202
Maddux, W. W., 282
Madey, S. F., 46
Maeda, E., 219
Maestripieri, D., 216
Magner, N. R., 353
Maheswaran, D., 99, 111
Mahler, H. I. M., 191
Mahoney, S., 227
Maio, G. R., 92, 98, 103
Maisonneuve, J., 195
Major, B., 137, 139, 144, 145, 146, 162
Makijani, M. G., 157
Malamuth, N. M., 311
Malone, B. E., 65
Malone, P. S., 71, 73
Maner, J. K., 198, 297
Manis, M. M., 8
Mann, L., 266
Manning, J. T., 225
Mannix, L. N., 201
Manstead, A. S. R., 100, 101, 167
Marcus, D. K., 199
Markey, P. M., 204
Markman, G. D., 72, 134
Markman, K. D., 359
Markus, H., 128, 132
Markus, H. R., 128, 141
Marques, J., 141
Martin, C. L., 176
Martin, L., 10
Martin, L. L., 52, 117
Martin, R., 220
Martinez, R., 201
Martinot, D., 157
Martz, J. M., 224, 239
Marx, R., 220
Maslach, C., 255
Mastekaasa, A., 234
Master, S., 225, 226
Maticka-Tydale, E., 226
Matsushima, R., 219, 221
Matz, D. C., 225
May, J. L., 193
May, K. A., 200
Mayer, J. D., 50, 284
Mayo, C., 66
McAdams, D. P., 290
McAndrew, F. T., 296

McArthur, L. Z., 165
McAuley, E., 132
McCabe, M. P., 235
McCall, M., 8
McClintock, C. G., 348
McClure, J., 71
McConahay, J. B., 176
McConnell, A. R., 164
McConnell, W., 308
McCoy, S. K., 145, 146
McCullough, M. E., 315, 327, 328
McCusker, C., 348
McDavid, J. W., 256
McDonald, F., 206
McDonald, H. E., 50
McDonald, R. D., 192
McGarty, C., 99
McGillis, D., 69
McGuire, C. V., 135
McGuire, S., 218, 220
McGuire, W. J., 115, 135
McHale, S. M., 218
McKelvie, S. J., 199, 201
McKinney, K. D., 179
McLaughlin, L., 236
McLaughlin-Volpe, T., 132, 340
McMillan, D., 33
McNulty, J. K., 44, 236, 238
McQuinn, R. D., 220
Mead, G. H., 137, 144
Medvec, V. H., 37, 46
Mehrabian, A., 202
Meier, B. P., 201
Mendelsohn, G. A., 73
Mendoza-Denton, R., 129
Meyers, S. A., 229
Miall, D., 216
Michael, R. T., 231
Michela, J. L., 70
Miedema, J., 282
Migdal, M. J., 345
Mikulincer, M., 217, 235, 287
Milanese, M., 226
Miles, S. M., 71
Milgram, S., 264, 265, 266
Miller, D. A., 167
Miller, D. T., 76, 100, 103, 138
Miller, L. C., 68, 225
Miller, N., 111, 161, 201, 257, 316, 326
Miller, P. J. E., 77
Miller, R. S., 199
Mills, J., 236
Milne, A. B., 162
Mirenberg, M. C., 14, 15
Miron, A. M., 167
Mitchell, J. P., 202
Mitchell, T. R., 259
MIT-report, 158
Mladinic, A., 156, 157
Modigliani, A., 267
Moffitt, T. E., 234
Moghaddam, F. M., 159
Monahan, J. L., 197

Mondloch, C. J., 190
Monin, B., 103, 197
Monteith, M. J., 155, 166
Montepare, J. M., 202
Montgomery, R., 235
Montoya, R. M., 207
Moore, D., 343
Moore, P. J., 191
Moore, T., 289
Moreland, R. L., 196
Morey, N., 202
Morgan, H. J., 227
Morris, M. W., 71
Morrison, E. W., 85
Morrison-Beedy, D., 120
Morrow, G. D., 238
Moscovici, S., 257
Mosley, N. R., 208
Mossakowski, K. N., 137
Mugny, G., 257
Mullen, B., 164, 345
Mullins, L. C., 222
Mummendey, A., 160
Munro, G. D., 99
Murnen, S. K., 205
Murphy, S. T., 197
Murray, L., 216
Murray, S. L., 224, 234
Musselman, L., 200
Mussweiler, T., 140
Mustari, L., 344
Myers, D. G., 356
Myers, L. R., 192
Mynard, H., 321

Nadler, A., 282, 291, 292
Nash, S. C., 235
National Institute for Occupational Safety
    and Health, 322
Neighbors, C., 128, 199
Neimeyer, R. A., 78
Nelson, D., 169, 205
Nemeroff, C., 47
Nemeroff, C. J., 202
Nemeth, C. J., 257, 355, 360
Neto, F., 220
Neuberg, S., 167
Neuberg, S. L., 79, 82, 84, 167, 197
Neuman, J. H., 322, 323
Neumann, R., 61
Newby-Clark, I. R., 43
Newcomb, T. M., 203, 206
Newman, L. S., 359
Newman, M. L., 66
Newsom, J. T., 197, 291
Newsweek Poll, 92
Newton, T. L., 238
Neyer, F. J., 218
Nida, S. A., 201
Niemann, Y. F., 131
Nienhuis, A. E., 101
Nisbett, R. E., 10, 74, 75, 142, 312, 313
Noel, J. G., 97, 141

Nolen-Hoeksema, S., 126
Norlander, T., 223
Novaco, R. W., 308
Nunn, J. S., 137
Nurius, P., 132
Nurmi, J.-E., 222
Nuss, C. K., 191
Nussbaum, S., 73
Nyman, L., 81

Oakes, P. J., 127, 128, 160, 165, 173
Oberlander, E., 217
O'Brien, L. T., 155, 173
O'Brien, M., 239
O'Connor, S. C., 190
O'Donnell, C. D., 78
O'Donohue, W., 78
Oettingen, G., 76
Ohbuchi, K., 308, 325
Ohman, A., 35, 42
Ohtsubo, Y., 355
O'Leary, V., 320, 322
Oleson, K. C., 33, 163, 294
Oliver-Rodriguez, J. C., 199
Olson, J. M., 92, 103
Olson, M. A., 193
Olweus, D., 320
O'Moore, M. N., 321
Onishi, M., 217
Onorato, R. S., 131
Oppermann, M., 226
Orbell, S., 106
Orenstein, L., 286
Orpen, C., 208
Osborne, J. W., 148
Österman, K., 316, 317
Ostrom, T., 344
O'Sullivan, C. S., 163
O'Sullivan, M., 15, 40, 65, 67
Ouellette, J. A., 42
Owen, A. W., 40
Owens, L., 317
Owren, M. J., 194
Oxley, Z. M., 157
Ozer, D. J., 204, 233

Packer, G., 313
Padavic, I., 139
Paez, D., 141
Paik, H., 309
Pak, A. W.-P., 199
Palmade, G., 196
Palmer, J., 204
Paolini, S., 179
Papageorgis, D., 115
Paquette, J. A., 220
Parasuraman, S., 159
Paris, M., 228
Park, J., 52
Parke, B., 163
Parker, S., 176
Parks, G., 346
Patience, R. A., 225

Patrick, H., 128, 199
Patterson, M., 141
Paul, E. L., 226
Paulhus, D. L., 85
Pavalko, E. K., 137
Pearson, C. M., 323
Pearson, K., 233
Pedersen, W. C., 225
Pederson, W. C., 326
Pelfrey, M., 292
Pelham, B. W., 14, 15
Pendry, L. F., 202
Pennebaker, J. W., 201
Penner, L., 169
Penner, L. A., 281, 290
Penrod, S., 311
Penton-Voak, I., 199
Perrett, D. I., 200
Perrew, P. L., 235
Pessin, J., 341
Peterson, R. S., 350
Peterson, V. S., 157
Petruska, R., 279
Pettigrew, T. F., 92, 165, 174, 179, 182
Pettijohn, T. E. F., 11
Petty, R., 113
Petty, R. E., 52, 92, 99, 100, 104, 107,
    111, 112
Petty, R. J., 93, 103, 104, 109
Phelps, E. A., 40
Phemister, S., 284
Pickett, C. L., 65, 191
Piercy, M., 202
Pietromonaco, P., 37
Pietromonaco, P. R., 219
Pihl, R. O., 319
Piliavin, J. A., 282
Pinel, E. C., 148
Pinker, S., 295
Pittman, T. S., 68
Pizarro, D., 275
Plant, E. A., 155, 161
Pleban, R., 140
Plog, A. E., 83
Poh, L. L., 174
Polivy, J., 132
Pollak, K. I., 131
Pollock, C. L., 261
Pomerantz, E. M., 225
Pontari, B. A., 86
Ponzetti, J. J. Jr., 221
Postmes, T., 131, 146, 147, 345
Poteat, G. M., 221
Poulous, R. W., 284
Pratkanis, A. R., 358
Pratto, F., 38, 179
Preiser, N., 134
Preister, J. R., 92
Prentice, D. A., 100, 103
Prins, K. S., 221
Pronin, E., 148
Pruitt, D. G., 347, 350, 351
Przybyla, D. P. J., 282

Puente, S., 314
Pusecker, P. A., 132
Putcha-Bhagavatula, A., 225
Pyszczynski, T., 76, 136, 154

Queller, S., 164
Quinn, D. M., 147
Quinn, J. M., 114

Rainey, D., 201
Rankin, C. T., 232, 234
Rapson, R. L., 215, 228
Ray, G. E., 221
Read, S. J., 68
Redersdorff, S., 157
Regan, P. C., 224, 229, 235
Reicher, S., 340
Reichmuth, C. J., 197
Reidhead, S., 141
Reis, H. T., 192, 215, 217, 237
Reisman, J. M., 222
Reiss, A. J., 309
Rempel, J. K., 77
Reno, R. R., 247, 250, 251
Rensberger, B., 229
Rentfrow, P. J., 204
Rentsch, J. R., 129
Reskin, B., 139
Reynolds, K. J., 128, 130
Rhodes, G., 200
Rhodewalt, F., 113
Rice, M. E., 304
Richard, F. D., 267
Richards, Z., 33, 164
Richardson, D., 25
Richardson, D. R., 303, 317
Richardson, D. S., 316
Ridley, M., 296
Riess, M., 119
Riggio, H. R., 239
Riggio, R. E., 202
Riordan, C. M., 78
Ritchie, L. D., 219
Ro, T., 190
Robins, R. W., 73, 135, 234
Robinson, R. J., 350
Robinson, L. A., 78
Robinson, M. D., 201
Robinson, P. H., 324
Robinson, R., 349
Robinson, R. J., 349
Roccas, S., 129, 339
Rochat, F., 267
Rocher, S., 163
Roese, N. J., 45
Rogers, R. J., 76
Rogers, R. W., 308
Roggman, L. A., 199, 200
Rohles, W. S., 37
Rokach, A., 220
Roland, E., 320
Romer, D., 280
Rosenbaum, M. E., 205

Rosenberg, E. L., 62
Rosenberg, M., 135
Rosenblood, L. K., 190
Rosenfield, H. W., 63
Rosenhan, D. L., 284, 285
Rosenthal, A. M., 276
Rosenthal, E., 218
Rosenthal, R., 34, 66, 67
Roskos-Ewoldsen, D. R., 103, 106
Rosnow, J., 25
Ross, D., 310
Ross, L., 76, 148
Ross, M., 7, 42, 43, 76, 132
Ross, S., 310
Rotenberg, K. J., 220, 222
Roth, J. A., 309
Rothermund, K., 207
Rothgerber, H., 165
Rothman, A. J., 36
Rotton, J., 9, 318
Rowatt, W. C., 85
Rowe, P. M., 190
Roy, M. M., 205
Rozell, D., 345
Rozin, P., 47, 62
Rubin, J. Z., 25
Rubin, Z., 228
Ruble, D. N., 235
Ruder, M., 15, 36, 52
Rudman, L. A., 171
Rueter, M. A., 234
Runtz, M. G., 78
Runyan, A. S., 157
Rusbult, C. E., 238, 239
Ruscher, J. B., 83
Rushton, J. P., 295, 296
Russell, C., 190
Russell, G. W., 288, 315
Russell, J. A., 62
Russell, J. M., 62
Russell, R. J. H., 296
Rutkowski, G. K., 280
Ruvolo, A. P., 218
Ruvolo, C. M., 218
Ryan, C. S., 163
Ryan, M., 130
Ryan, M. K., 130
Ryckman, R. M., 201, 208
Ryff, C. D., 134, 215

Sabini, J., 225, 226
Sadler, P., 204
Saenz, D. S., 147
Sager, K., 288
Sales, S. M., 342
Sally, D., 348
Salmela-Aro, K., 222
Salovey, P., 165, 253, 254, 275, 284, 285
Salvarani, G., 286
Samuels, S., 358
Sanders, G. S., 343
Sanders, J., 255
Sanders, M. R., 238

Sangrador, J. L., 231
Sani, F., 340
Sanitioso, R. B., 136
Sanna, L. J., 45, 132
Santee, R. T., 255
Sattler, D. N., 288
Savitsky, K., 37
Schachter, S., 53, 191, 196, 203, 229, 337
Schaller, M., 164, 295
Scheier, M. F., 221
Schein, V. E., 157
Scher, S. J., 352
Scherbaum, C., 147
Schimel, J., 208
Schlenker, B. R., 86, 119, 136, 293
Schlenker, R. B., 286
Schmid, R. E., 232
Schmitt, D. P., 10, 11, 229
Schmitt, E., 236
Schmitt, M. T., 126, 140, 145, 146, 159
Schneider, M. E., 292
Schradron, G., 163
Schreiber, H. J., 160
Schubert, T. W., 64
Schul, Y., 83
Schulz, R., 289
Schulz-Hardt, S., 359, 360
Schumacher, M., 201
Schusterman, R. J., 197
Schwartz, S. H., 338
Schwarz, N., 36, 50, 101
Schwarzer, R., 42
Scutt, D., 225
Searcy, E., 292
Sears, D. O., 93, 111, 175
Sechrist, G. B., 182
Sedikides, C., 81, 132, 139
Seery, M. D., 137
Segal, M. M., 196
Seligman, M. E. P., 76
Selim, J., 194, 216
Senecal, C., 235
Seta, C. E., 50
Seta, J. J., 50
Settles, I. H., 129
Shackelford, T. K., 10, 11, 235
Shah, J., 9, 263, 264
Shams, M., 220
Shanab, M. E., 266
Shannon, M. L., 201
Shapiro, A., 235
Shapiro, D. L., 353
Shapiro, J. P., 192
Sharp, M. J., 84
Shavelson, R. J., 129
Shaver, F. M., 231
Shaver, P. R., 217, 227
Shavitt, S., 99
Shaw, D., 218
Shaw, J. K., 283
Shaw, J. L., 282
Shaw, L. L., 294
Sheehan, E. P., 201

Name Index

SUBJECT INDEX

Note: Page numbers followed by *f* and *t* represent figures and tables respectively.

Communicators
    attractiveness of, 110, 110*f*
    persuasion and, 108–111
Companionate love, 230, 235
Comparative negligence, 359
Competence, context and, 128, 128*f*
Competition
    for resources, as prejudice source, 171–172, 172*f*
Competitive orientation, 348
Complementarity, 204, 204*f*
Compliance
    definition of, 247
    principles of, 258
    tactics
        based on commitment or consistency, 259–260, 260*f*
        based on reciprocity, 260–261
        based on scarcity, 261–262, 262*f*
Compliance professionals, 258
Computer dating websites, 227, 227*f*
Condescension, 308
Conflict
    causes of, 346, 349–350, 349*f*
    elements in, 349
    resolution of, 335, 350–351
Conformity, 246, 248*f*
    bases of, 252–253, 254*f*
    cohesiveness and, 250
    factors affecting, 250–251, 251*f*
    gender differences in, 256
    group size and, 250
    measuring, 253
    research on, 248–249, 248*f*
    resisting, 254–256
Consensual validation, 206
Consensus, 70
Consistency, 70, 258
Consultation, 268
Consultative techniques, 268–269
Consumate love, 231
Contact hypothesis, 179
Context
    competence and, 128, 128*f*
    perceptions of attractiveness and, 201
    self-evaluations and, 140–141, 140*f*
Contrast effect, 201
Contributory negligence, 359
Controllable factors, attribution and, 71
Controlled processing
    definition of, 38
    vs. automatic processing, 39–40
Cooperation, 335, 346–348
Cooperative orientation, 348
Core values, 6
Correlation, 17–19, 19*f*
Correlation, illusory, 164–165
Correspondence bias (fundamental attribution error)
    attributions about groups, 75, 75*f*
    cultural factors in, 74
    description of, 73–74, 74*f*
Correspondent inference, theory of, 68–69
Counterarguments, 113–115, 115*f*
Counterfactual thinking, 48
Covariation principle, 145
Credibility, of communicators, 109–110, 110*f*
Crime, workplace aggression and,
        321–323, 322*f*

Criticism
    destructive, 349, 349*f*
    rejection from out-group members, 357–358, 358*f*
Cultural context
    biological factors and, 10–11
    social behavior and, 9
    stigmatized identity and, 147
Cultural differences
    self-conceptions and, 129
Culture
    conformity and, 255
    correspondence bias and, 74
    friendships and, 219–220
Cultures of honor, 312–314, 312*f*, 313*f*

Deadline technique, 261–262, 262*f*
Death wish (thanatos), 303
Debriefing, 25
Deception
    definition of, 25
    recognition of, 64–67, 65*f*, 67*f*
Decision making
    definition of, 354
    in groups, 354–360, 356*f*, 358*f*, 360*f*
    process for, 355–356
    representativeness heuristic and, 36
    social decision schemes and, 355
Decision/commitment, 231
Defensive attribution, 79
Deindividuation, 344–345, 345*f*
Dependent variable, 20
Depression
    attribution and, 77–78, 78*f*
    cognition and, 50
Descriptive norms, 250
Desegregation, 93
Desensitizing effect, 311
Destructive criticism, 349, 349*f*
Destructive obedience, 266
    resisting effects of, 266–267, 267*f*
Deterrence value, of punishment, 324–325
Devil's advocate technique, 359, 360*f*
Differential respect, gender stereotypes and, 161
Diffusion of responsibility, 277
Disappointment, counterfactual thinking and, 46
Disasters, altruism and, 288, 288*f*
Discounting principle, 71, 72*f*
Discrimination, 145, 156
    definition of, 175
    evaluation differences and, 162–163
    vs. prejudice, 167
Disengagement, social rejection and, 222
Dismissing attachment style, 217, 218
Disobedient models, 267
Displaced aggression, 326
Dissimilarity, interpersonal attraction and, 190
Dissonance
    attitude change and, 118–119, 119*f*
    beneficial behavior changes and, 119–120
    less-leads-to-more effect, 118–119, 119*f*
    as universal human experience, 117–118
    unpleasantness of, 117, 117*f*
Dissonance reduction, 116–117
Dissonance theory, 116
Distinctiveness, 70
Distraction–conflict theory, 343

Distributive justice (equity; fairness), 352
Divorce, 9, 239
Dominant responses, 342
Door-in-the-face technique, 260–261
Downward social comparison, 138
Drive theory
    of aggression, 304–305, 304f
    of social facilitation, 342, 342f

Ease-of-use heuristic, 52
Ego threat, 315
Egocentricism, altruistic personality and, 288
Ego-defensive function, of attitudes, 100
Egoism, 291
Egotism, implicit, 18
Elaboration-likelihood model of persuasion, 111–112, 112f
Elite group, 4
Emblems, 63
Emergencies
    correct interpretation of, 279–280, 280f
    failure to notice, 277–279
    helping, decision-making for, 281
    necessary knowledge/skills to act, determining, 281
    pluralistic ignorance and, 279–280
    responding to, 275–276, 275f
    responsibility to provide help, 280–281, 280f
    steps to prosocial behavior, 276–281, 276f, 278f–280f
    time pressure and, 279, 279f
    unresponsiveness to, 275f, 276
    witnesses to, 276, 277, 278
Emergent group norms, 357
Emotional contagion, 61
Emotional distress, individual responses to, 286–287
Emotions
    aggression and, 308–309, 309f
    basic, 62
    combinations of, 62, 62f
    effect on attraction, 192–193
    interpersonal attraction and, 190
    prejudice and, 144–147
    prosocial behavior and, 284–285, 285f
Empathetic joy hypothesis, 295
Empathy
    affective component of, 286
    altruistic personality and, 288
    biological basis of, 286–287
    cognitive component of, 286
    development of, 286–287, 287f, 288f
    forgiveness and, 328
Empathy–altruism hypothesis, 294–295
Employee theft, 354, 354f
Encoding, 32–33
Entiativity, 335f, 336
Environment, behavior and, 9
ERPs (event-related potentials), 13–14, 136
Error, sources of, 7, 72–77
Ethnic slurs, exposure to, 177–178, 178f
Evaluation apprehension, 343
Evaluations
    instant, 197–198
    mutual, 208
    of social stimuli, 39–40, 40f
Event-related potentials (ERPs), 13–14, 136
Evolutionary perspective, 304
Evolutionary psychology, 10–11, 10f
Example
    learning by, 97, 97f

Exchange, 268
Excitation transfer theory, 308, 309f
Exhibitionism, high self-esteem and, 137
Expectancies, stereotype-based, violating, 157–158
Experimental methods, 19–22, 20f, 21f
Experimentation, 20–21, 20f
    confounding and, 21–22, 21f
    success, requirements for, 21–22, 21f
Explanation, 19
External causes, of attribution, 70
External factors
    behavior and, 68–69
    loneliness and, 222
External validity, 22
Extroverts, 86
Eye contact
    in deception, 65
    as nonverbal cue, 63

Faces, composite, attractiveness of, 199–201, 200f
Facial expressions, 62–63, 62f, 65–66
Fairness
    in groups, 335
    judgments
        rules for, 352–353
Fallacy(ies)
    planning, 42
False promises, 350
Family, 216–219
    composition, changes in, 235–236
Fear, 62
Fear appeals, 108–109, 108f, 109f
Fearful–avoidant attachment style, 217
Fighting instinct, 304
First impressions, 108, 108f
    motives for forming, 83–84
    schemas and, 81–82, 81f
First-shift rule, 355
Flattery, 85, 208, 259, 259f
"Flower children," 231, 231f
Foot-in-the-door technique, 259
Forced compliance, 118
Forewarning, 113–114
Forgiveness, 326–328, 328f
Friends, 30
Friendship
    close, 219
    compliance and, 258
    cross-group, 179
    gender and, 219f, 220
    vs. romance, 223–225, 224f
Frustration, aggression and, 307–308
Frustration–aggression hypothesis, 304–305, 304f
Fundamental attribution error, 73–74, 74f, 82
Future, forecasts for, 43

Galton, Sir Francis, 203
GAM (general aggression model), 305–306, 306f
Game-playing love, 230
Gay marriage. See Same-sex marriage
Gazes, 63
Gender
    friendships and, 220
Gender differences, 48
    in aggression, 316–317, 316f
    in bullying, 320–321, 320f
    in conformity, 256

in empathy, 287
in gestures, 64
in helping behaviors, 282
in mate selection, 225–226
in self-definition, 130, 130f
in self-esteem, 137–138
in social perception, 66–67, 67f
Gender stereotypes
accuracy of, 161
changes over time, 126–127
definition of, 156–157, 157t
differential respect and, 161
targets of, 159–161, 160f
women's intuition and, 66–67
General aggression model (GAM), 305–306, 306f
Generativity, 290
Genetic determinism model, 295–297
Genetic factors, empathy and, 286–287
Gestalt psychologists, 108
Gestures, 63–64, 64f
Glass ceiling, 157–158
Glass escalator, 158
Goals, superordinate, 351
Group decisions, improving, 359–360, 360f
Group differences, in self-concept, 129
Group equality, progress toward, 144–145, 144f
Group polarization, 356, 356f, 357
Group processes, 4
Group size, conformity and, 250
Groups, 334–335, 335f
    attributions about, correspondence bias in, 75, 75f
    benefits of joining, 338–339, 339f
    biased information processing in, 358–359
    cohesiveness of, 337–338
    coordination in, 346–351
    costs of membership, 339–340, 340f
    decision making in, 354–360, 356f, 358f, 360f
    differentiation of functions in, 336
    entiativity, 335f, 336
    failure to share information in, 359
    hierarchies in, 336–337, 337f
    joining, motives for, 340
    mere presence of others, 341, 342
    norms, 337
    perceived fairness in, 352–354, 354f
    social facilitation, 341–343, 341f
    splinter, 339–340, 340f
    withdrawal from, 339–340, 340f
Groupthink, 357–358

Handshakes, 202
Happiness, downside of, 51–52
Health messages, positive *vs.* negative, 108–109, 108f–109f
Helpfulness
    emotions and, 284–285
    empathy and, 286–288
    responsibility for problem and, 283
Helping
    as accomplishment, 295
    behaviors
        mimicry and, 282, 283f
        situational factors and, 282–284, 283f
    feeling of being helped, 291–292, 292f
    negative-state relief model and, 295
Heroism, 275–276, 275f

Heuristic
    anchoring and adjustment, 37–38, 38f
    availability, 36–37
    definition of, 31, 35
    mood and, 51–52, 52f
    representativeness, 36
Heuristic processing, 111–112, 112f
Hierarchies, in groups, 336–337, 337f
High school friends, 188–189
"Hippie" identity, 131
Hispanic identity, 132
Homosexuals, social norms and, 255–256
Hostile aggression, 315
Hostile attributional bias, 315
Hostile sexism, 160, 160f
Hostility, expressions of, workplace aggression and, 322
Human immunodeficiency virus (HIV), 231–232
Hypocrisy, 120

Ideal self, 12
Identity dilemma, 132
Identity function, of attitudes, 99–100, 100f
Identity interference, 129
Illusory correlation, 164–165
Imbalance, 206
Implicit associations, 169, 169f
Implicit bystander effect, 278
Implicit personality theories, 81–82, 81f
Implicit processes, 14–15
Implicit racial attitudes, measuring, 176–177, 176f
Implicit theories of personality, 61
Impression formation
    cognitive perspective and, 82–83
    definition of, 61
    effortless nature of, 80
    motives for, 83–84
Impression management (self-presentation)
    cognitive overload and, 85–86, 86f
    definition of, 61, 84, 85f
    self-regulation and, 141–142
    tactics, 115–116
    techniques for, 259, 259f
Impression motivation function, of attitudes, 100f, 101
Impulsivity, 316
Incidental feelings, 168
Incidental similarity, 259
Inclusive fitness, 296
Independent self-concept, 129
Independent variable, 20
Individualistic cultures, 74
Individualistic orientation, 348
Individuality, need to maintain, 255
Individuation, 255
Induced compliance, 118
Inequality, perceived, 155
Infants, communication of, 216, 217f
Inferences, 9, 61
Inferential prisons, stereotypes as, 164
Inferential statistics, 21–22
Infidelity, 237–238
Infidelity, sexual, 312–313, 313f
Influence, 4
Information
    concealing, 61
    negativity bias and, 41–42, 42f
    sharing, failures in groups, 359
Information gathering, inappropriate, 350

Possible selves, 132–133
Power, gestures of, 64
Preattribution, 326
Predictions, 17–18
Prejudice, 156
   based on category membership, 155
   behavioral consequences of, 147–148
   cognitive consequences of, 147
   contact hypothesis, 179
   definition of, 167
   development of, 167–168, 168f
   emotional consequences of, 144–147
   extreme forms of, 154, 155f
   as generic negative emotional response, 167–168, 168f
   justification/acceptability of, 155
   legitimized *vs.* illegitimate, 173, 173t
   against obesity, 201–202, 201f
   origins of, 170–175
   of others', exposure to, 177–178, 178f
   persistence of, 171, 171f
   reducing
      recategorization for, 180
      saying "no" to stereotypes, 180–181, 181f
      social influence and, 182
   self as target for, 144–148
   social learning view of, 179
   sources of, competition for resources, 171–172, 172f
   threats to self-esteem and, 170–171, 171f
   vs. discrimination, 167
Prejudice plausible condition, 145
Preoccupied attachment style, 217, 218
Pressure, 268
Price reductions, 261
Primates, need for affiliation and, 216, 216f
Priming
   for aggression, 306
   definition of, 36–37, 37f, 177
Primitive ancestors, reactions to strangers, 206–207
Prisoner's dilemma, 347
Private acceptance, *vs.* public conformity, 249
Proportion of similarity, 204, 205f
Prosocial behavior
   definition of, 274–275, 346
   emotions and, 284–285, 285f
   feeling of being helped, 291–292, 292f
   genetic determinism model, 295–297
   long-term commitment to, 289–292
   mimicry and, 282
   models, exposure to, 283–284, 284f
   motives for, 293–297, 293f, 294f, 296f
   personality variables and, 288
   positive and negative influences on, 296f
   self-interest and, 291
   steps to, 276–281, 276f, 278f–280f
Provocation, 308
Proximity
   interpersonal attraction and, 190
   repeated exposure and, 195–197, 196f
Psychological mechanisms, evolved, 10
Punishment, for aggression prevention/control, 323–325, 324f

Racial attitudes, implicit, measuring, 176–177, 176f
Racism
   modern, 175–176
Random assignment of participants to experimental conditions,
   20f, 21
Rational persuasion, 268

Reactance, 47, 113, 269
Realistic conflict theory, 171–172
Reasoned action, theory of, 105–106
Reasoning ability, limits on, 47–48
Recall, 33
Recategorization, 180
Receiving help, 291–292, 292f
Reciprocal altruism, 348
Reciprocal liking or disliking, 208
Reciprocity
   compliance and, 258, 260–261
   definition of, 347
Refutational defense condition, 115
Rejection, 131
Relatives, 30
Repeated exposure effect, interpersonal attraction and, 190,
   195–197, 196f
Reporting, 33
Representative sampling, 17
Representativeness heuristic, 36
Reproductive fitness, mate selection and, 225
Repulsion hypothesis, 205
Research methods, 16–22
   correlation and, 17–19, 19f
   experimental, 19–22, 20f, 21f
   working knowledge of, 16
Research results, interpretation of, 21–22
Respect, 161
Retrieval, 32–33
Retrieval cue, 50
Rewards, for "right views," 96–97
Risky shift, 355–356
Robberies, workplace aggression and, 321–323, 322f
The Robber's Cave, 172
Role models, 133
Roles, 336
Romance
   love, sex and, 231–232
   vs. friendship, 223–225, 224f
Romantic destiny, 226–227
Romantic relationships
   description of, 223–225, 224f
   mate selection, 225–226
   schemas in, 224, 224f
Rosenberg Self-Esteem Scale, 135, 135f, 136
Rudeness, 38–39
Rumination, 328

Same-sex marriages, 232, 233f
   attitudes toward, 232
Same-sex marriages, attitudes toward, 92, 255–256, 256f
Sampling, representative, 17
Scarcity, compliance and, 258, 261–262, 262f
Schemas
   definition of, 31, 32f, 161–162
   first impressions and, 81–82, 81f
   in romantic relationships, 224, 224f
   self-confirming nature of, 34
   social cognition and, 32–33
Science, definition of, 6, 7f
Scientific approach, adoption of, 6–7
Secure attachment style, 217
Security procedures, at airports, 154
Selection, 10, 10f
Selective altruism, 294, 294f
Selective avoidance, 114
Selective exposure, 114

PHOTO CREDITS

Chapter 1

Page 2: Jon Feingersh/Masterfile; 7 (left): Photo Researchers; 7 (right): Trevor Wood/Stone/Getty Images; 9 (left): Chuck Savage; 9 (right): Ronnie Kaufman/Corbis Bettmann; 13: Lester Lefkowitz/Stock Market/Corbis

Chapter 2

Page 28: Alex Mares-Manton/Getty Images; 32 (left): Rob Gage/Taxi/Getty Images; 32 (right): Chuck Savage; 34: Hulton Archive/Getty Images; 37: Bill Crump/Image Bank/Getty Images; 38: AP Wide World Photos; 40 (left): J. Curley/The Image Works; 40 (right): J.P. Laffont/Sigma/Gamma Press; 43: Michael Dwyer/Stock Boston; 46: Jeffrey Greenberg/PhotoEdit; 48: Dave King/Dorling Kindersley Media Library; 57 (left): Michael Prince/Corbis; 57 (right): Jutta Klee/Corbis

Chapter 3

Page 58: Andersen Ross/Photodisc/Getty Images; 60 (left): Hulton/Deutsch Collection/Corbis; 60 (right): AP Wide World Photos; 62 (left): Courtesy of Robert A. Baron; 62 (middle): Courtesy of Robert A. Baron; 62 (right): Courtesy of Robert A. Baron; 64 (left): Courtesy of Robert A. Baron; 64 (middle): Courtesy of Robert A. Baron; 64 (right): Courtesy of Robert A. Baron; 67 (top): Rommel Pecson/The Image Works; 67 (bottom left): Bob Daemmrich/PhotoEdit; 67 (bottomright): Larry Kolvoord/The Image Works; 77 (left): Dylan Martinez/Corbis; 77 (right): AP Wide World Photos; 78 (left) : Corbis Digital Stock; 78 (right): Steven Lunnetta/PhotoEdit; 80: Rob Lewine/Corbis; 86: Jim Bourg/Corbis/Reuters; 88: Corbis RF; 89: Kevork Djansezian/AP Wide World Photos

Chapter 4

Page 90: Bob Daemmrich/PhotoEdit; 93 (left): Tom McCarthy/PhotoEdit; 93 (right): Jim Bourg/Corbis/Reuters; 95: Mark Peterson/Corbis; 97: Amy Etra/PhotoEdit; 106: Dan McCoy/Rainbow; 107: Bernard Boutirt/Woodfin Camp & Associates; 108: A. Ramey/PhotoEdit; 110: Bonnie Kamin/PhotoEdit

Chapter 5

Page 124: Stone/Getty Images; 127: Hulton Archive/Getty Images; 128: Jonathan Nourok/Stone/Getty Images; 132: Yellow Dog Productions/Image Bank/Getty Images; 133 (top): Thea E. Linscombe; 133 (bottom): AP Wide World Photos; 135 (left): Kai Pfaffenbach/Corbis/Reuters; 135 (right): Corbis Digital Stock; 142: Dion Ogust/The Image Works

Chapter 6

Page 152: Gilles Mingasson/Liaison/Getty Images; 155 (top left): Gianluigi Guercia/AFP/Getty Images; 155 (top right): ABC, Inc. Photography; 155 (bottom): AP Wide World Photos; 159: Stephen Jaffe/AFP/Getty Images; 163: Ariel Skelley/Corbis; 168: Monika Graff/The Image Works; 172: Peter Turnley/Corbis

Chapter 7

Page 186: Peter Adams/Image Bank/Getty Images; 192 (top left): David Katzenstein/Corbis; 192 (top right): Nancy Richmond/The Image Works; 192 (bottom left): David Katzenstein/Corbis; 192 (bottom right): Tony Savino/The Image Works; 196: Spencer Grant/PhotoEdit; 198 (top left): Keline Howard/Sygma/Corbis; 198 (top right): Keline Howard/Sygma/Corbis; 198 (bottom): Larry Williams/Corbis; 200: Courtesy of Dr. Judith H. Langlois, Charles and Sarah Seay Regents Professor, Dept. of Psychology, University of Texas, Austin; 201: David Young-Wolff/PhotoEdit; 204: Alex Wong/Getty Images; 210 (left): Charles Gupton/Stock Market/Corbis; 210 (right): Bill Losh/Taxi/Getty Images

Chapter 8

Page 212: Jeremy Maude/Masterfile; 216: Peter Arnold; 217: Corbis RF; 219 (left): Courtesy of Robert A. Baron; 219 (right): Courtesy of Robert A. Baron; 224: Photo Network/Alamy; 227: Courtesy of Perfectmatch.com; 231: Tom Miner/The Image Works; 233: Terry Schmitt/Landov; 235: Michael Newman/PhotoEdit; 242 (left): George Shelley/Corbis; 242 (right): Mark Ludak/The Image Works

Chapter 9

Page 244: Colin Hawkins/Image Bank/Getty Images; 248 (top): AP Wide World Photos; 248 (bottom): Courtesy of the Archives of the History of Psychology; 251: Kayte Deioma/PhotoEdit; 256: AP Wide World Photos; 257: Sylvia Johnson/Woodfin Camp & Associates; 262: Rhoda Sidney/Stock Boston; 265: Alexandra Milgram; 267: North Wind Picture Archives

Chapter 10

Page 272: AP Wide World Photos; 275: Damir Sagol/Corbis/Reuters; 280: Sygma/Corbis; 284: David Young-Wolff/PhotoEdit; 287 (left): Allan Tannenbaum/The Image Works; 287 (right): Grigory Dukorg/Corbis/Reuters; 288: Jeff Greenberg/PhotoEdit; 289: Johnny Crawford/The Image Works; 292: Adrian Arbib/Corbis; 294: Corbis

Chapter 11

Page 300: Chris Anderson/Aurora & Quanta Productions; 303: AP Wide World Photos; 305 (left): Corbis/Reuters; 305 (right): Dex Images/Corbis; 312: Bejing New Picture/Elite Group Picture Desk/Kobal Collection; 316: Rick Gomez/Corbis; 320: Michael Newman/PhotoEdit; 324: Andrew Lichtenstein/Aurora & Quanta Productions; 328: Corbis Royalty Free; 331 (top): David Young-Wolff/PhotoEdit; 331 (middle): Gary Conner/PhotoEdit; 331 (bottom): Michael Newman/PhotoEdit

Chapter 12

Page 332: Tom Le Goff/Digital Vision/Getty Images; 335 (top): Jeff Greenberg/Omni-Photo Communications; 335 (bottom left): Don Spiro/Stone/Getty Images; 335 (bottom right): Rune Hellestad/Corbis; 337: Sherwin Crasto/Corbis; 339: Philip James Corwin/Corbis; 341: Neal Preston/Corbis; 345: Pawel Kopczynski/Corbis; 349: Amy Etra/PhotoEdit; 354: Courtesy of Robert A. Baron